IBM

International Technical Support Organization

Deployment Guide Series: IBM Tivoli Change and Configuration Management Database Configuration Discovery and Tracking v1.1

November 2006

SG24-7264-00

Note: Before using this information and the product it supports, read the information in "Notices" on page xiii.

First Edition (November 2006)

This edition applies to Version 1, Release 1 of IBM Tivoli Change Configuration Management Database (product number 5724-M19).

Note: This book is based on a pre-GA version of a product and might not apply when the product becomes generally available. We recommend that you consult the product documentation or follow-on versions of this book for more current information.

Contents

Notices

This information was developed for products and services offered in the U.S.A.

IBM may not offer the products, services, or features discussed in this document in other countries. Consult your local IBM representative for information on the products and services currently available in your area. Any reference to an IBM product, program, or service is not intended to state or imply that only that IBM product, program, or service may be used. Any functionally equivalent product, program, or service that does not infringe any IBM intellectual property right may be used instead. However, it is the user's responsibility to evaluate and verify the operation of any non-IBM product, program, or service.

IBM may have patents or pending patent applications covering subject matter described in this document. The furnishing of this document does not give you any license to these patents. You can send license inquiries, in writing, to:
IBM Director of Licensing, IBM Corporation, North Castle Drive Armonk, NY 10504-1785 U.S.A.

The following paragraph does not apply to the United Kingdom or any other country where such provisions are inconsistent with local law: INTERNATIONAL BUSINESS MACHINES CORPORATION PROVIDES THIS PUBLICATION "AS IS" WITHOUT WARRANTY OF ANY KIND, EITHER EXPRESS OR IMPLIED, INCLUDING, BUT NOT LIMITED TO, THE IMPLIED WARRANTIES OF NON-INFRINGEMENT, MERCHANTABILITY OR FITNESS FOR A PARTICULAR PURPOSE. Some states do not allow disclaimer of express or implied warranties in certain transactions, therefore, this statement may not apply to you.

This information could include technical inaccuracies or typographical errors. Changes are periodically made to the information herein; these changes will be incorporated in new editions of the publication. IBM may make improvements and/or changes in the product(s) and/or the program(s) described in this publication at any time without notice.

Any references in this information to non-IBM Web sites are provided for convenience only and do not in any manner serve as an endorsement of those Web sites. The materials at those Web sites are not part of the materials for this IBM product and use of those Web sites is at your own risk.

IBM may use or distribute any of the information you supply in any way it believes appropriate without incurring any obligation to you.

Information concerning non-IBM products was obtained from the suppliers of those products, their published announcements or other publicly available sources. IBM has not tested those products and cannot confirm the accuracy of performance, compatibility or any other claims related to non-IBM products. Questions on the capabilities of non-IBM products should be addressed to the suppliers of those products.

This information contains examples of data and reports used in daily business operations. To illustrate them as completely as possible, the examples include the names of individuals, companies, brands, and products. All of these names are fictitious and any similarity to the names and addresses used by an actual business enterprise is entirely coincidental.

COPYRIGHT LICENSE:
This information contains sample application programs in source language, which illustrates programming techniques on various operating platforms. You may copy, modify, and distribute these sample programs in any form without payment to IBM, for the purposes of developing, using, marketing or distributing application programs conforming to the application programming interface for the operating platform for which the sample programs are written. These examples have not been thoroughly tested under all conditions. IBM, therefore, cannot guarantee or imply reliability, serviceability, or function of these programs. You may copy, modify, and distribute these sample programs in any form without payment to IBM for the purposes of developing, using, marketing, or distributing application programs conforming to IBM's application programming interfaces.

Trademarks

The following terms are trademarks of the International Business Machines Corporation in the United States, other countries, or both:

Redbooks (logo) ™
ibm.com®
iSeries™
AIX®
AS/400®
Collation®
Confignia®
Database 2™
Domino®
DB2®
IBM®
Lotus®
OS/2®
Rational Unified Process®
Rational®
Redbooks™
Tivoli Enterprise™
Tivoli Enterprise Console®
Tivoli®
WebSphere®

The following terms are trademarks of other companies:

SAP, and SAP logos are trademarks or registered trademarks of SAP AG in Germany and in several other countries.

Snapshot, and the Network Appliance logo are trademarks or registered trademarks of Network Appliance, Inc. in the U.S. and other countries.

IT Infrastructure Library, IT Infrastructure Library is a registered trademark of the Central Computer and Telecommunications Agency which is now part of the Office of Government Commerce.

ITIL, is a registered trademark, and a registered community trademark of the Office of Government Commerce, and is registered in the U.S. Patent and Trademark Office.

iPlanet, EJB, IQ, Java, JavaScript, JavaServer, JavaSpaces, Jini, JDBC, JDK, JMX, JRE, JSP, JVM, J2EE, J2SE, Solaris, Streamline, Sun, SunOS, and all Java-based trademarks are trademarks of Sun Microsystems, Inc. in the United States, other countries, or both.

Active Directory, Microsoft, Visual Basic, Windows NT, Windows, and the Windows logo are trademarks of Microsoft Corporation in the United States, other countries, or both.

UNIX is a registered trademark of The Open Group in the United States and other countries.

Linux is a trademark of Linus Torvalds in the United States, other countries, or both.

Other company, product, or service names may be trademarks or service marks of others.

Preface

This IBM® Redbook focuses on the planning, deployment, and customization of IBM Tivoli Change and Configuration Management Database Configuration Discovery and Tracking v1.1 in small to medium and large environments.

This book covers installation, configuration, and operational considerations that are related to a stand-alone implementation of IBM Tivoli Change and Configuration Management Database Configuration Discovery and Tracking v1.1 and does not include topics that are related to the inter operability with the IBM Tivoli® Change Configuration Management Database Process Management and Integration Platform feature.

IBM Tivoli Change and Configuration Management Database Configuration Discovery and Tracking v1.1 (Configuration Discovery and Tracking) provides a Configuration Management Database (CMDB) to store configuration items about the corporations critical infrastructure. To automatically populate the CMDB with relevant configuration item data of the components and relationships in your IT infrastructure, an automated, agentless discovery method is provided.

Configuration Discovery and Tracking also federates data with other data either pre-existing, already stored in the customer environment in various tools or databases, or captured by other IBM, Tivoli, or third-party tools. Lastly, the Configuration Discovery and Tracking product provides analytics available by comparing like similar configuration items to each other to check for compliance, as well as keeping a comprehensive change history of configuration items to give an in depth look at change over time, or change history, and the ability to detect configuration drift.

This book covers the following topics:

- Introducing Configuration Discovery and Tracking
- Configuration Discovery and Tracking terminology
- Deploying Configuration Discovery and Tracking v1.1
- Step-by-step Configuration Discovery and Tracking
- Useful tools and utilities
- Populating and maintaining the Configuration Management database
- Consuming configuration and relationship data
- Tips, tricks, and troubleshooting

The information compiled in this book is targeted to the IT specialist who will install and customize IBM Tivoli Change and Configuration Management Database Configuration Discovery and Tracking v1.1.

Note: The material in this book is meant to be an adjunct to the User and the IBM Tivoli Change and Configuration Management Database v1.1: Administering the Configuration Discovery and Tracking feature. If you are interested in integrating the product with other applications, we expect that you are familiar with the *IBM Tivoli Change and Configuration Management Database Configuration Discovery and Tracking v1.1 SDK Guide.*

The team that wrote this redbook

This IBM Redbook was produced by a team of specialists from around the world working at the International Technical Support Organization (ITSO), Austin Center.

Morten Moeller is a Project Leader at the ITSO, Austin Center. He applies his extensive field experience as an IBM Certified IT Specialist to his work at the ITSO where he writes extensively on all areas of Systems Management. Before joining the ITSO, Morten worked in the Professional Services Organization of IBM Denmark as a Distributed Systems Management Specialist where he was involved in numerous projects designing and implementing systems management solutions for major customers of IBM Denmark.

James Bacon is a Technical Presales Specialist for the Americas GEO, based in Austin Texas. He has 14 years of experience in the IT field. He holds a degree in English from the University of Texas at Austin. His areas of expertise include four years IBM software group presales support, five years general network and application support, five years specializing in Software Delivery and machine imaging, and most recently TADDM.

Murtuza Choilawala is a Senior Software Engineer with IBM Tivoli. He is a IBM Certified IT Specialist working with Tivoli Global Response Team (GRT) helping customers resolve critical situations and provide technical support on various Tivoli products. He actively presents at various Tivoli Technical User Conferences and User Group meetings. He has 13 years of experience in information technology, the last six years with Tivoli. He has a Bachelors Degree in Computer Engineering, and a Diploma in Computer Engineering. Prior to joining Tivoli, he worked with iSeries™ platform. He has also been a Product Manager for AS/400® systems as an IBM Business Partner.

Petar Kadijevic is an Advisory IT Specialist at IBM Global Technology Services in Denmark with seven years of experience in the Systems Management and Service Management field. After completing studies of Social Science at Roskilde University Petar joined IBM in 1999 through a two-year trainee-ship and has in parallel completed several Computer Science courses at different educational institutions. His areas of expertise include Java™ programming, implementing Service Management solutions with Tivoli and Peregrine Systems products and ITIL® processes.

Charles R. Rich has held many position over the last 24 years in the IT industry. Most recently at Collation®, before its acquisition by IBM, Charles Rich was the Director of Field Sales Engineering. Prior to Collation, Charles Rich was the Director of the Application Management Product Line (in R&D) at EMC/SMARTS where he was responsible for technical product management and spearheaded the requirements and design of BSM & Application Management products, as well as contributing to several patents in that field. Prior to EMC/SMARTS Charles R. Rich has held positions including VP of Marketing at InterWorld and key positions at Tivoli, Stratus and Motorola.

Kulasekaran Satagopan is a Director of IT Governance Practice at **Megasoft Consultants, Inc.** in Virginia, USA. He has 13 years of experience in Information Technology. He holds a Masters degree in Business Administration and Bachelors degree in Electronics and Communication Engineering. He has Project Management Professional (PMP), Certified Quality Manager (CQM) and Certified Information Security Manager (CISM) certifications. His areas of expertise include process management, project management, software development and maintenance, infrastructure services management and information security. He has written extensively on process and project management, ITIL and information security. Megasoft is an advanced Business Partner of IBM and offers Tivoli centric solutions. Megasoft has extensive experience in implementing CCMDB in client locations and has developed CMDBConnect, an adapter for the CCMDB product to integrate with the Remedy product suite.

Thanks to the following people for their contributions to this project:

The ITSO editing team

Andy Barclay,
IBM Pre-Sales

Byron Todd, Sushma Patel, Shashank Joshi, Gierard Chandler, Laura Farley, John Jerney, Jim Collins, Mark Presland, Kevin Kingsbury, David Robinson
CCMDB Development
Tivoli Systems

Become a published author

Join us for a two- to six-week residency program! Help write an IBM Redbook that deals with specific products or solutions, while getting hands-on experience with leading-edge technologies. You will team with IBM technical professionals, Business Partners, or customers.

Your efforts will help increase product acceptance and customer satisfaction. As a bonus, you will develop a network of contacts in IBM development labs, and increase your productivity and marketability.

Find out more about the residency program, browse the residency index, and apply online at:

ibm.com/redbooks/residencies.html

Comments welcome

Your comments are important to us!

We want our Redbooks™ to be as helpful as possible. Send us your comments about this or other Redbooks in one of the following ways:

- Use the online **Contact us** review redbook form found at:

  ibm.com/redbooks

- Send your comments in an e-mail to:

  redbook@us.ibm.com

- Mail your comments to:

  IBM Corporation, International Technical Support Organization
  Dept. HYTD Mail Station P099
  2455 South Road
  Poughkeepsie, NY 12601-5400

1

Introducing Configuration Discovery and Tracking

This chapter discusses the overall IBM vision for IT Service Management, which is to provide our clients with the capability to understand their IT infrastructure and implement processes to help them manage IT in the same way as a business.

1.1 The four areas of IBM IT Service Management

To aid IT departments in running as proficiently as possible as businesses, IBM IT Service management concentrates on four areas of study:

- Technology integration and standards
- Improved collaboration among IT people spread across organizational silos
- Best-practices based process modules to enable automated process execution
- Sharing of business-critical IT information to improve decision making

In finding workable solutions to these areas, IBM solutions cover four key areas:

- Process Managers that provide automated ITIL-aligned workflows for key IT processes
- An open, standards-based IBM IT Service Management platform
- Integration between process tasks and Operational Management Products to automate the running of those tasks from the process flow
- Best practices to help pull it all together

At the heart of the IBM solution is the IBM Tivoli Change and Configuration Management Database Configuration Discovery and Tracking which provides rich details of configuration items (CIs) with automated, agentless discovery of assets and their application dependencies, as well as a Discovery Library technology to help use data from other sources. In addition, it provides the ability to audit and control configuration items with full configuration and change management processes, and acts as an integration platform for Operational Management Products.

Using the CCMDB as an integration platform for ITIL aligned process flows, customers can take advantage of the Process Managers for Release, Availability, and Information Lifecycle Management. Each of these process managers runs on top of the CCMDB and provides ITIL aligned process flows that can help customers manage their IT infrastructure like a business. Over time, IBM will develop and deliver more Process Manager modules to enhance the solution by incorporating facilities to control and automate more processes used in the IT organization.

1.2 IBM Tivoli Change and Configuration Management Database Configuration Discovery and Tracking overview

IBM Tivoli Change and Configuration Management Database Configuration Discovery and Tracking was created to provide an agentless deep discovery tool that auto-discovers applications and hardware in a complex computer server environment, the dependencies between these components, and tracks changes to them. It is the core component of IBM IT Service Management strategy, and also IBM Tivoli Unified Process (ITUP). Configuration Discovery and Tracking fills the role of Change Management Database, or CMDB, which is the definitive repository for configuration items in an Infrastructure Technology Information Library (ITIL) aligned IT model. ITIL is a best practices methodology evolved from a series of reference manuals that show the benefits of organizing IT services along business service lines.

IBM has further expanded the initial capabilities of Configuration Discovery and Tracking from its original debut to support its role in the IBM IT Service Management strategy, enhancing the database federation capability, expanding the methods of getting data in and out of the CMDB to integrate easily with other tools in the computing environment, and also creating a process engine and a series of process managers utilizing process modeling to ensure workflow consistency. Further, IBM has taken steps to ensure that Configuration Discovery and Tracking is able to use the power of the already existing line of operational managers available for handling specific IT challenges such as backup solutions (fulfilling the business continuity role for example) to provide a comprehensive solution consistent with IBM IT Service Management and ITUP.

The IT Infrastructure Library

The IT Infrastructure Library® (ITIL) is a series of reference books that provide best practices to transform the IT organization from a silo based organizational structure focused around technology concerns - to a dynamic organization focused on overall business goals. This structure moves information in a freer fashion between traditionally separate disciplines, such as database-, network-, system-, and application-management specialists. ITIL focuses on how components should be defined (Configuration Items), and once defined how they should interact to achieve business goals and to provide services to other aspects of the business. This makes IT a more usable commodity in the business, with more easily measured impacts and goals allowing greater use of technology to provide a competitive edge in the business.

For more details on the IT Infrastructure Library, refer to Appendix G, “Service management and the IT Infrastructure Library” on page 441.

The IBM Tivoli Unified Process

IBM Tivoli Unified Process (ITUP) is a roadmap for delivering ITIL based IT Service Management using existing Tivoli and IBM solutions as well as the new Process Managers, which are described in more detail in 1.4, "Process managers" on page 23.

ITUP links actual product names and capabilities with ITIL defined roles, responsibilities and processes - and complements the IBM Rational® Unified Process® (a logical method of application development) to provide a mechanism and a philosophy for customers to align their IT organization and processes along business service guidelines, and develop and implement applications with additional manageability factors built in to take full advantage of these new concepts. ITUP is available for download from this Web site:

```
http://www.ibm.com/software/tivoli/features/it-serv-mgmt/itup/
index.html
```

This site provides a brief overview of components, features, and how they interact with each other in the overall IBM IT Service Management strategy. ITUP is considered by IBM to be a definitive guide on how to implement ITIL in a modular yet comprehensive fashion using IBM solutions available today.

1.2.1 Why do I need IT Service Management?

The answer can be reduced to several points, which apply to today's complex networking environments, as exemplified by the typical enterprise application infrastructure depicted in Figure 1-1 on page 5.

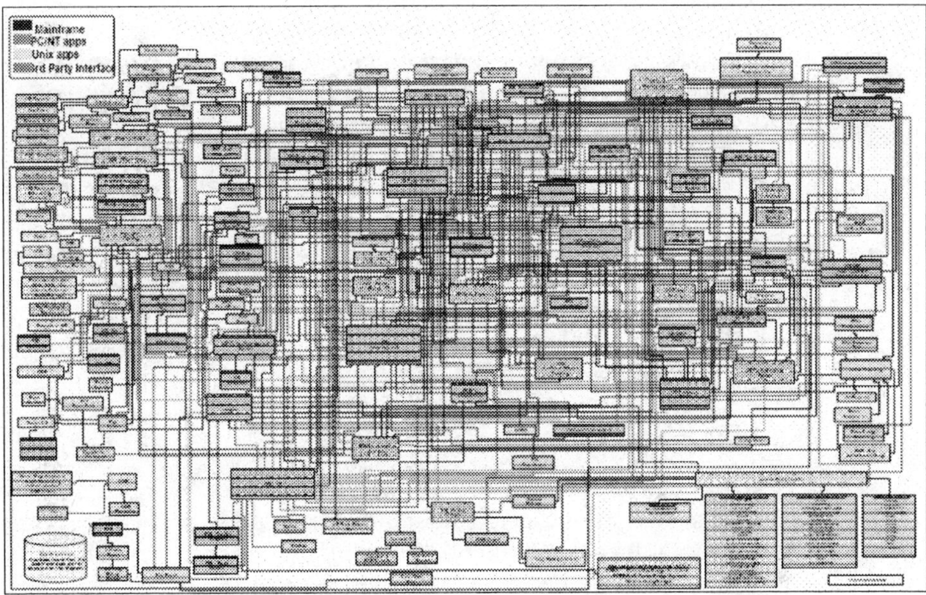

Figure 1-1 A network environment diagram adds to problem resolution time

You do not have to work at a very large company with thousands of employees to experience these particular examples. They exist in most IT Service Delivery organizations and require careful planning to avoid, often times undone, because of the need to accomplish a goal in an allotted time within an allotted budget. Just because some planning might have been incomplete does not mean that the IT Service Delivery is doomed, though. It does take some care and thoughtful planning and implementation to bring IT service around to a more manageable state, so that the administrators can spend more time improving service rather than spending an ever increasing amount of time maintaining their current levels of service.

To get a better idea of what contributes to the boredom that can set in for a typical systems administrator, and some of the continuing vexations that IT executives dread, we can make some simple observations about the state of the IT department.

Configuration management

Today's applications use reusable components to reduce turnaround time for developers. To take that concept further as it was popular and worked well, it was then applied to reusing application infrastructure components in entirety (such as databases) to create composite applications. While this in turn reduced the time to create large implementations which helped the IT department make contributions to the business side of the company, at times these composite applications become unwieldy to track. This is because they span multiple computers, and are comprised of multiple components, such as a Web server providing an easy to navigate user interface, linked to an application to providing a functional back-end, and a database to provide information and records for the other components to work with and store the results of that work. By itself, this leads to many, many servers to maintain which is in itself a point to consider. Patching 1, 2, 5, or even 10 machines can be accomplished with a minimum of fuss, but in iterations of 50 or more, it becomes desirable to have a repeatable, consistent method of doing this, either forcing automation though code, or rigid oversight through process control. This can be eased through application of the ITIL mind set and implementation according to ITUP. The first building block being IBM Tivoli Change and Configuration Management Database Configuration Discovery and Tracking.

Impact analysis

To place on top of this complexity through size and number of components, there has been a trend towards server consolidation, using multiprocessor machines to reduce the overall number of systems to manage, and also to harvest otherwise wasted CPU utilization for servers that might not have much load under a 1-server-1-application architecture.

However, this comes with its own dilemma, as it becomes even more difficult to provide accurate mapping of function to machine or application as several instances of databases or Web servers coexist on the same host machine, each capable of performing separate critical tasks in the environment. The use of Virtual Machines are also popular methods of recovering CPU and memory that would otherwise be wasted, but again it can complicate systems management. If it is difficult to determine the effect of taking a virtual machine or a host machine and associated applications down for servicing, it will lead to paralysis in the IT center, leading to security and performance vulnerability as patches are delayed, applications are not upgraded, and hardware upgrades are not performed to meet increased capacity requirements.

To better understand the relationships and dependencies between application-, infrastructure-, and system-components IBM Tivoli Change and Configuration Management Database Configuration Discovery and Tracking provides the visibility into the IT infrastructure to enhance greatly the Impact Analysis processes of change management in any environment. Figure 1-2 on page 7 depicts an example of the map for a business application named Order Management.

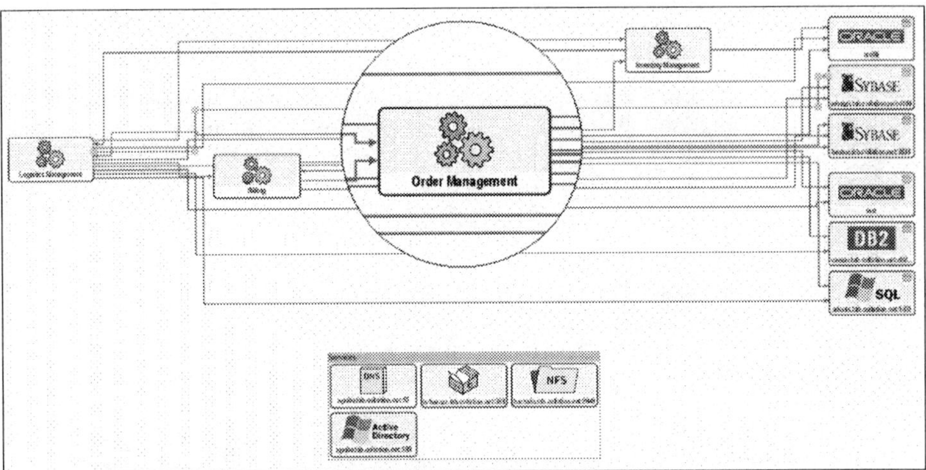

Figure 1-2 Aligning application maps along business lines reduces complexity

Change management

Another bone of contention which IT Service Management alleviates is providing process control to allow for Change Management. Change must occur in a production environment for many reasons as we mentioned, including security patches, operating system patching and upgrades as they go out of support, application introduction and retirement, or hardware and network upgrades.

The process for change management now is filled with review meetings, back out procedures, risk assessment meetings, and determination for which components will be worked on directly, and which will be affected by temporary unavailability of systems as well as code level compatibility after the change.

The need for consistency in these proceedings in turn leads to consistency in change process, and minimizing disruption caused by change, as well as clear records to determine cause and effect in troubleshooting for problem or incident management if those become necessary. Figure 1-3 on page 8 depicts the application map for Order Management highlighting changed components.

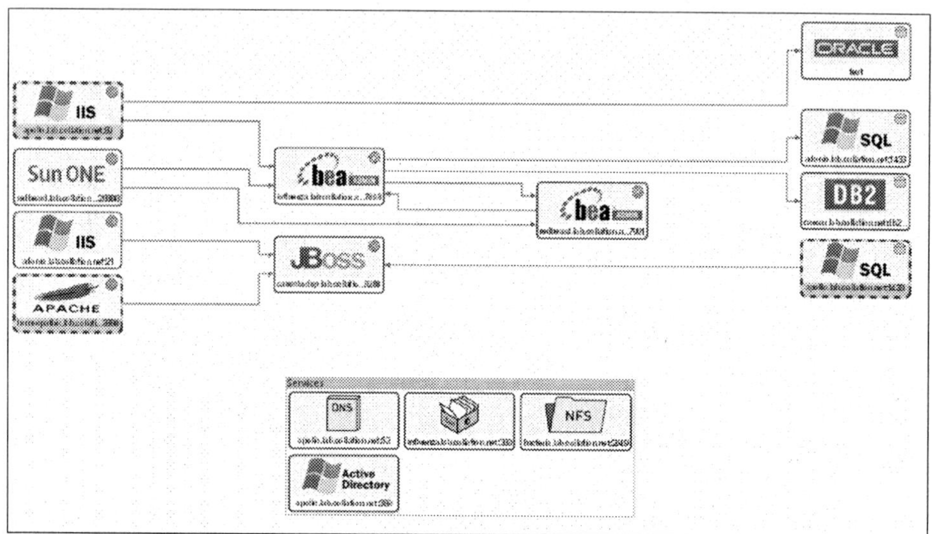

Figure 1-3 Change History reports quickly highlights change relationships

By levering the capabilities of IBM Tivoli Change and Configuration Management Database Configuration Discovery and Tracking it is ensured, that everyone has access to the same, updated information, which accurately reflects the state of the IT infrastructure, as exemplified by the Order Management Change History Report shown in Figure 1-4.

Change History: Results

Type	Component	Change	Date	Attribute	Old Value	New Value	Id
Apache	homeopathix.lab.collat	Updated	12/04/2004 15:01 PST	appDescriptors		/usr/local/apache/appd	13342
Apache	homeopathix.lab.collat	Updated	12/04/2004 15:01 PST	appDescriptors		/usr/local/apache//app	13342
ApacheWebContainer	homeopathix.lab.collat	Updated	12/04/2004 15:01 PST	ApacheWebContainer	/usr/local/apache/	/usr/local/apache	13342
ApacheWebContainer	homeopathix.lab.collat	Updated	12/04/2004 15:01 PST	ApacheWebContainer	15	20	13342
ApacheWebContainer	homeopathix.lab.collat	Updated	12/04/2004 15:01 PST	ApacheWebContainer	88	100	13342
ProcessPool	homeopathix.lab.collat	Updated	12/04/2004 15:01 PST	homeopathix.lab.collat	/usr/local/apache//bin	./httpd -d /usr/local/ap	13420

Figure 1-4 A deep level of detail on changes reveals old and new values

Reporting and auditing

Taking into account the inherent complexity in the original environment, adding into the need for change to occur in a predictable manner, there is another consideration which comes into play with regularity—the need to quantify what has happened (reporting), and increased scrutiny of these reports, auditing. Currently the effort entailed with just gathering the information and certifying its correctness in considerable, and it is a generally accepted truism that most data is obsolete almost before the ink dries on the report. There is, however, an increased awareness in today's IT world that there are significant auditing initiatives which must occur for certain industries, and the penalties for incorrect data can include jail time. Since these audit initiatives are conducted for different end goals, such as ensuring security of sensitive patient data, or access to critical applications is limited, or that code purchased is indeed running in the companies environment, very often the methods for gathering this information leads to conflicts of their own. Again this is a function that needs to be quantified and automated as much as possible to reduce potentially disastrous results. Figure 1-5 shows a sample drift report in which different versions of component configurations are compared, and differences highlighted.

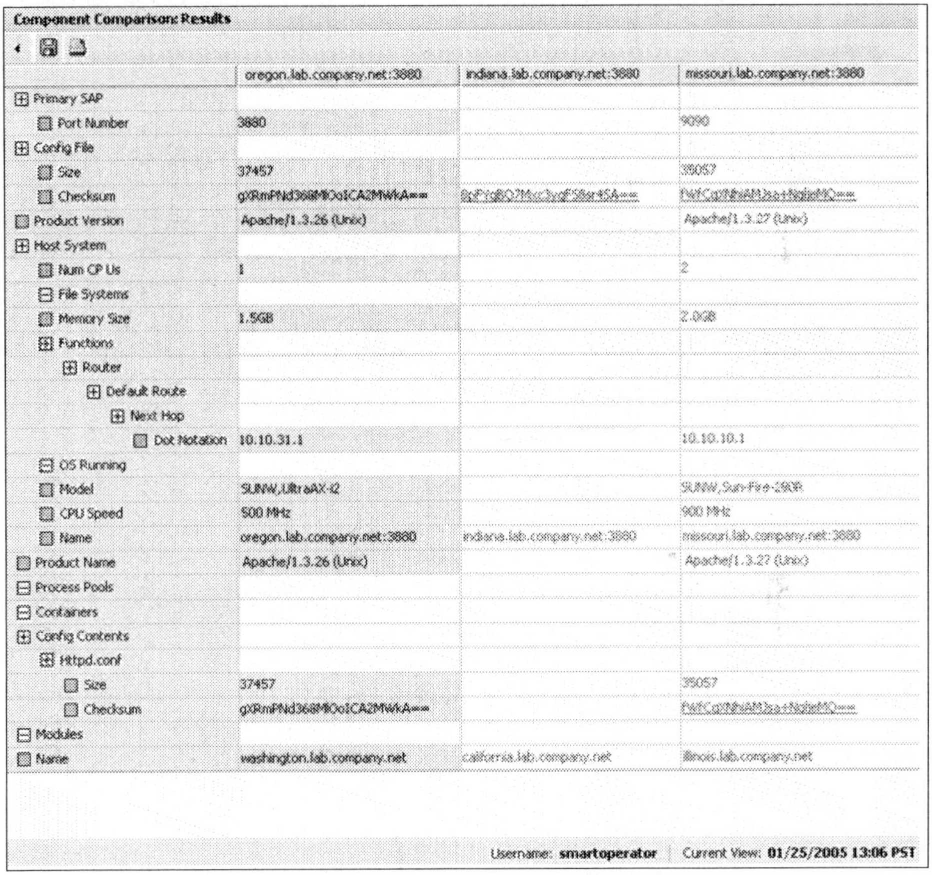

Component Comparison Results

	oregon.lab.company.net:3880	indiana.lab.company.net:3880	missouri.lab.company.net:3880
Primary SAP			
Port Number	3880		9090
Config File			
Size	37457		35057
Checksum	gXRmPNd368MOoICA2MWkA==	[illegible]	[illegible]
Product Version	Apache/1.3.26 (Unix)		Apache/1.3.27 (Unix)
Host System			
Num CP Us	1		2
File Systems			
Memory Size	1.5GB		2.0GB
Functions			
Router			
Default Route			
Next Hop			
Dot Notation	10.10.31.1		10.10.10.1
OS Running			
Model	SUNW,UltraAX-i2		SUNW,Sun-Fire-280R
CPU Speed	500 MHz		900 MHz
Name	oregon.lab.company.net:3880	indiana.lab.company.net:3880	missouri.lab.company.net:3880
Product Name	Apache/1.3.26 (Unix)		Apache/1.3.27 (Unix)
Process Pools			
Containers			
Config Contents			
Httpd.conf			
Size	37457		35057
Checksum	gXRmPNd368MOoICA2MWkA==		[illegible]
Modules			
Name	washington.lab.company.net	california.lab.company.net	illinois.lab.company.net

Username: **smartoperator** Current View: **01/25/2005 13:06 PST**

Figure 1-5 A comparison readily shows drift across configuration items

The tracking functions of IBM Tivoli Change and Configuration Management Database Configuration Discovery and Tracking provides the necessary capabilities to identify un-authorized changes to the infrastructure, which in turn will help you streamline your processes and the accountability of the entire IT organization.

1.2.2 IBM IT Service Management: the answer to your prayers

IBM IT Service Management addresses these needs through our process managers and operational managers, and the critical CMDB which provides access to the proper information to enable these components. Another avenue to pursue to further integrate Configuration Discovery and Tracking with third party applications is supplied by IBM in the Open Process Automation Library (OPAL). This is a catalog containing extensions for over 500 IBM Tivoli and Business Partner products, and contains information and executables useful in extending Configuration Discovery and Tracking in its IT Service Management role.

The Open Process Automation Library in brief

The Open Process Automation Library is a catalog of over 500 Tivoli and IBM Business Partner extensions designed to extend IT Service Management and process automation. Configuration Discovery and Tracking users will find executables and information about how to integrate Configuration Discovery and Tracking with third party products, as well as automation techniques to speed implementation of IT Service Management into your IT Department. There are also white papers which outline differences in techniques (agentless technologies versus agent-based solutions) and solution code for topics ranging from monitoring Apache Databases with ITM 6.1 to Tivoli and Micromuse event flow integration.

The resources available at OPAL can be further researched at the following IBM Web site:

`http://catalog.lotus.com/wps/portal/topal`

1.2.3 What Part does Configuration Discovery and Tracking play as the CMDB?

IBM Tivoli Change and Configuration Management Database Configuration Discovery and Tracking fulfills the role of the CMDB, plus more, but right now lets just take a look at core functionality as regards the configuration information central to keeping track of our efforts in the IT environment.

A Configuration Item (CI) is a basic unit of information describing a host machine, or an application, or instructions or documentation of process in our computing environment. A fundamental task which goes into managing these CIs is to determine the level of detail which is necessary to track function and dependencies between these CIs. The more information available, the more that can then be deduced about the CIs' role in the network environment. However that comes with a price as well, because the information must then be stored in a database accessible by the CMDB. Another overhead component is that the information for these items must be entered in some fashion. If this takes too long, it will render the starting information incorrect, or jeopardize the completion of the entry effort as other tasks become pressing in the day-to-day of the typical IT department. Configuration Discovery and Tracking resolves these two possibilities in that it performs auto discovery of CI information with a minimum of effort, and without agents that would have to be installed on each system, along with the overhead that entails. Configuration Discovery and Tracking also automates this discovery process, and allows it to be broken up by logical scopes to reduce the effort to manageable pieces. Furthermore, Configuration Discovery and Tracking gathers information that is running in memory to nullify the possibility that applications that can be started from command line with runtime flags that override configuration files will be entered incorrectly into the CMDB, as is possible if just scanning these configuration files alone would lead to. Configuration Discovery and Tracking can also federate multiple databases to consolidate existing information as well as avoid having to create a monolithic database with overhead and size constraints of its own.

Configuration Discovery and Tracking also has the capability to handle the central information broker role on CIs for the IT Service Management solution through API calls, real-time integration with select third party applications, and the use of Discovery Library Adapters (DLAs) and the bulk loader to capture DLA input from operational managers. Once this critical component is in place, the discussion can then shift to how it is supported with process managers and operational managers.

1.3 Why have a Change and Configuration Database?

With all vendors offering a configuration management database strategy and only a few offering true Configuration Management Database (CMDB) capability, it is critical to know the difference between a CMDB and a configuration database or asset/inventory database.[1]

1.3.1 The value of the CMDB

ITIL describes a CMDB as a core enabling technology for IT Service Management that accounts for all IT assets, provides accurate information to support other Service Management processes, provides a sound basis for Incident, Problem, Change, Configuration and Release Management and enables the verification (and correction) of records against the IT infrastructure. These individual records, or Configuration Items (CIs), contain details about the attributes, change history and nature of any relationships between them.

[1] The information in this section is mainly based on Gartner's report "CMDB or Configuration Database: Know the Difference", Author: Ronni J. Colville, Publication date: 13 March 2006

Sharing a common configuration database enables IT processes to flow across technology silos; this also ensures a more definitive and consistent source of configuration data across the enterprise. A CMDB improves management of the IT environment by providing a single source of truth to ensure data consistency and simplify integration between differing service management processes—it is essential for a real-time view of the IT environment, giving IT the ability to respond to business needs while controlling and securing the infrastructure.

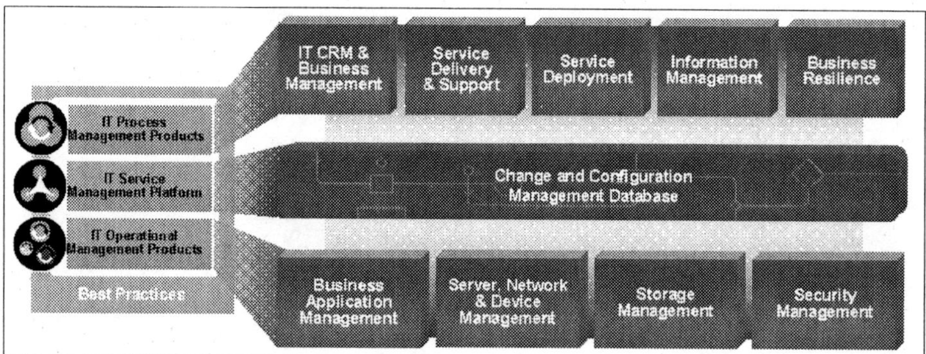

Figure 1-6 Everything references the CCMDB in the IT Service Management strategy

Challenges to building a CMDB

Every enterprise is buzzing about how to, when to, and who should build a CMDB. Even organizationally, there is a mixture of groups advocating that they should own the CMDB. But, clearly, a significant amount of building awareness is coming from the vendors. It seems that every vendor has a CMDB. So the real question is: Where to get the one that builds the platform for IT Service Management?

Creating and maintaining a comprehensive IBM IT Service Management CMDB that represents today's IT services and its infrastructure can be very challenging:

- IT infrastructure visibility challenges

  Distributed application architectures (such as J2EE™ and .NET) are very complex and are composed of several components that span several IT silos, software applications, systems, network, storage, and so forth. To completely represent the application infrastructure, the CMDB solution should provide the capability to represent a wide variety of infrastructure components. The CMDB should also provide the capability to extend the representation support customer specific components and configurations.

- Infrastructure change

  Data center infrastructures change constant. As a result, it is critical that the CMDB solution provides the capability to update the CMDB dynamically to accurately reflect the changing infrastructure and to maintain the freshness and accuracy of its data.

- Data integration challenges

  The CMDB represents a consolidation of heterogeneous data managed by different enterprise organizations. Many of these organizations enforce their own data ownership and security policies. Many of these applications also implement custom data update/synchronization polices, which vary significantly. Hence, to get widespread deployment, the CMDB solution should also support the security and data ownership policies of the application administrators. Furthermore, the CMDB architecture should support a wide variety of integration technologies to easily interface to the existing applications.

- Scale of data challenges

  Enterprise IT infrastructures can easily extend to thousand of servers and therefore the CMDB must scale to support very large IT environments. Furthermore, because the CMDB also aggregates several other IT-related data, the CMDB architecture should support the ability to support very large volumes of data effectively.

To support today's enterprise IT needs and objectives, further architectural requirements of the CMDB solution include the following:

- Data sharing

  Because all IT services depend on the CMDB, the CMDB solution should provide an abstraction interface to allow multiple applications to easily integrate and cost effectively to the underlying data store. Furthermore, since this data store needs to be integrated to a wide variety of applications and processes, the interface should be open and published.

- Platform services

  As the CMDB provides a common data platform, it should also provide the capability to develop and share common services. By using these services across all the applications, the CMDB implementation will eliminate the need to building custom capabilities at the application level.

- Rapid deployment

  The CMDB solution should be quickly deployed and with low overhead for customers to realize fast return on investment.

Building a CMDB with existing data stores

Contrary to the flood of marketing brochures, there is no CMDB per definition available today. Some vendors are developing a strategy with a set of application programming interfaces (APIs) layered onto current products that federate together the data between the products. Others have added capability to new releases that blends the data into one monolithic data store, and yet others are using established data stores to build out to include more data. But regardless of how the vendors are proposing to provide a CMDB solution, none provides all the features and functions needed for a comprehensive CMDB.

Because the IT Infrastructure Library (ITIL) does not prescribe a process to build the CMDB, enterprises implementing IBM IT Service Management have embarked on several different approaches to creating the CMDB:

- Manually created CMDB

  Many organizations that are starting out on IBM IT Service Management deployments begin by manually creating their CMDB. This approach might work well for very small IT organizations, where the IT staff laboriously documents the IT infrastructure and related data to create a home-grown CMDB. This approach however, does not work for today's typical application infrastructure, which is large, complex and ever changing. In these enterprises, it is impossible for manual approaches to keep up with the changes to accurately maintain the CMDB. Hence, manual CMDB creation and maintenance is not an option for most IT organizations trying to implement ITIL across their entire IT infrastructure.

- Process-created CMDB

  Most enterprises use IT processes to create and maintain CMDBs. Process-based approaches usually start out with manually creating a baseline CMDB or importing data from well-established processes around the Service Desk or Help Desk. After they are created, change management processes are used to control and update the infrastructure changes into the CMDB to maintain the accuracy of the CMDB. Unfortunately, because these changes are manually documented by the users and administrators of the solution, process-based solutions do not accurately capture the full details and the effects of changes. Furthermore, because many process-based approaches lack a structured service model, these solutions also do not provide analytic capabilities (such as impact analysis or historical change trends) to allow users to plan and execute changes accurately.

- ITIL-compliant CMDB

  Today, several ITIL-focused vendors offer out-of-the-box CMDBs. While these data stores offer a comprehensive and broad set of ITIL-compliant schema and model representation, they do not offer any capabilities or tools to populate these models. Customers who choose these solutions are stuck with the task of creating and maintaining these models, significantly impeding ITIL implementation.

Successful approach to building a CMDB

The CMDB represents the integration of several different enterprise applications and their data. Given the complexity and scale of the integration involved, it is critical that organizations take a phased approach to build the CMDB. Without a careful process, identifying an optimal starting point and then following a phased integration approach to integrate other applications, creating the CMDB will be very expensive and time-consuming.

At the core of ITIL are the IT applications and their supporting infrastructure components. Therefore, the ideal starting point to create the CMDB is a database of the IT application and its IT infrastructure. Today, there are several application discovery solutions that provide an unparalleled level of visibility into how the infrastructure actually delivers the applications on which the business relies. These solutions automatically create and maintain cross-tier maps of the application and its supporting infrastructure. These application maps also include the deep configuration values of the supporting infrastructure components and their run-time dependencies. After it is created, this database can be integrated to the other enterprise applications including:

- Process applications
- Organizational data applications

Besides discovery, the CMDB must provide the following critical functions, which distinguish the CMDB from other tools:

- *Reconciliation* ensures the data is coalesced; avoiding duplicates and enabling matching of configuration items from different sources.
- *Federation* brings in multiple data sources directly and also by linking to sources.
- *Mapping and visualization* enable a peer-to-peer and hierarchical view of the CIs.
- *Synchronization* ensures the same version of the truth across integrated systems.
- *Access controls* ensure only the right administration changes are made to the schema and access is monitored at the CI level.

Tools marketed as CMDBs that do not have all four critical functions will require significant human resources to provide them.

Reconciliation

Reconciliation is the ability to rationalize the same instance of a CI or component that might come into the CMDB from multiple sources. One discovery tool might see a UNIX® device by a hostname, another might discover it by an IP address, and additional technology by its Media Access Control (MAC) address. Reconciliation ensures that there is only one instance of this server with the right configuration data represented in the CMDB.

The most challenging aspect of reconciliation is to be able to determine that the same instance of a component or CI coming from different sources might have different naming conventions. Reconciliation also must include capability that checks the relationship for integrity to ensure that the managed linkages are both semantically and actually accurate. Therefore, the CMDB must ensure that the reconciliation engine can determine that multiple identities are actually the same component or CI to enable the CMDB to be the hub between different management tools.

Federation

Federation enables multiple data sources to feed some level of data or just link data stores and configuration repositories into the CMDB while the individual IT domain sources continue to maintain detailed configuration information about an infrastructure component. It is impossible to store and manage all configuration data of an enterprise in a single CMDB.

Federation is not just integration (as done in tools for discovery data) or the ability to bring data into a new data store (such as integrating device information into an asset tool). It is the ability to bring multiple data sources into a coalesced view where the various feeds come together to represent a view with relationships across components.

Mapping and visualization

Mapping and visualization provide the ability to illustrate logically and physically the peer-to-peer and hierarchical relationships between CIs. IT service management tools must discover applications, underlying servers, storage devices, and load balancers, as well as switching fabric to show peer-to-peer and hierarchical relationships across them. In addition, the visualization of the direction of the relationships is core to facilitate IT in managing business services.

Tools (such as Configuration Discovery and Tracking) can run as stand-alone dependency mapping discovery solutions. They build the foundation for a CMDB to be able to visualize all relationships across all CIs from a variety of federated data sources.

Mapping and visualization also includes reporting and analysis capabilities such as running reports to see what applications reside on specific resources or components.

Synchronization

Synchronization is the ability to update the CMDB with approved changes, as well as to identify changes that are not approved. After a baseline is established, comparisons are made against various sources. If inappropriate changes are detected, a notification is triggered to a change management workflow to alert the appropriate IT domain to investigate and potentially remedy the drifted configuration. This results in achieving the goals of closed-loop change control.

A CMDB enables the ability to provide input into the risk and impact analysis of a planned change with a view of the interdependencies of one IT component with respect to another (such as helping to understand the impact of a vulnerability in one application on all of its associated components). This capability will also be able to help IT organizations quickly identify when a system is not in its desired state, although the CMDB would be working in conjunction with its federated data sources to achieve this.

Access controls

Access controls ensure that only the appropriate roles (humans, as well as tools and systems) have read and write access to the information. This is a bigger requirement than one might think at first glance. Because of the federated nature of the information, updates to the CMDB might not update only the central store, but also likely cascade to the trusted source, or perform the reverse and report on the discrepancies.

CMDB is on the agenda

Today CMDB seems to be on every IT organization's to-do list. Some companies have very clear ideas of why they need to implement, but others are struggling to justify the investment.

As many organizations decide whether to embark on a CMDB, they struggle to identify the business case justification and to quantify the anticipated benefit. Whatever the driver, the business case justification for a CMDB is usually tied to high-visibility projects, such as security auditing, change management, process re-engineering (that is, ITIL), improving availability of mission-critical systems and compliance initiatives. The IT organization is challenged to correlate this data to provide better service management to the business and a more cohesive view of the IT infrastructure.

A practical approach for a successful implementation of a CMDB requires a federated data model with a consistent view that receives at least some data from element-specific tools (for example, desktop configuration management, server configuration management, network management, and storage management). However, many other feeds are required to build a comprehensive map of the entire infrastructure (for example, purchasing systems and asset management). The driver for this renewed focus on an integrated view is that IT must define services from end-user devices to servers, networks, storage, applications and data to better serve the ever-changing and dynamic nature of business needs.

CMDB enables IT Service Management

ITIL describes a CMDB as a core enabling technology for IT service management that:

- Accounts for all IT infrastructure assets and components
- Provides accurate information to support other service management processes
- Provides the basis for Incident, Problem, Change, Configuration and Release Management
- Enables the verification (and correction) of records against the infrastructure

These individual records, or Configuration Items (CIs), contain details about the attributes, change history, and nature of any interrelationships between them.

Sharing a federated configuration database enables IT processes to flow across technology management islands and ensures a more definitive and consistent source of cross-tier components, configuration data and interrelationships across the enterprise. A federated CMDB improves management of the IT environment by providing a source of truth to ensure data consistency and simplify integration between differing service management processes. A CMDB is essential for providing a Real-Time Infrastructure (RTI), giving IT the ability to respond to business needs while controlling and securing the infrastructure.

1.3.2 Using the CMDB to create the IBM IT Service Management Solution

IBM IT Service Management (ITSM) helps organizations better manage their IT infrastructure, to more effectively and efficiently deliver IT services. IBM can help ensure IT service continuity—optimizing IT costs by automating reactive IT management processes; create resilient IT services.

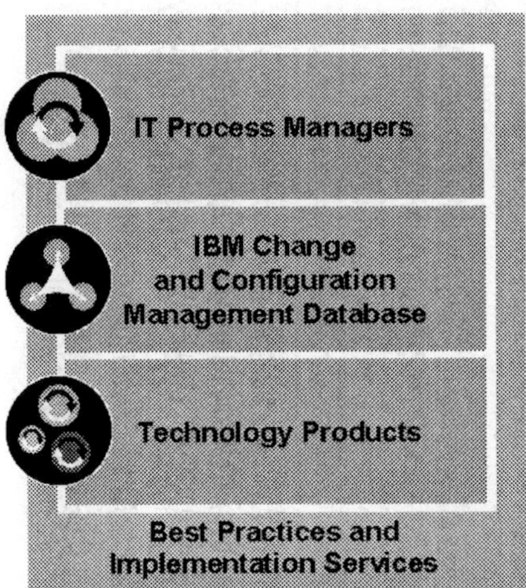

Figure 1-7 IBM IT Service Management Overview

At the intersection of business and technology is the road sign to the future. Compliance, complexity, speed of change, and cost are driving the need to evolve IT from a technology to a business focus. As these uniquely positioned to help customers meet business and IT challenges with products that use autonomic technology, service-oriented architecture, as well as process tools and deep consultative expertise which will enable them to realize faster time to value.

ITSM integrates processes, data, and tools

There are four capabilities IBM provides to customers when helping them delivering IT as a service with repeatable efficient processes:

- Automate specific tasks in a process with Tivoli and other IBM products.
- Standardize and share information across these tasks and tools with IBM IT Service Management platform which includes the Change and Configuration Management Database (CCMDB) concept.
- Address customer's pains with IBM Tivoli's process oriented solutions.
- IBM has used its experience and best practices into designing the above three solutions and IBM also provides packaging and installation services.

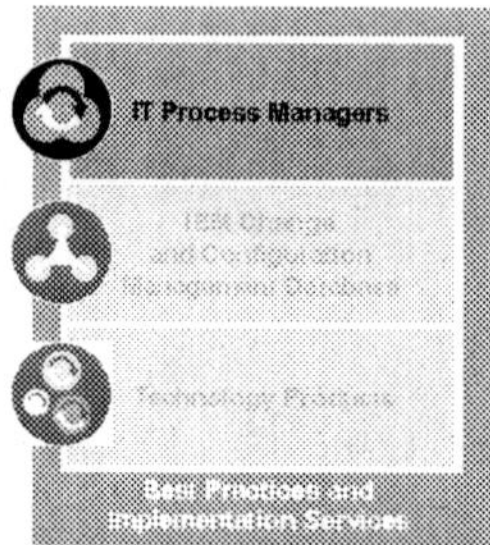

Figure 1-8 ITSM Process Managers

IT Process Management products

To further assist IT managers in their deployment of ITIL best practices, IBM has developed IBM Tivoli Process Managers. A collection of predefined, automation packages, Tivoli Process Managers outline the people, resources and information needed to create IT processes that are repeatable, measurable and efficient. Tivoli Process Managers include:

- Process modules – Predefined implemented processes
- Adapters – To integrate with current products
- SDK – Software Development Kit to customize and integrate with best-of-breed solutions

More details about Process Managers are provided in 1.4, “Process managers” on page 23.

IT Service Management platform

An essential component of the IBM IT Service Management infrastructure, IBM Tivoli’s Change and Configuration Management Database (CCMDB) delivers a federated view of the enterprise’s IT data, including information about hardware, software and the relationships between them. In addition, it provides a process foundation for the delivery of value-added solutions for release management, availability management and storage management. The Tivoli CCMDB also integrates IT service functions into a unified, automated infrastructure management platform, which helps IT organizations to:

- Consolidate information between disparate IT environments.
- Create synergy between different IT service management functions.
- Optimize the management of IT service demands.
- Maximize IT performance and ROI.

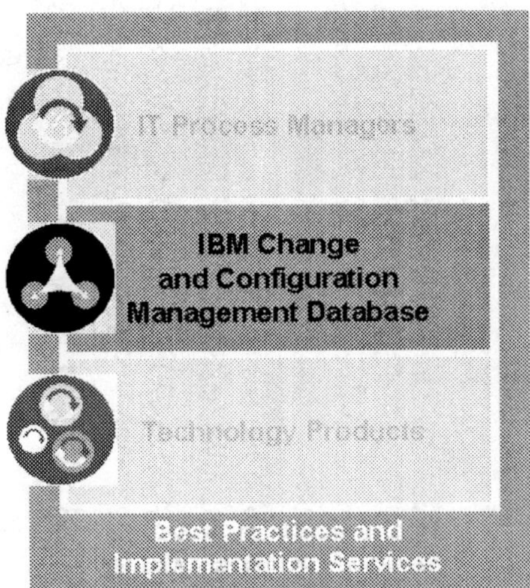

Figure 1-9 ITSM Change Configuration Management Database

On its own, the IBM Tivoli CCMDB provides a way to consistently collect, manage, distribute, and interpret management information and changes to the infrastructure. But the power of the combined database, workflow and modeling toolkit shows most clearly when it is used to simplify and integrate specific services and processes that formerly required extensive manual interventions to bridge gaps between people, platform and process silos.

IT Operational Management products

IBM product offerings use automation and virtualization technology, enabling IT organizations to further maximize IT efficiency. IBM component-based adoption models and roadmaps allow customers to integrate IT management processes on a time frame that best suits their business. Because IBM solutions are based on industry open standards, customers can optimize the processes they have now, and in the future.

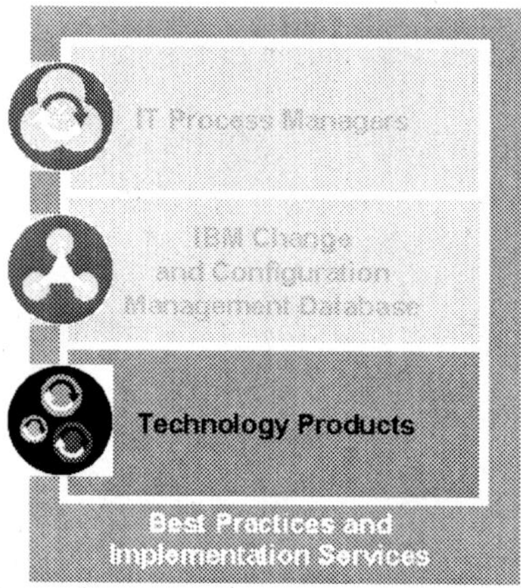

Figure 1-10 ITSM Operational Management products

IBM IT Service Management is built on a solid foundation of technology and products. For all practical purposes, Operational Management Products can be thought of as the standard IBM Tivoli products for Business Automation, Performance and Availability management, Provisioning and Orchestration, Storage and Security management. Further details of strategic Operational Management Products provided by IBM can be found in 1.5, "Operational managers" on page 26.

Best Practices And Implementation Services

IBM has used its experience and best practices to design the IT Service Management process accelerators, IBM Tivoli Change and Configuration Management Database, and its technology and products. IBM also provides consulting, packaging, and installation services.

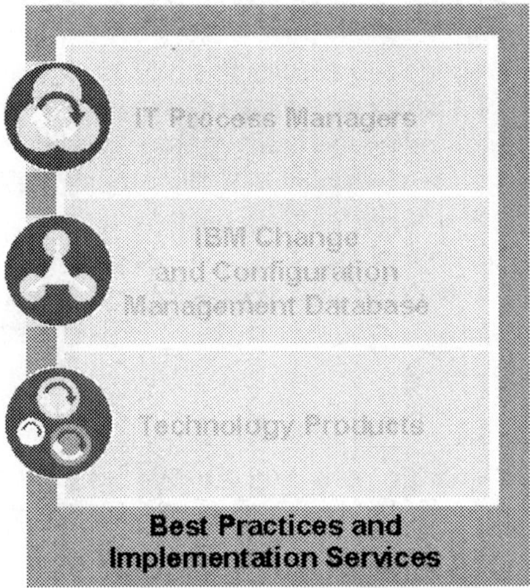

Figure 1-11 ITSM Best Practices

1.4 Process managers

Process managers are a part of IBM IT Service Management architecture and provide process solutions for organizing the approach to IT challenges. Three process managers of note are the Configuration manager, Change manager, and Release manager. We will go a little further in depth on each one, and explain a little bit more about the parts they play in IT Service Management.

1.4.1 Configuration manager

Configuration Management provides discovery of applications, hardware, and the dependencies between them, whether they are transactional, containment, or service dependencies. One primary function of Configuration Discovery and Tracking is generating and storing this information, as well as providing analytics to provide change history, comparison across like components, and versioning capability to assist in auditing efforts associated with the CMDB in ITIL best practices.

It should be noted that this function provides base-level information about the configuration items, which while detailed, is a different thrust than that of asset Management, which also focuses on accounting information, and often tracks leasing and retirement information of assets in the corporate computing environment. Also, Configuration Discovery and Tracking tracks dependencies between components, which Asset Management does not track.

The configuration manager also provides a central repository for configuration item information—Incident Management and Problem Management tools utilize this data to understand what components are involved in an outage and then to track down the root cause of a problem. This provides benefit in that it reduces the amount of time needed to resolve issues in both short term and long term fixes. Quick access to configuration item data by the appropriate people across disparate sources (usually referred to as silos in many large IT environments) allows them to quickly perform trend analysis, and approach a widespread IT problem systematically rather than the traditional method of working machine by machine or application by application until the root cause is discovered and applied throughout the network.

Configuration Item information is also extremely useful in the realms of change Management and Release Management, two other areas of focus according to ITIL principles. The configuration manager supplies Configuration Item information as a touchstone to understand the ramifications of proposed and completed changes, and these in turn update the CMDB with information about completed changes and deployed releases, keeping the CMDB information current and useful.

Service Level Management also uses the CMDB to store information, for its' ability to provide a measurement of how effective the IT department is in providing business services to the rest of the company, and allowing IT to accurately reflect the cost and usage of critical business services, such as e-mail, database storage, or network bandwidth usage to accept customer sales requests. These concerns tie into Availability Management which uses the CMDB to define areas of availability and unavailability, and also into Capacity Management which allows planning for future usage in a smooth transitional execution rather than allowing resources to run short and effectively hindering the business from maintaining any competitive edge it gains from its' use of technology.

1.4.2 Change Manager

The Change Manager tool in the IT Service Management and ITUP strategy utilizes the Configuration Item information stored in Configuration Discovery and Trackings' CMDB to provide the basic information needed such as machine configuration, application configuration, version levels and dependency mapping to ensure that the correct items are being used to implement proposed changes to the computing environment. The Change Manager itself includes a means of enforcing standard change methodology including scheduled change reviews, rollback plans in case the change does not work as expected, as well as emergency change procedures in response to security issues or critical application updates for industry competitiveness. The Change manager also provides utility for standard changes occurring within departmental policy and emergency change procedure for those falling outside of policy but still deemed necessary. The Change manager also provides control and management of implementing changes subsequently given approval.

The Change Management tool also interacts with other process managers in the IT service Management model. By sending approved Requests for Change (RFCs) to the Release Management tool, the Change Manager enables a smooth transition from planning to implementation. Change Management also interacts with Problem management by providing a structured framework for RFCs related to problem resolution, ensuring that emergency problem management does not degrade Configuration Item information in the CMDB by not reporting accurately the number and types of changes that occur to resolve a specific problem. Change Management also interacts with Availability and Capacity Management ensuring proper recording of proposed enhancements to infrastructure and configuration items through RFCs. Availability and Capacity management also assess RFCs in the Change manager to ensure that they do not negatively impact the current infrastructure, and that proper levels of availability and capacity are maintained to satisfy current service level agreements.

The Change manager also accepts input from the Financial management tool to ensure that costs attributed to a specific change remain within budget.

1.4.3 Release Manager

The Release Management tool is used in instances of a change large enough to require extra planning, as it can affect a large number of configuration items. This would include instances such as rolling out a new business application, a new set of Web servers to provide an enhanced user interface across multiple Web servers, or network upgrades to increase performance across specified business units or geographies. Release Management also involves adding configuration item information in the form of documentation and operating procedures, which would then be held in the CMDB for future reference.

Release Management consumes information from the Change manager in the form of RFCs, information from the CMDB to identify the proper configuration items to alter or deploy, and provides information to Incident management and Problem Management about errors identified during the release process.

1.4.4 How do the Process Managers integrate with Configuration Discovery and Tracking?

Process managers integrate with the CMDB using the process engine, and process models which ensure process execution consistency. Configuration Discovery and Trackings' CMDB utilizes an open and documented API and data model to enable the addition of information to the CMDB, and extension of the data model to capture configuration item information that the customer might feel is needed above and beyond the level of detail Configuration Discovery and Tracking already captures with its' out of the box sensors. Configuration Discovery and Tracking comes with over 200 sensors covering popular software application servers such as DB2®, WebSphere®, WebLogic, Oracle, Apache, as well as common Operating systems such as AIX®, SunOS™, HP, Windows®, and even routers. As well as these pre configured sensors, Configuration Discovery and Tracking allows the creation of custom server templates to allow definition of internally developed applications. There is also a lab in Perth, Australia dedicated to creating new sensors as well.

1.5 Operational managers

Operational managers are meant to address very specific IT challenges, such as Availability Management, which includes systems monitoring (IBM Tivoli Monitoring) or Event Management, which includes TEC and TBSM, which we will explain further in a later paragraphs. These managers provide a superior depth of functionality, generally carry out the functions described in process managers, and directly act on Configuration Items in Configuration Discovery and Tracking's CMDB. Operational Managers interact with data in the CMDB through Discovery Library Adapters and API calls, and also take advantage of a new bulk loader, which has been developed for the CCMDB in the June release. This bulk loader takes information from Discovery Library adapter books provided by the Operational managers named above and loads it into the CMDB to update large numbers of configuration items pertinent to the operational managers' role, and that information is then available for other processes to utilize as necessary.

The following links are related resources on the IBM World Wide Web:

- Configuration Management
- Incident Management
- Problem Management
- Change Management
- Release Management
- Financial Management
- Security Management

You can also visit (and download your own copy of) the IBM Tivoli Unified Process model:

`http://www.ibm.com/software/tivoli/features/it-serv-mgmt/itup/index.html`

Here you can find more details on how the features of each Operational Management Product supports your IT processes.

1.6 Roadmap for a successful ITSM implementation

To achieve an IT organization's short, mid-term and long-term objectives with the ITSM strategy, the focus should be based on the business values around the CCMDB and Process Managers.

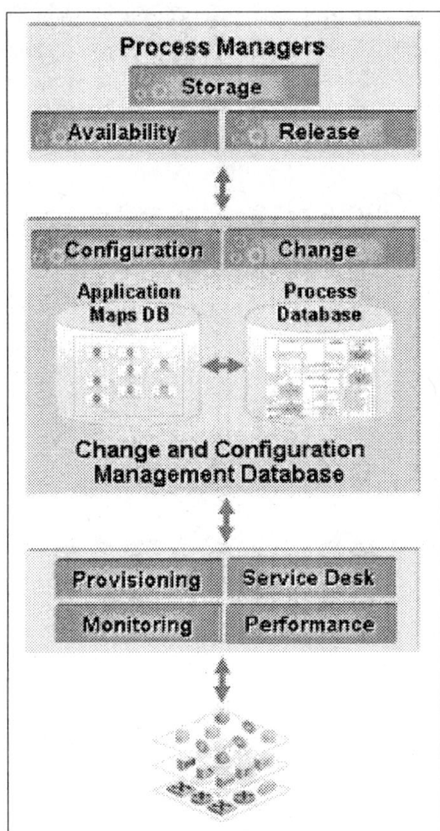

Figure 1-12 ITSM Strategy Roadmap

In a phased implementation of ITSM based on IBM CCMDB, deployment of IBM Tivoli Change and Configuration Management Database Configuration Discovery and Tracking is a natural first step. The three major phases are:

1. Visualizing the existing environment using Configuration Discovery and Tracking
2. Establish a federated CCMDB and integrate data with existing solutions

   and
3. Deploy IBM Tivoli Process Managers and Operational Managers

1.6.1 Visualizing the existing environment through Configuration Discovery and Tracking

For IT organizations to gain visibility and take action to optimize their application infrastructure, they need to understand what they have, including what the logical and physical locations are, what the interdependencies are; and most importantly, what the usage and demands are on a continuous basis.

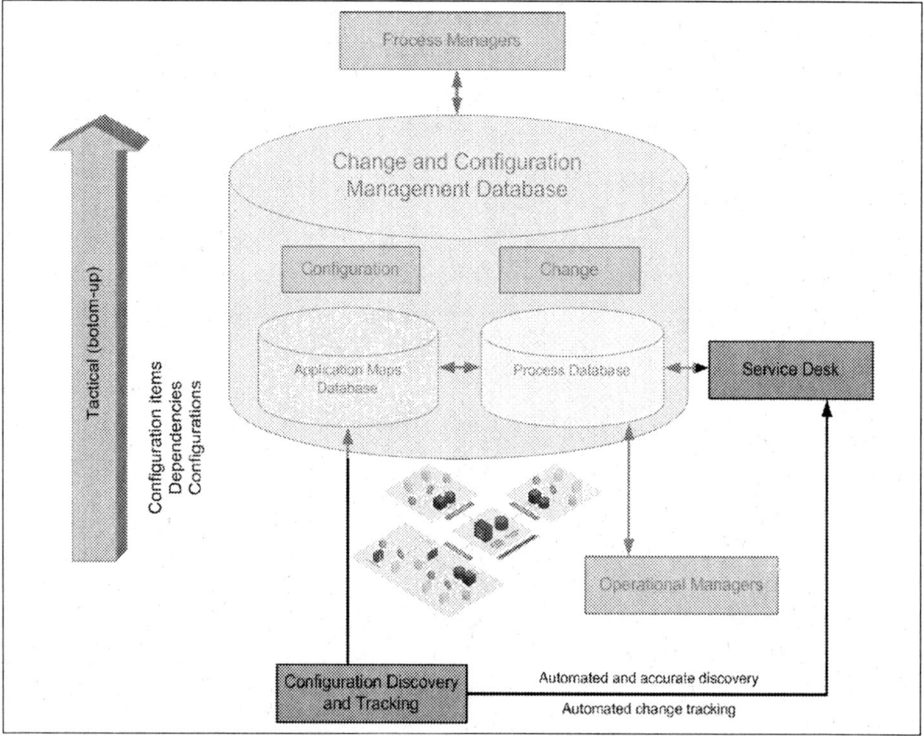

Figure 1-13 Application infrastructures and dependencies are unveiled

Benefits

With IBM Tivoli Change and Configuration Management Database Configuration Discovery and Tracking v1.1 and its predecessor product IBM Tivoli Application Discovery and Dependency Manager IBM has demonstrated how organizations can jump-start ITIL initiatives by first using agentless auto-discovery technologies to quickly and continuously populate a federated CMDB with an inventory of physical resources (network devices, hosts, storage devices), applications (software services) and the inter-dependencies of these resources and applications.

By implementing Configuration Discovery and Tracking, IBM Tivoli customers have achieved benefits like:

- Identified what service configurations look like (versus what they thought they looked like).
- Discovered and documented installations of applications for audit or compliance initiatives, such as Sarbanes-Oxley and Basel II.
- Built a service view of all of the components (such as networks, servers, application components and database servers) for better impact analysis or root-cause analysis.

Configuration Discovery and Tracking value

The most frequent need expressed by IT organization is the desire for a deeper understanding of how infrastructure components relate to each other. Organizations use this understanding to make more informed decisions during change impact assessment and during problem isolation.

This IT service dependency mapping of Configuration Discovery and Tracking addresses the need for information and understanding as well as the change, audit and compliance needs for many data centers and application environments. It is also integral to many other management disciplines.

1.6.2 Establishing a federated CCMDB and integrate data with existing solutions

Enterprises will continue to have a variety of drivers for CMDBs, which include:

- Cost efficiencies
- Process engineering initiatives around configuration and change management
- Audit and compliance initiatives
- Raised attention to security
- Increased change activity and IT and business alignment

As many IT organizations decide whether or not to implement a formal CMDB, they struggle to identify the business case justification and to quantify the anticipated benefit. When undertaking a CMDB, businesses have different drivers that led them to that decision, however, whatever the driver – the benefits seem to be clear:

- A real-time or near-real-time view of infrastructure components (also known as configuration items) and their dependencies within and across each other
- Improved risk assessment
- Improved root cause analysis
- More reliable change management
- Facilitates service management

Many organizations are looking to broaden discovery beyond servers and applications to more than just one more component. This could support the premise that these discovery tools are being used as a starting place for many CMDB initiatives, for two reasons.

- First, having accurate configuration data about infrastructure components is a critical requirement for any CMDB initiative.
- Second, with one-third of the first group presumably using this type of tool, they had already gained insight on one aspect of their data center, and now they were looking to broaden the dependency view.

IBM Tivoli CCMDB: The strategic approach

There is new awareness emerging in enterprises that is causing them to take a more detailed look at CMDB technology.

At the heart of ITSM lies the Change and Configuration Management Database (CCMDB). Much more than a simple registry of physical assets, it provides an accurate inventory of customers IT resources and the relationships between them.

An essential component of the IBM IT Service Management infrastructure, the IBM Tivoli CCMDB delivers a federated view of all your enterprise's IT data, including information about hardware, software, and the relationships between them. In addition, it provides a process foundation for the delivery of value-added solutions for release management, availability management and storage management.

The IBM Tivoli CCMDB also integrates IT service functions into a unified, automated infrastructure management platform, which helps customers to:

- Consolidate information between disparate IT environments
- Create synergy between different IT service management functions
- Optimize the management of IT service demands
- Maximize IT performance and ROI

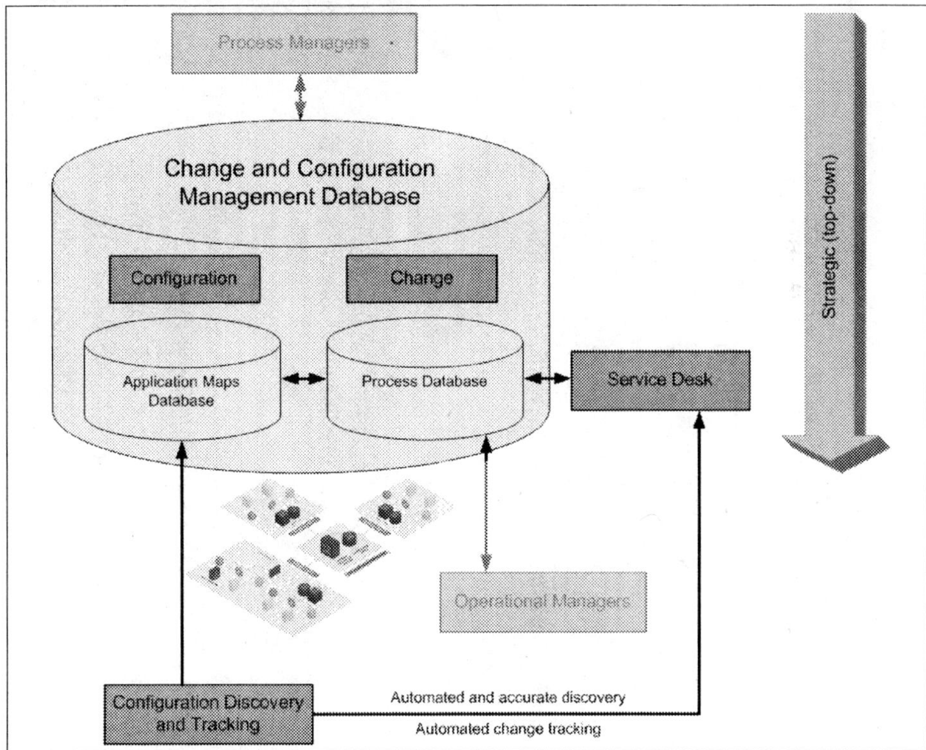

Figure 1-14 Streamline™ processes using IBM CCMBD and process managers

A CMDB strategy is central to the IT Service Management framework implementation described in the IT Infrastructure Library (ITIL) documents. ITIL outlines two main areas of this framework:

- Service support to enable effective delivery of IT Services
- Service delivery which outline the management of these services

Projects require this CI (Configuration Item) data in order to begin to take advantage of these best practice frameworks, therefore the need for the CMDB.

1.6.3 Deploying IBM Tivoli Process Managers and Operational Managers

By adopting a federated CMDB approach, IT organizations can use repositories throughout their environment through integration and utilization of open interfaces to share data. However, this is just a portion of the information needed and does not begin to give the organization the continuous application infrastructure data required to build their overall best-practice strategies.

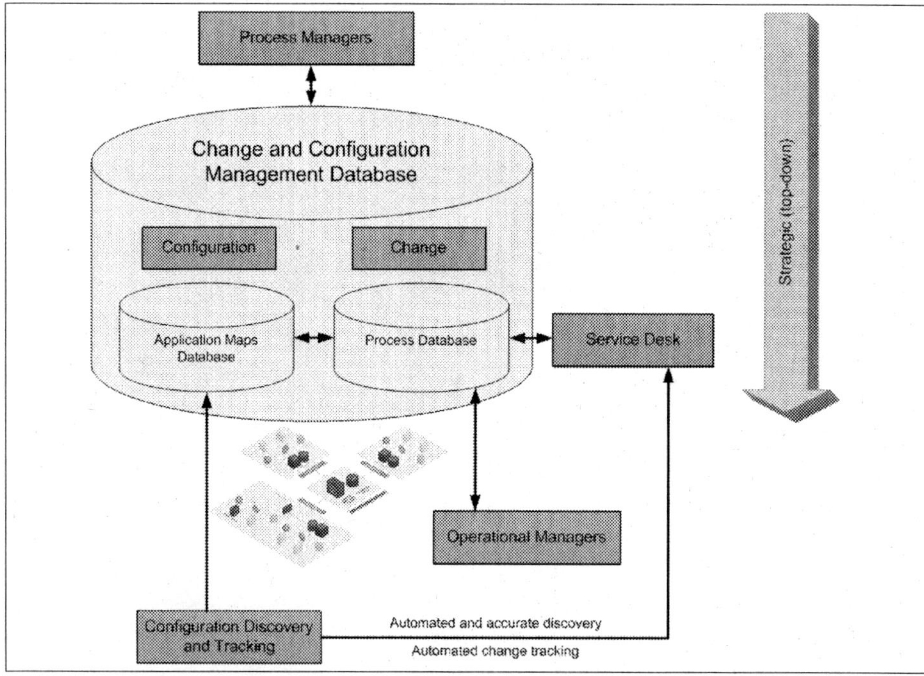

Figure 1-15 Automate processes through Operational Managers integration

To further assist IT managers in their deployment of ITIL best practices, IBM has developed IBM Tivoli Process Managers. A collection of predefined, automation packages, IBM Tivoli Process Managers outline the people, resources and information needed to create IT processes that are repeatable, measurable and efficient. For example, IBM Tivoli has designed process managers for three main components of the ITIL architecture—release management, availability management and storage management—which enable customization and allow for in-house or third-party product integration.

1.7 Discovery technologies: A brief comparison

The following provides a brief discussion on the benefits of using agentless technologies for discovery, and well as a comparison between discovery and inventorying technologies. For a more in-depth discussion of the differences and similarities of agent-based versus agentless discovery technologies, please see Appendix A, “Agent-based versus agentless application Discovery” on page 309.

1.7.1 Agent-based versus agentless discovery

Discovery solutions deliver two types of agents to discover and collect configuration information. The first is a *resident agent* which is installed on the target system to be managed and the second is *agentless,* which actively probes the target system without installing agent technology. The intent of this appendix is to compare both approaches.

Technology behind discovery solutions

There are two distinct approaches to building an automated discovery solution. Most discovery solution vendors have use the traditional monitoring technologies to provide an agent based solution to discover the underlying infrastructure components and create application maps. In this approach, the vendor expects the customer to install and manage a “small” application on each server/host that the user seeks to discover; the applications are persistently running and monitor updates.

There is, however, another approach to solving this problem. Many IT Infrastructure components offer standard protocol-based access and query mechanisms. These open and secure access protocols can be use to provide an agent-free discovery technology to automatically discover, create and maintain these application maps. Since this approach requires no agents, the customer does not have to deploy any application or manage their life cycle.

The choice of the underlying discovery technology: agent-based or agentless, significantly impacts the achievable Return on Investment (ROI) for the customer in terms of time and expense to deploy and maintain the solution, as well as other operational overheads to be aware of as one deploys the solution. The solution evaluator therefore should understand the differences between the approaches to quantify the value proposition of the solution.

Limitations of agent-based discovery solutions

Most of the current agent-based discovery solutions have severe limitations:

- Agent Installation and Configuration

  Agents require IT administration staff to install small applications on all hosts that they wish to discover. It is a non trivial task to manually deploy these applications in a large environment. Even when deployed through software distribution tools, agents require expensive post-distribution configuration (including kernel modifications in some cases).

- Agent Maintenance

  Agents require constant maintenance work; especially in today's data center environments which abounds with several OSs and disparate infrastructure components. In such a heterogeneous environment, just keeping track of the deployed agents and their OS compatibility is not a trivial task and allocates human resources. Also, every change in OS platform will force a fork-lift update to deployed agents and add significant costs to the ongoing maintenance.

- CPU and Network Resource Utilization

  Most agent-based solution vendors claim to use minimal CPU and network bandwidth. However small the footprint of an agent can be, this finite resource consumption can dramatically affect peak hours operations of the mission-critical applications being provided by the IT department.

- Quality Assurance

  In order to comply with a host of regulatory requirements, many enterprises IT organizations are mandating strict requirements on the IT infrastructure. In such infrastructures, proprietary applications can only be deployed once they have been thoroughly tested and qualified. This qualification process increases the total cost and time to deploy agent based solutions.

- Security

  Agent-based solutions are potential candidates to create security holes within an infrastructure, as they offer yet another mechanism for malicious users to exploit. This fact could add concerns for the security administrators who are already overburdened with ensuring security policies for the mission-critical applications.

Current distributed application technologies have advanced to a point where they can be easily discovered, queried and configured without requiring local instrumentation (for example the JMX™ instrumentation technology for J2EE application servers, WMI for Windows). The instrumentation supported by remote technologies, offer more breadth and depth of control as well as configuration data than what is offered through local, agent-based instrumentation.

Configuration Discovery and Tracking's agentless Discovery solution

IBM Tivoli Change and Configuration Management Database Configuration Discovery and Tracking provides complete enterprise visibility of all business critical applications. Configuration Discovery and Tracking application maps provide an accurate view of all business systems including their software, system and network tiers components, their runtime dependencies and configuration settings. At the core of Configuration Discovery and Tracking is an agent-free discovery engine that uses light-weight "discovery sensors" to automatically discover the infrastructure as well as create and maintain the application maps.

The benefits of Configuration Discovery and Tracking's agent-free discovery technology include:

- Rapid time to market

  Because Configuration Discovery and Tracking does not require the deployment of any agent application on the enterprise hosts, enterprises can be up and running with the application dependency discovery solution in a very short period of time; providing high Return on Investment (ROI). Upon installation, Configuration Discovery and Tracking's agent-free discovery starts building the enterprise application topography and can produce results rapidly. Unlike proprietary agents, Configuration Discovery and Tracking discovery sensors use standards protocols and pre-deployed utilities (such as SSH, SNMP, JMX, WMI, LDAP, SQL, and PS) to discover and query infrastructure components. Therefore, Configuration Discovery and Tracking require no time consuming configuration of the infrastructure for discovery.

- Low maintenance costs

  Configuration Discovery and Tracking uses standard discovery protocols and therefore requires no changes to support platform/OS upgrades. Support for applications components only requires Configuration Discovery and Tracking support for the new sensor, as opposed to the time and labor intensive task of upgrading hundreds on predeployed agents. Configuration Discovery and Tracking sensors can be easily extended in the field or added through the Configuration Discovery and Tracking sensor factory.

- Minimal Operational Impact

  Configuration Discovery and Tracking has been architected to consume minimal (typically less than 1%) CPU and network resources during its discovery process. Enterprises can easily schedule Configuration Discovery and Tracking discovery runs during off-peak hours (for example right after a midnight change window), to minimize the impact of the discovery process on the delivery of mission critical services. The Configuration Discovery and Tracking discovery schedules are typically limited to a specified subset of the infrastructure, thus allowing the customer to perform discovery on the infrastructure that matters most, while mitigating the resource impact of the discovery process.

- Enterprise Security Policy Compliance

  Configuration Discovery and Tracking has been architected to comply with common enterprise security policies. Configuration Discovery and Tracking sensors use standard and secure protocols such as SSH and WMI to discover and query the infrastructure components. Furthermore, because the sensors are not continuously running applications, they do not compromise the customer's security policies.

1.7.2 Application discovery versus inventory

IT executives should be encouraged to learn that, far from creating a redundancy, Application Discovery and Dependency Mapping solutions and Inventory/License Management solutions strategically complement one another. Each technology is providing different but synergistic benefits while using many of the same investments in software tools, implementation, and staff.

- Application Discovery and Dependency Mapping

  IT service dependency mapping tools such as Configuration Discovery and Tracking discover IT Configuration Items (CIs), everything from user devices to servers, networks, storage, operating system software, applications and databases. They also document and track the relationships between the CIs by automatically mapping dependencies from IT services (or business applications) down to the CIs that enable those services.

- Inventory Management

  Inventory management solutions provide automatic scanning and collecting information about the server and workplace enterprise hardware and software components.

- License Management and Metering

  License management enables achievement of a total software-asset management solution, enabling planning, management and optimization of enterprise wide software assets. With advanced software inventory, usage monitoring, contract and reporting capabilities, customers can know exactly what software licenses they have, which ones are being used and which ones they need. In addition, these offerings help organizations to efficiently manage the contractual and financial details of software contracts and agreements.

Table 1-1 Technology comparison - Discovery versus Inventory

	Application Discovery and Dependency Mapping[6]	Inventory Management	License Management and Metering
Product core capability	Build the foundation to create a comprehensive CMDB that identifies application and its infrastructure dependencies	Create a comprehensive inventory of installed hardware and software components	Enable planning, management and optimization of enterprise wide software assets
Product maturity	Early market deployments focused on ITSM initiatives	Mature market product	Mature market product
Scope of support	Primarily data center and server infrastructure	Server and client (desktop) infrastructure	Server and client (desktop) infrastructure
Infrastructure support	Focused on server infrastructure – supports hundreds of key data center components	Provides broad support for wide variety of infrastructure including desktop applications; thousands out-of-the-box signatures	Provides broad support for wide variety of infrastructure including desktop applications; thousands out-of-the-box signatures
Discovery technology	Agentless discovery technology	Agent-based discovery technology	Agent-based discovery technology
Discovery characteristics	Focused on running applications; no (out-of-the-box) discovery of installed components	Focused on installed applications	Focused on tracking usage metrics
Performance and scale	Optimized for Configuration item (CI) and configuration discovery	Optimized for asset/inventory discovery	Optimized for asset/inventory usage

1.8 Summary

In this chapter we obtained an introduction to the IBM Tivoli Change and Configuration Management Database Configuration Discovery and Tracking product and several important supporting structures IBM has positioned around it to integrate it into a working IT Service Management environment. We learned a little about ITIL and about ITUP, IBM Tivoli Unified Process model, and the benefits they can bring us. We learned about Process Managers, and how they use a process engine to activate process models which define workflow to deliver consistency in execution of tasks in the IT environment. We learned about Operational Managers which execute specialized functions in the IT environment and communicate with Configuration Discovery and Tracking in its' CMDB role, and about OPAL, a community effort designed to extend Configuration Discovery and Tracking and other IBM and Tivoli products. The following chapters will go into more depth of the inner workings of Configuration Discovery and Tracking, hopefully this introduction has served to illuminate why it would be of use and interest in your own IT environment.

1.8.1 Business benefits of CMDB

The business benefits of CMDB are described in the following sections.

CMDB provides visibility of the enterprise IT assets

CMDB discovers assets across the enterprise or a part of it and gets detailed configuration data of IT assets, including hardware, software and network and communication equipment. This data is useful to:

- Make informed decisions when making changes to the assets
- Reconcile asset data in asset and financial management systems
- Optimally utilize the available assets
- Plan for capacity augmentation
- Plan for service continuity and
- Plan for new releases.

CMDB maintains the change history of enterprise IT assets

CMDB maintains the history of all changes to every individual IT asset and includes new additions, modifications and deletions. The change history data is useful to:

- Verify if approved change requests have been implemented and
- Identify unauthorized changes.

CMDB provides information for asset dependencies

CMDB discovers and maintains the dependencies between IT assets and this is useful to:

- Perform impact analysis
- Perform risk analysis
- Plan for new releases and
- Plan for service continuity.

CMDB improves the performance of Process Managers

CMDB provides real time data on Configuration Items (CIs) to Process Managers[2] helping them become a more reliable and useful process infrastructure. For example, a change management system becomes more useful, if it can get real time asset dependency data from the CMDB to perform impact analysis.

CMDB helps organizations comply with ITIL

CMDB automates the most critical and difficult process management activity in the IT Infrastructure Library domain. It not only addresses the Configuration Management needs but also helps other process managers to perform efficiently and effectively.

[2] Process Managers are the IT service management tools for Change Management, Asset Management, SLA Management, Availability Management, Information Life Cycle Management, Configuration Management, Release Management etc.

2

Configuration Discovery and Tracking terminology

Today's IT organizations are under enormous pressure to deliver high levels of service with agility and efficiency. At the same time, they often find themselves in reactive mode, relying on inadequate tools and manual processes to solve problems that exist in an environment of rapidly increasing complexity and change. The complexity introduced by component architectures such as J2EE and .NET, increased virtualization of software, OS and networking layers as well as ever increasing business demands mean that having a shared understanding of how all of the IT infrastructure components are related and configured to actually deliver business applications is critical to IT's success[1]. Leading IT organization are now evaluating and implementing solutions to this problem using application mapping products such as IBM Tivoli Change and Configuration Management Database Configuration Discovery and Tracking (Configuration Discovery and Tracking). These solutions deliver a shared understanding of the components, dependencies and configuration of critical business applications. This visibility is critical in order to meet service level commitments, eliminate unanticipated change related problems, reduce problem resolution times, enforce technology consistency, process conformity and compliance policy and enable agile and responsive change.

[1] See Gartner (Colville) "Organizations Are Paying More Attention to Configuration Management" 31 March 2005; and Enterprise Management Associates, "The ITIL Configuration Management Database: Panacea or Pandora's Box?" December, 2004.

In order to achieve the necessary levels of visibility required, a solution must:

- Provide a fully automated and accurate application-centric view into the run-time structure of business applications including their software and hardware components, their cross-tier dependencies and configurations.
- Store these application maps and all of their associated data in a well defined application maps database that is:
  - Comprehensive enough to cover all common run-time datacenter components, yet flexible enough to meet the specific needs of each implementation
  - Detailed to include deep, run-time configuration and dependency information
  - Easily accessible and understood by operations personnel and
  - Programmatically sharable with other management and enterprise applications
- Scale to enterprise levels
- Provide its value rapidly, securely and at a low overhead.
- Deploy and work securely, consistent with enterprise security policies and infrastructure.

These are precisely the high level product requirements that drove the design and architecture of IBM flagship application mapping product, IBM Tivoli Application Dependency Discovery Manager (Configuration Discovery and Tracking). In order to meet these requirements, five critical design decisions were made in the architecture of Configuration Discovery and Tracking:

1. Build the product around a predefined, application-centric, standards based, extensible reference model, therefore eliminating the need for custom modeling with every implementation
2. Choose an agent-free approach to eliminating the performance and security risks and implementation and qualification expenses of deploying a new set of management agents
3. Publish a well-defined schema with a complete set of documented data and process level APIs, enabling rapid integration to existing management products and processes.
4. Provide the ability to federate and extend the application maps database, allowing the product to be deployed at enterprise scale.
5. Utilize existing secure protocols and standards, making implementation secure and straightforward.

The combination of these key design decisions translates into a solution that provides complete visibility into how the infrastructure delivers applications and services, can be securely and rapidly deployed, is easily integrated, scaled and extended, and whose overall cost of ownership is the lowest possible. Solutions lacking in any of these areas will face time and cost obstacles in successfully providing the visibility required to manage and improve service delivery.

This chapter intended to provide a technical evaluator with a detailed description of Configuration Discovery and Tracking's architecture and how the product works to deliver complete infrastructure visibility. It includes the following:

- An overview of the Configuration Discovery and Tracking architecture
- A detailed description of how the Configuration Discovery and Tracking product creates and maintains its application maps
- An explanation of the Configuration Discovery and Tracking APIs and integration capabilities
- An overview of the Configuration Discovery and Tracking deployment architecture
- A security, scalability and reliability overview

By deploying IBM Configuration Discovery and Tracking, organizations not only improve application availability and lower cost today, but they lay in the groundwork for building a truly scalable IT service management capability. The data and knowledge created by Configuration Discovery and Tracking is a key building block not only to improving service delivery and management, but to automating and enabling capabilities such as dynamic application provisioning, measurable and enforceable Service Level Agreements and effective IT Governance. The remainder of this paper will focus on how Configuration Discovery and Tracking is architected and works to deliver this capability.

2.1 Architecture overview

Configuration Discovery and Tracking's agent-free, model-driven architecture is depicted in Figure 2-1 on page 44. In this section, each element is briefly highlighted and described.

Next, 2.2, "Architectural details" on page 46 provides the details for each of the major architectural components, describing both the rationale for its design and an overview of its implementation, and explains how the pieces work together to populate the application mapping database and create and maintain application maps.

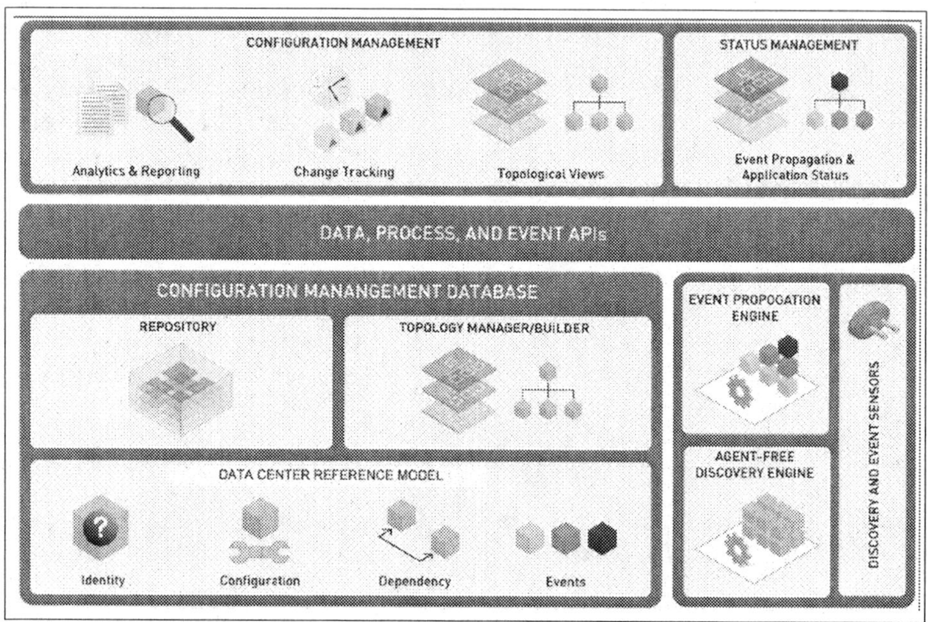

Figure 2-1 Configuration Discovery and Tracking Server Architecture

2.1.1 IBM Data Center Reference Model

This model represents the foundation of Configuration Discovery and Tracking and provides the definition for the data center applications and their supporting infrastructure components, cross-tier relationships and configuration attributes. Without a reference model, implementation would be dependent on expensive, time-consuming, incomplete and error-prone manual modeling. Configuration Discovery and Tracking provides out-of-the-box definitions for a wide variety of commonly deployed software applications, hosts, network devices and network services. The extensible reference model includes an event propagation model, which provides the underpinnings to interpret infrastructure component events in the context of the applications that they deliver.

2.1.2 Agent-free discovery engine

The discovery engine orchestrates and manages the discovery process. The engine instructs the *discovery sensors,* which are server-based components that use the knowledge built in the reference model to interrogate the data center components and gather the necessary information to build the application maps database.

2.1.3 Topology Manager and Builder

Upon completion of the discovery process, the topology manager consolidates the discovered data and generates a cross-tier topological representation of the application. The application topology includes its underlying infrastructure components (software, systems and network components), and their associated configurations and cross-tier dependencies.

2.1.4 Configuration Discovery and Tracking Application Map Database

The Configuration Discovery and Tracking database is a cross-tier representation of the application topology, its components and their configurations. The database also tracks and documents all configuration changes. The Configuration Discovery and Tracking database is optimized for both read and write access and supports extensive query capabilities.

2.1.5 Configuration Discovery and Tracking API

Configuration Discovery and Tracking's open and published API interfaces easily with third party ecosystem applications. The Configuration Discovery and Tracking API provides authenticated and secure access to the underlying Configuration Discovery and Tracking database (through the Data API) and the Configuration Discovery and Tracking process engines (through the Control API). Configuration Discovery and Tracking also provides an event API to import and export events to other management applications.

2.1.6 Configuration Discovery and Tracking user interface

Accessing the Configuration Discovery and Tracking database and the Configuration Discovery and Tracking Discovery engine through the Configuration Discovery and Tracking APIs, the Configuration Discovery and Tracking User Interface provides command and control of the Configuration Discovery and Tracking server, advanced topology visualization and management, and a robust set of change and configuration analytics.

2.1.7 Configuration Discovery and Tracking Application Status Manager

Using Configuration Discovery and Tracking's topology based event propagation model, the Application Status Manager imports component events from monitoring solutions through Configuration Discovery and Tracking event sensors. Events propagate within the context of their supporting business applications, providing near instantaneous impact of component level events on application health.

2.2 Architectural details

The following provides the details for each of the major architectural components, describing both the rationale for its design and an overview of its implementation, In addition, it is explained how the pieces work together to populate the application mapping database and create and maintain application maps.

2.2.1 The Data Center Reference model

The Configuration Discovery and Tracking Data Center Reference model represents a definition of data center infrastructure components, their cross-tier relationships and configuration attributes. The Data Center Reference Model is based on the DMTF's CIM object model. See

`http://www.dmtf.org`

For platform-specific extensions such as JSR773, see

`http://www.jcp.org/en/jsr/detail?id=77).`

The reference model includes a wide variety of object types, including software components (Web, application, and database servers), hosts and operating systems, network elements (routers, switches, load balancers, firewalls, and storage) and network services (LDAP, NFS, and DNS), and is easily extensible based on customer-specific needs.

The model representation for each component type includes:

- Signature

  The signature uniquely identifies the component type and its dependencies and configuration template.

- Configurations

  Configuration data elements include the static and the dynamic configurations of the component, the run time resources the component uses (for example, the JDBC™ connection pools or the JMS topic queue used by an application server, the patches deployed on a OS or the IP routing table of a network element) and the deployed application objects (for example, the EJBs and JSPs on an application server) that implement the business application and services.

- Dependencies

  Dependencies model the run-time relationships among the various components within the data center. Configuration Discovery and Tracking discovers and categorizes several types of cross-tier dependencies, including:

  – Transactional dependencies

    The logical connections (IP based) between the components of a distributed application. These connections represent the provider-consumer relationships between the components. For example, an application server is the consumer of a service provided by a database server.

  – Containment dependencies

    Cross-tier hierarchical relationships (for example, an application server is deployed on a host) as well as logical grouping relationships (such as a Web, application and database server make up a business application).

  – Service dependencies

    Network services upon which most infrastructure components depend (NFS, DNS, and LDAP services).

2.2.2 Agent-free discovery engine and process

Configuration Discovery and Tracking's agent-free discovery engine manages the overall discovery process. The discovery process collects the data needed to instantiate the Data Center Reference Model to represent the specific data center infrastructure. Core to the discovery process are lightweight discovery sensors, which build upon the Data Center Reference Model to comprehensively discover the infrastructure components, their configurations and dependencies. Discovery sensors use open and secure protocols and access mechanisms to discover the data center components. Furthermore, unlike persistent and invasive agents, discovery sensors are centrally deployed and managed and consume minimal bandwidth and CPU resources (<1% when active) in the target environment. The discovery engine provides a workflow framework to schedule, distribute, coordinate and manage the various discovery sensors.

Discovery requirements

Configuration Discovery and Tracking discovery requires a minimal set of discovery setup information:

- The discovery scope

  Typically a valid IP range, subnet or a specific address, the discovery scope signifies the span of the discovery process.

- Access lists

  Access lists specify the read-only access credentials needed to discover and query the components for its appropriate configuration attributes and dependencies. The access mechanism varies based on the type of components discovered, for example:

  - SNMP (Simple Network Management Protocol) community strings to discover the network elements
  - SSH (Secure Shell) to discover the configuration and dependencies of the Unix hosts/operating systems
  - WMI (Windows Management Interface) to discover Windows OS and its applications
  - Protocols (such as JMX, SQL, LDAP, and others) standard access mechanisms to discover application software

- Schedule

  The Configuration Discovery and Tracking discovery process can be executed on demand, as part of a schedule, or driven by events that are triggered externally.

The discovery process

Upon discovery initiation, the Configuration Discovery and Tracking discovery engine proceeds through a multi-step process:

1. The discovery engine uses standard protocols to inspect the defined discovery scope to identify the IP nodes (address) of all installed devices.
2. For each valid IP node in the set, Configuration Discovery and Tracking launches a discovery sensor. The discovery sensors discovers and categorizes the component type by matching it to the appropriate signatures in the Data Center Reference Model
3. The discovery sensors then query the component for its configurations and dependencies.
4. The discovery process is iterative—each discovery sensor run can spawn a subsequent discovery sensor (for example, a host discovery triggers the discovery of applications and services that reside on the host) until the entire infrastructure is discovered.
5. Upon completion of discovery, Configuration Discovery and Tracking processes the discovered component data to populate the Configuration Management Database and generate a topological representation of the infrastructure.

6. Subsequent discovery runs update the maps database and topologies, while maintaining a comprehensive change history of the infrastructure configuration and dependencies.

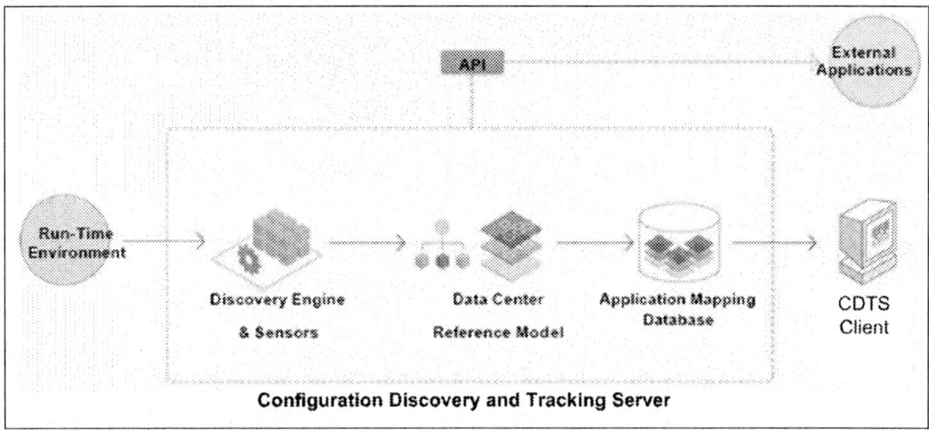

Figure 2-2 Configuration Discovery and Tracking

2.2.3 Discovery extensibility

IBM provides the broadest available out-of-the-box discovery coverage of any solution on the market. However, every datacenter has some unique or new requirements beyond those built into the Configuration Discovery and Tracking application. In order to meet the specific needs of each implementation, Configuration Discovery and Tracking's discovery coverage can be extended in three ways:

- Custom software components

  All running custom software processes are discovered out of the box by Configuration Discovery and Tracking. These discovered processes can subsequently be identified and categorized by their run-time signatures, allowing them to participate in configuration, change tracking and business service discovery. These custom server templates can be user created in minutes through the Configuration Discovery and Tracking User Interface and APIs.

- Off-the-shelf components

  Any data center elements not currently supported out-of-the box by existing Configuration Discovery and Tracking Discovery Sensors can be created in weeks by the IBM Sensor Factory. The IBM Sensor Factory is a set of flexible resources that can rapidly create, test and ship new Sensors independent of Configuration Discovery and Tracking's release cycle. The Factory is constantly creating new Sensors, and is scheduled based on customer demand.

- Existing or custom data sources

  Many customers have configuration data available in sources such as spreadsheets, files and other tools. The IBM Universal Data Sensor (UDS) allows for the scheduled importing and transformation of this data into the Configuration Discovery and Tracking model as part of the discovery process, allowing Configuration Discovery and Tracking to use existing data sources and management processes.

2.2.4 Business application discovery

In today's component architectures, business applications are composed of many interrelated software components. Currently, there is no standard way for the operations and service delivery teams to know what software components are a part of a given business application. IBM Configuration Discovery and Tracking provides two ways to automatically create and maintain these business application groupings

1. IBM Application Descriptors

   IBM Application Descriptors automate the process of creating and maintain business applications, by allowing developers or deployment managers to add simple XML files to application modules at the time of packaging, prior to deployment. IBM Application Descriptors are simple XML files that define business applications and the components that belong to them. Theses Application descriptors then allow Configuration Discovery and Tracking to automatically create and maintain the business application groupings. An example of an application descriptor file is shown in Figure 2-3 on page 50.

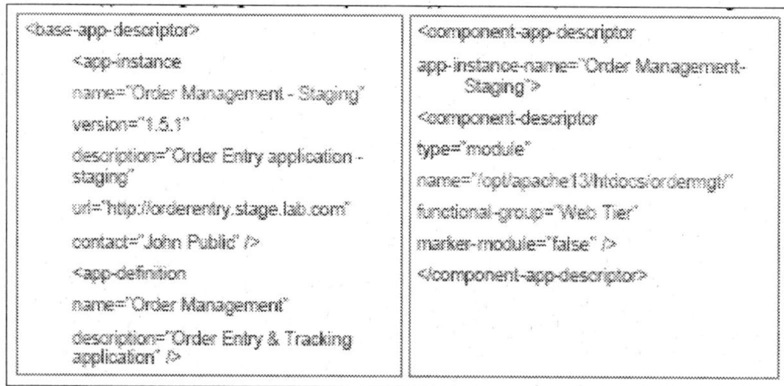

Figure 2-3 IBM application descriptors

2. Component and Application signatures templates

   In addition to application descriptors, Configuration Discovery and Tracking can also discover business applications by identifying component signatures, and designate matching custom components as *belonging to* a given business application or applications. The component templates specify the unique signature of the components by using combinations of items such as program names, ports and environment variables to classify the components; once classified, the business application template specifies the components that belong to the given business application. The components are then classified and grouped automatically during the discovery process. Representative component and application templates are show in Figure 2-4 on page 51. Custom Component and Application Templates define the components signature and application membership.

For example, in deploying a credit authorization application, which is composed of four components (Login Server, Gateway Server, BizLogic Server, and a Customer Database Server), Configuration Discovery and Tracking can use component and application templates to automate application discovery.

Based on unique signatures of the individual components (Example: An Apache application whose program name contains *login server*), Configuration Discovery and Tracking discovers and classifies the discovered servers as matching to the specific component templates. Based on the application template, the Discovery Engine adds the classified components to the credit authorization business application topology, thus eliminating any need to manually define application groupings. The component and application signature templates can be deployed in combination with the IBM Application Descriptors.

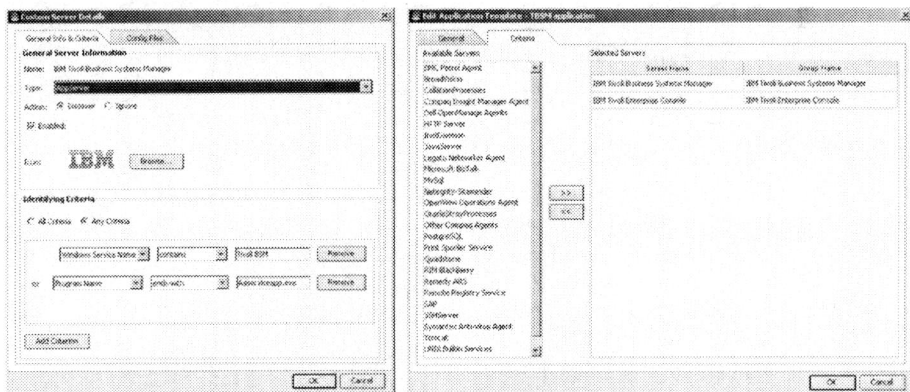

Figure 2-4 Custom component and application templates

2.3 Configuration Discovery and Tracking interfaces

IBM Tivoli Change and Configuration Management Database Configuration Discovery and Tracking provides several facilities for interfacing with the solution on both the operational level (initiating scans and manipulating data) and the data level (to synchronize several data sources). The following sections introduce these facilities.

2.3.1 Configuration Discovery and Tracking's provides open interfaces

The Configuration Discovery and Tracking API provides a secure and modular interface to the Configuration Discovery and Tracking database. The open and published API provides bindings such as Java, Web Services/SOAP and shell scripts. Configuration Discovery and Tracking enforces authenticated API access and upon authentication, all API clients are assigned access privileges, which authorize user actions. API access can also be encrypted through SSL to ensure maximum security. The capabilities of the API include the following:

- *Data APIs*, which provide access to the full application topologies including the components, their detailed configurations as well as their run-time dependencies. The Data APIs also provides access to Configuration Discovery and Tracking's change analytics and reporting. In addition, the data APIs allow for the import and storage of additional data pertaining to discovered components such as asset, financial and administrative information.
- *Control APIs*, which provide asynchronous access to the Configuration Discovery and Tracking discovery processes including discovery setup as well as the discovery scheduling and control. Using these APIs, third party solutions can control the Configuration Discovery and Tracking server, including initiation and abort of discovery runs.
- *Event APIs*, which allow the importing of third-party events into the Configuration Discovery and Tracking application topologies, exporting of change and state events from Configuration Discovery and Tracking to third-party consoles and products.

Using the APIs, IBM provides integrations to several leading ecosystem vendors, including Micromuse, Compuware, BMC Remedy, HP UP OpenView, and others. The Configuration Discovery and Tracking SDK includes sample integration code as well as integration tools that allow XML proficient programmers to easily implement custom integrations in the field.

2.3.2 Configuration Discovery and Tracking uses Discovery Library technology

As the CMDB becomes the central repository for configuration data for your IT components, chances are, that you want to load data which are already known and maintained by other management solutions into the CMDB (for example inventory data from Tivoli Configuration Manager, or monitoring probe data from IBM Tivoli Monitoring). Chances are, that you also might want to extract information from the CMDB to be loaded into operational systems management solutions (such as Tivoli Business Systems Manager or Tivoli Provisioning Manager) to reflect the most up-to-date configuration of the IT environment.

For these purposes IBM Tivoli Change and Configuration Management Database Configuration Discovery and Tracking supports the IBM Discovery Library technology which is based on the IdML industry standard format.

For each subsystem that supplies or consumes data, a *Discovery Library Adapter* must be created. Through the IBM in the Open Process Automation Library (OPAL) at:

`http://catalog.lotus.com/wps/portal/topal`

IBM along with Business Partners delivers , or will plan deliver, Discovery Library Adapters for specific solutions such as IBM Tivoli Business Systems Manager, IBM Tivoli Monitoring, IBM Tivoli Intelligent Orchestrator, IBM Tivoli Configuration Manager, Peregrine Service Desk, BMC Remedy, Relicore Clarity, Cendura, and many more.

Depending on the desired functionality (export, import, or both), a Discovery Library Adapter can consist of one or two components:

DLA Writer: A specialized program which extracts information from a system management solutions local data store, and generates a IdML formatted Discovery Library Book that can be read by DLA readers. The Discovery Library Adapter Writer is also knows as a DLA Author.

DLA Reader: A specialized program that reads Discovery Library Books, and inserts selected content (determined by the data needs of the system management solution) into the local data store of the solution.

In order to provide data to the Discovery Library, an author must map its local resource and relationship instance data to the IdML specification. This mapping can occur using an Extensible Stylesheet Language Transformation (XSLT) to generate an IdML file from the authors local format of the resources.

As shown in Figure 2-5, Configuration Discovery and Tracking provides its own general DLA Reader (known as the Bulk Loader) and DLA Writer (the api.sh utility).

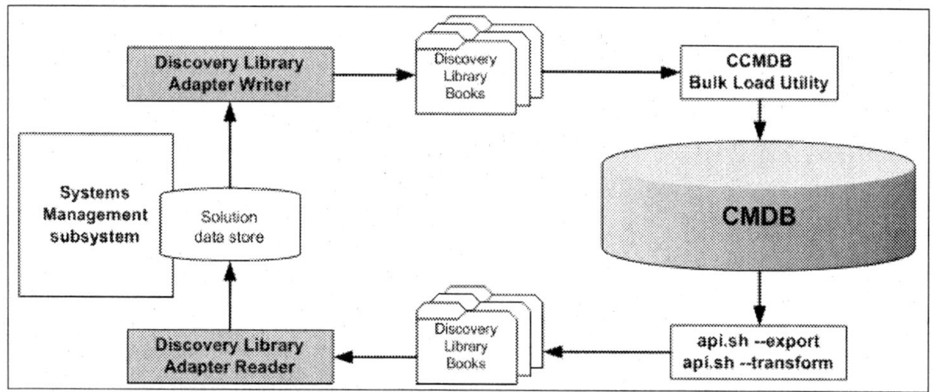

Figure 2-5 Discovery Library Adapter overview

The use of Discovery Library Adapters is asynchronous, and the generated DIscovery Library Books are stored on shared file system until consumed. It is the responsibility of the consumer (the DLA Readers) to keep track of which files have been read - and optionally delete them from the shared file system after successful processing.

2.3.3 Configuration Discovery and Tracking supports data federation

As enterprises embark on IT Service Management initiatives, IT managers are being asked to integrate several forms of data to provide actionable information to better manage their IT services. For example, the enterprise CIO might be interested in identifying the total investments in their mission critical applications or the CFO is looking to ensure that the financial applications are meeting regulatory compliance requirements. To satisfy these requests, IT managers must consolidate and correlate several different forms of data:

- Application infrastructure information (discovered and represented by application maps)
- Application asset information
- Financial data
- Application user information
- SLA metrics

Today, these data sets exist in heterogeneous applications and are managed by different organizations within the enterprise. Furthermore, the access control policies (who gets access to what data, as well as the application data *life cycle*, meaning how often the data is updated or refreshed, could differ dramatically across these applications. Hence, brute force consolidation of this data into a central repository is not an option. To work with these enterprise application integration issues, Configuration Discovery and Tracking offers an elegant data federation technology. Rather than consolidate data into one central repository, the Configuration Discovery and Tracking federation technology enables *just-in-time* access of data from these heterogeneous data stores to create accurate and consistent reports that can support the IT organization.

Configuration Discovery and Tracking's federation technology provides the following capabilities:

- Standard adapters

  The Configuration Discovery and Tracking federation platform provides *standard adapters* for several standard application data stores, including XML based databases, SQL databases, and csv/flat files. Each adapter securely stores the authentication credentials to access the datastore. Users can also build custom adapters as needed.

- Federation engine

  The *federation engine* allows users to create rules to access the datastore, to filter for the appropriate information (rows or XML data), and to *join* (correlate) these data streams to create the appropriate reports. The federation engine allows provides an API interface. Using the API interface, customers can write shell scripts and Java programs to access the federated datastores and create the reports.

- Reporting portal

  Configuration Discovery and Tracking a Web-based *reporting portal* for users to configure and view their reports. The Web-based portal is JSR 168 compliant and hence allows the reports to be easily shared within the enterprise. Users can also save custom reports and refresh them at prescheduled intervals to provide the most up-to-date information to the enterprise.

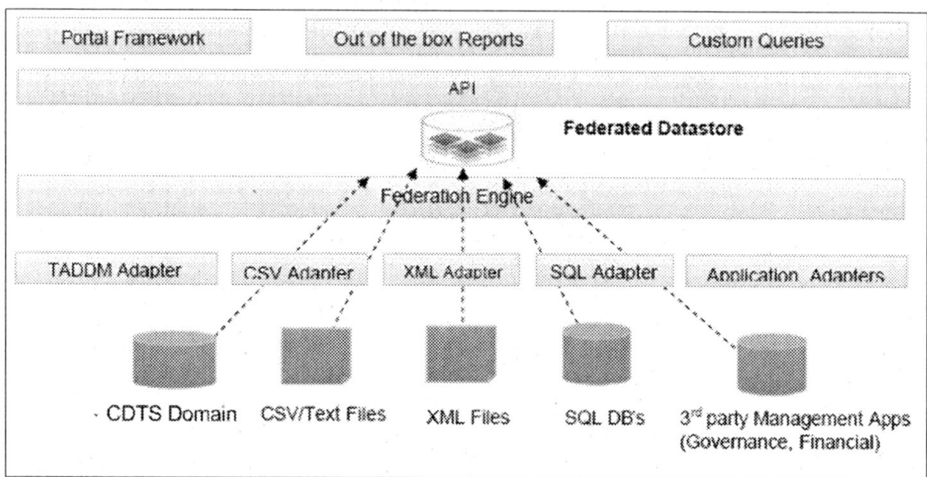

Figure 2-6 Configuration Discovery and Tracking interfaces

For more details regarding the Discovery Library Adapter support in Configuration Discovery and Tracking v1.1, refer to Appendix C, "Discovery Library overview" on page 387.

2.4 Configuration Discovery and Tracking Deployment Architecture

Designing your deployment of IBM Tivoli Change and Configuration Management Database Configuration Discovery and Tracking is a relatively simple matter. The architecture operates with only four basic components, which can be mixed and matched to meet the requirements of your environment. The four basic infrastructure components are:

- Configuration Discovery and Tracking *Database* is the Central Database hosting the CMDB. IBM Tivoli Change and Configuration Management Database Configuration Discovery and Tracking v1.1 supports DB2 UDB v8.2 and Oracle Database Server (8, 9, 10i/g).
- Configuration Discovery and Tracking *Server* is the main server hosting the Configuration Discovery and Tracking executables, and interfaces. IBM Tivoli Change and Configuration Management Database Configuration Discovery and Tracking v1.1 can be implemented on AIX 5.2, RedHat Enterprise Linux®

ES/AS 3.0, SUSE 9, or Solaris™ 2.8 or 2.9 with a minimum configuration of at least 2 CPUs (>1.5 GHz), 2 GB RAM and 2 GB of disk space.

The Configuration Discovery and Tracking server accesses the Configuration Discovery and Tracking Database through JDBC, and allows clients using the Product Console to access the server through HTTP or HTTPS.

- Configuration Discovery and Tracking Anchor *Host* is a distributed instance of the Configuration Discovery and Tracking Server (without the need for database access) that acts as a proxy for the Configuration Discovery and Tracking Server in order to overcome communication restrictions (for example because of firewall restrictions) or to relieve the central Configuration Discovery and Tracking Server of some of the workload.
- Configuration Discovery and Tracking Windows Gateway is a A Microsoft® Windows 2003 system acting as a Proxy Gateway between the Configuration Discovery and Tracking Server or local Anchor Host and any Windows systems to be discovered, which are not accessible through the SSH protocol. WinSSH needs to be installed on the Gateway, which in turn accesses the local WIndows systems through the WMI protocol.

  The hard and software requirements for the Windows 2003 server is a minimum configuration of at least 2 GB RAM, 2 CPUs, 1.5 Ghz CPU, 600 MB Free disk space.

In addition, IBM Tivoli Change and Configuration Management Database Configuration Discovery and Tracking provides two User Interfaces - one Web based for administration and reporting, and the Java based for operators. The interfaces are:

Domain Manager — The Web-based interface used for report generation and management of users and roles.

Product Console — A Java based fat client used by operators and administrative personnel that need access to the detailed configuration information in the database.

Both the Domain Manager and the Product Console can be run in normal or secure mode and are launched from a browser that has an active session with the Configuration Discovery and Tracking Servers Administrative Console page.

Important: For the most up-to-date information about hardware and software requirements for the various components, refer to the IBM Tivoli Change and Configuration Management Database v1.1: Administering the Configuration Discovery and Tracking feature and the IBM Tivoli Change and Configuration Management Database v1.1: Release Notes.

In large implementations, in which service centers are geographically dispersed—or business or LOB issues dictate this—the Configuration Discovery and Tracking environment can be split into several individual domains, which then can be controlled by an enterprise level Domain Manager, which in essence is nothing but another Configuration Discovery and Tracking Server with a special configuration.

The deployment architecture of IBM Tivoli Change and Configuration Management Database Configuration Discovery and Tracking scales easily - both horizontally (to provide faster scanning in a single domain) and vertically (to support geographically dispersed implementations) by replicating Configuration Discovery and Tracking Servers and Anchor Hosts.

2.4.1 Small Configuration Discovery and Tracking deployment and discovery

The typical starting Configuration Discovery and Tracking installation includes:

- Configuration Discovery and Tracking Server

  The Configuration Discovery and Tracking Server is installed on a AIX 5.2, Solaris 2.8 or 2.9 or RedHat Enterprise Linux ES/AS 3.0 or SUSE 9 with a minimum configuration of at least 2 CPUs (>1.5 GHz), 2 GB RAM and 2 GB of disk space.

- Configuration Discovery and Tracking database

  DB2 (UDB8.2), or Oracle Database Server (8, 9, 10i/g) or deployed on separate host/server.

- Configuration Discovery and Tracking client console

  Configuration Discovery and Tracking uses a browser-based client and requires no separate customer installation. The Configuration Discovery and Tracking client manages the Configuration Discovery and Tracking server and is the user portal to analyze the discovered application maps.

2.4.2 Windows infrastructure

Discovery Configuration Discovery and Tracking uses the secure Windows Management Interface (WMI) protocol to discover the Windows/.NET application infrastructure. Configuration Discovery and Tracking requires a dedicated Windows Gateway server that proxy's Configuration Discovery and Tracking server discovery protocols to the WMI protocol to discover the remote Windows infrastructure. The Windows Gateway servers requirements include:

- A Windows 2003 server with a minimum configuration of at least 2 GB RAM, 2 CPUs, 1.5 Ghz CPU, 600 MB Free disk space

- WMI accessible network connectivity to all remote Windows machines being discovered with local administrator access credentials
- SSH software to communicate between the Configuration Discovery and Tracking server and the Windows Gateway

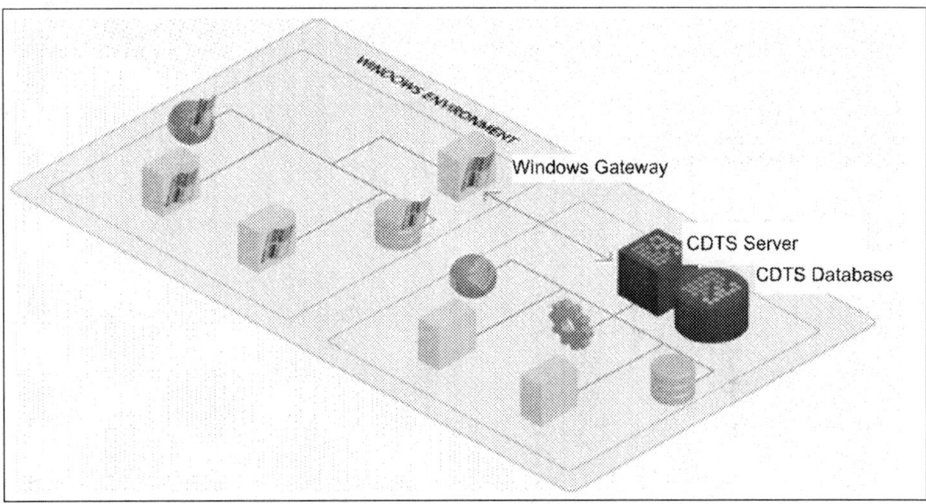

Figure 2-7 Configuration Discovery and Tracking Windows architecture

2.4.3 Configuration Discovery and Tracking discovery works transparently across firewalls

The basic Configuration Discovery and Tracking deployment requires network access to all the infrastructure elements within the specified IP scope. However, some applications can span firewall zones, where application infrastructure elements are separated by a firewall. For example, customer facing Web applications are deployed with a cluster of Web servers in a de-militarized zone (DMZ) with a firewall separating the DMZ from the back-end business and processing application. For security reasons, most enterprise IT policies do not permit opening ports in firewalls; some enterprises also implement restrictive filtering rules to block network access and to ensure secure communication.

Configuration Discovery and Tracking deployment architecture is designed to easily and securely work in such environments. To discover applications that span firewall *zones*, Configuration Discovery and Tracking automatically deploys *anchor servers* in the firewall zones. Anchor servers discover application infrastructure in the firewall zones; users only have to open a secure SSH port in the firewall to relay information to and from the central Configuration Discovery and Tracking server to the specified anchor server. The central Configuration Discovery and Tracking server consolidates the data from the anchor server to provide a comprehensive cross firewall view of the application infrastructure. Requirements for the Configuration Discovery and Tracking Anchor Server are:

- AIX 5.2, Solaris 2.8 or 2.9, or RedHat Enterprise Linux ES/AS 3.0 with minimum configuration of at least 2 CPUs (>900 MHz), 2 GB RAM and 800 MB of disk space
- SSH software to communicate to the central Configuration Discovery and Tracking server
- Network connectivity to the remote servers within the discovery scope in the firewall zone

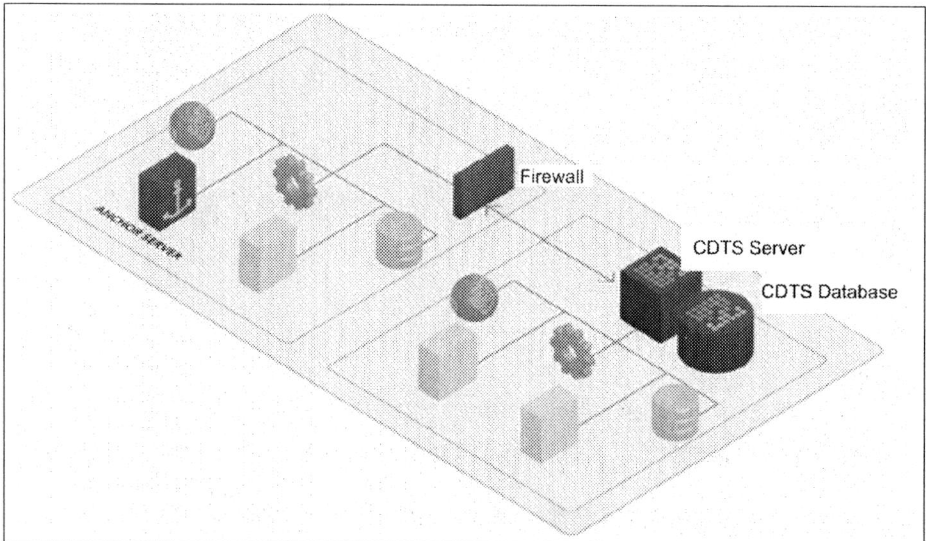

Figure 2-8 Configuration Discovery and Tracking works across firewall zones

2.4.4 Scaling Configuration Discovery and Tracking to meet enterprise visibility needs

IBM Configuration Discovery and Tracking is architected to modularly scale to very large data centers. A single Configuration Discovery and Tracking server can support around 10 000 physical servers.

> **Note:** A single physical server can host multiple software servers and can be connected to multiple network devices.

Customers can also tune Configuration Discovery and Tracking operating characteristics (that is, discovery engine thread counts, discovery sensor time-outs, and so on) as well as increased the Configuration Discovery and

Tracking server or Configuration Discovery and Tracking database resources (CPUs, memory, an so on) to achieve increased support for infrastructure discovery and storage.

While it is possible to scale Configuration Discovery and Tracking servers to support large enterprise environments, IBM offers a *domain-based,* best-practice deployment architecture to elegantly scale the solution to support several tens of thousands of infrastructure elements.

Most large enterprise environments are divided into *management domains* which represent the span of control of a given IT operations team. Domains can be based on organizational, functional, geographic boundaries, or combinations of these or other criteria. To support the operational needs of the domain, IBM recommends a standalone Configuration Discovery and Tracking server per management domain. Each Configuration Discovery and Tracking server is responsible for its own domain—it discovers and stores all configuration data for its local domain. Users of each management domain use the local Configuration Discovery and Tracking instance to manage the operational aspects of their domain, including running analytics such as change history, comparison and inventory reports. As an example, in Figure 2-9 a domain Configuration Discovery and Tracking server maps and manages the individual data centers -in Seattle, Los Angeles, and New York.

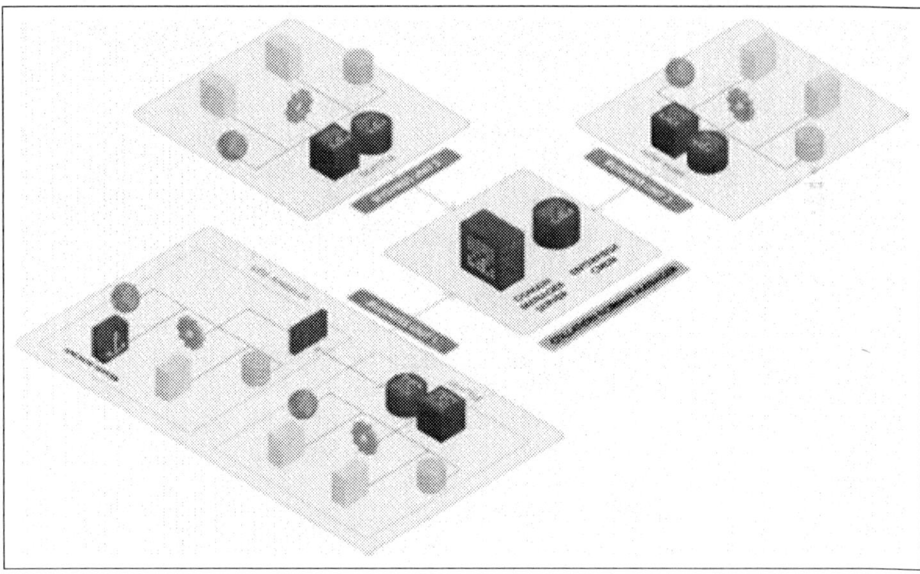

Figure 2-9 Configuration Discovery and Tracking domain-based scaling

However, IT organizations also have the need to have cross-domain views of their IT information. For example, the CIO might want to see an aggregate count of the enterprise wide Oracle deployments to ensure that the enterprise is compliant with its licensing contracts. To address this capability, IBM provides the Configuration Discovery and Tracking Domain Manager. The Configuration Discovery and Tracking Domain Manager federates data from the multiple local Configuration Discovery and Tracking server instances to provide a *rolled-up* single enterprise-wide repository of information. The federated architecture ensures that the data is not duplicated in multiple data stores—the Domain Manager stores references to the appropriate data in the local Configuration Discovery and Tracking server and access the data on as needed basis.

The IBM Domain Manager provides a Web based portal to administer the local domain servers and view and analyze the rolled up enterprise data. It also provides a query and reporting interface that you can customize, which allows data to be easily shared across the enterprise.

2.5 Configuration Discovery and Tracking Security

Unlike other solutions, Configuration Discovery and Tracking's discovery process does not require the deployment of persistent agents in the target environment. This approach not only eliminates the need to qualify and manage yet another set of agents, but also eliminates the security and support risks associated with deploying persistent agents in the data center infrastructure. The Configuration Discovery and Tracking discovery sensors use industry standard secure protocols to discover the infrastructure components and their configurations. The foundation of the Configuration Discovery and Tracking discovery process is built around the Secure Shell protocol (SSH)[2] the gold standard for secure enterprise data center communications. Configuration Discovery and Tracking uses SSH extensively to enforce strong authentication and encryption during the discovery process. In addition, Configuration Discovery and Tracking requires read-only access, and no write privileges.

Configuration Discovery and Tracking also ensures the security of access to its server and the underlying application map database. Access to the Configuration Discovery and Tracking server is only provided to users or applications with valid login/password credentials. Configuration Discovery and Tracking also supports and recommends certificate-based authentication over SSL protocol for the both user and API clients. Upon successful authentication, users are assigned multi-tiered roles which provide read as well as discovery action privileges. In addition, following an authenticated access to the Configuration Discovery and Tracking server, all user actions are tracked and logged and accessible for audit purposes. Configuration Discovery and Tracking's key security features are summarized in Table 2-1 on page 63.

[2] `http://www.ietf.org/html.charters/secsh-charter.html` and `http://www.openssh.com`

Table 2-1 Configuration Discovery and Tracking security features

Feature	Benefits
Agent-free discovery	Eliminates lengthy and costly qualification processes and risks of instrumenting operating systems and code
Utilizes SSH for host access	Authenticates and secures all discovery activity
Requires Read-only access	Creates no risk of unauthorized actions on discovered components
Complete logging of user activity	Enables security audits
Credentials required for user of API access	Eliminates unauthorized access to information or control
Automatically deployed anchor servers	Enables seamless discovery across firewall zones

2.6 Summary

IBM Tivoli Change and Configuration Management Database Configuration Discovery and Tracking's application mapping solution is an enterprise-class offering built on a standards-based data center reference model. The product performs agent-free discovery of the entire cross-tier application infrastructure, and feeds this information through the reference model to create specific application maps and build and maintains the associated application map database. These maps include all of the components that make up an application, and their run-time dependencies and deep configuration settings. This information, as well as its change over time, is stored in an extensible and open database.

Configuration Discovery and Tracking provides a full set of data, control and event APIs to allow this information to be used by existing and future management products and processes These APIs are supported by a complete and standard based Software Development Toolkit, allowing IT organizations to rapidly implement the specific integrations that they need.

Configuration Discovery and Tracking provides both horizontal and vertical scaling capabilities. Configuration Discovery and Tracking can be deployed flexibly across both management and security domains. By providing for all possible combinations of management and security requirements, Configuration Discovery and Tracking's deployment architecture can be custom fit to each organizations needs. Configuration Discovery and Tracking is also designed to meet the reliability and security requirements of the enterprise.

In summary, though thoughtful design choices, Configuration Discovery and Tracking offers an extensible, scalable and secure solution that delivers complete visibility into complex application infrastructures. By deploying Configuration Discovery and Tracking, organizations are improving the availability, consistency and agility of service delivery for their business critical applications.

3

Deploying Configuration Discovery and Tracking v1.1

This chapter discusses the planning, installation, and customization of a working IBM Tivoli Change and Configuration Management Database Configuration Discovery and Tracking v1.1 environment that is able to discover the infrastructure, application system components, and their dependencies.

We use a stand-alone installation of IBM Tivoli Change and Configuration Management Database Configuration Discovery and Tracking v1.1. However, we do not include the Configuration Discovery and Tracking feature as part of an IBM Change Configuration Management Database v1.1 installation.

The focus of this chapter is explaining the components for a small to medium-sized environment using a single domain server. For further details on Enterprise Server installation and interaction with different domain servers, refer to the *IBM Tivoli Change and Configuration Management Database v1.1: Planning Guide*.

3.1 Creating a deployment plan

Creating a deployment plan is essential to creating and installing a configuration and tracking environment. The basic considerations for creating a deployment plan are provided in the IBM Tivoli Change and Configuration Management Database v1.1: Planning Guide. This document covers all the planning considerations and provides scenarios for creating a comprehensive deployment plan. At a minimum, you need to gather the following information before installing any software:

- Base hardware and software requirements for IBM Tivoli Change and Configuration Management Database Configuration Discovery and Tracking v1.1.
- Whether the computer systems in your distributed network can support this new software, whether these systems can be upgraded to meet your business needs, or whether you will need new systems.
- Which Configuration Discovery and Tracking components to install on which computer systems in your distributed network to support your business needs and whether they have additional third-party software requirements.

For each system where you plan to install components of Configuration Discovery and Tracking, you should also provide the following information:

- Host name
- Operating system
- Available memory and available disk space
- Which components of IBM Tivoli Change and Configuration Management Database Configuration Discovery and Tracking to install

To help you create your deployment plan, you can use the information in the *Planning Worksheet* that is provided in the IBM Tivoli Change and Configuration Management Database v1.1: Planning Guide. After creating your deployment plan and before starting the installation of Configuration Discovery and Tracking v1.1 components, make sure you read the IBM Tivoli Change and Configuration Management Database v1.1: Release Notes accompanying the product.

3.1.1 Sizing your Configuration Discovery and Tracking environment

The following provides the best rule-of-thumb sizing recommendations available at the time of writing this book.

Configuration Discovery and Tracking Server sizing

The rule-of-thumb for Configuration Discovery and Tracking sizing is based on the number of Configuration Items (CIs) per host.

While there is no common industry agreement on the number of CIs per host, a good rule of thumb for CIs per host is around 100 per CPU. The greater the processing capacity of a system, the more likely it is that more business application components (CIs) will be hosted by the system. This translates to the following numbers:

1-CPU host	50 CIs
2-CPU host	100 CIs
4-CPU host	200 CIs

The rule of thumb for the number of CIs within a single Configuration Discovery and Tracking Domain is 500 000. That would allow timely processing of around:

10 000 hosts	If you have 50 CIs per host
5000 hosts	If you have 100 CIs per host
2500 hosts	If you have 200 CIs per host

Assumption: Discovery must complete reconciliation in less than 24 hours because it is seen as a task that might be run daily. So, it is unacceptable if Discovery takes more than 24 hours.

However, the Configuration Discovery and Tracking Server itself does not scale linearly beyond four CPUs.

Topology reconciliation is not a linear process

This means that the time it takes to reconcile does not increase two times when the number of CIs increases two times.

Increasing the number of CPUs on the system hosting the Configuration Discovery and Tracking Server appears at first as though it would decrease discovery time because of parallelism. However, because topology reconciliation is not linear, the knee in the curve is reached at around four CPUs.

Important: It is extremely unlikely that a true, managed domain would be bigger than 5000 hosts. So, a single Configuration Discovery and Tracking Server should suffice. This is so, because purchase of server hardware is usually decentralized and management of them follows suit. So, while the corporation might have 20 000 hosts, they do not need a single domain with a single CMDB to discover and store them. Real life experience says it will never be used that way.

A 4-CPU Configuration Discovery and Tracking Server cannot process more than 1,000,000 (one million) objects, not CIs, in less than 24 hours.

One million objects translates to 400 objects per host which equals 2500 4-CPU hosts per Configuration Discovery and Tracking Domain, assuming a 1-2 ratio of model objects to CIs. You can think about it on one of two ways:

- 1 000 000 / 400 = 2500 4-CPU hosts
- 1 000 000 / 200 = 5000 2-CPU hosts

Think of topology reconciliation as an n^x matrix. We do not know in advance how many dependencies there could be and it could keep expanding as we discover in a tightly meshed environment where there are many dependent application components. The amount of dependencies is not directly related to the number of CIs. It could be orders of magnitude more. If this is highly meshed, we are increasing in complexity in an exponential manner. This takes a lot of processing time, and experience has shown that we hit about 24 hours with one million objects. Adding more CPUs does not reduce that time.

The actual Sensor discovery part is linear and more CPUs does help there; however, it turns into *hurry up and wait* when the reconciliation phase in memory is reached and the perceived advantage of the additional CPUs only contributes a small amount to the total time.

Also, different environments behave differently. A large notebook computer population might reconcile linear since the notebooks likely have no dependencies on each other, therefore very little mesh.

Database sizing considerations

To calculate CMDB database size, use the rule of thumb: 2 MB per host.

For example, the following numbers of hosts work out to these database sizes:

5000 hosts:	10 GB
10 000 hosts:	20 GB

From an actual, large scale implementation the following numbers were realized:

```
Having been running weekly discoveries of about 2500 hosts and network
devices for 14 months uses about 7 GB of space.
```

The reason that the planning information cannot be better qualified is that the determining factor, besides the number of hosts and devices, is the number of components that will be discovered in the environment and the rate of change. Both of these factors can vary tremendously from one environment to another. In addition, the size of an individual component varies as well. For example, how many EJBs are deployed in a WebSphere Application Server, or how many tables exist in a database? Using Custom Server Templates and Computer System Templates to collect and track files can also greatly influence the capacity requirements of the CMDB.

In an Enterprise configuration, the ECMDB is sized to do an initial synchronization of five million objects within a 24-hour period. At about an average processing time per object of 20 ms, five million objects are processed in 100 000 seconds, or 27.7 hours.

- The Enterprise CMDB should be able to do an incremental synchronization at a rate of two seconds per model object.
- A query on a top-level model object should return in less than four seconds.
- Synchronization between multiple CMDBs should be serialized.
- Five million Model Objects equals 100 000 servers at an average of 50 Model Objects per host.
- A Domain CMDB can scale to 500 000 Model Objects, either 2500 hosts for a 4 CPU host or 5000 for a 2 CPU host).
- An Enterprise CMDB should be able to handle up to 50 Domains assuming number of model objects is not exceeded.

3.1.2 Security considerations

In order to be able to access the target systems of the discovery, the Configuration Discovery and Tracking Server need to have an entry defined in the Access List which contains the credentials (user ID/password) that will be used for the following:

UNIX targets
: Login using the SSH protocol and execute the **lsof** command to extract system information. The user ID must be a member of the `sys` group or have similar system-wide privileges.

Windows targets
: Execute WMI requests to extract system information. The user ID must be member of the `Administrators` group or have similar system-wide privileges.

Anchor Hosts
: Same as Unix targets. In addition this account is used as the owner of the Anchor Host binaries (stored in the user's home directory) and processes.

Windows Gateway
: Login using SSH, and execute WMI calls locally and against Windows target systems. Windows Gateway executables are stored in the home directory of this user. The user ID must be member of the `Administrators` group or have similar system-wide privileges.

These credentials, also known as the *service account*, can naturally be shared between multiple systems if they apply each UNIX-based target system that will be a target of the discovery.

3.1.3 Communications

When running, the Configuration Discovery and Tracking solution uses the protocols shown in Table 3-1.

Table 3-1 Communication protocols

Component	Server	Anchor Host	Windows Gateway	Unix target	Windows target	Network Device
Server	n/a	SSH[a] RMI	SSH	SSH	n/a	SNMP SSH/Telnet
Anchor Host	n/a	SSH[a] RMI	SSH	SSH	n/a	SNMP
Windows Gateway	n/a	n/a	n/a	n/a	RPC/WMI	n/a
Product Console	HTTP HTTPS					
Domain Manager	9430					

a. Used only for discovery of the anchor host system and deployment of the Anchor host executables.

The default port numbers that must be open in the firewalls between the various Configuration Discovery and Tracking infrastructure components are:

SSH	22
Telnet	23
RPC/WMI	135 - DCOM is used under the covers
SNMP	161
HTTP	9430 - Portal and Domain Manager
HTTP/HTTPS	9433 - Product Console
RMI	Configurable for each Anchor Host

It is your responsibility to open the necessary ports in the firewalls that the Configuration Discovery and Tracking communication traverses.

Internally within the Configuration Discovery and Tracking Server, the following ports in Table 3-2 on page 71 are used to facilitate communication between the various components of the Configuration Discovery and Tracking Server itself.

Table 3-2 Configuration Discovery and Tracking Server port usage

Functional area	Description	port #
GUI	Port used for Tomcat shutdown command	5637
	Web Server HTTP port to use without SSL	9430
	Web Server HTTPS port to use with SSL	9431
	Naming service JNDI lookup port	9432
	Naming service RMI registry port	9433
	RMI data port to use with SSL	9434
	RMI data port to use without SSL	9435
API	Port for collation API	9530
	Port for SSL API	9531
Enterprise ports	Security Manager port	9540
	Topology Manager port	9550
	API Server port	9560
	Change Manager port	9450
	Report Server port	9580
Miscellaneous ports	RMI daemon port	1098
	Unicast discovery port	4160
	Tivoli SNMP trap agent	9162
	Unknown	9902

3.2 Component installation prerequisites

For information about the software and hardware requirements for all components used in a IBM Tivoli Change and Configuration Management Database Configuration Discovery and Tracking environment, see 2.4, "Configuration Discovery and Tracking Deployment Architecture" on page 56. In this section we look at the prerequisites needed to implement these components.

3.2.1 Configuration Discovery and Tracking Server

Before deploying the server code for Configuration Discovery and Tracking Server, you must have either a local or remote database server installed. You can configure Configuration Discovery and Tracking to use the following external databases to store information collected during the discovery process:

- IBM UDB DB2 v8.2.x
- IBM DB2 Client v8.2.x
- Oracle 9i or 10g

> **Note:** When using an Oracle database, you must create an Oracle instance and corresponding database account.

Creation of the database can be done prior to the installation or the Configuration Discovery and Tracking Installer will create it for you. If you plan to install the database prior to installation or on a remote system after you have installed theConfiguration Discovery and Tracking Server. the following script `make_db2_db.sh` can be used. After installation of the Configuration Discovery and Tracking Server, the `make_db2_db.sh` script - shown in Example 3-1 is available in the `${COLLATION_HOME}/dist/support/bin` directory.

Example 3-1 CMDB database creation - make_db2_db.sh

```
#!/bin/sh

if test -z "$1"
then
        echo "Usage: $0 <database_name>"
        exit 1
fi

db2 drop database $1
db2 create db $1
db2 <<EOF
connect to $1
create bufferpool buf32k immediate size 384 pagesize 32k
create tablespace userspace2 pagesize 32k managed by system using
('usercont2') bufferpool buf32k
create large tablespace largespace2 pagesize 32k managed by database
using (file 'largedata' 2560) bufferpool buf32k
create system temporary tablespace largetemp2 pagesize 32k managed by
system using ('systemp2') bufferpool buf32k
update db cfg using APP_CTL_HEAP_SZ 1024
update db cfg using LOGFILSIZ 4096
update db cfg using LOGPRIMARY 6
```

```
update db cfg using LOGSECOND 20
update db cfg using LOCKLIST 1500
update db cfg using MAXLOCKS 35
update db cfg using CATALOGCACHE_SZ 384
update db cfg using PCKCACHESZ 512
update db cfg using AVG_APPLS 3
update db cfg using SORTHEAP 1024
update db cfg using LOGBUFSZ 512
update db cfg using NUM_IOCLEANERS 3
update db cfg using NUM_IOSERVERS 5
update db cfg using DFT_DEGREE ANY
disconnect $1
quit
EOF

db2set DB2_EVALUNCOMMITTED=YES
```

The make_db2_db.sh script creates the database, bufferpools and tablespaces used by the Configuration Discovery and Tracking Server. The default name of the database is cmdb. This value can be changed to your preference.

The make_db2_db.sh script can be run directly from the Configuration Discovery and Tracking Server, and requires the database instance hosting the database to have been created in advance. Make sure that you have sourced the db2profile of the database user or are logged in as the database user.

If your database are hosted by a remote system, make sure that you have the IBM DB2 Client v8.2.x installed on the Configuration Discovery and Tracking Server system and perform the following preparation steps:

1. At the system hosting the DB2 instance create a database named cmdb:
   a. Login as the DB2 instance owner
   b. create the database named cmdb using the following command:
      `db2 create database cmdb`
2. At the Configuration Discovery and Tracking Server, catalog the DB2 Instance host and the database, using the following commands:

   ```
   db2 catalog tcpip node cmdbhost remote <db2_instance_host> service
   <db2_instance_port>

   db2 catalog catabase cmdb as cmdb at node cmdbhost authorization
   server
   ```

3. Comment out the two lines in the make_db2_db.sh script that drops and creates the database:

```
#db2 drop database $1
#db2 create db $1
```

When using the installer to create your database, you can see the results of database creation by looking at the log files under ${COLLATION_HOME}/installLogs. The database creation log files are:

- cdb_cr_db2_stderr.log
- cdb_cr_db2_stdout.log

External Oracle database configuration

Follow these steps to create and configure your Oracle environment:

1. Create an Oracle instance with a recommended tablespace of at least 500 MB for every 100 servers that will be discovered.
2. Create an Oracle user with connect and resource roles. You can use the following command to create the Oracle users `coll_usr` and `coll_arch`:

```
create user coll_usr identified by coll_usr_pw;
grant connect, resource, select_catalog_role to coll_usr;

create user coll_arch identified by coll_arch_pw;
grant connect, resource, select_catalog_role to coll_arch;
```

If you perform the Oracle setup after installing the Configuration Discovery and Tracking Server, a script to create the Oracle users is available here:

${COLLATION_HOME}/dist/support/bin/make_ora_user.sh

Note: The actual tables within the database are created when the server starts the first time. Servers DBInit process creates those approximately 1200+ tables.

3.3 Installing IBM Tivoli Change and Configuration Management Database Configuration Discovery and Tracking v1.1

You can install CMDB Configuration Discover and Tracking using the GUI or using the silent installation. Installation of Configuration Discovery and Tracking Server is supported on the following operating systems:

- RedHat Advance Server 3.0, 4.0
- SuSE Linux Enterprise Server 9.0
- AIX 5.2, 5.3
- Solaris 8, 9, 10

IBM Tivoli Change and Configuration Management Database Configuration Discovery and Tracking v1.1 needs its own user ID to start itself and run commands after the product is installed. During the installation, the wizard will create a user ID for you. The newly created user ID will not have a password assigned to it. If you want, you can create this ID prior to installation.

> **Important:** The installation procedure described in the following sections is based on the stand-alone installation of IBM Tivoli Change and Configuration Management Database Configuration Discovery and Tracking v1.1 and does not include the steps needed to install Configuration Discovery and Tracking as part of a full CCMDB implementation.
>
> If you install Configuration Discovery and Tracking v1.1 as part of a single system installation of IBM Tivoli Change Control and Configuration Management Database v1.1, the sequence and dialog content might be slightly different than described here.

To launch the installation wizard, mount the installation media (the CCMDB DVD for the platform on which you are installing) on the system where you want to install the Configuration Discovery and Tracking Server, and start the installation script by logging in as root and execute the appropriate setup<platform>.bin file for your operating system from the CMDB subdirectory. For example, for a Linux operating system:

```
/media/cdrom1/CMDB/setupLinux.bin
```

The first action performed by the installation wizard is to copy the executables needed to launch a Java Virtual Machine on your system. By default these files are placed in the /tmp directory. If you want to download the Java Virtual Machine to a directory other than the /tmp directory, enter:

```
./setup<interp>.bin -is:tempdir directory
```

Where `directory` is the directory to where you download the Java Virtual Machine.

During the installation, you can select to perform a *Typical* or a *Custom* installation. For both types of installation the first few steps are common.

3.3.1 Common installation steps

After the installation program is started as specified in 3.3, "Installing IBM Tivoli Change and Configuration Management Database Configuration Discovery and Tracking v1.1" on page 75, you must accept the license agreement and specify the location for installation.

The default location the product will be installed in is /opt/IBM/cmdb. This can be changed as seen in Figure 3-1.

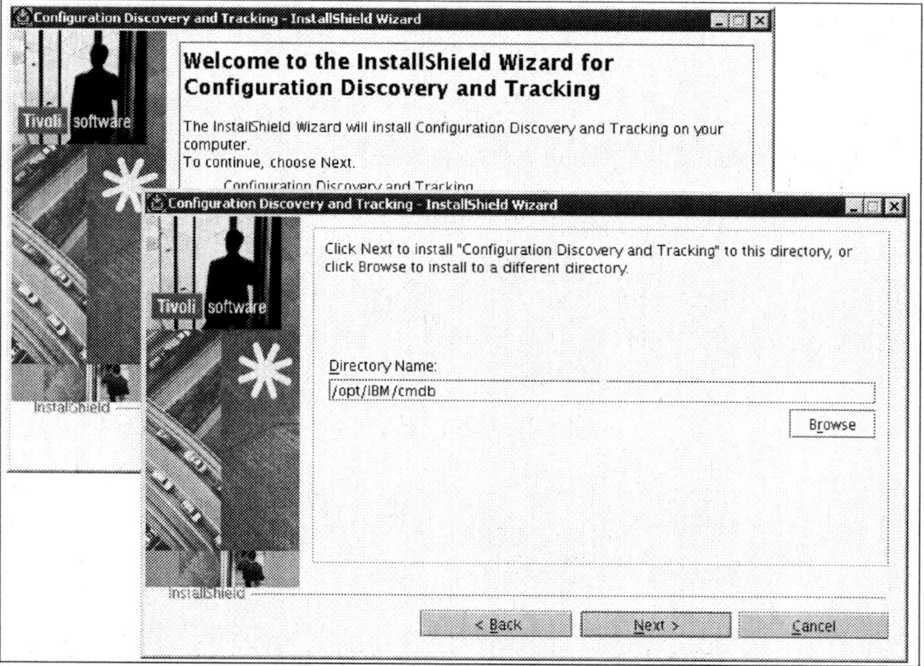

Figure 3-1 Configuration Discovery and Tracking Installation wizard: Location

When you have specified the location, you are prompted to define the user ID to be used to own the Configuration Discovery and Tracking files and processes. This user is created by the installation wizard for you. If you want, a predefined system user ID can also be used. Figure 3-2 on page 77 shows that we used a user ID for the Configuration Discovery and Tracking user named `itaddm`.

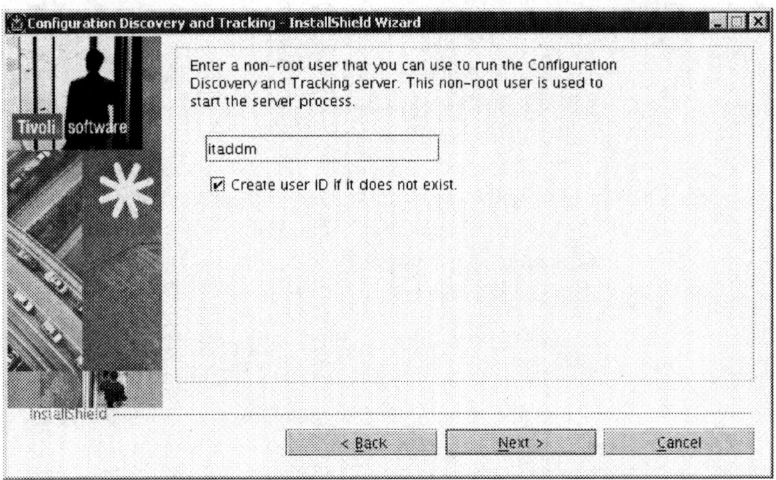

Figure 3-2 Configuration Discovery and Tracking Server installation: User

Next you are presented with a choice of either performing a Typical or a Custom installation as shown in Figure 3-3 on page 79.

The installation provides you with choice of installing DB2 if DB2 is not installed locally or a remote instance is not defined. Using the **Typical** installation path, DB2 is the only database choice. In addition, the typical installation will use default values for internal ports and startup settings for Configuration Discovery and Tracking. The following section 3.3.2, "Typical installation" on page 78 provides a walk-through of the typical installation.

If Oracle is your preferred database choice, you install Configuration Discovery and Tracking as part of a CCMDB installation, or you want to customize Configuration Discovery and Tracking configuration parameters, you should select the **Custom** installation. A walk-through of the custom installation is provided in 3.3.3, "Custom installation" on page 81.

3.3.2 Typical installation

When typical installation is selected during the installation of IBM Tivoli Change and Configuration Management Database Configuration Discovery and Tracking v1.1, the following actions take place:

1. Select to install DB2 or not to install DB2. The typical installation path only supports DB2 database.
   a. If you select to install DB2 during Configuration Discovery and Tracking install, a dialog box prompts you to specify where to install DB2 UDB and the user ID and password of the DB2 instance user.
   b. If you select not to install DB2 during Configuration Discovery and Tracking installation, a dialog box prompts you for the existing DB2 instance user ID and password information. This dialog also allows you to create the CMDB database during installation or postpone the task, and create it manually after the installation.
2. If DB2 installation is selected, the Configuration Discovery and Tracking installer calls the DB2 database installer in silent mode.
3. If the DB2 install completed successfully (or you select not to install DB2), the Configuration Discovery and Tracking installer invokes the install.sh to install the CMDB server. There is no ECMDB in the typical path.
4. If the Configuration Discovery and Tracking Server install completed successfully, the installer starts the Configuration Discovery and Tracking Server.
5. Upon completing the installation, a summary panel displays a successful or failed status.

The following instructions detail these steps:

1. Choose the **Typical** installation type, as in Figure 3-3 and press **Next**.

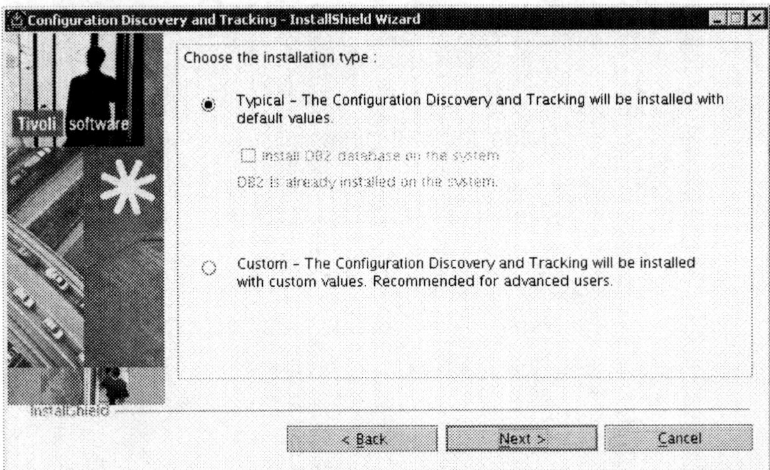

Figure 3-3 Configuration Discovery and Tracking Server installation: Typical

   This will take you to the next installation dialog box in which you define the DB2 parameters.

2. Supply the DB2 configuration parameters that apply to your environment. The settings we used are shown in Figure 3-4.

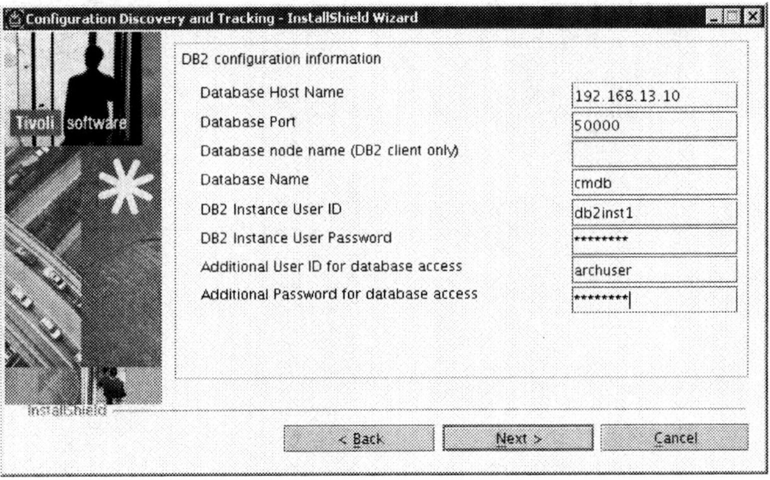

Figure 3-4 Configuration Discovery and Tracking server installation: DB2

Here we define the following attributes:

Database Host name
: Name of the DB2server or IP address

Database Port
: Database listening port

Database node name
: Define for DB2 clients

Database name
: Name of the database created to store Configuration Discovery and Tracking information

DB2 instance user ID
: Name of the DB2 instance owner by default db2inst1

DB2 instance password
: Enter password for DB2 instance owner

Additional ID for database access
: By default `archuser` is created

Additional password for database access
: Password for above user ID

Press **Next** to continue to the Typical installation.

3. Confirm your parameters for the Typical installation. The parameters should be similar to the ones shown in Figure 3-5.

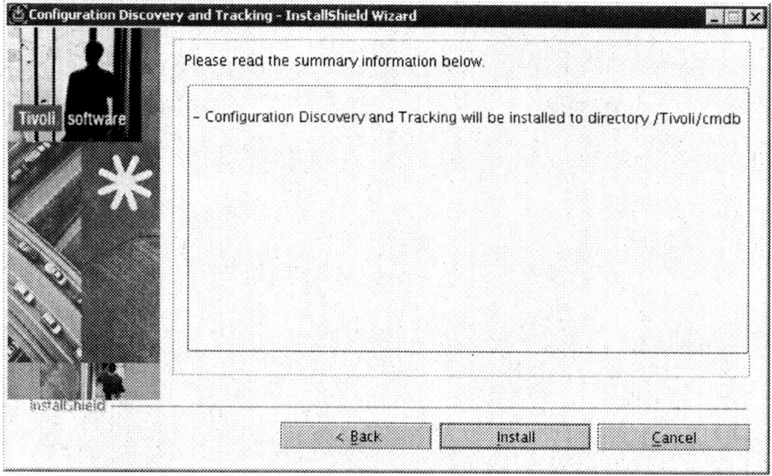

Figure 3-5 Configuration Discovery and Tracking Server installation: Summary

Click **Install** on this screen to deploy the product.

3.3.3 Custom installation

When you select the Custom installation path during the installation of IBM Tivoli Change and Configuration Management Database Configuration Discovery and Tracking v1.1, the following actions will take place.

1. Select to install CMDB or ECMDB (Enterprise CMDB).
2. Default configuration parameters are accepted and modified in several dialog boxes.
3. The database type, either DB2 or Oracle, is determined. If DB2 is selected, the user can select to install DB2 server during CMDB install.
   a. For DB2, the user can select to create CMDB database during CMDB install or manually create it after the install.
   b. For Oracle, the user can select to create the runtime connection Oracle user ID during CMDB install or manually create it after the install.
4. User can modify the default communication ports.
5. The installer validates the provided parameters, and, if all requirements are satisfied, allows user to continue with the installation process. If the option **Start server after install is finished** is selected, the installer attempts to connect to the database. In this case, the installer will not continue if the database connection cannot be established.
6. If DB2 installation is selected, the Configuration Discovery and Tracking installer calls the DB2 database installer in silent mode.
7. If the DB2 installation completed successfully or you selected not to install DB2, the CMDB installer invokes the install.sh to install the CMDB server.
8. If the option **Start server after install is finished** is selected and the CMDB server installation completed successfully, the installer starts the server.
9. Upon completing the installation, a summary panel displays the successful or failed status.

The key advantages of using Custom installation are:

- You can chose either DB2 or Oracle as your database.
- You can change default ports for various components.
- You can choose the installation to be a Domain server or a Enterprise server.
- You can define if the Configuration Discovery and Tracking Server needs to start at boot or not. It also allows control of starting the server after installation.

In this section we go through the step-by-step installation dialog boxes for a Custom installation.

1. As seen in 3.3.1, “Common installation steps” on page 76, the initial dialog boxes are similar for Typical and Custom installation types, so here we start from the installation type selection dialog shown in Figure 3-6.

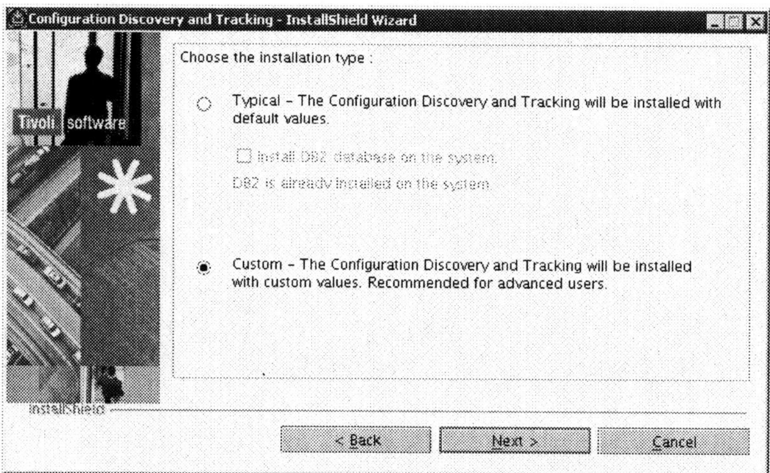

Figure 3-6 Configuration Discovery and Tracking Custom installation

   Select **Custom Installation**, and click **Next** to proceed.

2. The next two dialog boxes allow you to customize the various ports on which the Configuration Discovery and Tracking components communicate. As seen in Figure 3-7, you can change the port numbers if there is a conflict or there are specific needs in you environment.

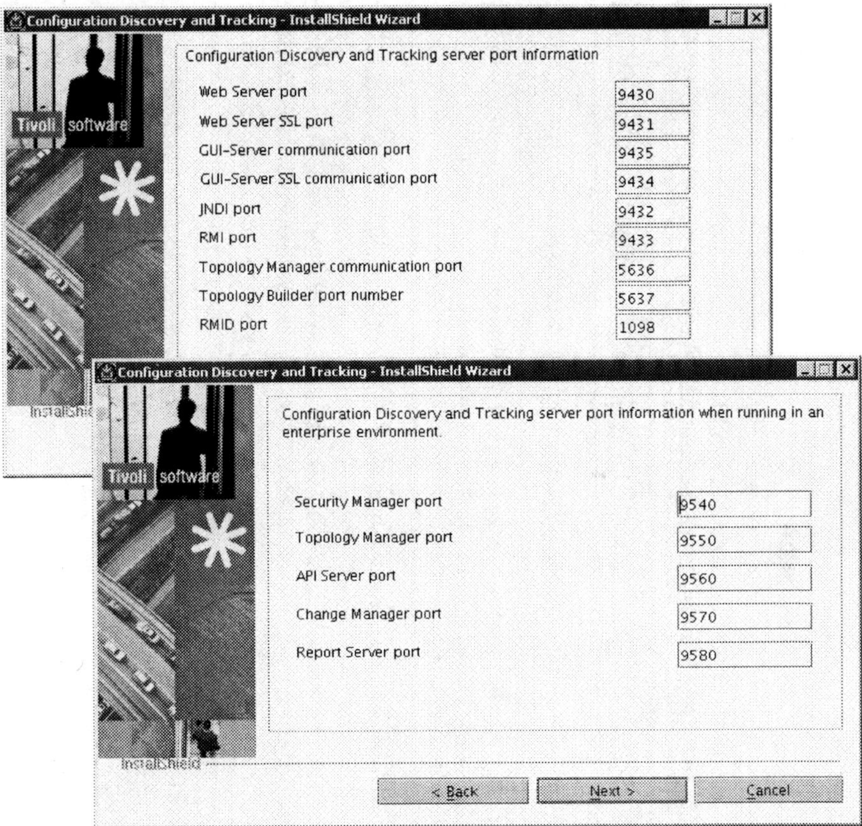

Figure 3-7 Configuration Discovery and Tracking Custom Server: Ports

Click **Next** if the default port numbers, or **OK** if port numbers have been modified, in order to continue the Configuration Discovery and Tracking Server configuration.

3. The next dialog box, shown in Figure 3-8 on page 84, allows you to configure the Configuration Discovery and Tracking server information.

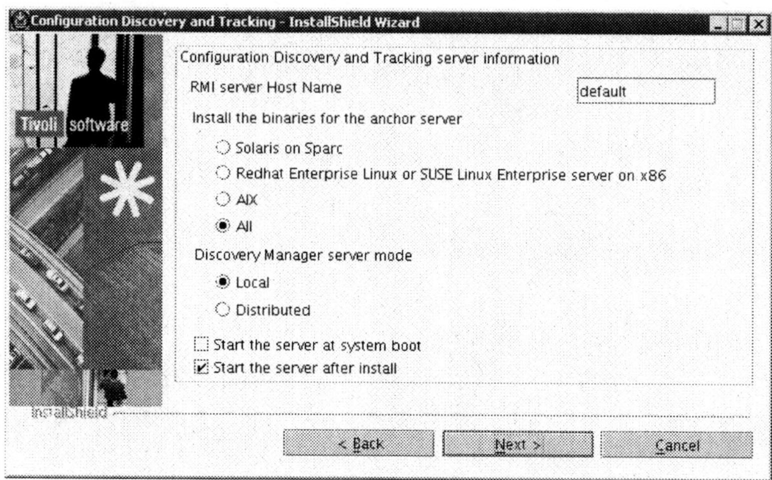

Figure 3-8 Configuration Discovery and Tracking Custom server: Server

The meaning of the parameters you can modify is:

- RMI Server Host Name

  The default value is `default`.

  When the Product Console is launched, it starts communicating with the Configuration Discovery and Tracking Server using the RMI protocol, in order to obtain information about where certain services are running. Access to these services are necessary for the Product Console to work correctly.

  If the RMI Server Host Name is set to `default`, the Product Console attempts to connect to the Configuration Discovery and Tracking Server at the address from which the Product Console was originally downloaded. Normally this is correct, however, sometimes it is not.

  Depending on your DNS configuration and the Configuration Discovery and Tracking Server the address returned to the Product Console might be incorrect—for example `127.0.0.1`—and in this case the local workstation will attempt to contact the server at that address (which is your workstation, itself). When this happens, you will get an error message saying `server is not running or not reachable`.

  Another case when `a value of default` is not appropriate is if the Configuration Discovery and Tracking Servers are accessed through a NAT device.

  After installation, you can modify this parameter by editing the value of the `com.collation.clientproxy.rmi.server.hostname` parameter in the `${COLLATION_HOME}/etc/collation.properties` file.

– Install the binaries for the anchor server

  Allows you to control which binaries you will copy to the file system on the Configuration Discovery and Tracking Server in order to be able to deploy Anchor Serves to specific platforms. Select binaries for the platforms to which you expect to deploy Anchor Hosts.

In addition you can control the startup options of the Configuration Discovery and Tracking Server at system boot and immediately after installation. By default, server startup at system boot is disabled and server startup after installation is enabled.

Supply the values that best match your preferences and click **Next**.

4. Configuration Discovery and Tracking Server can communicate with CCMDB (Change and Configuration Management Database) which is comprised of Configuration Discovery and Tracking and PMIP (Process Management Integration Platform). The next dialog box, shown in Figure 3-9, allows you to define the PMIP Server.

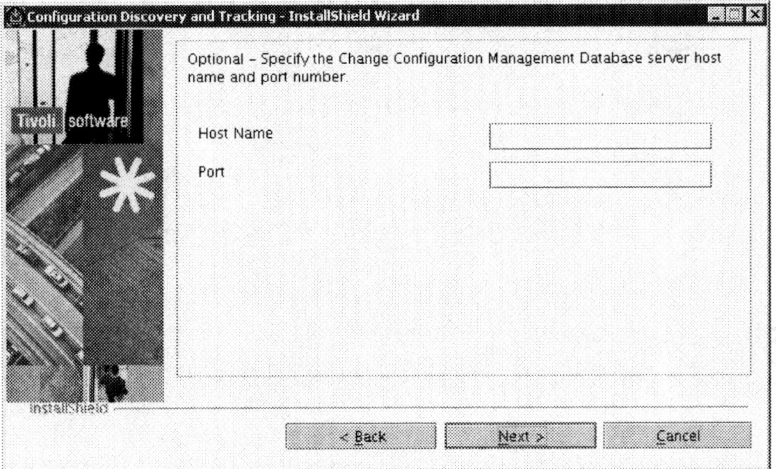

Figure 3-9 Configuration Discovery and Tracking Custom server: CCMDB

Supply the hostname or IP address of the PMIP Server and the port used to connect to it - or leave these fields empty if you do not want to integrate this instance of the Configuration Discovery and Tracking Server with PMIP.

Press **Next** to continue.

5. The following dialog boxes allow you to work with your database of choice, either DB2 or Oracle. The Installation Wizard can deploy DB2 for you if it is not already installed. Figure 3-9 on page 85 shows a couple of the deployment dialog boxes.

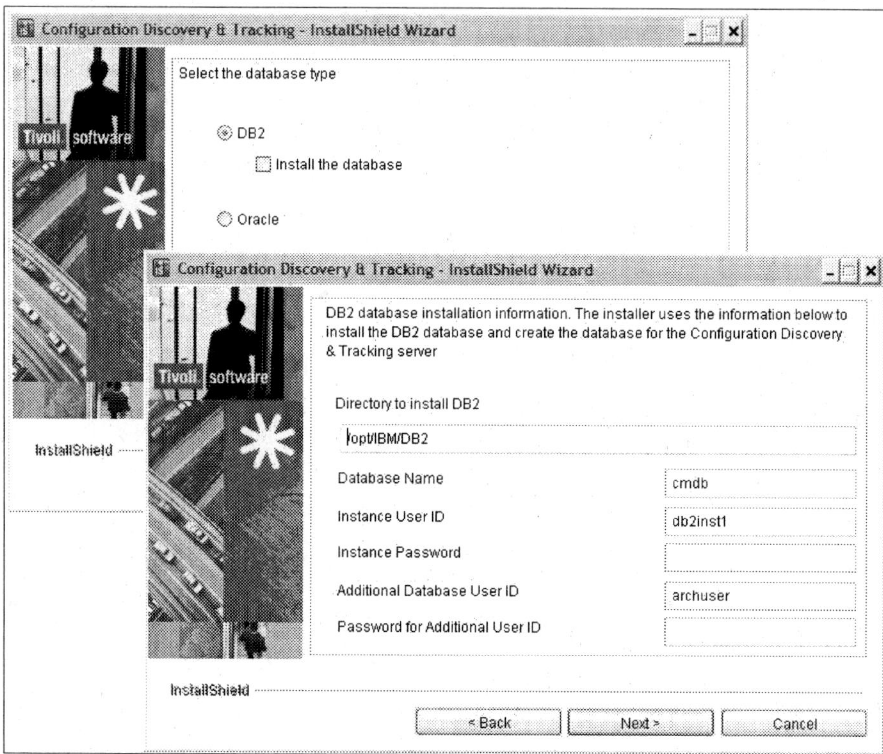

Figure 3-10 Configuration Discovery and Tracking Custom server installation: DB2

To configure a DB2 database and optionally have DB2 installed as part of the process, follow the instructions provided in step 2 on page 79.

The dialog shown in Figure 3-11 on page 87 is presented when the database type chosen is Oracle. You can choose to create the Oracle runtime user ID during installation or create it manually after the installation has completed, in which case you should follow the procedure described in “External Oracle database configuration” on page 74.

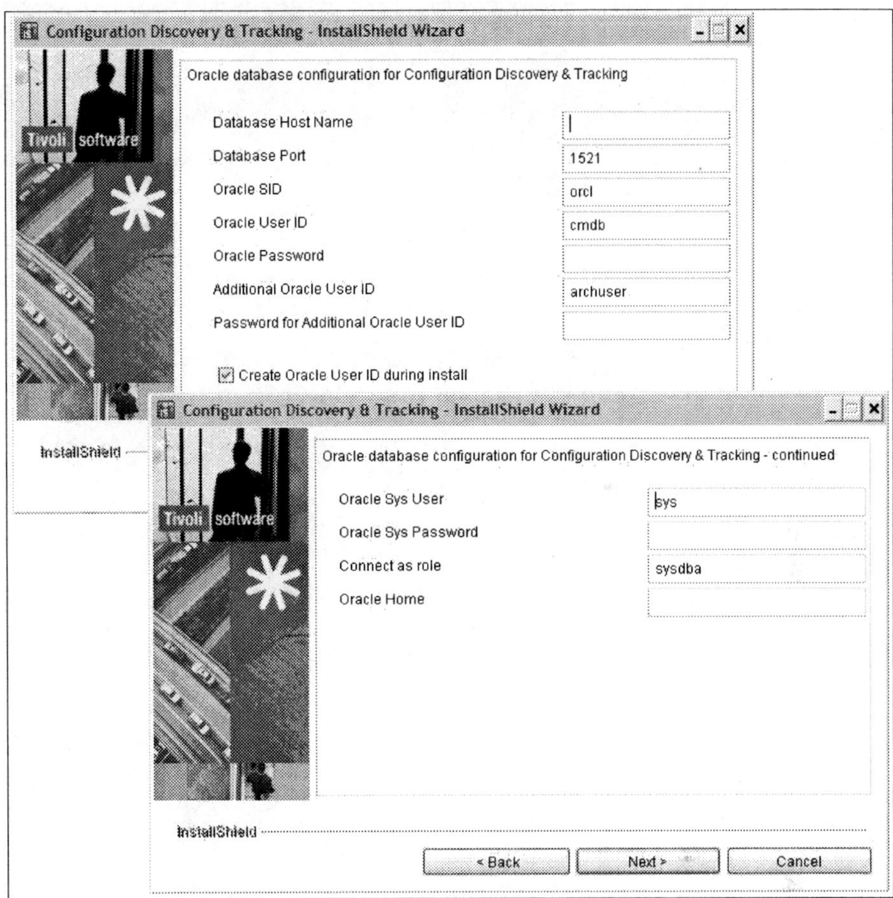

Figure 3-11 Configuration Discovery and Tracking Custom installation: Oracle

Press **Next** to continue.

6. Finally the summary dialog box opens, similar to the one shown in Figure 3-5 on page 80. Press **Install**, and wait for the confirmation of the successful installation.

3.4 Installation verification and server status

After installing the Configuration Discovery and Tracking feature, you can verify the operation of the Configuration Discovery and Tracking Portal and the Product Console on a computer in the network.

1. Test the status of the Configuration Discovery and Tracking server.

   a. In the /opt/IBM/cmdb/dist/bin (default installation directory), type:

   ```
   ./control status
   ```

   You should see the following message, if the server has started. It takes a while for all the services to start.

   ```
   DBInit: Started
   Tomcat: Started
   GigaSpaces: Started
   Discover: Started
   EventsCore: Started
   Topology: Started
   Proxy: Started
   DiscoverAdmin: Started

   TADDM: Running
   ```

   > **Note:** The control binary needs to be run as the user running the Configuration Discovery and Tracking Server. If you are signed on as root you might get the following error message
   >
   > ```
   > [root@vmw07g01 /]# /Tivoli/cmdb/dist/bin/control status
   > ERROR: This script must NOT be run as root
   > ```
   >
   > Root can still use the old method of checking server status or stopping and starting the server by executing the command:
   >
   > ```
   > /etc/init.d/collation status
   > ```

   b. To stop the Configuration Discovery and Tracking server, type:

   ```
   ./control stop
   ```

   c. To start the Configuration Discovery and Tracking server, type:

   ```
   ./control start
   ```

2. Testing the Product Console involves installing Java Web Start and the Java Runtime Environment (JRE™).

   Open a Web browser, then enter the URL and port number of the system where you installed the Configuration Discovery and Tracking server. For example, you could enter something similar to the following:

   ```
   http://vmw07g01.grt.com:9430
   ```

   You should see the Configuration Discovery and Tracking Portal in you browser, just like the one shown in Figure 3-12.

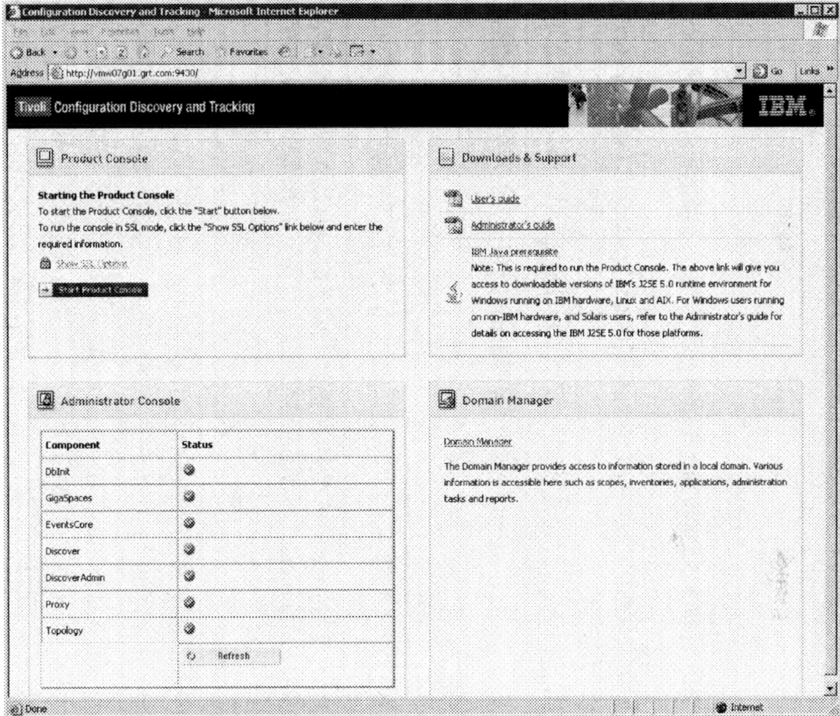

Figure 3-12 Configuration Discovery and Tracking start page

From the Configuration Discovery and Tracking Portal, the following functions are available:

- The Administrator Console view and the status of the server
- A button to start the Product Console
- A link to the Domain Manager

Before running the Product Console for the first time, you must have Java 2 Standard Edition 5.0 installed on the local machine. You can download and install Java 2 Standard Edition 5.0 by completing the following steps:

a. Click the **IBM Java prerequisites** link if you are on an AIX, Windows, or Linux client.

   A Web page opens, enabling you to download the installation program for J2SE/JRE version 5.0.

b. If you are on a Solaris client, the J2SE™ download is available from the Configuration Discovery and Tracking DVD.

   i. Go to /collation/solaris.zip.

   ii. Decompress the file.

   iii. Go to the ${COLLATION_HOME}/external/jdk subdirectory.

   In that directory, there is a file called jdk-1.5.0-SunOS-sparc.zip. This is the JDK™ version 5.0 for Solaris sparc (for Solaris v8, 9, and 10).

c. Download and run the J2SE installation program.

d. Close and restart the Web browser. Ensure that every browser window is closed before restarting the browser.

3. When using SSL, click the **Show SSL Options** link and enter the required information. Using SSL encrypts all data transmitted between the Product Console and the Configuration Discovery and Tracking server. Further details are provided in 4.1.3, "Launching the Product Console" on page 108.

4. Click **Start Product Console** to install and start the Product Console. To login to the Product Console for the first time, you can use the user ID `administrator` and the password `collation`.

3.4.1 Keeping your database responsive

In order to keep the database responsive, you will periodically have to update the statistics of the system catalogs, so the database manager will have the most up-to-date information regarding the contents of the database and the distribution of key values.

Configuration Discovery and Tracking provides two scripts to help you update the statistics of the tables. Both scripts reside in the `${COLLATION_HOME}/bin` directory:

runstats_db2_catalog.sql
: db2 control statements used to update the system catalog tables

gen_db_stats.jy
: Jython script that generates the sql statements necessary to update the statistics of the user tables in the CMDB.

To execute these scripts you must login as the instance owner of the CMDB. Example 3-2 shows the commands used in our environment to update the statistics for both the system catalog and the user tables in the CMDB.

Example 3-2 Updating database statistics

```
## logon as the CMDB instance owner
su - cmdb
## connect to the CMDB database
db2 connect to cmdb
## update statistics of the system catalog
db2 -tvf /opt/IBM/cmdb/dist/bin/runstats_db2_catalog.sql
## generate sql statements for update of the user tables
/opt/IBM/cmdb/dist/bin/gen_db_stats.jy > /tmp/runstats_db2.ddl
## update statistics of the user tables
db2 -tvf /tmp/runstats_db2.ddl
## disconnect from the database
db2 disconnect cmdb
## logout
exit
```

3.5 Silent installation of Configuration Discovery and Tracking Server

IBM Tivoli Change and Configuration Management Database Configuration Discovery and Tracking v1.1 Server can also be installed silently. For more information about silently installing Configuration Discovery and Tracking server refer to the IBM Tivoli Change and Configuration Management Database v1.1: Installing the Configuration Discovery and Tracking feature.

3.6 Deploying Windows Gateways

As explained in 2.4.2, "Windows infrastructure" on page 58, Configuration Discovery and Tracking requires you to specify a Windows system to serve as a gateway server in order to discover information about Windows-based systems running in your environment. This gateway server should be in the same firewall zone as the discovered Windows hosts, and must have SSH access from the Configuration Discovery and Tracking server.

You do not need to configure Windows gateways during the installation process. You can use the Configuration Discovery and Tracking console to configure which hosts will serve as Windows gateways on your network.

Figure 3-13 illustrates the network architecture when using two Windows gateways to assist in the discovery of Windows-based systems.

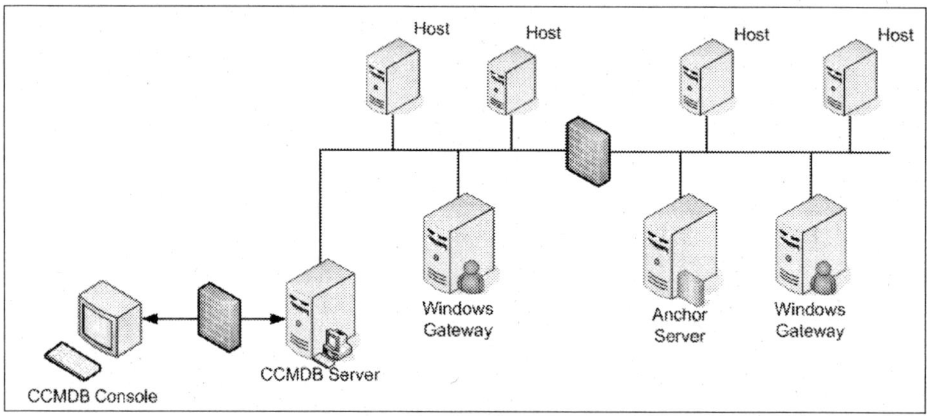

Figure 3-13 Windows gateway Configuration

When using a gateway server, Configuration Discovery and Tracking is able to discover the following systems:

- Windows computer systems running Windows 2000/2003/XP
- Windows-hosted databases, including Microsoft SQLServer
- Web servers and J2EE/.NET containers, including IIS, Apache, iPlanet™, WebLogic, and WebSphere
- Network infrastructure, such as Active Directory® 2000/2003, DNS
- Custom services

> **Note:** WMI must be available on all Windows hosts that will be discovered. WMI is available by default on Windows 2000 systems and higher, and available as an option for Windows NT® and Windows 98/95-based systems.

In order to discover components, each discovery server must be able to communicate with other computer hosts and network devices. In cases when a firewall prevents direct access from the discovery server to certain hosts or devices, you can specify a computer system that does have access to the hosts or devices to be an anchor host. An anchor host acts similar to a proxy to assist in the discovery process.

You do not need to configure anchor hosts during the installation process, but you should include anchor hosts in your installation plan and verify the system requirements for candidate machines. Following installation, you can use the Configuration Discovery and Tracking console to configure which hosts will serve as anchor hosts on your network.

3.6.1 Setting up SSH connectivity to Windows Gateways

IBM Tivoli Change and Configuration Management Database Configuration Discovery and Tracking depends on Windows Management Instrumentation (WMI)[1] to access and discover Windows System components.

In order for the discovery to work, you need to have an Access List entry defining the user ID and password of a user account (local or domain) who is a member of the Administrators group of each target system. Naturally, target systems using the same credentials can share one Access List entry.

Setting up SSH connectivity to Windows Gateways

Before configuring the gateway server, ensure that it meets the following prerequisites:

- The gateway server must be a Windows 2003 Server.
- WSH version 5.6 is required. This is installed by default with Windows 2003 Server.

Steps to configure a Windows Gateway Server:

1. Create an admin account: required a user which is a member of the local Administrators group.
2. Install Bitvise WinSSHD 4.06a or later on the Windows Gateway.

   You can download Bitvise WinSSHD with a trial license at:

   `http://www.bitvise.com/download-area.html`

   a. Run the WinSSHD installer program. This will start up the WinSSHD control panel. Click the button that starts the server.

[1] For further details on WMI see `http://www.microsoft.com/whdc/system/pnppwr/wmi`

b. WinSSHD has a host lockout feature that must be disabled. In the WinSSHD control panel, go to the **Settings** tab, and click **Edit/View Settings**. Now, select **Session**, and set the value of the following two variables to ‘0’:
   - IP blocking - window duration (s)
   - IP blocking - lockout time (s)

3. If the account you plan to use for Configuration Discovery and Tracking discovery is a domain account, you will need to set up a virtual group and a virtual account. To enable the account collation2 in the LAB2 domain, you would do the following:

   a. First, create a virtual group called `collation2`. Go to the WinSSHD control panel, open the **Settings** tab, and click **Edit/View Settings**. Expand **Access Control** in the tree on the left-hand side, and select **Virtual Groups**. From the details window, click **Add**, and provide the following information:

Group	`collation2`
Windows account domain	`LAB2`
Windows account name	`collation2`
Login allowed	Selected
(everything else	Keep the default values.

   Click **OK** to create the virtual group.

   b. Next, create a virtual account called `collation2`. From the WinSSHD navigation tree, select **Virtual Accounts**, click the **Add** button in the details window. Provide the following information:

Virtual account name	`collation2`
Virtual account password	Click and set the password
Use default Windows account	Checked
(everything else	Keep the default values.

   Click **OK** to create the virtual account.

4. You can restrict ssh host access to the Windows Gateway. In the WinSSHD control panel, open the **Settings** tab, and click **Edit/View Settings**. Expand **Access Control** in the tree on the left-hand side, and select **Hosts: IP rules**. From the details window, delete the 0.0.0.0/0 entry and add entries for the IP addresses of the Configuration Discovery and Tracking Server and Anchor Hosts that will initiate ssh communication with this Windows Gateway.

Note: Other versions of SSH might work but have not been tested and are not supported.

Note: WMI must be available on all Windows hosts that will be discovered. WMI is available by default on Windows 2000 systems and higher, and available as an option for Windows NT and Windows 98/95- based systems.

3.6.2 Configuring Windows Gateway

After installing WinSSH on the Windows 2003 Server which will become our Windows Gateway, the next step is to define the machine in the Configuration Discovery and Tracking server.

1. From the **Product Console** under the **Discovery** tab click **Anchors and Gateways**.
2. This will bring up a window where you are allowed to add a Anchor or Windows Gateway. Enter the following information:
   a. Under **Type** select **Windows Gateway**.
   b. Select either the IP address and fill in the Windows Gateways IP address or select Host name and fill in the host name.
   c. **Scope to search for host,** allows you to define Windows Gateways utilization. You can select the Gateway to be used for all addresses by specifying **Entire Scope** or limit its usage to define scope by selecting **Limit to specified scope**

Figure 3-14 depicts the dialog boxes and steps described here.

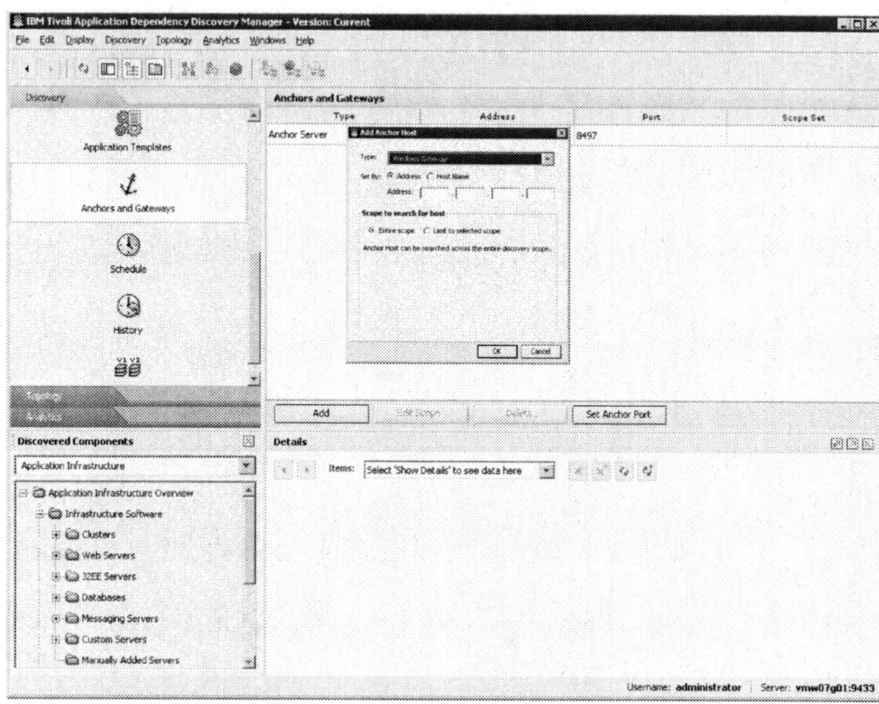

Figure 3-14 Windows Gateway

3.6.3 Anchor hosts

In order to discover components, the Configuration Discovery and Tracking Server must be able to communicate with other computer hosts and network devices. In cases where a firewall prevents direct access from the Configuration Discovery and Tracking server to certain hosts or devices, you can specify a computer system that does have access to the hosts or devices to be an anchor host. An anchor host acts similar to a proxy to assist in the discovery process.

You do not need to configure anchor hosts during the installation process. You can use the Configuration Discovery and Tracking console to configure which hosts will serve as anchor hosts on your network.

Figure 3-15 illustrates the network architecture when using a single anchor host to assist in the discovery of an adjacent firewall zone.

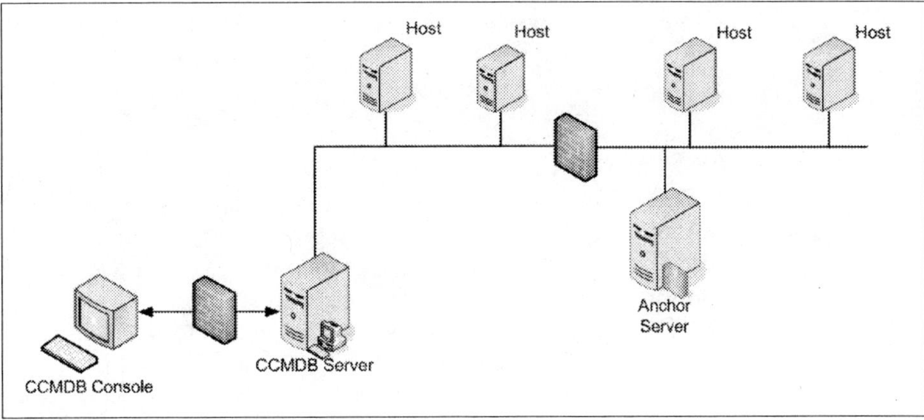

Figure 3-15 Anchor Host Configuration

Deploying an anchor host

Anchor host is automatically deployed on the next scan after it is defined. As seen in Figure 3-14 on page 96 we deploy the anchor host:

1. From the **Product Console** under the **Discovery** tab click **Anchors and Gateways**.
2. This opens a window where you are allowed to add a Anchor or Windows gateway. Enter the following information:
   a. Under **Type** select **Anchor Server**.
   b. Select either the IP address and fill in the Anchor Server's IP address or select Host name and fill in the host name.
   c. **Scope to search for host,** allows you to define Windows Gateways utilization. You can select the gateway to be used for all addresses by specifying **Entire Scope** or limit its usage to define scope by selecting **Limit to specified scope.**

After you define the previous settings on the next discovery, the Configuration Discovery and Tracking Server will find the anchor server and deploy Anchor Server code to the Anchor Server machine. By default, the files are installed in the $HOME directory of the user which has access to this Anchor Server. The user is defined in the Access List.

The users $HOME directory Configuration Discovery and Tracking will create a coll4.0 directory. This directory needs approximately 1 GB of space to deploy all the java and binary files required for the Anchor Server.

Note: If you have a slow connection between the Configuration Discovery and Tracking Server and the new to be Anchor Server it could take a long time for all the files to be laid down.

Anchor host communication

On each discovery run where anchors are specified, Configuration Discovery and Tracking Server tries to connect to any running anchor servers and, failing that, will try to start one. All communication is tunneled through SSH, so that only port 22 needs to be opened. A local port is needed for port forwarding through SSH. The Anchor Server will listen on that port to which SSH will forward. Almost all communication is serialized Java objects, so that the remote JRE better be the same version of the JRE as is running on the Configuration Discovery and Tracking Server. Locally, a listening port 8497 is opened, which receives network traffic from the local SSH server.

Anchor host logs

During installation, Configuration Discovery and Tracking Servers writes anchor server deployment errors to the error.log file. The error.lof file is by default located in the /opt/IBM/cmdb/dist/logs directory.

After the server is deployed, Anchor Server writes logs in the $HOME/coll4.0/log directory where $HOME is the home directory of the user used to deploy Anchor Server. The user is picked from the access list defined on the Configuration Discovery and Tracking Server.

3.7 Uninstalling Configuration Discovery and Tracking Server

To uninstall the Configuration Discovery and Tracking server, run the uninstallation script. You can find the uninstallation script in the root directory the Configuration Discovery and Tracking. For example:

```
${COLLATION_HOME}/../_uninst/uninstall.bin
```

This command launches the Uninstall Wizard is shown in Figure 3-16.

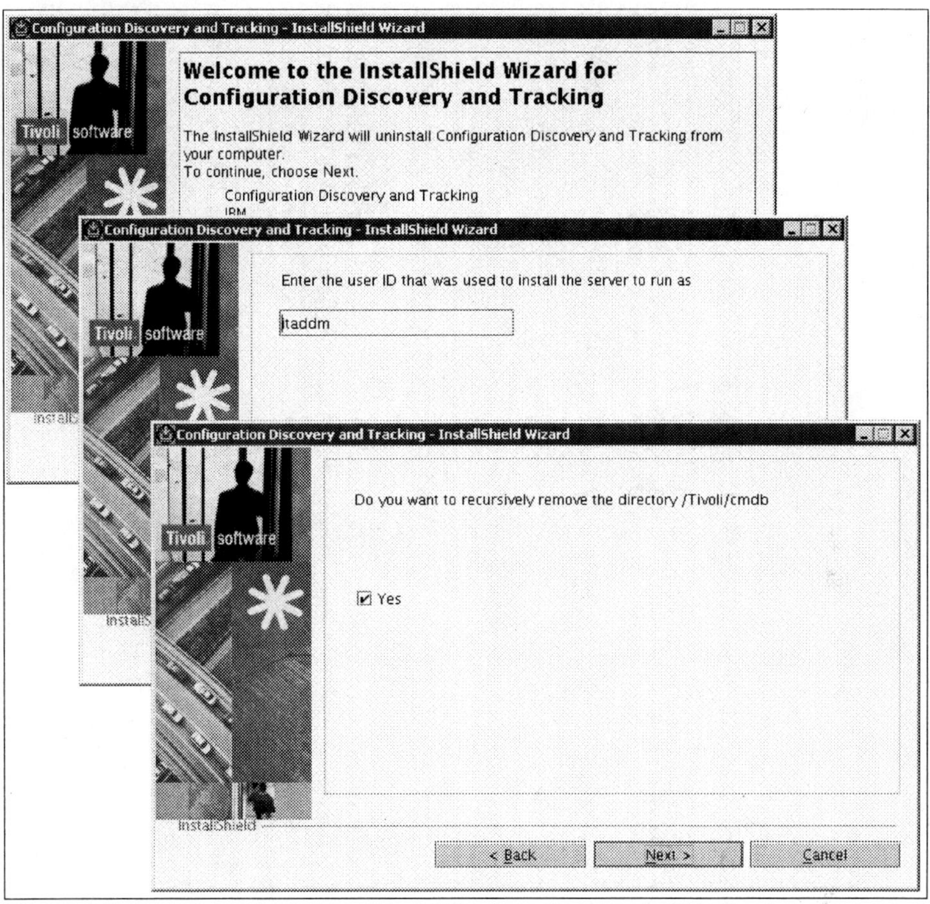

Figure 3-16 Configuration Discovery and Tracking Server uninstall wizard

4

Step-by-step Configuration Discovery and Tracking

This chapter tells you step-by-step how to set up your newly established Configuration Discovery and Tracking environment to discover simple three-tiered application, including discovering the dependencies between each of the components and the related hardware and networking resources.

4.1 Initial administration

After installation the IBM Tivoli Change and Configuration Management Database Configuration Discovery and Tracking v1.1 should be ready to use, provided that the server has been started.

To verify that Configuration Discovery and Tracking Server status, direct your browser to the following URL:

```
http://<your_server_hostname_or_ip-address>:9430
```

Verify that you can access the Configuration Discovery and Tracking Portal. Your browser should display a dialog box similar to the one shown in Figure 4-1.

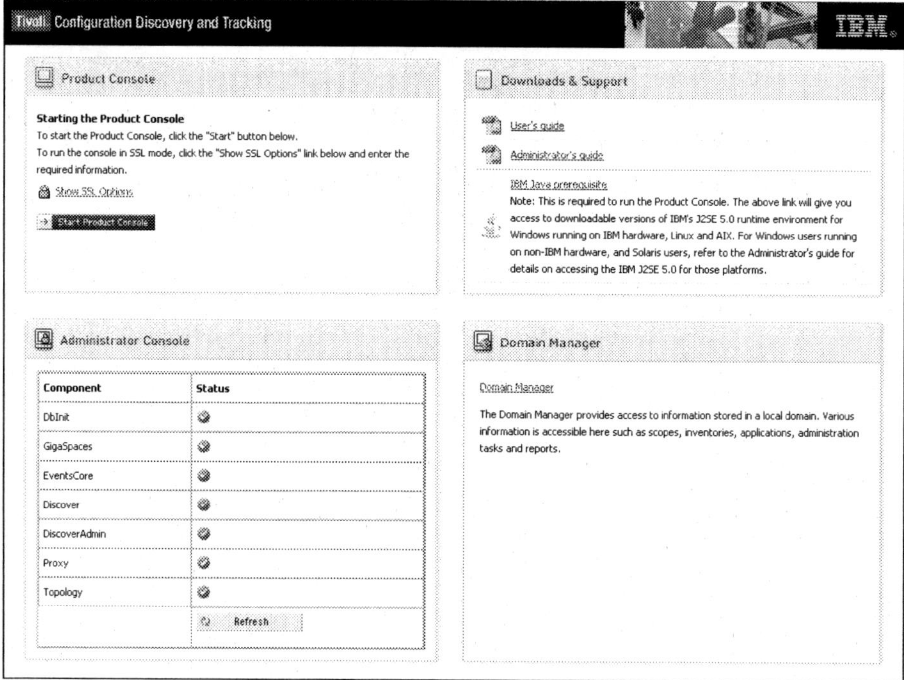

Figure 4-1 Configuration Discovery and Tracking Web Portal

Here you see that all the components of the Configuration Discovery and Tracking Server are operational (green and checked).

Upon installation, Configuration Discovery and Tracking has a few users defined which allows you to use and administer the environment. Without customization, the users in Table 4-1 on page 103 are available for use.

Table 4-1 Default Configuration Discovery and Tracking users

User ID	Password	Roles
administrator	collation	supervisor
operator	collation	operator

The authorizations of the predefined roles are listed in Table 4-2.

Table 4-2 Default Configuration Discovery and Tracking roles

Privilege	Role			Description
	Supervisor	Administrator	Operator	
Admin		x		Allows the user to administer the Configuration Discovery and Tracking environment, including the management of user accounts
Discover	x	x		Allows the user to initiate discoveries
Read	x	x	x	Allows the user to read data from the CMDB
Update	x	x		Allows the user to create and modify objects in the CMDB

The Portal is the first interface all users will see, but to set up user accounts and control authorizations (role assignments), the system administrators must use the **Domain Manager** link to access the administrative functions. To log in to the Domain Manager for the first time, use the administrator account (Figure 4-2).

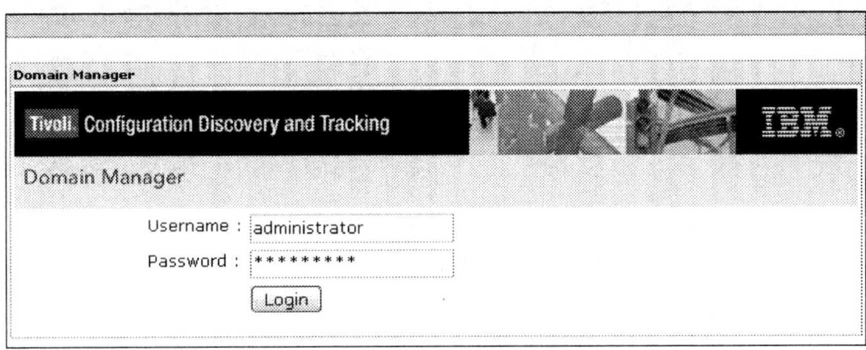

Figure 4-2 Configuration Discovery and Tracking Domain Manager login

4.1.1 Create roles

Initially there are no particular reasons to define custom roles, however if it is required in your particular environment, you should create the necessary roles prior to defining new user accounts. From the Domain Manager, navigate to the Administration section of the navigation pane (at the bottom), and click the **Roles** icon. Then, from the Roles dialog, click **Create Role**.

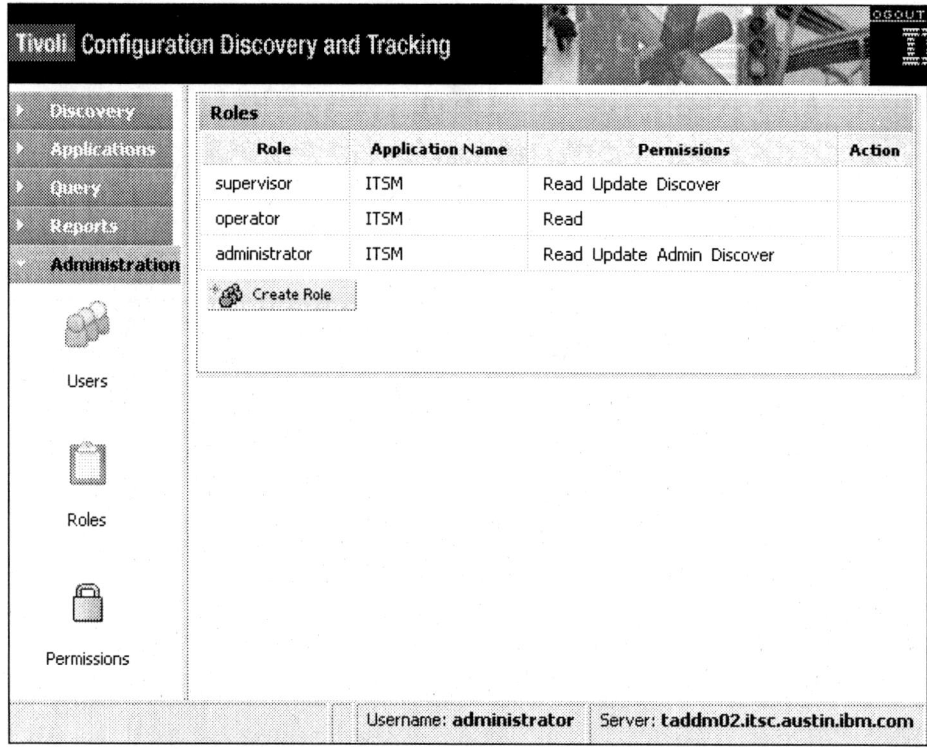

Figure 4-3 Create new role

A *role* is made up of any combination of the four permissions described in Table 4-2 on page 103: Admin, Discover, Read, and Update.

To create the role, provide a name, select the desired combination of permissions, and click **Create Role**. Figure 4-4 on page 105 shows the creation of a role name d ITSO All Roles, and in Figure 4-5 on page 105 you see that is was created.

In the next section, you will use the roles when defining new users.

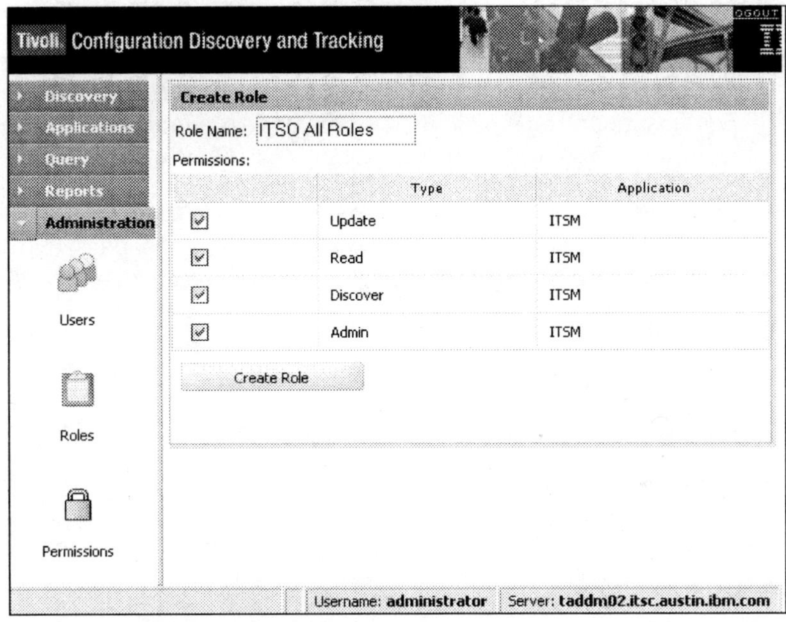

Figure 4-4 Assign role permissions

Figure 4-5 New role created

4.1.2 Create users

Creating and maintaining user IDs in Configuration Discovery and Tracking is just as simple as managing Roles. From the Domain Manager, navigate to the Administration section of the navigation pane (at the bottom), and click the **Users** icon. Then, from the Users dialog box, click **Create User**.

First, in the General Information section of the Create User dialog box, you must supply the user base data, ID, name, e-mail address, password, and time-out, as shown in Figure 4-6. Note that only user ID, password, and time-out are required.

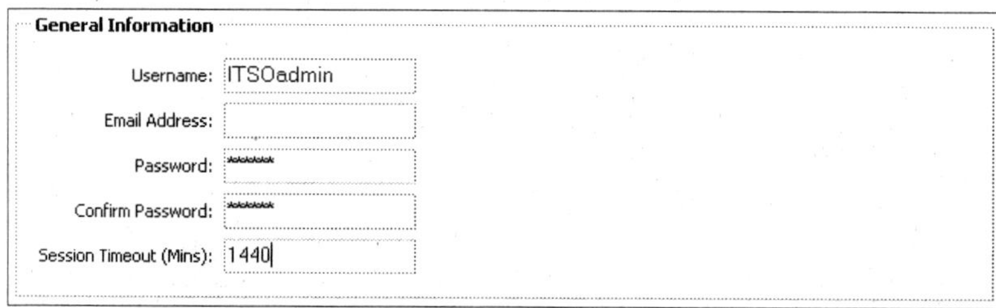

Figure 4-6 Defining user base data

In the Required Role section of the Create User dialog box, you must assign a role and an access Collection to the user.

Collections are basically nothing but a group of resources that the user is allowed to access and are maintained form the Product Console. If a collection has been tagged as an Access Collection, it can be used to determine which objects a user can access. Only one Access Collection, the DefaultAccessCollection which includes all objects, is available immediately after installation.

Figure 4-7 shows that we assigned the **ITSO All Roles** role to the new user, and allowed the user to access all the objects in the **DefaultAccessCollection**.

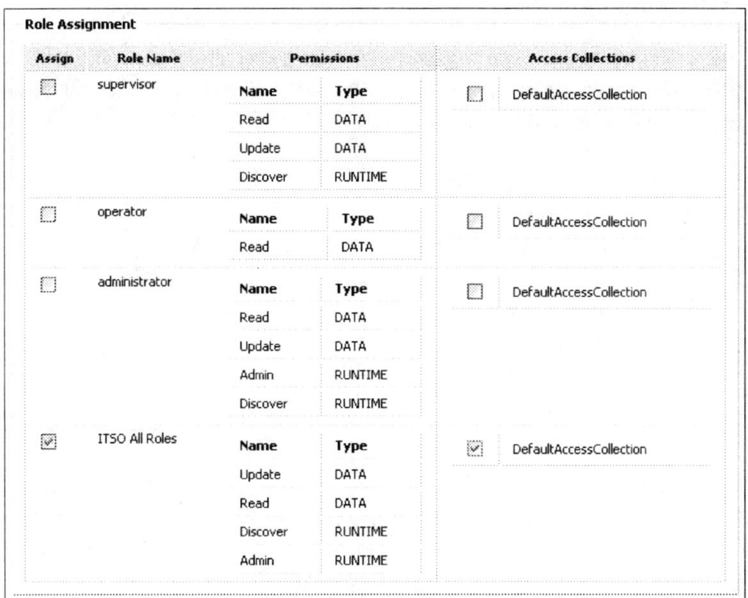

Figure 4-7 Defining user roles and access collection

When you have finished the user definition, press **Create User**, and the user will appear in the users list, as shown in Figure 4-8.

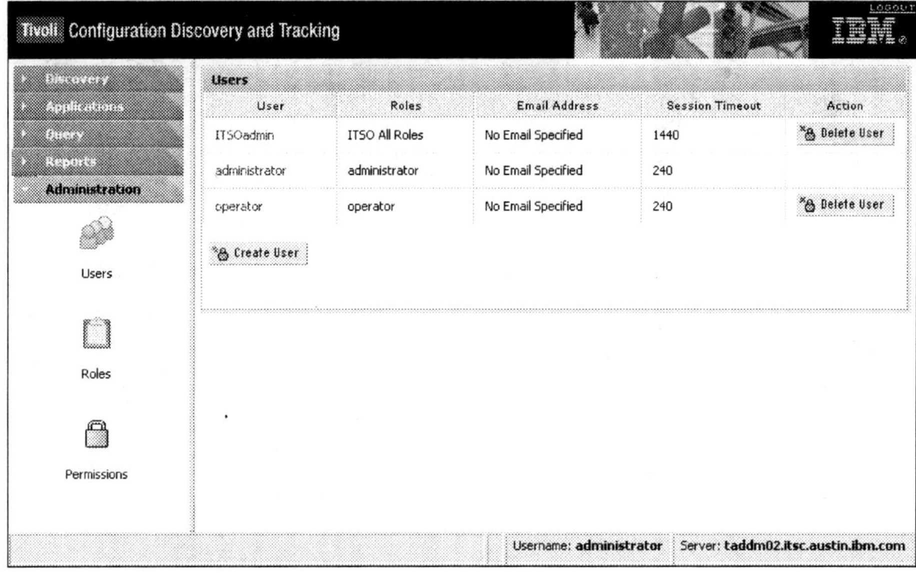

Figure 4-8 User created

4.1.3 Launching the Product Console

Having defined the roles, and user IDs needed to support our initial setup, the next step is to open the Product Console in order to start the discovery process an investigate features of Configuration Discovery and Tracking.

To open the Product Console, launch the IBM Tivoli Change and Configuration Management Database Configuration Discovery and Tracking portal. Point your browser to this URL:

```
http://<your_server_address_or_name>:9430)
```

Before continuing, you should stop and consider a few issues.

- You must have the IBM Java Runtime Environment (JRE) version 1.5 installed. You can verify the current version of your JRE by issuing the java **-version** command. If the reported version is different from IBM Java Runtime Environment v1.5, you can use the link on the IBM Tivoli Change and Configuration Management Database Configuration Discovery and Tracking Portal page, shown to the left in Figure 4-9 on page 109, to download and install the correct JRE.
- Consider downloading the certificate used to establish the session between the Product Console and the a Configuration Discovery and Tracking Portal using the Secure Socket Layer (SSL) protocol. By using the SSL protocol, all communication between the Product Console and the Configuration Discovery and Tracking Server will be encrypted, which might be a requirement in your organization, especially if your responsibilities include defining Access List entries (user ID and password combinations)

  To download the certificate to your workstation and configure you browser with the information needed to find the certificate when needed, click **Show SSL Options**. Then, specify the directory in which the certificate will be stored on your workstation, and click **Download Trust Store**. In the example shown in Figure 4-9, the directory where the certificate will be stored is c:\collation\certs.

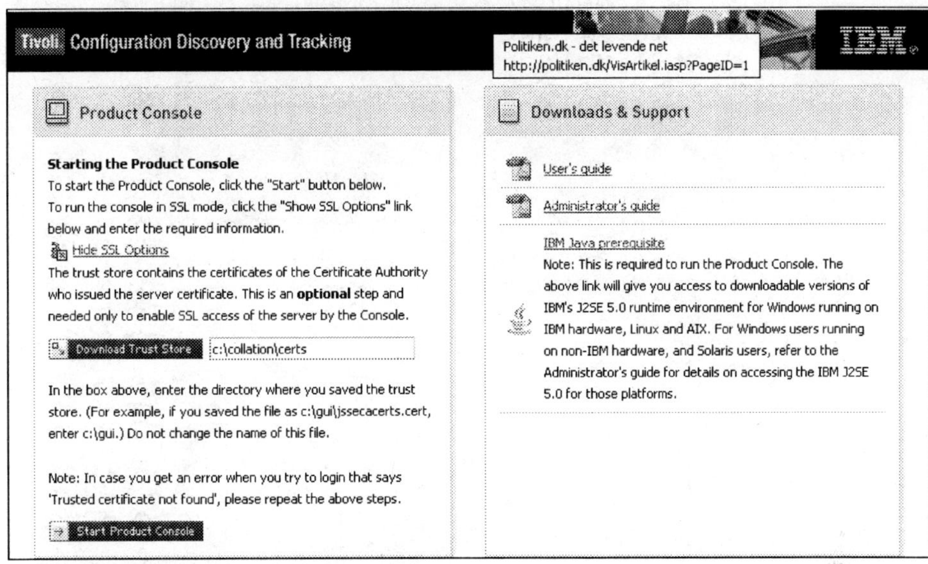

Figure 4-9 Product Console preparation links

After successful download, you can start the Product console by clicking the **Start Product Console** link. The Product Console java files are downloaded to a temporary location on your workstation, and you are prompted to decide whether or not to start the Product Console automatically using the Java Web Start (`javaws`) program, as in Figure 4-10.

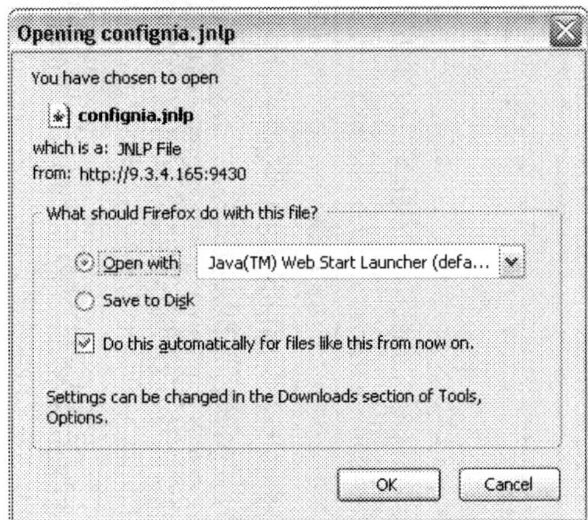

Figure 4-10 Automatic start the Product Console using Java Web Start

If your browser has not been set up to do this, follow the procedure described in 7.3.1, "Launching the Product Console" on page 254 to configure your browser to do this automatically. After Downloading the Product Console files, the login dialog box shown in Figure 4-11 is displayed.

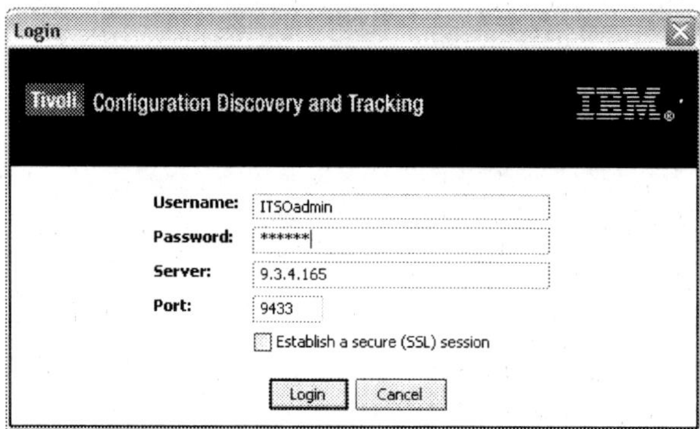

Figure 4-11 Product Console Login prompt

Besides suppling the credentials of a valid user ID and password combination, you have the option to specify whether or not the SSL protocol should be used. It is recommended that you always use SSL.

For your first login, you might want to use the credentials of one of the two system defined users `administrator` or `operator`. The password for both of these users is `collation`. Figure 4-11 shows that we used the new user created in 4.1.2, "Create users" on page 106.

4.2 Discovering your business application

The application used in this section is a test-implementation of Tivoli Intelligent Orchestrator in a single-system configuration. This implies that a single system hosts the following infrastructure components:

- DB2 UDB Enterprise Server v8.2
- IBM Tivoli Directory Server v5.2
- IBM WebSphere Application Server v5.1

On top of which, IBM Tivoli Intelligent Orchestrator v3.1 is installed.

Figure 4-12 depicts the application system setup along with the naming and relationships used in our test environment.

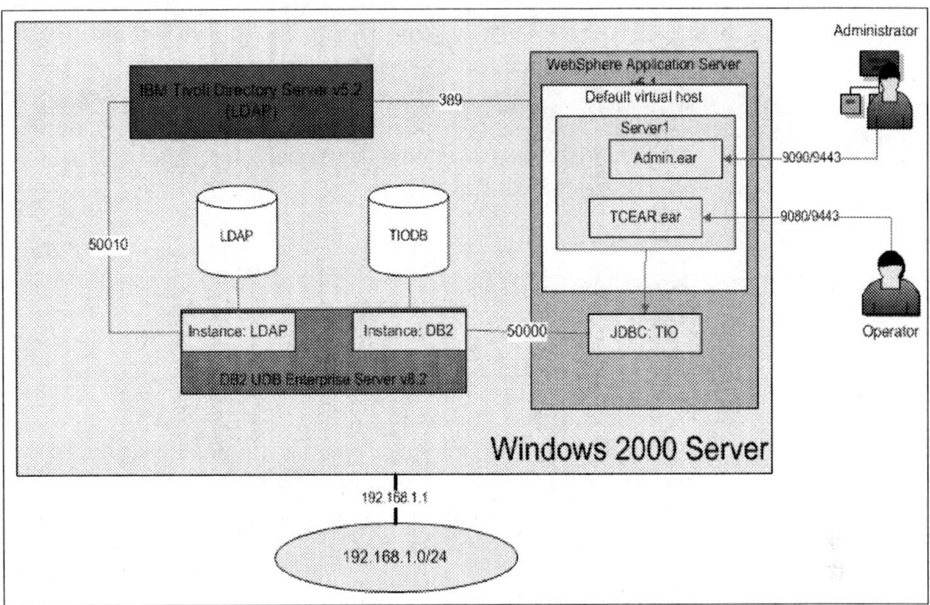

Figure 4-12 Tivoli Intelligent Orchestrator infrastructure and components

In the following sections, it is assumed that the discovery and tracking infrastructure, including users, authorizations, roles, gateways and anchor hosts, has been established, and that it is operational. Figure 4-13 shows the infrastructure needed in our environment, which was established in accordance with the instructions provided in Chapter 3, "Deploying Configuration Discovery and Tracking v1.1" on page 65.

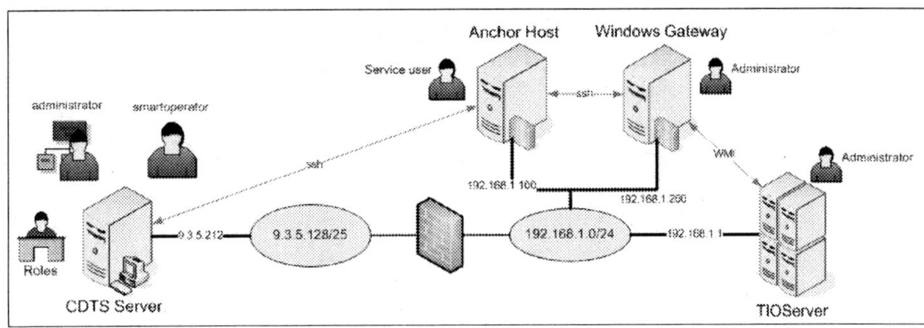

Figure 4-13 Required discovery and tracking infrastructure

The prerequisite Configuration Discovery and Tracking definitions that are assumed to be in place before setting out to discover the Tivoli Intelligent Orchestrator application environment are:

- Users, Roles and authentications
- Anchor hosts and Windows Gateways, including Access List entries necessary for normal operation

The tasks required to discover the Tivoli Intelligent Orchestrator related components and relationships and those tasks needed to define application components, business systems, and business services to IBM Tivoli Change and Configuration Management Database Configuration Discovery and Tracking in order to facilitate management, are:

1. Define the scope (optional).
2. Define Access List entries for infrastructure components.
3. Define custom servers.
4. Define Application templates.
5. Define Business Application.
6. Define Business Services.
7. Perform discovery.

All of these steps are covered in more detail in the following sections.

4.2.1 Define the scope

The first optional step in discovering the TIO environment is to make sure that the IP addresses of the systems hosting the application components are defined in a scope, so they can be discovered.

Scopes are used to define subsets of your infrastructure that will be the target of a discovery process, thus allowing you to discover only a limited number of systems. For easy management, scopes are grouped in Scope Sets. Scopes can be made up of subnet-, IP range-, or individual IP address or hostname definitions allowing you to group systems and devices as you want.

In our environment, we decided to define a scope named TIO_ScopeSet, in which only the one system (which hosts all the TIO application components) is known. This was primarily in order to create a nimble test environment and to be able to create access list entries that apply only to the tioserver environment.

> **Note:** In a more realistic environment, you will most likely have to define more than one system to your scope to cover all the components of the application system, in particular if you plan to discover clustered application systems.

Create a Scope Set

All scopes reside in *Scope Sets*, collections of individual scopes. At least one Scope Set must exit. To create a Scope Set, open the Scope dialog box by selection **Discovery → Scope** from the menu bar of the Product Console, and press **Add Set**. Now, provide a name for the Scope Set, and press **OK**, as in Figure 4-14.

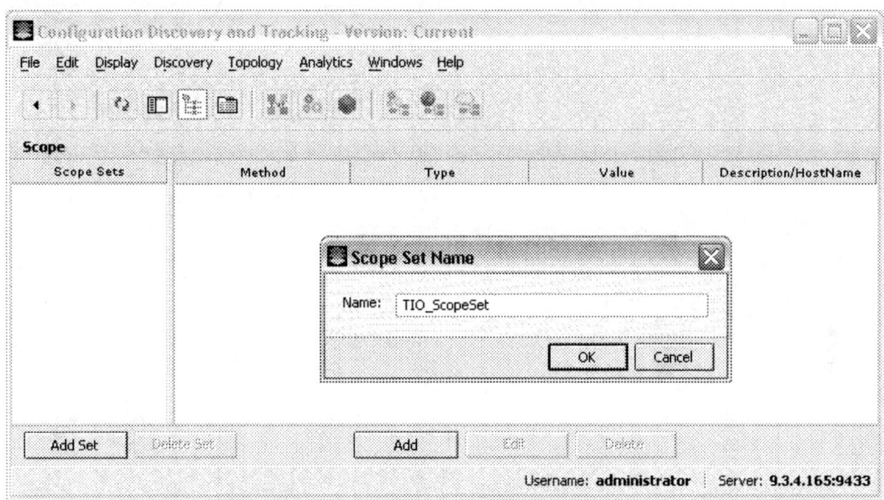

Figure 4-14 Create Scope Set

Figure 4-14 shows that we named our first Scope Set `TIO_ScopeSet`.

Create a Scope

To define the TIO_ScopeSet scope you can use the Product Console or prepare a flat file to be imported using the **loadscope** command. Refer to B.3.2, "loadscope - the scope import utility" on page 369 or the CDTS Users Guide for more details on defining scopes and using the loadscope utility.

Using the loadscope utility we prepared a flat file named `/tmp/TIOServer.scope` with only one line containing the IP address of the system hosting the tioserver system:

```
9.3.5.216
```

We created the TIO_ScopeSet scope with the following commands:

```
export COLLATION_HOME=/opt/IBM/cmdb/dist
${COLLATION_HOME}/bin/loadscope.jy -u administrator -p collation \
-s TIO_ScopeSet load /tmp/TIOServer.scope
```

You can verify the scope creation by looking at the Product Console, as shown in Figure 4-15.

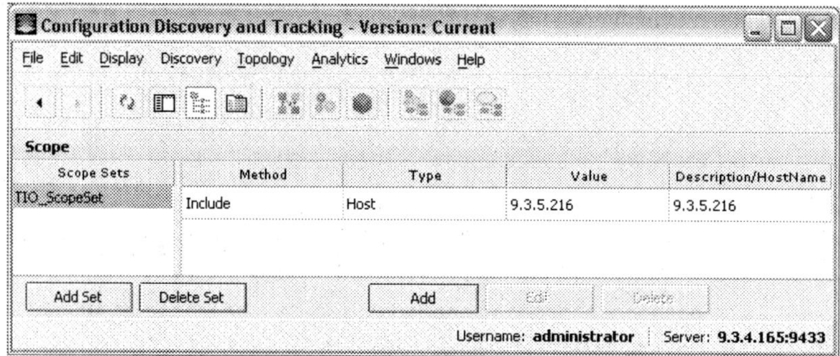

Figure 4-15 The TIOServer.scope scope

To verify that your scope includes the expected systems, you can use some of the tools described in B.4, "Support tools" on page 374 to verify your newly created scope.

4.2.2 The initial discovery

When a scope includes all the IP addresses we want to inspect, in our case just a single one, we can initiate a discovery to see which data are captured by Configuration Discovery and Tracking even before we have provided credentials to connect to components to gather detailed component data.

To initiate the discovery, open the Discovery Overview dialog box by selecting **Discovery → Overview**. From the Overview dialog box, click **Run Discovery**, and select the scope of devices to be discovered. In the example shown in Figure 4-16 we used only the newly created scope 9.3.5.216 from the TIO_ScopeSet.

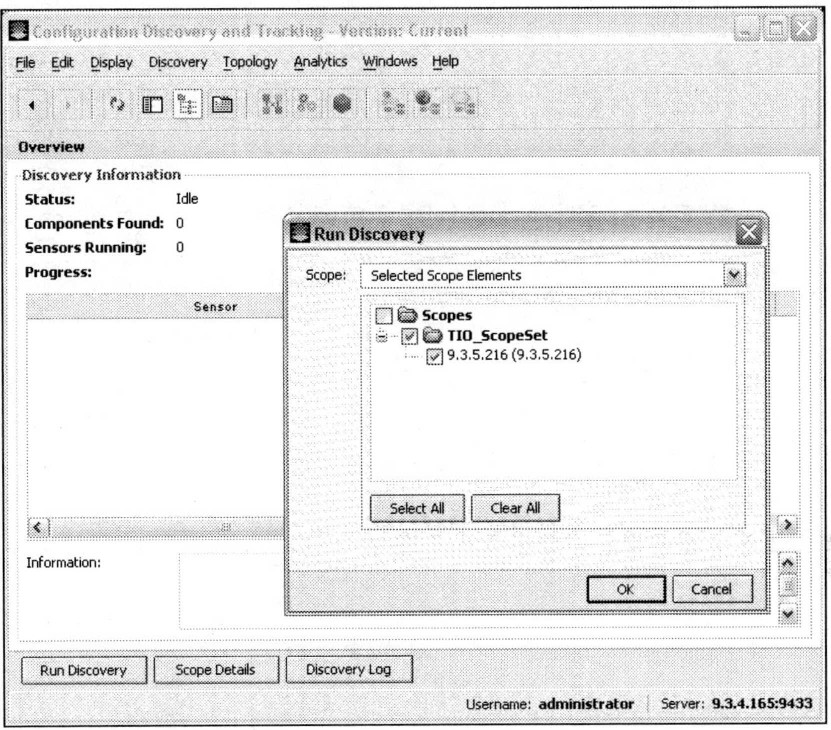

Figure 4-16 Initiating the discovery

While the discovery is running you can follow the deployment and execution status of sensors in the Overview dialog box. The same information will be logged to the discovery log, available after the discovery in the Discovery History dialog box. Figure 4-17 on page 116 show the execution log for our initial scan.

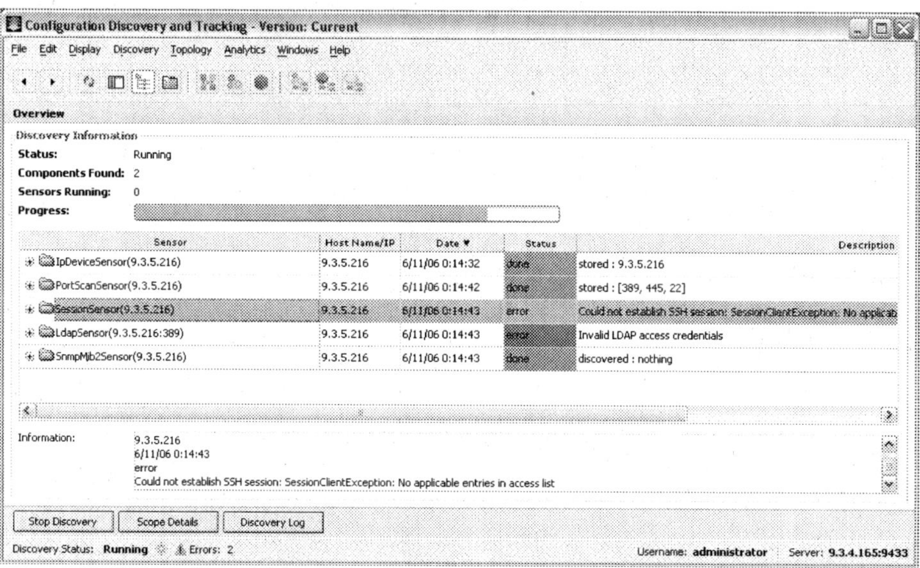

Figure 4-17 Initial scan discovery log

Figure 4-17 reveals, that only a few of the build in sensors actually were executed, and thus, only IP device information was discovered. The reason for this is found in the highlighted log entry for the SessionSensor, which did not successfully establish a SSH session with the system behind the IP address 9.3.5.216. This was expected because, at this point, we had not provided any Access List entries containing credentials to be used to authenticate with the device.

The reason that the execution of the SessionSensor was attempted at all is found in the results of the PortScanSensor execution in the top of the list. Here you see that the IP device on address 9.3.5.216 has ports 22, 389, and 445 open. Additionally, because port 22 is used by the SSH daemon, Configuration Discovery and Tracking tries to open a SSH session and execute the SessionSensor to gather more details. Similarly, the second line in the discovery log shows that the LdapSensor is kicked in, because the IP device is listening on port 389, which is the commonly used LDAP port. Again we see that no valid access credentials have been provided.

All the information gathered by Configuration Discovery and Tracking at this point, relates to the *raw* IP device. Figure 4-18 on page 117 shows that the only component that was discovered is registered as Other IP Device because no further details could be discovered for lack of access to the device. By opening the Details dialog box for the 9.3.5.216 device, you see not a lot of information besides the IP address, which was the starting point for this simple discovery.

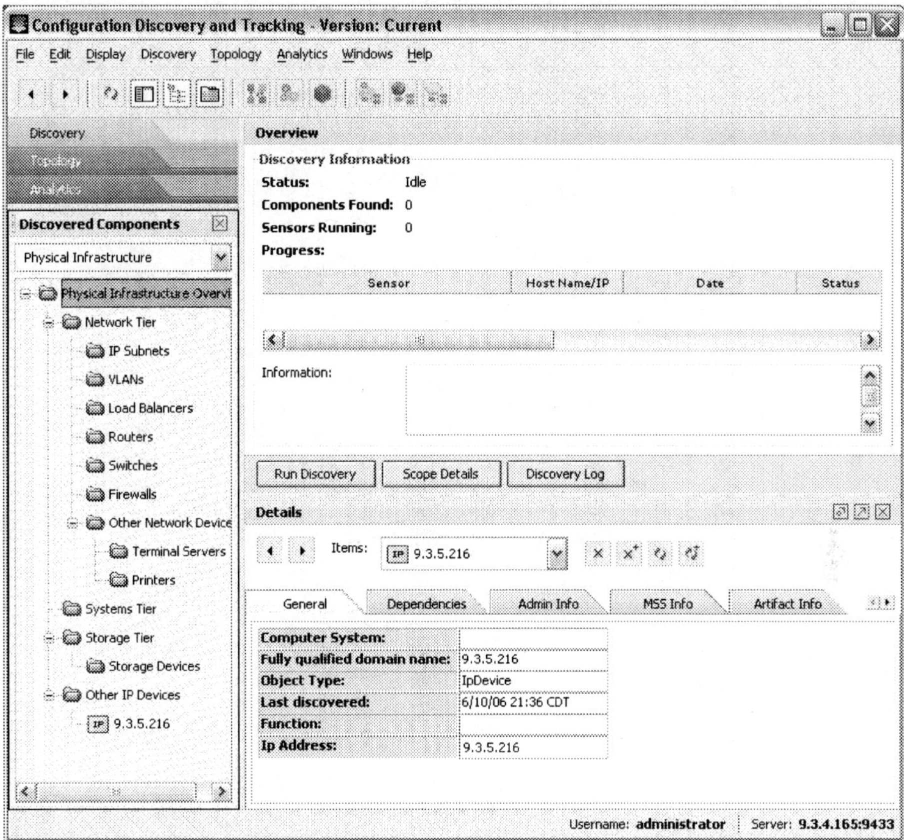

Figure 4-18 Other IP Device discovered details

To get further into the details of the components hosted on the 9.3.5.216 device, you have to define Access List entries, which will help Configuration Discovery and Tracking authenticate against the OS and subsystems on the device.

4.2.3 Define Access List entries for infrastructure components

To enable Configuration Discovery and Tracking to discover the details of the infrastructure components, you have to provide details of the credentials to use to connect to each type of resource. The credentials are sorted in the Access List, which allows you to specify different sets of credentials for each of the resource types listed in Table 4-3 on page 118.

Table 4-3 Access list entry requirements per component

Resource type	Credentials	REMARKS
Application Server	User ID and password needed to access the Application Server. For secure WebSphere servers, additional SSL certificate key and trust files - along with the pass phrases required to open them - must be specified.	Used to access Application Servers administrative functions through the JMX protocol on top of SOAP.
Cisco Device	User ID, password, and enablement password defined for the device	
Cisco Works	User ID and password of a user authorized to login and operate Cisco Works	Used to access Cisco Works form the host on which it is running.
ComputerSystem	User ID, password or key.	Used to access Unix systems including Anchor Hosts.
ComuterSystem (Windows)	User ID, password or key of a user who is member of the Administrators group of the Windows Gateway	Used to access Windows Gateways through SSH from the Configuration Discovery and Tracking server (or Anchor Hosts)
	User ID, and password of a user who is member of the Administrators group on the target system	Used to access Windows target systems through WMI from the Windows Gateways
Database	User ID and password of the database instance owner	Used to access database instances from the target system itself or to add authentication to windows WMI calls.
LDAP server	User ID and password of the root user	Used to access LDAP directories. User ID is typically the string `cn=root` or something similar.
Network Element (SNMP)	Read community name	Community name defined on the target system used to access the Management Information Blocks through the SNMP protocol.

In the Access List, you can specify several entries for each component type, allowing you specify, for example, several different user ID and password combinations used to establish SSH sessions to your systems. When defining more entries for the same type of component, be aware that Configuration Discovery and Tracking processes the entries top-down. So for performance reasons, you should keep the entries that will be used the most at the top of the list. Another way to speed up execution, is to limit certain Access List entries to specific scopes, thereby forcing Configuration Discovery and Tracking to only try these credentials if discovering the specific scope defined for the Access List entries.

To create Access List entries, open the Access List dialog box by selecting **Discovery → Access List** from the menu bar of the Product Console. Click **Add** to create a new entry, select component type, and provide the user ID and password (or key) details required to access one or more instances of that component type in your infrastructure. Figure 4-19 shows our password-based Access List entry for accessing the Linux operating system behind the 9.3.5.216 IP address.

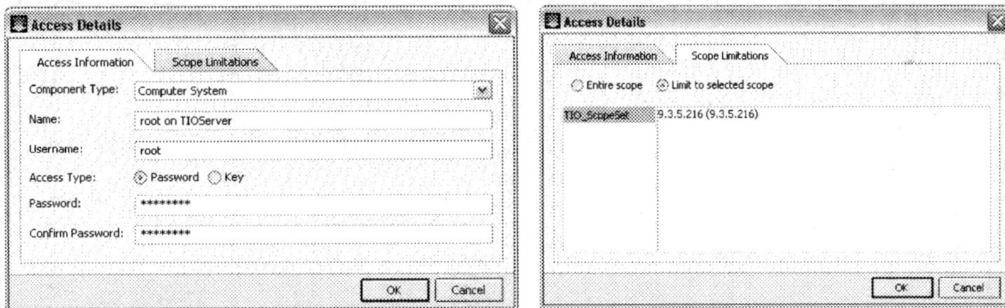

Figure 4-19 Computer System Access List entry with scope limitations

4.2.4 Discovering ComputerSystem Components

With this Access List entry, which will allow us to establish an SSH session with the tioserver computer system, we are ready to launch another discovery. This time, we use the API command line script to start the discovery:

```
export COLLATION_HOME=/opt/IBM/cmdb/dist
${COLLATION_HOME}/sdk/bin/api.sh -u administrator -p collation \
discover start 9.3.5.216
```

> **Note:** When initiating a discovery using the api.sh script, you do not have to have any scopes defined. The last parameters specify the hosts, ranges, and subnets that are the targets for the discovery.

For more details on using the api.sh script to control discoveries, refer to B.2.2, “api discovery: controlling discoveries” on page 348 or the IBM Tivoli Change and Configuration Management Database Configuration Discovery and Tracking v1.1 SDK Guide.

The log for this discovery (with valid credentials for the ComputerSystems within the scope) is shown in Figure 4-20.

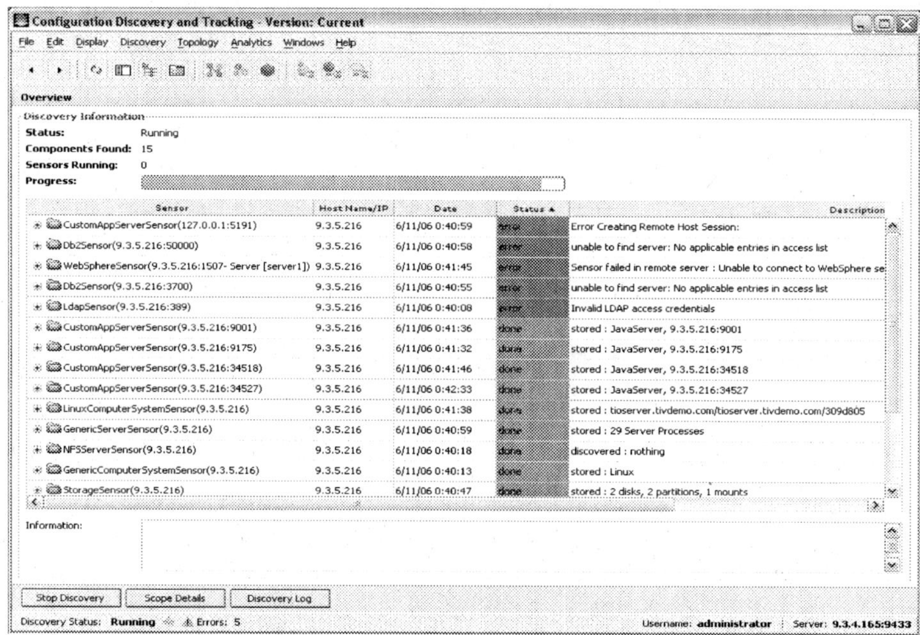

Figure 4-20 Configuration Discovery and Tracking ComputerSystem discovery

From this discovery log we see that this time around a total of 15 components were discovered, compared to the 2 components of the previous scan. This time Configuration Discovery and Tracking could successfully log in to the ComputerSystem and discover additional information such as hardware and operating system details, active sessions, and even selected subsystems. Again we see that because of missing access credentials the subsystem sensors (Db2, WebSphere, LDAP, and so on) all failed.

The information discovered from the ComputerSystem, by the particular sensors related to the discovered components, is far too extensive to discuss in detail here. However, Figure 4-21 on page 121 depicts the main categories of ComputerSystem related information, and the general details as well as the dependencies discovered. Remember that because of the missing Access Lists, not all details are being discovered yet.

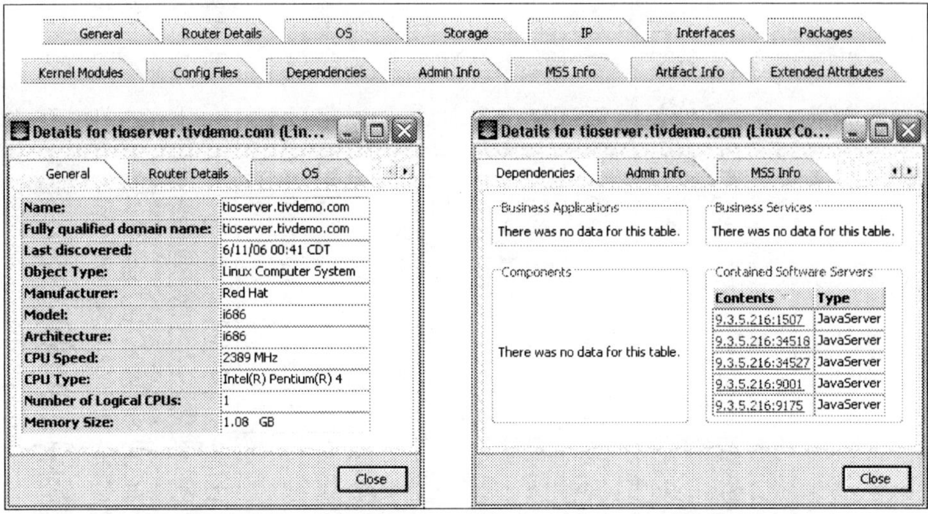

Figure 4-21 Discovered ComputerSystem attributed - including dependencies

When looking at the right-hand side of Figure 4-21, you can see that on the 9.3.5.216 IP device , which we know is a ComputerSystem named tioserver.tivdemo.com, Configuration Discovery and Tracking discovered five running Java processes with active sessions. Because no information has been provided to characterize these processes further, they are, for the time being, registered as JavaServer™ components.

The category of JavaServer is assigned because the Custom Server Template provided out-of-the -box by the name of JavaServer by default identifies all processes where the program ends with `java`, `java.exe` or `jre`. Because this Custom Server Template is enabled and specifies that we want to *discover* rather than *ignore* the processes, all java processes running on ComputerSystems within the selected Scope will be added to the topology as JavaServer objects.

More important than the type of the object is that they were discovered, and that they are being registered as Software Servers hosted by the tioserver.tivdemo.com ComputerSystem.

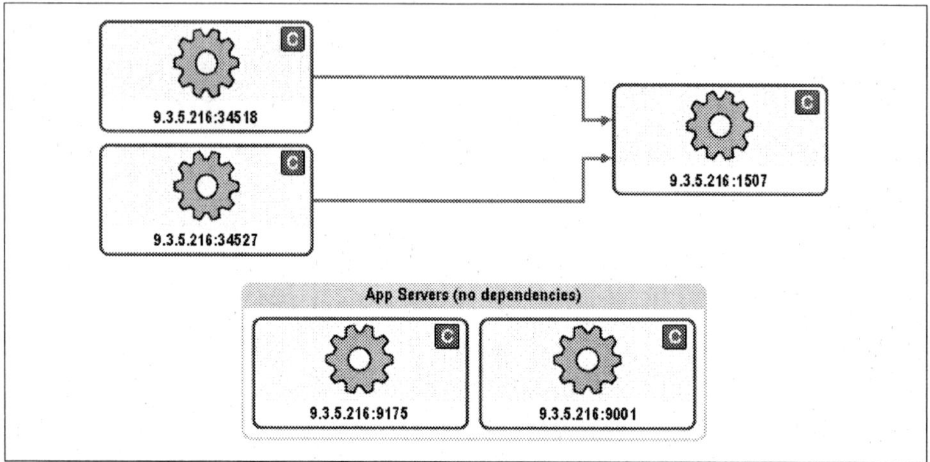

Figure 4-22 Discovered application-level components and dependencies

In addition, by looking on the Topology map shown in Figure 4-22 Configuration Discovery and Tracking discovered, that some of these JavaServer components are actually in session, thus depend on each other. By right-clicking on the server on port 1507, and selecting **Component Dependencies**, the following information in Figure 4-23 is revealed.

Dependencies List

Dependency Type	Participation	Other object Name	Created By
Transactional	Provider	9.3.5.216:34527	Discovered
Transactional	Provider	9.3.5.216:34518	Discovered

Add

Remove

Details

Close

Figure 4-23 Application Server Component dependencies

All of this information is critical when we drill down further, because we can use it to clearly identify the hard- and software components involved in provisioning the various logical server components of a business application system.

4.2.5 Discovering the infrastructure component credentials

To discover the configuration details of the infrastructure components hosted by the tioserver.tivdemo.com, we must make sure that the individual component sensors can connect to the servers to extract the desired information. This involves defining the missing Access List entries for each of the following component types, which was identified in one of two ways:

- By inspecting the discovery log for errors indicating wrong or missing credentials
- By identifying the different server components by looking on the infrastructure architecture diagram in Figure 4-12 on page 111

The component types for which we must define Access List entries are:

- Database (DB2)
- LDAP server
- Network Element (SNMP)
- Application Server (WebSphere)

Credentials for SNMP access

SNMP is enabled in our sample infrastructure, so naturally we want to extract as much information as possible from the SNMP Management Information Blocks. To do this, we need the read community name defined on the tioserver system. Figure 4-24 shows how we defined the SNMP Access List entry.

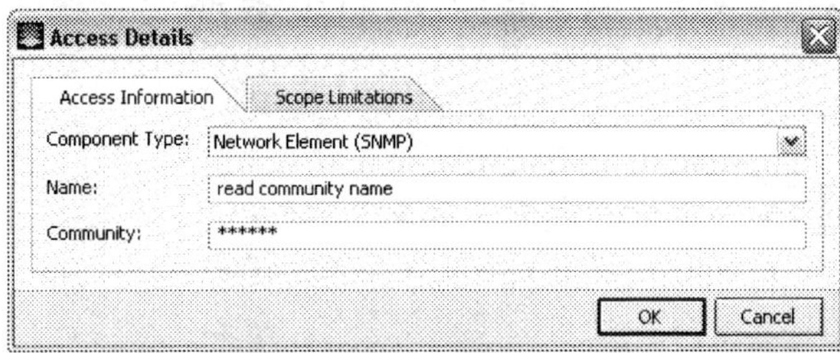

Figure 4-24 SNMP Access List entry

LDAP Component credentials

Our tioserver system hosts, among other servers components, an IBM Directory Server, which implements an LDAP directory used for user authorization by IBM Tivoli Intelligent Orchestrator. To discover the details of this LDAP implementation, we have to set up credentials that allows Configuration Discovery and Tracking to extract information from the LDAP directory.

In our implementation, the root user of the LDAP directory is named cn=root, so this is the user we select when defining the Access List entry for our LDAP Server - as shown in Figure 4-25 on page 124.

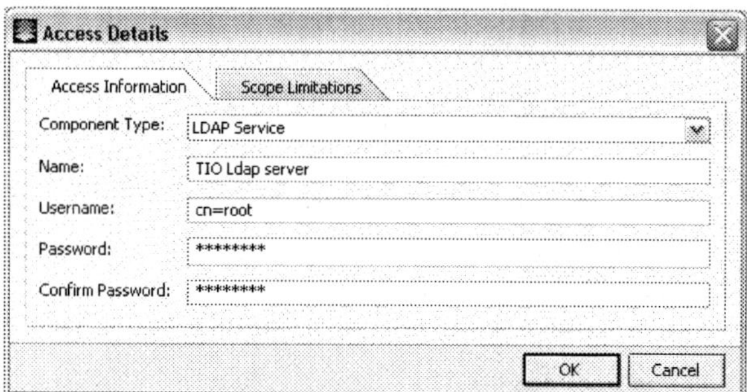

Figure 4-25 Setting up LDAP Access List entries

Defining DB2 Database component credentials

To successfully access the two databases in our infrastructure, we must define credentials for a user ID that has administrative access to the database instances. In our case, we have no common user that can access both database instances, so we will have to create two Access List entries. For ease of use, we use the user ID of the DB2 instance owners. Figure 4-26 shows the Access List entry for the `tiodb` database.

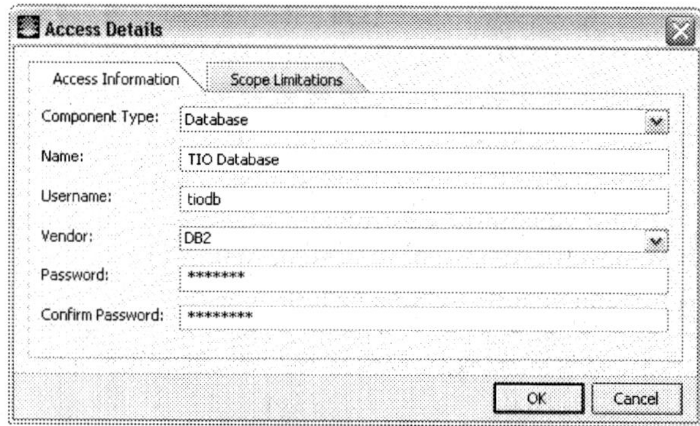

Figure 4-26 DB2 Database Access List entry

WebSphere Application Server Credential definition

Finally, to be able to discover the configuration details of the WebSphere Application Server that hosts the IBM Tivoli Intelligent Orchestrator application we have to create yet another Access List entry, this time for the `AppServer` object type.

The user ID and password combination must have been defined within the WebSphere Application Server environment as a valid user with administrative privileges. To test and verify that the user can access the WebSphere

Application Server environment, direct your browser to the following URL and log in:

```
http:<your_WAS_server>:9090/admin
```

Figure 4-27 shows that the administrative user used to login to the WebSphere Application Server hosted on the tioserver system is named `wasadmin`.

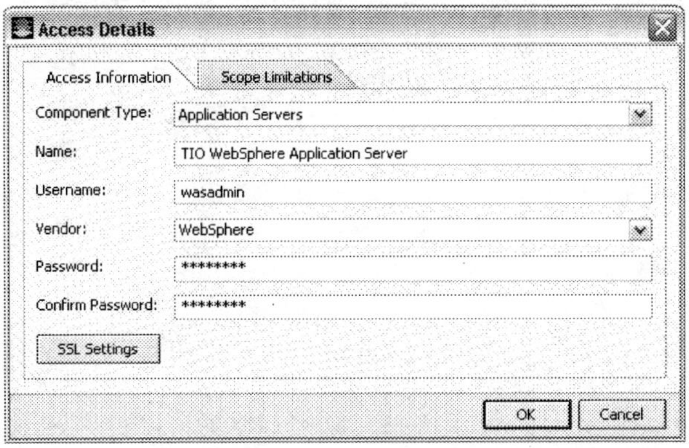

Figure 4-27 WebSphere Access List entry - base data

If you receive the following error from the WebSphereSensor during discovery:

```
Sensor failed in remote server : javax/management/ObjectName
```

You are missing the required files needed on the Configuration Discovery and Tracking server for WebSphere Application Server discovery. Ask your CCMDB administrator to install WebSphere Application Server, or copy the entire content of the ${WAS_HOME} directory of an existing WebSphere Application Server v5 or v6 installation to the Configuration Discovery and Tracking server. Remind your administrator install or copy the files while logged in as the user ID that runs the Configuration Discovery and Tracking Server. This will ensure that the Configuration Discovery and Tracking processes can access the files. Finally, to inform the Configuration Discovery and Tracking server about the location of the WebSphere Application Server files, update the com.collation.websphere.root.dir in the collation.properties file by providing the location of the newly created WebSphere libraries - either relative to the ${COLLATION_HOME} directory or fully qualified. If the WebSphere Application Server files were coped to /opt/IBM/WebSphere and the ${COLLATION_HOME} is /opt/IBM/CCMDB/cmdb you can use either of the two notations shown:

- com.collation.websphere.root.dir=/opt/IBM/WebSphere
- com.collation.websphere.root.dir=../../WebSphere

After restarting the Configuration Discovery and Tracking Server, WebSphere discovery will succeed, provided that the correct Access List entries have been created.

If, as in our case, your WebSphere Application environment is set up to enforce security, you also have to import the SSL trust and key certificates in order to successfully connect to the WebSphere Application Server. If you do not perform this step, you might get the following error message:

```
Sensor failed in remote server : Unable to connect to WebSphere
server at 9.3.5.216:8880 - ADMC0016E: Could not create SOAP
Connector to connect to host 9.3.5.216 at port 8880
```

The trust and key certificate files reside on the WebSphere Application Server - typically in the ${WAS_HOME}/AppServer/etc directory, and the default names are:

Key certificate file:	DummyServerKeyFile.jks
Trust certificate file:	DummyServerTrustFile.jks

In addition to having to access these files, either directly through the Product Console running at the WebSphere Application Server, or from the local file system at the Configuration Discovery and Tracking server to which the files might have been copied, you also have to supply the fingerprint of the files. The fingerprint, also known as the *Key Store Pass Phrase*, can be considered as a password required to open the certificate files. Figure 4-28 shows the SSL definitions for our WebSphere Application Server. In our case, the Key certificate and trust certificate files were copied to the Configuration Discovery and Tracking Server prior to creating the Access List entry.

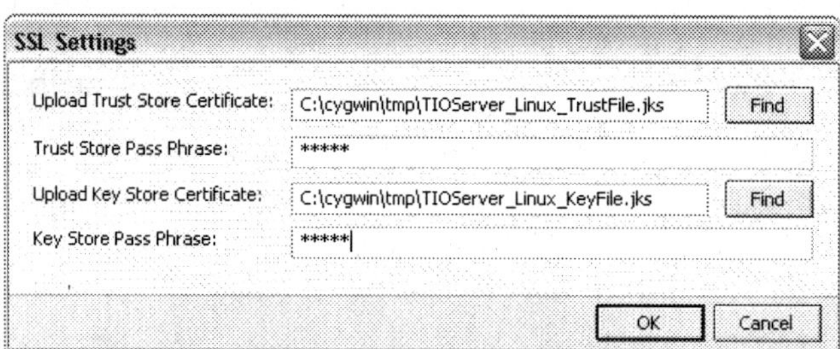

Figure 4-28 WebSphere Access List entry - SSL information

Your WebSphere Application Server administrator can supply both the names of the certificate files as well as the fingerprints required for you to define the Access List entries for your WebSphere servers.

Access List entries needed to discover the components

Figure 4-29 summarizes the Access List requirements needed to discover all the components of the IBM Tivoli Intelligent Orchestrator solution hosted on the tioserver system.

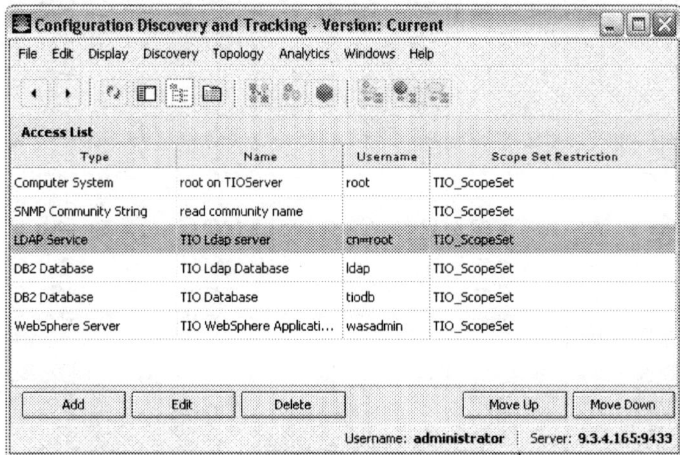

Figure 4-29 Access List entries required to discover the tioserver infrastructure

Before running the discovery again, you might want to verify the Access list entries you have just created. Naturally, you could just run a discovery and check the discovery log for errors, but, especially in a production environment, this can take quite a while. You can use the tools described in B.4, “Support tools” on page 374 to verify your newly created Access List entries.

To initiate another discovery of the systems defined within the TIO_SscopeSet, which basically only includes the tioserver system (at 9.3.5.261), either:

- Issue the following command:

  ```
  ${COLLATION_HOME}/sdk/bin/api.sh -u administrator -p collation
  discover start TIO_ScopeSet
  ```

- Use the Product Console, and select **Discovery** → **Overview**, and press **Run Discovery**. On the Run Discovery dialog, select the **TIO_ScopeSet**, and press **OK**.

The discovery is executed again. During the execution, you will see many more sensors executing successfully. If you look at Figure 4-30 on page 128, you will notice that both two instances of the DB2Sensor, and one instance of the WebSphereSensor has completed successfully because this time around the Access List entries needed to authenticate with these infrastructure components had been provided.

Sensor	Host Name/IP	Date ▼	Status	D
StorageSensor(9.3.5.216)	tioserver	6/30/06 21:16:42	done	stored : 2 disks, 2 partitions, 1 mounts
CustomAppServerSensor(9.3.5.216:34068)	tioserver	tioserver 0/06 21:16:53	done	stored : JavaServer, 9.3.5.216:34068
GenericServerSensor(9.3.5.216)	tioserver	6/30/06 21:16:53	done	stored : 19 Server Processes
CustomAppServerSensor(9.3.5.216:34061)	tioserver	6/30/06 21:16:53	done	stored : JavaServer, 9.3.5.216:34061
CustomAppServerSensor(9.3.5.216:9175)	tioserver	6/30/06 21:16:54	done	stored : JavaServer, 9.3.5.216:9175
CustomAppServerSensor(127.0.0.1:5191)	tioserver	6/30/06 21:16:54	done	stored : JavaServer, 9.3.5.216:5191
ApacheServerSensor(9.3.5.216:80)	tioserver	6/30/06 21:17:15	done	stored : 1 server bound to 0.0.0.0:80
AnchorSensor(anchor: @9.3.5.212:8497)	anchor	6/30/06 21:17:49	done	stored : #2 on no address
LinuxComputerSystemSensor(9.3.5.216)	tioserver	6/30/06 21:17:50	done	stored : tioserver.tivdemo.com/tioserver.tivdemo.com/30
IpDeviceSensor(9.3.5.216)	tioserver	6/30/06 21:17:55	done	stored : 9.3.5.216
PortScanSensor(9.3.5.216)	tioserver	6/30/06 21:18:00	done	stored : [389, 445, 22]
Db2Sensor(9.3.5.216:50000)	tioserver	6/30/06 21:20:16	done	stored : 1 systems
Db2Sensor(9.3.5.216:3700)	tioserver	6/30/06 21:20:18	done	stored : 1 systems
WebSphereSensor(9.3.5.216:1507- Server [server...	tioserver	6/30/06 21:21:29	done	stored : Cell: tioserver, Type: STANDALONE, 1 nodes, 1 s

Figure 4-30 Discovery with Access List entries for all components

Upon completion of the discovery, you can see the components and relationships depicted in Figure 4-31 if you take a look at the Application Topology by selecting **Topology → Application Infrastructure**.

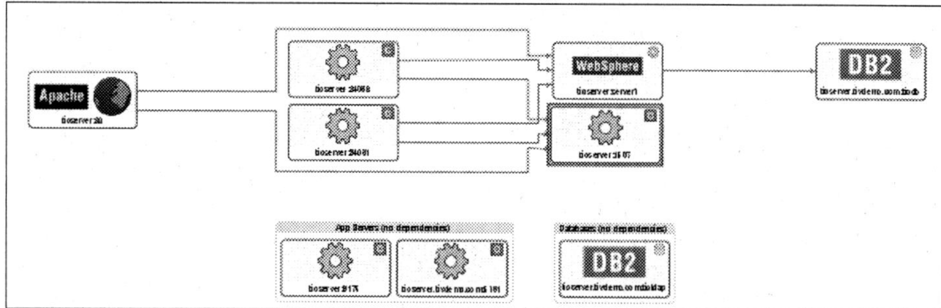

Figure 4-31 Application Topology after discovery with correct Access List

Compared to the application topology from the first discovery (shown in Figure 4-22 on page 122) we now get both the expected WebSphere Application Server and two DB2 Instances shown in the topology. We even see the relationships between the two previously discovered JavaServer objects (on the left hand side of Figure 4-31) and the new WebSphere object (`tioserver:server1`), as well as the jdbc connection between the WebSphere server and the database.

In addition, you see that the JavaServer object from the initial discovery labeled `9.3.5.216:1507` still persists even though, if you look at the **Details** for the WebSphere object (`tioserver:server1`), under the **Runtime** you will see that

Configuration Discovery and Tracking has discovered that the WebSphere server actually listens on the following ports:

```
1507 2809 5557 5559 8880 9043 9080 9090 9443 9511 9512 9513 34176
34182 34188 36952 44041 44042 44043 44044 44136 44139 44176 44182
60710
```

The lowest portnumber was the one used to create the label for the JavaServer object.

Identifying dormant components

Because Configuration Discovery and Tracking discovery is cumulative, meaning that previously discovered objects will not be removed automatically if they are not found in subsequent discoveries, the JavaServer labeled `9.3.5.216:1507` will persist in the topology until manually deleted by an administrator.

To help the administrator identify components that are no longer present in the infrastructure, Configuration Discovery and Tracking can be instructed to assign a status of `dormant` to objects that have not been discovered since a specific point in time. Dormant components can be viewed in the Dormant Components report from **Analytics → Dormant Components**. In addition, objects that have been tagged as dormant might be hidden from the topology view by checking the **Hide 'Dormant' Components** in the topology view options (Figure 4-32) and supplying a cut-off date in the Dormant after: field. To access the topology view options, select **Topology → Options**.

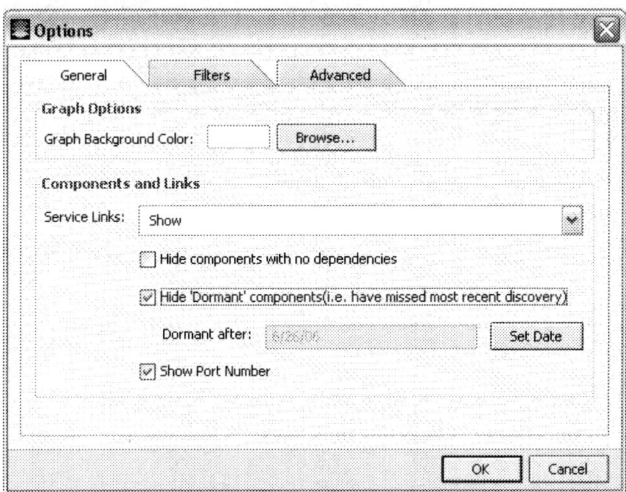

Figure 4-32 Controlling display of dormant components

The cut-off date provided in the Topology settings will be compared to the Last Modified Time attribute for each object, and those objects with a Last Modified Time prior or equal to the cut-off date will be marked as dormant.

For more details on running the Dormant Components report, refer to 6.8.3, "Generate a dormant components report" on page 235.

Deleting components

Because the 9.3.5.216:1507 JavaServer is now obsolete, we want to delete it from the topology. To achieve this, we simply right-click the object in the topology view or the discovered components view and select **Delete**.

After rebuilding the topology after the deletion, the topology now looks like the one shown in Figure 4-33.

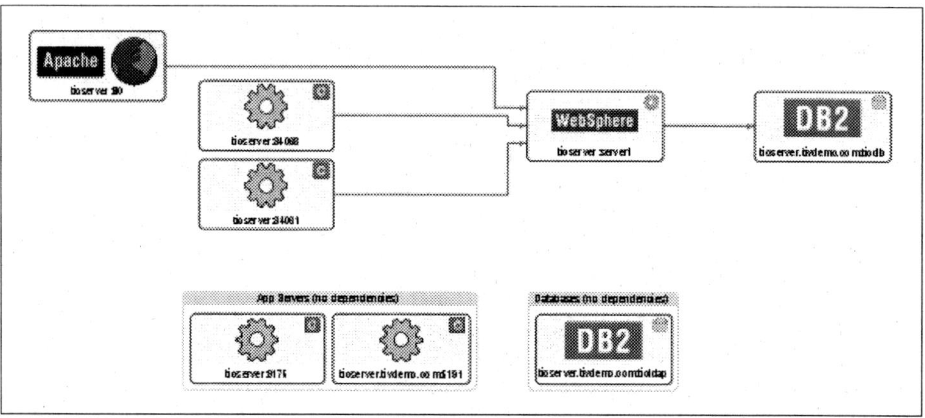

Figure 4-33 Discovered application topology

This topology reveals that the relationships between the WebSphere server and both the Apache and the database instance `tiodb` was discovered just automatically. Looking at the **Dependencies** tab of the Details page for the WebSphere server, we see all four dependencies, as shown in Figure 4-34 on page 131.

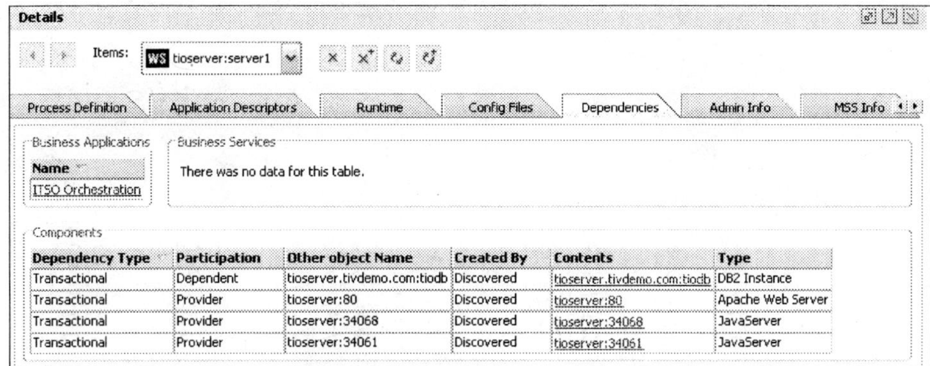

Figure 4-34 WebSphere Server dependencies

In addition, we can see all the configuration details for all the components discovered. As an example, we take a look at the **Resources** tab of the WebSphere server instance details, and see all the resources known to the server instance in Figure 4-35.

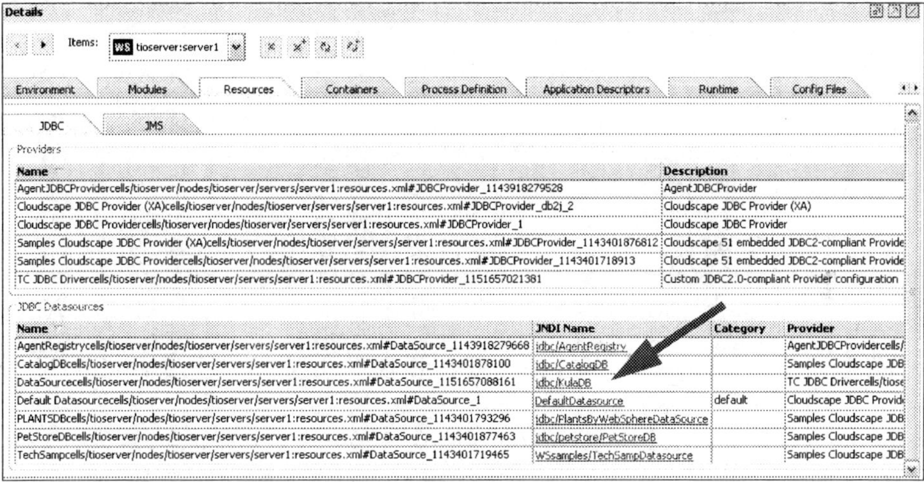

Figure 4-35 WebSphere server instance resources

And by clicking the `jdbc/KulaDB` resource name link, we can drill down into the details of the defined jdbc resource and see how it is defined, as in Figure 4-36 on page 132.

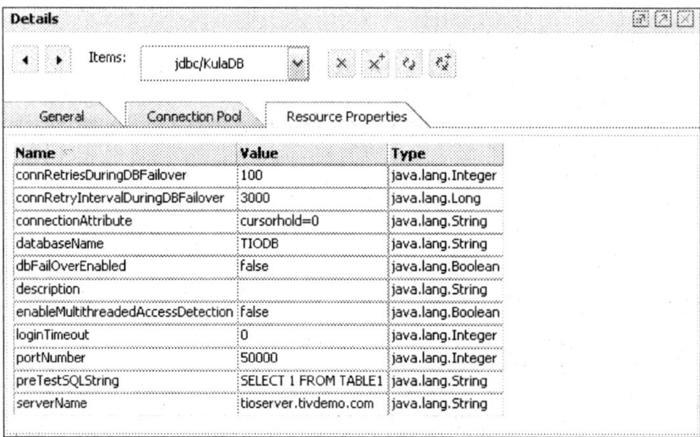

Name	Value	Type
connRetriesDuringDBFailover	100	java.lang.Integer
connRetryIntervalDuringDBFailover	3000	java.lang.Long
connectionAttribute	cursorhold=0	java.lang.String
databaseName	TIODB	java.lang.String
dbFailOverEnabled	false	java.lang.Boolean
description		java.lang.String
enableMultithreadedAccessDetection	false	java.lang.Boolean
loginTimeout	0	java.lang.Integer
portNumber	50000	java.lang.Integer
preTestSQLString	SELECT 1 FROM TABLE1	java.lang.String
serverName	tioserver.tivdemo.com	java.lang.String

Figure 4-36 WebSphere jdcb resource details

Should any of these parameters change before the next discovery, these changes will be recorded, and the jdbc object will be tagged as having been changed.

4.2.6 Define custom server templates

Looking at the topology represented in Figure 4-33 on page 130, we notice that there are still some generic JavaServer objects. These actually represent processes running on the tioserver system that are part of the Tivoli Intelligent Orchestrator application. Besides the TCEAR.ear module running inside the tioserver:server1 WebSphere server, Tivoli Intelligent Orchestrator starts four java processes to provide the services to the solution. As shown in the topology, only two of these are in constant communication with the WebSphere server. As a result, the dependencies are discovered. Knowing the internals of the Tivoli Intelligent Orchestrator solution, we can already say that the started java processes represent the following TIO related servers:

- PolicyEngine
- DeploymentEngine
- AgentShellServer
- HelpSystem

Instead of seeing generic JavaServer servers in the topology, we would like to be able to assign specific object types to each of these processes, so at a later point we will be able to easily identify new instances of these application-specific server processes and automatically create new, complete application instances of new Tivoli Intelligent Orchestrator servers added to the infrastructure. To do this, we must define four new Custom Server Templates, one for each Tivoli Intelligent Orchestrator server process. Custom Server Templates are used to help Configuration Discovery and Tracking register discovered processes as specific object types by applying filters identifying the individual object type.

The filters used within Custom Server Templates are made up by combining one or more criteria, values for one of the following attributes of the processes discovered by Configuration Discovery and Tracking, either as the combination of all the criteria or just any one of them:

- Program name
- Argument
- Environment
- Port
- Windows Service Name

The comparison operators used to evaluate the discovered attribute with the specified value can be one of:

- is
- is-not
- contains
- does-not-contain
- starts-with
- does-not-starts-with
- ends-with
- does-not-ends-with
- regular expression

Each Custom Server Template should have a unique combination of the filter, and they are processed in the order in which they appear in the list of Custom Server Template definitions. Consider these two Custom Server Template definitions where *Generic 94* appears prior to the *TMR Server* definition in the list of Custom Server Templates (as shown in Table 4-4).

Table 4-4 Custom Server Template definitions

Name	Generic 94	TMR Server
Criteria Type	Any	All
Port	is 94	is 94
Program Name	ends with *generic*	contains *tivoli*

In the event that a discovery identifies a running process with a program name of `/opt/Tivoli/bin/tivoli` which is listening on port 94 no TMR Server objects ever be registered, because port 94 is caught by the Generic 94 Custom Server Template definition.

Now, we return to our Tivoli Intelligent Orchestrator environment, in which we want to define Custom Server Templates that identifies the four processes needed by the solution. We already know, since they were all registered as JavaServer objects, that the running process ends with the string `java`, so we need some other way of differentiating them. Because the ports used are allocated dynamically, we use a string in the arguments for the processes to make the distinction between each of the servers and, to avoid overlap with other (future) servers with similar names (such as PolicyEngine) and the resulting misregistration, we use a string within the environment which identifies our solution as much as possible.

The information represented in Table 4-5 was compiled from looking at the RunTime details for each of the discovered server processes. An example is shown in Figure 4-37 on page 135.

Table 4-5 Tivoli Intelligent Orchestrator custom server templates

Custom Server Template name	**Criteria**		
	Program name ends-with	**Environment contains**	**Argument contains**
TIO PolicyEngine	*java*	*TIO_SERVER* is *server1*	PolicyEngine
TIO DeploymentEngine			DeploymentEngine
TIO AgentShellServer			AgentShellServer
TIO HelpSystemServer			infocenterApplication

We could create the Custom Server Template definitions from scratch by selecting **Discover → Custom Servers** and using the **Add** button. However, because we have already discovered the servers, remember they were registered as JavaServer objects, we will use the inventory reporting function to easily find the attributes needed to create unique filters.

Select **Analytics** → **Inventory**, select the **Other Servers** category, and **Run Report**. The report shown in Figure 4-37 opens.

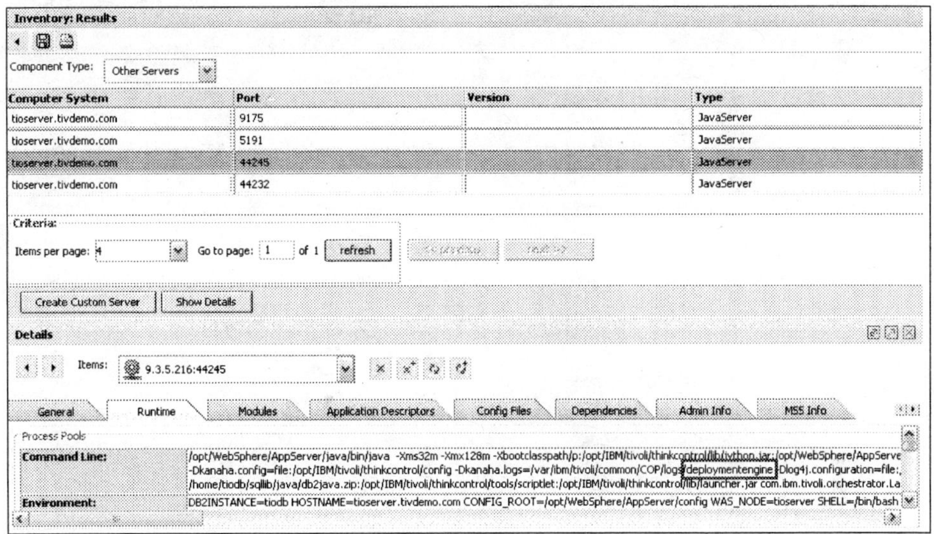

Figure 4-37 Other Servers Inventory report

By selecting a server and clicking the **CreateCustom Server** button, the Custom Server Details dialog box will be opened, as shown in Figure 4-38.

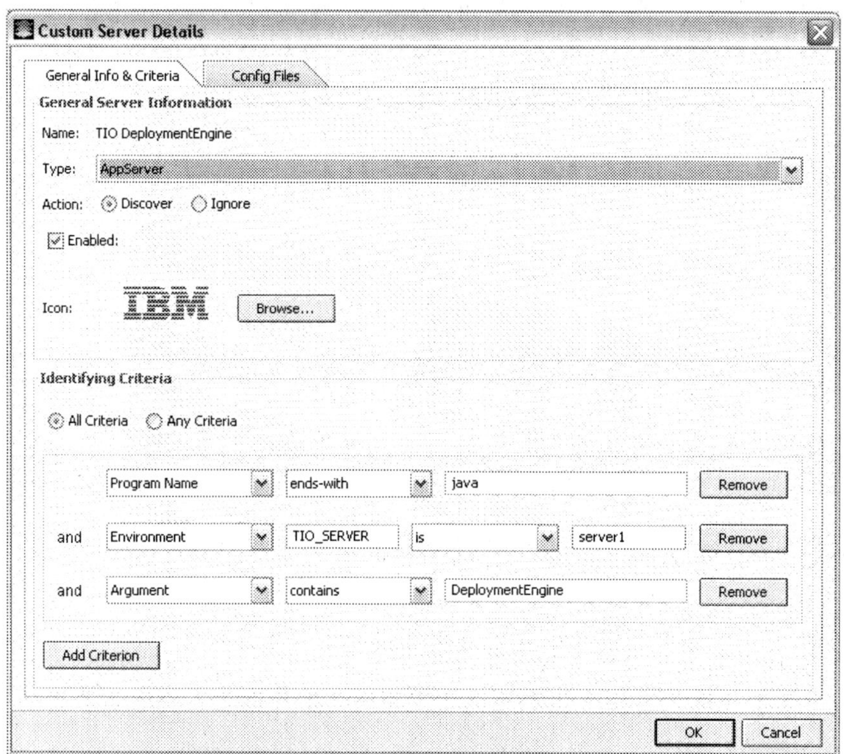

Figure 4-38 Defining your Custom Server Template

Now, we repeated this process for all four TIO server processes. Alternatively, we might have used the Product Console to create the first Custom Server Template, and then used the `templateloader` program (with the `export` parameter) to export the template to a flat file. This file could have been copied, and modified to be used as input for following templateloader...import executions. More details about the templateloader program are located in B.3.3, "templateloader: the template import/export utility" on page 373.

When new Custom Server Templates are defined, either manually or through importing them, they will automatically be added to the end of the list. Because the JavaServer template appears prior to our new templates, the TIO server processes will be caught by this and the new templates will not take effect, unless they appear in the list of Custom Server Templates prior to the JavaServer template. Therefore, we have to move the JavaServer template to the very bottom of the list, as shown in Figure 4-39 on page 137, before initiating yet another discovery to get the java processes registered correctly.

Custom Servers					
Enabled	Icon	Name	Type	Action	Config Files
true		Windows Builtin Services	AppServer	Ignore	
true	IBM	TIO DeploymentEngine	AppServer	Discover	
true	IBM	TIO PolicyEngine	AppServer	Discover	
true	IBM	TIO AgentShellServer	AppServer	Discover	
true	IBM	TIO HelpSystemServer	AppServer	Discover	
true		JavaServer	AppServer	Discover	$PWD/

Add | Edit | Copy | Delete | Move Up | Move Down

Figure 4-39 Sequencing the AppServer Custom Server Templates

Upon completion of the discovery, notice that the icons of the server have changed according to the ones we assigned to the Custom Server Templates for the Tivoli Intelligent Orchestrator solution, as shown in Figure 4-40.

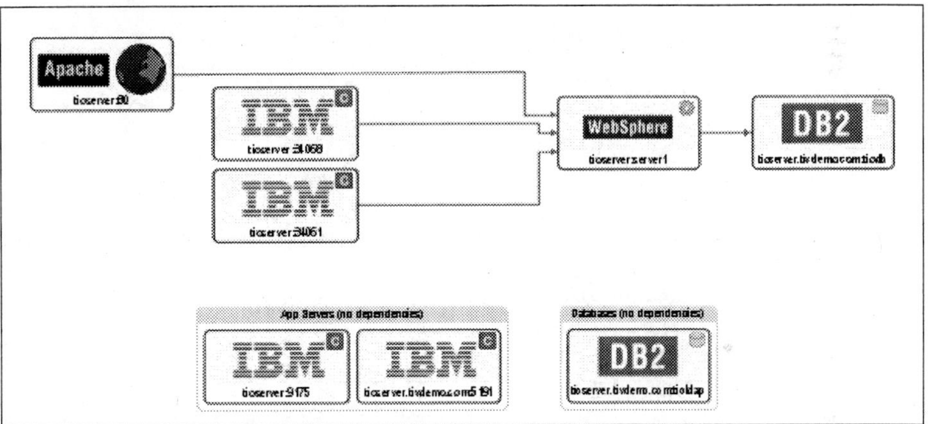

Figure 4-40 Tivoli Intelligent Orchestrator server components topology

The proper registration is further documented by looking at the Discovered Components dialog box, which shows that one instance of each of the Custom Servers Templates we expected was discovered (Figure 4-41 on page 138).

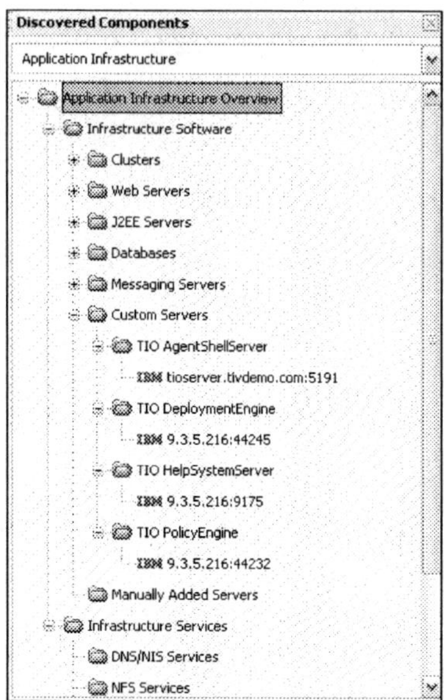

Figure 4-41 Discovered TIO Custom Server instances

Services

The pre-GA version of the product used to develop this book did not automatically discover the relationship between our WebSphere Application Server and the LDAP service automatically. Neither did it discover the relationship between the LDAP service and the database used to store the security information.

To make up for this, so we will be able to recognize these dependencies for example when performing an impact analysis on a change to the LDAP database, we defined a Custom Server Template which maps the LDAP Service named `tioserver:389`. Figure 4-42 on page 139 shows the definitions of the Custom Server Template.

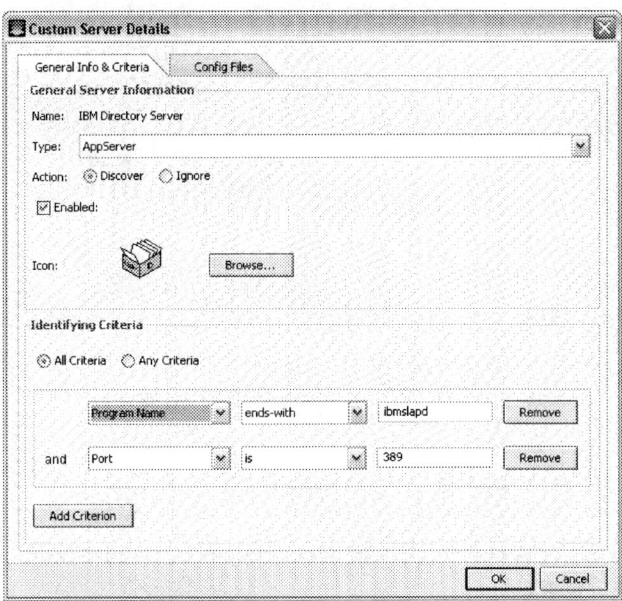

Figure 4-42 Custom Server Template mapping the tioldap:389 service

Once this IBM Directory Server Custom Server has been discovered, we can manually add the relationships to the `tioldap` database instance and the `tioserver:389` ldap service, in order to record all the dependencies in our infrastructure.

Manually adding Dependencies

A dependency between two objects consists of a *Provider* and *Dependent*. Typically a database server assumes only the Provider role, the J2EE servers are dependents of Databases and a providers to Web Server, and Web Servers are normally only dependents.

Dependencies come in two varieties:

Transactional
: Transactional dependencies occur between application components such as Web servers, application servers, and databases. The dependent component issues requests to the provider component in order to perform certain functions, such as JDBC calls from a J2EE server to a database. In this case, the provider is often referred to as a *server* and the dependent as a *console.*

Service
: Service dependencies occur between application components and infrastructure services such as DNS, LDAP, and NFS. The provider is the infrastructure

service, and the dependent component requests system services from the provider, such as a request to map a DNS name to an IP address.

In the case of the IBM Directory Server in our environment, we want to make the topology reflect the relationship between the LDAP server (represented by the `tioserver:389` instance of the IBM Directory Server Custom Server) and the database instance `tioserver.tivdemo.com:tioldap`. By right-clicking the `tioserver:389` object and selecting **Component Dependencies**, you see an overview of the dependencies related to this object. To create a relationship manually click **Add**, and provide the details. Figure 4-43 shows the definition of the LDAP server-database instance relationship for our environment.

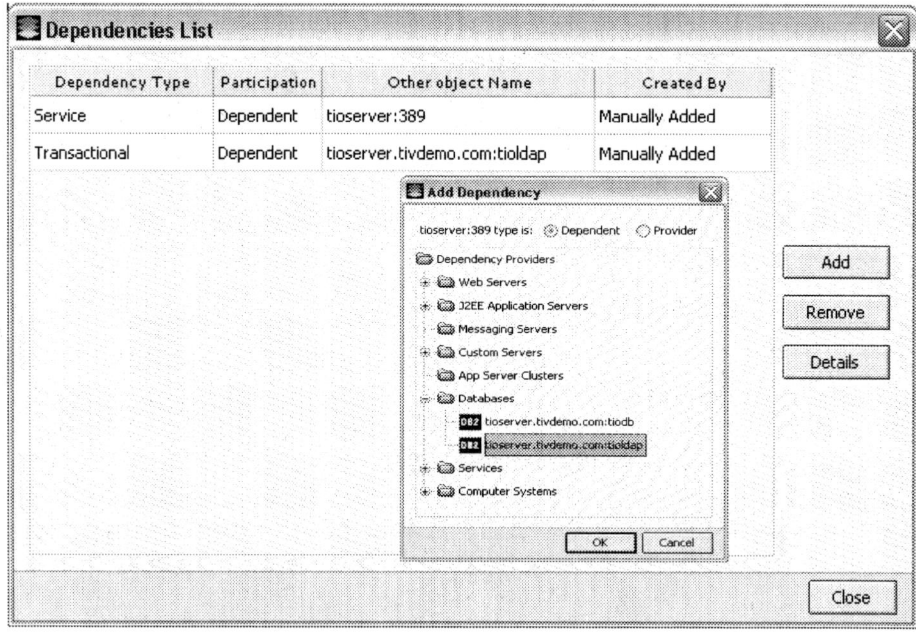

Figure 4-43 Manually adding dependencies

Notice that when defining the dependency, the object for which you define the dependency becomes the anchor point for the definition, and for this you have to specify the type: Dependent or Provider. In the dependency overview, these values translate to a dependency type or *transactional* or *service*. In our LDAP server-database instance relationship, the LDAP server (`tioserver:389`) is the dependent, and the database instance (`tioserver.tivdemo.ibm.com:tioldap`) automatically becomes the provider. This relationship is depicted in Figure 4-44 on page 141 by the arrow pointing from the IBM Directory object to the DB2 object.

As seen in Figure 4-43 on page 140 we also defined a dependency between the IBM Directory Server Custom Server instance named tioserver:389 and the discovered LDAP service named `tioserver:389`. This relationship is also visible in Figure 4-44.

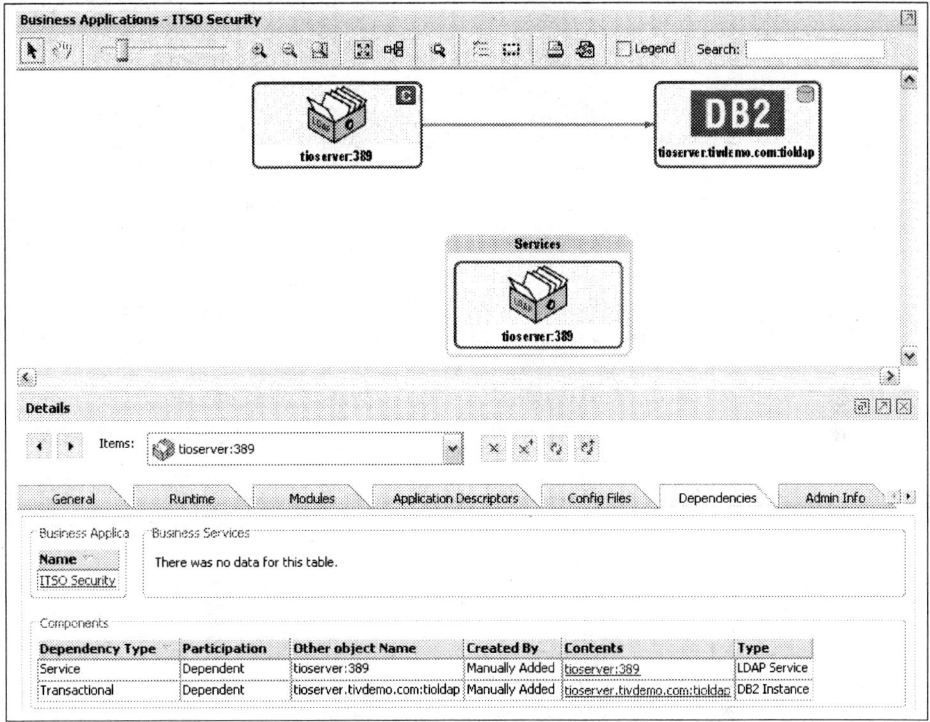

Dependency Type	Participation	Other object Name	Created By	Contents	Type
Service	Dependent	tioserver:389	Manually Added	tioserver:389	LDAP Service
Transactional	Dependent	tioserver.tivdemo.com:tioldap	Manually Added	tioserver.tivdemo.com:tioldap	DB2 Instance

Figure 4-44 Topology with WebSphere server - database instance relationship

Looking at Figure 4-44, notice that the relationship between the service and the Custom Server is not represented by a dependency arrow. The reason for this is the design team has chosen not to show these, because of all the possible dependencies to infrastructure services such as LDAP, DNS, and NFS servers. Depicting these relationships would most likely add to the confusion rather than help visualize the important dependencies.

4.2.7 Defining Business Applications

Now that we have registered an instance of the IBM Directory Custom Server, we want to create register the entire LDAP system (Custom Server, database and LDAP service) as a separate Business Application entity, in order to be able to reference it from various Business Services, which basically are collections of

Business Applications that participate to provide a unique business service such as CRM or Home Banking.

Business Applications can be created in one of three ways:

- Manually through the Product Console
- Semi-automated by means of an Application Template
- Automated using *Descriptor* files which are deployed onto the actual systems hosting the application components.

The main difference between the three methods are, that the manual way creates a static definition of a Business Application. Even if new components are added, these will not be reflected in the Business System definition. Using the semi-automated method, the Business Application definition is based on a set of Custom Server Template definitions, and all instances of these Custom Servers will be automatically added to the Business Application. This method works fine if all instances of Custom Servers belong to the same Business System, however if two separate instances of a Custom Server in fact belongs to two different Business Application instances, this method falls short. To automatically discover and register different instances of similar Business Applications, the third - descriptor file based - method is recommended.

The first two methods are outlined in the following sections. For information about how to set up and use descriptor files, refer to 5.1.8, “Automatically discovering Business Application instances” on page 182.

Manual Business Application definition

To create a Business Application, open the Product Console, and select **Edit → Create Business Application**. This will take you through three dialog boxes, in which you define the basic data to identify and describe the application, and associate the prediscovered components of which the application is made.

First you have to provide the Business Application identification data. Figure 4-45 on page 143 shows the attributes we used for defining the LDAP service, represented by the IBM Directory Server Custom Server Template.

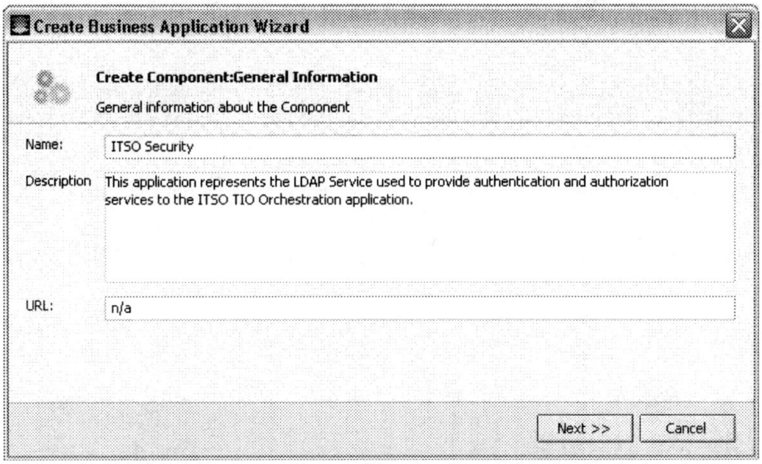

Create Business Application Wizard

Create Component:General Information

General information about the Component

Name: ITSO Security

Description: This application represents the LDAP Service used to provide authentication and authorization services to the ITSO TIO Orchestration application.

URL: n/a

Next >> Cancel

Figure 4-45 Naming and describing a Business Application

Press **Next**, and you are prompted to select application components. The components you want to add have to have been discovered prior to defining the Business Application. Figure 4-46 shows the addition of the IBM Directory Server Custom Server object instance named `tioserver:389` and the DB2 database instance `tioserver.tivdemo.com:tioldap`.

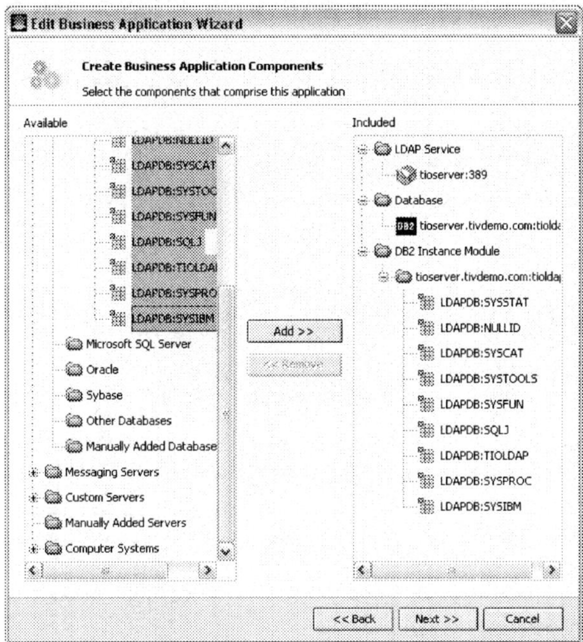

Figure 4-46 Adding components to a Business Application

Note: As shown in Figure 4-46 on page 143 you should note that, when defining your Business Application, you have to possibility to define the individual resources hosted by the servers, which were identified by the respective sensors.

When adding components, you can assign them to different user-defined functional groups that are used to group similar components within the Business Application—and across Business Applications—thus allowing you to group and track components by any function you choose, not just by the server type. For example, suppose you want particular servers to be dedicated to front-end processing, and particular servers to be dedicated to back-end processing. You can group the Apache servers that are part of the business application into two functional groups: FrontEndGroup and BackEndGroup.

When you press **Next**, you are prompted to supply administrative information such as contacts, location, and so forth about the Business Application, as in Figure 4-47.

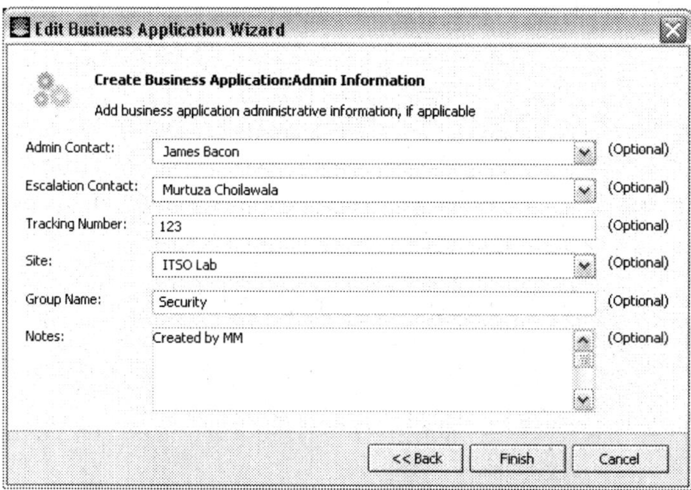

Figure 4-47 Defining Contacts for a Business Application

Finally, when you press **Finish**, the application is created, and you can use the Physical Topology view of the Business Application to verify your definitions, as in Figure 4-48 on page 145.

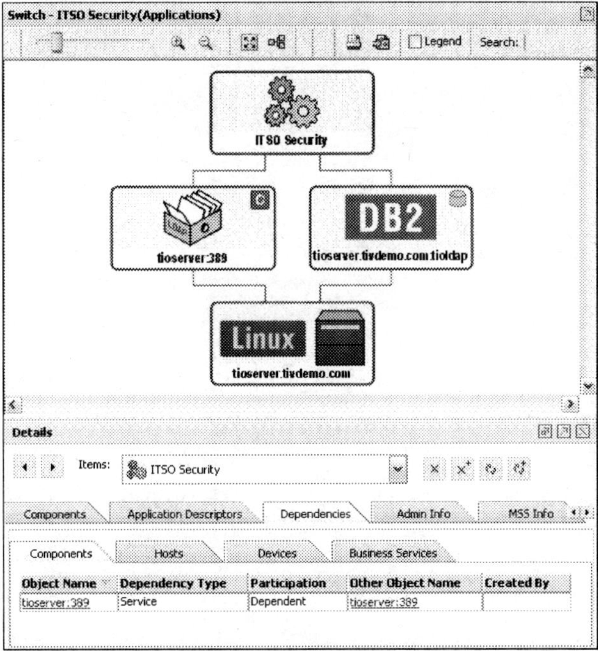

Figure 4-48 Business Application - Physical Topology

Defining an Application Template based Business Application

If your Business Application is comprised of components that are discovered through Custom Server Template definitions, the Application Template offers the facilities to automatically add all the servers to an application.

Creation of the Application Template is similar to the Business Application definition. However, instead of adding individual, discovered resources to the application, you add Custom Server Template types. Upon discovery, the Application Template based Business Application will be populated with all the components that have been *mapped* by the associated Custom Server Templates.

The following text shows the definition of a Business Application based on an Application template named ITSO TIO. For convenience, we reuse the Custom Server Templates that are defined in 4.2.6, "Define custom server templates" on page 132.

To create an Application Template, open the Product Console, and select **Discovery → Application Templates** and press the **Add** button. In the **General** section, enter the same type of identification and contact information as was provided for the statically defined Business Application. Figure 4-49 on page 146 shows the definition of an Application template for the ITSO Tivoli Intelligent Orchestrator implementation by the name of `ITSO TIO`.

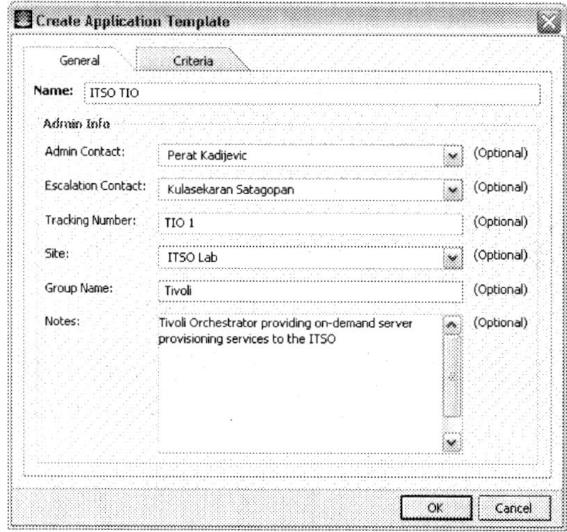

Figure 4-49 Naming an Application template

Next, go to the **Criteria** section, and select the Custom Server object types to which you have automatically assigned to this Application. In Figure 4-50 you can see that we selected the four `TIO...` Custom Server types which were created previously. See 4.2.6, "Define custom server templates" on page 132.

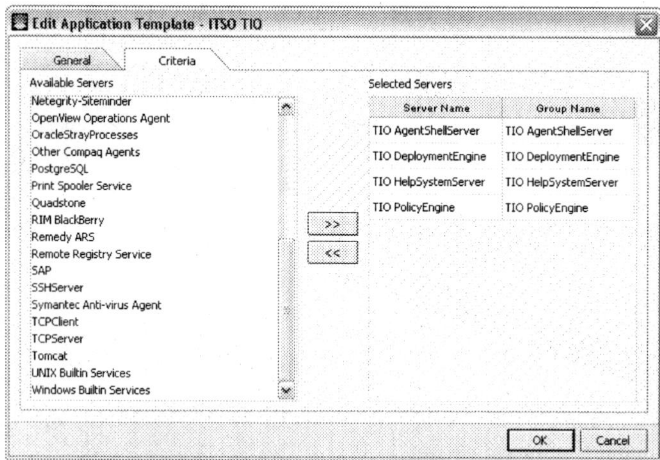

Figure 4-50 Selecting Custom Server Template types for Application Template

When you press **OK**, the Application Template is created. After the next discovery, the Business Application will be populated with all the instances of the

Custom Server types that were associated with the Application Template. Figure 4-51 shows the discovered Physical Topology and components of the ITSO TIO Business Application.

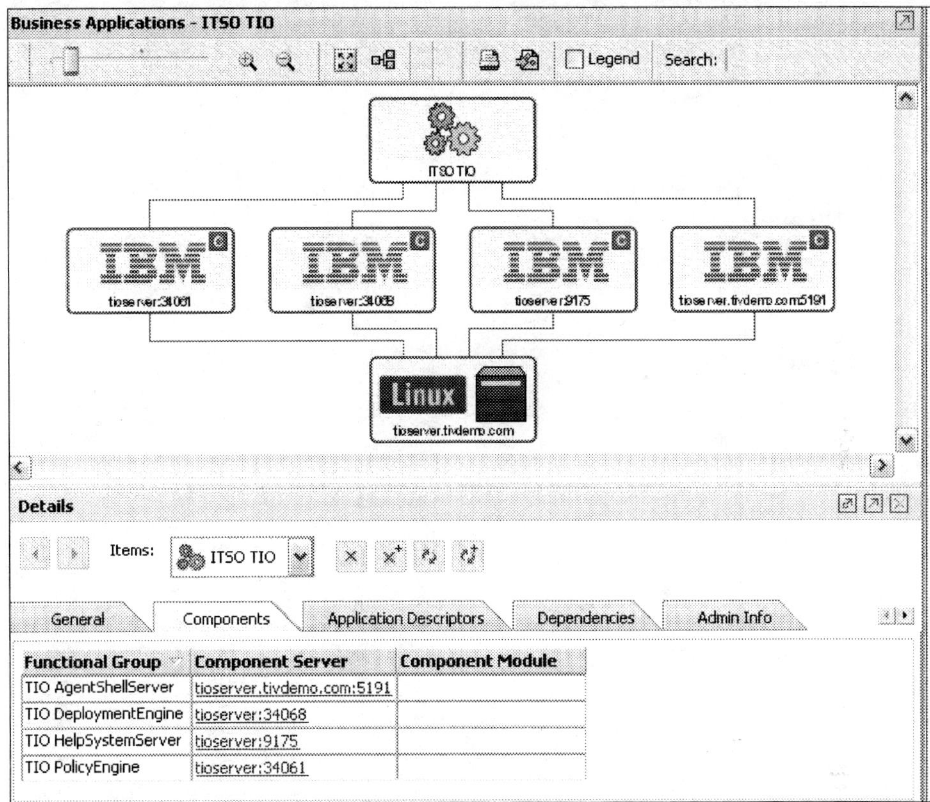

Figure 4-51 Components of the ITSO TIO Business Application

Business Applications defined from descriptor files

As already stated, the recommended way to automatically discover Business Applications is by using descriptor files. For more information about how to create and use descriptor files, see 5.1.8, "Automatically discovering Business Application instances" on page 182. However, to spur your interest, Figure 4-52 on page 148 shows the ITSO Orchestration Business Application discovered using this technology.

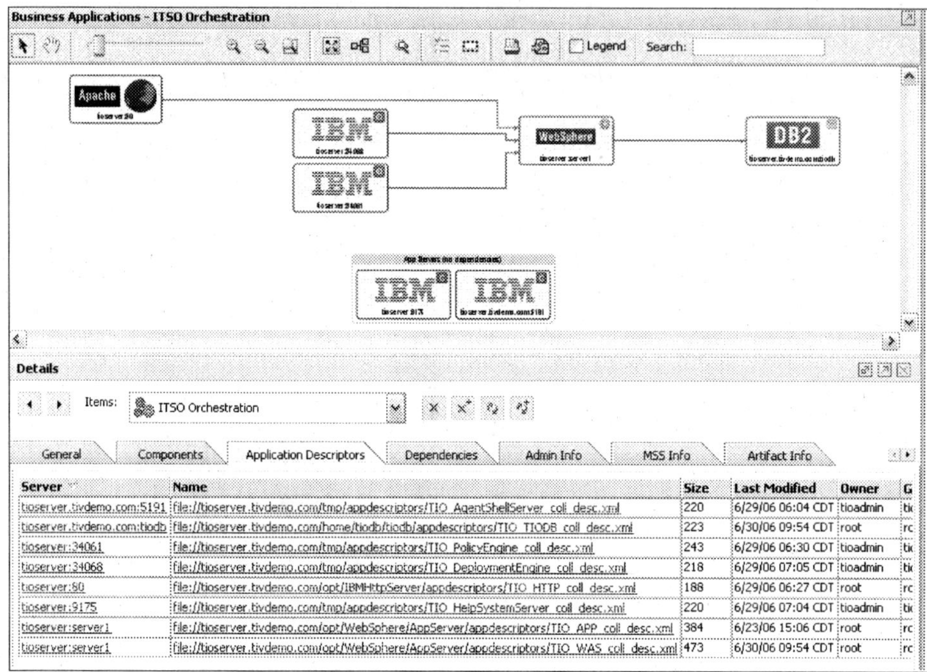

Figure 4-52 Business Application discovered from descriptor files

4.2.8 Defining Business Services

The top level in the component hierarchy of Configuration Discovery and Tracking is the Business Service. Business Services can contain any number of the lower level resources, from Business Applications to ear modules in a WebSphere server or specific configuration files on systems. The purpose of the Business Service object is to consolidate multiple lower-level objects and their relationships in order to perform reporting and analysis considering all related resources easily.

The procedure for defining a Business Service is similar to that of defining a Business Application. The only difference, apart from the object type, is that Business Applications can be members of Business Systems.

5

Populating and maintaining the Configuration Management database

This chapter describes how components, configuration data, and dependencies are discovered and programatically fed into the IBM Tivoli Change and Configuration Management Database Configuration Discovery and Tracking (CCMDB) database from both the built-in sensors, the customizeable object definitions such as Custom Servers and Computer Systems, loading of Discovery Library Books generated by external solutions (such as IBM Tivoli Monitoring, and IBM Tivoli Business Systems Manager), as well as the various APIs provided by Configuration Discovery and Tracking.

Configuration Discovery and Tracking provides a variety of specialized sensors that cover most of the infrastructure components used in large enterprises today. But in order to support custom applications and special cases, the openness of the CCMDB architecture allows for additional ways to automatically feed data into the solution. This chapter describes these options, starting with feeds related to discoveries and then presenting how to manipulate the database from external systems. The main topics covered are:

- Discovery
- Importing Discovery Library Books
- Providing input programmatically

5.1 Discovery

This section describes how data are fed into CCMDB during discovery. Discovery is the heart of IBM Tivoli Change and Configuration Management Database Configuration Discovery and Tracking and the primary way of populating the CMDB. This section presents how the discovery mechanism of Configuration Discovery and Tracking is conducted. Moreover, this chapter takes you through how to use the Custom Server and Computer System sensor templates so that IBM Tivoli Change and Configuration Management Database Configuration Discovery and Tracking can include even uncommon and homemade applications and services in the IT infrastructure.

5.1.1 Understanding Discoveries

Being a key feature of IBM Tivoli Change and Configuration Management Database Configuration Discovery and Tracking, the discovery process is worthwhile understanding.

From a high-level point of view the discovery performs the following tasks:

1. Initially the discovery is kicked off either manually through the GUI, by an API call, or as a result of a schedule that has been set up.
2. The discovery engine inspects the defined discovery scope to identify the IP addresses of the network infrastructure.
3. For each valid IP node, CCMDB launches discovery sensors which match the discovered components to defined signatures in the Data Center Reference Model.
4. The sensors query the components for configuration data and dependencies.
5. Upon completion of discovery, CCMDB populates the database and generates the topology of the infrastructure. As subsequent discoveries are run, IBM Tivoli Change and Configuration Management Database Configuration Discovery and Tracking will detect changes, providing a sophisticated change history.

As shown in Figure 5-1 on page 151, there are three main components of discovery in the Configuration Discovery and Tracking product.

- First, there are the discovery sensors that query the network to discover what data center components exist in the environment.
- Second, there is the topology subsystem that manages model object data from the discovery sensors. As data is discovered, each sensor converts the discovered data into model object results and passes them to the topology

subsystem. The topology manager then processes the result objects and persists them to the database.

- The final component of the discovery process is the UI component. This consists of the GUI, also known as the Product Console, and the API subsystem. The GUI and the API gives the user access to discovered data either in a topology or a model object representation.

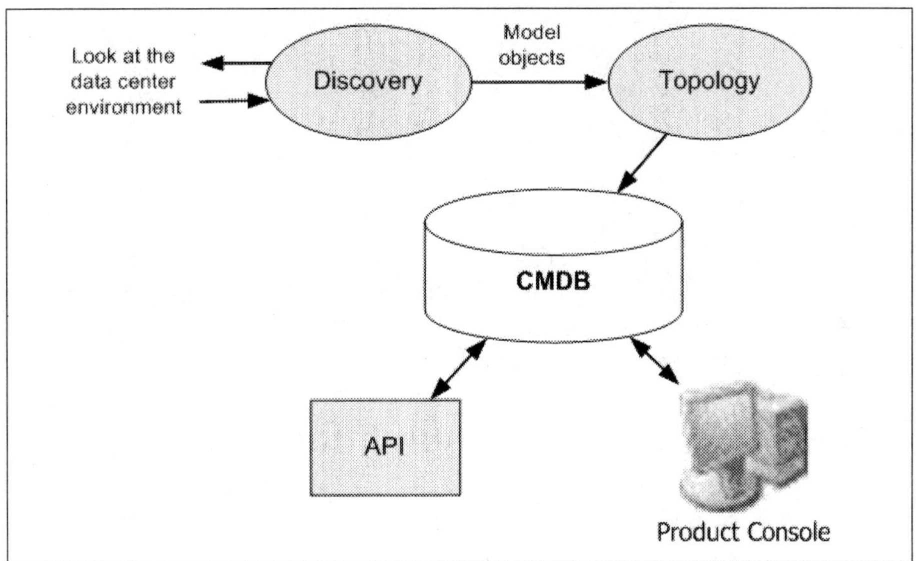

Figure 5-1 Sensor components

The following sections go one step further into the discovery process, providing a deeper understanding which can be useful if you find yourself in a need of troubleshooting or performance tuning of IBM Tivoli Change and Configuration Management Database Configuration Discovery and Tracking.

5.1.2 Sensor overview

Sensors provide the Configuration Discovery and Tracking product with an agent-free application discovery and dependency mapping facility to discover all aspects of your data center environment. They provide a structured way to query and analyze infrastructure data by querying devices in the network and logging discovered data about each device and any software installed on it.

The discovery sensors collect the data needed to represent the specific data center infrastructure. They are lightweight and designed to discover the infrastructure components and their configurations and dependencies. Discovery sensors use open and secure protocols and access mechanisms to discover the data center components.

Furthermore, unlike persistent and invasive agents, discovery sensors are centrally deployed and managed, consuming minimal bandwidth and CPU resources (<1% when active) in the target environment. The discovery engine provides a workflow framework to schedule, distribute, coordinate and manage the various discovery sensors.

Appendix D, "Supported sensors" on page 421 details the sensors that (at the time of writing) are delivered with IBM Tivoli Change and Configuration Management Database Configuration Discovery and Tracking v1.1.

5.1.3 The Discovery process in detail

The basic discovery flow can be seen in Figure 5-2. From the GUI or from the API, a discovery can be initiated by specifying an initial scope or seed. This initial seed is typically an IP address or a range of IP addresses to discover. The seed provides a starting-point for the discovery engine.

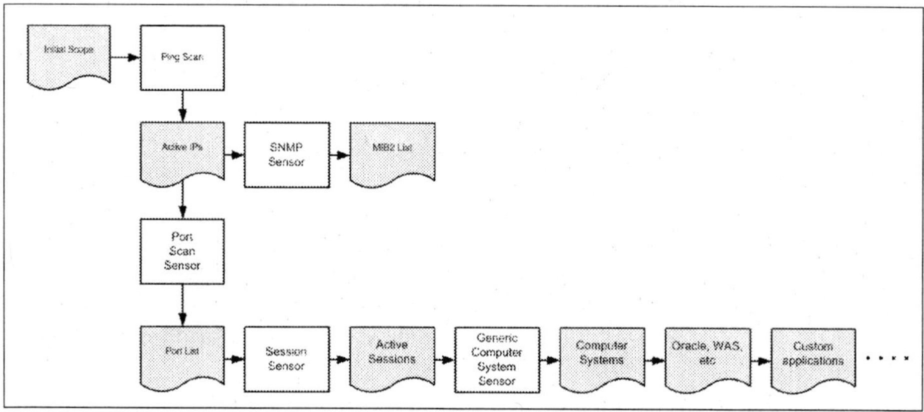

Figure 5-2 Sensor Discovery process

During discovery, seeds are placed in a JavaSpaces™. This permits all running processes to have shared access to the data stored in the JavaSpaces, but the JavaSpaces provides a transactionally secure implementation for sharing the data. JavaSpaces is closely tied to the Jini™ architecture. Read about Jini and JavaSpaces at this Web site:

`http://www.jini.org`

1. The discovery engine extracts the scope from the JavaSpaces and first executes a parallel `ping`, whereby it basically tries to contact each IP address in the seed IP range. If an IP address responds, it is added to a list of known

active IP addresses and a new seed is placed in the JavaSpaces. If the ping times-out, that IP address will be ignored for further discovery.

2. For each seed generated from the Ping Scan, the discovery engine will execute a Port Scan for certain ports such as ssh (22), telnet (23), and WMI to scan each individual IP address. If the port scan is successful, the IP address and port number become a seed for further discovery. If the port scan for an IP address is unsuccessful, communication with that IP address is attempted with SNMP to discover if the device is a, MIB2-compliant device.

3. Each seed generated by the Port Scan will become subject to a Session sensor which tries to establish a session by logging into the device using the seed port. If successful, the IP address, port number and session become a seed for further discovery.

   First, a Generic Computer System Sensor is launched to determine the type of the operating system. If successfully, new seeds are created and put in the JavaSpaces.

   These seeds will be used by the discovery engine to execute operating system specific sensors discovering details about the operating system including a list of process names running on the system. The process names will be used by the discovery engine to generate yet more seeds and run specific software application sensors. As each sensor completes, the result can be generation of more seeds driving additional sensors.

   This process is done recursively until all aspects of the system have been discovered.

   All of this activity is performed in parallel. For example, the Port Scan can run against one system while an operating system sensor is running on another. Sensors are run on a first-come-first-served basis as seeds are deposited into the JavaSpaces.

Figure 5-3 on page 154 shows the steps that seed a discovery, generate results, generate news seeds from generated results, and finally stores results in the database.

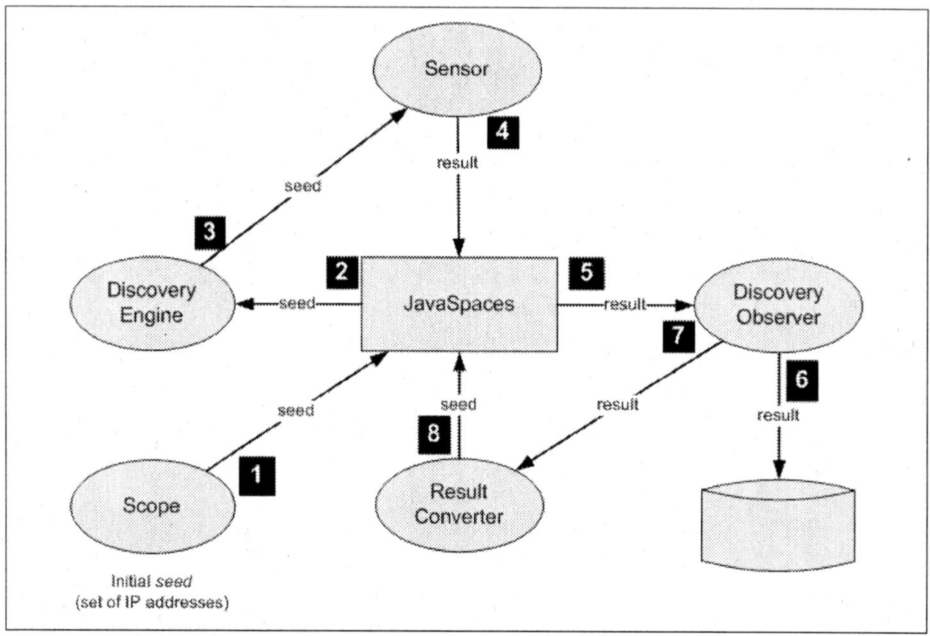

Figure 5-3 Sensor Discovery Process

The detailed steps in the Discovery Process are:

1. An initial scope (seed) is specified for a discovery run either through the GUI, an API call, or triggered by a defined schedule. This initial scope becomes the first seed for the discovery run, and is placed into the JavaSpaces.
2. The discovery engine detects a new seed in the JavaSpaces, and extracts the seed.
3. Based on the seed, the discovery engine starts the appropriate sensor.
4. The sensor performs its discovery. Results are written back to the JavaSpaces.
5. The Discovery Observer detects that a result has been placed in the JavaSpaces and extracts the result.
6. The Discovery Observer persists the result to the database.
7. If there is a Result Converter associated with the sensor, the Discovery Observer will pass the result to that Result Converter.
8. The Result Converter parses the result and might generate new seeds. These seeds are put back in the Java Spaces and step 2 can then reoccur. The latter can reiterate until there are no more seeds and no more running sensors.

This completes the discussion of the discovery process. Although much of the described functionality occurs behind the scene, it is useful to have a detailed knowledge when diving into discovery tuning and troubleshooting.

5.1.4 Planning for Discovery

As is the case for many other activities, you should not start your discovery process without just a tiny bit of planning. This is recommended in order for you to:

- Optimize discovery efficiency by creating a scope structure that allows you to limit your discoveries to a specific subset of your infrastructure, which represents only the part of the infrastructure that you want to discover, for example a single LOB, a group of similar business applications, or a functional group.
- Optimize discovery execution times by creating Access List entries that allow you to access target systems in the most efficient way.
- Identify the additional executables required to successfully discover details from all the components in your infrastructure.

Setting up Scopes

When defining your scopes to Configuration Discovery and Tracking, you should try to define them as logical groups in which all dependencies can be resolved. This will ensure the granularity necessary to perform incremental discoveries in a timely fashion. In addition, you should consider how the user credentials needed to access the systems in the scope might be applied to the group. By allocating separate Access List entries to your individual scopes, you greatly reduce the processing needed to access the hosts in your scope.

As mentioned in 4.2.1, “Define the scope” on page 112, scopes can be defined from the Product Console or can be imported from a flat file. See B.3.2, “loadscope - the scope import utility” for more details on the import function.

Instead of using scopes or specific IP addresses when initiating a discovery, the Product Console allows you to specify any combination of already discovered resources. Figure 5-4 on page 156 shows such a discovery initiation in which the resources related to the Business Application named TCP Application and the systems hosting the two selected database instances will be dynamically included in the scope for this discovery.

When a component-based discovery is initiated, the systems hosting the selected components are added as seeds, and the proper credentials to be used to access the hosts are found by inspecting the scope definitions and find the Access List entries associated with the scopes in which the IP address of the hosts are included.

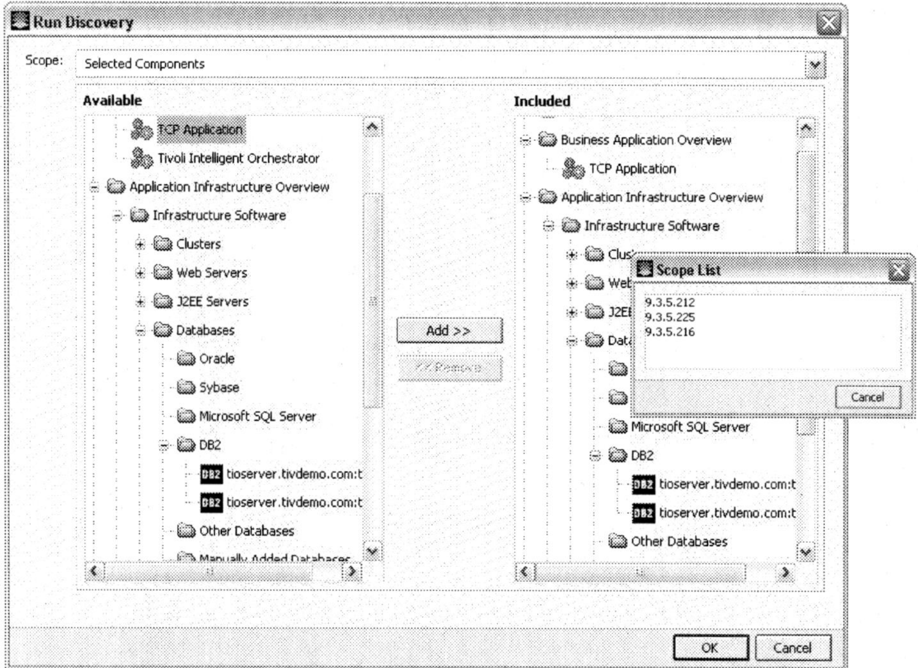

Figure 5-4 Select discovery targets by component

To be able to select components rather than scopes, click the **Selected Components** scope specification at the top of the Run Discovery dialog box.

Setting up credentials

In 4.2.3, “Define Access List entries for infrastructure components” on page 117 we provide a detailed discussion of how to set up Access List entries and how to relate them to scopes.

In addition, you should be aware of the processing sequence performed by the Configuration Discovery and Tracking Server when accessing devices. The order of processing is:

1. SSH access is attempted using the public key of the user owning the Configuration Discovery and Tracking Server processes.

2. If this fails, the Configuration Discovery and Tracking Server will try all the Access List entries within the scopes defined for the system that has keys defined.
3. Finally, if the Configuration Discovery and Tracking server still has been unable to establish a session, all the password-based Access List entries within the scopes for the IP address of the host is attempted.

This implies that if you already have a public key infrastructure for SSH deployed to your servers, the management effort maintaining Access List entries for ComputerSystems should be minimal.

In Windows environments, you can also consider using domain users for your access list instead of local users to minimize Access List maintenance.

Before initiating a discovery immediately after you have defined new Anchor Hosts and Windows Gateways to the environment, you might want to verify that the SSH and WMI connections are correctly configured. To verify SSH and WMI access to your targets, or the Anchor Hosts and Windows Gateways themselves, you can use the tools provided in the ${COLLATION_HOME}/support/bin directory. In particular you should look at `testssh.py` and `testwmi.jy` which are described in more detail in B.4.9, "testssh.py" and B.4.10, "testwmi.jy" on page 384.

Configuring for Discovery of Web and application servers

In addition to providing a valid set of credentials in your Access List that allows you to access the Web and application servers, for WebSphere servers you must make specific executable, required to examine the subsystems, available to the Configuration Discovery and Tracking Server.

To do this, you can extract the file named CMDB_WebSphere.zip form the installation media (in the /CMDB/sdk directory) to the Configuration Discovery and Tracking installation directory, usually /opt/IBM/cmdb.

Assuming that you installed IBM Tivoli Change and Configuration Management Database Configuration Discovery and Tracking v1.1 to the `/opt/IBM/cmdb` directory and you have mounted the installation media CD/DVD on `/media/cdrom`, you can use the following command to extract the required binaries:

```
unzip /media/cdrom/CMDB/sdk/CMDB_WebSphere.zip -d /opt/IBM/cmdb
```

For more information, consult the IBM Tivoli Change and Configuration Management Database v1.1: Release Notes.

In the even you do want to add the support for Web and application servers in a more controlled fashion, the Table 5-1 outlines the procedure for configuring each of the supported Web and application servers.

Table 5-1 Configuring Web and application servers

Web Application Server	Configuration
IBM WebSphere Application Server	To enable IBM WebSphere Application Server discovery, you must make a WebSphere installation available to the Configuration Discovery and Tracking Server - either locally or through an NFS mount. For example, if you installed WebSphere into /opt/WebSphere on the Configuration Discovery and Tracking Server, then the installation creates a directory called /opt/websphere/AppServer. To inform Configuration Discovery and Tracking Server of the location of the WebSphere Application Server executables, edit the ${COLLATION_HOME}/etc/collation.properties file, and set the com.IBM.websphere.root.dir property as follows: com.IBM.websphere.root.dir=/opt/WebSphere/AppServer If you plan to discover WebSphere Application Server instances through an Anchor Host, ensure that the WebSphere Application Server executables are available to the Anchor Host itself. The directory where the WebSphere Application Server binaries are installed should be the same as the value specified for the com.collation.websphere.root.dir property in the collation.properties file on the Configuration Discovery and Tracking Server.
BEA WebLogic	To enable BEA WebLogic discovery, copy weblogic.jar and webservices.jar from a WebLogic distribution to ${COLLATION_HOME}/lib. The Configuration Discovery and Tracking Server requires the WebLogic system login and password for the Product Console.
JBoss	To enable JBoss discovery, copy jbossall-client.jar and jboss-jmx.jar from a JBoss distribution to ${COLLATION_HOME}/lib/jboss/<version number>. The <version> should be 325 or 402 depending on the JBoss versions 3.2.5 or 4.0.2. The Configuration Discovery and Tracking Server requires the JBoss system login and password for the Product Console.
Lotus® Domino®	The Configuration Discovery and Tracking requires the following to access Domino servers: ► IIOP server must be running on at least one Domino server per Domino domain ► A default user
Apache Web server	The Configuration Discovery and Tracking Sever requires read permission to Apache configuration files, such as httpd.conf.
Sun™ iPlanet Web server	The Configuration Discovery and Tracking Server requires read permission to the iPlanet configuration files.

Web Application Server	Configuration
Microsoft IIS	No access requirements. The user account already established on the host is sufficient.

Configuring an Oracle Application server

The discovery of an Oracle Application server uses jar files that are included with the Oracle Application server. These jar files are not included in the Configuration Discovery and Tracking Server installation. There is a property in the `${COLLATION_HOME}/etc/collation.properties` file to enable you to point to an existing installation of the Oracle Application server. Example 5-1 contains the associated text that is in the collation.properties file:

Example 5-1 Collation.properties file for Oracle

```
# Location of the root directory for Oracle Application Server
# on the Configuration Discovery and Tracking Server
# 1. An example is /home/oracle/product/10.1.3/OracleAS_1
# 2. A relative directory is relative to com.collation.home
# 3. This directory (and its subdirectories) must be accessible
#    for the user under which the server runs, usually the
#    collation user.
# 4. Ignore if you do not intend to discover an Oracle Application
#    server.
```

Edit the following line in the collation.properties file:

```
com.collation.oracleapp.root.dir=lib/oracleapp
```

In an Oracle Application server installation, the directories that contain the required jar files are owned by the oracle user with permissions: `rwx------`. This means no user apart from the owner (usually `oracle`) can access these directories. If the Configuration Discovery and Tracking Server is run using the oracle user, then these directories are accessible. However, if this is not the case, then you must complete the following actions:

Change the directory permissions of these directories to rwxr--r-- (711) so that all users can access the following directories:

- <OracleAppServerHome>
- <OracleAppServerHome>/j2ee
- <OracleAppServerHome>/j2ee/home
- <OracleAppServerHome>/opmn
- <OracleAppServerHome>/opmn/lib,

An example of <oracleAppServerHome> is:

/home/oracle/product/10.1.3/OracleAS_1

Configuring for deep discovery of WebSphere

By default, the discovery of WebSphere Application server configuration details does not include the collection of the following attributes:

- Deployment descriptors for J2EE applications and modules
- WebSphere variables
- Shared libraries
- Custom properties

In the event you need to extract these to keep them under Change Control, you can change the value of the `com.collation.websphere.deep.discovery.setting` property in the `${COLLATION_HOME}/etc/collation.properties` file to `true`.

> **Note:** You should be aware that the implications of enabling deep discovery of you WebSphere Application Servers will increase both the discovery time and the space requirements for the CMDB.
>
> Also note, that this setting applies to all of your WebSphere Application Server instances. Deep discovery is enabled for either `all` or `none`.

5.1.5 Discovering with built-in facilities

As described previously, discovery is based on a set of specialized sensors, which are built to provide two types of information for the components that they support:

- Configuration data for specific components
- Seeds for subcomponents to be discovered by other sensors

IBM Tivoli Change and Configuration Management Database Configuration Discovery and Tracking is shipped with many build-in sensors. Appendix D, “Supported sensors” on page 421 provides details on the sensors delivered with the product.

These sensors cannot be modified but can be disabled and enabled as needed, see "Disabling sensors" on page 265. IBM will continuously develop new sensors based on customer needs. One of these specialized sensors is the CustomServerSensor, which mission is to discover (or exclude) custom defined server processes, that has been defined through the definition (and enablement) of one or more Custom Server templates.

Essentially, the CustomServerSensor is a built-in sensor which cannot be modified. However, it provides the means to influence which components are being discovered, including custom servers that are not discovered by the standard sensors.

Custom Server templates

The definition of specific Custom Server templates (found in the **Discovery** menu) provides a way to easily extend your discovery to include server processes that are not discovered by the standard sensors.

When planning to use Custom Server Templates, you should remember that only processes with an active TCP listening port can be detected. Stand-alone programs that do not communicate with clients will not be discovered. The programs to be discovered can be vendor-provided software or a custom program.

The following section takes you through a small example of how to setup a Custom Server template for a homemade program in order enable Configuration Discovery and Tracking to discover active instances.

Example 5-2 shows a small Java program named TCPServer, which acts as a dummy server doing nothing but listening on port 37645.

Example 5-2 A simple TCPServer Java program acting as a server

```
import java.io.BufferedReader;
import java.io.InputStreamReader;
import java.net.ServerSocket;
import java.net.Socket;
import java.util.Date;

public class TCPServer {
  public static void main(String args[]) {
     int port = 37645; // default port
     try {
       if (args.length > 0) {
        port = Integer.parseInt(args[0]);
       }
      ServerSocket serversocket = new ServerSocket(port);
```

```
      System.out.println("Server started at " + new Date());
      System.out.print("Listening on port: " + port);
      System.out.println(". Waiting for data!");
      Socket socket = serversocket.accept(); // Now listening
      BufferedReader reader = new BufferedReader(new
InputStreamReader(socket.getInputStream()));
      String line = reader.readLine();
      while (line != null) {
        System.out.println("Client says: " + line);
        line = reader.readLine();
      }
      System.out.println("Got it all. Goodbye!");
      System.out.println("Server stopped at " + new Date());
      socket.close();
      serversocket.close();
     } catch (Exception e) {
      System.out.println("Usage: TCPServer <port>");
     }
  }
}
```

The TCPServer Java program can be compiled and started by issuing the following commands (assuming you have Java SDK v1.4.2 or later installed).

```
javac TCPServer.java
java -Dclasspath=<directory_of_TCPServer.class> TCPServer
```

Assuming that the TCPServer program is running on a host in your environment for which you have configured scope and credentials, you can define a matching Custom Server template easily through the Product Console.

1. Go to **Discovery → Custom Servers**.
2. In the Custom Servers window click **Add**.

   You will be presented with a window where the details of the Custom Server must be provided.
3. To define the TCPServer program by the name of TCPServer, we provided the following criteria:

   - Process name ends-with `java`
   - Argument ends-with `TCPServer`
   - Port is `37645`

   See Figure 5-5 on page 163.

Note: What really distinguishes one Custom Server template from another is the criteria defined for each individual Custom Server template. The name, though it must be unique, is only used for identification purposes.

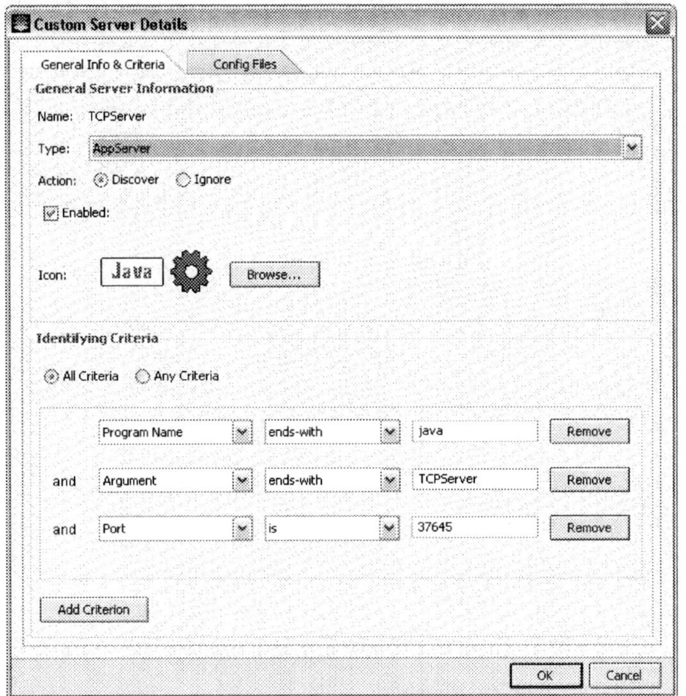

Figure 5-5 TCPServer Custom Server template Details

Note: The order in which the Custom Server templates appear in the list is important. When the CustomServerSensor executes as part of a discovery, the Custom Server templates are applied by the Configuration Discovery and Tracking in the top-down order they are presented in the Product Console. Therefore, you have to make sure that Custom Server definitions are not being masked by other definitions.

For example, if you have a Custom Server template that looks for process names starting with `java`, and it appears prior to the TCPServer template defined above, the TCPServer will never be identified by the discovery, because our running TCPServer program will be caught by the less restrictive template, which only looks for `java*` processes. This prevents the `java TCPServer listening on port 37645` template from being applied because the less restrictive `java*` definition already was applied.

For this reason, it is strongly recommended that the most restrictive Custom Server templates appear at the top of the Custom Server template hierarchy.

Note: In addition, be aware that all Custom Server templates with an action of `ignore` are applied first, independent of their location in the list of Custom Server templates.

In addition discovering instances of the TCPServer custom server we will also like to control the content of certain files related to the TCPServer. On deployment of the TCPServer, we deployed the files `TCPServer.class` and a `TCPServer.properties` (which is not used by the program) file to the `/tmp` directory on the target system. To place these files under change control so we can track changes to the TCPServer, we add them to the Custom Server Template, by modifying the template, and using the **Config Files** tab on the Custom Server Details dialog box.

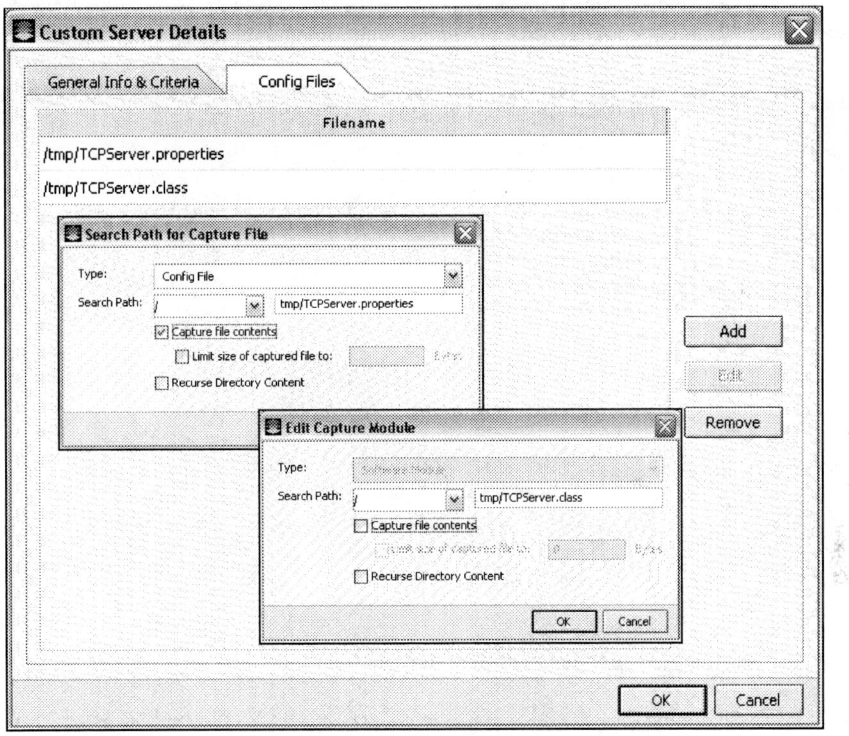

Figure 5-6 Adding configuration files to a Custom Server template

For all instances of the TCPServer, we want to register the TCPServer.class file as a Software Module hosted by the server, and the TCPServer.properties file as a normal configuration file. By selecting Software Module and Config File respectively, we achieve our goal. In addition, by enabling **Capture FIle Contents**, we ensure that changes to the file are being tracked. For the TCPServer this option is only enabled for the TCPServer.properties file because the .class file is binary, and we only want to know if it has changed, not necessarily what the changes were. However, for the .properties file (a plain text file) we want to know the nature of the changes as they occur.

Before running a discovery (which would now result in finding and displaying a stand alone TCPServer) complete this example by adding a TCPClient. In order for the TCPClient to be discovered it needs to be listening on a TCP port. Example 5-3 lists a sample java client program that interacts with the TCPServer program shown in Example 5-2 on page 161.

Example 5-3 A simple TCPClient Java program, listening on TCP port.

```
import java.io.*;
import java.net.*;
import java.util.Date;

public class TCPClient {

   public static void main(String[] args) {
      String serverhostname = "";
      try {
         serverhostname = args[0];
         int serverport = Integer.parseInt(args[1]);
         int seconds = Integer.parseInt(args[2]);
         Socket socket;
         PrintWriter writer;
         System.out.println("Client started at " + new Date());
         socket = new Socket(serverhostname, serverport);

         // The Client has to have a listening port as well
         Thread anotherThread = new NewThread();
         anotherThread.start();

         writer = new PrintWriter(socket.getOutputStream());
         writer.write("I will go to sleep.\n");
         writer.flush();
         while (seconds > 0) {
            Thread.sleep(20000);
            System.out.println("  Zzzz Zzzz (" + new Date() + ")");
            writer.write("Zzzz Zzzz (" + new Date() + ")\n");
            writer.flush();
            seconds -= 20;
         }
         writer.write("I woke up again.\n");
         writer.close();
         anotherThread.interrupt();
         System.out.println("Client stopped at " + new Date());
      } catch (IOException e) {
         System.err.println("Could not connect to " + serverhostname);
      } catch (Exception e) {
         System.out.println("Usage: TCPClient <hostname> <port> 
<keep-alive-time>");
      }
   }
}
```

```
class NewThread extends Thread {
   ServerSocket serversocket;

   public void run() {
      try {
         serversocket = new ServerSocket(37646);
         serversocket.accept();
      } catch (Exception e) {
      } // ignoring exception in this example
   }

   public void interrupt() {
      super.interrupt();
      try {
         serversocket.close();
      } catch (Exception e) {
      } // ignoring exception in this example
   }
}
```

The TCPClient program can be compiled and run by issuing the following commands (assuming you have Java SDK 1.4.2 or later installed).

```
javac TCPClient.java
java -Dclasspath=<directory_of_TCPServer.class> TCPClient \
<hostname> <port> <keep-alive-time>
```

Where the following terms are defined as:

hostname	The host name or IP address of the TCPServer
port	The port of the TCPServer.
keep-alive-time	The amount of time in seconds that you want to keep the communication a live.

Similarly to defining the TCPServer as a Custom Server you can now define a Custom Server for TCPClient. Open the Product Console, and follow these simple steps:

1. Go to **Discovery → Custom Servers**.
2. Find and select the TCPServer and click **Copy**.
3. Give the copy a new name, `TCPClient`.
4. Select the TCPClient Custom Server template and click **Edit**.

5. Change the Identifying criteria to the following:
   - Process name ends-with `java`
   - Argument contains `TCPClient`
   - Argument contains `37645`

   Click **OK.**

Your new Custom Server template for the TCPClient should look similar to the one shown in Figure 5-7.

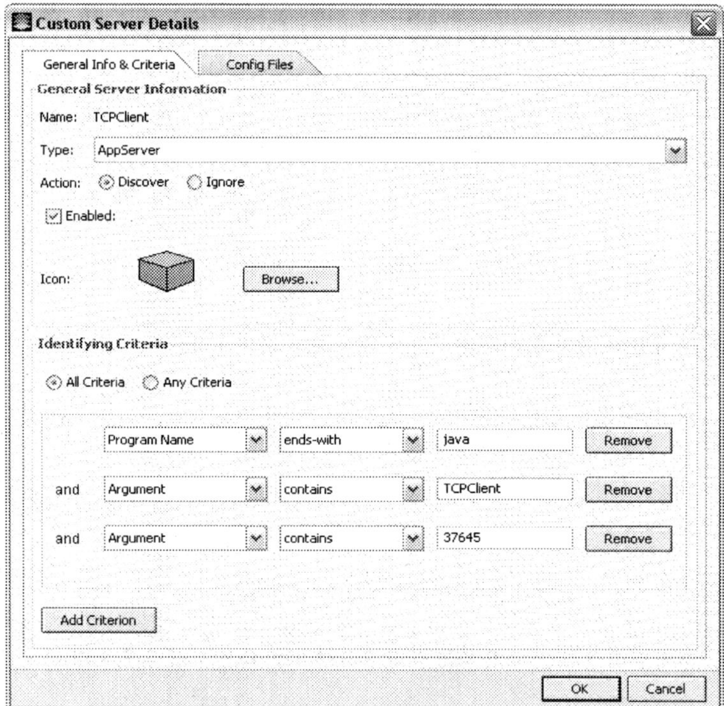

Figure 5-7 TCPClient Custom Server template

To enable change control of the files making up the TCPClient, you have to update the Config Files of the TCPClient. The two entries that were defined for the TCPServer also apply to the TCPClient, with the exception that the filenames are TCPClient.class and TCPClient.properties (Table 5-2). After updating the filenames the TCPClient Custom Server Template should include the following Config Files.

Table 5-2 TCP Client Config Files under Change Control

File name	Type	Search Path	Capture File content
tmp/TCPClient.class	Software Module	/	disabled
tmp/TCPClient.properties	Config File	/	enabled

Now it is time to perform the discovery. Make sure the TCPServer and TCPClient are started and communicating (see the messages on the console) and then go to **Discovery → Run Discovery**. Select a scope that includes the hosts where TCPServer and TCPClient are running and click **OK**.

When the discovery is complete, IBM Tivoli Change and Configuration Management Database Configuration Discovery and Tracking creates the topology in Figure 5-8.

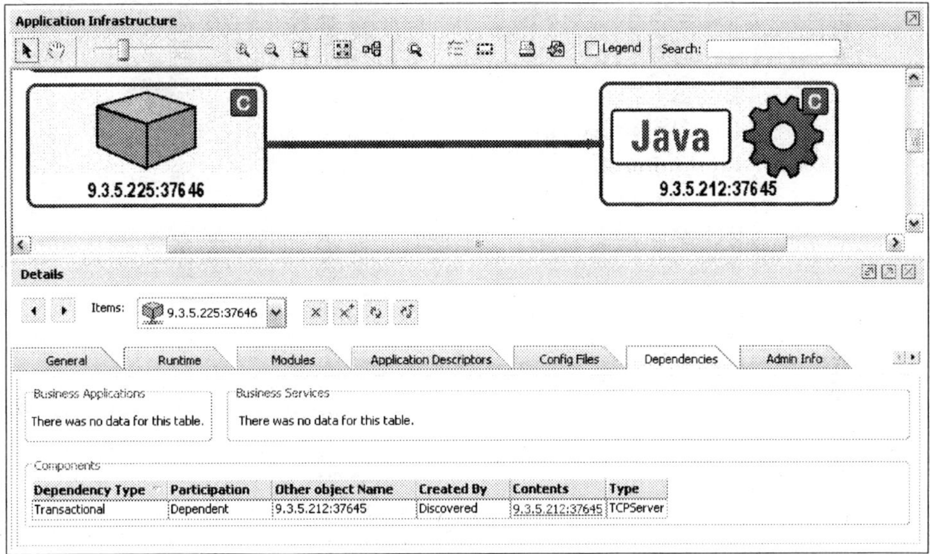

Figure 5-8 The Application Infrastructure Topology view

In the , you see that Configuration Discovery and Tracking has discovered both Java programs: the TCPServer which listens on port 37645 to the right, and the TCPClient to the left.

By right-clicking one of the components and selecting **Show Dependencies** Configuration Discovery and Tracking highlights the line between the components. In addition, Figure 5-8 on page 169 shows that the TCPClient has been selected, and the configuration details are shown in the Details window

(Figure 5-9). On the **Dependencies** tab you can see the reference to the TCPServer.

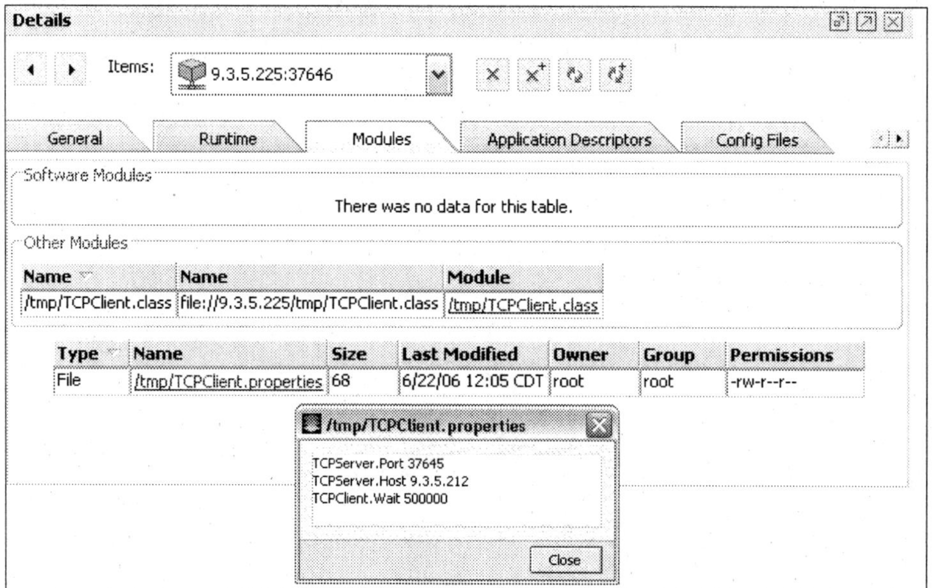

Figure 5-9 TCPClient Modules and Config Files

Looking at the **Modules** tab for either of the components, you will see that the .class files have been added, and the **Config Files** tab reveals that .properties files have been discovered. The contents can be viewed by clicking on the link.

Computer Systems templates

Basically, the Computer Systems template found in the menu **Discovery → Computer Systems** work the same way as the Custom Servers just described. Therefore, setting up a custom Computer System is not detailed here, but the reason for mentioning the Computer Systems templates is that the more advanced features described in the next section also applies for Computer System templates.

5.1.6 Extending discovery through Custom Server templates

Custom Server templates provides an easy way of extending the functionality of the discovery. Basically, each Custom Server template can be extended to gather more information about the target system whenever the template is matched during a discovery. There are three functions of the extensibility:

1. Execute a command on the target system which's output populates an attribute of the data model.

2. Execute a command on the target system with output stored as a Config File.
3. Execute a jython script. This feature gives you full control in manipulating the component.

The extensibility commands for a Custom Server Sensor are triggered based on the existence of a file with the same name as the Custom Server template. The file must be located in the ${COLLATION_HOME}/etc/templates/commands directory.

To continue the example of the TCPServer, to extend the functionality of the Custom Server template, in order to populate custom attributes, we have to create the file:

${COLLATION_HOME}/etc/templates/commands/TCPServer

Based on the content of the newly crated file, we can instruct Configuration Discovery and Tracking to populate an attribute, store the output of a command execution, or execute a jython script on the Configuration Discovery and Tracking Server, which can perform any action we need. The following provides guidance on how to implement each of these functionaities.

> **Note:** The criteria of the Custom Server template have to be matched before the functions are actually executed. In other words, even though a previous discovery have recognized a specific target host before, the functions above will only execute if the program(s) is still running (that is "matching" the template) during the discovery execution.

Populating an Attribute using from a command

To populate an attribute of the discovered instance of the TCPServer Custom Server, add a line to the ${COLLATION_HOME}/etc/templates/commands/TCPServer file similar to the following:

```
CMD:<attribute name>=<command>
```

Where the following attributes are defined as:

attribute-name
: The name of an attribute defined in the data model for the component type that was assigned to the Custom Server template.

command
: A valid operating system command for the platform hosting the component discovered by the Custom Server template.

When TCPServer was defined it was specified to be of the type `AppServer`. Therefore, the attributes available will be only those that apply to the AppServer data model object. Consulting the data model javadoc for the AppServer interface of the com.collation.platform.model.topology.app package, the Field Summary reveals which attributes can be set. Look for the methods starting with the string `set`. Figure 5-10 shows a subset of the set-methods available for the AppServer object type.

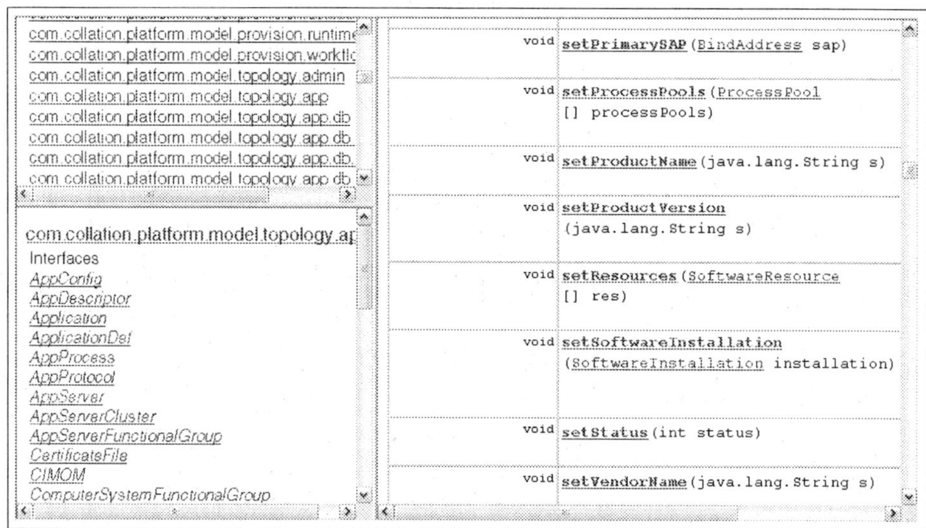

Figure 5-10 CMDB Data Model java doc for AppServer interface

Tip: To access the data model javadocs, unpack the `${COLLATION_HOME}/sdk/doc/model/model-javadoc.tar.gz` file to a location of your choice, and open the index.html file in your browser.

You should notice, that one restriction applies. Since an operating system command returns a string to standard out, only attributes of type String (java.lang.String) can be manipulated or set. In other words: *only set methods that take a String as argument can be used.* If you want to set more complex data types you will need to use the SCRIPT function described later.

Example 5-4 shows the use of the CMD function. By adding the lines shown to the ${COLLATION_HOME}/etc/templates/commands/TCPServer file, we set the values of the `productVersion`, `productName`, and `vendorName` attributes by echoing strings in a command shell environment on the hosting platform.

Example 5-4 TCPServer Custom Server extension using CMDs

```
CMD:productVersion=/bin/echo "TCPServer Version 1"
CMD:productName=/bin/echo "Simple TCPServer by ITSO"
CMD:vendorName=/bin/echo "TCPServer ITSO Vendor"
```

This example only shows the use of the **echo** command to set the attribute values to predefined static strings. Naturally, any command, program, or script for which the user ID defined in the Access List entry used to access the system has been authorized to execute can be used to generate the value for the attribute.

After running a discovery, our discovered instance of the TCPServer AppServer component will be updated with the values shown here. The fact that changes have occurred is immediately visible in the Product Console. If you display the Application Topology, and select **Topology → Show Changes** you will see the TCPServer object indicating that changes have been detected (Figure 5-11).

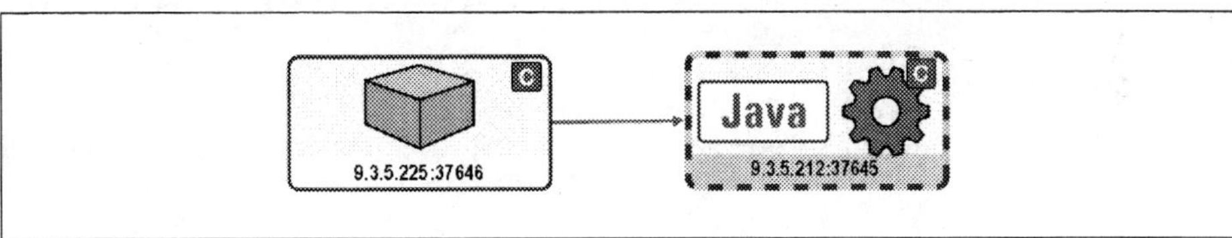

Figure 5-11 Application Topology indicating chances

The attributes which have been changed are, in our case, not visible in the details window of the Product Console, because these attributes have not been added to the user interface. To verify that the attributes have actually been updated, you should.execute a Change History report on the TCPServer (by right-clicking the TCPServer object and selecting **Change History**), and you will see the values as shown in Figure 5-12.

Change History: Results

Component	Type	Change	Date	Attribute	Old Value	New Value	Id
9.3.5.212:37645	AppServer	Created	6/21/06 15:35 CDT				1AA2FFD4F7B43644B664A544DBE8E88F
9.3.5.212:37645	AppServer	Updated	6/21/06 22:41 CDT				1AA2FFD4F7B43644B664A544DBE8E88F
taddm01:37645	AppServer	Updated	6/21/06 22:41 CDT	productName		Simple TCPServer by ITSO	1AA2FFD4F7B43644B664A544DBE8E88F
taddm01:37645	AppServer	Updated	6/21/06 22:41 CDT	vendorName		TCPServer ITSO Vendor	1AA2FFD4F7B43644B664A544DBE8E88F
taddm01:37645	AppServer	Updated	6/21/06 22:41 CDT	productVersion		TCPServer Version 1	1AA2FFD4F7B43644B664A544DBE8E88F

Show Details

Figure 5-12 Change History report showing updated attributes

Information similar to what is shown in Figure 5-12 can also be gathered through the `api.sh` command line interface. You will need two `api.sh` commands to accomplish this - one to find the Guid of the AppServer, and one to find the changes.

To find the Guid, use a find command to select AppServers with an `objectType` of `TCPServer`, as in Example 5-5.

Example 5-5 api.sh command to find TCPServer AppServers

```
C:\collation\sdk\bin>api -u administrator -p collation -H 9.3.4.165 find
--depth 0 "Select * from AppServer where obj
ectType == 'TCPServer'"
<?xml version="1.0" encoding="ISO-8859-1"?>
...
  <AppServer array="1" guid="1AA2FFD4F7B43644B664A544DBE8E88F"
        lastModified="1150980927780"
  xsi:type="coll:com.collation.platform.model.topology.app.AppServer"/>
</results>
```

Using the Guid identified in the **find** api command, you can now find the changes using the api **changes** command, as in Example 5-6.

Example 5-6 api.sh changes command to fine changes to a specific TCPServer

```
C:\collation\sdk\bin>api -u administrator -p collation -H 9.3.4.165 changes
1AA2FFD4F7B43644B664A544DBE8E88F "06/06/2006
 06:00:00 pm"
<?xml version="1.0" encoding="UTF-8"?>
<changes>
  <change Attribute="" Change="Updated" Component="9.3.5.212:37645"
        Date="Wed Jun 21 22:41:43 CDT 2006"
        Id="1AA2FFD4F7B43644B664A544DBE8E88F" Type="AppServer">
        <Old_Value><![CDATA[]]></Old_Value>
        <New_Value><![CDATA[]]></New_Value>
    <causes>
      <change Attribute="productName" Change="Updated"
                Component="taddm01:37645"
                Date="Wed Jun 21 22:41:43 CDT 2006"
                Id="1AA2FFD4F7B43644B664A544DBE8E88F" Type="AppServer">
                <Old_Value><![CDATA[]]></Old_Value>
                <New_Value><![CDATA[Simple TCPServer by ITSO]]></New_Value>
      </change>
      <change Attribute="vendorName" Change="Updated"
                Component="taddm01:37645"
                Date="Wed Jun 21 22:41:43 CDT 2006"
                Id="1AA2FFD4F7B43644B664A544DBE8E88F" Type="AppServer">
                <Old_Value><![CDATA[]]></Old_Value>
                <New_Value><![CDATA[TCPServer ITSO Vendor]]></New_Value>
      </change>
      <change Attribute="productVersion" Change="Updated"
```

```
                Component="taddm01:37645"
                Date="Wed Jun 21 22:41:43 CDT 2006"
                Id="1AA2FFD4F7B43644B664A544DBE8E88F" Type="AppServer">
                <Old_Value><![CDATA[]]></Old_Value>
                <New_Value><![CDATA[TCPServer Version 1]]></New_Value>
      </change>
    </causes>
  </change>
</changes>
```

Using variables in the CMD statement

Three variables are supported in the extension file which allow the executed command to be relative to the discovered process

`${COLL_PROGPATH}` Expands to the name of the directory where the program was found. If for example the command specifies `/usr/local/bin/foobar -c /var/etc/foobar.conf` the content of the ${COLL_PROGPATH} variable will be `/usr/local/bin`

`${COLL_PROGNAME}` Expands to the last component of argv[0] of the command line. If for example the command specifies `/usr/local/bin/foobar -c /var/etc/foobar.conf` the content of the ${COLL_PROGNAME} variable will be `foobar`.

`${COLL_CMDLINE}` Expands to the whole command line, including any arguments. If for example the command specifies `/usr/local/bin/foobar -c /var/etc/foobar.conf` the content of the ${COLL_CMDLINE} variable will be `/usr/local/bin/foobar -c /var/etc/foobar.conf`.

These variables can be used creatively, for example to find the version of `sshd` which is running on a system. In this case, you know that you need to execute the command **`ssh -V`** to acquire that information, but you are not sure where the ssh program is installed, primarily because the location of the ssh executable is different for different operating system platforms. The locations might be similar to these:

Linux	/usr/sbin/sshd
Solaris	/usr/local/sbin/sshd
AIX	/opt/software/sbin/sshd
Windows	C:\cygwin\bin

To find the actual location you could write a separate custom server template for each location, or you could use the following:

```
CMD:productVersion=$COLL_PROGPATH/ssh -V 2>&1 |awk -F" " '{print $3}'
```

Depending on the hosting environment for your Custom Server, the resulting value of the productVersion attribute would become either one of the values shown previously.

Populating a virtual Config File using a command

In addition to setting attribute values based on the execution of commands on the target system, the Custom Server Template command file also allow you to create a virtual Config File, type the following syntax into the Custom Server Template command file:

```
CMD:CONFCONTENT.<name of config file>=<command>
```

This function is similar to the previous, but instead of saving the output of a command into a specific attribute of the component data model, the output is saved as a virtual, nonexisting, Config File.

In the following example, the `/etc/hosts` and the `/etc/services` files are concatenated and printed as a virtual Config File named `hostAndServices`, which is stored in the CMDB as a configuration file. This will allow you to inspect the content directly from the **Config Files** tab in the **Details** pane of the Product Console.

To achieve this, the following line could be appended to the ${COLLATION_HOME}/etc/templates/commands/TCPServer file:

```
CMD:CONFCONTENT.hostAndServices=cat /etc/services /etc/hosts
```

After running a discovery, the Change History reveals that a new DataFile object has been added as a member of the TCPServer object (Figure 5-13).

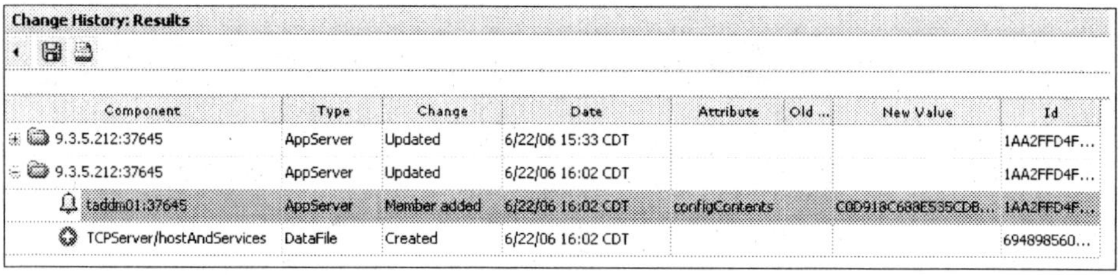

Change History: Results

Component	Type	Change	Date	Attribute	Old ...	New Value	Id
9.3.5.212:37645	AppServer	Updated	6/22/06 15:33 CDT				1AA2FFD4F...
9.3.5.212:37645	AppServer	Updated	6/22/06 16:02 CDT				1AA2FFD4F...
taddm01:37645	AppServer	Member added	6/22/06 16:02 CDT	configContents		C0D918C688E535CDB...	1AA2FFD4F...
TCPServer/hostAndServices	DataFile	Created	6/22/06 16:02 CDT				694898560...

Figure 5-13 Change History showing addition of a DataFile

The new Config File shows up on the **Config Files** tab in the **Details** pane, as shown in Figure 5-14.

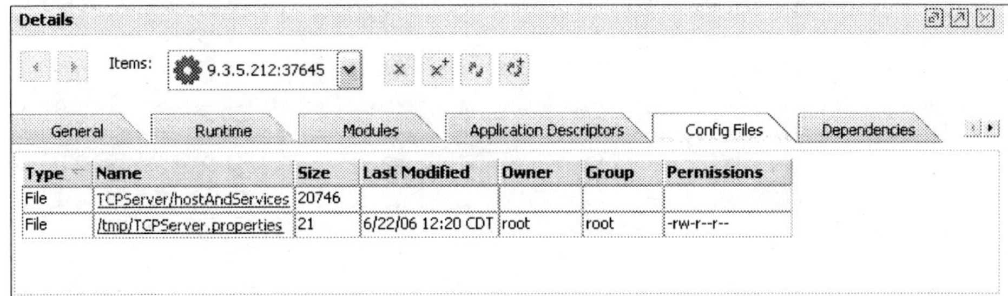

Type	Name	Size	Last Modified	Owner	Group	Permissions
File	TCPServer/hostAndServices	20746				
File	/tmp/TCPServer.properties	21	6/22/06 12:20 CDT	root	root	-rw-r--r--

Figure 5-14 Discovered virtual configuration file

Remember that the TCPServer/hostAndServices configuration file is a virtual Config File. There is no physical file called hostAndServices but it is captured and treated by Configuration Discovery and Tracking exactly like any other configuration file that might have been selected for configuration control by being added to the Config Files section of the Custom Server Template. You can click the link in the Product Console to see the content.

This also means, that if you make changes to either /etc/hosts or /etc/services, which are detected during a subsequent discovery, Configuration Discovery and Tracking will report the hostsAndServices file as having been changed. To test this, you can edit a line in the /etc/hosts file appending `ADDED_A_DUMMY_HOST`, as shown here.

Change the first version of this line the the last version:

```
9.3.4.174    taddm99 taddm.itsc.austin.ibm.com
9.3.4.174    taddm99 taddm.itsc.austin.ibm.com ADDED_DUMMY_HOST
```

After running a new discovery, you can see the new value in the virtual Config File but you will also see the changes reflected in the Change History Report, as in Figure 5-15.

Change History: Results

Component	Type	Change	Date	Attribute	Old Value	New Value	Id
9.3.5.212:37645	AppServer	Updated	6/22/06 12:15 CDT				1AA2FFD4F7B4...
TCPServer/hostAndServices	DataFile	Updated	6/22/06 12:15 CDT				694898560D403...
TCPServer/hostAndServices	DataFile	Updated	6/22/06 12:15 CDT	content	# /etc/services:# $Id:...	# /etc/services:# $Id:...	694898560D403...
TCPServer/hostAndServices	DataFile	Updated	6/22/06 12:15 CDT	size	20746	20763	694898560D403...
TCPServer/hostAndServices	DataFile	Updated	6/22/06 12:15 CDT	checksum	AWdJ1Srjc9z82zCW9...	zS5BaP2uD3X+Ti8PPO...	694898560D403...

Diff | Show Details

Figure 5-15 Change History report indicating configuration file changes

By selecting the line with the `content` attribute, you can click the **Diff** button Configuration Discovery and Tracking will show exactly what and where the change has occurred (Figure 5-16).

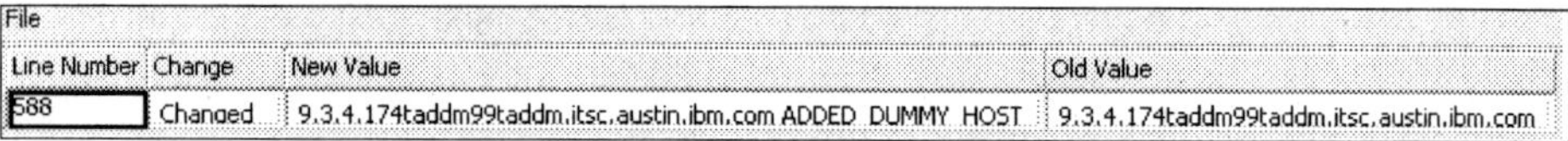
File

Line Number	Change	New Value	Old Value
588	Changed	9.3.4.174taddm99taddm.itsc.austin.ibm.com ADDED DUMMY HOST	9.3.4.174taddm99taddm.itsc.austin.ibm.com

Figure 5-16 Actual changes to a configuration file discovered

Collecting attribute values through a jython script

Using the command functions described earlier provides a simple yet powerful way of enhancing the functionality of Custom Server Sensor to meet a specific need. If further control and manipulation is needed the Jython Script option is available. More information regarding the Jython language and Jython scripting can be found at this Web site:

```
http://www.jython.org
```

To execute a jython script type the following syntax into the Custom Server template command file;

```
SCRIPT:<location of script>
```

If the path of the location of the script starts with a / (forward slash) it is assumed to be absolute. If the path does not start with a forward slash, then it is assumed to be relative to ${COLLATION_HOME}. For the sake of clarity, it is recommended that you give the Jython file the same name as the Custom Server template, with an extension of .py, and put it in the same location.

> **Note:** Jython script files *must* have the extension .py (and not .jy which, in other contexts, is a widely used extension for jython scripts).

In the Custom Server Template command file you simply specify the location of the script to be executed. For example, in the ${COLLATION_HOME}/etc/templates/commands/TCPServer file we added:

```
SCRIPT:/usr/local/collation/dist/etc/templates/commands/TCPServer.py
```

Contrary to the command (CMD) functions the SCRIPT options does not execute on the target hosts but on the Configuration Discovery and Tracking Server itself. However, the script has a hashmap available for manipulation called `targets`. In addition other objects are made available to the script. These are described in Table 5-3.

Table 5-3 Template target array keys available to custom Jython script

Template type	Key	Value
Custom Servers	result	The CustomAppServerResult object
	seed	The CustomAppServerSeed object
	environment	The environment variables hashmap
	osobject	The osobject (Which can be used to execute remote commands)
Computer Systems	result	The ComputerSystemResult object
	seed	The ComputerSystemSeed object
	osobject	The osobject (Which can be used to execute remote commands)
	system	ComputerSystem
	contentarray	ComputerSystem ConfigContent

Using the osobject

If needed, you can execute a remote command on the target host by using the following lines:

```
os_handle = target.get("osobject");
os_handle.executeCommand("myCommand");
```

Using the environment

If needed, you can use the system environment settings by using the following lines:

```
env = target.get("environment")
path = env.get("PATH")
```

Continuing the example of the TCPServer, Example 5-7 shows the content of a simple TCPServer.py script, which sets the value of the name attribute to the concatenated value of `TCPServer on <hostname> in <timezone>`, where the host name and time zone values are picked you from the target system during execution.

Example 5-7 Jython script to set attributes during Custom Server discovery

```
# Getting the result object
result = targets.get('result');

# get the handle for the target
os_handle = targets.get('osobject');

#build command to extrace timezone and hostname
command = str('zone=`date +%Z`; host=`hostname`;echo  $host in $zone');
# execute command
value = os_handle.executeCommand(command);
# prepend TCPServer to value
value = 'TIOServer at ' + str(value);

# Getting the AppServer
appServer = result.getServer();
# set the value for the name attribute
appServer.setName(value)
```

Note: Remember that all files described here are read by the TADDM Server process which is run by the operating system user specified during installation. Therefore, all files must be readable and executable by that user.

Another important note is that if a command hangs during execution, the sensor will time out and the component will not be discovered.

5.1.7 Discovering Business Applications

So far we have focused on discovering hardware and software components. Fundamentally, in a modern enterprise IT environment, components do not provide business value by themselves, but in concert with each other the business realizes benefits. So, to group one or more components into Business Applications (which in turn can be grouped into Business Services) we elevate the configuration discovery and tracking capabilities to report on a higher level than just the components.

As described in 4.2.7, "Defining Business Applications" on page 141 Business Applications canbe defined manually through the Product Console, by linking specific Custom Server Components to a Business Application. However, this can be automated by using an Application Template to hold information about the components we want to associate with a particular Business Application. The Business Application will automatically be populated with components based on Custom Server Templates that are associated with the Application Template. In addition, basic information such as contacts, site, and so forth can be defined in the Application Template.

Upon discovery, all the discovered components that matches the associated Custom Server Templates will be registered as components of the application.

Because only Custom Server Templates can be associated with an Application Template, you have to define Custom Server Templates for infrastructure components such as WebSphere Application Servers, and DB2 Databases that you want to associate with specific Application Templates. Naturally, you must apply application-specific criteria in these Custom Server Templates to differentiate on instance of the specific object type from another. Often you can use environment variables or process arguments to make that distinction.

Figure 5-17 depicts the Application Template defined for a `TCP Test` application system that consist of out `TCPServer` and `TCPClient` components, for which we have already created Custom Server templates.

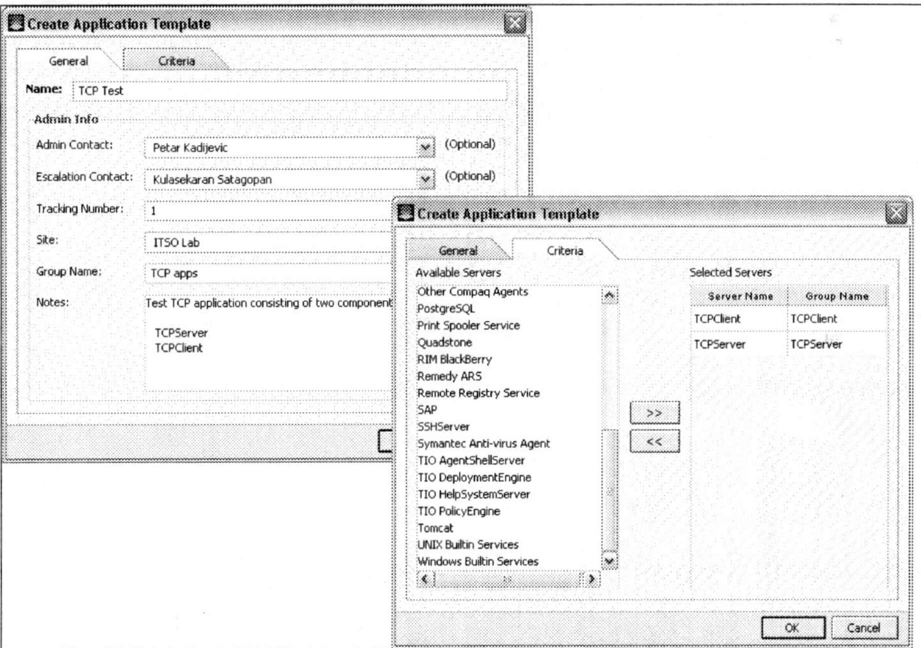

Figure 5-17 TCP Test Application Template

After running a discovery, we notice that a new Business Application named `TCP Test` has been created. By right-clicking it, and selecting **Show Software Topology**, we see components having been automatically associated with the Business Application, as shown in Figure 5-18.

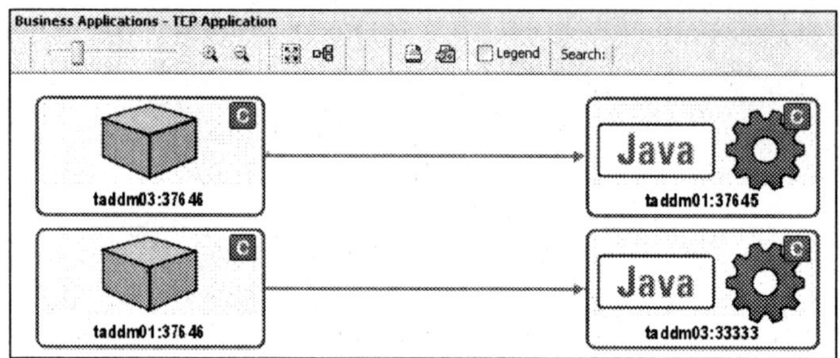

Figure 5-18 TCP Test software topology

The software topology actually reveals that on each of the servers taddm01 and taddm03 we have a TCPServer and a TCPClient component running, and that the client on one system has a dependency to the server on the other system.

To verify this, we can look at the physical topology, shown in Figure 5-19, which confirm our findings.

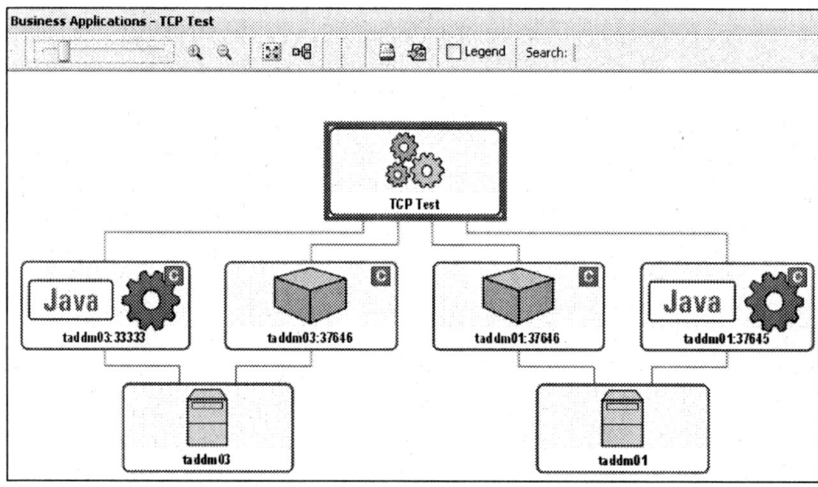

Figure 5-19 Business Application physical topology

5.1.8 Automatically discovering Business Application instances

In addition to using the Application templates and Custom server Templates to automatically discover Business Applications, Configuration Discovery and Tracking can automatically discover your Business Application Instances based on special descriptor files that might have been deployed to predefined locations in the file systems of your servers along with the deployment of the application code, or at a later point in time. Contrary to automatically discovering your

Business Applications based on Application Templates, which cannot tell the difference between multiple instances of similar application systems, the Application Descriptor Files allow you to specify specific instance names of the same applications implemented by similar components.

The following provides an example on how to define and deploy descriptor files. More details are available in IBM Tivoli Change and Configuration Management Database v1.1: Configuring Configuration Discovery and Tracking.

To use Application Descriptor Files to discover your Business Applications, you have to deploy two different types of files: Application Descriptor Files and Component Descriptor Files. Most modern application life cycle tools allow you to create these files as part of the application development processes, but you can also create and deploy them after the applications have been deployed.

Application descriptor files

The Application Descriptor Files define your application system and the specific instances you want to define. Example 5-8 shows the Application Descriptor File for an application instance named `TCP Test 1 at ITSO` which is a `TCP Test` application system.

Example 5-8 Application descriptor file for application TCP Test 1

```
<base-app-descriptor>
  <app-instance
     name="TCP Test 1 at ITSO"
     version="1.1"
     description="Testing TCP dependencies at the ITSO"
     url="http://TCPTest1.ITSO.org"
     contact="Petar Kadijevic" />
  <app-definition
    name="TCP Test"
    description="Testing TCP Dependency discovery"/>
</base-app-descriptor>
```

This application file must be distributed along with a random component of the application system. When a sensor discovers the Component Descriptor File, it will automatically look for an Application Descriptor File, and transfer both files back to the Configuration Discovery and Tracking Server for processing. If multiple Application Descriptor Files are found for the same application, the most recent one is used.

Component descriptor flles

After the application instance has been defined, you must create the Component Descriptor Files that specify the components that belong to an application instance. Example 5-9 shows the Component Descriptor File for the TCPServer component that belongs to the TCP Test 1 at ITSO application instance.

Example 5-9 Component descriptor file for TCPServer server in TCP Test 1

```
<component-app-descriptor
  app-instance-name="TCP Test 1 at ITSO">
  <component-descriptor
    type="server"
    name="TCPServer"
    functional-group="TCP Server"
    marker-module="false" />
</component-app-descriptor>
```

Notice that the Component Descriptor File points to the specific application instance defined in the Application Descriptor File, and that it points to a specific application component, *server* or *module,* that is part of the application.

For generic application components , as is the case in this example, the type should be server. If, however, you are defining components that are hosted by a J2EE server, you can use the *module* type, provided that the name of the component is actually discovered in the J2EE hosting environment.

Example 5-10 shows the module definition of the TCPClient application component that is part of the TCP Test 1 at ITSO application instance.

Example 5-10 Component descriptor file for the TCPClient module in TCP Test 1

```
<component-app-descriptor
  app-instance-name="TCP Test 1 at ITSO">
  <component-descriptor
    type="module"
    name="TCPClient.class"
    functional-group="TCP Client"
    marker-module="false" />
</component-app-descriptor>
```

The location of these files is important in order for the sensors to discover the information. It is unique for each component and depends on a combination of your environment variables set for the process that owns the component to be discovered and the type of resource you are discovering.

Configuration Discovery and Tracking determines the location of the Component Descriptor Files descriptor using the following order of precedence:

- The COLL_APP_DESC_DIR environment variable (if set)

- The `COLL_APP_DESC_DIR` command line argument (if specified)
- Specific subdirectories of the server, used only in cases when neither the environment variable or command line argument is specified.

Table 5-4 outlines the default directory locations based on the server.

Table 5-4 Default Application Descriptor File locations

Server type	supported modules	Default directory
WebSphere	J2EE applications Web modules EJB™ modules connector modules.	<WAS_home_dir>/appdescriptors Example: `/opt/WebSphere/AppServer/appdescriptors`
WebLogic		<WebLogic_home_dir>/appdescriptors
JBoss		<JBoss_home_dir>/appdescriptors
IPlanet	Servlets, JSP™ pages	<server_root_dir>/appdescriptors
Apache	Modules	<server_root_dir>/appdescriptors Example: `/opt/IBMHttpServer/appdescriptors`
Microsoft IIS	Virtual hosts	<server_home_dir>/appdescriptors
Oracle	Users	<oracle_home>/<instance_name>/appdescriptors
Sybase/Sybase IQ™	Databases	<sybase_home>/appdescriptors
SQLServer		<SQLServer_home>/appdescriptors
DB2		<instance_home>/<database>/appdescriptors Example: /home/db2inst1/cmdb/appdescriptors
Domino Server		<domino_home>/appdescriptors
Custom Server	User-supplied through template definition	User-supplied through template definition Supported modules: .

All servers support static-content modules. Web servers support static-content modules directly, while other servers support the modules using custom templates. In the case of managed servers, such as J2EE servers which are managed by the J2EE domain, the location of the application descriptor directory is at the level of the Administration Server or Domain Manager.

The contents specified in that directory are used as the super-set of all possible mappings for all managed servers. For each managed server (depending on which modules are discovered as deployed), the Component Descriptor is processed for inclusion of those modules in the application.

Discovering Application instances

In 5.1.7, "Discovering Business Applications" on page 180 we discovered two instances of the TCP Test application both made up of a set of TCPServer and TCPClient components. Assuming that each set represent a specific instance of a Customer Relationship Management application, one for LOB1 and the other for LOB2, there is no way that we can distinguish between the two by looking at the topologies.

However, if we deploy Application and Component Descriptor Files to each of the two systems involved, and instruct the Custom Server Templates for TCPServer and TCPClient to look for the descriptor files, we can differentiate the two. This is what we did:

1. We created two Application Descriptor Files similar to the one shown in Example 5-8 on page 183 and placed them in the `/tmp/appdescriptors` of each of the systems. Both files were named `TCP_APP_coll_dscr.xml`, and one identified an application instance named `TCP Test 1 at ITSO` (as in the example) and the other identified an application instance named `TCP Test 2 at ITSO`.
2. We created the Component Descriptor Files for the TCPServer components. Both were named `TCP_Server_coll_desc.xml`, and was placed in the same location as the Application Descriptor files, `/tmp/appdescriptors`. On one system, the TCPServer Component Descriptor File referenced the application instance `TCP Test 1 at ITSO`, surprisingly, on the other system the `TCP_Server_coll_desc.xml` file referenced `TCP Test 2 at ITSO` application instance. Example 5-9 on page 184 shows the sample content of the `TCP_Server_coll_desc.xml files`.
3. We repeated the process for TCPServer Component Descriptor Files to create the TCPClient descriptor files. These were named `TCP_Client_coll_desc.xml`, their sample content shown in Example 5-10 on page 184, and each one referenced the application instance not already referenced by the TCPServer descriptor files. Table 5-5 shows the locations and application instance affinities of the components:

Table 5-5 Application instance relationships for TCP Test applications

System	Application	TCPServer	TCPClient
taddm01	TCP Test 1 at ITSO	TCP Test 1 at ITSO	TCP Test 2 at ITSO
taddm03	TCP Test 2 at ITSO	TCP Test 2 at ITSO	TCP Test 1 at ITSO

4. We had to update the TCPServer and TCPCLient Custom Server Templates to instruct them to look for the descriptor files. Using the **Config Files** section of the Custom Server Template definitions we added a Application Descriptor File definition to each of the TCPServer and TCPClient templates, as shown in Figure 5-20.

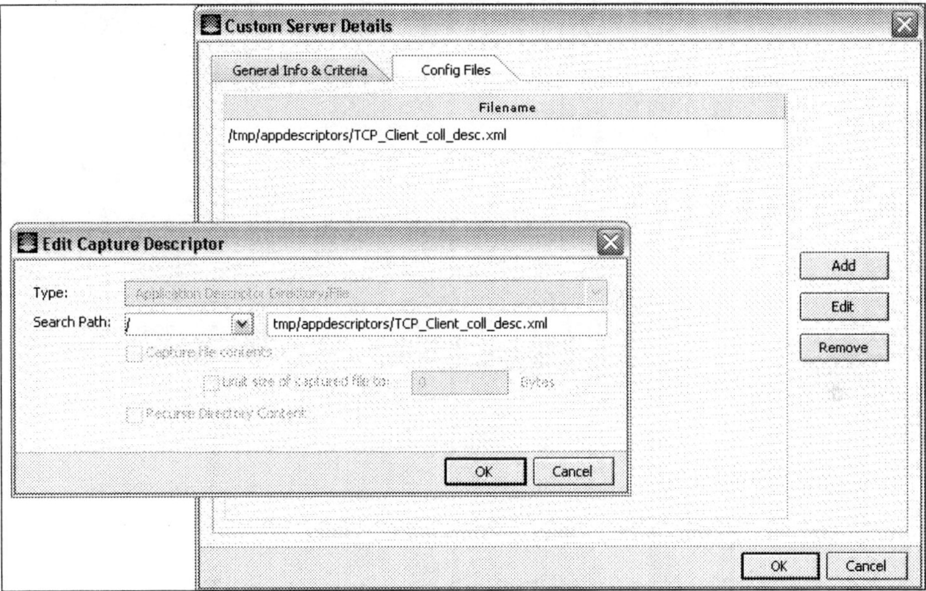

Figure 5-20 Adding Application Descriptor Files to Custom Server Template

The Application Descriptor FIles referenced in the two Custom Server Templates were:

TCPServer	`/tmp/appdescriptors/TCP_Server_coll_desc.xml`
TCPClient	`/tmp/appdescriptors/TCP_Client_coll_desc.xml`

5. We were ready to run the discovery, and see that the two new Business Applications `TCP Test 1 at ITSO` and `TCP Test 2 at ITSO` was created as expected, as in Figure 5-21 on page 188.

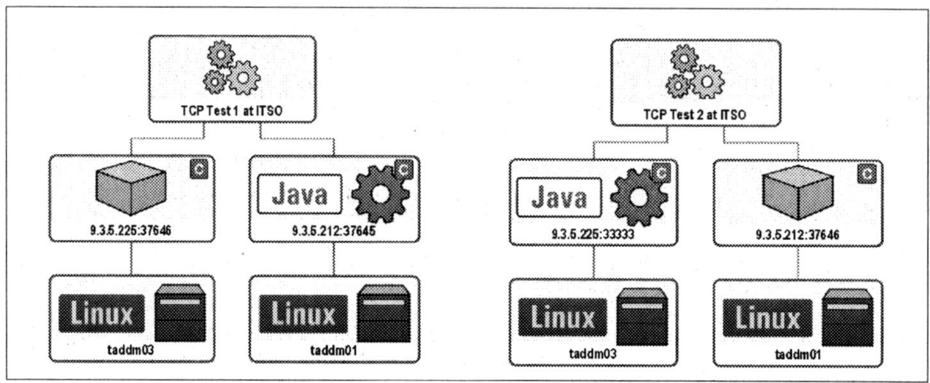

Figure 5-21 Business Applications

6. In order to be able to report on any of the instances, we create a Business Service named `TCP Test`, that groups all the instances of the `TCP Test...` application instances.

   The Business Service is created manually from the PRoduct Console. Select **Edit →Create Business Service**, as in Figure 5-22.

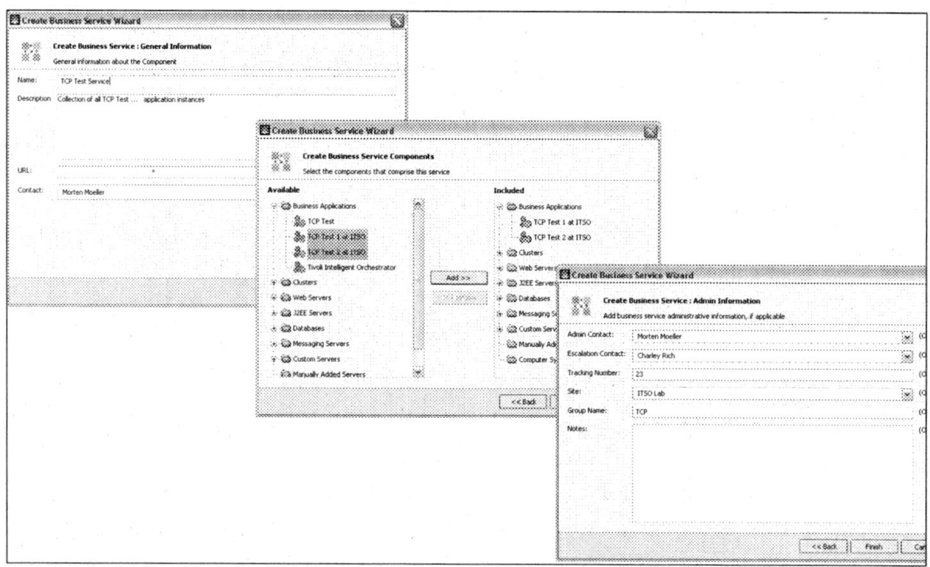

Figure 5-22 Creating the TCP Test Service Business Service

The topology of the Business Service reveals that both application instances are represented and the details shows all four expected components (Figure 5-23 on page 189).

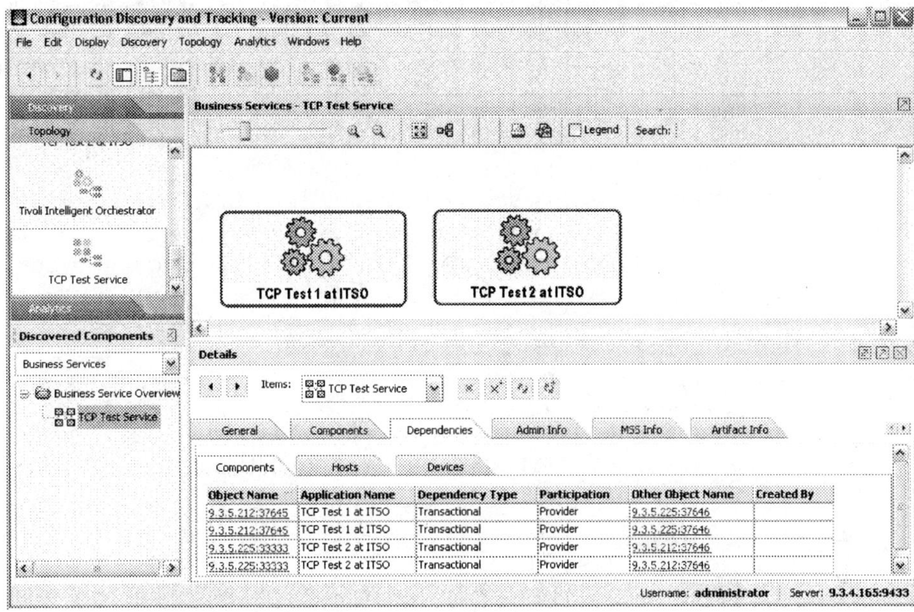

Figure 5-23 TCP Test Service topology and details

5.2 Importing Discovery Library Books

As described in 2.3.2, “Configuration Discovery and Tracking uses Discovery Library technology” on page 53, the Discovery Library technology is key component of Configuration Discovery and Tracking for data exchange with other management system servers (MSS) such as IBM Tivoli Monitoring, IBM Tivoli Business Systems Manager, IBM Tivoli Configuration Manager, or IBM Tivoli Provisioning Manager and IBM Tivoli Intelligent Orchestrator, just to name a few.

As described in detail in Appendix C, “Discovery Library overview” on page 387 the Discovery Library technology is based on two basic components, an author (or writer) and a reader. The author is responsible for extracting data from the proprietary format and structure used by the MSS, to create standardized IdML formatted XML documents (so called Discovery Library Books) containing the relevant information. The responsibility of the reader, is to load the IdML formatted documents into the data structures used by the MSS, in our case Configuration Discovery and Tracking. Naturally this process can be reversed, in order to extract data from the CMDB to be imported into for example the Data Center Model of Tivoli Provisioning Manager. The combination of Discovery author and reader components are often referred to as a Discovery Library Adapter (DLA).

Over time, most DLAs will be delivered as integral parts of the various IBM MSS solutions, either in new versions, as part of FixPacks, or through the IBM Open Process Automation Library (OPAL) which is accessible at this Web site:

`http://catalog.lotus.com/wps/portal/topal`

Configuration Discovery and Tracking provides a generic DLA reader that is capable of loading several books into the CMDB at a time. Therefore, it is also referred to as the *BulkLoader*. As any other DL reader, the BulkLoader is keeps track of the imported books for logging and auditing purposes.

5.2.1 Creating a Discovery Library book

The only Discovery Library Adapter available to us during the development of this book was the DLA for IBM Tivoli Monitoring v6.1. In our test environment, we established an ITM MSS, and used the DLA to extract ITM managed information regarding the systems in our infrastructure.

A quick look at the ITM Tivoli Enterprise™ Portal, Figure 5-24, shows the systems which have been instrumented to be monitored by ITM.

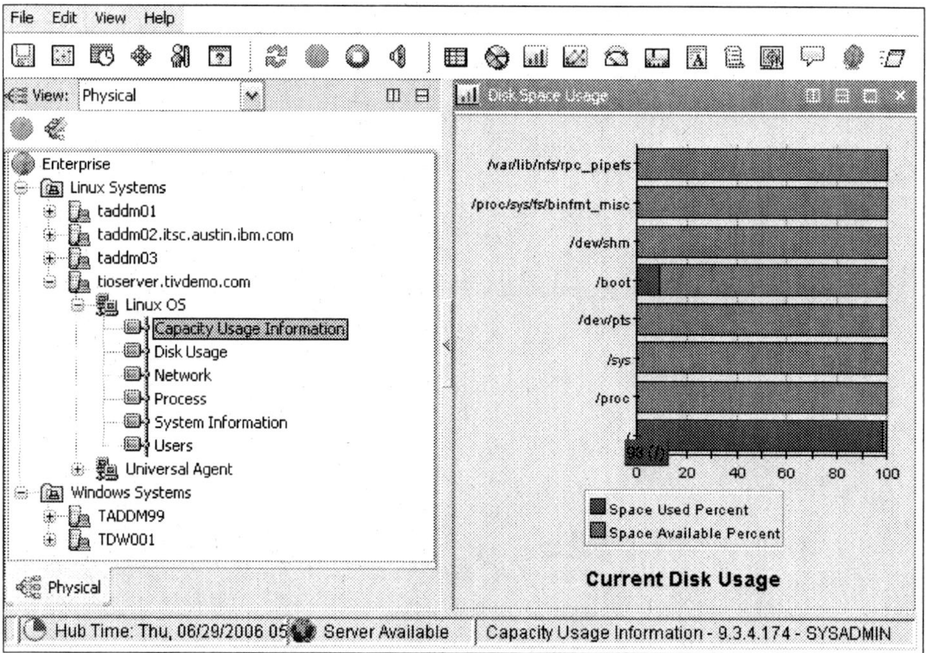

Figure 5-24 Tivoli Enterprise Portal showing the monitored computer systems

To install the DLA Author on the ITM system, copy the following files to the `%CANDLE_HOME%\cnps` directory where the TEPS is running, for example `C:\ibm\tivoli\ITM\CNPS`

- kfwTmsDla.exe
- kfwIDMLBrowse.htm

These files will be shipped in this directory with ITM FixPack 3.

Then, to run the TMS DLA to generate the Discovery Library Book, follow these steps:

1. Open a command prompt and go to the CNPS directory where `kfwTmsDla.exe` was installed.
2. Issue the command in Example 5-11 to see the optional parameters.

Example 5-11 Displaying KfwTmsDla.exe parameters

```
C:\IBM\Tivoli\ITM\CNPS>KfwTmsDla.exe /?

TMS Discovery Library Adapter Command Line Utility.

Usage:  KfwTmsDla [/?][/b][/d][/l][/o orgname][/s][/x outputfile]
Options:
    /?              Display this help screen.
    /b              Launch html browse utility on completion of the
                    discovery.
    /d              Create diagnostic file during discovery process.
    /l              Discover Logical Views.
    /o orgname      Organization GlobalName will be set to orgname.
    /s              Discover HTTPS URL rather than HTTP URL..
    /x outputfile   Create XML file of name outputfile.
```

3. Issue `kfwTmsDla.exe` (with optional parameters if desired) and a Discovery Library IDML XML file will be created by default in a subdirectory of the CNPS directory called `tmsdla`.

   > **Note:** For `kfwTmsDla.exe` to execute successfully, the ITM Tivoli Enterprise Portal Server (TEPS) has to be active and communicating with the ITM Hub Tivoli Enterprise Management Server (TEMS).

   We opted to view the resulting book in the browser tool, so the command we used to generate the book was:

   ```
   C:\IBM\Tivoli\ITM\CNPS>KfwTmsDla.exe /b /o ITSO
   ```

Upon completion, the browser was automatically opened to show the results. A wealth of information is discovered, including information about the management system server itself. See Figure 5-25. For a summary of classes and links, see Figure 5-26.

cdm:process.ManagementSoftwareSystem

CDMSchemaVersion	2.3
sourceContactInfo	http://taddm99.itsc.austin.ibm.com:1920
cdm:Hostname	taddm99.itsc.austin.ibm.com
cdm:Label	TEPS taddm99.itsc.austin.ibm.com
cdm:ManufacturerName	IBM
cdm:MSSName	ibm-cdm:///CDMMSS/Hostname=taddm99.itsc.austin.ibm.com,Manufacturer=IBM+ProductName=IBM Tivoli Monitoring Services
cdm:ProductName	IBM Tivoli Monitoring Services
cdm:ProductVersion	6.1.0
Comment	TMSDLA Build: v1.0.0 Jun 13 2006 15:40:48

Figure 5-25 DLA Book generation results - MSS information

Class and Link Summary

Class	Count
cdm:app.TMSAgent	14
cdm:net.Fqdn	6
cdm:net.IpInterface	6
cdm:net.IpV4Address	6
cdm:process.Organization	1
cdm:sys.ComputerSystem	6
cdm:sys.linux.Linux	4
cdm:sys.windows.WindowsOperatingSystem	2
Total Class Instances	**45**

Link	Count
cdm:assignedTo	6
cdm:bindsTo	6
cdm:contains	6
cdm:federates	13
cdm:installedOn	20
cdm:runsOn	6
Total Link Instances	**57**

Figure 5-26 DLA Book generation results - Class and Link Summary

4. By default the DLA Book name will be in Discovery Library file format `<DLA-author>.<fully-qualified-hostname>.<timestamp>.refresh.xml`, for example:

```
TMSDISC100.taddm99.itsc.austin.ibm.com.2006-06-29T18.14.22Z.refresh.xml
```

The DLA Book file can now be transferred to the Discovery Library File Store available to the Configuration Discovery and Tracking Server (either automatically or manually) and loaded into CMDB with the Discovery Library Bulk Loader. We transferred it manually to our Configuration Discovery and Tracking Server in the `/tmp/dlaBooks` directory.

5. Import the book into the CMDB using the BulkLoader. Some customization is necessary. Details on how to customize the BulkLoader are provided in B.3.1, "loadidml: the bulk loader" on page 362.

   To run the bulk loader loadidml.sh script you must log in as the user running the Configuration Discovery and Tracking Server. If you are not sure which user has been set up to do this, you can find the name of the user in the `com.collation.unixuser` parameter of the `${COLLATION_HOME}/etc/collation.properties` file. In our case, the user ID is `itaddm`.

   In addition, the loadidml.sh script must have the anchor directory of the Configuration Discovery and Tracking files defined in the `COLLATION_HOME` variable. In our case, this is `/opt/IBM/cmdb/dist`.

   The only required parameter for the `loadidml` program is the `-f` parameter. This parameter specifies the directory and, optionally, the fully qualified file name from which to read the DLA books to be loaded. If no filename is provided, all the files with the .xml extension in the specified directory will be loaded.

   To import all the DLA books in the `/tmp/dlaBooks` directory, we used the commands in Example 5-12.

Example 5-12 Importing all DLA books into /tmp/dlaBooks

```
[taddm@taddm02 bin]$ export COLLATION_HOME=/opt/IBM/cmdb/dist
[taddm@taddm02 bin]$ ${COLLATION_HOME}/bin/loadidml.sh -f /tmp/dlaBooks
Bulk Load Program starting.
Bulk Load Program running....
Bulk Load Program running.
Bulk Load Program succeeded. Return code is: 0
0
Bulk Load Program ending.
```

   Upon successful import, the bulk directory or the directory referenced by the `com.ibm.cdb.bulk.workdir` parameter in the ${COLLATION_HOME}/bulkload.properties file will contain copies of the imported files, and information in the `processedfiles.list` file about the imported files.

   To verify the results of the bulk load, you can check the log files (with the .results extension) in the `${COLLATION_HOME}/bulk/results` directory.

6. After import of the ITM Discovery Library Book, we selected **Edit →MSS** from the Product Console to see that a new MSS system had been defined in the CMDB (Figure 5-27 on page 194).

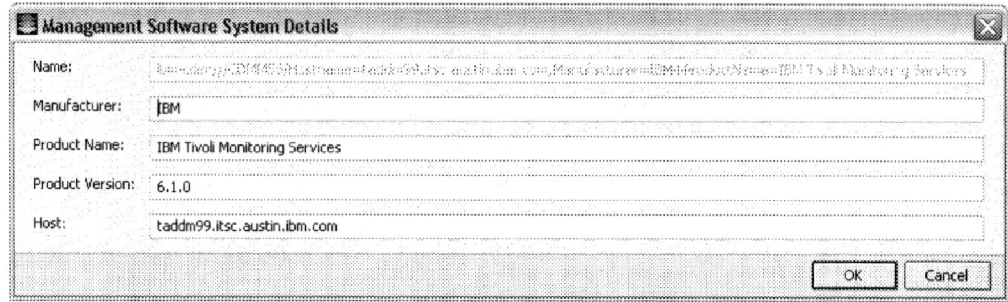

Figure 5-27 New Management System Server

In addition, we see that two new ComputerSystems have been introduced in Figure 5-28.

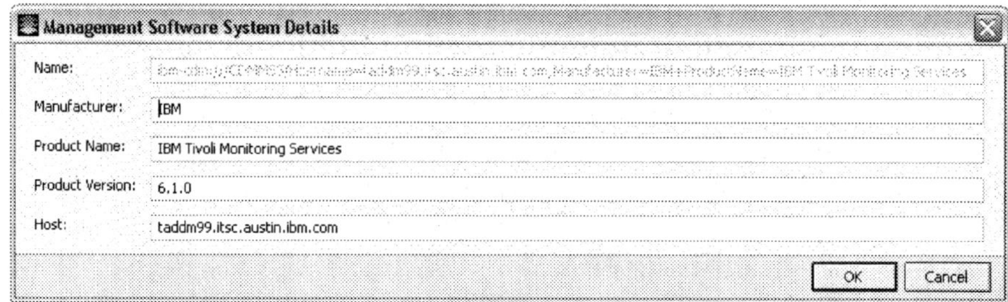

Figure 5-28 New Management System Server

Figure 5-29 shows that a new ComputerSystem named taddm99 has been created, and that it is related to the ITM MSS from which the DLA Book was created.

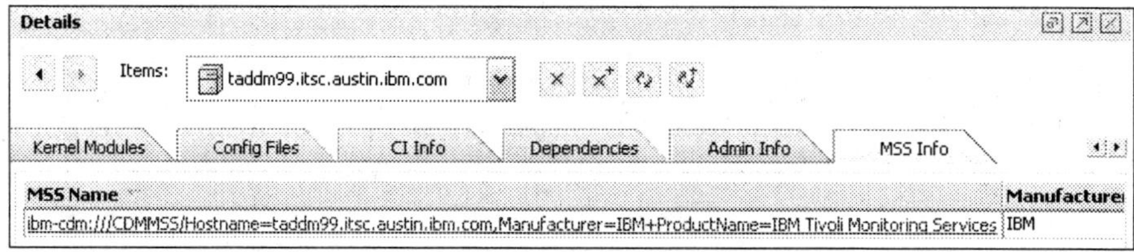

Figure 5-29 The ComputerSystem Details MSS section

5.3 Providing input programmatically

IBM Tivoli Change and Configuration Management Database Configuration Discovery and Tracking v1.1 provides several ways of maintaining the CMDB programatically. The different options each support different integration needs and are invoked from different environments:

- The Command line environment is primarily used to implement lightly-integrated automation solutions and for process automation
- The SOAP environment is primarily used for building on-the-glass integration between solutions such as IBM CCMBD and an off-the-shelf Service Desk solution.
- The EJB environment is used for low-level application integration to home-grown application and service-oriented architecture (SOA) services.

5.3.1 Command Line

The primary tool to be used in this environment is the api script, which, as described in B.2.9, "Using api.sh from remote systems" on page 358, can be implemented on a remote system. One example if this is hosting the IBM Tivoli Enterprise Console® event management system.

From an integration point of view, the command line interface offers the following advantages and disadvantages:

- Advantages
  - Easy to use.
  - Easy to integrate with other systems through a well proven technology provided by the Operating System, standard in/out/error.
- Disadvantages
  - The command line interface does not expose all feature of the IBM Tivoli Change and Configuration Management Database Configuration Discovery and Tracking APIs.
  - Because the command line interface return strings of XML, it requires thorough skills for parsing and manipulation XML (such as through xsl and scripting) if advanced functionality is needed.

Updating using the api.sh

If you are to update an object in the IBM Tivoli Change and Configuration Management Database Configuration Discovery and Tracking using the **api.sh** you need to provide an XML file that describes that data is to be imported. If you do not have this file, an easy way to retrieve it is by issuing the **api.sh** command with the find action, for example:

```
api.sh -u administrator -p collation find --depth 1 "SELECT * FROM
ComputerSystem WHERE displayName=='taddm02.itsc.austin.ibm.com'" >
/tmp/taddm02.xml
```

Note that the output is redirected to a file, taddm02.xml, and the content of taddm02.xml could look similar to Example 5-13.

Example 5-13 Content of taddm02.xml


```
<?xml version="1.0" encoding="ISO-8859-1"?>
<results
        xmlns="urn:www-collation-com:1.0"
        xmlns:coll="urn:www-collation-com:1.0"
        xmlns:xsi="http://www.w3.org/2001/XMLSchema-instance"
        xsi:schemaLocation="urn:www-collation-com:1.0
              urn:www-collation-com:1.0/results.xsd">
    <ComputerSystem array="1"
guid="58E6E62D0DD2322787FAC082FDD98673"
        lastModified="1148402976945"
xsi:type="coll:com.collation.platform.model.topology.sys.linux.Linux
UnitaryComputerSystem">
        <displayName>taddm02.itsc.austin.ibm.com</displayName>
        <contextIp>9.3.5.216</contextIp>
        <CDMSource>taddm02.itsc.austin.ibm.com</CDMSource>
        <name>taddm02.itsc.austin.ibm.com</name>
        <type>ComputerSystem</type>
        <systemId>309a504</systemId>
        <signature>9.3.4.165(00112506F51F)</signature>
        <fqdn>taddm02.itsc.austin.ibm.com</fqdn>
<OSInstalled array="1" guid="943F09E7C6B23675A9E196CEFD9E0851"
            lastModified="1148402976947"
            parent="58E6E62D0DD2322787FAC082FDD98673"
xsi:type="coll:com.collation.platform.model.topology.sys.linux.Linux
"/>
        <OSRunning guid="943F09E7C6B23675A9E196CEFD9E0851"
            lastModified="1148402976947"
            parent="58E6E62D0DD2322787FAC082FDD98673"
xsi:type="coll:com.collation.platform.model.topology.sys.linux.Linux
"/>
    </ComputerSystem>
</results>
```

You can now open taddm02.xml in an editor and change or insert a value. In Example 5-14 an extra line `<manufacturer>MyManufacturer</manufacturer>` is inserted to the file so that it now looks like this.

Example 5-14 Edited taddm02.xml

```
<?xml version="1.0" encoding="ISO-8859-1"?>
<results
        xmlns="urn:www-collation-com:1.0"
        xmlns:coll="urn:www-collation-com:1.0"
        xmlns:xsi="http://www.w3.org/2001/XMLSchema-instance"
        xsi:schemaLocation="urn:www-collation-com:1.0
              urn:www-collation-com:1.0/results.xsd">
    <ComputerSystem array="1"
guid="58E6E62D0DD2322787FAC082FDD98673"
        lastModified="1148402976945"
xsi:type="coll:com.collation.platform.model.topology.sys.linux.Linux
UnitaryComputerSystem">
        <displayName>taddm02.itsc.austin.ibm.com</displayName>
        <contextIp>9.3.5.216</contextIp>
        <CDMSource>taddm02.itsc.austin.ibm.com</CDMSource>
        <name>taddm02.itsc.austin.ibm.com</name>
        <type>ComputerSystem</type>
        <systemId>309a504</systemId>
        <signature>9.3.4.165(00112506F51F)</signature>
        <fqdn>taddm02.itsc.austin.ibm.com</fqdn>
        <manufacturer>MyManufacturer</manufacturer>
        <OSInstalled array="1"
guid="943F09E7C6B23675A9E196CEFD9E0851"
            lastModified="1148402976947"
            parent="58E6E62D0DD2322787FAC082FDD98673"
xsi:type="coll:com.collation.platform.model.topology.sys.linux.Linux
"/>
        <OSRunning guid="943F09E7C6B23675A9E196CEFD9E0851"
            lastModified="1148402976947"
            parent="58E6E62D0DD2322787FAC082FDD98673"
xsi:type="coll:com.collation.platform.model.topology.sys.linux.Linux
"/>
    </ComputerSystem>
</results>
```

Notice the new line in bold. Now run the **api.sh** with the import option:

```
api.sh -H 9.3.4.165 -u administrtor -p collation import taddm02.xml
```

After the import the Product Console reflects the changes, as in Figure 5-30.

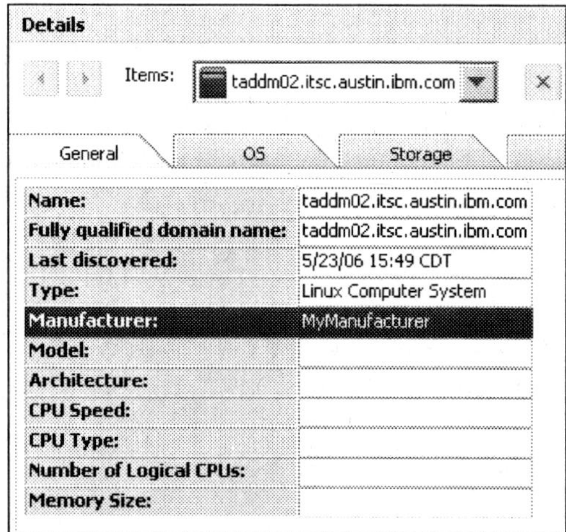

Figure 5-30 New objects imported by api.sh

Inserting using api.sh

If you want to populate the database with new objects, you can make use of an existing XML structure, modify it, then import it into IBM Tivoli Change and Configuration Management Database Configuration Discovery and Tracking. For example, the newobject.txt in Example 5-15, has been created based on the taddm02.xml file mentioned before.

Example 5-15 Newobject.txt file

```
<?xml version="1.0" encoding="ISO-8859-1"?>
<results
        xmlns="urn:www-collation-com:1.0"
        xmlns:coll="urn:www-collation-com:1.0"
        xmlns:xsi="http://www.w3.org/2001/XMLSchema-instance"
        xsi:schemaLocation="urn:www-collation-com:1.0
              urn:www-collation-com:1.0/results.xsd">
    <ComputerSystem
xsi:type="coll:com.collation.platform.model.topology.sys.linux.Linux
UnitaryComputerSystem">
        <CDMSource>NEWOBJECT.itsc.austin.ibm.com</CDMSource>
        <displayName>NEWOBJECT.itsc.austin.ibm.com</displayName>
        <contextIp>9.3.5.226</contextIp>
        <CDMSource>NEWOBJECT.itsc.austin.ibm.com</CDMSource>
        <name>NEWOBJECT.itsc.austin.ibm.com</name>
        <type>ComputerSystem</type>
         <signature>NEWOBJECT signature</signature>
```

```
        <fqdn>NEWOBJECT.itsc.austin.ibm.com</fqdn>
    </ComputerSystem>
</results>
```

Notice that the array, Guid, and lastModified attributes of the ComputerSystem tag has been removed (along with, for space saving reasons, the child elements OSInstalled and OSRunning). Again after the import the Product Console should reflect the new object, as shown in Figure 5-31.

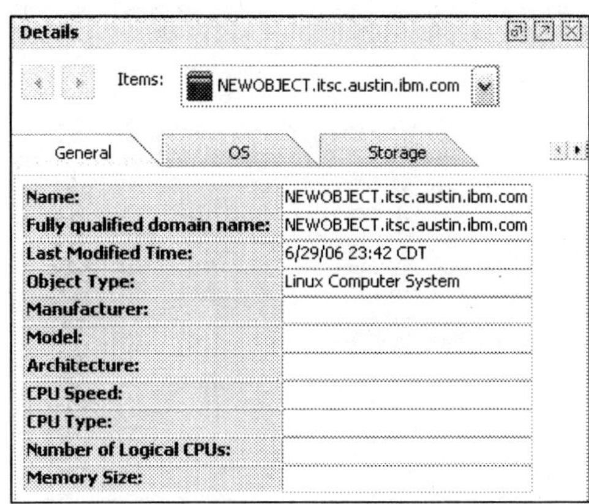

Figure 5-31 NEWOBJECT imported through the api import function

5.3.2 The SOAP/Web Services interfaces

Configuration Discovery and Tracking also provides a Web Service/SOAP interface through the Web Services Description Language (WSDL) available by pointing to the following URL: `http://<CTS server>:9430/axis`. Although there are three WSDLs available, this section covers only the CollationService because this is the one containing SOAP calls accessing and manipulating data in the Configuration Discovery and Tracking. The CollationService WSDL is accessed directly at:

```
http://<taddm server>:9430/axis/services/CollationService?wsdl
```

A Web Services Description Language (WSDL) is basically a standard format that describes what SOAP Calls (services) are available at a given server, in this case the IBM Tivoli Change and Configuration Management Database Configuration Discovery and Tracking server. The WSDL is defined in XML and has no bindings to any particular programming language. Consequently, many different tools, or IDEs (Integrated Development Environment) can assist in transforming the WSDL file into concrete client code of a particular language. In most modern IDEs there will be a wizard or similar that takes the URL of the WSDL as an input and then turns the WSDL into client code. This is, for example, the case for Rational Application Developer, which is an IBM Eclipse-based IDE that can transform a WSDL into java client code. Refer to the relevant Rational Application Developer documentation or the RedPaper “WebSphere Studio V5 Overview and Architecture”, SG24-3742 for information about how to use the “Create Web Service Client” Wizard.

The SOAP/Web Services interface offers the following advantages and disadvantages:

- Advantages
  - Standard technology that can be deployed in a service-oriented architecture (SOA).
  - Independent of programming language.
- Disadvantages
  - Only limited functionality of the api command.
  - Data from the Configuration Discovery and Tracking is return as XML strings that you have to parse and handle yourself.
  - Requires knowledge of WSDL on how to generate client code from an IDE.

Assume that Rational Application Developer has created a packaged called com.ibm.axis.services.CollationService and a class (among a few others) called SoapServiceProxy which will expose the soap calls defined in the WSDL as java methods. The following list shows the essential methods:

- `login()`
- `logout()`
- `abortDiscovery()`
- `getStatus()`
- `clearTopology()`
- `rebuildTopology()`
- `find()`
- `findBasedOnChange()`
- `getClassNames()`
- `insert()`
- `getChangeHistory()`
- `createVersion()`
- `deleteVersion()`
- `getAllVersions()`
- `exportData()`
- `importData()`

You might notice that both an `insert()` and an `importData()` call is available. The two calls have much in common, in fact, the only functional difference between the two is that the `insert()` call takes an XML String as an argument, while the `import()` call takes a path to an XML file as a parameter. Therefore, the `insert()` goes hand in hand with find() which returns an XML string and `import()` goes hand in hand with exportData() which places a file on the Configuration Discovery and Tracking Server at a path specified. Other than that, the list of SOAP calls is tightly connected to the actions available through the **`api.sh`** command line api. Basically, it is the same functionality just exposed as an Web service. Therefore, you can refer to IBM Tivoli Change and Configuration Management Database Configuration Discovery and Tracking v1.1 SDK Guide for more details.

5.3.3 Native Java API

To use the native Java API to communicate with the CMDB api server, it is necessary to include the following jar files, which can be found in the `$COLLATION_HOME}/sdk/lib` directory.

api-client.jar	Java api implementations.
api-dep.jar	External dependent jars. Might conflict with some classes in embedded environments. See below.
platform-model.jar	Model interfaces and implementation classes.

In certain embedded environments, the classes which exist in the api-dep.jar file can interfere with existing classes. As a convenience, this jar has been broken out into its constituent parts in the `${COLLATION_HOME}/sdk/lib` directory:

log4j.jar	Apache logging routines.
jini-ext.jar	Jini network utilities.
reggie.jar	Jini lookup service.
jargs.jar	Command line parsing for api.sh.

See more in the javadoc for com.collation.proxy.api.client.DataApi.

The native Java interface offers the following advantages and disadvantages:

- Advantages
  - Full featured access to the IBM Tivoli Change and Configuration Management Database Configuration Discovery and Tracking APIs
  - You can retrieve true Java objects (as opposed to an XML string) that represent the Configuration Discovery and Tracking data model, thereby, having full and clean access to components data and relationships.
  - You can still retrieve data as XML.

- Disadvantages
  - You are tied to the Java programming language. However, you can use scripting languages such as JavaScript™ or Jython that can interact with native Java.
  - Requires knowledge of Java programming.

In the following sections, we provide a few simple examples on using the JavaAPI from a Windows based environment. For more details, refer to the IBM Tivoli Change and Configuration Management Database Configuration Discovery and Tracking v1.1 SDK Guide.

Setting up the environment.

Follow the instructions provided in Appendix B.2.9, "Using api.sh from remote systems" on page 358 to establish your runtime environment.

You can optionally modify the com.collation.LogFile property of the collation.properties file - <apiroot>\etc\collation.properties - to a logfile of your choice, for example. <apiroot>\\log\\TADDMclient.log. In the Windows environment you can use either the forward slash (/) or double backslaches (\\) as the directory delimiter.

Verifying connection

To verify your setup, compile and run the following java code in Example 5-16.

Example 5-16 TestConnection.java source code

```
import com.collation.proxy.api.client.ApiConnection;
import com.collation.proxy.api.client.ApiSession;
import com.collation.proxy.api.client.CMDBApi;

public class TestConnection {

   public static void main(String[] args) throws Exception {
      if (args.length < 4) {
         System.out.println("Usage: TestConnection <hostname> <port>
<username> <password>");
         System.exit(1);
      }
      ApiConnection conn = ApiConnection.getConnection(args[0], Integer
            .parseInt(args[1]), null, false);
      ApiSession session = ApiSession.getSession(conn, args[2],
args[3],
            ApiSession.DEFAULT_VERSION);
      CMDBApi api = session.createCMDBApi();
```

```
        System.out.println("Discovery is: " + api.getStatus());
    }
}
```

To compile the code, use the following commands:

```
set COLLATION_HOME=<apiroot>
javac -cp %COLLATION_HOME%\lib\api-client.jar;. TestConnection.java
```

And to test the connectivity to your Configuration Discovery and Tracking server, execute the TestConnection program with the following two commands:

```
set COLLATION_HOME=<apiroot>
java -Dcom.collation.home=%COLLATION_HOMME% -cp
lib\api-client.jar;lib\api-dep.jar;. TestConnection <server ip-address>
<server port> <userid> <password>
```

> **Note:** The `-D` option for the collation home directory is required.

In our test environment, where the default administrator credentials were still active, we used the following:

```
set COLLATION_HOME="C:\taddm51winAPI"
java -Dcom.collation.home=%COLLATION_HOME% -cp
%COLLATION_HOME%\lib\api-client.jar;%COLLATION_HOME%\lib\api-dep.jar;.
TestConnection 9.3.4.165 9530 administrator collation
```

The code simply connects to TADDM and asks if a discovery is running. The output of the program should look similar to the following:

```
2006-06-14 03:18:51,752  [main]  INFO client.ApiPool - ResourcePool is
null for Host: 9.3.4.165 Port: 9530
......
Discovery is: Idle
```

GetUpdAttribue

After the connectivity has been verified, you can test the following program (GetUpdAttribute.java), which shows how retrieve and update single attributes of any object in the CMDB trough the use of the native Java api.

Example 5-17 GetUpdAttribute.java JavaAPI sample code

```
import java.lang.reflect.InvocationTargetException;
import java.lang.reflect.Method;

import com.collation.platform.model.AttributeNotSetException;
import com.collation.platform.model.ModelObject;
```

```
import com.collation.proxy.api.client.ApiConnection;
import com.collation.proxy.api.client.ApiException;
import com.collation.proxy.api.client.ApiSession;
import com.collation.proxy.api.client.CMDBApi;

public class GetUpdAttribute {

   public static void main(String[] args) throws Exception {
      String usage = "Usage: TestConnection <hostname> <port>
<username> <password> <datatype> <where-clause> <attribute> [get|upd
<newvalue>]";

      if (args.length < 8) {
         System.out.println(usage);
         System.exit(1);
      }
      if (!(args[7].equals("upd") || args[7].equals("get"))) {
         System.out.println(usage);
         System.out.println("   The 8th argument must be \"upd\" or
\"get\"");
         System.exit(1);
      }
      if (args.length > 7 && args[7].equals("upd") && args.length < 9)
{
         System.out.println(usage);
         System.out.println("   When using \"upd\" you must provide
<newvalue>");
         System.exit(1);
      }

      // Variable / Arguments
      String hostname = args[0];
      int port = Integer.parseInt(args[1]);
      String username = args[2];
      String password = args[3];
      String type = args[4];
      String condition = args[5];
      String attribute = args[6];
      String action = args[7];
      String newvalue = "";
      if (args.length > 8) {
         newvalue = args[8];
      }

      CMDBApi api = null;
```

```
      ApiSession session = null;
      try {
         ApiConnection conn = ApiConnection.getConnection(hostname,
port, null, false);
         session = ApiSession.getSession(conn, username, password,
ApiSession.DEFAULT_VERSION);
         api = session.createCMDBApi();

         String query = "SELECT * FROM " + type + " WHERE " +
condition;
         ModelObject mo[] = api.find(query, -1, null, null);
         if (mo != null && mo.length == 1) {
            Class c = Class.forName(type);

            Method method = c.getMethod("get" + attribute, new
Class[0]);
            String returnType = method.getReturnType().getName();
            String oldval = getOldvalue(returnType, method, mo[0]);

            if (returnType.equals("java.lang.String") &&
action.equals("upd")) {
               Method updmethod = c.getMethod("set" + attribute,
Class.forName("java.lang.String"));
               updmethod.invoke(mo[0], newvalue);
            }
            if (returnType.equals("int") && action.equals("upd")) {
               Method updmethod = c.getMethod("set" + attribute,
Integer.TYPE);
               updmethod.invoke(mo[0], Integer.parseInt(newvalue));
            }
            if (returnType.equals("long") && action.equals("upd")) {
               Method updmethod = c.getMethod("set" + attribute,
Long.TYPE);
               updmethod.invoke(mo[0], Long.parseLong(newvalue));
            }
            if (returnType.equals("double") && action.equals("upd")) {
               Method updmethod = c.getMethod("set" + attribute,
Double.TYPE);
               updmethod.invoke(mo[0], Double.parseDouble(newvalue));
            }
            if (returnType.equals("float") && action.equals("upd")) {
               Method updmethod = c.getMethod("set" + attribute,
Float.TYPE);
               updmethod.invoke(mo[0], Float.parseFloat(newvalue));
            }
```

```
            api.update(mo[0], mo[0].getGuid());
            outputResponse(returnType, method, action, attribute,
oldval, newvalue, mo[0]);

         } else {
            System.out
                  .println("GetUpdAttributes found "
                        + mo.length
                        + " Components matching your WHERE-CLAUSE. You
can only use GetUpdAttributes with a WHERE-CLAUSE that identifies a
single Component");
         }

      } catch (ApiException ae) {
         System.err.println("Api Exception:" + ae);
         ae.printStackTrace();
      } finally {
         try {
            if (api != null) {
               api.close();
            }
            if (session != null) {
               session.close();
            }
         } catch (Exception ex) {
            System.err.println("Exception:" + ex);
            ex.printStackTrace();
         }
      }
   }

   private static String getOldvalue(String returnType, Method method,
ModelObject mo) throws IllegalArgumentException,
         IllegalAccessException {
      String oldval = "";

      try {
         if (returnType.equals("java.lang.String")) {
            oldval = (String) method.invoke(mo, new Object[0]);
         }
         if (returnType.equals("int")) {
            oldval = ((Integer) method.invoke(mo, new
Object[0])).toString();
         }
         if (returnType.equals("long")) {
```

```
            oldval = ((Long) method.invoke(mo, new
Object[0])).toString();
         }
         if (returnType.equals("double")) {
            oldval = ((Double) method.invoke(mo, new
Object[0])).toString();
         }
         if (returnType.equals("float")) {
            oldval = ((Float) method.invoke(mo, new
Object[0])).toString();
         }
      } catch (InvocationTargetException anse) {
         if
(anse.getTargetException().getMessage().startsWith("Attribute not
set")) {
            oldval = "N/A (was not set in TADDM)";
         } else {
            System.out.println("ERROR: " +
anse.getTargetException().getMessage());
            anse.printStackTrace();
         }
      }
      return oldval;
   }

   private static void outputResponse(String returnType, Method method,
String action, String attribute, String oldval,
         String newvalue, ModelObject mo) throws
AttributeNotSetException, IllegalArgumentException,
         IllegalAccessException {
      if (action.equals("get")) {
         System.out.println("The " + attribute + " value of GUID " +
mo.getGuid() + " is: " + oldval);
      }
      if (action.equals("upd")) {
         System.out.println("The " + attribute + " value of GUID " +
mo.getGuid() + " is changed from \"" + oldval
               + "\" to \"" + newvalue + "\"");
      }
   }
}
```

To compile the sample code, use the java compiler as you did to create the TestConnection.jar:

```
set COLLATION_HOME=<apiroot>
javac -cp %COLLATION_HOME%\lib\api-client.jar;. GetUpdAttribute.java
```

The syntax for running GetUpdAttribute is;

```
Usage: TestConnection <hostname> <port> <username> <password>
<datatype> <where- clause> <attribute> [get|upd <newvalue>]
```

Some examples of running GetUpdAttribute are:

- Getting the Primary Mac address from a Computer System (Example 5-18)

Example 5-18 GetUpdAttribute for the Mac address

```
set COLLATION_HOME=<apiroot>
java -Dcom.collation.home=%COLLATION_HOME% -cp
%COLLATION_HOME%\lib\api-client.jar;%COLLATION_HOME%\lib\api-dep.jar
;%COLLATION_HOME%\lib\platform-model.jar;. GetUpdAttribute 9.3.4.165
9530 administrator collation
com.collation.platform.model.topology.sys.ComputerSystem
"displayName == \"tioserver.tivdemo.com\"" PrimaryMACAddress get
```

It produces output similar to Example 5-19.

Example 5-19 Output from GetUpdAttribute for the Mac address

```
2006-08-14 03:38:14,797  [main]  INFO client.ApiPool -
ResourcePool is null for Host: 9.3.4.165 Port: 9530
...
The PrimaryMACAddress value of GUID
E424D7FFF50D3E0FB5687CAA7DE75AC4 is: 000C29743C5A
...
```

- Getting the number of CPUs from a Computer System (Example 5-20)

Example 5-20 GetUpdAttribute for the number of CPUs

```
set COLLATION_HOME=<apiroot>
java -Dcom.collation.home=%COLLATION_HOME% -cp
%COLLATION_HOME%\lib\api-client.jar;%COLLATION_HOME%\lib\api-dep.jar
;%COLLATION_HOME%\lib\platform-model.jar;. GetUpdAttribute 9.3.4.165
9530 administrator collation
com.collation.platform.model.topology.sys.ComputerSystem
"displayName starts-with \"tio\"" NumCPUs get
```

- Updating the number of CPUs of a Computer System (Example 5-21)

Example 5-21 GetUpdAttribute for updating the number of CPUs

```
set COLLATION_HOME=<apiroot>
java -Dcom.collation.home=%COLLATION_HOME% -cp
%COLLATION_HOME%\lib\api-client.jar;%COLLATION_HOME%\lib\api-dep.jar
;%COLLATION_HOME%\lib\platform-model.jar;. GetUpdAttribute 9.3.4.165
9530 administrator collation
com.collation.platform.model.topology.sys.ComputerSystem
"displayName starts-with \"tio\"" NumCPUs upd 1
```

- Getting the Title from a Contact Information (Example 5-22)

Example 5-22 GetUpdAttribute for a TItle

```
set COLLATION_HOME=<apiroot>
java -Dcom.collation.home=%COLLATION_HOME% -cp
%COLLATION_HOME%\lib\api-client.jar;%COLLATION_HOME%\lib\api-dep.jar
;%COLLATION_HOME%\lib\platform-model.jar;. GetUpdAttribute 9.3.4.165
9530 administrator collation
com.collation.platform.model.topology.admin.ContactInfo "name ==
\"Peter Peterson\"" Title get
```

- Updating the Title of a Contact Information (Example 5-23)

Example 5-23 GetUpdAttribute for updating a Title

```
set COLLATION_HOME=<apiroot>
java -Dcom.collation.home=%COLLATION_HOME% -cp
%COLLATION_HOME%\lib\api-client.jar;%COLLATION_HOME%\lib\api-dep.jar
;%COLLATION_HOME%\lib\platform-model.jar;. GetUpdAttribute 9.3.4.165
9530 administrator collation
com.collation.platform.model.topology.admin.ContactInfo "name ==
\"Peter Peterson\"" Title upd "TADDM Administrator"
```

- Updating the e-mail Address of a Contact Information (Example 5-24)

Example 5-24 GetUpdAttribute for updating an e-mail address

```
set COLLATION_HOME=<apiroot>
java -Dcom.collation.home=%COLLATION_HOME% -cp
%COLLATION_HOME%\lib\api-client.jar;%COLLATION_HOME%\lib\api-dep.jar
;%COLLATION_HOME%\lib\platform-model.jar;. GetUpdAttribute 9.3.4.165
9530 administrator collation
com.collation.platform.model.topology.admin.ContactInfo "name ==
\"Peter Peterson\"" Email upd peter@peterson.com
```

6

Consuming configuration and relationship data

In this chapter, we look at the options provided by Configuration Discovery and Tracking for integration, study the integration needs of IT service management tools with Configuration Discovery and Tracking, and look at some real world scenarios with the help of use cases. We also take a look at the different reports available and how to generate Custom Queries.

6.1 Integration plans

IBM Tivoli Change and Configuration Management Database Configuration Discovery and Tracking v1.1 (Configuration Discovery and Tracking) is designed to integrate into the highly complex infrastructure in a modern data center environment. To facilitate rapid integration, Configuration Discovery and Tracking provides a complete Software development Kit (SDK), including a full set of data, process, and event APIs. Configuration Discovery and Tracking also has integration with other IBM and other vendor-provided management applications.

Over time, more integration modules will be provided by IBM through the IBM Tivoli Open Process Automation Library (OPAL) at the following Web site:

`http://catalog.lotus.com/wps/portal/topal`

At the time of writing, the plans are to provide integration modules for the following tools, within two-three months of the product's general availability:

- IBM INFOMAN
- IBM Tivoli Composite Application Manager for SOA
- IBM NetView/390
- SAP® R4.x
- Tivoli Business Systems Manager v3.1
- Tivoli Configuration Manager v4.2.3 and later
- IBM Tivoli Monitoring v6.0 and later
- Tivoli Productivity Center v3.1
- Tivoli Provisioning Manager v5.1
- Tivoli Service Level Advisor v2.1
- Tivoli Storage Manager v5.3
- IBM Z/OS (CICS/DB2/IMS)
- BMC Remedy
- Peregrine Service Desk v5.

6.2 Integration reports

IBM Tivoli Change and Configuration Management Database Configuration Discovery and Tracking v1.1 provides several types of reports that contain detailed information about the components in an infrastructure, and about the changes that have occurred in components over a specified time period. CCMDB also provides a Custom Query facility to generate customized reports.

6.3 Introduction

Configuration Discovery and Tracking discovers the default configurations of all identified Configuration Items (CIs) across the network and stores them in the CMDB. This database has the information about each individual component which might be required by the other IT service management tools. However, it is more that likely that the CMDB data needs to be mapped to the IT Service Management tools' specific and often unique data structures. The data needs vary with the processes and technology (tools and level of customizing involved) adopted by an enterprise aligned to its business goals.

The following list represents possible scenarios that pose challenges to integrating Configuration Discovery and Tracking with an organization's IT service management tools:

- The organization might have a heterogeneous environment with its service management tools custom built or with one or more custom off-the-shelf (COTS) products from one or more vendors.
- The extent of customizing of the COTS products depends on the unique needs of the organization.
- The IT service management tools might be integrated or not integrated.
- Individual service management disciplines might be completely or partially automated or can remain manual with word processor and spreadsheet-based templates.
- The organization might have adopted Information Technology Infrastructure Library (ITIL), IBM Tivoli Unified Process (ITUP), Microsoft Operations framework (MOF) or any other standard or framework with similar but unique data needs or might not have any structured processes.
- The organization might have standardized processes and thereby standardized workflows across the organization or might have different work flows for different projects and functions.
- The organization might have a standard tool to address a particular discipline or might have different tools used by different groups for the same discipline. For example, in an enterprise, the Java applications production team might use a custom-built tool, the SAP production team might use its native Change Transport System, and the Peoplesoft production team can use a customized, third-party product, all managing the release of the respective applications.

The real time data from Configuration Discovery and Tracking helps the IT service management tools to be more efficient and effective. Here are a few examples of the benefits that Configuration Discovery and Tracking provides:

- Real-time asset configuration and dependency details which are useful for a Change Management application to conduct impact analysis.
- Real-time change exceptions that can be used to validate the changes made in the change management system and detect unauthorized changes that are not in the change management system.
- Data to help in Asset Management function to have real-time asset configuration information and dependencies. It can help track the location, utility, as well as the commissioning and decommissioning of assets.
- Data to help in Service Desk function in determining the asset configuration, availability, and dependency details to resolve service requests.
- Information for the problem management function to diagnose and resolve problems.

6.4 Integration options

IBM Tivoli Change and Configuration Management Database Configuration Discovery and Tracking has two standard, out-of-the-box integration facilities namely, Discovery Library Adapters (DLA) and Software Development Kit (SDK). The other integration options include IBM Tivoli Directory Integrator (ITDI).

Figure 6-1 depicts the options currently available to generate reports and integrate with other databases.

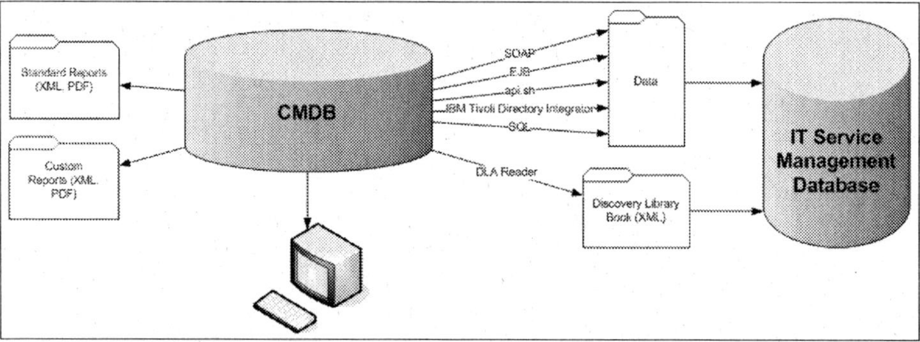

Figure 6-1 Integration options

6.4.1 Integration using Discovery Library Adapters

The IBM Discovery Library consists of a set of reusable tools that discover resources from IBM and third-party software. Use the Discovery Library tools to communicate discovery and the relationships between discovered resources within the enterprise. The Discovery Library tools include the following:

- Discovery Library XML schema specification, called the Identity Markup Language (IdML)

  The Discovery Library includes an XML schema to describe instances of relationships and resources from data sources.

- Discovery Library Components (IBM and third-party software) that extract and transform data to the XML schema specification
- The books, or XML files that contain discovery information including identity of resources and their relationships
- A set of recommended practices for deploying, loading information into, utilizing and managing the Discovery Library

For more information about Discovery Library Adapters (DLAs) refer to Appendix C, "Discovery Library overview" on page 387.

6.4.2 Integration using Software Development Kit

IBM Tivoli Change and Configuration Management Database Configuration Discovery and Tracking Software Development Kit (SDK) offers comprehensive access to the Configuration Discovery and Tracking application map and its discovery process, enabling you to:

- Protect implementation investment by using a market-proven, open, and standards-based integration SDK.
- Ensure success of IT management initiatives by cost effectively sharing and reusing Configuration Discovery and Tracking's application maps across all management applications.
- Improve accuracy of management solutions by integrating real-time and accurate application maps.
- Use Configuration Discovery and Tracking's built-in adapters and integrations for quick time-to-market deployments.

Core to the Configuration Discovery and Tracking SDK are a set of documented APIs that include the following:

- *Topology API* provides comprehensive access to Configuration Discovery and Tracking application maps including the discovered applications, their components, configurations and dependencies.

- *Control API* provides complete control of Configuration Discovery and Tracking's discovery process and its life cycle (start/stop/abort of discovery).

The Configuration Discovery and Tracking SDK package also includes the following:

- A built-in Java SDK library, enabling you to securely access the Configuration Discovery and Tracking Server.
- The SDK library, including a Command Line Interface (CLI) and a Web Services/SOAP wrapper
- Complete documentation of the Configuration Discovery and Tracking model, schema, and SDK library
- Integration tool, including libraries for XQuery and XSLT
- Code integration examples including sample transformation modules to convert and integrate Configuration Discovery and Tracking's data model to third party application data representations.

The integration options available in the SDK package include:

- Command Line Interface (CLI)

  The api.sh command is a shell script wrapper around the DataAPI, and implements the CLI of the Configuration Discovery and Tracking SDK. The command provides all the functionality from the convenience of a UNIX shell.

- SOAP

  SOAP is a simple, light-weight XML protocol for exchanging structured and typed information about the Web. It is used extensively in exchanging data between applications.

  SOAP can be used to link CCMDB with disparate systems, for example programs written in different languages and running on different operating systems. It is quick and easy to implement and supports interoperability. However, SOAP commands consume higher processing power as the process of converting the data into text and parsing them back into data structures at the receiving end and tags make the SOAP messages bigger than conventional messages.

  For more information, visit:

  `http://www.w3.org`

- EJB

For more information about the Software Development Kit (SDK) refer to the IBM Tivoli Change and Configuration Management Database Configuration Discovery and Tracking v1.1 SDK Guide.

6.4.3 Integration using Tivoli Directory Integrator

IBM Tivoli Directory Integrator synchronizes identity data residing in databases, directories and other corporate applications.

By serving as a flexible, synchronization layer between a company's data sources, IBM Tivoli Directory Integrator eliminates the need for a centralized datastore. IBM Tivoli Directory Integrator helps ease the process by connecting to data from the various repositories throughout the organization.

With some built-in connectors, an open-architecture Java development environment to extend or modify these connectors and tools to apply logic to data as data is processed, IBM Tivoli Directory Integrator can help you by:

- Synchronizing and exchanging information between applications
- Managing data across a variety of data sources providing the consistent data infrastructure needed for a wide variety of applications
- Creating the authoritative data spaces needed to expose only trustworthy data to advanced software applications such as Web services

IBM Tivoli Directory Integrator helps you get users, systems and applications online and productive fast, reduce costs and maximize return on investment. IBM Tivoli Directory Integrator software architecture includes:

- An AssemblyLine methodology that builds a compound information object from connected information sources, performs modifications on received data, or creates new entries altogether and adds, updates, an deletes the new information object to the assigned destinations.
- An Event Handler framework that adds to the flexibility of Directory Integrator by providing the ability to wait for, and react to, specific events that have taken place in the infrastructure, such as changes in a directory, arriving e-mails, records updated in certain databases, incoming HTML pages from a Web server or browser, arriving Web services-based Simple Object Access Protocol (SOAP) messages, as well as other types of events defined by the user.
- Connectors to support numerous protocols and access mechanisms are included with the product or can be easily created or modified.
- Parsers to interpret and translate information from a byte stream into a structure information object, where each piece of information is accessible by name. You can also translate a structured information object into a byte stream.
- Hooks to enable the definition of certain actions to be executed under specific circumstances, or at desired points in the execution of the AssemblyLine process.

The plug-and-play functionality of these IBM Tivoli Directory Integrator components facilitate rapid prototyping and implementation of intelligent data flows. Additionally it is possible to extend virtually all of these integration components (for example, Connectors, Parsers, and EventHandlers), functions, and attributes through Java scripts. IBM Tivoli Directory Integrator supports JavaScript and Perl plug-in scripting languages that can be used with every AssemblyLine, Parser, and Connector.

Table 6-1 details IBM Tivoli Directory Integrator's features and related advantages and benefits.

Table 6-1 Advantages and benefits of IBM Tivoli Directory Integrator

Features	Advantages	Benefits
Broad Platform Support	Runs on Windows, UNIX, and Linux	Fits into the widest variety of heterogeneous customer environments without disruption, regardless of operating system or directories in use today.
Open Architecture	Full featured Java API accessible through built-in scripting engine	Build powerful integration solutions with little scripting.
Nonpersistent data store	Scalable, flexible architecture	Uses existing investments in directory and identity repositories. Flexibility and scalability more efficient than solutions that demand the centralization of all resources.
Standards & Web Services support	Tivoli Directory Integrator supports most standard protocols, transports, APIs and formats, like JDBC, LDAP, JMS, JNDI and XML, and interacts seamlessly with a wide array of repositories and technologies	Integrates seamlessly with a wide variety of repositories and technologies and enables integration with new and existing Web Services in the enterprise.
Offers scheduled synchronization or integrated event-condition-action paradigm and event handlers	Can operate independently of data systems or react real time to business process events	Offers great flexibility for synchronization.
Includes Directory Server	Flexibility in deployment	Can be used as an enterprise directory and connected to disparate data sources by Tivoli Directory Integrator.

6.5 Comparison of the integration options

A comparison of the integration options available for integrating CCMDB with other ITSM products is provided in Table 6-2.

Table 6-2 Comparing integration options

Integration Option	Advantages	Disadvantages	When to use
Discovery Library Adapters	► These adapters are available out-of-the-box and can be installed, and configured quickly ► These adapters are developed to meet the data requirements of ITSM tools	► These adapters are available only for a few ITSM tools currently. However more adapters will be developed in future ► These adapters work only on a batch mode on prescheduled, event-based, or on an as-needed basis. The data is not available real time	This adapter is best used when integrating with tools for which: ► DLA writers are readily available ► Need minimal customizing ► Data requirements are not real time ► Integration is required in quick time ► Need to minimize native environment interruptions
Using SDK: Command Line Interface			This is best used when real time information from CMDB is required
Java API - including EJB			This is best used when real time information from CMDB is required
Using SDK: SOAP			This is best used when real time information from CMDB is required
IBM Tivoli Directory Integrator	TDI integration provides real time information from Configuration Discovery and Tracking and the ITSM tools		This is best used when real time information from CMDB is required

6.6 Integration points

Today, various CMDBs are available with ITIL-compatible, preconfigured tools that integrate with supporting applications. This capability lowers the cost to deploy services and increases their effectiveness. For example, the Service Desk captures events from a variety of different sources. Events are filtered, standardized, and prioritized based on severity, scope of problem, or business impact. This action provides the functionality to open a trouble ticket that the support staff can prioritize, based on the goals and priorities of the ITIL processes used to filter events. The process is automated and much more repeatable, and eliminates the manual burden typically associated with prioritizing and filtering.

Today, many organizations consider the ability to manage Configuration Items (CIs) to be the primary step for getting started with configuration management. Using a CMDB for asset management can significantly reduce costs. Without a CMDB, organizations run the risk of over-provisioning because they cannot track which assets are used for which purposes, or which availability and service problems relate to certain types of assets.

Table 6-3 lists how the CMDB data is used by various IT Service Management functions.

Table 6-3 Configuration Discovery and Tracking data use by function

ITSM functions	Configuration Discovery and Tracking Data		
	Asset Configuration Details	**Asset Dependency Details**	**Asset Change History Details**
Change Management	► Helps perform initial diagnosis ► Helps take proceed, defer, reject decision ► Comparison of configuration data between two discoveries of an asset helps in identifying unauthorized changes	► Helps classify RFCs ► Helps prioritize RFCs ► Helps perform impact analysis ► Helps perform risk analysis ► Helps develop Test Cases ► Helps in planning and releasing changes	► Helps in reconciliation of RFCs against the actual changes made to an asset

ITSM functions	Configuration Discovery and Tracking Data		
	Asset Configuration Details	**Asset Dependency Details**	**Asset Change History Details**
Configuration Management	► Helps identify all Configuration Items (CIs) ► Helps identify and maintain configuration information of all CIs ► Helps reconcile the CIs related data in the CMDB against the discovered data	► Helps identify and maintain asset dependencies of all CIs	► Helps in change control of all CIs ► Provides change history of all CIs
Release Management	► Helps in planning and making releases ► Helps in designing and setting up the production landscape ► Helps in planning and making roll backs	► Helps in planning and making releases ► Helps in planning and making roll backs	None
Service Desk	► Helps perform initial diagnosis ► Helps take proceed, defer, reject decision	► Helps to classify Service Requests ► Helps to prioritize Service Requests	► Helps in root cause analysis
Problem Management	► Helps perform initial diagnosis ► Helps take proceed, defer, reject decision	► Helps in root cause analysis ► Helps in impact analysis ► Helps to classify Problem Tickets ► Helps to prioritize Problem Tickets	► Helps in root cause analysis
Incident Management	► Helps perform initial diagnosis ► Helps take proceed, defer, reject decision	► Helps in root cause analysis ► Helps in impact analysis ► Helps to classify Incident Tickets ► Helps to prioritize Incident Tickets	► Helps in root cause analysis

<table>
<tr><th rowspan="2">ITSM functions</th><th colspan="3">Configuration Discovery and Tracking Data</th></tr>
<tr><th>Asset Configuration Details</th><th>Asset Dependency Details</th><th>Asset Change History Details</th></tr>
<tr><td>Service Level Management</td><td>Helps develop Service Level Agreements (with business units), Operating Level Agreements (with other internal IT organizations or functions) and External Contracts (with external clients and vendors)</td><td>Helps to develop Service Level Agreements (with business units), Operating Level Agreements (with other internal IT organizations or functions) and External Contracts (with external clients and vendors)</td><td>None</td></tr>
<tr><td>Capacity Management</td><td>Helps optimize capacity planning, with assets inventory and configuration information</td><td>Helps in capacity planning</td><td>None</td></tr>
<tr><td>Availability Management</td><td>Helps in prioritizing and planning for the assets that need maximum protection, redundancy, security and back-up</td><td>Helps in prioritizing and planning for the assets that need maximum protection, redundancy, security and back-up</td><td>None</td></tr>
<tr><td>Service Continuity Management</td><td>► Helps in prioritizing and planning for the assets that need maximum protection, redundancy, security and back-up
► Helps in prioritizing assets that need to be up and running earliest in times of disaster</td><td>► Helps in prioritizing and planning for the assets that need maximum protection, redundancy, security and back-up
► Helps in prioritizing assets that need to be up and running earliest in times of disaster</td><td>None</td></tr>
<tr><td>Financial Management</td><td>Assets identified by Configuration Discovery and Tracking along with its financial details in the Asset Management system are the basis for data validation and reconciliation in the Financial Management System</td><td>None</td><td>None</td></tr>
</table>

6.7 Typical integration road map

IBM recommends the following road map when integrating Configuration Discovery and Tracking with other tools:

1. Develop integration plan
2. Identify integration needs
3. Determine integration methods
4. Develop integration architecture
5. Configure integration
6. Develop new integration components
7. Implement integration components

Each of these implementation steps produces deliverables, which document the integration plan, specifications, architecture, test cases and test reports.

6.7.1 Develop integration plan

Develop an integration plan that details the following items:

1. Define the scope of work.

   Describe what is within scope and what is excluded from the scope of work.

2. Estimate the time, effort, and budget.
3. Plan the resource requirements.

   Define the staff and infrastructure resources required to execute the work.

4. Plan the activities.
5. Develop a project schedule.

   Document the plan in the Integration Plan document. Get it reviewed and approved by the stakeholders.

Figure 6-2 on page 224 depicts the planning tasks involved in integrating Configuration Discovery and Tracking with other tools.

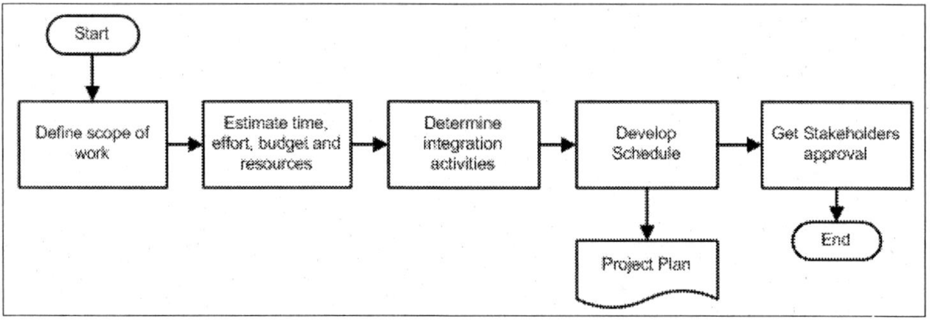

Figure 6-2 Develop integration plan

6.7.2 Identify integration needs

The integration needs of other ITSM tools with Configuration Discovery and Tracking are driven by the process needs which in turn are driven by the business needs. In this step you:

1. Understand the integration points between Configuration Discovery and Tracking and the ITSM tools.

   Identify the data needed for the ITSM tools and map it to Configuration Discovery and Tracking data fields.

2. Determine how you will use these data elements in each of the ITSM tools.

   The integration needs are identified and documented by a Business Analyst(s) on discussing with the clients and other project stakeholders. An Integration Specification document is developed by the Business Analyst, which is reviewed first by the Project Lead and other Project Team Members before it is approved by the external stakeholders.

Figure 6-3 on page 225 depicts a step-by-step approach to identifying the integration needs.

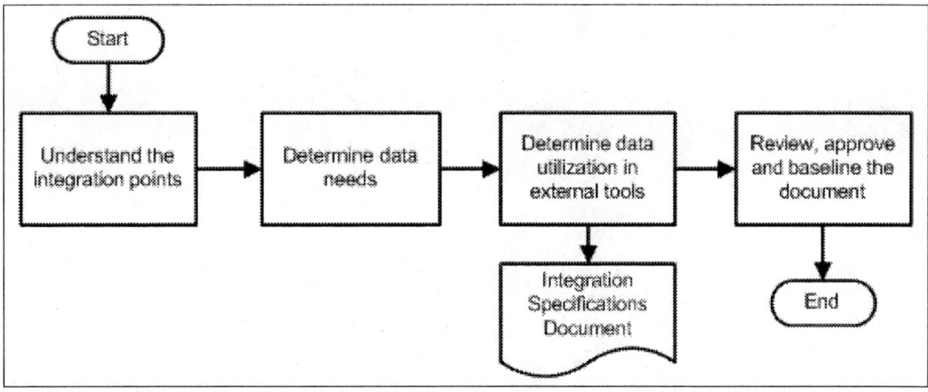

Figure 6-3 Identify the integration needs

6.7.3 Determine integration methods

Configuration Discovery and Tracking offers a host of integration options to pull and push data with other ITSM tools. Configuration Discovery and Tracking has ready-to-use *integration components* for some of the ITSM tools, including some IBM Tivoli tools, and other vendors' service management systems. In the real world, we can have a heterogeneous environment, with ITSM tools for which Configuration Discovery and Tracking has integration components and others that have to be integrated using Configuration Discovery and Tracking's SDK (Software Development Kit). Refer to 5.3, "Providing input programmatically" on page 194 and IBM Tivoli Change and Configuration Management Database Configuration Discovery and Tracking v1.1 SDK Guide for more information about integration and SDK options.

1. Identify integration components.

   Identify the ITSM tools for which there are out of the box integration solutions available with Configuration Discovery and Tracking. Evaluate, if the out of the both solution address all the integration needs defined.

2. Define new integration specifications.
3. Identify, evaluate and select the appropriate integration option.

   Study the integration options available with Configuration Discovery and Tracking (primarily the SDK) and also with the ITSM tools and select the appropriate integration option.

Document these integration options in the Integration Specifications document. Get the project lead's approval of the document.

Figure 6-4 details the process steps involved in determining the integration methods to be adopted in integrating Configuration Discovery and Tracking with other tools.

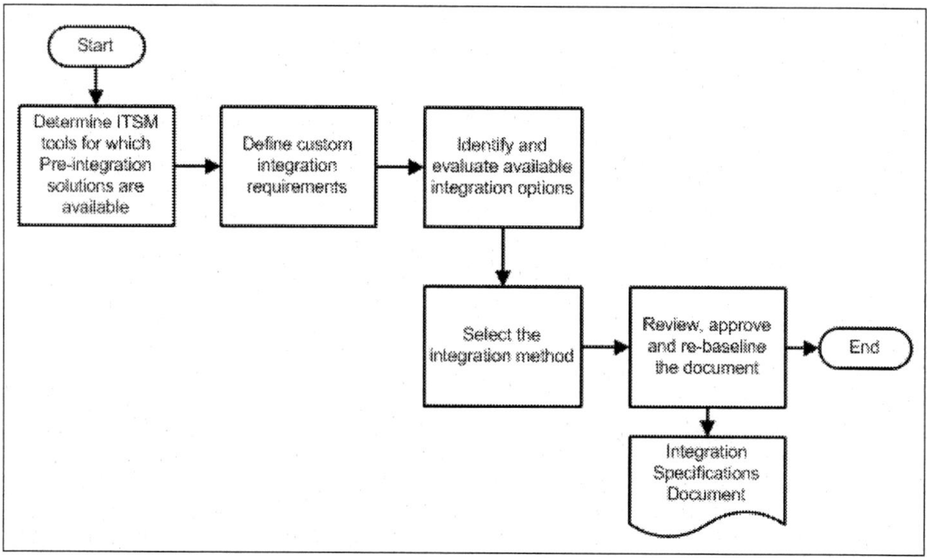

Figure 6-4 Determine the integration methods

6.7.4 Develop integration architecture

In developing the integration architecture, follow these steps:

1. Based on the integration options identified in step 2 on page 225, evaluate and choose the appropriate technologies for integration.
2. Develop the technical architecture depicting the chosen integration option, the technologies to develop the integration scripts, and the associated communication protocols.
3. Evaluate the architecture against identified criteria including performance considerations, skills availability and cost, effort and schedule implications to name a few.
4. Develop the deployment architecture depicting the production landscape to host the integration components.

Document the integration architecture in the Integration Specifications document.

Figure 6-5 on page 227 explains the tasks involved in developing the integration architecture.

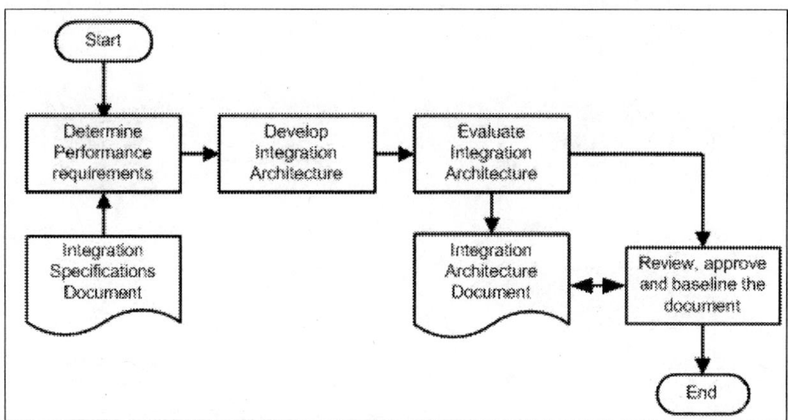

Figure 6-5 Develop integration architecture

6.7.5 Configure integration

First the integration components are configured and tested. The key steps include:

1. Configure the integration components.
2. Develop test cases.

   Develop test cases and document them in the test case document.
3. Test the integration components.

Figure 6-6 on page 228 explains the configuration and testing of existing integration components.

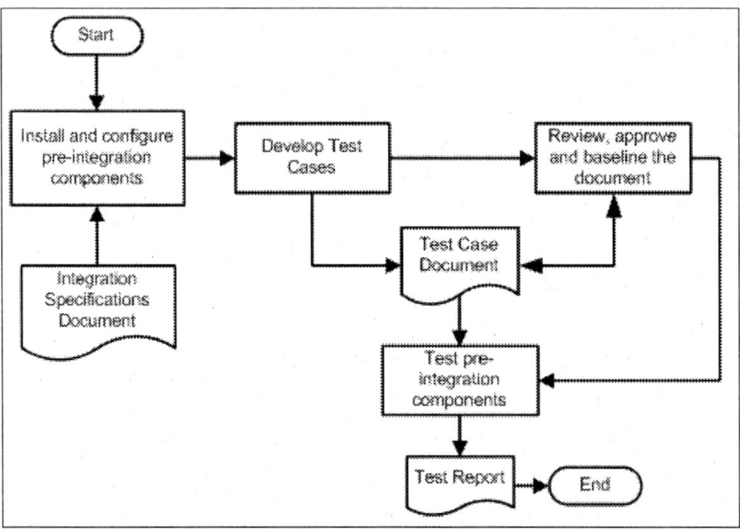

Figure 6-6 Configure integration components

6.7.6 Develop new integration components

The process steps to develop and test new integration components include:

1. Develop new integration components.
2. Develop test cases.
3. Review, approve and baseline the test cases.
4. Test the new integration components.

   Perform unit, integration and performance testing on the new integration components, using the test cases and produce the test report(s).

Figure 6-7 on page 229 depicts the steps to develop and test new integration components.

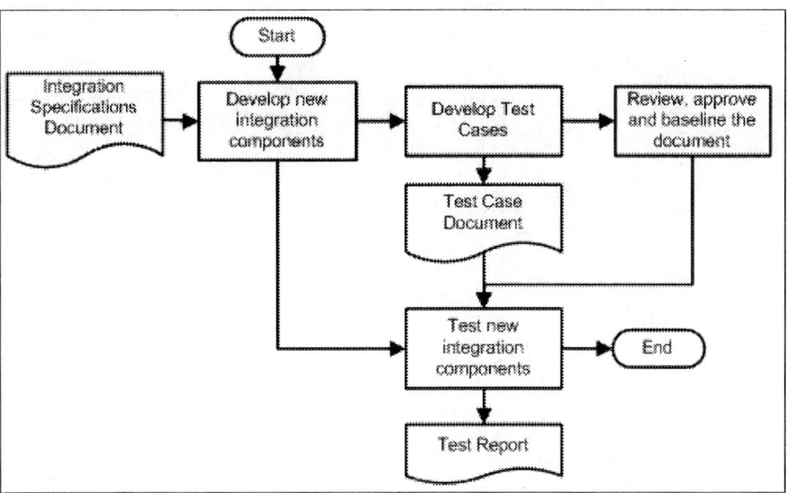

Figure 6-7 Develop new integration components

6.7.7 Implement integration components

The process steps involved in implementing the integration components include:

1. Create a Build.

   Tag the relevant integration components (with the correct versions) and create a build. Optionally, a Release Note can be produced detailing the integration components in the build.

2. Move the Build to the staging area.
3. Develop test cases.

   Primarily System and Performance testing are done at this stage and relevant test cases need to be developed.

4. Review, approve and baseline the test cases.
5. Test the Build in the staging area.

   Test the Build in the staging area using the test cases (primarily system testing and performance testing) and produce the relevant test report(s).

6. Install and configure the Build in the production environment.
7. Review the test reports and approve to Go Live.
8. Go live!

Figure 6-8 on page 230 details the steps leading to the implementation, testing and Go Live of the integration components.

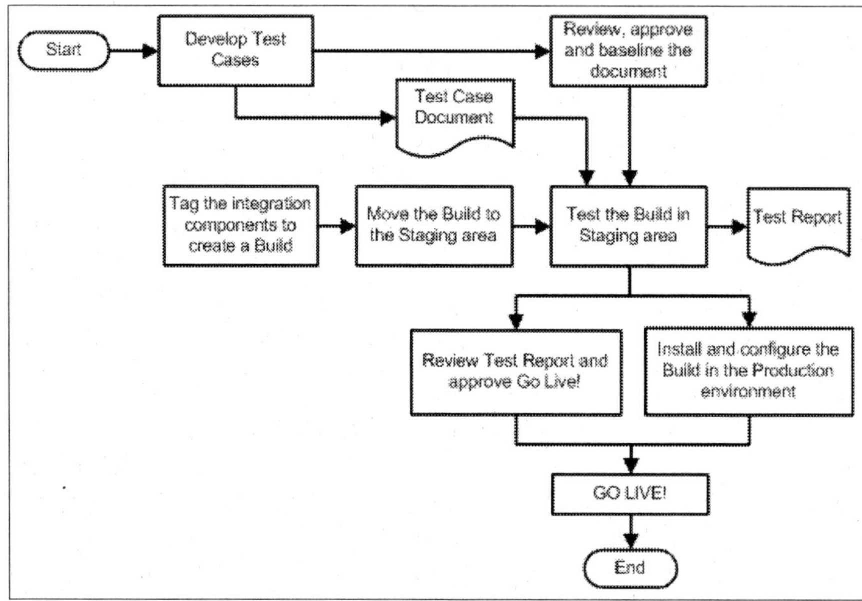

Figure 6-8 Implement integration components

6.8 Configuration Discovery and Tracking reports

IBM Tivoli Change and Configuration Management Database Configuration Discovery and Tracking provides several types of reports that contain detailed information about the components in an infrastructure, and about the changes that have occurred in components over a specified time period. Creating IBM Tivoli Change and Configuration Management Database Configuration Discovery and Tracking reports is quick and easy.

IBM Tivoli Change and Configuration Management Database Configuration Discovery and Tracking also provides a Custom Query option to custom develop reports to the unique needs of an organization.

Table 6-4 describes the tasks you can complete using the analytics features of IBM Tivoli Change and Configuration Management Database Configuration Discovery and Tracking Console:

Table 6-4 Configuration Discovery and Tracking analytical reports

Report	Description
Inventory	Contains detailed inventory information about all components or a specific type of component. For example, instead of using manual documentation methods, you can use the Inventory Report to quickly and easily document all components or specific types of components, such as all Web servers.
Change History	Contains detailed information about changes in all components, or in a specific type of component, over a specified period of time. You can use the Change History report for troubleshooting when you need to determine precisely which components have changed in a given time period.
Dormant Components	Contains components that IBM Tivoli Change and Configuration Management Database Configuration Discovery and Tracking can no longer access during the discovery process. You can use this list to manually remove components that are no longer present in your environment.
Component Comparison	Contains detailed information about the changes in an individual component and its related components over a specified period of time.
Data Center Drift	Contains a consolidated summary of changes throughout your environment for the following categories: services, hosts, software servers, and network elements. The report also displays a graphical representation of the aggregate information, enabling you to identify configuration change trends and patterns.
Application Drift	Contains a consolidated summary of changes to specific business applications throughout your environment, enabling you to identify trends and patterns of configuration changes.
Switch Topology	Contains consolidated information about switch-level (OSI Layer 2) dependencies for switches, business applications, and business services.

6.8.1 Generating an inventory report

To generate an inventory report, follow these steps:

1. To be able to specify which components to include in your inventory report, select **Analytics** → **Inventory** from the menu bar, as shown in Figure 6-9.

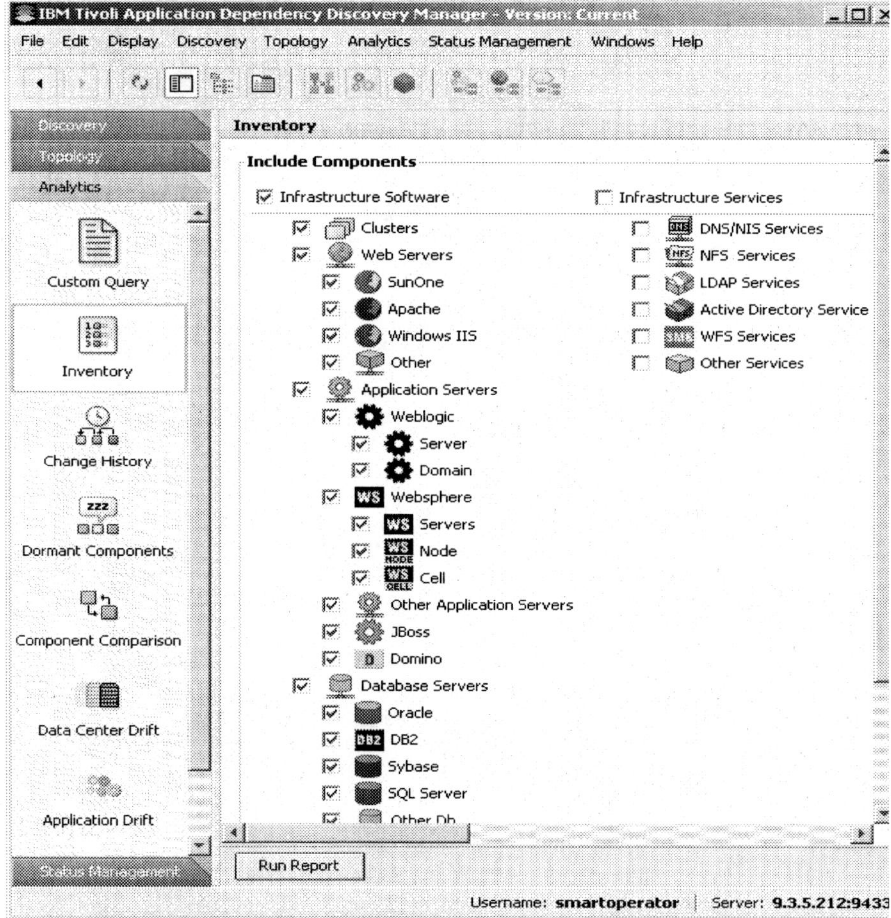

Figure 6-9 Inventory report query

2. Choose the components for which you need the inventory details and click the **Run Report** button, as shown above.

3. You can print and save the report using the **Print** and **Save** options in the inventory results screen, as shown in Figure 6-10.

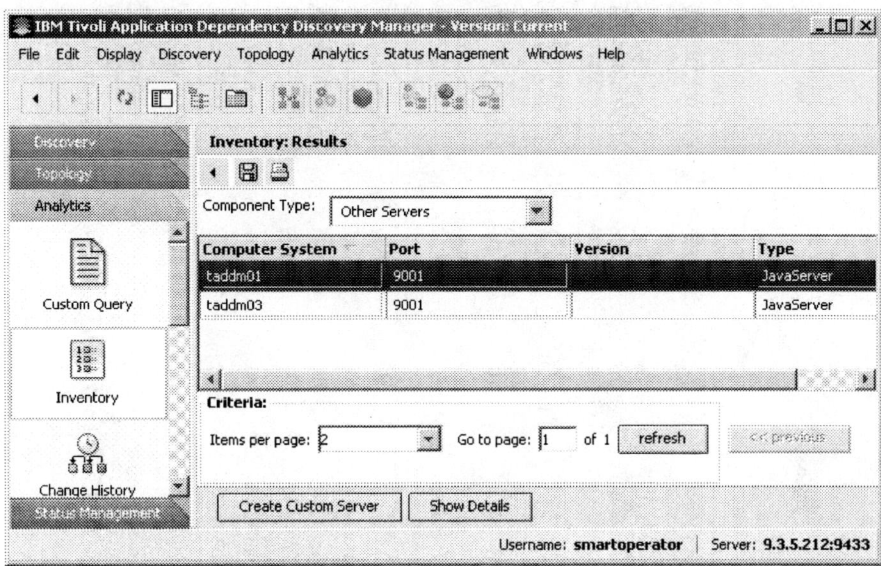

Figure 6-10 Inventory Results

6.8.2 Generating a change history report

To generate a change history report, use the following procedure:

1. To be able to specify the date range and components to include in your Change History report, select **Analytics → Change History** from the menu bar, as shown in Figure 6-11.

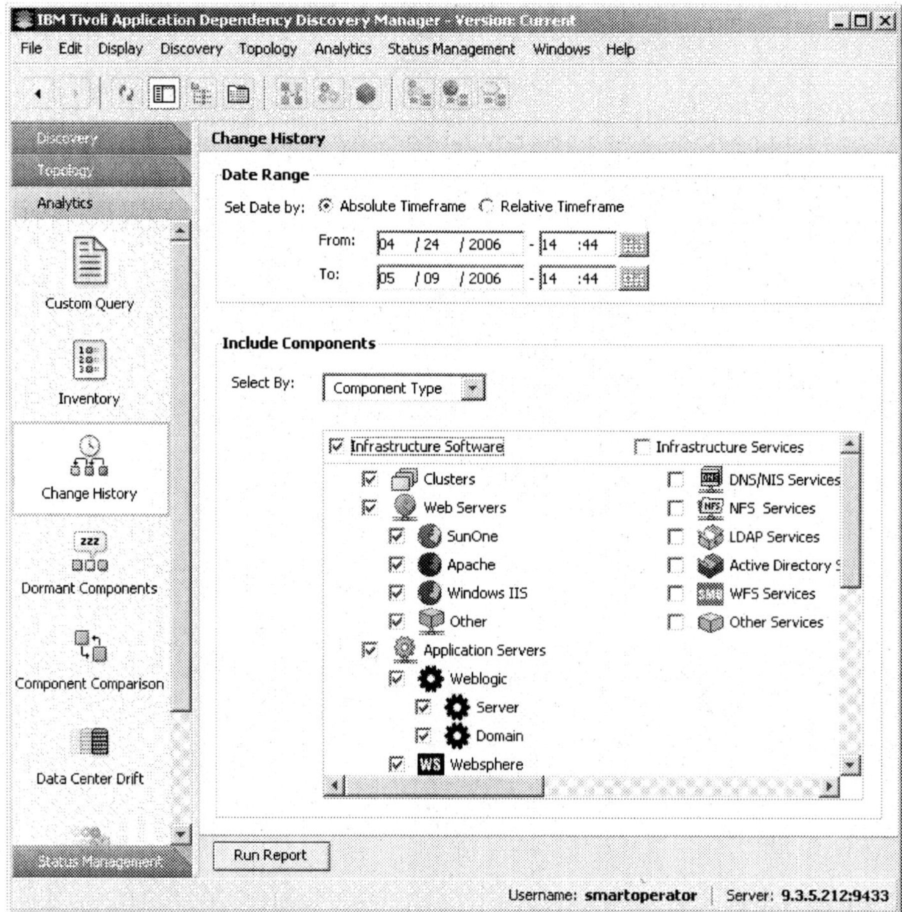

Figure 6-11 Change History query

2. Choose the Date Range and whether you need Absolute Time frame or Related Time frame, select the components to be included in the change history report and click the **Run Report** button, as shown above.

3. You can print and save the report using the **Print** and **Save** options in the Change History results screen, as shown in Figure 6-12.

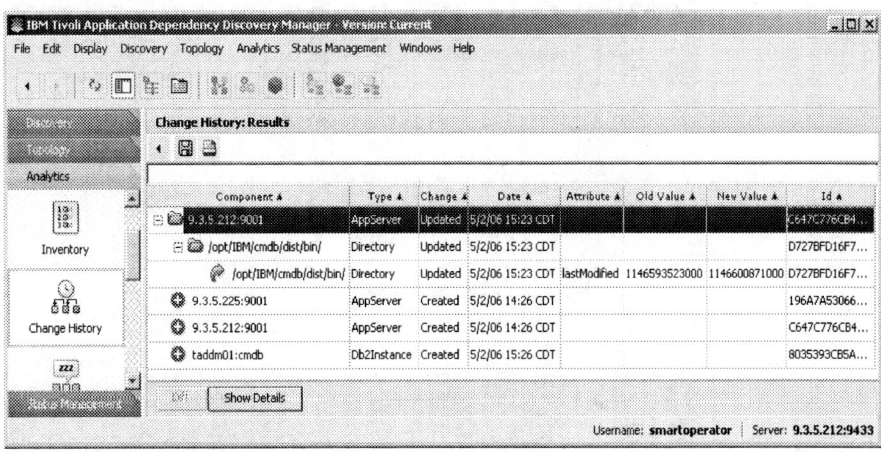

Figure 6-12 Change History report

6.8.3 Generate a dormant components report

The following steps demonstrate how to generate a dormant components report:

1. To be able to specify the date range and components to include in your Change History report, select **Analytics** → **Dormant Components** from the menu bar, as shown in Figure 6-13.

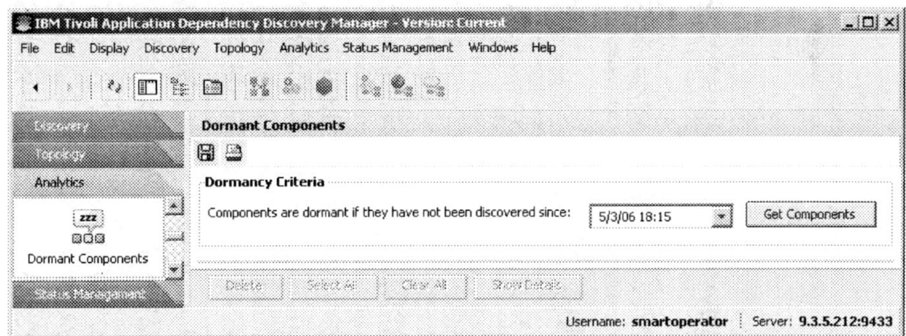

Figure 6-13 Dormant Components query

2. Choose the Dormancy Criteria and click the **Get Components** button, as shown here.

3. You can print and save the report using the **Print** and **Save** options in the Dormant Components results screen, as shown in Figure 6-14.

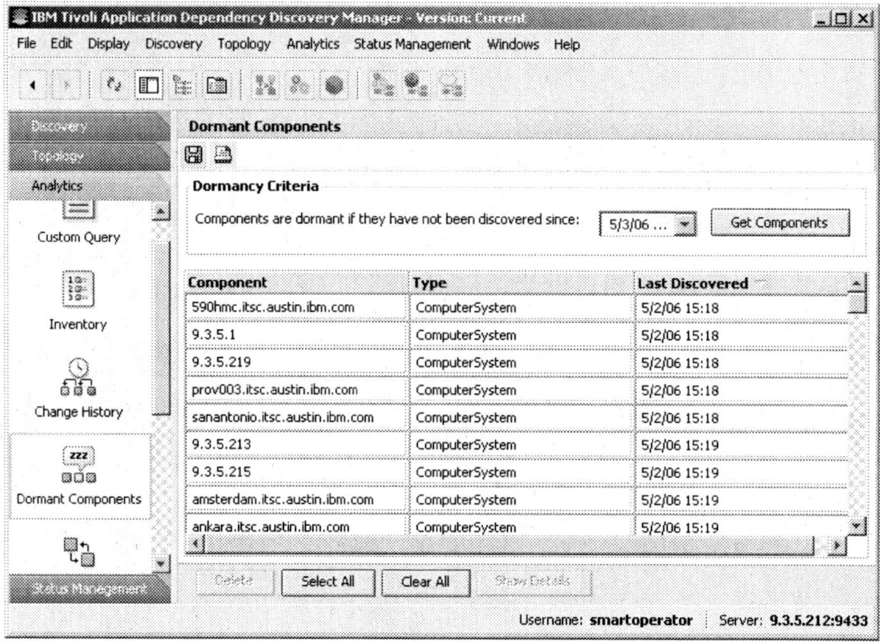

Figure 6-14 Dormant Components report

6.8.4 Generate a component comparison report

Follow these steps to generate a component comparison report:

1. To be able to specify the components to compare in your Components Comparison report, select **Analytics → Component Comparison** from the menu bar, as shown in Figure 6-15.

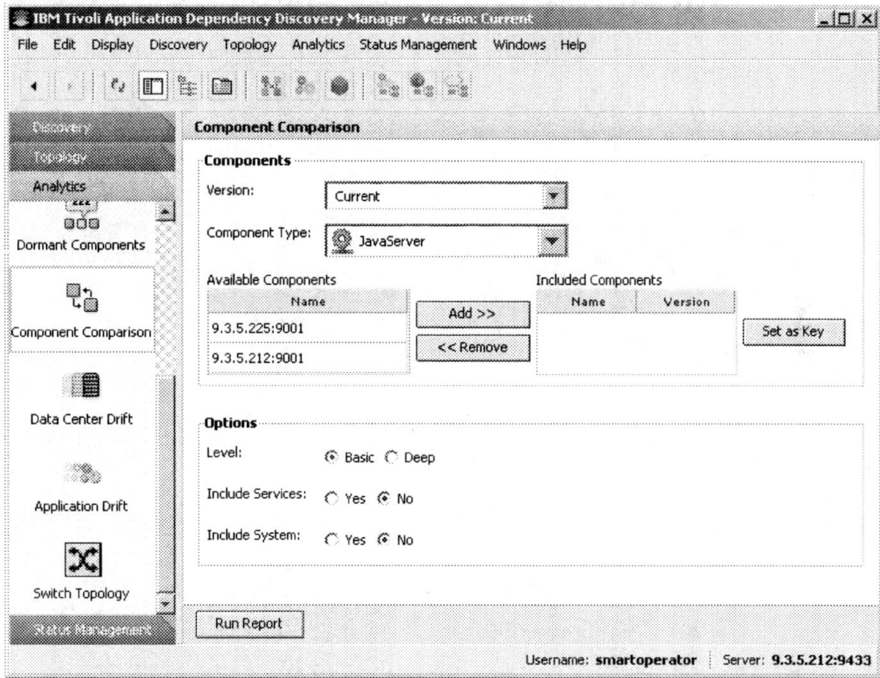

Figure 6-15 Component Comparison query

2. Choose Version of Discovery, Component Type, Included Components from the Available Components and the Key, as shown here.
3. In the options column, choose the Level of comparison details, and **Include Services** and **Include Systems** as shown here.
4. Click **Run Report** to generate the Component Comparison report.

5. You can save the report as XML and PDF and Print it using the options shown in Figure 6-16.

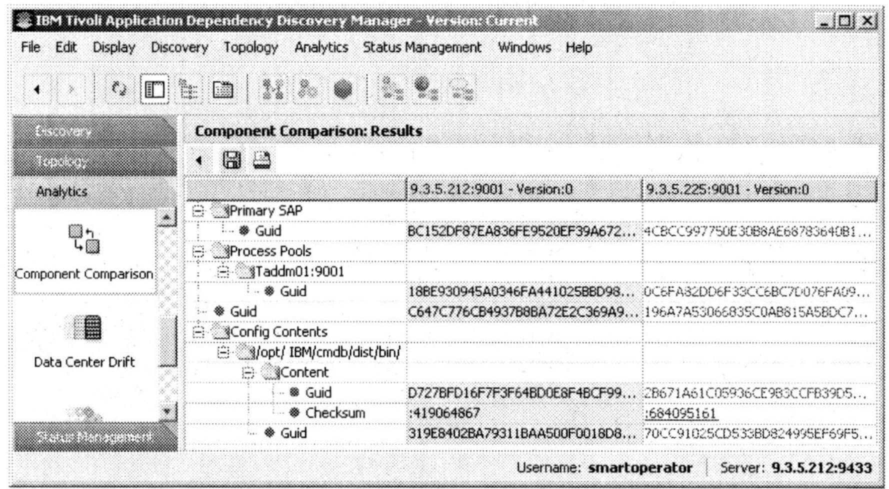

Figure 6-16 Component Comparison Report

6.8.5 Generating Data Center Drift Report

To generate the Data Center Drift report, follow these steps:

1. To be able to set the timing and frequency for the Data Center Drift report, select **Analytics** → **Data Center Drift** from the menu bar, as shown in Figure 6-17.

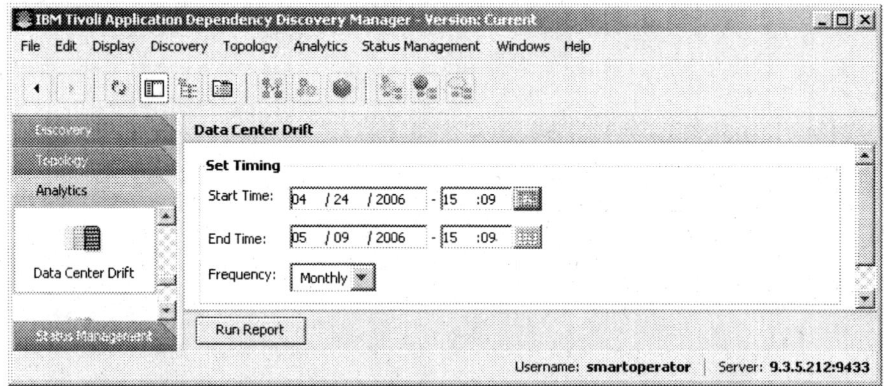

Figure 6-17 Data Center Drift query

2. Choose the Start and End Date, Time, and Frequency, as shown. Then click the **Run Report** button.
3. The Data Center Drift results can be seen in two formats:
   - Tabular format as shown in Figure 6-18.
   - Graphical format as shown in Figure 6-19 on page 240.
4. To save the report as an XML or PDF document or print the report, use the options shown in Figure 6-18 and Figure 6-19.

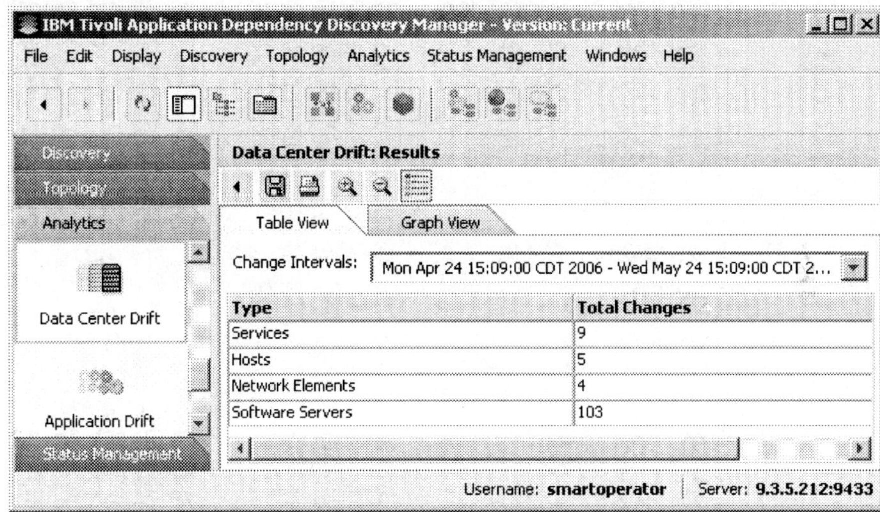

Figure 6-18 Data Center Drift Results (Table View)

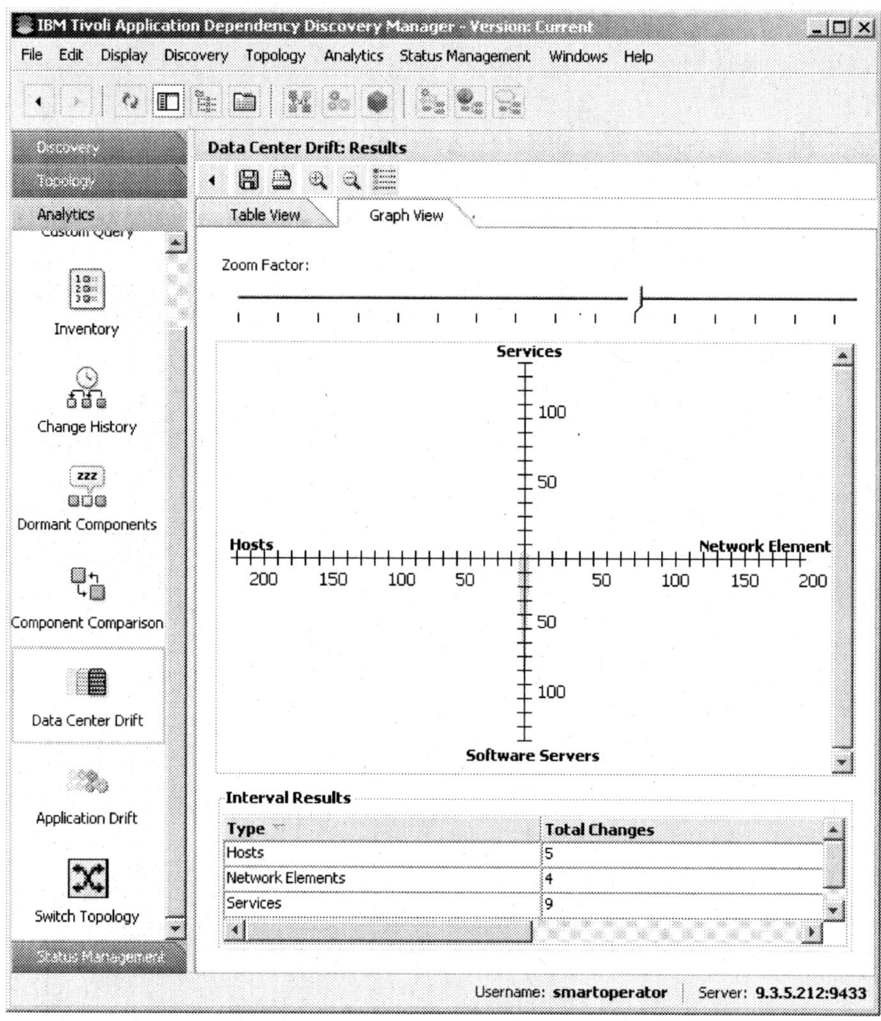

Figure 6-19 Data Center Drift Results (Graphical View)

6.8.6 Generating an application drift report

The following steps guide you through the creation of an application drift report:

1. To be able to set the timing, select the frequency and application for the Application Drift report, select **Analytics** → **Application Drift** from the menu bar, as shown in Figure 6-20.

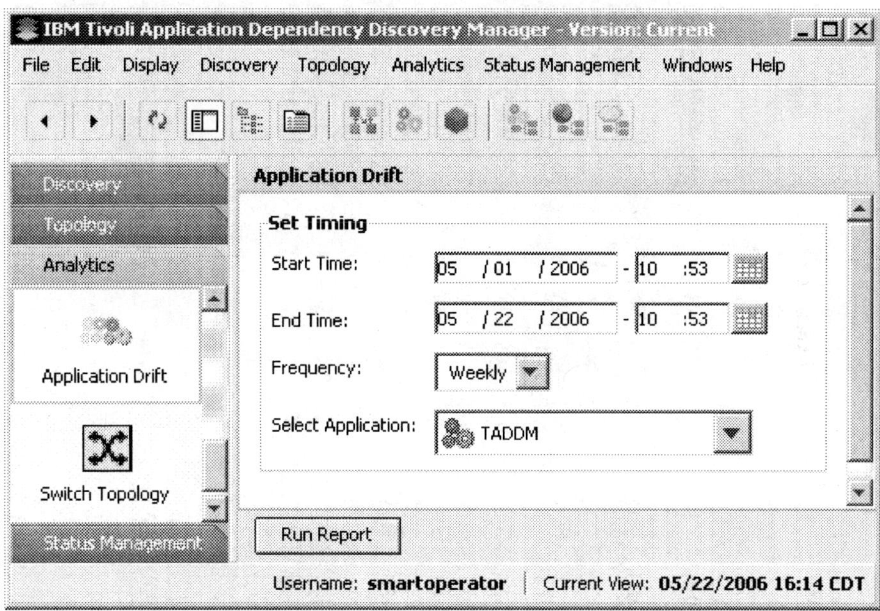

Figure 6-20 Application Drift query

2. Choose the Start and End Date and Time, the Frequency and the Application, as shown above and click the **Run Report** button.
3. To save the report as an XML or PDF document or print the report using the **Print** and **Save** options shown in Figure 6-21.

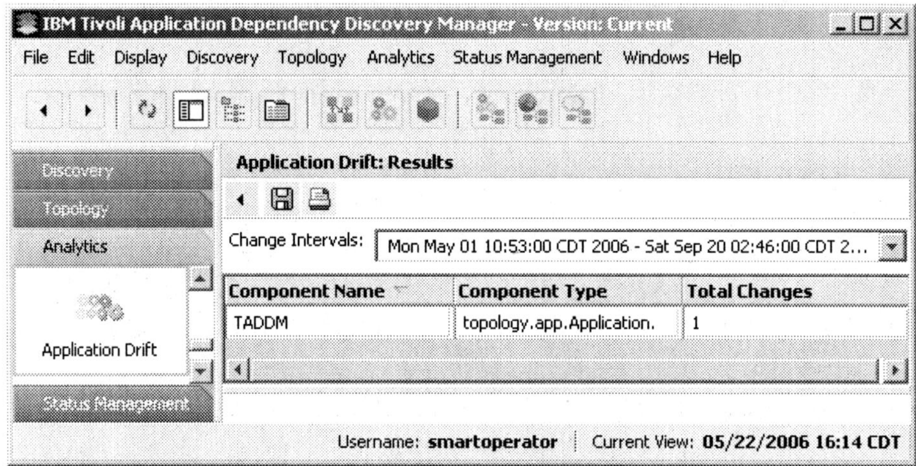

Figure 6-21 Application Drift Results

6.8.7 Generating a switch topology report

Follow these steps to generate a switch topology report:

1. To be able to select the report type, component and the available options for the Switch Topology report, select **Analytics** → **Switch Topology** from the menu bar, as shown in Figure 6-22.

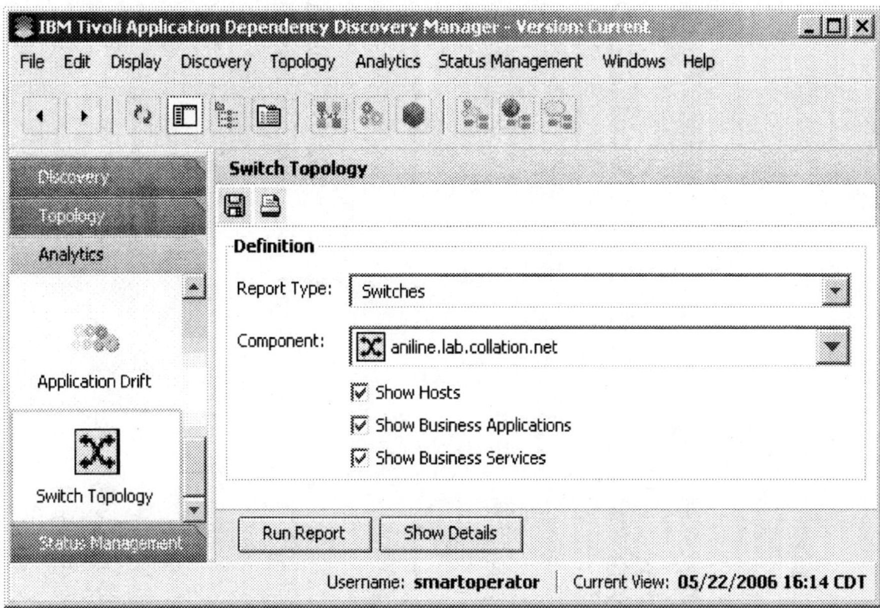

Figure 6-22 Switch Topology Query

2. Choose the following:
   a. **Report Type** from Switches, Business Applications or Business Services
   b. Components
   c. Choose the options: **Show Hosts**, **Show Business Applications**, **Show Business Services**, as applicable.
3. Click **Run Report**.
4. Save the report as an XML or PDF document, or print the report using the **Print** and **Save** options as shown in Figure 6-23 on page 244.

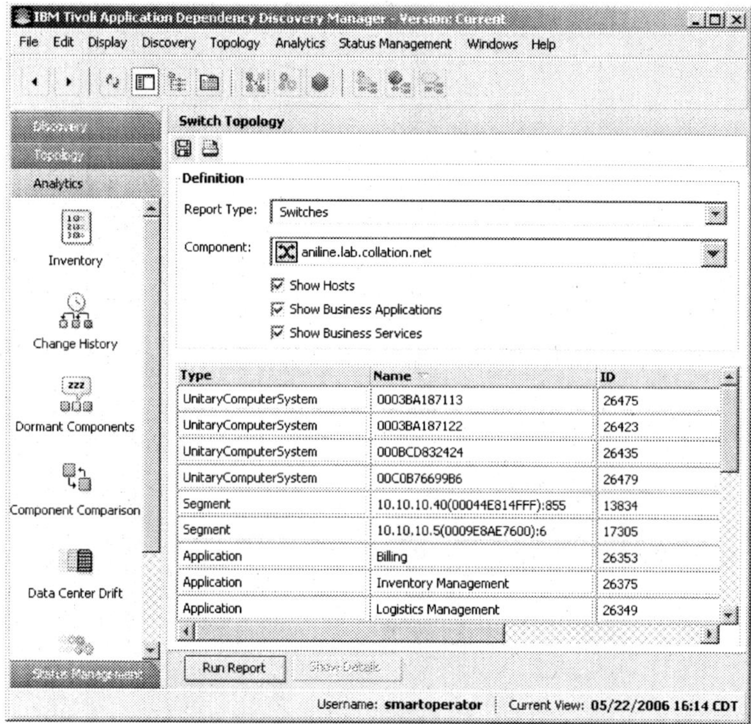

Figure 6-23 Switch Topology Results

6.8.8 Generating custom reports

To generate a Custom Query report, use the following procedure:

1. To be able to choose a saved query or to create a new query and run the Custom Query, select **Analytics** → **Custom Query** from the menu bar, as shown in Figure 6-24 on page 245.

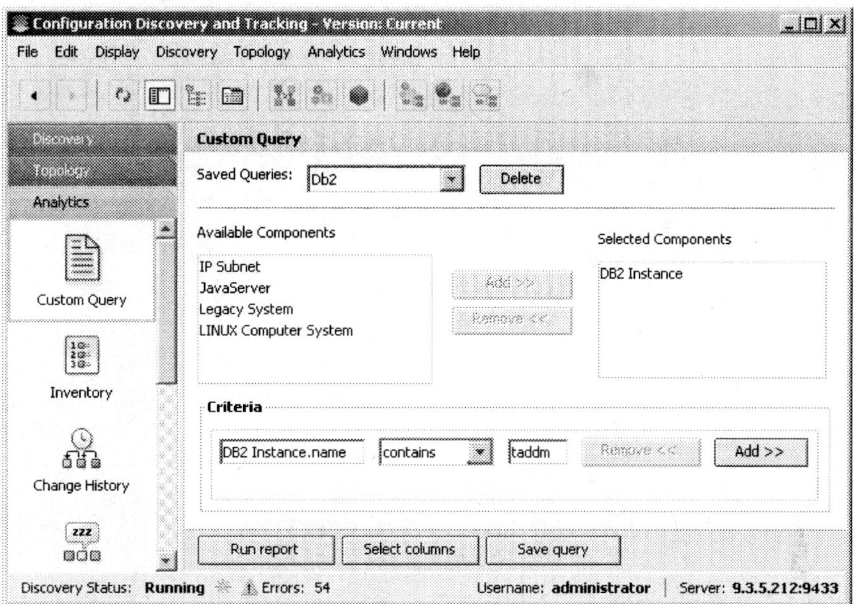

Figure 6-24 Custom Query dialog box

2. To run an existing query, choose a **Saved Query** and click **Run Report**.
3. To create a new query:
   a. Add the components from the **Available Components** column to the **Selected Components** column.
   b. Enter the Query **Criteria** for individual components.
   c. Using the **Select Columns** button, choose the component attributes.
   d. Choose one of the available options (equals, not equals, null, not null, contains, and so on) and the relevant value.
   e. You can add additional criteria by using the **Add** button.
4. To save the Query, click the **Save query** button.
5. To run the Query, click the **Run query** button.
6. To save the report as an XML or PDF document, or print the report using the **Print** and **Save** options in the Custom Query Results page.

7

Tips, tricks, and troubleshooting

This chapter contains a collection of tips, tricks, and troubleshooting guidance to help you resolve issues and problems you might encounter in installing, customizing, and using IBM Tivoli Change and Configuration Management Database Configuration Discovery and Tracking v1.1.

7.1 Log files

IBM Tivoli Change and Configuration Management Database Configuration Discovery and Tracking v1.1 provides comprehensive logging features that allows you to narrow down any problems you might experience.

7.1.1 Installation log files

The installation log files are located in the installLogs subdirectory in the location in which you installed the product, which is typically /opt/IBM/cmdb. The names of the files produced during installation are self-explanatory. The files are:

```
cdb_cr_db2_stderr.log
cdb_cr_db2_stdout.log
cdb_install.log
cdb_install_stderr.log
cdb_install_stdout.log
cdb_modify_archpwd.log
```

7.1.2 Discovery log files

When IBM Tivoli Change and Configuration Management Database Configuration Discovery and Tracking is performing a discovery, a Discovery Log is visible in the Product Console in the menu **Discovery** → **Overview**. When an active discovery completes, the Discovery Activity Log is immediately moved to the History tab in the Discovery pane in menu **Discovery** → **History** where a history of these are kept.

The number of kept histories can be changed by modifying the `com.collation.number.persist.discovery.run` property in the ${COLLATION_HOME}/dist/etc/collation.properties file. The default is 10.

The Discovery Log in the Product Console is a synopsis of the actual log files that are produced during a discovery. The main log files of interest are the error.log in the dist/log directory and the DiscoverManager.log in the dist/log/service directory. These log files can be controlled by settings in the dist/etc/collation.properties file as shown in Table 7-1 on page 249.

Table 7-1 collation.properties log options

Property	Description
com.collation.log.level	The log level. Set this to DEBUG when troubleshooting and analyzing for performance tuning. When done be sure to set the value back to the default of INFO. Running the Configuration Discovery and Tracking server with DEBUG turned on produces extensive output and reduce performance.
com.collation.log.filecount	Number of log files before rollover. Together with the com.collation.log.filesize this setting basically dictates how much log history you want to preserve. Default is 5.
com.collation.log.filesize	Dictates the size in MB before a log file is subject to rollover. Default is 20 MB.
`com.collation.number.persist.discovery.run`	Number of discovery runs to persist. These are viewable to users in the GUI. Default is 10.

All log files are located in the dist/log or dist/log/services directory. The following files are primarily interesting for *startup* problems;

- ${COLLATION_HOME}/dist/log/control.log
- ${COLLATION_HOME}/dist/log/tomcat.log
- ${COLLATION_HOME}/dist/log/error.log

For *discovery* problems the primary log file is:

${COLLATION_HOME}/dist/log/services/DiscoverManager.log

For application servers for WebSphere, Weblogic, and so on, also look for local-anchor<hostname>.log.

As mentioned previously, the discovery is performed in parallel. In other words, the discovery is *multi-threaded*, meaning that one type or instance of sensor can be running on one host simultaneously with another type/instance of sensor running on a different system. All sensors are providing information to the log files at runtime and consequently the log files can be difficult to follow. Therefore, when looking in the DiscoverManager.log is would be a good approach to jump to the bottom of the file and find the sensor you are interested in and identify the

ThreadNumber. The following example is an example of line in the log finding a sensor that has timed out:

```
2006-05-13 23:42:36,104 DiscoverManager [TIMEOUT_DiscoverWorker-9]
DEBUG session.AbstractSessionClient - ssh session inactivity for too
long....
```

In this example, the ThreadNumber is 9. Therefore, the following command would be useful to extract only log entries for that specific sensor:

```
cat DiscoverManager.log | grep DiscoverWorker-9 > DiscoverWorker-9.log
```

7.1.3 Troubleshooting hanging discoveries

If discoveries are continuously hanging, it might be because old serialized seeds and results are still left. You can clean this up by removing all the *.ser files from the ${COLLATION_HOME}/dist/var/dwitem and ${COLLATION_HOME}/dist/var/scwitem directories. The commands to achieve this are:

```
rm -rf ${COLLATION_HOME}/dist/var/dwitem/*.ser
rm -rf ${COLLATION_HOME}/dist/var/scwitem/*.ser
```

7.2 Configuration Discovery and Tracking Server operations

To verify the operational state of your Configuration Discovery and Tracking Server, issue the service collation status command from a command-line on the Configuration Discovery and Tracking itself. If all subcomponents are running, you should expect output similar to Example 7-1.

Example 7-1 Service collation status results

```
[root@taddm ~]# service collation status
DbInit: Started
Tomcat: Started
GigaSpaces: Started
Discover: Started
EventsCore: Started
Topology: Started
DiscoverAdmin: Started
Proxy: Started

TADDM: Running
```

Alternatively, you can direct your browser to this URL:

```
http://<your_Configuration Discovery and Tracking_Server>:9430
```

Verify the operational state of the server components. They should all be green, as shown in Figure 7-1.

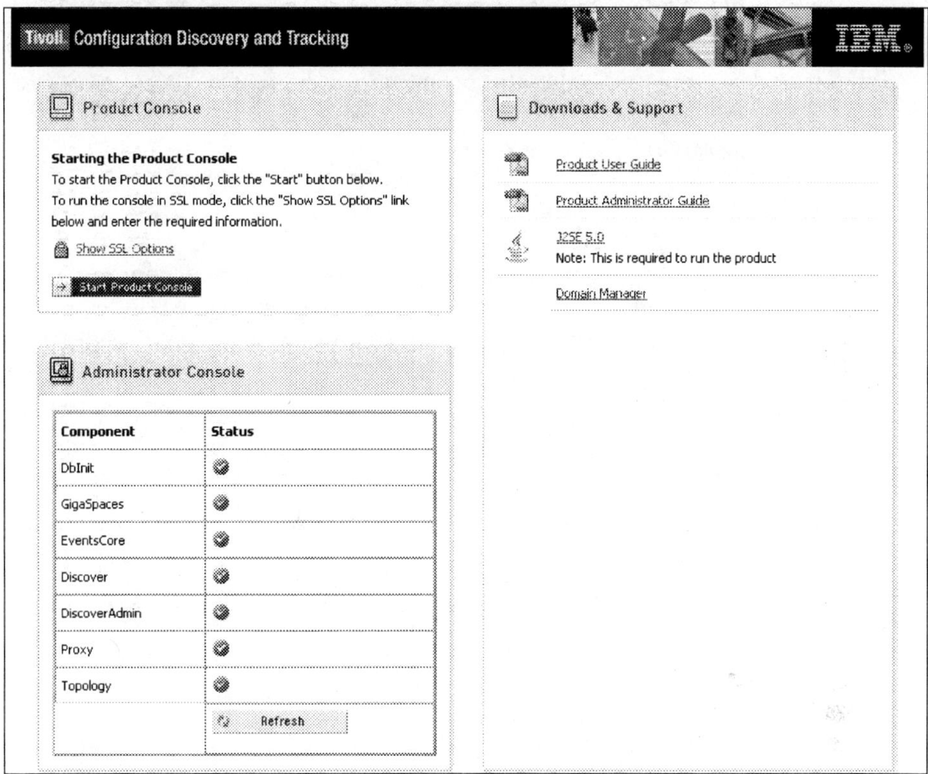

Figure 7-1 Configuration Discovery and Tracking Server console

7.2.1 Tuning the Configuration Discovery and Tracking for performance

There are several ways to improve the performance of Configuration Discovery and Tracking. Here are a few of the most common ways:

- Do not run the database on the same machine as the Configuration Discovery and Tracking Server.
- A corollary of this is to ensure that access to the database server uses a different network interface than the sensors are using to communicate with devices in the scope.

- Configuration Discovery and Tracking is tuned for a 2-CPU, 2 GB system. If you have more CPUs or memory, you can change the thread settings in collation.properties, as shown in Example 7-2.

Example 7-2 Changing the settings in collation.properties

```
#Max number of discover worker threads
com.collation.discover.dwcount=16
# Max number of seed creators
com.collation.discover.sccount=2
# Max Number of Agent selectors
com.collation.discover.ascount=1
# Number of TopoPump threads in discover observer
com.collation.discover.observer.topopumpcount=2
```

  There is no magic formula for determining optimum values for these thread counts. A lot of it is determined by how sparse your subnets are and how your firewalls are configured. Here are a few general rules of thumb:

  - If all your CPUs are not saturated during a discovery run, then you should increase the `dwcount` by a few threads, and try again. Also note that if you increase this thread count when your CPUs are saturated, the sensors will start to timeout and you will not get complete discovery results.
  - If you increase the `dwcount` by a few threads and still do not get increased CPU usage, then bump the `sccount` by 1 and try again.
  - Never change the value for the `ascount` parameter.
  - The `topopumpcount` controls the storage speed. It is safe to set this to the number of CPUs on the system.

DB2 database tuning

Set the instance variable DB2_EVALUNCOMMITTED=YES, as in:

```
db2set DB2_EVALUNMOMMITTED=YES
```

Set the database configuration parameter MAXLOCKS=90 (percentual amount of lock space used by a single application):

```
db2 connect to <database_name>
db2 update db cfg using MAXLOCKS 90
```

For more DB2 tuning advice, refer to Appendix E, “Top DB2 performance tips” on page 425.

7.2.2 Server not started automatically

If the Configuration Discovery and Tracking Server does not start automatically, you should check the following settings.

Check autostart settings

To verify that your system has been set-up to start the Configuration Discovery and Tracking Server during startup, use the `chkconfig --list collation` command to see at which OS-startup levels has the service should be active. The normal setting would look like the following:

```
[root@taddm bin]# chkconfig --list collation
collation 0:off   1:off   2:on    3:on    4:on    5:on    6:off
```

To disable automatic start of the Configuration Discovery and Tracking Server at OS-startup levels 2, 3, 4 and 5, use the following command:

```
[root@taddm bin]# chkconfig --level 2345 collation off
```

To verify your new settings, issue a new **chkconfig --list** command:

```
[root@taddm bin]# chkconfig --list collation
collation 0:off   1:off   2:off   3:off   4:off   5:off   6:off
```

Starting and stopping the Configuration Discovery and Tracking Server

You can use the built-in service interface in Linux to start, stop, and query the status of your Configuration Discovery and Tracking Server.

- To start the server, use:

  ```
  service collation start
  ```

- To stop the server, use:

  ```
  service collation stop
  ```

- To get the server status, use:

  ```
  service collation status
  ```

  The output from this command (Example 7-3) will give you the status of each of the servers' subcomponents:

Example 7-3 Service collation status output

```
[root@taddm ~]# service collation status
DbInit: Started
Tomcat: Started
GigaSpaces: Started
```

```
Discover: Started
EventsCore: Started
Topology: Started
DiscoverAdmin: Started
Proxy: Started

TADDM: Running
```

7.2.3 DBInit failed

Make sure that the database instance is started, and verify database connectivity using the **testjdbc** utility described at B.4.2, "testjdbc.jy" on page 376.

7.2.4 Server start is slow

Clean-out content of ${COLLATION_HOME}/var/dwitem and ${COLLATION_HOME}/var/scwitem which might have been left over from previous discoveries.

7.3 Product Console

The ports in Table 7-2 are used by the Product Console.

Table 7-2 Communication ports used by the Product Console

Port	Protocol	Use
9430	TCP	Initial Web page and Administrator Console non-SSL
9431	TCP	Initial Web page and Administrator Console over SSL
9433	TCP	RMI Naming Service
9434	TCP	Required only for SSL communication
9435	TCP	Required only for non-SSL communication

If you specified different ports during the Configuration Discovery and Tracking installation process, you must open those ports.

7.3.1 Launching the Product Console

You might encounter problems when trying to start the Product Console from a Linux system using the Mozilla browser. The typical error symptom is a message indicating that Mozilla does not know how to handle jnlp files. The reason behind this behavior is, most likely, that Mozilla has not been configured to launch jnlp files with Java Web start.

To configure Mozilla to launch jnlp files with javaws, perform the following steps:

1. Add a helper application to Mozilla to start jnlp files with Java Web start.
2. Find or install the javaws program on the same computer on which you are running Mozilla.
3. Open Mozilla, and select **Edit** → **Preferences** → **Helper Applications**.
4. Supply the following values:

MIME Type:	`application/x-java-jnlp-file`
Description:	`Java webstart`
Extension:	`jnlp`
Open it with:	The fully qualified path to your javaws program (This line should be the path to your javaws application.)

> **Note:** The Java Web start program, javaws, is shipped with Configuration Discovery and Tracking in the ${COLLATION_HOME}/external/ directory. Find the appropriate jdk 1.5.0 javaws for your platform in one of the subdirectories.

7.3.2 Configuration Discovery and Tracking Server is not running or is not rechargable

If you receive the message shown in Figure 7-2 while trying to start the Product Console from your workstation, your Configuration Discovery and Tracking Server might have been configured to only allow connections from the local host.

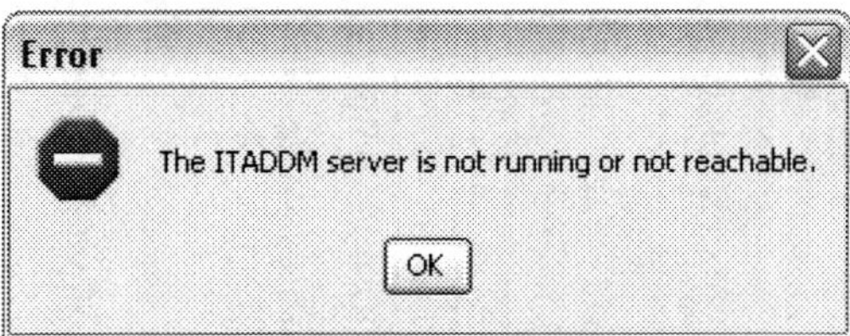

Figure 7-2 Configuration Discovery and Tracking Server is not reachable

You can remedy the situation by changing the value for `allowlocalhostonly` from the default value of true to `false` in the ${COLLATION_HOME}/etc/collation.properties file, as in Example 7-4.

Example 7-4 Changing the allowlocalhostonly property to false

```
# Only allow connections to the internal services if they come from
local host
# Do not change this setting to false in production environments.
Its insecure
com.collation.allowlocalhostonly=false
```

Restart the server whenever you modify the properties file.

You should also look at the value for the `rmi.server.hostname` setting in the collation.properties file (Example 7-5).

Another reason for not being able to access the Configuration Discovery and Tracking Server might be that you cannot resolve its host name. If the rmi.server.hostname setting is set to a value of default, the Configuration Discovery and Tracking Server will lookup its own host name (from a DNS or the local hosts file) and instruct the Product Console to connect to this IP name. If, for one reason or another, the workstation from where your try to launch the Product Console cannot resolve the name, it will appear as though the Configuration Discovery and Tracking Server is unavailable.

To resolve this situation, you can provide the IP address of the Configuration Discovery and Tracking Server as the value for the rmi.server.hostname, in which case no names need to be resolved. Product Console should be able to find the Configuration Discovery and Tracking Server, provided that the proper network routing has been established.

Example 7-5 Checking the rmi.server.hostname setting

```
# if the next property is set to an ip address, then the clientproxy
# will set the java.rmi.server.hostname
# If the property is set to "default", then clientproxy will NOT
# set the java.rmi.server.hostname
com.collation.clientproxy.rmi.server.hostname=192.168.1.54
```

7.3.3 Accessing the Configuration Discovery and Tracking server in an SSH tunnelling environment

Set the rmi.server.hostname to the host name of the Configuration Discovery and Tracking server.

```
rmi.server.hostname=Configuration Discovery and Tracking.domain
```

Set the same name in the client hosts file but set the IP address to your tunnel IP address:

```
Configuration Discovery and Tracking.domain tunnel.ip.address
```

In this way the Configuration Discovery and Tracking server will be able to resolve Configuration Discovery and Tracking.domain to its local IP address but the client will resolve Configuration Discovery and Tracking.domain to the IP address of the tunnel.

When the client connects, the Configuration Discovery and Tracking server will send Configuration Discovery and Tracking.domain to the client. The client will connect to the tunnel IP address and be tunnelled through.

7.3.4 Encrypt data transmissions when setting up access list

The Configuration Discovery and Tracking interface normally uses HTTP to transmit data from the user interface to the Configuration Discovery and Tracking server. When setting up the access list that contains user accounts and passwords you should use SSL to avoid transmitting this data in clear text.

Configure SSL mode for the product console:

1. Start the Product Console.
2. Select **Show SSL Options**.
3. Click **download trust store** and save the certificates that are transferred from the Configuration Discovery and Tracking server on your local hard drive.

4. Enter the location of the certificates on your hard drive, as shown in Figure 7-3.

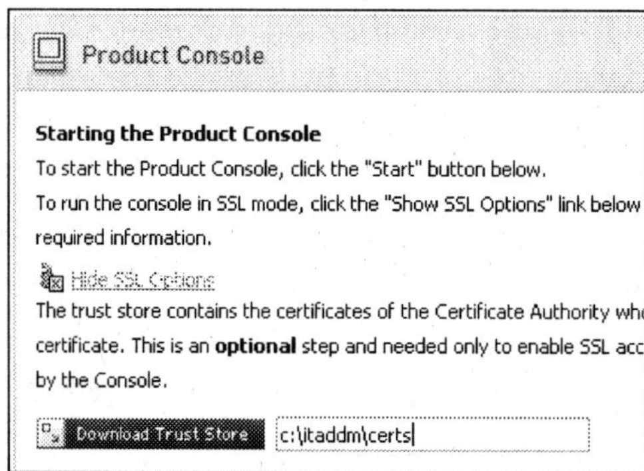

Figure 7-3 Download credentials used for SSL connection

5. Choose **Start Product Console**.The login screen opens (Figure 7-4).
6. Select **Establish a secure (SSL) session** and log in.

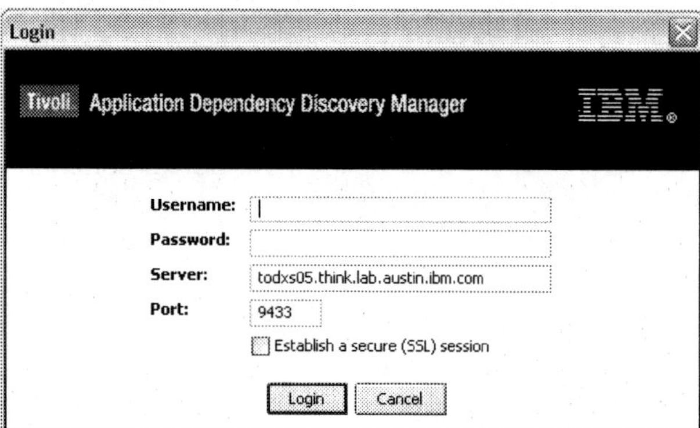

Figure 7-4 Secure SSL login to Configuration Discovery and Tracking server

This option encrypts all data, including all login names and passwords, before transmitting the data over the network. Using the SSL option is especially important when setting up the access list. You must enter the path to the certificates every time you wish to start the Configuration Discovery and Tracking Product Console in SSL mode.

7.4 Infrastructure connectivity

The following tips are provided to help you resolve infrastructure connectivity issues.

7.4.1 Verifying that a UNIX system is able to be discovered

The following sections discuss the steps needed to verify that a UNIX system can be discovered by Configuration Discovery and Tracking.

Access

Create a Service account. Configure the account to be a member of the sys group and use /bin/sh as the shell for this account.

SSH, protocol version 1 or 2 must be installed and access tested from the Configuration Discovery and Tracking server. If using key-based authentication, install public keys on all the hosts. Use SSH from the Configuration Discovery and Tracking command line to verify that the login and password or the key and passphrase work properly.

Software

Configuration Discovery and Tracking software requires the program **lsof** to be installed on all host computers

Table 7-3 specifies detailed runtime requirements for each supported UNIX platform.

Table 7-3 UNIX runtime requirements for enabling discovery

Platform	Requirement
AIX	User must be in group system and sys which allows read access to /dev/mem and /dev/kmem or "sudo" access for lsof
HPUX	lsof must be setuid root or "sudo" access for lsof
Linux	lsof must be setuid root or "sudo" access for lsof
Solaris	User running lsof must be in sys group or lsof must be setgid sys or "sudo" access for lsof

7.4.2 Verifying access to a computer system through ssh

In order to check access without having to run a discovery, use the `testssh.py` script located in ${COLLATION_HOME}/support. You must set the `COLLATION_HOME` environment variable prior to executing the command `testssh.py script-` as shown here:

```
export COLLATION_HOME=/opt/IBM/dist
${COLLATION_HOME}/support/bin/testssh.py <ipaddress | hostname> \
hostname
```

The `COLLATION_HOME` environment variable outputs the host name of the system to which you are testing the connectivity. You will know quickly whether access is working.

7.4.3 Verifying WMI access to a target system

You can use the **`testwmi`** and **`wmiexec`** WMI tools that are described in B.4.10, "testwmi.jy" and B.4.11, "wmiexec.jy" on page 385 to verify WMI functionality.

To verify that your WMI environment is set up correctly, log in to your Windows Gateway system, or systems, and from the \WINDOWS\system32 directory, issue the following command:

```
cscript prnjobs.vbs -l -s <remotehostname> -u <rempteAdminUserID> -w
<remoteAdminPassword>
```

If your WMI is set up correctly, you get a message stating how many print jobs reside on the host name specified. Of course, this is just an example. Other WMI functions can be used as well.

To verify that the Configuration Discovery and Tracking Server can issue the WMI call over the SSH protocol successfully, log on to the Configuration Discovery and Tracking server as the user defined for the server, for example `taddm` (or su to the user from the root user), and issue the following command:

```
ssh -l <user> -p <AnchorPort>@<windowsGW> cscript
%systemroot%\\system32%\\prnjobs.vbs -l -s <remotehostname> -u
<rempteAdminUserID> -w <remoteAdminPassword>
```

The following text shows how to verify WMI access to the target systems both the local to the Configuration Discovery and Tracking server and remotely (through an Anchor host).

Consider the following infrastructure setup in Table 7-4.

Table 7-4 Sample infrastructure setup

role	IP address	account	password
Configuration Discovery and Tracking Server	9.3.4.165	taddm	smartway
Local Windows Gateway	9.3.4.174	Administrator	smartway
Local Windows target	9.3.4.172	Administrator	smartway
Anchor Host	9.3.5.212	root	swj43r
Remote Windows Gateway	9.3.5.252	Administrator	swj43r
Remote Windows target	9.3.5.216	Administrator	swj43r

- Local logged into the Configuration Discovery and Tracking server as the root user:

```
su - taddm
ssh Admin@9.3.4.174 cscript %SystemRoot%\\system32\\prnjobs.vbs \
-l -s 9.3.4.172 -u Administrator -w smartway
```

- Remote logged into the Configuration Discovery and Tracking server as the root user:

```
su - taddm
ssh root@9.4.5.212 "ssh Adminstrator@9.3.4.252 \
cscript %SystemRoot%\\system32\\prnjobs.vbs \
-l -s 9.3.4.172 -u Administrator -w swj43r"
```

7.5 Discovery

Use the following tips to resolve issues related to discovery.

7.5.1 Tuning discoveries

Depending on your environment, discovery can be time-consuming. First of all, it is important to understand that IBM Tivoli Change and Configuration Management Database Configuration Discovery and Tracking is designed so that discovery affects the discovered systems (production servers, and so forth) as little as impossible.

The activities involved in making the discoveries perform the best way possible are focused in three areas:

- Optimizing the infrastructure
- Tuning the Configuration Discovery and Tracking Server configuration
- Disabling sensors

Optimizing the infrastructure

Take these steps to optimize your infrastructure:

1. Ensure that the Configuration Discovery and Tracking server is sized with the minimum requirements described in the IBM Tivoli Change and Configuration Management Database Configuration Discovery and Tracking documentation.
2. It is highly recommended that you run the database on a machine separate from the Configuration Discovery and Tracking server.
3. It is advisable that the Configuration Discovery and Tracking uses one network interface to communicate with the database server and another to communicate with the devices in the discovery scope.

Tuning the Configuration Discovery and Tracking Server configuration

When Configuration Discovery and Tracking is initially installed, the default discovery-related settings of the ${COLLATION_HOME}/dist/etc/collation.properties file are tuned for a Configuration Discovery and Tracking server with two CPUs and two GB RAM. The most important settings related to discovery performance in this file are listed in Table 7-5.

Table 7-5 Performance properties in the collation.properties file

Setting	Description
com.collation.discover.dwcount	Maximum number of discovery worker threads. By increasing this value, the Discovery Engine spawns another process that detects and extracts seeds. Default is 16.
com.collation.discover.sccount	Maximum number of seed creators threads. By increasing this value, more seeds are placed in the JavaSpaces. Default is 2.

Setting	Description
com.collation.discover.observer.topopumpcount	Number of TopoPump threads in the Discovery Observer. This effectively controls the storage speed. Converting results to objects and writing the results to the database is time-consuming. By increasing this value, you can shorten discovery time, however, if you see a large number of storage errors you should decrease the value. It is generally safe to set this to the number of CPUs on the system. Default is 4.

However, even if the server is so configured, these settings are not unalterable because determining the optimal settings depends highly on the network environment, including firewalls, subnets, and so forth. Therefore, the following approach is advisable for any installation in order to decrease discovery time:

1. During a discovery run, monitor the CPUs' usage of the Configuration Discovery and Tracking server. If the CPUs are not fully utilized, then you could increase the `dwcount` by a few threads, and rerun and remonitor the discovery. Alternatively, if the CPUs are too busy or memory usage is exhausted, there is a risk of sensors starting to timeout and result in incomplete discovery results. In this case try decreasing the value of the `dwcount` parameter.
2. If increasing the `dwcount` did not impact the utilization of the CPUs, it might be because that the seed creation is slow. Increase the `sccount` by 1 and try again.
3. The `topopumpcount` controls the storage speed. It is safe to set this to the number of CPUs on the system.

This is the main rule. However, with a general understanding of the discovery mechanism (see 5.1.3, "The Discovery process in detail" on page 152) together with an understanding of analyzing the logfiles (see 7.1.2, "Discovery log files" on page 248). Table 7-6 on page 264, which includes other discovery-related settings, can assist you in determining the best setup for your environment.

Table 7-6 Discovery options

Property	Description
com.collation.discover.dwcount	Maximum number of discovery worker threads. By increasing this value, the Discovery Engine spawns another process that detects and extracts seeds. Default is 16.
com.collation.discover.sccount	Maximum number of seed creators threads. By increasing this value, more seeds are placed in the JavaSpaces. Default is 2.
com.collation.discover.ascount	Maximum number of Agent selectors. This setting should never be changed. Default is 1.
com.collation.discover.observer.topopumpcount	Number of TopoPump threads in the Discovery Observer. This effectively controls the storage speed. Converting results to objects and writing the results to the database is time-consuming. By increasing this value you can shorten discovery time, however, if you see a large number of storage errors you should decrease the value. It is generally safe to set this to the number of CPUs on the system. Default is 4.
com.collation.discover.observer.topopumptimeout	Timeout in milliseconds for the TopoPump watchdog timer. This is the maximum time allowed for storing a single result. Default is 1800000.
com.collation.discover.observer.topopumpstorageattempts	Number of times TopoPump will try to store a result. Default is 8.
com.collation.discover.observer.topopumpBackoffBase	Base amount of time to wait when a TopoPump storage attempt fails. Default is 30.
com.collation.discover.observer.topopumpBackoffDelta	Variable delta amount of time to wait when a TopoPump storage attempt fails. Default is 30.
com.collation.discover.javaspace.mem	Memory size in MB used for the java space. Default is 256.
com.collation.discover.DefaultAgentTimeout	The default timeout sensor time out. This setting helps prevent runaway sensors. If the time-out value expires during a sensor's run, that sensor will be terminated. In addition, each sensor has a timeout property in collation.properties. If more than one sensor is timing out, consider changing the default timeout for all sensors. Default is 600000.

After modifying any parameter in the collation.properties file, you must restart the server.

Disabling sensors

Another way of reducing discovery time is to disable sensors that you know are not used in your environment. For instance, if you know that you do not have any Nokia Snmp devices in your environment, you could simple disable the NokiaSnmpSensor. Each sensor has a corresponding XML file located in the ${COLLATION_HOME}/dist/etc/discover-sensors directory. To enable or disable sensors, you must modify the sensor's enabled tag accordingly.

Example 7-6 displays the content of the NokiaSnmpSensor.xml file.

Example 7-6 Sample sensor XML file

```
<?xml version="1.0" encoding="UTF-8"?>
<results>
    <AgentConfiguration
xsi:type="coll:com.collation.platform.model.discovery.agent.AgentConfig
uration">
        <enabled>true</enabled>
        <familyName>DiscoverSensor</familyName>
        <name>NokiaSnmpSensor</name>
<seedClassName>com.collation.discover.seed.net.NokiaSnmpSeed</seedClass
Name>
<agentClassName>com.collation.discover.agent.net.NokiaSnmpAgent</agentC
lassName>
    </AgentConfiguration>
</results>
```

Disable the sensor simply by changing the value of the <enabled> tag from true to `false`. Because the Nokia Snmp sensor will no longer be run, discovery time will shorten.

> **Important:** It is vital to be aware of the logical dependencies between sensors. As described earlier, some sensors create seeds that start other sensors. If you disable a sensor that create seeds, these seeds will no longer be placed in the JavaSpace and, as a result, not be invoked.

7.5.2 Error messages that might occur during discovery

Table 7-7 through Table 7-16 on page 271 describe some of the most common problems related to the execution of sensors.

Table 7-7 General Errors (Applicable to all sensors)

Message	Reason	Remedy
Sensor killed due to time quota overrun	This error occurs when the Sensor takes too long for discovery. The Sensor could be hanging due to a network protocol error.	To remedy this, the Sensor timeout can be increased by increasing the timeout for the sensor in the collation.properties file.
Sensor failed in remote server, <message>	This error occurs when the sensor running in a remote anchor fails.	The <message> suggests the possible reason for the failure.
Unexpected sensor error.	This error occurs when there is an error in the discovery which has not been anticipated.	Report this as a bug to Configuration Discovery and Tracking Support.
Authorization error and Authentication error	This error occurs because the credentials provided for the element are not valid.	Make sure the appropriate credentials are provided.
Storage error	This error is caused by an incomplete discovery of some key attributes of elements.	Report this as a bug to Configuration Discovery and Tracking Support.
Could not determine remote OS: SessionClientException: WMI Session Error: Exception caught in main: The remote procedure call failed.	At that particular instance, cannot access remote host.	Re-run discover against this host.
Could not create session to gateway x.x.x.x for x.x.x.x: SessionClientException: Failure preparing gateway: exit status 1) Called by Discovery Manager	Gateway preparation is failed due to time outs.	Check the access and retry the discovery.

Table 7-8 Generic server sensor

Message	Reason	Remedy
Unable to discover Processes and Connections : Command lsof -i failed	This error occurs because: 1. The lsof utility is not available on the remote server. 2. The lsof utility is not set up with the correct path.	To correct this error: 1. Check whether lsof is in the path. The path used is specified in collation.properties using the property : com.collation.discover.agent.path.<systype> 2. Check the lsof permissions to make sure the suid-root bit is set.

Table 7-9 Apache sensor

Message	Reason	Remedy
Error Executing : /usr/local/apache/bin/httpd -V	This message occurs when the httpd executable does not have permissions for the user to execute it. This execution is needed to find several compile-time options of the httpd server. It does not start the server, but merely prints the information out.	Change the permission on httpd to be executable by the user, or give the user more privileges.
Apache httpd path [/usr/lib/ab2/dweb/sunos5/bin/dwhttpd] does not contain /httpd	This message is SUN's answerbook running in their Java Web server.	

Table 7-10 DB2 sensor

Message	Reason	Remedy
DB2Sensor: unable to find sensor: null	DB2 cannot be discovered when running on Windows.	none

Table 7-11 Domino sensor

Message	Reason	Remedy
Could not find an IIOP server to deep discover server: helios/collation from domain: collationDomain	This means that the IIOP server in Domino server cluster is not enabled. This is required for Configuration Discovery and Tracking to discover Domino.	Start the IIOP server for one of the Domino servers
storage error	Server name could not be read from notes.ini	Ensure the ServerName property exists in notes.ini and collation account can read this file

Table 7-12 LDAP Sensor

Message	Reason	Remedy
Invalid LDAP Credentials	The Access provided for LDAP servers is incorrect or non-existent.	Provide the correct Access for LDAP Servers.

Table 7-13 Oracle Sensor

Message	Reason	Remedy
unable to find servers: no Oracle servers found	There was an error finding the instances of Oracle. The problem could be incorrect or inadequate access.	Provide the correct Access for Oracle Servers and make sure the user has select_catalog role.
Unable to find servers: No Oracle Servers found	Oracle cannot be discovered when running on Windows	none

Table 7-14 Session Sensor

Message	Reason	Remedy
Authorization failed	This means that none of the authentication methods (SSH1, SSH2, WMI) were successful in reaching the remote host.	Make sure the authentication provided for the host access is correct. Test it from the command line.

Message	Reason	Remedy
TestSession failed after 0 seconds: SessionClientException: WMI session error: connect: The RPC server is unavailable.	The WMI server is either unreachable or is not really a WMI port (Sometimes there are other servers listening on the DCE port - for instance Hp Openview.	
TestSession failed after 27 seconds: SessionClientException: WMI session error: Exception caught in main: Shutting Down	This is an intermittent issue with some WMI calls.	The remedy is to simply retry the discovery of this component.
Error Creating Remote Host Session:	At that particular instance, cannot access remote host.	Retry the discovery of this host.
Sensor timeout		Retry the discovery of this host.

Message	Reason	Remedy
Could not connect (This server does not support ssh1, connect to ssh2 enabledError in creating SSH2 Session to saemcol01@x.x.x.x: SSH2FatalException: Key exchange failed: No match in kex params 'enc-algorithms-cli2srv', or Could not connect (Sorry, server does not support the 'blowfish-cbc' cipher.Error in creating SSH2 Session to coll@x.x.x.x: SSH2FatalException: Key exchange failed: No match in kex params 'enc-algorithms-cli2srv', our's: blowfish-cbc, peer's: aes128-cbc,3des-cbc,aes 192-cbc,aes256-cbcError in creating SSH2 Session to saemcol01@138.220.3.19 5: SSH2FatalException: Key exchange failed:	Configuration Discovery and Tracking supports only blowfish cipher ; device does not support blowfish	none
Could not connect (This server does not support ssh1, connect to ssh2 enabled	Configuration Discovery and Tracking tried both ssh2 and ssh1 and neither of those protocols worked on port 22	
Server closed connection	Some Systems run IDS servers that listen on port 22 and record the connection attempt	
SessionSensor: could not execute os.getHostId	This suggests a problem on the windows gateway server. Possible reasons are the disk where windows is installed is full.	Check if the file system on the gateway is full and delete unwanted files.

Table 7-15 SnmpMib2Sensor

Message	Reason	Remedy
Snmp request timed out	The snmp agent on the remote is not running	Start the snmp agent on the device if discovery through snmp is desired.

Table 7-16 WebSphere Sensor

<table>
<tr><th>Message</th><th>Reason</th><th>Remedy</th></tr>
<tr><td>Unable to connect to WebSphere server at x.x.x.x:8880 - ADMC0016E: Could not create SOAP Connector</td><td>The access provided is incorrect. This could be a problem with the access or the SSL key certificates which are provided</td><td>Make sure the SSL keys are correctly entered and the Passphrase is correct.</td></tr>
<tr><td>Sensor failed in remote server: Error: WebSphere root directory might not be set properly.</td><td rowspan="2">WebSphere jar files neither installed nor located</td><td rowspan="2">Install the WebSphere jar files onto the Configuration Discovery and Tracking Server
(or NFS mount them), and change the property com.collation.websphere.root.dir in collation.properties to point to them.</td></tr>
<tr><td>Sensor failed in remote server : javax/management/ObjectName</td></tr>
<tr><td>Timeout errors communicating with WebSphere JMX connector, check server/host/network health and retry discovery</td><td>jmx service rejects queries 3 times ; sometimes it is a access or insufficient privileges</td><td>ensure JMX user has admin privileges</td></tr>
</table>

7.5.3 Path incorrect for discovery

Many sensors assume certain paths for running commands. If your environment is different, you can add the path to the command to the environment used by discovery by editing the collation.properties file.

The path is a property in collation.properties. It is passed verbatim to the shell when a session is created, which means you can actually use semicolons to add arbitrary directories. The path property can be specified for your entire environment, for particular platforms, or for specific IP addresses.

Using AIX as an example, the property path is:

```
com.collation.discover.agent.path.AIX=/usr/local/bin:/bin:/user/bin:/us
r/X11R6/bin:/etc:/usr/sbin
```

For an entire environment, the property path becomes:

```
com.collation.discover.agent.path.AIX=/usr/local/bin:/bin:/user/bin:/us
r/X11R6/bin:/etc:/usr/sbin;export
LD_LIBRARY_PATH=/opt/Oracle/OracleAS10g/lib
```

For inclusion in this book, we had to break the path lines here. Remember, the path is all on one line.

You can set properties in the collation.properties files for specific operating systems, IP addresses, or combinations of operating systems and IP addresses. Just copy the com.collation.discover.agent.path property and tack the OS and the IP address to the end of it.

So if you want to specify it by IP, do this:

```
com.collation.discover.agent.path.10.10.250.3=/usr/local/bin:/bin:/user
/bin:/usr/X11R6/bin:/etc:/usr/sbin;export
LD_LIBRARY_PATH=/opt/Oracle/OracleAS10g/lib
```

For inclusion in this book, we had to break the path lines here. Remember, the path is all on one line.

7.5.4 Server components are not discovered

If some of your expected server components are not discovered, the following steps can be helpful in order to narrow down the problem:

1. Verify that the computer system hosting the server is within the selected scope for the discovery and has been discovered.
2. Verify access to the system through a ComputerSystem ACL.
3. Verify access to the server through the <serverType> ACL.
4. Verify that the server is operational.
5. Check the settings in Custom Servers to verify if any enabled Custom Server definition has a set of criteria that overlaps and matches your expected server signature (process names, parameters, environment values, and so on) *and* has an action setting of DISABLE.
6. Check the settings in Custom Server templates to verify if any enabled Custom Server template definition, which has an Action setting of Discover, *and* a set of criteria that overlaps (but are less restrictive than) your expected

server signature (process names, parameters, environment values, and so forth) appears earlier in the list of Custom Server templates than the template you expect to identify your custom server.

7.5.5 No computer systems are discovered

Follow these steps if no systems are discovered:

1. Verify that the computer system is within the selected scope for the discovery.
2. Verify access to the system through a ComputerSystem ACL.
3. Verify that the server is operational.
4. Check the networking definitions (host name resolution and routing) from the Configuration Discovery and Tracking server (or the Anchor Host) to ensure connectivity between the server and the target system. You can use the **ping** and **traceroute** commands in your problem determination.

7.5.6 Expected files are not discovered from Computer Systems

Check the settings in Computer Systems to verify if any enabled Computer System definition has a set of criteria that overlaps your expected server signature (OSName) and has a setting of DISABLED.

Check that the ComputerSystem definition that matches your expected server signature includes the desired files.

7.6 Troubleshooting custom server templates

The following section provides guidance on solving problems related to the use of Custom Server Templates.

7.6.1 No software is discovered on a UNIX/Linux system

If a discovery does not return the expected results regarding software components on Linux and UNIX systems, the reason might be that lsof is not working correctly or your Custom Server Template hierarchy filters out the expected components.

To remedy this situation, do one of the following:

- Verify that lsof is working correctly

  It MUST be able to print out information about all the processes on the system. The most reliable way to ensure this is to enable sudo access to lsof by the Configuration Discovery and Tracking Service account.

- Verify the Custom Server Template matching.

  Remember, all ignore templates match first. Likely there is an ignore template that matches the process you want first.

  Try disabling all the ignore templates and rerunning the discovery.

  It MUST be able to print out information about all the processes on the system. The most reliable way to ensure this is to enable sudo access to lsof by the Configuration Discovery and Tracking Service account.

- Custom Server template is not matching.

  Remember, all ignore templates match first. Likely there is an ignore template that matches the process you want first

  Try disabling all the ignore templates and retrying the discover.

7.6.2 About the Discover or Ignore radio button

Choose **Discover** when you want to categorize a process.

Choose **ignore** to suppress a process (and its dependencies) from being shown in Configuration Discovery and Tracking.

All ignore templates happen prior to any discover templates.

7.6.3 Dependencies not being discovered?

Configuration Discovery and Tracking discovers dependencies in two ways:

- By looking at the TCP connections listed by lsof
- By looking at the configuration of some programs (JDBC resources returned by JMX)

In the first case, only TCP connections that are present at the time when the discovery runs the `lsof` command will be discovered.

Eventually, a discovery will catch those connections established, and the dependencies will be created.

If you do not want to wait that long, create a manual connection.

Once the connection is discovered, the manual connection is promoted to a transactional dependency.

7.6.4 Software process not discovered?

Discovery of some applications requires an entry in the access list. See this Web site and search for *access list* for details:

http://www-306.ibm.com/software/sysmgmt/products/support/IBMTivoliChangeandConfigurationManagementDatabase.html

Only processes with TCP connections are discovered. Run **lsof/netstat** to verify if the process you are interested in has a TCP connection. Processes with no TCP listening ports are discarded by default. However, there are properties that can be changed in collation.properties to cause non-listening processes to be discovered. The properties are:

- com.collation.platform.os.UnixOs.forcedServerList
- com.collation.platform.os.WindowsOs.forcedServerList

If you add <process name> to this list, you will be able to discover a host that does not have a listening port. For example, if you want to discover perl processes, you could modify the property to:

```
com.collation.platform.os.UnixOs.forcedServerList=bash;perl
```

7.6.5 Dependency between two software processes not shown

If you know that two processes communicate through TCP and the connection is not shown, be aware that:

- Connections between Software servers are detected only if the TCP connection is established at the time the discovery is run.
- The connection might be discovered eventually after a series of discovery runs, or a manual connection can be created.

7.6.6 Connections between software processes on the same machine not shown?

By default, servers with listening ports on loopback interfaces are suppressed. This is controlled by the property:

```
com.collation.platform.os.ignoreLoopbackProcesses=true
```

To enable discovery of dependencies established on the loopback adapter, ensure that the value for this property is `true`.

7.6.7 Runtime tab Environment section for an application empty?

The **ps** command on Linux needs to be **setuid** or **sudo** access must be granted to the Configuration Discovery and Tracking Service Account.

On HP-UX, the **system-V ps** command is unable to show environment variables.

7.7 Application ServerDiscovery

Consult the following tips to solve issues related to discovery of application server discovery.

7.7.1 Which authorizations are required?

Table 7-17 details the required access permissions for discovery of various application server components.

Table 7-17 Access requirements for Application Server discovery

Web Servers	Apache	Read permission for apache configuration files (httpd.conf) and execute permission for httpd or Apache.exe binary.
	iPlanet	Read permission to the iPlanet configuration files (IPlanet version 4.x & above supported) and execute permission for ns-httpd binary.
	Microsoft IIS	No access requirements. User account already set up on the host is sufficient.

Application Servers	Weblogic	Weblogic Server login/pw for the console. (Weblogic 6.x and above supported)
	WebSphere WebSphere 5.x is supported	WebSphere server installed on the Configuration Discovery and Tracking Server. This is for access to WebSphere libraries that cannot be distributed with Configuration Discovery and Tracking. ► If security is disabled then no user accounts are needed. ► If security is enabled then a Web console admin user, password and client side SSL certificates are needed ► If this user is Administrator then Configuration Discovery and Tracking discovers all config data. ► If this user is not Administrator (e.g. monitor) then Configuration Discovery and Tracking discovers all configuration data except Security configurations
	Lotus Domino Version 6.0 and above supported	IIOP server and Web server must be running on at least one Domino Server per Domino Domain ► Create a default user
	JBoss	JBoss Console login and password are needed.
Databases	Oracle	A user account with select_catalog_role privileges (Oracle 8i, Oracle 9i, and Oracle 10g supported)
	DB2	A user account with access to the database
	Sybase	A user account that is a member of sa-role. Sybase IQ user is member of DBA. (grant select on sysengines to public)
	SQL Server	A user with public role in the master DB and every other database to be discovered
Other Servers	PeopleSoft	Read permission for configuration files
	SAP	Read permission for configuration files
	Documentum	Read permission for configuration files

7.7.2 Verifying discovery of WebSphere Application Servers with security enabled

To verify that a WebSphere Application Server is able to be discovered when security is enabled on the server, perform the following:

Create an Access List entry with the Web console admin user and password *plus* the client-side SSL certificates.

Configuration Discovery and Tracking requires console user with an Administrator role to be able to discover fully all configuration data for WebSphere.

Verifying the account

To verify that the user is an Administrator user, you can run the following command on the WebSphere server:

```
cd $WAS_ROOT_DIR/bin
./wsadmin.sh -user userid -password password -c '$AdminConfig list
Security'
```

The output from this command should be similar to the following line, representing successful access to the security config data, to which only Administrators have access.

```
(cells/mycell:security.xml#Security_1)
```

Uploading the SSL certificates

To upload the SSL certificates to the Configuration Discovery and Tracking server, you must be able to access the certificate trust and key-store files that reside on the WebSphere Application Server. The default location for these files is:

```
${WAS_HOME}/etc
```

Because the Product Console most likely runs from your local workstation, you should temporarily copy the trust and key-store files to your local workstation, so you can access them from the FileSelection dialog box that is presented to you when defining the Access List entry for the WebSphere Application Server.

7.7.3 Discover WebSphere servers using an anchor server

WebSphere discovery requires WebSphere libraries.

To discover WebSphere servers, you must have WebSphere installed and the following property in the collation.properties file pointed to the location of the installation:

```
com.collation.websphere.root.dir=lib/websphere/5.0
```

The directory specified in this property must be correct for WebSphere Application Server installed on the Configuration Discovery and Tracking server and for WebSphere Application Server installed on any anchor servers.

7.7.4 WebSphere Server discovery with multiple, deployed SSL certificates

There are two ways to discover WebSphere servers with multiple SSL certificates deployed. Create Access List entries for each individual server, and limit the scope for each entry, or merge the certificates into one set of key- and trust-store files.

Scope limit access entries

Define a set of distinct WebSphere access entries for each set of SSL certificates and scope-limit it so that it is tried on the appropriate servers. This will ensure that the first access entry tried will have the correct SSL certifications and will work.

Merge SSL certificates

Define a single WebSphere access entry that contains a merged set of SSL certificates by doing the following:

1. Collect each distinct server-side SSL key file that you want to merge.
2. Go to a machine which has WebSphere and start the ikeyman utility. You can find it in the $WAS_ROOT/bin directory (ikeyman.sh / ikeyman.bat). Note that this utility brings up a GUI, so you will need to be able to launch it on your screen.
3. Load each server-side key file into ikeyman, then extract the server's public key into a .arm file, e.g. server1.arm, server2.arm, and so forth. You should be able to view this key under the Personal Certificates drop-down in ikeyman after you load the file. Usually the key is shown by default.
4. When all the keys have been extracted, create a new trust file. Delete all the default certificates that are added, then use the **Add** button to add each of the .arm files.
5. The trust file created in step 3 contains all the public keys of the servers that need to be connected. You can upload this file to the SSL auth for WebSphere. For the key file, you can use one of the client-side key files from

one of the servers. This file only contains a single personal certificate, that of the client.

7.7.5 Verifying discovery of database servers

The following shows how you can verify that a database server is able to be discovered.

- DB2

  Use the DB2 command line tool.

- Oracle

  Use sqlplus to make sure the following command can be executed:

  ```
  select * from dba_data_files;
  ```

- SQL Server

  Verify that the following SQL commands successfully execute:

  ```
  select name, filename from sysdatabases
  select config, value from syscurconfigs
  select spid, cmd from sysprocesses
  ```

7.8 Networking devices

The following sections show troubleshooting tips for networking devices.

7.8.1 MIBs used by SNMP Sensors

Table 7-18 on page 281 lists the MIBs and objects detected by specific SNMP Sensors.

Table 7-18 MIBs and objects detected by specific SNMP Sensors

Sensor	MIB	Object Name
SnmpMib2Sensor	MIB2 (RFC1213) Interfaces Bridge	sysDescr sysObjectID sysContact sysName sysLocation ifTable ifXTable ifStackTable ifMauTable ifMauAutoNegTable ipAddrTable ipRouteTable ipForwarding dot1dBasePortTable
AlteonPortSensor	Alteon	agPortCurrentCfgTable agPortInfoTable
AlteonSnmpSensor	Alteon	agVirtServerTable agRealServerTable agRealServerGroupTable agVirtServiceTable
AlteonVlanSensor	Alteon	agCurCfgTable agPortCurCfgTable
BridgeSnmpSensor	Bridge	dot1dTpFdbTable dot1dTpPortTable
BigIPPortSensor	F5	(TBD)
BigIPSnmpSensor	F5	(TBD)
BigIPVlanSensor	F5	(TBD)
CheckPointSnmpSensor	CheckPoint	fwPropertiesTable
CdpSensor	Cisco	cdpGlobalDeviceId cdpCacheTable
CiscoPortSensor	Cisco	c2900PortTable portTable
CiscoVlanSensor	Cisco	vlanMemberShipTable managementDomainTable vtpVlanTable vlanTrunkPortTable

Sensor	MIB	Object Name
EntityMibSensor	Entity	(TBD)
ExtremeVlanSensor	Extreme	extremeVlanIfTable extremeVlanEncapsIfTable ifStackTable
HostResourcesSensor	HostResources	hrStorageTable hrDeviceTable hrSWInstalledTable
LanManagerSnmpSensor	LanManager	svSvcTable
NetcreenSnmpSensor	Netscreen	mipTable serviceTable vipConfigTable vipServerTable
NokiaSnmpSensor	Nokia	rsACLTable rsRuleTable

7.8.2 Access List Specification for Cisco Telnet Access

There are three different possible user configurations on a Cisco router. They each need a different treatment in the access list setup.

- Password only

  This is the default setup. When you telnet into the box, you only get a password prompt. To reach enable mode, you need to give the enable command and enter the enable password.

  Specify the following in the access list:

  - user = default
  - password
  - enable password

- Non-privileged user

  In this case a user has been defined on the box. When you telnet into the box, you get a user name prompt and password prompt. To reach enable mode, you still need to give the enable command and enter the enable password.

  Specify the following in the access list:

  - user
  - password
  - enable password

- Privileged user

  In this case a user has been defined on the router with privilege level 15. When you telnet into the box, you get a user name prompt and password prompt. When you log in you are automatically in enable mode.

  Specify the following in the access list:

  - user
  - password
  - enable password = default

7.9 How-tos

The following sections provide information about achieving specific objectives.

7.9.1 How to add custom icons

There are three steps to creating custom icons in Configuration Discovery and Tracking:

1. Create three svg icons to display the item in the graph:

   icon_"familyname"_state.svg used when a state change occurs
   icon_"familyname"_default.svg used for the standard view of the icon
   icon_"familyname"_dormant.svg used when the item is shown as dormant

   The graphics type of these files *must* be RBG-Alpha 1-layer.

   Place these icons in your installation directory under this directory:

   `${COLLATION_HOME}/dist/images/custom`

2. Create a single png icon to be used as the tooltip icon. Name it `"familyname"_tooltip.png.`

   Place these icons in your installation directory under this directory

   `${COLLATION_HOME}/dist/images/custom/tooltip directory`

3. Create a png icon to be used in the tree. Name it `"familyname".png`, and place it in your installation directory under this directory:

   `${COLLATION_HOME}/dist/images/custom/tree`

   The variable `"familyname"` can be any string you like. For example: apache, apache_state.svg, apache_tooltip.png, apache.png.

7.9.2 WMI Access without Administrator Account

Instructions for working around the lack of an administrator account to use WMI to discovery Windows machines.

There are a set of dlls that need to be installed on discovered nodes. Administrator accounts can install them automatically, but you can install them manually if you do not have an administrator account.

The automated install uses a script called GetVersionAndInstall.js (or in the some versions, InstallProvider.js), which can be found under ${COLLATION_HOME}/dist/lib/ms/gateway. If you look there, you will see that the following files are installed on each target:

- Win32_Confignia.dll
- Win32_Confignia.mof
- ConfigniaLog.dll
- aports.dll
- msvcr71.dll

If you do not have administrator access you can do one of the following two things:

1. Install the files and sets WMI permissions by hand.
2. Do an initial discovery with an Administrator account, which will automatically install the WMI provider on the various nodes. Subsequent discoveries can be run with a non-administrator user.

7.9.3 Adding new elements to the details panel

This section discusses how to add new elements.

XML files

Most of the details panel is defined in three different XML files, with certain exceptions. The XML files of interest are:

- Screenlayout.xml

  This XML file is physically located under the src tree in gui/client/resources directory. The XML Schema for this XML file is in proxy.clientproxy.common.meta.screenlayout.xsd

  This XML file contains the following information:

  - For a given model object (defined by its fully qualified class name), the tabs that are to be shown.
  - Each tab either has recursive tabs or it has tables inside the tabs.

  - Every leaf tab (no more recursions) contains one or more tables. If there is more than one table, then the tab contains information of how these tables are laid out in screen.
  - Each table (tabdata in the XML file) has an user facing display name and an unique name. This unique name is the key to get the information of what should be shown inside each of these tables.
- Screencontent.xml

  This file is physically located under gui/client/resources/screencontent.xml. The XML schema for this file is in proxy.clientproxy.common.meta.screencontent.xsd

  For each of the unique names in the tabdata sections in Screenlayout.xml, there should be an entry in the Screencontent.xml file.

  The Screencontent.xml file contains information about what are the fields to be displayed in each table inside the tabs.

  Each element in this XML file (tableContent) contains the following information:

  - Type of table: Is this a property sheet or a multi-row or multi-column table.
  - What are the various fields to be shown in each table? Starting at the top-level ModelObject, how does one navigate to get to those fields?
  - How should each field be rendered? Is it a simple text entry, is it a list of entries to be shown in a drop down box? Is it a special type of entry such as memory (interpret data and show it in MB), is it a link and so on.
- Attributenames.xml

  This file is physically located under gui/client/resources/attributenames.xml. The XML schema for this file is in proxy.clientproxy.common.meta.screenlayout.xsd

  There must be a user-facing term for each attribute we show to users. This XML file consists of the mapping of an attribute name in a model object to its user-facing term.

  Each entry in the screencontent.xml must have an entry in the attributenames.xml. The attributenames.xml file is used not only by details panel, but also by comparison report and change history report.

Sample code

Consider the details panel for ApacheServer. Layout information is shown in Example 7-7.

Example 7-7 Details panel ApacheServer code

```
<layout
name="com.collation.platform.model.topology.app.web.apache.ApacheSer
ver" hasAdminInfo="true" displayName="Apache Server">
      <tab name="General">
            <tabdata name="ApacheServer.General"
displayName="General"/>
        </tab>
        <tab name="Configuration" layout="verticalPanels">
            <tabdata name="ApacheServer.SSL" displayName="SSL"/>
            <tabdata name="ApacheServer.Server"
displayName="Server"/>
        </tab>
        <tab name="Virtual Hosts">
            <tabdata name="ApacheServer.VirtualHosts"
displayName="Virtual Hosts"/>
        </tab>
        <tab name="Modules">
            <tab name="Apache Modules">
                <tabdata name="ApacheServer.Modules"
displayName="Modules"/>
            </tab>
            <tab name="Other">
                <tabdata name="AppServer.StaticModules"
displayName="Other Modules"/>
            </tab>
        </tab>
        <tab name="Application Descriptors">
            <tabdata name="AppServer.ApplicationDescriptors"
displayName="Application Descriptors"/>
        </tab>
        <tab name="Runtime" layout="verticalPanels">
            <tabdata name="AppServer.Runtime"
displayName="Runtime"/>
            <tabdata name="AppServer.Ports" displayName="Ports"/>
            <tabdata name="AppServer.Connections"
displayName="Connections"/>
        </tab>
        <tab name="Config Files">
            <tabdata name="AppServer.ConfigFiles"
displayName="Config Files"/>
        </tab>
    </layout>
```

The details panel for ApacheServer is uniquely identified by the name field in the XML snippet layout. The details panel has the following top level tabs: `General`, `VirtualHosts`, `Modules`, `Application Descriptors`, `Runtime` and `Config Files`.

The `Modules` tab has nested tabs inside them.

`Configuration` tab has more than 1 table to be shown inside the tab. The layout value `"verticalPanels"` tells that these panels should be layered vertically one below the other. The accepted values for layout are defined in the XSD file screenlayout.xsd.

For each of these tables (tabdata), the attribute `name` tells what to search for in the screencontent.xml file.

Tabs added automatically

Not all tabs have to be entered in this XML file. Some tabs such as dependencies, admin info, MSS info, and so on are added automatically by the details manager. In the case of Computer System details panels, the tabs for functions such as Router, Load Balancer, and so forth are added automatically as well.

Content information

This section discusses Name / Value property sheet-type tables. Consider the content for the general tab, displayed in Example 7-8.

Example 7-8 General tab properties

```
<tableContent name="ApacheServer.General"
className="com.collation.platform.model.topology.app.web.apache.Apac
heServer">
        <field>
            <plain fieldName="displayName"/>
        </field>
        <field>
            <plain fieldName="objectType" displayType="type"/>
            <plain fieldName="lastObjectModified"
displayType="date"/>
        </field>
        <field>
            <plain fieldName="productName"/>
        </field>
        <field>
            <plain fieldName="productVersion"/>
        </field>
        <field>
            <plain fieldName="vendorName"/>
```

```
        </field>
        <field>
            <nested fieldName="host"
className="com.collation.platform.model.topology.sys.ComputerSystem"
>
                <plain fieldName="displayName" displayType="popup"/>
            </nested>
        </field>
        <field>
            <nested fieldName="primarySAP"
className="com.collation.platform.model.topology.net.BindAddress">
                <nested fieldName="primaryIpAddress"
className="com.collation.platform.model.topology.net.IpAddress">
                    <plain fieldName="dotNotation"/>
                </nested>
            </nested>
        </field>
        <field>
            <nested fieldName="primarySAP"
className="com.collation.platform.model.topology.net.BindAddress">
                <plain fieldName="portNumber"/>
            </nested>
        </field>
        <field hidden="true">
            <nested fieldName="processPools"
className="com.collation.platform.model.topology.app.ProcessPool">
                <plain fieldName="displayName"/>
                <plain fieldName="cmdLine"/>
                <plain fieldName="env"/>
                <nested
className="com.collation.platform.model.topology.sys.RuntimeProcess"
fieldName="runtimeProcesses">
                    <plain fieldName="displayName"/>
                    <nested fieldName="ports"
className="com.collation.platform.model.topology.net.BindAddress">
                        <nested fieldName="ipAddress"
className="com.collation.platform.model.topology.net.IpAddress">
                            <plain fieldName="displayName"/>
                        </nested>
                    </nested>
                    <nested fieldName="connections"
className="com.collation.platform.model.topology.net.LogicalConnecti
on">
                        <plain fieldName="displayName"/>
                    </nested>
```

```
                </nested>
            </nested>
        </field>
        <field>
            <nested
className="com.collation.platform.model.topology.app.ConfigFile"
fieldName="configFile">
                <plain fieldName="realFile"/>
            </nested>
        </field>
        <field hidden="true">
            <nested fieldName="processPools"
className="com.collation.platform.model.topology.app.ProcessPool">
                <nested fieldName="executable"
className="com.collation.platform.model.topology.sys.DataFile">
                    <plain fieldName="displayName"/>
                </nested>
            </nested>
        </field>
        <field hidden="true">
            <nested fieldName="configContents"
className="com.collation.platform.model.topology.app.AppConfig">
                <nested fieldName="content"
className="com.collation.platform.model.topology.core.LogicalContent
">
                    <plain fieldName="displayName"/>
                </nested>
            </nested>
        </field>
 </tableContent>
```

This table is a name/value property sheet type table. We know this because otherwise there would be an attribute called "layout".

The field element in XML illustrates a grouping of one or more attributes to be shown. The field element contains one or more <plain> elements and / or one or more <nested> elements.

The <plain> elements are primitive attributes in the object model. The <nested> elements are complex / non-primitive attributes in the object model.

For instance, `"displayName"` is a primitive field in the object model. ApacheServer has a method called `getDisplayName()` which returns the displayName of the apache server. The field name follows the javabean syntax of naming. For example, if the object model contains a method called getDisplayName() and a method called setDisplayName(Strings), then the field is of type String and name displayName.

Note: For a method name getDDD(), the attribute name is DDD and not dDD. The fieldName entered here is case-sensitive.

For nested elements, consider the following code snippet in Example 7-9.

Example 7-9 Nested elements

```
<field>
  <nested fieldName="host"
    className="com.collation.platform.model.topology.sys.ComputerSys
tem">
    <plain fieldName="displayName" displayType="popup"/>
  </nested>
</field>
```

ApacheServer has an attribute called host, which is of a type ComputerSystem. This code snippet tells the details manage to do the following.

apacheServer.getHost().getDisplayName().

Every <nested> element *must* end up with leaf <plain> elements. Details manager shows only <plain> elements. If the field to show is three levels deep, then there must be three levels of <nested> elements that end in a <plain> element.

When defining a <nested> element, the className *must* be mentioned. This tells details manager, if it performs a getHost() on the Apache server, it should expect an instance of class ComputerSystem.

- displayType

  Notice the attribute displayType in <plain> fields. The various values that this field can use are defined in the screencontent.xsd file. This field indicates how the data should be shown, that is simple String, as a popup (only other model objects can be pop-ups), list of entries and so on.

- hidden type

  In certain cases, the in built table generators won't be sufficient. This usually happens when details manager has to execute custom queries to the database (it cannot retrieve all the data through the java object interface) or if the information to be shown is not in a straightforward object reference. In such cases, we define "custom" generators. The fields defined as "hidden" are not shown to the end user, but the field must be defined so that the details manager prefetches information from the database before starting to render the details panel.

Only the fields mentioned in these tabdata entries are retrieved from the database. Since this is driven by the object tree, in the absence of such a mechanism, there is a risk of retrieving data recursively, thereby sucking all the data from the database.

- Multiple-row tables

  In some cases, we want to show multiple rows of data. This is usually the case for array attributes. For array attributes, we might want to expand them to show certain fields in a table format, instead of showing them in a drop down list.

  Consider the Modules tab displayed in Example 7-10.

Example 7-10 Modules tab code

```
<tableContent name="ApacheServer.Modules" layout="table"
className="com.collation.platform.model.topology.app.web.apache.Apac
heServer">
  <field>
    <nested
      className="com.collation.platform.model.topology.app.web.apach
e.ApacheModule" fieldName="modules">
      <plain fieldName="name"/>
      <plain fieldName="fileName"/>
    </nested>
  </field>
</tableContent>
```

  This code snippet tells the details manager to do the following:

  - Create a table with multiple rows, based on the number of elements returned by the `getModules()` call.
  - For each module, do a `getName()` and a `getFileName()` and show them as columns.

Whenever you have an array attribute and if we want to show one or more attributes of the array elements in a table format, set the `layout="table"` attribute in the <tableContent>. Whenever you define such a <tableContent>, there must be at least one <nested> element which is of array type and that should contain one or more <plain> fields to be displayed.

Custom generators

In most cases, the prebuilt generators for property entries and tables can generate the tables. In some cases, where the default behavior is not useful, you can specify custom generators, as in Example 7-11.

Example 7-11 Custom generator

```
<tableContent name="ApacheServer.SSL"
className="com.collation.platform.model.topology.app.web.apache.Apac
heServer" layout="singleColumn"
generator="com.collation.proxy.clientproxy.common.detail.custom.apac
he.ApacheServerSSLPanelGenerator">
  <field>
    <nested fieldName="containers"
className="com.collation.platform.model.topology.app.web.apache.Apac
heWebContainer" flattenData="true">
      <nested fieldName="sslSettings"
className="com.collation.platform.model.topology.app.web.apache.Apac
heGlobalSSLSettings">
        <plain fieldName="connectRandomSeed"/>
        <plain fieldName="mutex"/>
        <plain fieldName="passPhraseDialog"/>
        <plain fieldName="sessionCache"/>
        <plain fieldName="startupRandomSeed"/>
      </nested>
    </nested>
  </field>
</tableContent>
```

In the code snippet here for the ApacheServer SSL table, the custom server generator ApacheServerSSLPanelGenerator will be invoked. All the custom generators are in the package proxy.clientproxy.common.detail.custom. Take a look at this package for various custom generators.

The <field> entry inside these custom generators must contain all the fields that the custom generators will access. If the fields are not present either here or as a <hidden> field in other tabs of the model object, the custom generator will not have access to the data at runtime. Details manager parses these XML files and only fetches the attributes mentioned in the <plain> fields before it passes the data to the runtime table generator. It is important to mention the fields in the XML file, even if it is a custom generator.

Attribute names

This section discusses coding for attribute names (Example 7-12).

Example 7-12 Attributes

```
<attribute name="displayName" displayName="Server Name"
className="com.collation.platform.model.topology.app.web.apache.Apac
heServer"/>
<attribute name="productName" displayName="Product Name"
className="com.collation.platform.model.topology.app.web.apache.Apac
heServer"/>
<attribute name="productVersion" displayName="Product Version"
className="com.collation.platform.model.topology.app.web.apache.Apac
heServer"/>
<attribute name="vendorName" displayName="Vendor Name"
className="com.collation.platform.model.topology.app.web.apache.Apac
heServer"/>
```

For each <plain> entry in the screencontent.xml, an entry must be present in the attributenames.xml file. In this file, we enter the user facing terms to the user for the attribute names.

For example, the "displayName" attribute in Apache server is resolved to "Server Name" and shown to the user in the GUI.

Unit tests

Any changes to these XML files must be carefully done. Since breaking these XML files can break the GUI functionality, before checking in any changes to any of the three XML files, run unit tests on these files.

In the gui/client directory, do the following:

```
ant jarLocal testAllXml
```

The testAllXml target makes sure the XML files are well formed, they are valid, that the entries in screenlayout.xml are in sync with screencontent.xml. In addition, it also validates the <nested> and <plain> fields against the object model to make sure they are in sync. Finally, it also ensures that for each entry in the screencontent.xml file, there exists an entry in the attributenames.xml file.

Run these unit tests without fail before checking in any of this code.

7.10 Frequently asked questions

The following sections addresses some of the most frequently asked questions regarding IBM Tivoli Change and Configuration Management Database Configuration Discovery and Tracking v1.1.

7.10.1 Is Configuration Discovery and Tracking a 32-bit or 64 bit application?

Configuration Discovery and Tracking is agnostic to this. Java byte code is bit-length agnostic. Only the 32- or 64 bit-ness of the JVM™, itself counts.

7.10.2 Is the Van Dyke Shell supported?

No, it is not supported in either IBM Tivoli Change and Configuration Management Database Configuration Discovery and Tracking v1.1.

If Vshell actually responded with Windows NT then all would have been well. The problem was that Vshell does not support command concatenation with "&&" like the Unix shells and cmd.exe do, so our attempt to run **uname** failed.

7.10.3 What is the unique signature of hosts?

Example 7-13 is from ${COLLATION_HOME}/sdk/doc.

Example 7-13 Component signatures

```
0="signature"
1="manufacturer,model,serialNumber" 2="systemBoardUUID"
3="primaryMACAddress"
4="hostSystem,VMID"
5="managedSystemName"
```

7.10.4 Is there an object in the data model with a Site attribute?

In other words, how do you run a query that returns all CIs that have a location = "100 Main Street NY"

Yes, there is a Admin data model object with a "site" attribute for the location info.

7.10.5 Is there a way to load scope without doing it with the GUI?

Yes, there is a utility for doing exactly that: loading scope in bulk from the command line. The script is called loadscope.jy and can be found in the ${COLLATION_HOME}/bin directory.

For more details, refer to B.3.2, "loadscope - the scope import utility" on page 369.

7.10.6 How do I use the API from the command line?

Refer to B.2, "The command line interface: api.sh" on page 340.

7.10.7 How do I know which classes the api.sh command supports?

They are all listed in the SDK doc, which can be found in ${COLLATION_HOME}/sdk/doc. Bring up the index.html file in a browser and view them.

The following is an example using api.sh to list all objects of type `DominoServer`:

```
./api.sh -u userid -p password find DominoServer > domino.xml
```

You can substitute one of the following classes below for the above example of Domino Server. The domino.xml entry above is just a filename to create to store the results in.

Other high-level objects classes are:

Oracle:	Oracle Server
WebSphere:	WebSphereCell, WebSphereServer, WebSphereNode
Windows:	WindowsComputerSystem
AIX:	AixUnitaryComputerSystem
Linux:	LinuxUnitaryComputerSystem
LDAP:	Service

7.10.8 Can I replicate the access credentials to another server?

Yes, this can be done by copying a couple of files from the source system to the target system, and updating the value for a parameter in the collation.properties file on the target system.

Copy the following files from the source system to similar locations on the target system, over-writing any files that already might exist on the target system:

- `${COLLATION_HOME}/etc/auth`
- `${COLLATION_HOME}/etc/userdata.xml file`

Update the value of the `com.collation.security.internal parameter` in the `${COLLATION_HOME}/etc/collation.propertirs file` on the target to the match the value found in the source system. This value is an encryption key generated at install time.

7.10.9 Does dependency mapping work for custom servers?

Yes, when you write a Custom Server Template, you are categorizing a running process. The **lsof** command that Configuration Discovery and Tracking runs also determines any connections to this process (or netstat on Windows). There is nothing special about how dependencies are determined for custom server processes.

7.10.10 Icon arrangement in the business applications map

Why are the databases' icons displayed on the left when it would seem as though they are already represented in the business application icons? The answer is our designers believe that databases are most likely shared between business applications, so it would be helpful to see that relationship on the main screen.

7.10.11 What if I am not allowed to run lsof?

Your can run `lsof` manually and save its output to a file, for example /tmp/lsoffile.

Change the values of the com.collation.discover.agent.command.lsof.<platform> line(s) in ${COLLATION_HOME}/etc/collation.properties file to `cat /tmp/lsoffile`, or whatever the real filename is.

Also, see the next question.

7.10.12 How can I manually capture dependencies ?

Wrap your **cat** command into a script, for example `/tmp/runlsof`. The contents of the script should be:

```
#!/bin/sh
cat /tmp/lsof.out
```

Then place this script in a directory, for example `/tmp`, and modify your property as follows:

```
com.collation.discover.agent.command.lsof.HP-UX=/tmp/runlsof
```

Make sure you rerun the **lsof** script periodically, for example every 10 minutes.

This should work. The reason a direct substitution of the **lsof** command is failing is because the code expects some arguments to the **lsof** command that are not accepted by the **cat** command.

Note: On Solaris, you want to put the lsof.out file in a directory other than /tmp, which is cleaned out during every reboot.

This assumes that your lsof.out file contains the output of the following command:

```
lsof -nP -i –C
```

7.10.13 Is sys group sufficient privilege on HP/UX 11.11 to run lsof?

On Hp/UX 11.0 it is sufficient; however on 11.11 it is not sufficient. You might have to setuid root on lsof for it to work.

The main page for **lsof** actually states that for Hp/UX 11.11 and 11.23, setuid is recommended.

The first and rarer permission is setuid-root. It comes into effect when **lsof** is executed. Its effective UID is then root, while its real (that of the logged-on user) UID is not. The **lsof** distribution recommends that versions for these dialects run setuid-root: HP-UX 11.11 and 11.23.

7.10.14 Must other ports besides the one for SSH be open for a Windows Gateway to function appropriately?

The Configuration Discovery and Tracking server needs port 135, used by the DCOM Service Control Manager, open so that it can determine if there is a Windows system there.

This is a result of the following parts of discovery:

- How can you determine if there is a computer system at a particular IP address?
- How can you determine what type of authentication should be used on that computer system?

The answers that Configuration Discovery and Tracking used are:

- Configuration Discovery and Tracking make TCP connections to selected ports. If any response (accept, connection refused) is returned, then Configuration Discovery and Tracking knows there is something there.
- Then Configuration Discovery and Tracking try port 22 and port 135 to make sure those ports are open. If 22 is open, Configuration Discovery and Tracking tries to connect to that port through mindterm and tries to determine the type of UNIX system. If it returns windows in the uname, then it is thought

to be Windows. If port 22 is not open, but port 135 is open, Configuration Discovery and Tracking attempts discovery as a Windows system.

- If port 22 is not open, and port 135 is not open, thenConfiguration Discovery and Tracking attempt SNMP discovery.

7.10.15 How do I manually test access to WebLogic?

To test WebLogic access, in a browser window type: `ipaddress:port/console`. If you see a WebLogic screen, then it worked.

This is often necessary when the WebLogic Sensor did not discover an instance of WebLogic and you needed to test whether it is running and is accessible from your location.

7.10.16 How do I check if all necessary files have been deployed to a Windows Gateway?

The list of Gateway Server Required Files is:

- Win32_Confignia.mof
- Win32_Confignia.dll
- aports.dll
- ConfigniaLog.dll
- msvcr71.dll
- InstallProvider.js
- InstallProvider.wsf
- InstallProvider.bat

If the files are on the Configuration Discovery and Tracking Server, then check on the gateway under c:\windows\temp\Confignia®.xxx, in particular, Confignia.38163108.

Another good thing to try next is to remove all the temp\Confignia.xxx directories on the gateway, start a new discovery on the gateway. then examine the discovery results, logs, and the newly created Confignia.xxx directory.

7.10.17 What is the default SSL passphrase for WebSphere Application Server?

The default passphrase for WebSphere Application Server is `WebAS`.

> **Note:** You can use 5.0 setting in collation.properties for WebSphere jars even if the customer is using 5.1

7.10.18 Correcting too many time-outs during discovery for DB2 databases

One method is to decrease the threadcount (to have less discovery processes running at the same time) and increase the timeouts.

For example, change the following parameters in ${COLLATION_HOME}/etc/collation.properties:

```
com.collation.SshSessionCommandTimeout=120000
com.collation.discover.DefaultAgentTimeout=600000
com.collation.discover.dwcount=4
```

7.10.19 Do Anchors or Gateways initiate a callback to the Server?

SSH connections from Configuration Discovery and Tracking Server to an Anchor Host are only initiated from the Configuration Discovery and Tracking Server and never from the Anchor Host back to the Configuration Discovery and Tracking Server.

7.10.20 Granularity of dormancy analysis

The granularity is at the Managed Object level. Having said that, it really depends on the sensor granularity. In the situation of the WebSphere Application Server server, the sensor brings in all the JVM information at the same time, so do not expect to see dormancy for one and not the other unless the object does not exist any more.

Regarding installed Software Packages, Configuration Discovery and Tracking replaces the list. So yes, if it does not exist anymore, it will be replaced with the new list (blob object).

7.10.21 Cannot remotely connect to the server

Check that the Configuration Discovery and Tracking Server that in the /etc/hosts file (or equivalent) that local host and host name are not the same.

If you cannot change the host file, then edit collation.properties.

```
com.collation.rmi.server.hostname = default
```

Change this value to the actual IP address or host name and then restart the server.

7.10.22 Unavailable DNS server hosts with IP addresses and no host names

Edit the /etc/hosts file on the computer on which Configuration Discovery and Tracking Server is running. Add the IP address/host name pairs for the hosts that are discovered by just IP address and rerun discovery.

Be certain the local /etc/nsswitch.conf file on the Configuration Discovery and Tracking Server has both files and DNS files entries.

7.10.23 Verify the Linux version

This information is located at:

- `/etc/redhat-release` (RedHat)
- `/etc/SuSE-release` (SUSE)

7.10.24 Discovery runs slowly

If DNS is not set, discovery can be slowed down. A workaround is to start the named service, the DNS daemon, on the Configuration Discovery and Tracking Server. Then make sure that the Configuration Discovery and Tracking server is pointed to itself for name resolution in the `/etc/resolv.conf` file.

7.10.25 Lots of sensor timeouts in log file

Increase the timeouts in ${COLLATION_HOME}/etc/collation.properties file.

The default timeout for all sensors is 60,000 milliseconds. which equals one minute.

7.10.26 Are you getting an lsof failure in the log?

Check the following:

1. SSH to that host.
2. Run the **`lsof -nP`** command.

   if this returns nothing you have a problem. Use these workarounds:

   - Check permissions on lsof and make sure it is executable.
   - Try sudo. This must be enabled without a password. See the sudoers file.

     i. `vi sudo` (a script file). Enter:

        ```
        coll (use your collation account UID) ALL-NOPASSWD
        ```

```
NOPASSWD=/usr/sbin/lsof (your path may be different)
```

ii. Run **sudo lsof -nP -i** (on Linux).

If this works:

iii. Add an entry to collation.properties for this specific host(s) with a sudo lsof (it will be clear in the file), and restart server

iv. collation account must be part of sys group

```
setuid root on lsof (but a lot of customers won't enable this)
```

7.10.27 Product Console disappears and does not come back

Check your home directory for a file(s) hs_error*. If you see this error, it means that your JVM crashed.

7.10.28 Weird GUI behavior such as show details does nothing

Java cache is confused. Clear the Web start cache and restart the Product Console.

7.10.29 Configuration Discovery and Tracking Server will not start

Make sure that IPv6 is not running. Currently, IBM Tivoli Change and Configuration Management Database Configuration Discovery and Tracking v1.1 is incompatible with IPv6.

Here is a workaround if IPv6 is running:

- Add "alias net-pf-10 off" to `/etc/modules.conf` and then reboot.

7.10.30 Need to know what encryption is used

BlowFish and, optionally, DES. Credentials are encrypted on both the wire and disk using the following encryption methods: md5 hash, single DES, cbc mode, pkcs5padding.

Client can also use SSL to connect to the Configuration Discovery and Tracking Server.

7.10.31 Configuration Discovery and Tracking language

The language used to write Configuration Discovery and Tracking language is almost 100% Java with some VB script for Windows and some JavaScript and Jython scripting. There is no C++.

7.10.32 LSOF issues

The lsof program is usually found in either of two directories:

- /usr/sbin/lsof
- /usr/local/bin/lsof

Tuning lsof as the given user must enable you to view processes belonging to other users.

Collation Service Account must be in the sys group on Solaris, AIX and HP. If your system administrators do not allow this, you can use one of the three alternative methods listed here to assign the proper authorities to the Collation Service Account:

- Collation service account has sudo (or equivalent) access to lsof. You must change collation.properties.

  ```
  com.collation.discover.agent.command.lsof.Linux=sudo lsof
  ```

- Run the **cron** script and dump to a file (on a schedule). See the prior tip.
- Run setuid lsof: This is the least desirable because patches can reset this and some versions of lsof will reset effective uid upon execution.

7.10.33 Migrate the database on Oracle to a new instance

To migrate the database, follow these steps:

1. Shutdown Configuration Discovery and Tracking.
2. DBA's copy our schema and user name/password to the new Oracle instance.
3. Update our JDBC connection strings in ${COLLATION_HOME}/etc/collation.properties. The two lines that must be updated are:
   - "com.collation.db.url="
   - "com.collation.db.archive.url=".
4. It will probably be obvious to your DBAs what to change on these two lines (the server name, port, and Oracle SID).
5. Start Configuration Discovery and Tracking.

7.10.34 How to test WMI access

To test WMI on a Windows Gateway, perform the following steps:

1. Log in to the Windows 2003 Server Gateway system.
2. Go to the %SystemRoot%system32 directory.
3. Execute the following command:

   ```
   cscript prnjobs.vbs -l -s <remote_host>
   ```

   Replace <remote_host> with one you want to access with WMI. The output should be similar to:

   ```
   C;\Windows\system32>cscript prnjobs.bs -l -s localhost
   Microsoft Windows Script Host Version 5.6
   Copyright.....

   Number of print jobs enumerated 0
   ```

4. Execute the `wmimgmt.msc` program to ensure that the Windows Gateway account is a member of the administrator's group on the host or hosts to be discovered'
   - Use the WMI control to add all access for the administrator group for the CIMV2 and DEFAULT namespaces.

For more details on debugging WMI, refer to Appendix F, "Solving WMI Access Denied errors" on page 437.

7.10.35 Extract and reuse templates and the namespace

To extract and reuse Custom Server Templates, use the API export and import functions. The **api** command is located in ${COLLATION_HOME}/sdk/bin.

The necessary steps are:

1. Find the Guid of the template to be exported:

   ```
   api.sh -u administrator -p collation find --depth=0 "Select name
   from <template_type> where displayName =='<your_template_name>'"
   ```

   <template_type> can be one of:

Template	specifies Custom Server Templates
ApplicationTemplate	specifies Application Templates
ComputerSystemTemplate	specifies Computer System Templates

   In the resulting xml file, identify the Guid of the template you want to export.

2. Export the template to an xml file

```
api.sh -u administrator -p collation find --depth=-1 "Select * from
<template_type> where guid =='<your_template_guid>'" >
<your_xml_file_directory>
```

3. To import, use the **api** import function to import the previously exported xml files:

```
api.sh -u administrator -p collation import
[ <your_xml_file_directory> | <your_xml_file_name> ]
```

7.10.36 How to test SSH

A script designed to verify SSH connections, named testssh.py. is located in ${COLLATION_HOME}/support/bin.

```
testssh <ip> <command>
```

For more details, see B.4.9, "testssh.py" on page 384

7.10.37 Set up LDAP for Configuration Discovery and Tracking?

Here is a short summary of our LDAP support follows:

- IBM Tivoli Change and Configuration Management Database Configuration Discovery and Tracking v1.1 support both anonymous authentication as well as password-based authentication with an external LDAP server.
- The LDAP Server host name, port, base DN and bind DN and password (required for password-based authentication) are configurable in collation.properties. Also configurable is the specific naming attribute that can be searched for to match the UID, as in Example 7-14.

Example 7-14 LDAP parameters in collation.properties

```
#==============================
# LDAP Authentication
#==============================
com.collation.security.auth.ldapAuthenticationEnabled=false
com.collation.security.auth.ldapHostName=ldap.eng.collation.net
com.collation.security.auth.ldapPortNumber=389
com.collation.security.auth.ldapBaseDN=ou=People,dc=Collation,dc=net
#Properties for Simple Authentication
#com.collation.security.auth.ldapBindDN=uid=ruser,dc=Collation,dc=net
#com.collation.security.auth.ldapBindPassword=XXXX
# ldap naming attribute for username for treesearch
```

```
com.collation.security.auth.ldapUIDNamingAttribute=uid
```

- If LDAP authentication is enabled, then Configuration Discovery and Tracking bypasses the internal authentication for all external users except administrator, who is always authenticated locally.
- Internal users (users internal to our subsystems) are authenticated locally as well.
- Users that will be authenticated using an external LDAP server will still need to be created locally for authorization purposes and other Configuration Discovery and Tracking specific configurations such as Client session timeouts and association with Roles and Access Collections.
- Administrator password and internal user passwords are hashed when stored locally (md5 hash).
- LDAP configuration is recommended in ECMDB and Domain setups as user passwords on ECMDB and Domain match with no special work should ECMDB not be reachable from a Domain during an authentication.

7.10.38 Are multiple active sessions allowed?

IBM Tivoli Change and Configuration Management Database Configuration Discovery and Tracking v1.1 currently allow any number of users to login using the same user ID and password.

7.10.39 Users automatically logged out after x minutes of inactivity

Configuration Discovery and Tracking supports this function. The timeout can be specified on a per user basis when the user is created.

7.10.40 Password rules

Many monitoring programs enforce a minimum six-character, mixed-case, alphanumeric password. These passwords must have at least one numeric and one alpha of each case (upper and lower) in the password (fixed by LDAP).

IBM Tivoli Change and Configuration Management Database Configuration Discovery and Tracking v1.1 do not enforce any password length or composition requirements, however, this can be enforced by an LDAP implementation.

7.10.41 Are password record or playback techniques used?

IBM Tivoli Change and Configuration Management Database Configuration Discovery and Tracking v1.1 does not use password playback.

7.10.42 Can you force Password change on Initial Login?

IBM Tivoli Change and Configuration Management Database Configuration Discovery and Tracking v1.1 do not currently have this capability.

7.10.43 Can you force Password change at set interval?

IBM Tivoli Change and Configuration Management Database Configuration Discovery and Tracking v1.1 does not currently have this capability

7.10.44 Can you disable password after three failed logon attempts?

IBM Tivoli Change and Configuration Management Database Configuration Discovery and Tracking v1.1 does not currently have this capability.

7.10.45 Can you disable a password after a set interval of inactivity?

IBM Tivoli Change and Configuration Management Database Configuration Discovery and Tracking v1.1 doe not currently have this capability.

7.10.46 Can you log all login attempts and retain for a defined time period?

IBM Tivoli Change and Configuration Management Database Configuration Discovery and Tracking v1.1 does this today.

7.10.47 Are passwords transmitted in clear between the user interface and server ?

IBM Tivoli Change and Configuration Management Database Configuration Discovery and Tracking v1.1 support the ability to use SSL or non-SSL. If SSL is chosen, then Configuration Discovery and Tracking will encrypt to the level required. Currently, there is no way to enforce SSL logins only. In other words, Configuration Discovery and Tracking have SSL capabilities, but users are not forced to use it.

7.10.48 Are passwords are not stored in clear on the server?

IBM Tivoli Change and Configuration Management Database Configuration Discovery and Tracking v1.1 encrypt all passwords and credential information: md5 hash, single DES, cbc mode, pkcs5padding.

7.10.49 Integration with Netegrity for Single Sign-On

IBM Tivoli Change and Configuration Management Database Configuration Discovery and Tracking v1.1 supports LDAP authentication for single sign-on. If Netegrity supports that, we will work to make it available.

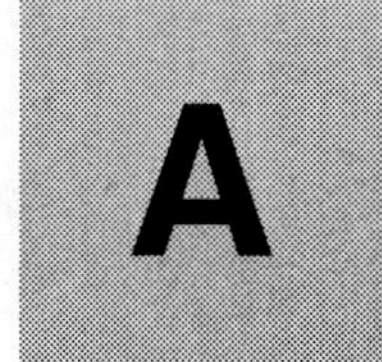

Agent-based versus agentless application Discovery

How you measure matters; measurement is meaning. In the world of quantum mechanics, the physicist Walter Heisenberg, said that all *measurement is meaning*[1], implying that the process of how you measure a quantity cannot be separated from the result. This insight into the workings of our physical world is applicable to the virtual world of information technology (IT), specifically to automated application discovery. There are multiple ways to measure (agent versus agentless). Which method you select and how it performs its measurement influences the result returned. The requirements for your business activity should guide you as to which is optimal for your needs.

This appendix clarifies the values and costs inherent in the two competing approaches for automated discovery:

- The traditional autonomous agent deployed to each host
- The newer, so-called agentless approach

From this discussion, you should be better able to make an educated choice as to which approach is better for your needs.

[1] 1 Quantum Mechanics, 1925-1927: The Uncertainty Relations by Walter Heisenberg 2

While both approaches have their values and their costs, it is proposed that the agentless approach offers the more appropriate methodology, at the least cost for automated discovery of application topology and configuration data and thus, is the better choice for this task.

A.1 Accelerators: The Rate of Change for Applications in the Enterprise

While the network management world is fairly mature in its procedures and its established methods of discovery and monitoring are almost universally accepted, the application management world is far less mature and its methodologies differ widely between vendors and across users.

In addition to variance in methodologies, in many industries the intricacies of applications themselves change regularly at a seemingly accelerating rate. You might ask why they change so frequently? The answer lies in the definition of what applications are and how they differ from networks.

According to the online computer dictionary, Webopedia, an *application* is defined as: *A program or group of programs designed for end users.*

`http://www.webopedia.com`

You can add to that definition a further refinement stating that applications are really designed for a business in order to provide a service for end users.

Applications are specifically aligned to the business needs of a firm and thus as the needs and requirements of both the business and end users are better understood or evolve, in accordance the applications themselves must change. It is almost like an evolutionary approach for applications. This is especially true in firms where technology is the essential enabler of their key differentiators. Typically, this differentiator is an application of technology to deliver a unique service enabling the firm to offer greater value than their competition. Using technology in this way is often referred to as the "bet your business model". This model can almost mimic a natural selection process - if the application does not adapt to changing customer needs, extinction (going out of business) is next. Today, this effect is seen most frequently in the financial services industry, where application innovation is often the delivery vehicle of key competitive advantage and the harbinger of longevity.

A.1.1 Effect of the Regulatory Industry on Compliance

The recent rise of the compliance[2] and regulatory industry and the rather adverse penalties for noncompliance (jail time) that accompany it, have caused most businesses to initiate an internal review of their application inventory more comprehensive than anything other than perhaps the year 2000 effort. While that turned out to be somewhat of a nonevent, compliance is here, real, and must be ascertained. The alternatives are not attractive.

However, compliance is really nothing new to the trading industry with its tight relationship with the Securities and Exchange Commission (SEC). Applications such as SIAC's DisplayBook application that specialty traders use on the New York Stock Exchange can change intra-day based on SEC requirements.

DisplayBook reduces the time a specialist requires to complete a trade. For further details see these Web sites:

`http://www.siac.com/corporate_overview/highlights.html`

This puts a tremendous strain on the process of moving applications from development, to Quality Assurance, to production. Not obvious, but just as important is the strain it puts on operations and their need to know what applications are deployed, where they are deployed, their topologies and dependencies. Of course, this leads to a similar strain on the vendors of tools which can auto discover this vital information. As a result, a difficult problem to begin with becomes exacerbated by a high rate of change, resulting in a spiraling process where the same problem-type must be solved over and over again. Another example of this same effect is the public insurance industry which due to its regulation by each of the 50 states in the USA, is said to have fifty masters. As a result, these firms release a new version of their applications every six to eight weeks.

The first need in preparation for compliance is to know what you have. Next , how it is configured, including who has access to it. And finally, on what is it dependent?. Tools that automate the acquisition of this information are necessary to manage the effect compliance has on the IT infrastructure of a business.

[2] Examples of externally imposed compliancy include: HIPPA, GLBA, SOX and many others

A.2 Agents as a means of application data acquisition

In this section, we examine why use agents in the first place?

A.2.1 In the beginning there were agents and they were good

The traditional methodology for NSM (network and systems management) instrumentation has been the ubiquitous *agent*. While the dictionary definition of agent has many variations, there are several that are very interesting:

- *A spy* or *one that acts or has the power or authority to act*. See the dictionary.com Web site for further information.

  `http://dictionary.reference.com/search?q=agent`

- The computer dictionary, Webopedia has a more industry-relevant definition:

  A program that performs some information gathering or processing task in the background. Typically, an agent is given a very small and well-defined task.

  `http://www.webopedia.com/TERM/a/agent.html`

The definition of agent as spy is very relevant here as this is essentially what it does; an agent spies on the host on which it is installed and the applications running there. As a spy with a specific mission, using the dictionary definition of it having a small and well defined task, this agent is aware of activity on its host, but rarely is it aware of the big picture of how this host relates to others in kind.

The analyst firm Gartner[3] says that *all agent architecture require some form of a high-level manager* to provide command and control; however, agents vary in how independent the agent is from the manager. *The agent/manager paradigm is the traditional management architecture.*

A.2.2 The Agent: Automation in response to a rise in complexity

In the earlier days of computing when mainframes ruled the world (at least the IT part of it) the controversy and pertinent differences between an agent versus an agentless approach to discovery were nonexistent. Why was this so? At that time, everything was self-contained in a large single host, the mainframe. While it is true that mainframes could be linked together into a lose affiliation of cross-domain clusters, this was rarely done.

But, the advent of Client Server[4] changed everything...

---

[3] Agentless NSM Technology: Panacea or Problem by Gartner

[4] Webopedia (`http://www.webopedia.com`): A network architecture in which each computer or process on the network is either a client or a server.

A.2.3 The financial imperative towards distribution

There was now a financial imperative forcing distribution of application functionality out across smaller computing platforms. "Put the processing out where the user is" became the mantra.

The price of these smaller computing platforms enabling Client/Server architectures was below the budget radar and could be purchased at the department level. This enabled a proliferation of hosts in a somewhat uncontrollable manner resulting in a very surprising result - lack of clarity as to what was deployed, what was installed on it and what it depended on. It was not unusual for vendors at this period in time to ask a user, "how many servers do you have and where are they located", only to receive a "sheep-ish" smile and a quiet, "I think I have *n* servers installed in North America, but wait a minute that is not counting... and the recent changes...well, I hate to admit it, I am not really sure."

However, the cost of managing these distributed platforms was not widely considered at the time of their implementation. Thus, it was the big surprise at its end that it cost so much to monitor this environment that it might have actually outweighed the cost benefit of the smaller computing platforms.

The approach initiated to monitor distributed applications led to the advent of the agent[5]. In the beginning, agents were not especially flexible; however, today this has evolved such that the agents themselves are specialized, remotely configurable and can even contain their own knowledge databases of information about specific devices and applications.

However, the approach of the agent is an outside one looking in, where the agent observes the activity on a host and uses this to infer what is really going on based on its knowledge base and then report this back to the central server. Agents can store information when there is a network discontinuity and then forward this to the server when connectivity is resumed.

Agents might also take action when a problem occurs. Although much touted by vendors of these agents, this capability is rarely utilized in a production environment as few businesses are willing to trust this capability to an autonomous process as the potential exists for cause of even greater problems.

In their first incarnation, these agents were used to monitor availability and performance. Today there is renewed focus, due to the pressures of compliancy, on discovering what it is deployed, how it is configured and on what it is dependent.

---

[5] In this paper, we are not referring to the SNMP agent, due to its limited adoption for application usage. This is, of course, contrary to its overwhelming success in the network world.

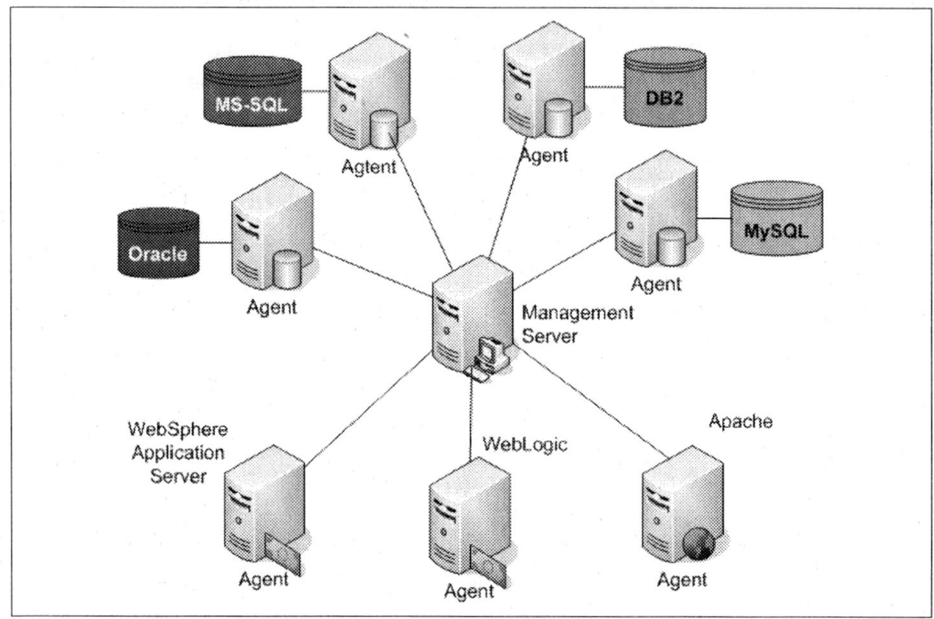

Figure A-1 Typical agent architecture with a hub-spoke layout

A.3 The impact of n-Tier architectures

n-Tier[6] architectures are typically three tier architectures with the tiers corresponding to:

Presentation/Access	Through Web servers
Business Logic	Through application servers
Data	Through relational databases

The complexity of the n-Tier environment is high for three reasons:

1. A rapidly increasing mixture of components or moving parts
2. An unregulated and ever growing user base
3. Decreasing times between releases of ever more sophisticated applications

The complexity of n-Tier architectures transcends the technical and crosses into the organizational and political as each tier is typically "owned" and managed by different units within the corporation. This results in separate technical management architectures for each tier and a decided lack of clarity as to the

[6] Webopedia - N-tier *application architecture* provides a model for developers to create a flexible and reusable application. By breaking up an application into tiers, developers only have to modify or add a specific layer, rather than have to rewrite the entire application over, if they decide to change technologies or scale up.

topology across tiers and across the different business applications these tiers underlie.

The complexity of the application now dramatically increases as the number of moving parts has increased. This architecture makes it very difficult for an agent (or multiple agents) to acquire a clear view as to how all the "parts" fit together. We end up with a specialist view, with separate agents for the Web servers, application servers, databases and the applications that rely on them. Unfortunately, as a result of mirroring the organizational structure of the business, we end up with stovepipe management architecture with a decidedly less than clear understanding of the topology.

A.4 Using an agent for application discovery

Using agents for discovery of application topology has some strong positives as well negatives. The advantages of using agent-based discovery are described in Table A-1.

Table A-1 Advantages of agent-based discovery

	Advantages of agent-based discovery
Real-time Monitoring	Agents are the tool closest to the application (or other monitored object) and thus can provide a continuous stream of information about it and therefore are the only choice if the requirement is real-time topology discovery.
Low Net Utilization	Agents also do not require direction and can run semi-autonomously thus maintaining low network utilization.
High-Availability	In addition, Agents can run while the management server is down and forward their results when it is up - thus surviving an outage.
Maturity	Sophistication as technology available for over 20 years. Agent architectures can be sophisticated with Master Agents providing shared services across registered Subagents and specialized Subagents that are easier to develop and modify.
Depth of Data Retrieved	Agents can retrieve a considerable amount of data about an application.
Optimized log file reading	A local agent, since it is always present, can have the OS wake it up when a new event is written to a log file.
WANs	Across a WAN a local agent with local intelligence might be more effective avoiding the problem of network latency, than an agentless connection that spans the WAN and perhaps performs more slowly.

Table A-2 lists the disadvantages of using agent-based discovery technology.

Table A-2 Disadvantages of Agent-based Discovery

	Disadvantages of Agent-based Discovery
Resource Depletion	A local agent uses up valuable resources on a host, such as Memory, CPU, Disk and network bandwidth. Its constant presence might adversely effect the operation of the host.
High Total Cost of Ownership	Higher than agentless systems. Acquisition costs of agent-based management systems are generally higher, and regardless of their design, agents are pieces of software that must be purchased, installed and maintained on each managed system, resulting in higher operational expenses. Greater implementation times for these systems also results in a longer time-to-value than for agentless systems[a].
Incompatibilities between agents	Since agents are application or host specific, it is often necessary to deploy multiple agents to the same host. Introducing a new one on a host with others can be disruptive as it is unlikely that your particular combination of agents has been tested to ensure against compatibility issues.
Need for Software Distribution Service	Local agents must be deployed to multiple hosts and then re-deployed when new versions are available. This requires a software distribution program and accommodation of its need for resources and management.
Requirement for Patching Process	Local agents need to be repeatedly patched and this requires a patch management process and accommodation of its need for resources and management.
Reliability Questions	Agents require their own monitoring to ensure that they are running or one can't tell the difference between no response from an agent because there is nothing to learn or no response because the agent is malfunctioning.
2-way TCP connectivity might be problematic	To accept command. & control from the console, agents needs a 2-way connection. That means the agents have to deal with DHCP and changing IP address, multi-homed hosts and firewall rules which conspiring together might make this difficult to accomplish.
Political Bombshell[b]	Asking management for yet another agent can be problematic as historically agents might have caused problems and executives have long memories.

a. EMA, May 2003

b. The CMDB Landscape: Market Directions, Vendor Solutions and IT Deployments A Research Report Prepared by EMA June 2005

A.4.1 Additional issues to consider when using an agent

In addition to the advantages and disadvantages of using agent-based discovery technology that are listed in Table A-1 and Table A-2, you should consider the following.

Making more work for yourself

Agent sophistication comes at a price. The agent, the ultimate (at the time of its inception) tool of management, itself became yet another object to be managed and monitored. There is no roll-off in cost as you grow—the more hosts you have the more agents you will need. Most often the discussion on agents or agentless focuses on resource utilization and while that can be an issue (see below); the real issue is total cost of ownership. It simply costs more, over the lifetime of an application, to manage through agents as opposed to using the agentless approach. The following paragraphs below will explore these issues.

Resource utilization

While the original goal of agents and the dictionary definition of a "small, but well defined process; their rise in sophistication eventually led to the dreaded condition of "bloat." Maturity in the software industry often leads to more and more features being added to a product to meet the requirements of long-standing customers and to close a large sales deal. This always leads to larger and larger program sizes (hence bloat) to accommodate these new features which many times have questionable value to the mass market for this product.

A larger program eventually leads to a rise in consumption of memory, disk and CPU which are the staples of a host, which when overly used results in degradation to all applications that this host provides. Coupled with the hidden dependencies other applications on other hosts have with this host can result in a cascading degradation.

This is an example of the uncertainty principle (as mentioned earlier: measurement is (or imparts) meaning)—every act of measurement impacts the thing being measured or the medical maxim "do no harm." But, agents can do harm. This can happen as a result of insufficient compatibility testing. It is very difficult to test the all the permutations of agents and applications and avoid unplanned, incompatible interactions between agents and new programs running on the same host.

Deployment

Agents are typically distributed to the hosts they are monitoring. This means that a software distribution program must be utilized to transfer the agents and their configuration files to these remote hosts. In many organizations such as a financial trading floor, this could be thousands of destinations.

Unfortunately, it is virtually impossible to ensure that all destinations receive the agents. In a large network with thousands of hosts, it is almost certain that at any one time, some hosts are down, others are not accessible through the network and as a result a one-shot deployment of the agents to all destinations will never happen. This means that distribution will have to be iterative and there will be a period of time where the environment is inconsistent (some hosts have agents and others do not (or some have different versions)—hardly a move in the direction of compliance.

Version updates

Unfortunately, the deployment process is not a one time event. Agents require updating as the sources they monitor change. In business, in order to stay competitive, applications change frequently and thus the intelligence of the agent requires retooling.

As agents are updated by their vendors, new versions must be deployed into your environment[7]. These new versions must also first be deployed to a lab and after passing certification tests, be deployed to production. Unfortunately, again all permutations cannot be tested in advance and often there is a harmful interaction between a new version of an agent and an application. Then, all the agents need to be removed and rolled back to the prior version.

Patch Updates

As problems are reported with a new release of an agent, patches are issued which must be tested and then deployed to the agents. The same problems with version updates can occur often again leaving behind an inconsistent environment.

Security

Many agents require root access in order to perform their activities. In recent years this has lessened; however, in some environments there can still be a requirement to grant the agent root access.

Who watches the watcher?

It is difficult to discriminate between the situation where there aren't any problems and one where there are problems, but the agent is malfunctioning and as a result, is not reporting any problems.

To protect against this condition, one must implement watchdog agents[8]. These are agents that watch the other agents. Unfortunately, this is a process without

[7] Vendors often require their clients to upgrade after a certain amount of time, by deprecating support for their agents, in order to lower their support costs by decreasing the number of product versions they must support.

[8] This problem has been attempted to be solved with the addition of a keep-alive protocol, which can fail, keeping alive the dead and purporting the alive to be otherwise.

end as eventually, as one scales, watchdogs will be needed for the watchdogs ad infinitum.

MSPs

The typical MSP (Management Service Provider) manages their customer's remote data centers through the Web and many not have the authority to place agents on their customer's hosts.

Web Services

In a Web Services environment, shared by dynamic trading partners, agents will not be a viable management option. It is unlikely that business partners will have the rights to place agents on the infrastructure underlying their partner's services.

Result: A Stovepipe view

Agents often present a silo or stovepipe view with a very deep vertical view of an application, but not the horizontal big picture with its relationships to other applications.

A.5 Agentless Discovery

The rise of Web Applications and eCommerce led to the need for an agentless approach to application management. These applications were often outsourced to Application Service Providers (ASPs). In order to ensure "quality of service" to their customers, Service Level Agreements (SLAs) were instituted to specify required performance levels for items such as end-to-end transaction rate. The instrumentation for measuring transaction rate was something called a synthetic transaction which emulates a user by attempting to remotely log onto a Web page and execute a Web transaction. Users of these systems were by definition customers and not employees of the seller. Therefore, an agent sitting on the seller's Web Servers could not effectively emulate this type of user. Thus, the need arose for executing these transactions from outside the firewall, thereby simulating access from a remote location and emulating more closely the real user. This was the beginning of the agentless approach.

As the complexity of eCommerce increased and its adoption of n-Tier as its preferred architecture became widespread, the need for discovery of application topology increased beyond the capabilities of current management architectures.

The analyst firm Gartner[9] says that, "An agentless solution is a polling engine that collects data through remote calls to a server or device, but it never installs software on them".

[9] Agentless NSM Technology: Panacea or Problem

The new architectures did initiate a change which was the new focus on "managing what matters". This was the result of the initiatives to better align IT and the business so that the key performance indicators for each would be focused on the same goal. Agents, as used prior to this change, were focused on acquiring a great deal of information, but in almost a one-to-one manner on a very specific resource. As IT attempted to implement the concept of managing what matters, they began to use the agentless approach as a way of monitoring an entire business service and later as a way of discovering the topology of that service. One could say that it is impossible to measure the user's viewpoint on quality of service by utilizing a measuring tool (agent) on the same host that is providing the service. This method is trapped by the uncertainty principle mentioned earlier and doomed to produce results that are skewed by its method of measurement. By its very nature, the agentless approach is better suited for measuring the quality of a business service and producing a measurement that is in accord with user experience.

In a similar manner, this is the better tool for "taking a step back" and capturing the topology of the entire business service. In that manner the tool being used (agentless) is able to capture the whole application as a member of the whole business service and not just the part residing on a specific host. This produces in-context data which is less expensive to process and utilize as it directly addresses the same business goal IT is required to solve: "what infrastructure underlies e.g. the Funds Transfer application." In-context data is directly usable for analytics and does not require costly processing using rules to piece it together into a whole - a daunting task. Importantly, this agentless approach is capable of producing in-context data or intelligence instead of just mere data.

Table A-3 illustrates the Gartner Group's view on agent versus agentless approaches[10]. Their report was written in 2002 and was reflective of the relative immaturity at that time of the agentless approach. In 2002 it was used mostly for remote Web transactions.

Table A-3 Relative Strengths of Agent-based versus agentless architectures

Feature	Agent	Agentless
Cost		X
Maintenance		X
Deployment Speed		X
Depth of Function	X	
Network Load	X	
Local Server Load		X

[10] Agentless NSM Technology: Panacea or Problem? 11/15/2002

Feature	Agent	Agentless
Continuous Operations	X	X
Command and Control	X	

The Gartner report was focused on evaluating methodologies for fault monitoring and thus their conclusions were based on those requirements and not those of application discovery. See Table A-4 and Table A-5.

Table A-4 Advantages of so-called agentless discovery

	Advantages of So-called Agentless Discovery
Less impact on your infrastructure	In terms of the usage of your host's memory, disk & CPU resources
Non-intrusive	No compatibility problems with agents already deployed on a discovered host
Less expensive	Low maintenance -little requirement for time spent in planning how this will be managed, execution of your plan and impact on your staff
Lean	No need for Software Distribution and Distributed Patching
Self-contained	No need for agents to monitor agents
An end-to-end view of the discovered application	Produced by emulating a user

Table A-5 Disadvantages of Agentless Discovery

	Disadvantages of Agentless Discovery
Limited functionality	Historically, limited to Web Transactions (but, no longer).
Limited in scope	Historically, light in depth of functionality (but, no longer).
Not real-time	Due to its centrally initiated nature, automatic real-time discovery is not available.
Can have an impact on network utilization	When used at a high frequency.
Not autonomous	Does not provide a highly available service. Technology fails if network is down.
More network Traffic	Theoretically, this approach could cause more network traffic than agents.

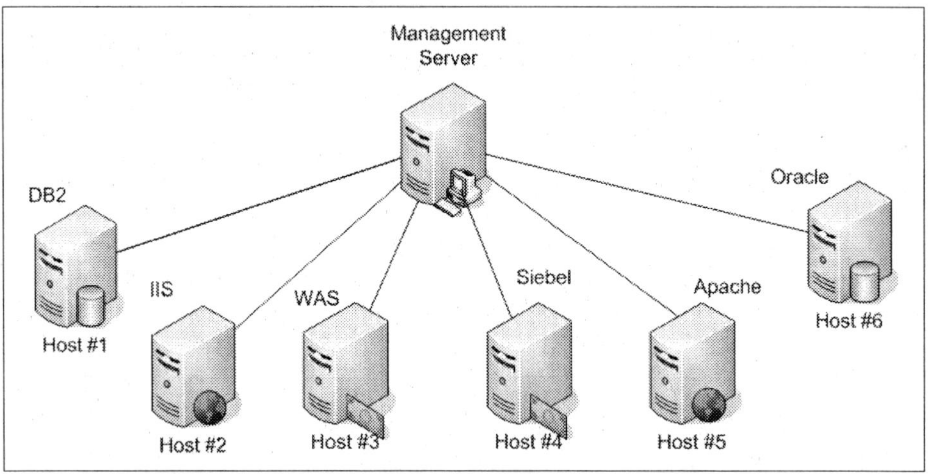

Figure A-2 Example of Discovery through an agentless approach

A.6 A variation: Network appliances for agentless discovery

In recent times a new approach to agentless monitoring has been the re-purposing of network appliances used for traffic management and layer seven content-based routing as tools for discovering application topology.

Typically, these devices sit on a spanned port on a switch and thus are able to passively observe all traffic that the switch sees. Of course, in order to see all traffic in the enterprise many appliances must be deployed each on a different switch after an analysis is done as to the minimum set of switches necessary to see all production traffic. In addition, these appliances must share a repository in order to aggregate their disparate data.

From their position on a switch these appliances are able to dynamically observe connections between applications and assuming both ends of the connection are visible to this switch; the appliance can construct a representation of an application topology.

The advantage of this approach is that a network appliance does not require software to be installed thus delivering a low TCO. *TCO* is defined as total cost of ownership over the lifetime of an application including: purchase price, upgrade costs, maintenance, support and training. However, there are also some built-in limitations to this method. Most importantly, from its position on the switch the appliance can see application topology; however, it has no way of knowing what the applications are. All it knows is that an application on port *n* residing on a host with an IP address of *x*, has a connection to an application on port *o*, residing on a host with an IP address of *y*. This is not especially helpful as it does nothing to further align the goals of IT with the business.

To get around this limitation the appliance vendors added a feature called "deep packet inspection" in order to look into the data being sent and try to find something identifying the host and the application name. This is a viable approach if the customer is not using encryption; however, in many industries businesses use encryption both in front of and behind the firewall. Financial Services is one industry that is very strict about maintaining encryption even within the bounds of the corporation and behind the firewall. With encryption turned on, the network appliance is back to discovering connections with no visibility as to what is connecting. With the recent upsurge in requirements for compliance, security and protecting the privacy of customers, depending on encryption being turned off might end up being a dead-end approach.

To surmount this drawback, the network discovery appliance vendors offer agents as an option. The agents do enable them to identify hosts and applications; however, at a cost to the customer in line with the traditional agent vendors. Customers of the network discovery appliances will now have to deploy agents, update them, patch them and monitor them. This alternative the network discovery appliance vendors are being forced to offer effectively withers away any advantages in low TCO they initially might have had.

A.7 A new approach: A hybrid called the sensor

The sensor is a new variation on the agentless methodology that achieves the depth of the local agent's discovery without incurring its cost. This is a best of both worlds synthesis referred to by the analyst firm, Enterprise Management Associates (EMA) as a *soft agent*[11].

This new approach, the Sensor, emulates a user running locally and is actually local to the monitored host, just like an agent, but only for a brief period of time. As a result, it accomplishes the requisite, deep depth of discovery, but without the high cost of installation and maintenance. The Sensor can provide the richness of data of the agent, but avoids the ongoing costs.

[11] The CMDB Landscape: Market Directions, Vendor Solutions and IT Deployments A Research Report Prepared by EMA June 2005

A.7.1 The Sensor and how it works

The Sensor functions by utilizing secure network connections, encrypted access credentials and host native utilities. In this way it is safe to use and provides the exact same data acquisition that a user (or an agent) could acquire "sitting" locally on the box. It has the insiders view as a result of "asking" the host and the applications how they are configured and who they are talking to. This is in marked contrast to the agent approach which is the "outsider looking in" and trying to infer from what is observed. But most importantly, there is no need to install anything permanent on each host that would require ongoing maintenance.

The Sensor functions in the following way:

- A secure connection is made to the host about to be discovered using a secure protocol such as SSH.
- SSH uses credentials that enable read-only access to system information (without root access), but does not necessitate access to application data or customer information.
- Once the SSH session is achieved, it invokes native OS utilities that return all the running processes on this host, their environments and arguments. It also captures all of the open ports and which processes are currently communicating on them.
- Using these native utilities, the sensor is able to "inventory" the host as to its configuration, software and patches installed, applications it is hosting and running processes.
- Differently configured Sensors, using appropriate credentials can log onto whatever applications are found on this host, such as Oracle or WebSphere. This application specific Sensor, upon logging into the application, can "ask" the application itself how it is configured. This is very important in terms of acquiring an accurate configuration, since many applications such as Oracle utilize the concept of a running configuration (using `spfile`) which might differ significantly from the configuration described in a configuration file.
- Once the host and application topology and configuration details are acquired, they are sent back to a central management server and the SSH session is terminated.
- Upon termination, the connection is severed with nothing left on the discovered host to be maintained.

Since this same Sensor-driven process is simultaneously occurring on other hosts, the process at "the other end" of each port is captured and using correlation back at the central server, a topology can be "stitched" together that accurately portrays the dependencies between applications.

Figure A-3 illustrates a Sensor in action. The data captured by the Sensor is reformatted according to schema in the CIM model (Data Center Reference Model) and then stored in a CMDB.

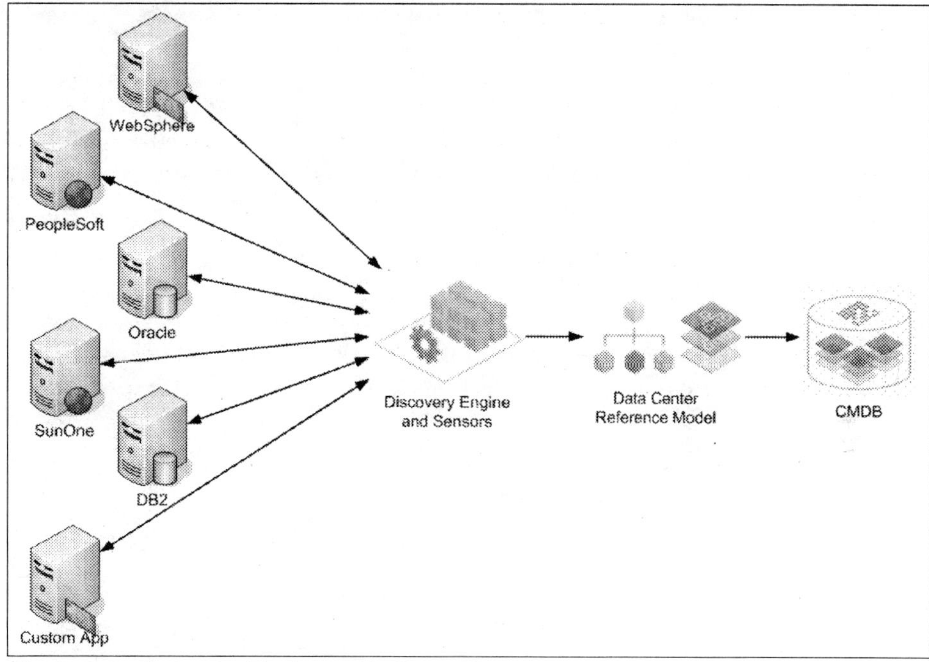

Figure A-3 Sensors - The best of both worlds

A.7.2 Remote management protocols

A relatively new direction has been the efforts at standardization around remote discovery protocols. Two well known ones are JMX (Java Management Extensions - JSR 77) and WMI (Windows Management Instrumentation) from Microsoft that is based on the DMTF standard called WBEM and includes the CIM (Common Information Model). Remote Management protocols are an excellent source of application data that augment the agentless approach to discovery of application topology.

Java Management Extensions Technology is a new feature in version 5.0 of the Java Platform, Standard Edition (J2SE). JMX technology provides a simple, standard way of managing resources such as applications, devices, and services. Because JMX technology is dynamic, you can use it to monitor and manage resources as they are created, installed and implemented. You can also use JMX technology to monitor and manage the Java Virtual Machine.

The advantage of JMX is that it is relatively standard amongst the major J2EE Application Server vendors such as IBM, BEA, Oracle, and SAP. It is also built into their products and does not require any special installation and it can be accessed remotely. JMX is an excellent source of information about J2EE application servers which have become the platform of choice for large-scale business applications.

WMI is an excellent source of data concerning Windows servers, applications and even desktops. Like JMX it does not require an installation as it is built into today's Windows Servers and accessible as an add-on service on Windows XP desktops.

WMI has access to both local and remote Windows events and configurations and is combined with a query language for the Common Information Model (CIM). The ability to easily script these solutions in Visual Basic® or using Windows Scripting Host (WSH) adds an often-requested dimension to Windows management. Table A-6 lists the advantages of Sensors.

Table A-6 Advantages of Sensors

	Advantages of Sensors (also called soft-agents)
Depth of Data Retrieved	Sensors can retrieve as much data about an application as is necessary
Cooperative	Can work in conjunction with existing earlier agents using them as just another data source - no "forklift" upgrade is required for earlier agents
An inside view of an applications configuration	Achieved by logging on to each application and requesting from them, their configuration produces the greatest accuracy
Model Driven Provides Context	Sensors understand what an Oracle DB or a Siebel application is and thus understand what information pieces to acquire and their relationship to the whole
Uses Remote Management Protocols	To gather application and platform specific data providing deep and deep information at a low cost
Security	Sensors encrypt all credentials with no requirement for root access
Less expensive	Low maintenance -little time spent in planning how this will be managed, execution of your plan and in calculating the impact on your staff
Lean	No need for the Software Distribution and Distributed Patching of agents

	Advantages of Sensors (also called soft-agents)
Self contained	No need for agents to monitor agents
Results	A deep end-to-end view of the discovered applications, their configurations and their dependencies

Table A-7 lists the disadvantages of using sensor-based discovery technology.

Table A-7 Disadvantages of Sensors (or soft-agents)

	Disadvantages of Sensors (or soft-agents)
Political Hurdle	Sensors require that you acquire and then maintain over time access credentials to all the important business applications and hosts in your enterprise. While not a technology problem as they can be maintained in encrypted form, this does present a "people management" problem as often users are loath to give out this information.

A.8 The politics of agents

In addition to the technical hurdles to be considered when selecting agents or the agentless approach there are often political aspects to be considered. In a recent publication by EMA Associates after interviewing their clients they had this to say: "agents came up as a concern, agentless is best from a political perspective. Soft Agents (Sensors) that involve logging into a box with privileged commands are the next most acceptable. And then full agents are often a political bombshell."[12] Apparently, in addition to identifying the best technical solution with the lowest TCO to address their need, IT must also take into account the historical perspectives their senior management might hold about past agent implementations.

A.9 Decide based on your requirements

All proper application design is done predicated on what the requirements are. Often when discussing the trade-offs between agents and the agentless approach, the implied assumption is that we are talking about fault management. And when the requirements are fault-management, many of the advantages of the agent are valid. However, the requirements discussed in the paper are for discovery of application topology and configuration data. This need has different requirements than fault management and thus, a comparison between the agent

[12] The CMDB Landscape: Market Directions, Vendor Solutions and IT Deployments A Research Report Prepared by EMA June 2005

versus agentless should be decided based on what *your* requirements are. While any set of requirements can be debatable, the standard set of requirements from customers for acquisition of application topology and configuration data, includes the following:

1. Be able to schedule a discovery of a logical portion of an enterprise's IP address space.
2. Be able to set reasonable frequencies of re-discovery. For example, shift-change updates, end-of-day updates and weekly updates
3. There is no requirement for real-time updates .

When there is no requirement for real-time updates, many of the advantages the agent has are no longer relevant to this problem. They are certainly relevant to other problem spaces such as fault-management. However, the problem space we are discussing is discovery of application topology and not fault-management.

Agent features *not* relevant here include the following:

- Real-time discovery
- High availability

With those advantages now properly classified as non-relevant to this set of requirements, it has hopefully, been made clear in this paper that the Sensor approach can provide all of the applicable value that agents do, but with the advantage of providing it at a lower total cost of ownership.

A.10 It is not all or nothing

If you already have agents deployed, your investment in them can be protected. Legacy agents can act as data sources to Sensors and can augment the discovery of topology and configuration that Sensors acquire.

The agent and agentless approach can work together to provide some very interesting and unique value. The agentless approach to discovery can be used as a means to identify where monitoring Agents need to be deployed in order to optimize the provisioning process. Conversely, when the need for real-time discovery is present, agents can be used to identify the initialization of new applications that run infrequently and might not be running when the agentless discovery process is scheduled.

Be careful to remember that it is too easy to confuse ends with means. Consider the choice between agent and agentless as the key decision. Most important is the value provided and the cost incurred to achieve it. It is the results that count.

A.11 Conclusion

There are many approaches to solving problems and it is best to begin by clearly defining your requirements in order to solve the right problem. For the requirements of Discovering Application Topology and Configuration data, the Sensor (agentless) approach is the best in that it has the depth of functionality needed, the flexibility to adapt to the complexity of today's n-Tier world and at the same time it is able to do all of this at a lower cost than the alternatives. The future is often uncertain; however, several things are definite: complexity will increase, change will accelerate and a push for compliance will be constant. The approach that best deals with these requirements today and one that will remain future-proof tomorrow is believed to be the Sensor.

B

Useful tools and utilities

This appendix introduces the command line based interface as well as some of the most useful tools and utilities that are provided with IBM Tivoli Change and Configuration Management Database Configuration Discovery and Tracking v1.1. Besides the main command line interface, the api.sh script, the following utilities are covered:

- loadidml: the bulk loader
- loadscope - the scope import utility
- templateloader: the template import/export utility

However, before going into details about each of the utilities, a general understanding of the CMDB data model is required. A description of the Data Model and its use is provided in B.1, "CMDB data model overview" on page 332.

In addition, the following test and verification tools are described:

- testhang.jy
- testjdbc.jy
- testos.jy
- testping.jy
- testportmap.jy
- testportscan.jy
- testsnmp.jy
- testssh.py
- testwmi.jy
- wmiexec.jy

B.1 CMDB data model overview

The IBM Tivoli Change and Configuration Management Database Configuration Discovery and Tracking CMDB employs 750+ classes to represent the internal model of discovered elements. This overview will document only the significant, top level objects and how the DataAPI represents this using XML.

All discovery data which is displayed in the Configuration Discovery and Tracking Product Console is accessible using this API interface. The data model contains discovered objects of each element type (for example computer systems, and IP interfaces) with corresponding details as contained objects (such as operating system, and configuration values). Data is represented as java model objects, or an XML format, with most contained objects embedded within the object or XML document, which makes navigation easier. In addition, the PresentationAPI is provided which contains all top level objects and their inter-relationships which roughly correspond to the structure of the Configuration Discovery and Tracking Product Console. Internally, the Configuration Discovery and Tracking data model is an object oriented tree-like structure of objects, which is persisted into a relational database. When converting to XML, the DataAPI will *flatten* the structure into an XML string, so that objects which are referenced multiple times will be duplicated within the document. The resulting XML document will be somewhat larger than the original data, which should be easier to search using tools such as XQuery or XSLT.

The data store consists mostly of the following types of objects:

AppServer	All software services are derived from this class (for example, ApacheServer, Db2Instance)
ComputerSystem	All computer hosts are derived from this class (for example, LinuxUnitaryComputerSystem, Windows, and so forth)
Application	A collection of objects making a single application
BusinessService	A collection of applications
AppServerCluster	A collection of AppServers

Dependencies between objects are not represented by direct references to objects but by independent dependency objects, which connect providers with dependent services using object IDs.

- IpDependency
- ServiceDependency
- SystemDependency
- TransactionalDependency
- Relationships

B.1.2, “Accessing Data Model objects - examples” on page 334 provides examples on how to join these objects together into a single query.

B.1.1 CMDB XML object model format

The `DataApi.findXML()`, which is used by the api.sh command line script, always returns an XML document containing a list of all objects of the chosen class. The root element will be called `results`, as a single root element is required for all XML documents. The XML output format will be as shown in Example B-1.

Example: B-1 XML output format from DataApi.find()

```
<?xml version="1.0" encoding="ISO-8859-1"?>
  <!-- query: "model object query" -->
  <results
    xmlns="urn:www-collation-com:1.0"
    xmlns:coll="urn:www-collation-com:1.0"
    xmlns:xsi="http://www.w3.org/2001/XMLSchema-instance"
    xsi:schemaLocation="urn:www-collation-com:1.0
       urn:www-collation-com:1.0/results.xsd" >
    <abbreviated_searched_class_name
      class="full class name"
      array="N"
      LINK="link id"
      Guid="unique model object id">
      <property_name1>"text value"</property_name1>
      ...
      <property_nameX
         class="full class name"
        Guid="unique model object id">
        <property_name1>"text value"</property_name1>
        ...
        <property_nameN>"text value"</property_nameN>
      <property_nameX/>
      ...
      <property_nameN>"text value"</property_nameN>
      <property_nameQ/>
    </abbreviated_searched_class_name>
  </results>
```

The following formatting rules apply:

- Query might be null.
- `property_nameX` is a ModelObject.
- `property_nameQ` is an example of a null element.
- `abbreviated_searched_class_name` is the searched for class name and not the actual class name.
- `class` and `Guid` are XML attributes and are not represented as separate elements.
- if the element is part of an array, `N` is its index
- LINKs are only used with infinite depth and sparse tree generation, LINKs are references to previously visited model objects. XPath/XSLT queries do not easily support LINK nodes.

XML is a hierarchical model, allowing no cycles. To convert model objects to XML, our model must be *flattened*, so that any cycles will result in duplicate entries in the XML. Thus it is necessary to supply a `depth` whenever converting from model objects to XML. A depth of 2 is often adequate. The CMDB data model is not deep, nor very interconnected, as most data elements are stand alone. Cycles in the model occur with parent pointers and explicit Guids. Often links between models, such as LogicalDependency, are represented by storing Guids, which are modeled as shallow model objects. When these objects are pursued, a cycle might result.

B.1.2 Accessing Data Model objects - examples

This section provides a few simple examples on how to access data in the CMDB either through the DataAPI.find() method, the api.sh script or native java objects. Since the api.sh command line interface uses the DataApi.find() method under the covers, both way of querying the database will provide the same results.

Example 1: Quick query on the model

List all computers with more than one CPU.

DataApi

```
DataApi api = session.getDataApi();
String str = api.findXML("SELECT name FROM ComputerSystem WHERE
numCPUs > 1", 2, null);
```

CommandLine

```
${COLLATION_HOME}/sdk/bin/api.sh -u administrator -p collation find
--depth 0 "Select * from ComputerSystem WHERE numCPUs > 1"
```

Results

The results of this query are displayed in Example 7-15.

Example 7-15 Output of listing all computers with more than on CPU

```
<?xml version="1.0" encoding="UTF-8"?>
 <results>
 <ComputerSystem array="1" id="guid"
   lastModified="time"
xsi:type="coll:com.collation.platform.model.topology.sys.ComputerSys
tem">
   <name>caesar.lab.collation.net</name>
 </ComputerSystem>
 <ComputerSystem array="2" id="guid"
   lastModified="time"
xsi:type="coll:com.collation.platform.model.topology.sys.ComputerSys
tem">
   <name>pancea.lab.collation.net</name>
 </ComputerSystem>
 <ComputerSystem array="3" id="guid"
   lastModified="time"
xsi:type="coll:com.collation.platform.model.topology.sys.ComputerSys
tem">
   <name>demo.lab.collation.net</name>
 </ComputerSystem>
 <ComputerSystem array="4" id="guid"
   lastModified="time"
xsi:type="coll:com.collation.platform.model.topology.sys.ComputerSys
tem">
   <name>whatzit.lab.collation.net</name>
 </ComputerSystem>
 <ComputerSystem array="5" id="guid"
   lastModified="time"
xsi:type="coll:com.collation.platform.model.topology.sys.ComputerSys
tem">
   <name>manikin.lab.collation.net</name>
 </ComputerSystem>
 <ComputerSystem array="6" id="guid"
   lastModified="time"
xsi:type="coll:com.collation.platform.model.topology.sys.ComputerSys
tem">
   <name>cleopatra.lab.collation.net</name>
 </ComputerSystem>
 </results>
```

Using Java objects

The following Java stub can be used to query the CMDB from a Java program:

```
ModelObject[] objs = api.find("SELECT name FROM ComputerSystem WHERE
numCPUs > 1", 2, null);
for (int i = 0; i < objs.length; i++) {
 System.out.println("name: " + ((ComputerSystem)objs[i]).getName());
}
```

Results

```
name: caesar.lab.collation.net
name: panacea.lab.collation.net
name: demo.lab.collation.net
name: whatzit.lab.collation.net
name: manikin.lab.collation.net
name: cleopatra.lab.collation.net
```

Note: Each ComputerSystem object will only have a single attribute set: The `name`, which was specified in the SELECT list. If "SELECT *" were used, all attributes, down to a depth of 2, would be returned. Please consult the JavaDocs for further details.

Example 2: Establishing a Session and Object Creation

The following code can be used to establish a session between your application and the Configuration Discovery and Tracking Server.

```
ApiConnection conn = ApiConnection.getConnection("localhost",
false);
ApiSession sess = ApiSession.getSession(conn, "user", "pass",
  ApiSession.DEFAULT_VERSION);
DataApi api = sess.getDataApi();
```

Note the split between connections and sessions. Think of connection as sockets, and sessions as both an active login, and as an API factory.

```
ComputerSystem sys = (ComputerSystem)ModelObjectFactory.
              newInstance("ComputerSystem");
sys.setSignature("10.10.10.10(0003BA137931)");
sys.setCPUSpeed(3600000000);
sys.setNumCPUs(19);
api.update(sys, null);
```

ComputerSystem might not have been the best the example, as the key used here, signature, has a non-obvious value. This will create and or update the given object within the CMDB.

```
sess.release();
conn.release();
```

It's necessary to clean up the session and connection when you're done with them. In this case, they're returned to their respective pools. Otherwise, connection/session time-outs and destructors will also close sessions and connections.

Java object model format

Java objects represent the model using simple bean objects with set() and get() methods for each attribute in the interface. There is also a has() method for each attribute, which shows whether or not the attribute is set, This is different than being set to null. Each get() method will throw an AttributeNotSetException if the corresponding has() method is false.

A subset of ModelObject, the root of all model objects. This is an abstract class. Using the api.sh is usually an exercise in using the model, so please refer to the model documentation when reading this CMDB API documentation. Here is a subset of the ModelObject class.

```
public interface ModelObject extends Serializable {of the ModelObject class.
  public Guid getGuid() ; // Returns the primary Guid of the object
  public String getDisplayName() ; // Returns a name string suitable for display in a UI.
  public String getObjectType() ; // Returns the type of object
  public String getSourceToken() ; // Returns the source token of object
  public String getDescription() ; // Returns a description of the object
  public int getAdminState() ; // Returns the administrative state of the object
  public Map getAllAttributes(); // Returns all attribute values in a Map.
                                 // Any attribute that has not been loaded will not be returned.
  public String getCreatedBy() ; // Returns a string identifying how the object was created
  public long getLastModifiedTime() ; // Returns the last modified time
  public String getLastModifiedBy() ; // Returns a string identifying how the object was last
                                      // modified
}
```

Java objects returned by find(), join() and executeQuery() will, by default, be plain old java objects, which are concrete implementations derived from com.collation.platform.model.ModelObject. Optionally, they might be RMI proxies, dynamic proxies for non model representations of external data. They will be compiled with the "`-target 1.4`" option to make them compatible with Java 1.4 or greater.

JavaDocs of the model can be found in the `${COLLATION_HOME}/sdk/doc` directory of the product distribution. See B.2.1, "Using api.sh find to query the database" on page 344 for instructions on how to access them.

B.1.3 Model Query Language

The find() methods accept a SQL like query string which specifies the model object class, or other data sources, their attributes and a filter expression to limit the selected objects. In it's simplest form, it names a single model class, such as:

```
ComputerSystem.
```

In this example, this query would return all instances of this class.

The class name might be fully qualified, as:

```
com.collation.platform.model.topology.sys.ComputerSystem
```

or it might be of the simple form:

```
ComputerSystem.
```

There are currently three model classes whose short form is ambiguous:

- AgentConfiguration
- SSLSettings
- WebModule

Some model objects are not selectable as they are abstract, or simply because no instances exist. There are no queries to find all instances of all objects.

The structure of a query is roughly:

```
SELECT attribute-list FROM data-sources [ WHERE expression ]
```

Where `data-sources` is a comma separated list of model object class names, or external data sources. A data source might be qualified by a domain-name, which is a running instances of the CMDB. The expression looks like:

```
member-name OP expression [ ... ]
```

Where a member name might be any attribute of any selected data source and might include dot separated members. An example:

```
SELECT name, model, numCPUs FROM ComputerSystem WHERE
OSRunning.OSName == 'Linux'
```

`OSRunning` is an OperatingSystem object referenced by a ComputerSystem and `OSName` is a primitive member of OperatingSystem.

Array membership might be queried with the EXISTS operator. For example:

```
SELECT * FROM ComputerSystem WHERE EXISTS
(ipInterfaces.ipNetwork.name ends-with '.ibm.com' )
```

This matches all computers systems which have an interface listening on "ibm.com".

The EXISTS expression can be any expression which refers to any array attributes of a class in the FROM list. At least one attribute must be an array in order to use the EXISTS expression.

Joins

At the moment, inner joins are supported against other model objects. Other join types, such as combinations of right outer or left outer are not currently supported and are not supported against model objects from external data sources. Joins are only supported with:

```
#join(String,int,Guid),
#findXML(String,int,Guid),
#executeQuery(String,Guid).
```

This is because joins might return sets of model objects of different sizes. For example:

```
SELECT Db2Server.*, OracleInstance.* from Db2Server, OracleInstance
WHERE Db2Server.port == OracleInstance.port
```

This could return the output in Example B-2.

Example: B-2 Data returned from a MQL join operation

```
{  { Db2Server1, Oracle1 },
   { Db2Server1, Oracle2 },
   { Db2Server2, NULL },
   { Db2Server3, Oracle1 },
   { Db2Server3, Oracle2 }
}.
```

This is currently not supported, only inner joins are supported, which means only one type of model object will be returned. For example:

```
SELECT Db2Server.* FROM Db2Server, OracleInstance WHERE
Db2Server.port == OracleInstance.port
```

This returns all Db2Server model objects where the port number from Db2Server and the port number from OracleInstance are equal.

External data sources

To specify external data sources to pull data from the following syntax might be used:

```
SELECT * from denver:ComputerSystem WHERE numCPUs > 4
```

This will return all of the computer system model objects from the `denver` server where the number of CPUs is greater than 4.

External data returned by the Java object model find() methods will be packaged into dynamic proxy model objects whose members will be available either by Java reflection or by using ModelObject.getAllAttributes().

B.2 The command line interface: api.sh

The primary command line tool for interacting with IBM Tivoli Change and Configuration Management Database Configuration Discovery and Tracking is the api.sh script, which resides in the `${COLLATION_HOME}/sdk/bin` directory.If executed from any other directory than `${COLLATION_HOME}/sdk/bin`, you have to export the `${COLLATION_HOME}` variable - typically pointing to `/opt/IBM/cmdb/dist` —prior to execution.

The api.sh script allows you to both query the CMDB and import data from external XML files. In addition, functions to control discoveries, versions, and the topology are provided. The following list summarizes the capabilities of the api.sh script:

find	Find a set of topology objects. Returns an XML representation
discover	Query, start or abort a discovery run
changes	Get the changes for a topology object.Returns an XML representation
export	Make a backup copy of the top level model objects in the database
import	Merge backup data into the current database
delete	Delete object from the database
version	Perform version functions
topology	Clear or rebuild the topology

The general syntax of the calls to the command line api.sh are:

```
api.sh OPTIONS COMMAND COMMAND-PARAMETERS COMMAND-OPTIONS
```

The OPTIONS are used to authenticate with the Configuration Discovery and Tracking server, and contains both optional and mandatory parameters:

The mandatory parameters are:

-u, --user	<user to run the api command as>
-p, --password	<password that authenticates this user>

The optional parameters are:

-H, --host	<host the Configuration Discovery and Tracking Server is installed on, defaults to "localhost">
-P, --port	<port the Configuration Discovery and Tracking Server is listening on, defaults to "9530">

The COMMAND section allows you to specify what to do. The supported commands are:

find	Find a set of topology objects. Returns an XML representation
discover	Start or abort a discovery run
changes	Get the changes for a topology object
export	Make a backup copy of the top level model objects in the database
import	Merge backup data into the current database
delete	Delete object from the database
version	Perform version functions
topology	Clear or rebuild the topology

For each of the commands, you can supply a set of COMMAND-PARAMETERS:

changes
```
<guid> <from-date1> [<to-date1>]]
```

delete
```
<guid>
```

discover
```
start [--name <run name>] <element1> <element2> ...
   <element-n>
abort
status
```

export
```
[<MSS-SECTION>] [--maxfilesize <size>]
<local directory to write to>
```

find
```
<FORMATTING OPTIONS>
--changetype <type2> --from <from-date1>
[--end <end-date1>] <root3>
--guid <object guid>
<MSS-SECTION> <MQL QUERY>
```

[1] date format: MM/dd/yy hh:mm:ss AM|PM

[2] changetype : 0=created, 1=updated, 2=deleted, 3=creates and updates, 4=all changes

import `[-T, --topo] [--timeout`[4]`<time in seconds>] [<MSS-SECTION>] <local directory to read from>`

topology `clear`
`rebuild`

version `<-c | --create> <version name> <version description>`
`<-e | --createempty> <version name> <version description>]`
`<-d | --delete> <version id or version name>]`
`getall`

`COMMAND-OPTIONS` include:

`<FORMATTING-OPTIONS>`

`[--depth <depth>] [--indent <num-spaces>] [--transform <xsl file>]`

Where:

depth Specifies the level of details returned. The following values are valid:
-1: all data
0: guid and name
1 - 4: more and more details based upon the object type

indent specifies the number of blank spaces to be added in front of each line of the output based on the level of the object in the object model hierarchy.

transform XSL file to control the transformation from XML to another format.

<MSS-SECTION> [--mssguid <mss guid> I --mssname <mss name>]

mss guid the guid of the Management Software Server to target
mss name the name of the Management Software System

<MQL QUERY>

`SELECT attribute-list FROM class_list { WHERE [expression | exists_expr] }`

Where:

attribute_list	attrib {, attrib}* I all
attrib	{class .} [<an attribute of a class> I all]
class_list	domain_class {, domain_class }*

[3] For a list of valid model object types, see the IBM Tivoli Change and Configuration Management Database Configuration Discovery and Tracking v1.1 SDK Guide or java documentation on the Configuration Discovery and Tracking Server at $COLLATION_HOME/sdk/doc/model/index.html?com/collation/platform/model/ModelObject.html

[4] timeout should only be used for extremely large file sizes. If set, the current running processes will be disabled

domain_class {domain_list} class

class <a model object class>

domain_list domain {, domain}* :

domain <the server from which to pull data from, default: local database>

exists_expr exists(array_attrib op value)

expression [attrib op value | attrib post-op | pre-op (attrib)] {logical_op expression}*

value <data value>

array_attrib <series of attributes where at least the second to last attribute is an array >

op != | == | > | < | >= | <= | contains | starts-with | ends-with | equals | not-equals

logical_op AND | OR | && | ||

post_op is-null | is-not-null

pre_op lower | upper

all *

> **Note:** The attribute can contain wildcard characters all keywords (SELECT, FROM, WHERE, and so forth) are case insensitive.

The currently supported expression operators are listed in Table B-1.

Table B-1 Data model query language expression operators

Token	Operator name	Precedence
	dot selection	5
!	unary not	4
upper()	function	4
lower()	function	4
()	parentheses	4
is-null	is null	3
is-not-null	is not null	3
equals	equals	2
not-equals	not equals	2
starts-with	starts-with	2
ends-with	ends-with	2
contains	contains-with	2

Token	Operator name	Precedence
==	equals	2
!=	not equals	2
>	greater than	2
>=	greater or equal	2
<	less than	2
<=	less or equal	2
or	logical or	1
and	logical and	1

Higher precedence values have greater precedence.

Restriction: Other SQL SELECT operators or features, such as GROUP BY, HAVING, ORDER BY, DISTINCT, nested SELECTS, IN, BETWEEN, aggregates, etcetera, are not supported.

Important: When using the api.sh script find command (or a SOAP call) to query the CMDB, the results will always be returned in an XML file format, and the selection of individual attributes to be returned is controlled by the --depth argument and NOT attribute-list specified in the select statement.

B.2.1 Using api.sh find to query the database

The api.sh script can be used to produce an XML file with pre-selected attributes of the objects in the database.

Using the `find` command, the `--depth` parameter defines the level of detail provided. Even though the filter in the select phrase can specify certain attributes, these will only be returned if the `DataApi.find()` method is called from a Java program - which is not the case when using the api.sh script.

As described above, the find command can specify either an object class, for example ComputerSystem or AppServer. To see which top-level objects are supported, unpack and open the `model-javadoc` file in the `${COLLATION_HOME}/sdk/doc/model` directory.

```
# cd /opt/IBM/cmdb/dist/sdk/doc/model
# tar -zxvf model-javadoc.tar.gz
```

Now, the model-javadocs have been unpacked, and you can open the `index.html` file your browser, by selecting the following url:

```
file:///opt/IBM/cmdb/dist/sdk/doc/model/index.html.
```

From here, select the package `com.collation.platform.model` and open the `ModelObject` interface. In the main pane you will see a list of all the ModelObjects, which can be referenced in an api.sh **find** command.

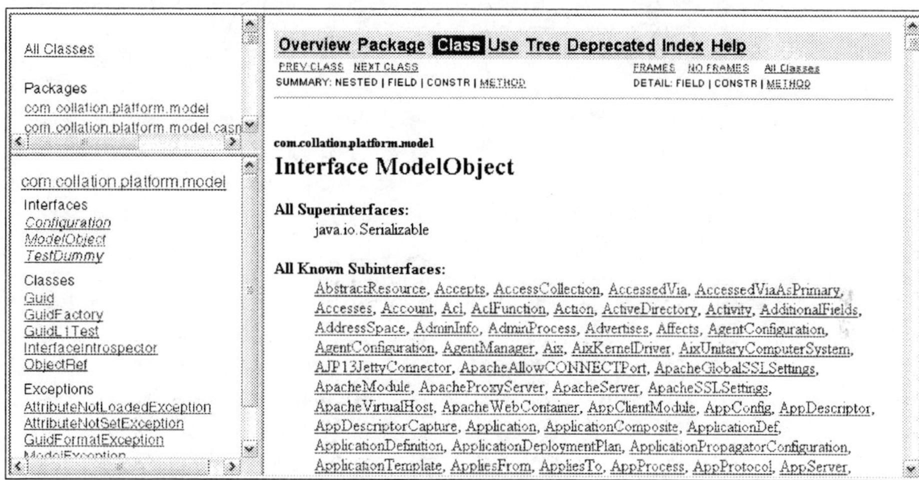

Figure B-1 Top level objects in the CMDB data model

Example: Finding the Guid of a ComputerSystem

To find the Guid of a ComputerSystem named `tioserver.tivdemo.com`, issue the following command:

```
./api.sh -H 9.3.4.165 -u administrator -p collation \
find --depth 0 "SELECT * from ComputerSystem where name ==
'taddm02.tivdemo.com'"
```

or

```
./api.sh -H 9.3.4.165 -u administrator -p collation \
find --depth 0 "SELECT * from ComputerSystem where name starts_with
'tioserver'"
```

Both of the two find commands above will return an XML file containing the basic information of the selected ComputerSystem. Because the depth was set to 0 only the most basic information - such as name and Guid - will be provided.

In order to extract the Guid from the resulting XML file, you should parse the XML file using `xslt`. A script to retrieve the Guid of a ComputerSystem from the fully qualified name would look like this:

```
#!/bin/bash
ip_name=$1
export COLLATION_HOME=/opt/IBM/cmdb/dist
${COLLATION_HOME}/sdk/bin/api.sh -u administrator -p collation find
--depth 0 “Select name from ComputerSystem where fqdn='$ip_name'” >
CompouerSystem0.xml
${COLLATION_HOME}/sdk/bin/xslt -xsl ComputerSystem0.xsl
```

Notice that the file that controls the XSL transformation (`ComputerSystem0.xlt`) contains the hard coded name of the input file (`ComputerSystem0.xml`), and has been developed to parse the exact number of parameters provided in the XML file. In case you change the depth, you will have to develop a new XLT file to parse the input file correctly.

In our example, the XLT file controlling the transformation looks like the one shown in Example B-3. Notice, that it has been designed to transform an XML file that contains only one ComputerSystem definition. If multiple ComputerSystems are present in the XML file, there are no separators between the different Guids. This behavior was specifically created to support automation scripting.

Example: B-3 ComputerSystem0.xmt file for extracting Guid from a api XML file

```
<xsl:stylesheet
    xmlns:xsl="http://www.w3.org/1999/XSL/Transform"
    xmlns="urn:www-collation-com:1.0"
    xmlns:coll="urn:www-collation-com:1.0"
    version="1.0">
    <xsl:output method="text"/>
    <xsl:strip-space elements="*"/>
    <xsl:template match="/">
        <xsl:apply-templates
select="document('ComputerSystem0.xml')/coll:results"/>
    </xsl:template>
    <xsl:template match="coll:ComputerSystem">
        <xsl:value-of select="@guid"/>
    </xsl:template>
</xsl:stylesheet>
```

Using the sample script and the ComputerSystem0.xsl file to control the transformation, the following output will be produced:

```
E424D7FFF50D3E0FB5687CAA7DE75AC4
```

This represents the Guid of the server named `tioserver`.

To get more details from more systems, you should increase the depth, and change the filtering criteria in the select statement. In addition, do not forget to supply a transformation file that matches your requirements.

To get a comma separated list of selected ComputerSystem attribute for all systems which name starts with the character `t`, you can use the following commands:

```
api -u administrator -p collation find --depth 2 "Select  * from
ComputerSystem where displayName contains 't'" > ComputerSystem2.xml
xslt -xsl ComputerSystem2.xsl
```

Provided you use the ComputerSytem2.xsl transformation file shown in Example B-4, the output from this command is:

```
Guid,Name,signature,CPU Model,Memory,OSName,OSVersion
E424D7FFF50D3E0FB5687CAA7DE75AC4,tioserver.tivdemo.com,9.3.5.216(000
C29743C5A),i686,1159725056,Linux,Red Hat Enterprise
Linux ES release 4 (Nahant Update 3),
C39430F15C5033E6AD7266D41D8EA4FD,taddm03,9.3.5.225(00112506F80B),i68
6,1049624576,Linux,Red Hat Enterprise Linux ES relea
se 4 (Nahant Update 3),
C43FC0D3B85C3E52A02D93CB1C02EAC5,taddm01,9.3.5.212(0011250D31BA),i68
6,2114977792,Linux,Red Hat Enterprise Linux ES relea
se 4 (Nahant Update 3),
```

Example: B-4 ComputerSystem2.xsl transformation file

```
<xsl:stylesheet
    xmlns:xsl="http://www.w3.org/1999/XSL/Transform"
    xmlns="urn:www-collation-com:1.0"
    xmlns:coll="urn:www-collation-com:1.0"
    version="1.0">
    <xsl:output method="text"/>
    <xsl:strip-space elements="*"/>

    <xsl:variable name="nl">
        <xsl:text>
</xsl:text>
    </xsl:variable>

    <xsl:template match="/">
        <xsl:text>Guid,Name,signature,CPU
Model,Memory,OSName,OSVersion</xsl:text>
        <xsl:value-of select="$nl"/>
```

```
        <xsl:apply-templates
select="document('ComputerSystem1.xml')/coll:results"/>
    </xsl:template>

    <xsl:template match="coll:ComputerSystem">
        <xsl:value-of select="@guid"/><xsl:text>,</xsl:text>
        <xsl:value-of select="coll:name"/><xsl:text>,</xsl:text>
        <xsl:value-of
select="coll:signature"/><xsl:text>,</xsl:text>
        <xsl:value-of select="coll:model"/><xsl:text>,</xsl:text>
        <xsl:value-of
select="coll:memorySize"/><xsl:text>,</xsl:text>
        <xsl:value-of
select="coll:OSRunning/coll:name"/><xsl:text>,</xsl:text>
        <xsl:value-of
select="coll:OSRunning/coll:OSVersion"/><xsl:text>,</xsl:text>
        <!--  -->
        <xsl:value-of select="$nl"/>
        <!-- -->
    </xsl:template>
</xsl:stylesheet>
```

B.2.2 api discovery: controlling discoveries

In addition to providing an interface to extract data from the CMDB, the api.sh script also provides facilities to control discoveries, as well as performing other administrative functions.

The syntax is:

```
api.sh OPTIONS discover
    start [--name <run-name>] <scope-element1> ... <scope-element-n>
    | status | abort
```

where OPTIONS is made up of:

Mandatory:

```
-u, --user          <user to run the api command as>
-p, --password      <password that authenticates this user>
```

Optional:

```
-H, --host          <host the Configuration Discovery and Tracking
                    Server is installed on, defaults to "localhost">
-P, --port          <port the Configuration Discovery and Tracking
                    Server is listening on, defaults to "9530">
```

and

```
<run-name>            An optional, descriptive name to be assigned to the
                      discovery.
<scope-element>       Name of a ScopeSet, or a valid IP address
```

The following shows how to use the api scripts `discover start` parameter to start a new discovery on a predefined scopeset and a single IP device.

```
[root@taddm02 bin]# ./api.sh -u administrator -p collation /
discover start --name "Initial Discovery" TIO_ScopeSet 9.3.5.216
Started
```

Use the `status` parameter to inquire if an active discovery is running.

```
[root@taddm02 bin]# ./api.sh -u administrator -p collation /
discover status
Running
```

To stop an active discovery, use the `abort` parameter:

```
[root@taddm02 bin]# ./api.sh -u administrator -p collation /
discover abort
Aborted
```

B.2.3 api change: unveiling changes

To generate an XML file of the changes that has been applied to an within a specific time period object you can call the `api` script using the `changes` parameter. The syntax is:

```
api.sh OPTIONS changes <guid> <from-date> [<to-date>]]
```

where `OPTIONS` is made up of:

Mandatory:

```
-u, --user          <user to run the api command as>
-p, --password      <password that authenticates this user>
```

Optional:

```
-H, --host          <host the Configuration Discovery and Tracking
                    Server is installed on, defaults to "localhost">
-P, --port          <port the Configuration Discovery and Tracking
                    Server is listening on, defaults to "9530">
```

and

<guid> The Guid of the object for which you like to see the changes.
<from-date> Start time stamp - - MM/dd/yy hh:mm:ss [ap]m.
<to-date> End time stamp - MM/dd/yy hh:mm:ss [ap]m

Example B-5 shows how to use the api.sh script's changes parameter to generate a XML file containing all the changes applied to an AppServer since 1 a.m. at 21 May 2006.

Example: B-5 XML output for api.sh AppServer changes by date

```
[root@taddm02 bin]# ./api.sh -u administrator -p collation -H 9.3.4.165
changes 1AA2FFD4F7B43644B664A544DBE8E88F "05/21/06 0
1:00:00 am"
<?xml version="1.0" encoding="UTF-8"?>
<changes>
    <change Attribute="" Change="Created" Component="9.3.5.212:37645"
        Date="Wed Jun 28 16:15:17 CDT 2006"
        Id="1AA2FFD4F7B43644B664A544DBE8E88F" Type="AppServer">
        <Old_Value><![CDATA[]]></Old_Value>
        <New_Value><![CDATA[]]></New_Value>
    </change>
    <change Attribute="" Change="Updated" Component="9.3.5.212:37645"
        Date="Wed Jun 28 16:15:17 CDT 2006"
        Id="1AA2FFD4F7B43644B664A544DBE8E88F" Type="AppServer">
        <Old_Value><![CDATA[]]></Old_Value>
        <New_Value><![CDATA[]]></New_Value>
        <causes>
            <change Attribute="" Change="Created"
                Component="TCPServer/hostAndServices"
                Date="Wed Jun 28 16:15:17 CDT 2006"
                Id="694898560D4035E098613D924E3B7813" Type="DataFile">
                <Old_Value><![CDATA[]]></Old_Value>
                <New_Value><![CDATA[]]></New_Value>
            </change>
        </causes>
    </change>
    <change Attribute="" Change="Updated" Component="9.3.5.212:37645"
        Date="Thu Jun 29 02:20:35 CDT 2006"
        Id="1AA2FFD4F7B43644B664A544DBE8E88F" Type="AppServer">
        <Old_Value><![CDATA[]]></Old_Value>
        <New_Value><![CDATA[]]></New_Value>
        <causes>
            <change Attribute="configContents" Change="Member added"
                Component="taddm01:37645"
                Date="Thu Jun 29 02:20:35 CDT 2006"
                Id="1AA2FFD4F7B43644B664A544DBE8E88F" Type="AppServer">
                <Old_Value><![CDATA[]]></Old_Value>
```

```
<New_Value><![CDATA[4A4E23A1A41832E69F3735FBF229232E]]></New_Value>
            </change>
            <change Attribute="" Change="Created"
                Component="/tmp/TCPServer.properties"
                Date="Thu Jun 29 02:20:35 CDT 2006"
                Id="FC02C99C10F93A0DADC43026A1AD6184" Type="ConfigFile">
                <Old_Value><![CDATA[]]></Old_Value>
                <New_Value><![CDATA[]]></New_Value>
            </change>
        </causes>
    </change>
</changes>
```

B.2.4 api version - managing versions

You can use the api.sh script to manage—create, list, and delete—the versions of your topology. This is performed by using the `version` parameter. The syntax is:

```
api.sh OPTIONS version
        getall |
        -c. --create <version name> <version description> |
        -e, --createempty  <version name> <version description> |
        -d, --delete <version id or name>
```

where `OPTIONS` is made up of:

Mandatory:

```
-u, --user          <user to run the api command as>
-p, --password      <password that authenticates this user>
```

Optional:

```
-H, --host          <host the Configuration Discovery and Tracking
                    Server is installed on, defaults to "localhost">
-P, --port          <port the Configuration Discovery and Tracking
                    Server is listening on, defaults to "9530">
```

and

`<version name>`	A name to be used to identify the version.
`<version description>`	A description of the version.
`<version id or name>`	The id (obtained using the `getall` option) or the name of the version

The following shows how to create a new version named `Redbook Test v1`.

```
[root@taddm02 bin]# ./api -u administrator -p collation /
version -c "Redbook Test v1" "Redbook environment"
Created Version Object with id : 1
```

The following demonstrates how to delete a version named `Redbook Test v2`:

```
[root@taddm02 bin]# ./api -u administrator -p collation /
version -d "Redbook Test v2"
Deleted Version Object with id : 2
```

To list the versions, use the `getall` parameter:

```
[root@taddm02 bin]# ./api -u administrator -p collation /
version getall
ID        Name
--        ---------------------
1         Redbook Test v1
3         Redbook Test v3
```

B.2.5 api delete - deleting objects from the command line

To delete object from the database you have to provide a the global unique id (Guid) of the object you want to delete, and call the `api.sh` script with the `delete` option, parsing the `Guid` as a parameter.

```
api.sh OPTIONS delete <Guid>
```

where `OPTIONS` is made up of:

Mandatory:

```
-u, --user          <user to run the api command as>
-p, --password      <password that authenticates this user>
```

Optional:

```
-H, --host          <host the Configuration Discovery and Tracking
                    Server is installed on, defaults to "localhost">
-P, --port          <port the Configuration Discovery and Tracking
                    Server is listening on, defaults to "9530">
```

The following example shows how to delete a Business Application named TCP Application from the database. The Guid was picked up by the following query

```
api ...find /
"select * from Application where displlayName == 'TCP Application'"
```

which returned the value 28A87D535F4F359891C5D52258DEB58E.

```
export COLLATION_HOME=/opt/IBM/cmdb/dist
${COLLATION_HOME}/sdk/bin/api -u administrator -p collation /
delete 28A87D535F4F359891C5D52258DEB58E
Deleted
```

B.2.6 api topology - managing topologies

To rebuild or clear the topology in your CMDB, you can use the api.sh script with the topology clear or topology rebuild parameters

The syntax is:

```
api.sh OPTIONS topology <clear | rebuild>
```

where OPTIONS is made up of:

Mandatory:

```
-u, --user          <user to run the api command as>
-p, --password      <password that authenticates this user>
```

Optional:

```
-H, --host          <host the Configuration Discovery and Tracking
                    Server is installed on, defaults to "localhost">
-P, --port          <port the Configuration Discovery and Tracking
                    Server is listening on, defaults to "9530">
```

The following example shows how to clear the topology:

```
export COLLATION_HOME=/opt/IBM/cmdb/dist
${COLLATION_HOME}/sdk/bin/api -u administrator -p collation /
topology clear
Topology cleared
```

Note: When you clear the topology, you only operate on the current level - meaning that the topology of previously saved versions will persist.

Use the following call to the api.sh script to rebuild your topology:

```
export COLLATION_HOME=/opt/IBM/cmdb/dist
${COLLATION_HOME}/sdk/bin/api -u administrator -p collation /
topology rebuild
Topology rebuildt
```

B.2.7 api export - extracting data from the CMDB

IBM Tivoli Change and Configuration Management Database Configuration Discovery and Tracking provides a facility to export the top level objects in the CMDB to external XML files. This facility might be used in backup, and migration scenarios, as well as by custom developed Discovery Library Authors to externalize data in a structured way for later processing.

The api.sh script is used to produce the external files my means of the `export` parameter. The syntax is:

```
api.sh OPTIONS export [--mssguid <mss_guid> | --mssname <mss_name>]
                      [--maxfilesize <size>] <export_directory>
```

where `OPTIONS` is made up of:

Mandatory:

```
-u, --user          <user to run the api command as>
-p, --password      <password that authenticates this user>
```

Optional:

```
-H, --host          <host the Configuration Discovery and Tracking
                    Server is installed on, defaults to "localhost">
-P, --port          <port the Configuration Discovery and Tracking
                    Server is listening on, defaults to "9530">
```

and

`<mss_guid>`	represents the Guid of the Management Software System that *owns* the resources.
`<mss_name>`	represents the name of the Management Software System that *owns* the resources.
<size>	represents the maximum size (in bytes) for any one file. Note, that if the size specified does not accommodate all the data to be exported, you data might be invalidated.
`<export_directory>`	points to a directory in which the exported data are stored.

The following example shows how we exported the content of our CMDB to external XML files in the /tmp/cmdbexp directory:

```
[root@taddm02 bin]# ./api.sh -u administrator -p collation /
export /tmp/cmdbexp
Export complete
```

The files produced in the /tmp/cmdbexp directory are listed in Example B-6.

Example: B-6 Files in the /tmp/cmdbexp directory

```
com.collation.platform.model.Configuration.xml
com.collation.platform.model.discovery.scope.ScopeElement.xml
com.collation.platform.model.discovery.scope.Scope.xml
com.collation.platform.model.discovery.template.ApplicationTemplate.xml
com.collation.platform.model.discovery.template.TemplateGroup.xml
com.collation.platform.model.discovery.template.Template.xml
com.collation.platform.model.domain.CMDBDomain.xml
com.collation.platform.model.topology.admin.AdminInfo.xml
com.collation.platform.model.topology.admin.ContactInfo.xml
com.collation.platform.model.topology.admin.SiteInfo.xml
com.collation.platform.model.topology.app.AppDescriptor.xml
com.collation.platform.model.topology.app.ApplicationDef.xml
com.collation.platform.model.topology.app.AppProtocol.xml
com.collation.platform.model.topology.app.AppServerCluster.xml
com.collation.platform.model.topology.app.AppServer.xml
com.collation.platform.model.topology.app.db.db2.Db2System.xml
com.collation.platform.model.topology.app.db.oracle.OracleServer.xml
com.collation.platform.model.topology.app.DefinitiveSoftwareLibrary.xml
com.collation.platform.model.topology.app.j2ee.J2EEDomain.xml
com.collation.platform.model.topology.app.j2ee.jboss.JBossMessageCache.xml
com.collation.platform.model.topology.app.j2ee.jboss.JBossPersistenceManage
r.xml
com.collation.platform.model.topology.app.j2ee.websphere.WebSphereClusterMe
mber.xml
com.collation.platform.model.topology.app.j2ee.websphere.WebSphereNamedEndp
oint.xml
com.collation.platform.model.topology.app.j2ee.websphere.WebSphereNode.xml
com.collation.platform.model.topology.app.j2ee.websphere.WebSphereSessionTu
ningParams.x
com.collation.platform.model.topology.app.j2ee.websphere.WebSphereSharedLib
rary.xml
com.collation.platform.model.topology.app.j2ee.websphere.WebSphereVariable.
xml
com.collation.platform.model.topology.app.lotus.DominoDomain.xml
com.collation.platform.model.topology.app.Probe.xml
com.collation.platform.model.topology.app.SoftwareImage.xml
com.collation.platform.model.topology.app.SoftwareModification.xml
com.collation.platform.model.topology.app.SoftwareModule.xml
```

```
com.collation.platform.model.topology.app.SoftwareProduct.xml
com.collation.platform.model.topology.app.web.iis.IIsParameter.xml
com.collation.platform.model.topology.core.Collection.xml
com.collation.platform.model.topology.core.Relationship.xml
com.collation.platform.model.topology.dev.ControlledBy.xml
com.collation.platform.model.topology.extattrib.UserData.xml
com.collation.platform.model.topology.meta.EnumerationType.xml
com.collation.platform.model.topology.meta.UserDataMeta.xml
com.collation.platform.model.topology.net.BindAddress.xml
com.collation.platform.model.topology.net.Fqdn.xml
com.collation.platform.model.topology.net.IpAddress.xml
com.collation.platform.model.topology.net.IpNetwork.xml
com.collation.platform.model.topology.net.LogicalConnection.xml
com.collation.platform.model.topology.net.NetworkService.xml
com.collation.platform.model.topology.net.Segment.xml
com.collation.platform.model.topology.net.TcpConnection.xml
com.collation.platform.model.topology.net.TransportEndpoint.xml
com.collation.platform.model.topology.net.VlanInterface.xml
com.collation.platform.model.topology.phys.physpkg.PhysicalPackage.xml
com.collation.platform.model.topology.process.AbstractResource.xml
com.collation.platform.model.topology.process.Account.xml
com.collation.platform.model.topology.process.Activity.xml
com.collation.platform.model.topology.process.BusinessSchedule.xml
com.collation.platform.model.topology.process.Capability.xml
com.collation.platform.model.topology.process.CompositeDef.xml
com.collation.platform.model.topology.process.Customer.xml
com.collation.platform.model.topology.process.Document.xml
com.collation.platform.model.topology.process.igs.Monitor.xml
com.collation.platform.model.topology.process.igs.ProbeScript.xml
com.collation.platform.model.topology.process.Interface.xml
com.collation.platform.model.topology.process.itil.IncidentRecordProxy.xml
com.collation.platform.model.topology.process.itil.ReleaseRecordProxy.xml
com.collation.platform.model.topology.process.itil.RFCProxy.xml
com.collation.platform.model.topology.process.ManagementSoftwareSystem.xml
com.collation.platform.model.topology.process.MSSObjectLink.xml
com.collation.platform.model.topology.process.Objective.xml
com.collation.platform.model.topology.process.OrganizationalEntity.xml
com.collation.platform.model.topology.process.Partner.xml
com.collation.platform.model.topology.process.Permission.xml
com.collation.platform.model.topology.process.PersonRole.xml
com.collation.platform.model.topology.process.Repository.xml
com.collation.platform.model.topology.process.Role.xml
com.collation.platform.model.topology.process.ServiceProvider.xml
com.collation.platform.model.topology.process.Supplier.xml
com.collation.platform.model.topology.process.UserDefinedValue.xml
com.collation.platform.model.topology.storage.Fabric.xml
com.collation.platform.model.topology.storage.StoragePool.xml
com.collation.platform.model.topology.storage.ZoneMember.xml
com.collation.platform.model.topology.sys.ComputerSystemCluster.xml
```

```
com.collation.platform.model.topology.sys.ComputerSystem.xml
com.collation.platform.model.topology.sys.DNSLookup.xml
com.collation.platform.model.topology.sys.FileSystemContent.xml
com.collation.platform.model.topology.sys.ITSystem.xml
com.collation.platform.model.topology.sys.KernelDriver.xml
com.collation.platform.model.topology.sys.RuntimeProcess.xml
com.collation.platform.model.topology.sys.ServiceAccessPoint.xml
com.collation.platform.model.topology.sys.Service.xml
com.collation.platform.model.topology.sys.SoftwarePatch.xml
com.collation.platform.model.topology.sys.zOS.Subsystem.xml
com.collation.platform.model.topology.sys.zOS.Sysplex.xml
com.collation.platform.model.workflow.TaskRuntime.xml
com.collation.platform.model.workflow.Task.xml
com.collation.platform.model.workflow.Transition.xml
com.collation.platform.model.workflow.WorkflowRuntime.xml
com.collation.platform.model.workflow.Workflow.xml
```

B.2.8 api import - loading data into the CMDB

After export, chances are that you want to import the data into you own CMBD or transfer the data to another CMDB for import.

To merge the content of previously exported XML files into the CMDB, use the api.sh script with the `import` parameter. The syntax is:

```
api.sh OPTIONS import [-T, --topo] [--timeout <time in seconds>]
                      [--mssguid <mssguid> | --mssname <mssname>]
                      <import_directory | XML_file>
```

Where `OPTIONS` is made up of:

Mandatory:

```
-u, --user          <user to run the api command as>
-p, --password      <password that authenticates this user>
```

Optional:

```
-H, --host          <host the Configuration Discovery and Tracking
                    Server is installed on, defaults to "localhost">
-P, --port          <port the Configuration Discovery and Tracking
                    Server is listening on, defaults to "9530">
```

and

-T or --topo	instructs Configuration Discovery and Tracking to rebuild the topology after successful import.
<time in seconds>	timeout at which the import will be aborted. **Note:** Only use for extremely large file sizes, since this will disable processes currently running.
<mss_guid>	represents the Guid of the Management Software System that *owns* the resources.
<mss_name>	represents the name of the Management Software System that *owns* the resources.
<import_directory>	points to a directory in which the previously exported XML files are stored.
<XML_file>	Specifies the fully qualified filename of a single XML file to be imported.

The following example demonstrates how to import Custom Server Template definitions from the file:

`com.collation.platform.model.discovery.template.ApplicationTemplate.xml`

and rebuild the topology after import:

```
[root@taddm02 bin]# ./api.sh -u administrator -p collation import -T
/tmp/cmdbexp/com.collation.platform.model.discovery.template
.ApplicationTemplate.xml
Import complete
Topology rebuilt
```

To import all the files in the `/tmp/cmdbexp` directory (without topology rebuild) use a command similar to the following:

```
[root@taddm02 bin]# ./api.sh -u administrator -p collation /
import /tmp/cmdbexp
Import complete
```

B.2.9 Using api.sh from remote systems

To be able to use the command line interface from remote systems, you have to make the classes used by the api.sh script available on the remote system, and set up few environment variables needed to help the api.sh script find the required resources.

The following describes the steps necessary:

1. Install Java Runtime Environment version 1.5
2. Create the directory structure
3. Copy resources from the Configuration Discovery and Tracking server
4. Set up the runtime environment

Install Java Runtime Environment version 1.5

The api.sh requires JRE v1.5 to operate correctly. To install this on the target system, download the code from either of these Web sites:

```
http://www.ibm.com/developerworks/java/jdk
http://java.sun.com/javase/downloads
```

Follow the installation instructions for your platform provided by the vendor.

Create the directory structure

The api.sh script expects to find the required resources in a directory structure similar to this:

```
<apiroot-dir> /sdk
                 /bin
                 /etc
                 /lib
                 /log
```

After you have decided what your `apiroot` directory will be, create the required structure by issuing the following command:

```
mkdir -p <apiroot>/sdk/bin <apiroot>/sdk/etc <apiroot>/sdk/lib
<apiroot>/sdk/log
```

Copy resources from the Configuration Discovery and Tracking server

Copy the files listed in Table B-2 from the specified location on the Configuration Discovery and Tracking server to the newly created directory structure on the remote system.

Table B-2 Resources to be copied tor remote execution of api.sh

file name	source location	target location
api.sh	$COLLATION_HOME/dist/sdk/bin	<apiroot-dir>/sdk/bin

file name	source location	target location
collation.properties	$COLLATION_HOME/dist/sdk/etc	<apiroot-dir>/sdk/etc
log4j.xml		
policy.all		
api-client.jar	$COLLATION_HOME/dist/sdk/lib	<apiroot-dir>/sdk/lib
api-dep.jar		
api-dl.jar		
platform-model.jar		
xalan.jar		
saxon7.jr	$COLLATION_HOME/dist/sdk/lib	<apiroot-dir>/lib

Set up the runtime environment

The final step is to ensure that the correct runtime environment is set up.

This requires the following two environment variables to be defined and exported

COLLATION_HOME pointer to your `apiroot` directory
JAVA_HOME pointer to the root directory of your JRE environment

If these variables have been exported already from you user profile, you are good to go, otherwise you can export them manually each time you want to start the api.sh script. Alternatively, use the recommended method of hard coding these variables in the script. We suggest that you add the following two lines to lines immediately following the first line (`#!/bin/sh`) to your api.sh script:

```
export COLLATION_HOME=<your apiroot-directory>
export JAVA_HOME=<your java 1.5.0 jre home directory>
```

In our RedHat Linux environment the first three lines of the api.sh script look similar to this:

```
#!/bin/sh
export COLLATION_HOME=/opt/IBM/cmdb/dist
export JAVA_HOME=/opt/IBMJava2-150/jre
...
```

Create a Windows version of the api.sh script

If you want the use the api.sh script from a Windows environment, you must create a new api.cmd script with the content shown in Example B-7.

Example: B-7 api.cmd to use API functions from a remote Windows system

```
@echo off
REM set environment variables
set COLLATION_HOME=%~dp0..\..
set ROOT=%COLLATION_HOME%\sdk
set LOG=%ROOT%\log\api-client.log
set
CLASSPATH=.;..;"%ROOT%\lib\api-client.jar";"%ROOT%\lib\api-dep.jar";"%R
OOT%\lib\platform-model.jar";"%ROOT%\lib\api-dl.jar"

REM ensure that the log directory exists
mkdir "%ROOT%\log" >nul 2>&1

REM call the api
"%JAVA_HOME%java" -Xmx1024M -ea -Dcom.collation.home="%ROOT%"
-classpath %CLASSPATH% com.collation.proxy.api.client.ApiCLI %*%
```

Note: In the api.cmd, we set up %COLLTION_HOME% automatically, and it is assumed that the correct java executable is found on the path. However, if the %JAVA_HOME% variable exists, it will be used.

Test the remote api.sh script

To verify the functionality of your api.sh script, you can issue the following command which lists the build-in Custom Server Template named CollationProcesses:

```
<your_api_path>/api -u administrator -p collation -H
<your_server_address> find --depth 0 “select * from template where
name == ‘CollationProcesses’”
```

From our a Windows workstation, we issued the following:

```
C:\collation\sdk\bin>api -u administrator -p collation -H
192.168.1.54 find --depth 0 "Select name from Template where name ==
'CollationProcesses'"
```

We received the following result in Example B-8.

Example: B-8 Testing the api.sh script output

```
<?xml version="1.0" encoding="ISO-8859-1"?>
<results
    xmlns="urn:www-collation-com:1.0"
    xmlns:coll="urn:www-collation-com:1.0"
    xmlns:xsi="http://www.w3.org/2001/XMLSchema-instance"
    xsi:schemaLocation="urn:www-collation-com:1.0
       urn:www-collation-com:1.0/results.xsd">
  <Template array="1" guid="6094801D97573C53BE834D7A425486E4"
    lastModified="1149586892456"
xsi:type="coll:com.collation.platform.model.discovery.template.AppSe
rverTemplate"/>
</results>
```

B.3 Useful utilities

The following utility programs and scripts are available in the ${COLLATION_HOME}/bin directory:

- loadidml: the bulk loader
- loadscope - the scope import utility
- templateloader: the template import/export utility

B.3.1 loadidml: the bulk loader

The loadidml.sh script loads Discovery Library Books into the CMDB. This script is also know as the bulk loader, because it has been designed to import the contents of a specific Discovery Library Book - or the content of multiple Discovery Library Books residing in the same directory. Prior to invoking the bulk loader program, it is the administrators responsibility to make the Discovery Library Books available the bulk loader, either by copying the books to a directory on the Configuration Discovery and Tracking Server, or by mounting a network file system hosting the books from the Configuration Discovery and Tracking Server.

The loadidml script, reads the books, imports data into the CMDB, and logs the results in the bulk loader `results` directory. In addition, the bulk loader logs error messages etc. in the ${COLLATION_HOME}/log/bulkloader.log file - as shown in Figure B-2.

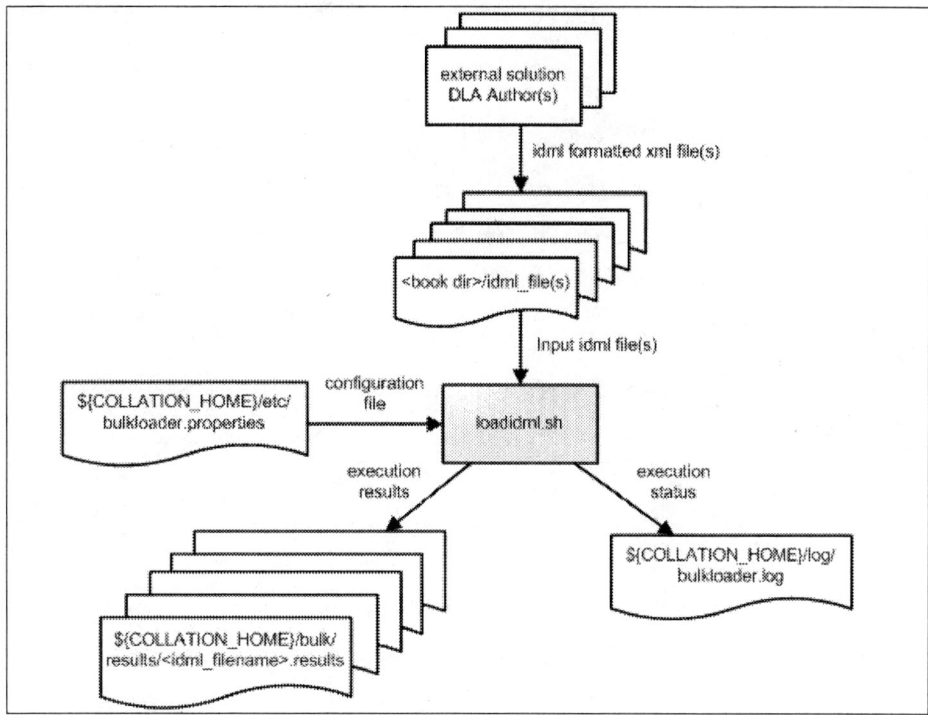

Figure B-2 loadidml input and output files

To ensure data consistency, only one bulk loader program can run at a time. Therefore the bulk loader has been designed to only be executed at the Configuration Discovery and Tracking Server - and to ensure proper authorizations, the program must be executed from the same user that runs the Configuration Discovery and Tracking Server processes.

In addition, all the directories used to store log and result files have to exist prior to executing the loadidml script for the first time. These can be customized through manipulation of the configuration settings defined in the `${COLLATION_HOME}/etc/bulkloader.properties` file.

How to run the bulk loader

To configure and run the bulk loader program, complete the steps described below:

1. Check the ${COLLATION_HOME}/etc/bulkload.properties file for accuracy. You should not need to change anything in the file if you want to accept the defaults.

   – com.ibm.cdb.bulk.workdir=bulk

     This is the directory the bulk loader uses to copy files before loading them. The default directory is relative to the top level directory of the directory referenced by the ${COLLATION_HOME} variable. Typically this would be /opt/IBM/cmdb/dist.

   – com.ibm.cdb.bulk.workdir.cleanup=false

     Specifies whether the working directory should be cleaned up after the load completes.

   – com.ibm.cdb.bulk.processedfiles.cleanup=30

     Number of days to keep files in the processed files list.

   – com.ibm.cdb.bulk.retrycount=5

     Number of times to retry loading a file if a discovery is currently in progress.

   – com.ibm.cdb.bulk.retrydelay=600

     Number of seconds in between retries while a discovery is in progress.

   – com.ibm.cdb.bulk.resultsdir=bulk/results

     Directory to write the results files created during the load of a file. The default directory is relative to the top level directory referenced by the ${COLLATION_HOME} variable. Typically this would be /opt/IBM/cmdb/dist.

   – com.ibm.cdb.bulk.stats.enabled=false

     Whether statistics gathering of the bulk loader will be performed. Turning on statistics decreases performance and increases log and result file sizes.

   Do not change any other settings in the properties file not specifically mentioned here. Other settings can be ignored.

2. Verify that the working directory and the results directory mentioned in the bulkload.properties file are valid.

   The working and results directories must pre-exist or the bulk loader will not run. It will not automatically create these directories.

The directories should be created using the same user that will be used to run the bulk loader. This user should be the same user used to start and stop the Configuration Discovery and Tracking Server. If the bulk loader does not have permissions to read and write from the working and results directories, the bulk loader will not be able to run.

If you wish to use different directories, you must create these manually and update the properties file.

3. Run the bulk loader.

   Log in as the user used to start and stop the Configuration Discovery and Tracking Server. You cannot run the bulk load program as another user.

```
su - taddm
export ${COLLATION_HOME}=/opt/IBM/cmdb/dist
cd dist/bin
./loadidml.sh -f <path_to_idml_file> -h <hostname> -u <userid> -p
<passwd> -o
```

   where

-f <path_to_idml_file>	REQUIRED Points to a fully qualified path to the input file or a directory that contains input XML files. The directory where the input file is placed must not be the same as the working directory of the bulk loader. If a shared directory is used to stage input files or if files are copied to a local directory, the directory where input files are staged cannot be the same as the working, results or log directory of the bulk load program.
-h <hostname>	Specifies the hostname of the Configuration Discovery and Tracking Server
-u <userid>	Specifies the user ID to be used to authenticate with the Configuration Discovery and Tracking Server
-p <password>	Specified the password used to authenticate with the Configuration Discovery and Tracking Server.
-o	Instructs the bulk load program to override the processed files file and load the IdML file(s).

The `-u` and `-p` parameters are optional. A user ID and password should only be supplied if the user ID has the correct permissions (full update and read privileges) and is defined in the Configuration Discovery and Tracking Server as a valid user. The `-h` parameter should only be used in case you experience problems resolving the IP name of the Configuration Discovery and Tracking Server.

If the bulk load program does not run, consult the messages on the console and the messages in the bulkload.log file. The log file is located in the ${COLLATION_HOME}/log directory

4. After the bulk load program runs, check the results file for problems during the bulk load. It will be located in the `resultsdir` directory configured in the bulkload.properties file.

   ```
   cd ${COLLATION_HOME}/bulk/results
   ```

   Look for a file with an .results extension and named the same as the IdML. If, for example, the name of the imported IdML file is `test.xml`, the name of the results file will be `test.results`:

   Important entries in this file are marked with SUCCESS and FAILURE tags. Percentage successful messages are also recorded if statistics are enabled. FAILURES are for individual objects and do not necessarily indicate a failure of the entire file.

5. To process the same book again after the first initial load, either use the **`-o`** flag, or remove the specific entry from the `processedfiles.list` file - or, if you are confident you know what you are doing, the entire file can be deleted).

   The `processedfiles.list` file is located in the working directory specified in the bulkload.properties file.

6. If the bulk load program indicates another bulk load program is already running, and you know this is not the case, go to the working directory and delete the `.bllock` file and try again. Remember that this file is a hidden file because it starts with a period. Deleting this file should only be done if you are positive that another bulk load program is not already running.

   You might also need to delete this file if you pressed `<control-c>` during the execution of the loadidml.sh script - also known s the bulk load program.

> **Note:** Always consult the bulkload.log file because it might contain additional details about the message.

The meaning of the various return codes from the bulk load program are listed in Table B-3.

Table B-3 .loadidml return codes

Return Code	Description
0	Successful run, there still might be objects that did not load
1	An unknown error occurred

Return Code	Description
2	The COLLATION_HOME property was incorrectly set in the environment
3	An invalid command line parameter was detected
4	A login error occurred
5	The input XML file contained an error but processing continued
6	The input XML file contained an error and processing stopped
7	An internal error occurred while parsing the XML file
8	An internal API error occurred while processing the XML file and processing continued
9	An internal API error occurred while processing the file and processing stopped
10	A copy of the bulk load program is already running
11	An internal service is busy and the bulk load program cannot run now
12	An internal service is busy and the bulk load program cannot run now
13	An invalid setting was found in the properties file or a property is missing
14	The file was already processed and will not be processed again
15	The API server could not be contacted

The following example shows how we loaded information from a Windows based ITM Server using the Discovery Library book, which will be distributed as part of the ITM v6.1 FixPack 3.

To install the TMS Discovery Library driver for Windows, copy the following files to the %CANDLE_HOME%\cnps directory where the TEPS is running (for example C:\ibm\tivoli\ITM\CNPS):

- kfwTmsDla.exe
- kfwIDMLBrowse.htm

These files will be shipped in this directory with ITM FixPack 3.

The To run the TMS Discovery Library Adapter:

1. Open a command prompt and go to the CNPS directory where kfwTmsDla.exe was installed into.
2. Issue the following command to see the optional parameters:

   ```
   kfwTmsDla /?
   ```

3. Issue kfwTmsDla.exe (with optional parameters if desired) and a Discovery Library IDML XML file will be created by default in a subdirectory of the CNPS directory called tmsdla.

   > **Note:** For kfwTmsDla.exe to execute successfully, the ITM Tivoli Enterprise Portal Server (TEPS) has to be active and communicating with the ITM Hub Tivoli Enterprise Management Server (TEMS).

4. By default the Discovery Library Book name will be in Discovery Library file format <DLA-author>.<fully-qualified-hostname>.<timestamp>.refresh.xml - for example:

   ```
   TMSDISC100.taddm99.itsc.austin.ibm.com.2006-06-19T13.45.11Z.refresh.xml
   ```

5. The Discovery Library Book file can now be transferred to the Discovery Library File Store available to the Configuration Discovery and Tracking Server (either automatically or manually) and loaded into CMDB through the Discovery Library Bulk Loader.

   To run the bulk loader—the loadidml.sh script—you have to login as the user running the Configuration Discovery and Tracking Server. If you are not sure which user has been set up to do this, you can find the name of the user in the com.collation.unixuser parameter of the ${COLLATION_HOME}/etc/collation.properties file. In our case, the user ID is taddm.

   In addition, the loadidml.sh script needs the have the anchor directory of the Configuration Discovery and Tracking files defined in the COLLATION_HOME variable. In our case this is /opt/IBM/cmdb/dist.

   The only required parameter for the loadidml program is the -f parameter. This parameter specifies the directory - and optionally the fully qualified file name - from which to read the Discovery Library books to be loaded. If no filename is provided, all the files with the .xml extension in the specified directory will be loaded.

So, to import all the Discovery Library books in the /tmp/dlaBooks directory, we used the following commands:

```
[taddm@taddm02 bin]$ export COLLATION_HOME=/opt/IBM/cmdb/dist
[taddm@taddm02 bin]$ ${COLLATION_HOME}/bin/loadidml.sh -f
/tmp/dlaBooks
Bulk Load Program starting.
Bulk Load Program running.
...
Bulk Load Program running.
Bulk Load Program succeeded. Return code is: 0
0
Bulk Load Program ending.
```

6. Upon successful import, the bulk loader working directory or the directory referenced by the com.ibm.cdb.bulk.workdir parameter in the ${COLLATION_HOME}/bulkload.properties file will contain copies of the imported Discovery Library Book files, and information in the processedfiles.list file about the imported files.

B.3.2 loadscope - the scope import utility

You can use the loadscope utility from ${COLLATION_HOME}/bin to load scopes into scope sets from a pre-prepared file, and to delete scope sets.

```
loadscope.jy [-d] -u <userid> -p <password> -s <ScopeSet> clear|load
<scopefile>
```

Where:

`-u <userid>`	Specifies the user ID to be used to authenticate with the Configuration Discovery and Tracking Server
`-p <password>`	Specifies the password for the user ID used to authenticate with the Configuration Discovery and Tracking Server
`-s <ScopeSet>`	Specifies the Scope Set to which is the target of the manipulation. If the specified ScopeSet does not exist prior to the execution of loadscope.jy script, it will be created.
`clear | load`	Instructs Configuration Discovery and Tracking to clear (empty) the scope set, or load the content of the `<scopefile>` into the scope set.
`<scopefile>`	Specifies a file containing scope(s) to be loaded into the scope set.

-d Optional.
Specifies that you want to debug the command. The -d option is only valid in conjunction with the load option, and when used, the results of the processing is stored in a XML file named tmp<number>loadscope.xml in the /tmp directory.

The format of the scope file is:

```
scope,[exclude_scope:exclude_scope...],[description]
```

where scope takes one of the following three forms:

subnet scopes	subnet address/netmask For example:1.2.3.4/255.255.255.0
address scopes	host IP address. For example: 1.2.3.4
range scopes	IP address range. For example: 1.2.3.4-5.6.7.8

The scope file can contain any number of scopes and the scopes can be any combination of the above three types. Obviously, address scopes should not have exclusions.

The -s <ScopeSet> and <scopefile> are not needed for the clear operation.

In the following data sets, we show how the prepare a simple scope file defining four scopes:

ITSO_LAB	a subnet-scope with range and host exceptions
CTS Server	a host scope
Windows Gateways	a range scope
Anchor Hosts	a range scope with host exceptions

The scope file - stored in /tmp/test.scope - has the following content:

```
9.3.5.0/255.255.255.0,9.3.5.20-9.3.5.29:9.3.5.67,ITSO Lab
9.3.4.165,,CTS Server
9.3.4.174-9.3.4.175,,Windows Gateways
9.3.4.180-9.2.4.185,9.3.4.183,Anchor Hosts
```

To verify it, we used the -d option to see the XML generated by the loadscope.jy utility in Example B-9.

Example: B-9 Using the loadscope.jy utility

```
[root@taddm02 bin]# ${COLLATION_HOME}/bin/loadscope.jy -d -u
administrator -p collation -s "Test Scope" load /tmp/test.scope
...
Processing:  9.3.5.0/255.255.255.0[9.3.5.20-9.3.5.29,9.3.5.67], ITSO
Lab
Successfully parsed
Processing:  9.3.4.165,,CTS Server
Successfully parsed
Processing:  9.3.4.174-9.3.4.175,,Windows Gateways
Successfully parsed
Processing:  9.3.4.180-9.2.4.185,[9.3.4.183],Anchor Hosts
Successfully parsed
Processing:
DEBUG--> XML stored in  /tmp/tmp2loadscope.xml
```

The XML file which was generated based on the `test.scope` is shown in Example B-10.

Example: B-10 loadscope XML output

```
<?xml version="1.0" encoding="UTF-8"?>
<results
        xmlns="urn:www-collation-com:1.0"
        xmlns:coll="urn:www-collation-com:1.0"
        xmlns:xsi="http://www.w3.org/2001/XMLSchema-instance"
        xsi:schemaLocation="urn:www-collation-com:1.0
        urn:www-collation-com:1.0/results.xsd">
        <Scope array="1"
xsi:type="coll:com.collation.platform.model.discovery.scope.Scope">
                <displayName>Test Scope</displayName>
                <name>Test Scope</name>
                <elements array="1"
xsi:type="coll:com.collation.platform.model.discovery.scope.IpRangeS
cope">
                        <displayName> ITSO Lab</displayName>
                        <name> ITSO Lab</name>

<keyGuid>1150297702691115029770269111502</keyGuid>
                <excludes array="1"
xsi:type="coll:com.collation.platform.model.discovery.scope.IpAddres
sScope">
```

```
                        <displayName>9.3.5.67]</displayName>
                        <name>9.3.5.67]</name>

<keyGuid>11502977026911150297702691115 02</keyGuid>
                        <ip>9.3.5.67]</ip>
                </excludes>

<start>9.3.5.0/255.255.255.0[9.3.5.20</start>
                        <end>9.3.5.29</end>
                </elements>
                <elements array="2"
xsi:type="coll:com.collation.platform.model.discovery.scope.IpAddres
sScope">
                        <displayName>CTS Server</displayName>
                        <name>CTS Server</name>

<keyGuid>11502977026911150297702691115 02</keyGuid>
                        <ip>9.3.4.165</ip>
                </elements>
                <elements array="3"
xsi:type="coll:com.collation.platform.model.discovery.scope.IpRangeS
cope">
                        <displayName>Windows Gateways</displayName>
                        <name>Windows Gateways</name>

<keyGuid>11502977026911150297702691115 02</keyGuid>
                        <start>9.3.4.174</start>
                        <end>9.3.4.175</end>
                </elements>
                <elements array="4"
xsi:type="coll:com.collation.platform.model.discovery.scope.IpRangeS
cope">
                        <displayName>Anchor Hosts</displayName>
                        <name>Anchor Hosts</name>

<keyGuid>11502977026911150297702691115 02</keyGuid>
                <excludes array="1"
xsi:type="coll:com.collation.platform.model.discovery.scope.IpAddres
sScope">
                        <displayName>[9.3.4.183]</displayName>
                        <name>[9.3.4.183]</name>

<keyGuid>11502977026911150297702691115 02</keyGuid>
                        <ip>[9.3.4.183]</ip>
                </excludes>
```

```
                        <start>9.3.4.180</start>
                        <end>9.2.4.185</end>
                </elements>
        </Scope>
</results>
```

To import the scope, we simply repeated the command, omitting the -d option, as in Example B-11.

Example: B-11 Importing the scope with the -d option

```
[root@taddm02 bin]# ${COLLATION_HOME}/bin/loadscope.jy /
-u administrator -p collation -s "Test Scope" load /tmp/test.scope
...
Processing:  9.3.5.0/255.255.255.0[9.3.5.20-9.3.5.29,9.3.5.67], ITSO
Lab
Successfully parsed
Processing:  9.3.4.165,,CTS Server
Successfully parsed
Processing:  9.3.4.174-9.3.4.175,,Windows Gateways
Successfully parsed
Processing:  9.3.4.180-9.2.4.185,[9.3.4.183],Anchor Hosts
Successfully parsed
Processing:
```

B.3.3 templateloader: the template import/export utility

Use the templateloader to import and export Application and Custom Server Templates:

```
Usage: templateloader.jy -u username -p password -t Template
import|export template_file
```

Example B-12 demonstrates how to export the TCPServer Custom Server Template definition to a file maned /tmp/TCPTest.template.

Example: B-12 Exporting the TCPServer Custom Server Template definition

```
[root@taddm02 bin]# ./templateloader.jy -u administrator -p
collation -t TCPServer export /tmp/TCPServer.template
Looking for extension descriptor for  TCPServer
Searching extension descriptor for extension scripts.
Found extension script  TCPServer.py
Could not connect to ITADD
```

Attention: In the version of IBM Tivoli Change and Configuration Management Database Configuration Discovery and Tracking v1.1 used to create this book, the templateloader.jy script was not running correctly. As a result, we cannot provide examples of its use.

B.4 Support tools

The following tools are provided with IBM Tivoli Change and Configuration Management Database Configuration Discovery and Tracking v1.1 on an as-is basis. The purpose of these tools is to help test and debug problems with the Configuration Discovery and Tracking setup and use.

All of the following tools can be found in the ${COLLATION_HOME}/support/bin directory. The most important tools, which are covered in the following sections, are:

testhang.jy	Helps determine if hanging sessions can be cancelled.
testjdbc.jy	Test database access through JDBC.
testos.jy	returns all the operating system details from a specific system.
testping.jy	returns the number of active IP interfaces within specified scope.
testportmap.jy	Provides the entire list active ports on a host.
testportscan.jy	Determines which session ports a target system is listening to - and thereby which protocols are supported.
testprimaryip.jy	Returns the primary IP address of a multi-homed host.
testsnmp.jy	Verifies the read community name used to access the SNMP MIB at a host.
testssh.py	Executes a command on a host using SSH.
testwmi.jy	Verifies that WMI is installed on a system.
wmiexec.jy	Executes a command on a Windows based system.

B.4.1 testhang.jy

Use this script to verify that hanging sessions with a Unix host are successfully backed out.

```
Usage : testhang.jy <ip>
```

This script requires valid Access List entries and Anchor Hosts and Windows Gateways to access the target device. See Example B-13.

Example: B-13 Using testhang.jy

```
[root@taddm02 bin]# ./testhang.jy  9.3.5.212
Testing ...:9.3.5.212
...
2006-06-27 17:54:55,370  [main]  INFO session.SessionFactory -
getNewSession(9.3.5.212) portList=null
2006-06-27 17:55:05,484  [main]  INFO util.PortScanner - PortScanner: scan
for 9.3.5.212 complete; returning: [22]
2006-06-27 17:55:10,488  [main]  INFO session.Ssh2SessionClient -
9.3.5.212: SSH version=[SSH-1.99-OpenSSH_3.9p1] reuse=true
2006-06-27 17:57:10,663  [main]  ERROR session.SshSessionClient -
readAsString: IOException: InputStreamPipe closed after 0 bytes
2006-06-27 17:57:10,663  [main]  WARN session.SshSessionClient - Command
[cat] failed in session ssh2:/root@9.3.5.212: timed out a
fter 120.003 seconds
Execute Failed
2006-06-27 17:57:10,892  [main]  INFO session.Ssh2SessionClient -
9.3.5.212: SSH version=[SSH-1.99-OpenSSH_3.9p1] reuse=true
Result is :anaconda-ks.cfg
anchor-setup.sh
coll
coll4.0
Desktop
dlmgr_.pro
install.log
install.log.syslog
InstallShield

Result is :total 116
-rw-r--r--  1 root root  1216 Apr 25 12:07 anaconda-ks.cfg
-rw-r--r--  1 root root  2308 Jun 20 12:05 anchor-setup.sh
drwxr-xr-x  3 root root  4096 May  2 14:25 coll
drwx------  8 root root  4096 Jun 20 12:05 coll4.0
drwxr-xr-x  3 root root  4096 Apr 27 10:11 Desktop
-rw-r--r--  1 root root    15 Apr 25 16:23 dlmgr_.pro
-rw-r--r--  1 root root 56590 Apr 25 12:07 install.log
-rw-r--r--  1 root root  9506 Apr 25 12:07 install.log.syslog
drwxr-xr-x  3 root root  4096 May  2 13:07 InstallShield
```

B.4.2 testjdbc.jy

Use this script to verity jdbc connectivity to a database.

```
Usage : testjdbc.jy {d[b2]|o[oracle]|s[ybase]} {ip|host} port user
password {oracle SID|sybase db|db2 db}
```

Example B-14 shows a successful attempt to connect to the TIO database (tiodb), owned by the instance listening on port 50000, on the tioserver system (9.3.5.216) using the credentials of the tioadmin user (tioadmin/smartway):

Example: B-14 Using testjdbc.jy to connect to tiodb

```
[root@taddm02 bin]# ./testjdbc.jy db2 9.3.5.216 50000 tioadmin
smartway tiodb
Testing ...:db2 9.3.5.216 50000 tioadmin smartway
optional SID/db:tiodb
Establishing DB2 connection
Connection string: jdbc:db2://9.3.5.216:50000/tiodb
Connection successful.
Version: 8020400
```

B.4.3 testos.jy

Use the testos.jy script to verify that Configuration Discovery and Tracking can access operating system information about a system, identified by the IP address.

The testos.jy program is invoked using the IP address as the only argument:

```
Usage : testos.jy <ip>
```

This script requires valid Access List entries and Anchor Hosts and Windows Gateways to access the target device. See Example B-15.

Example: B-15 Using testos.jy

```
[root@taddm02 bin]# ./testos.jy 9.3.5.212 ls
Testing os layer on ip 9.3.5.212
...
2006-06-28 08:53:12,741  [main]  INFO session.SessionFactory -
getNewSession(9.3.5.212) portList=null
2006-06-28 08:53:22,847  [main]  INFO util.PortScanner - PortScanner: scan
for 9.3.5.212 complete; returning: [22]
2006-06-28 08:53:27,248  [main]  INFO session.Ssh2SessionClient -
9.3.5.212: SSH version=[SSH-1.99-OpenSSH_3.9p1] reuse=true
[testos] computer system: ... before
```

```
2006-06-28 08:53:27,999  [main]  INFO ip.SystemSigner - System signature
set to: 9.3.5.212(0011250D31BA)
[testos] computer system:
{signature=9.3.5.212(0011250D31BA);type=ComputerSystem;systemId=7f0100;OSRu
nning=interface com.collation
.platform.model.topology.sys.linux.Linux;fqdn=taddm01;name=taddm01}
[testos] opsys: ... before
[testos] opsys: {osId=1;OSName=Linux;name=Linux;parent=interface
com.collation.platform.model.topology.sys.linux.LinuxUnitaryCompu
terSystem}
[testos] command: kill: kill
[testos] command: port map: lsof -nP -i | awk '{print $2, $8, $9}' | sort
-k 2 | uniq -f 1
[testos] command: ps users: ps auxw
[testos] hostid: 7f0100
[testos] hostname: taddm01
[testos] architecture: i686

[testos] kernel architecture: i686
[testos] kernel version: 2.6.9-34.ELsmp
[testos] pid to runtime process map: {}
[testos] computer model: i686

[testos] computer system:
{signature=9.3.5.212(0011250D31BA);type=ComputerSystem;systemId=7f0100;OSRu
nning=interface com.collation
.platform.model.topology.sys.linux.Linux;fqdn=taddm01;name=taddm01}
[testos] CPU speed: 2993.323

[testos] CPU type: Intel(R) Pentium(R) 4
[testos] Number of CPUs: 2

2006-06-28 08:53:28,936  [SSH2TransportRX]  WARN collation.stderr - mount
clntudp_create: RPC: Program not registered
[testos] exported NFS file systems:
[testos] network interfaces: [9.3.5.212]
[testos] ip forwarding?: 0
[testos] ip interfaces: array([{ipNetwork=interface
com.collation.platform.model.topology.net.IpNetwork;L2Interface=interface
com.
collation.platform.model.topology.net.L2Interface;ipAddress=interface
com.collation.platform.model.topology.net.IpAddress}, {ipNet
work=interface
com.collation.platform.model.topology.net.IpNetwork;L2Interface=interface
com.collation.platform.model.topology.net
.L2Interface;ipAddress=interface
com.collation.platform.model.topology.net.IpAddress}],
com.collation.platform.model.topology.net.
IpInterface)
```

```
[testos] manufacturer: Red Hat
[testos] memory size: 2017

[testos] nmap: /opt/IBM/cmdb/dist/external/nmap/Linux/nmap
[testos] os name: Linux
[testos] os path:
PATH=$PATH:/usr/local/bin:/bin:/usr/bin:/usr/sbin:/sbin:/usr/X11R6/bin;
[testos] os type: 2
[testos] os version: Red Hat Enterprise Linux ES release 4 (Nahant Update
3)
except...
[testos] computer system: ... before
[testos] computer system:
{signature=9.3.5.212(0011250D31BA);type=ComputerSystem;systemId=7f0100;OSRu
nning=interface com.collation
.platform.model.topology.sys.linux.Linux;fqdn=taddm01;name=taddm01}
[testos] opsys: ... before
[testos] opsys: {osId=1;OSName=Linux;name=Linux;parent=interface
com.collation.platform.model.topology.sys.linux.LinuxUnitaryCompu
terSystem}
[testos] command: kill: kill
[testos] command: port map: lsof -nP -i | awk '{print $2, $8, $9}' | sort
-k 2 | uniq -f 1
[testos] command: ps users: ps auxw
[testos] hostid: 7f0100
[testos] hostname: taddm01
[testos] architecture: i686

[testos] kernel architecture: i686
[testos] kernel version: 2.6.9-34.ELsmp
[testos] pid to runtime process map: {}
[testos] computer model: i686

[testos] computer system:
{signature=9.3.5.212(0011250D31BA);type=ComputerSystem;systemId=7f0100;OSRu
nning=interface com.collation
.platform.model.topology.sys.linux.Linux;fqdn=taddm01;name=taddm01}
[testos] CPU speed: 2993.323

[testos] CPU type: Intel(R) Pentium(R) 4
[testos] Number of CPUs: 2

[testos] exported NFS file systems:
[testos] network interfaces: [9.3.5.212]
[testos] ip forwarding?: 0
[testos] ip interfaces: array([{ipNetwork=interface
com.collation.platform.model.topology.net.IpNetwork;L2Interface=interface
com.
```

```
collation.platform.model.topology.net.L2Interface;ipAddress=interface
com.collation.platform.model.topology.net.IpAddress}, {ipNet
work=interface
com.collation.platform.model.topology.net.IpNetwork;L2Interface=interface
com.collation.platform.model.topology.net
.L2Interface;ipAddress=interface
com.collation.platform.model.topology.net.IpAddress}],
com.collation.platform.model.topology.net.
IpInterface)
[testos] manufacturer: Red Hat
[testos] memory size: 2017

[testos] nmap: /opt/IBM/cmdb/dist/external/nmap/Linux/nmap
[testos] os name: Linux
[testos] os path:
PATH=$PATH:/usr/local/bin:/bin:/usr/bin:/usr/sbin:/sbin:/usr/X11R6/bin;
[testos] os type: 2
[testos] os version: Red Hat Enterprise Linux ES release 4 (Nahant Update
3)
```

B.4.4 testping.jy

The testping script is used to get the number of IP interfaces that are currently active in a specific scope. The scope might identify a single IP device, a subnet, or a range.

The testping.jy program is invoked using the scope type and IP addresses or subnet and netmask information as arguments:

```
Usage: testping.jy -t type <address info>
 -t ip <ipaddress>
 -t net <network> <netmask>
 -t range <startip> <endip>
```

To get the number of active IP interfaces on specific host, use ip <ipaddress> invocation:

```
[root@taddm bin]# ./testping.jy -t ip 9.3.5.216
Ping type is: ip
responder count: 1
```

To see how many IP interfaces are responding from a specific subnet, use the net <subnet> <netmask> invocation:

```
[root@taddm bin]# ./testping.jy -t net 9.3.5.0 255.255.255.0
Ping type is: net
responder count: 74
```

And to get the number of active IP interfaces within range, you can use the range `<startip> <endip>` notation:

```
[root@taddm bin]# ./testping.jy -t range 9.3.5.1 9.3.5.100
Ping type is: range
responder count: 45
```

B.4.5 testportmap.jy

Use this script to see which ports are active on a device.

```
Usage: testportmap.jy <ip>
```

This script requires valid Access List entries and Anchor Hosts and Windows Gateways to access the target device. See Example B-16.

Example: B-16 Using testportmap.jy

```
[root@taddm02 bin]# ./testportmap.jy 9.3.5.225
Testing portmap on ip 9.3.5.225
...
2006-06-27 16:38:31,867  [main]  INFO session.SessionFactory -
getNewSession(9.3.5.225) portList=null
2006-06-27 16:38:41,972  [main]  INFO util.PortScanner - PortScanner: scan
for 9.3.5.225 complete; returning: [22]
2006-06-27 16:38:46,295  [main]  INFO session.Ssh2SessionClient -
9.3.5.225: SSH version=[SSH-1.99-OpenSSH_3.9p1] reuse=true
Result is:
2540 *:111
2540 *:111 (LISTEN)
2783 *:113 (LISTEN)
2802 127.0.0.1:25 (LISTEN)
20827 127.0.0.1:32774->127.0.0.1:32774
24470 127.0.0.1:631 (LISTEN)
20827 *:1920 (LISTEN)
2768 *:22 (LISTEN)
2560 *:32768
2560 *:32769 (LISTEN)
20827 *:32836 (LISTEN)
20827 *:32837 (LISTEN)
20827 *:3661 (LISTEN)
29192 *:37646 (LISTEN)
3873 *:523
3873 *:523 (LISTEN)
20827 *:6014 (LISTEN)
2560 *:616
24470 *:631
2476 *:68
8405 9.3.5.225:22->9.3.4.165:35843 (ESTABLISHED)
```

```
20827 9.3.5.225:32838->9.3.4.174:1918 (ESTABLISHED)
29192 9.3.5.225:32977->9.3.5.212:37645 (ESTABLISHED)
PID NODE NAME
```

B.4.6 testportscan.jy

Use this tool to verify if the device is listening any of the following ports:

port	**protocol**
22	sshd
23	telnet
135	DCOM

In order to determine which protocol to use to access the system.

```
Usage: testportscan.jy <ip> [<wait-time> <attempts>]
```

Example B-17 shows how to determine which of the ports - `22, 23, or 135` - the host on IP address `9.3.5.174` listens. Between each of the four attempts, that script will wait 2 seconds.

Example: B-17 Using testportscan.jy

```
[root@taddm02 bin]# ./testportscan.jy 9.3.5.174 2 4
Testing portscan on ip 9.3.5.174 with 4 attempts and a waittime of 2
seconds.
2006-06-27 17:20:41,371  [main]  INFO util.PortScanner - PortScanner:
scan for 9.3.5.174 complete; returning: [23, 22]
2006-06-27 17:20:49,394  [main]  INFO util.PortScanner - PortScanner:
scan for 9.3.5.174 complete; returning: [23, 22]
2006-06-27 17:20:57,424  [main]  INFO util.PortScanner - PortScanner:
scan for 9.3.5.174 complete; returning: [23, 22]
2006-06-27 17:21:05,441  [main]  INFO util.PortScanner - PortScanner:
scan for 9.3.5.174 complete; returning: [23, 22]
[root@taddm02 bin]# ./testportscan.jy 9.3.4.174 1 4
Testing portscan on ip 9.3.4.174 with 4 attempts and a waittime of 1
seconds.
```

Important: If you receive an error similar to the following:

```
Traceback (innermost last):
  File "./testportscan.jy", line 41, in ?
TypeError: com.collation.platform.util.PortScanner(): 1st arg
can't be coerced to String
```

You should change the line in the script that reads:

```
scanner = PortScanner(ia, waittime, numAttempts)
```

to

```
scanner = PortScanner(ip, waittime, numAttempts)
```

You might experience that the script never ends. To correct this, use the script in Example B-18, which shows a working version of the testportscan.jy script. In the code listed, changes compared to the version delivered with the GA code of IBM Tivoli Change and Configuration Management Database Configuration Discovery and Tracking v1.1 are highlighted in **bold**.

Example: B-18 testportscan.jy

```
#!/usr/bin/env ./jython_coll
## $Id: testportscan.jy,v 1.3 2005/03/22 22:15:24 jbarrera Exp $
## Copyright 2001-2005 Collation Inc. All Rights Reserved
## This software is the proprietary information of Collation Inc.
# Use is subject to license terms.
#
import sys
import string
import java

from java.lang import *
from java.net import InetAddress
from java.util import Collections

from com.collation.platform.util import PortScanner

try:
        ip = sys.argv[1]
        try:
                arg2 = sys.argv[2]
        except:
                arg2 = "10"
        try:
                arg3 = sys.argv[3]
```

```
		except:
			arg3 = "3"
		waittime = 1000 * string.atoi(arg2)
		numAttempts = string.atoi(arg3)
		print "Testing portscan on ip", ip, "with", numAttempts,
"attempts and a waittime of", arg2, "seconds."
except:
		print "Usage: testportscan <ip> <waittime-in-seconds>
<num_attempts>"
		System.exit(0)

oldlist = None
ia = InetAddress.getByName(ip)

i = numAttempts;
while i >= 1:
		i = i - 1;
		scanner = PortScanner(ip, waittime, numAttempts)
		ports = [ 22, 23, 135 ]
		list = scanner.scanPorts(ports)
		Collections.sort(list)
		if oldlist != None and not list.equals(oldlist):
			print "*** lists are different!"
			print "old: ", oldlist
			print "new: ", list
			break
		oldlist = list
System.exit(0)
```

B.4.7 testprimaryip.jy

Use this tools to get the primary IP address of a multi-homed device.

```
Usage: testprimaryip.jy <ip>
```

Requires valid Access List entries and Anchor Hosts and Windows Gateways to access the target device.

Example:

```
[root@taddm02 bin]# ./testprimaryip.jy 9.3.5.252
Testing :  9.3.5.252
Primary IP :  9.3.5.252
```

B.4.8 testsnmp.jy

Use this script to verify the community name used to access the SMNP MIB at a target system:

```
Usage: testsnmp.jy -h <host> -c <community>
```

Example:

```
[root@taddm02 bin]# ./testsnmp.jy -h 9.3.5.216 -c public
Testing 9.3.5.216 with community public
GET of .1.3.6.1.2.1.1.5.0 returned tioserver.tivdemo.com
```

B.4.9 testssh.py

Use this utility to verify SSH access to a system.

The testssh.py script uses the Access List credentials to access a system in your infrastructure, and execute a command specified on invocation.

```
Usage : testssh.py <ip> <command>
```

To get the universal time and date settings for a system, you can use the following:

```
[root@taddm02 bin]# ./testssh.py 9.3.5.216 "date -u"
Testing ...:9.3.5.216 date -u
...
Result is :Sat Jun 17 01:01:06 UTC 2006
```

Note: If the command passed to testssh.py is made up of more that one word, enclose the entire command in double-quotes.

B.4.10 testwmi.jy

This script can be used to verify the WMI connectivity between a Windows Gateway and a Windows target.

The testwmi script uses the Access List credentials to access the Windows based system, so it will fail unless proper Access List entries to connect to both the Windows Gateway (using SSH) and the target system does not exist.

```
Usage : testwmi.jy <ip>
```

See Example B-19.

Example: B-19 Using testwmi.jy

```
[root@taddm02 bin]# ./testwmi.jy 9.3.4.174
Testing WMI on host 9.3.4.174
...
2006-06-27 16:28:47,785  [main]  INFO session.SessionFactory -
getNewSession(9.3.4.174) portList=null
2006-06-27 16:28:57,888  [main]  INFO util.PortScanner - PortScanner: scan for
9.3.4.174 complete; returning: [135]
2006-06-27 16:29:06,875  [main]  INFO util.PortScanner - PortScanner: scan for
9.3.5.252 complete; returning: [22]
2006-06-27 16:29:07,868  [main]  INFO session.Ssh2SessionClient - 9.3.5.252: SSH
version=[SSH-2.0-1.75 sshlib: WinSSHD 4.13] reuse
=true
2006-06-27 16:29:08,526  [main]  INFO session.UnscopedGateway -
Gateway.prepare(9.3.5.252): first attempt
2006-06-27 16:29:11,043  [main]  INFO session.UnscopedGateway -
Gateway.prepare(9.3.5.252): succeeded!
2006-06-27 16:29:11,531  [main]  INFO session.AbstractWindowsSessionClient -
GetDesiredVersion returns version 20060607 after 0 se
conds.
2006-06-27 16:29:12,093  [main]  INFO session.AbstractWindowsSessionClient -
GetVersion returns version 20060607 after 0 seconds.
2006-06-27 16:29:12,719  [main]  INFO session.AbstractWindowsSessionClient -
GetVersion returns version 20060607 after 0 seconds.
```

B.4.11 wmiexec.jy

The wmiexec script can be used to execute a command on a Windows based target system using the WMI protocol.

The wmiexec script uses the Access List credentials to access the Windows based system, so it will fail unless proper Access List entries to connect to both the Windows Gateway (using SSH) and the target system does not exist.

```
Usage : wmiexec.jy <ip> <command>
```

Example B-20 shows how we execute the hostname command on a remote system 9.3.5.174 through a Windows Gateway (9.3.5.252).

Example: B-20 Using wmiexe.jy

```
[root@taddm02 bin]# ./wmiexec.jy 9.3.4.174 "hostname"
Testing ...:9.3.4.174 hostname
...
2006-06-27 16:26:31,528  [main]  INFO util.PortScanner - PortScanner: scan for
9.3.5.252 complete; returning: [22]
2006-06-27 16:26:32,692  [main]  INFO session.Ssh2SessionClient - 9.3.5.252: SSH
version=[SSH-2.0-1.75 sshlib: WinSSHD 4.13] reuse
=true
2006-06-27 16:26:33,320  [main]  INFO session.UnscopedGateway -
Gateway.prepare(9.3.5.252): first attempt
2006-06-27 16:26:35,729  [main]  INFO session.UnscopedGateway -
Gateway.prepare(9.3.5.252): succeeded!
2006-06-27 16:26:36,216  [main]  INFO session.AbstractWindowsSessionClient -
GetDesiredVersion returns version 20060607 after 0 seconds.
2006-06-27 16:26:36,734  [main]  INFO session.AbstractWindowsSessionClient -
GetVersion returns version 20060607 after 0 seconds.
2006-06-27 16:26:37,390  [main]  INFO session.AbstractWindowsSessionClient -
GetVersion returns version 20060607 after 0 seconds.
Result is :taddm99
```

C

Discovery Library overview

The IBM Tivoli Discovery Library, is a core a component of the IBM Tivoli Change Configuration Management Database solution, which brings together various technologies that perform automatic discovery of resources and their relationships for transactions, applications and business processes.

The following provides a description of the Discovery Library technology and the various architectural components it is made up off.

C.1 Introduction

The IBM Discovery Library consists of a set of reusable tools that discover resources from IBM and vendor software. Use the Discovery Library tools to communicate discovery and the relationships between discovered resources within the enterprise. The Discovery Library tools includes the following:

- Discovery Library XML schema specification, called the Identity Markup Language (IdML). The Discovery Library includes an XML schema to describe instances of relationships and resources from data sources.
- Discovery Library Components (IBM and third party software) that extract and transform data to the XML schema specification.
- The Discovery Library Books, or XML files that contain discovery information including identity of resources and their relationships.
- A set of recommended practices for deploying, loading information into, utilizing, and managing the Discovery Library.

The Discovery Library tools are reusable for various products. For example, the tools can be used to populate IBM Tivoli Business Systems Manager 3.1 (TBSM) and the same data might be fed into other applications through the Configuration Management Database (CMDB).

The following scenario describes integration of an existing data source into a vendor product:

1. Define the model mapping from the data source model to the Common Data Model (CDM).
2. Create the application that implements the model mapping:
   a. Process the data sources existing model.
   b. Parse that into a set of invocations that drives a CDM modeled back-end.
3. Implement the selected back-end to create operations and instance records in Discovery Library IdML format that specify a reader to create, modify, or delete instances.

C.1.1 Interaction with the Discovery Library

Figure C-1 represents the high-level interactions that occur between actors and the Discovery Library.

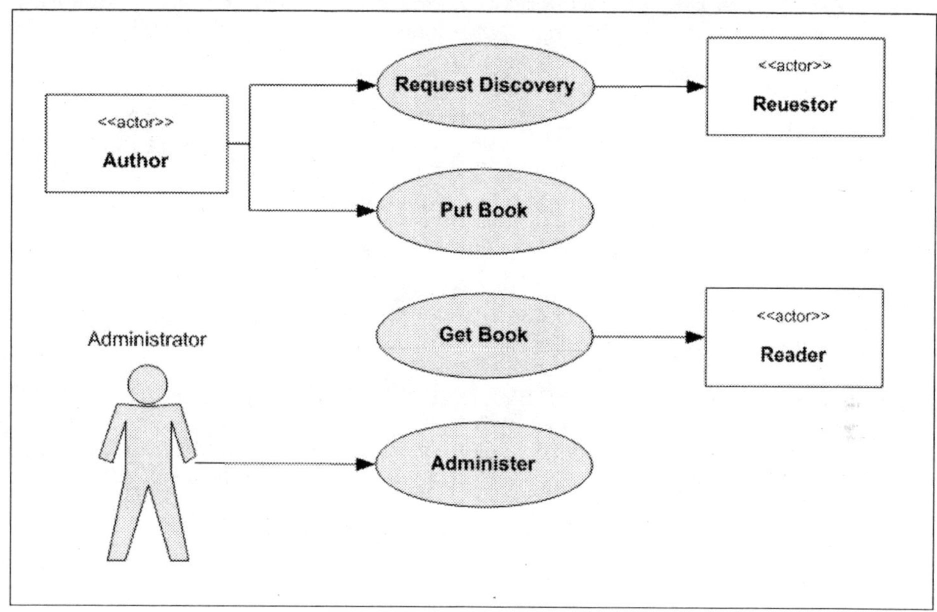

Figure C-1 Actors interactions

Actors

The following list describes actors that interact with the Discovery Library:

Author
: The author is the actor that obtains the source data of interest from the data source (also known as a management software system). The author produces books (XML files) that contain the source data and requests updates to the Discovery Library. Authors can also provide a capability for discovery updates to be requested. At this level of the specification there is no assertion that discovery updates must be dynamic or on-demand. The data source must make its resource/relationship data available through a supported interface such as API, database schema, or file format.

Requester
: The requestor is the actor that coordinates requests for authors to perform discoveries. Requestors must have the capability to interact with the author to request any supported type of discovery. Requestors must also have the capability to request any supported type of discovery. In a single deployment, the design assumes a one-to-many relationship between an instance

of the requestor and instances of the author. The design recommends that an author is controlled by one requestor at a time. The Discovery Library views coordination of requests to occur outside the Discovery Library. See the "Request Discovery use case" on page 416 for a case description of how the requestor fulfills the role of a discovery orchestrator across multiple authors.

Reader
: The reader is the actor that retrieves books to read from the Discovery Library. While reading the books, the reader performs the specified operations on resources and relationships contained in the book.

Administrator
: The administrator maintains the Discovery Library, ensuring that it is available to other actors. Each Discovery Library instance has one administrator.

C.1.2 Discovery Library system level use cases

The following list and describes the types of interaction, or use cases, that can occur between an actor and the Discovery Library:

Request Discovery
: The Request Discovery use case captures the communication between the requester and the author.

Put Book
: The Put Book use case captures all interaction between the author and the Discovery Library that are involved with adding content from the author's domain.

Get Book
: The Get Book use case describes how books and information about books are retrieved from the library. The Get Book use case is an interaction between the reader and the Discovery Library. The author does not communicate with this use case because it is based on content that is in the library at the time the use case occurs.

Administer
: The Administer use case describes all of the ways in which the Discovery Library is maintained. The Administer use case covers all functions not described by the previous use cases.

See C.4, "Use Cases" on page 413 for more information about uses cases.

C.1.3 Discovery Library schema

The Discovery Library XML schema is called IdML. IdML is an extension of the Common Data Model XML schema developed by IBM. Its extensions specify characteristics of specific Discovery Library adapters, such as the class types that a specified discovery adapter can find and report, as well as characteristics of specific instances of discovery like the type of discovery, and the time that a discovery ran.

The best practices provide guidance with using the IdML schema, including help in determining the either of the following items:

- Which resource and relationship classes to use to represent typical components in a business system.
- Which mechanisms enhance the ability successfully to route status information to the resources described in IdML.Consider the schema terms and conditions to ensure optimal results from a well-controlled environment.

C.1.4 Adapters

The Discovery Library adapters exploit mechanisms that are implemented by the sources of discovered information (such as transaction topology views) to extract specific information about resources and resource relationships. The Discovery Library adapters transform the native source information into an IdML-schema-compliant data file that readers can process for their domain-specific purposes. The goal of the information from the adapters is to discover and keep current the sets of resources and relationships that comprise business applications and support for business processes. The solutions wrap the Discovery Library adapters they need in an infrastructure that provides functions such as deployment, configuration, command and control, and communication. The Discovery Library provides a common API for the creation of XML files against the IdML specification.

C.1.5 Discovery Library books

A Discovery Library book is self-contained in that it uniquely identifies the author of the discovery data, when the data was generated, and the resources and relationships specified in the book. All instances in the book have sufficient identifying information that a reader can render into its own representation. A book is represented as one XML file in the Discovery Library. A Discovery Library book carries time stamp information to chronologically sequence multiple files from an author.

A Discovery Library book can describe either complete or delta discoveries. A complete discovery includes a declaration by the author that the set of instances and relationships in the book are the full set of entities that are in the domain of the authors at the time of discovery with the constraints of the authors observation algorithm. A complete discovery can therefore be used by a reader to compare to a previously read complete discovery from the author to determine which entities the author believes no longer exist in the domain. This is the refresh tag described in "IdML Schema" on page 399.

A delta discovery can include operations to delete or modify previously announced instances and relationships. A delta discovery carries sufficient time stamp information so that it is clear what previous state it has changed from.

The IdML-schema-compliant data files contain the information that readers can process for their domain-specific purposes. Each file represents view of the resources and relationships as seem by a single discovery adapter. Readers of the Discovery Library data integrate these views into the context of their environment for relevant information.

C.2 Discovery architecture overview

Figure C-2 displays the operational flow of the Discovery Library, the main actors and components of the Discovery Library, and the exploiting solution:

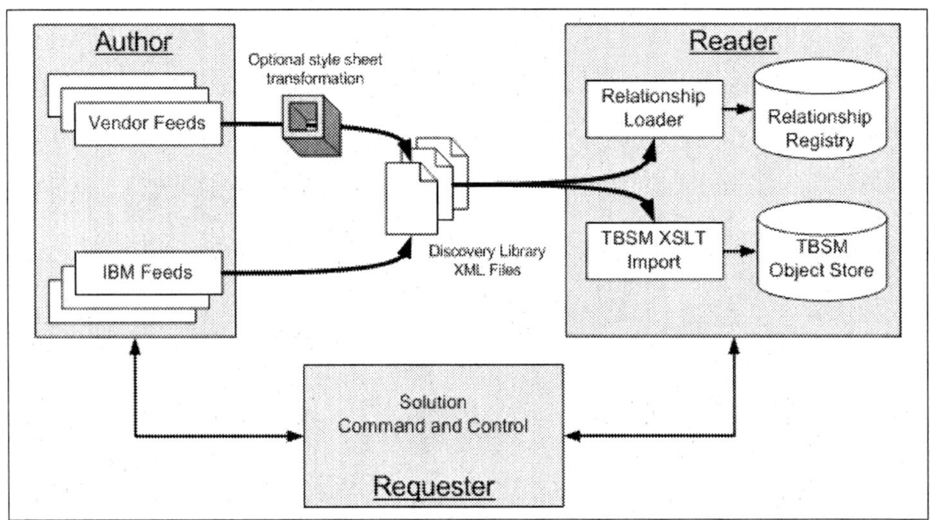

Figure C-2 Discovery Library Environment

IBM and vendors supply authors. Authors produce IdML, either natively or by using a transformation process, and make their IdML files available to the consuming solutions called readers.

The authors in Figure C-2 are Discovery Library adapters. An author is a runtime component that accomplishes integration by using interfaces and classes provided by the Discovery Library. Authors are composed of code that reads native resource and relationship information from data sources and produces IdML from that information.

Tivoli Business Systems Manager and the Relationship Loader are the readers in Figure C-2 on page 392. The Bulk Load Utility loads books into the Configuration Management Database. These readers are outside the scope of the Discovery Library. Readers apply filters and processing to books to acquire useful content.

Each Discovery Library feed must produce its own system design document that includes operations details and flow of data from the source to the Discovery Library. Each product that exploits the Discovery Library is responsible for producing a design document that addresses deployment, configuration, and management of Discovery Library modules appropriate to their environment.

Figure C-3 displays a detailed view of the Discovery Library.

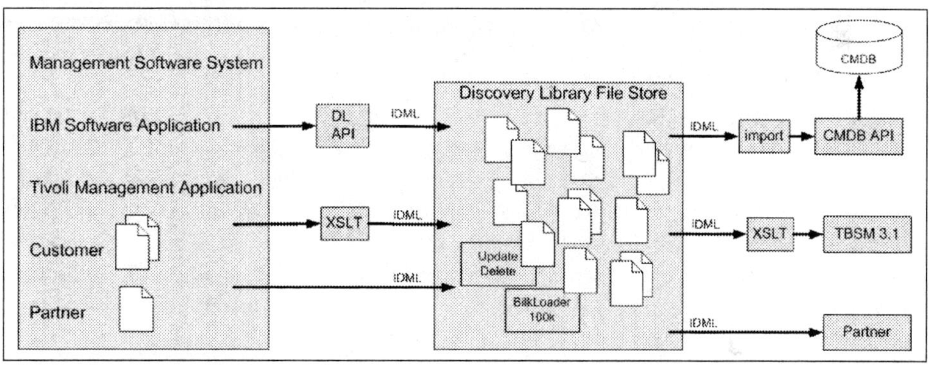

Figure C-3 Discovery Library File Store

C.2.1 Authors

There are two types of authors: a *Discovery Library Integrator* and a *Discovery Library Adapter*. A Discovery Library Integrator does not use the IdML Production API or the Discovery Library Adapter API. The following criteria determine whether the author is a Discovery Library integrator or a Discovery Library adapter:

- The application environment on which the author exists.
- The level of integration the author needs.

An job of the author is complete when it places the book in the Discovery Library File Store. A book should not be modified by any author or reader.

The Discovery Library provides a series of flows for applications in the author role to provide data to the Discovery Library. In order to provide data to the

Discovery Library, an author must map its local resource and relationship instance data to the IdML specification. This mapping can occur using an eXtensible Stylesheet Language Transform (XSLT) to generate an IdML file from the authors local format of the resources. This mapping must occur before the file is placed into the Discovery Library. If an author knows how to normalize the instance data (elements and their relationships) to the IdML specification, the author generates the IdML file and place the file in an administrator-configured location. This location holds Discovery Library IdML files from multiple authors. This administratively configured location is called the Discovery Library File Store. The Discovery Library File Store holds IdML file information, but it does not provide infrastructure or access to or facilitate interaction with the files in the Discovery Library File Store.

The Discovery Library contains an IdML Production API that generates an IdML file based on author input. The author makes API calls to generate an XML file.

The API calls `create`, `update`, and `delete` on resource or relationship instances. When appropriately called, this API opens and closes an XML file and places the resulting file in the Discovery Library through the output stream provided by the Discovery Library adapter.

A *Discovery Library Integrator* is an author that produces IdML files for the Discovery Library File Store. An integrator accepts no external command or control requests. This author generates a book for the Discovery Library at a frequency determined by the author. The Discovery Library Integrator is both the author and requestor. This author must have a flow in place to provide the book to the Discovery Library File Store. No other communications flow exists between a Discovery Library Integrator and the Discovery Library. The Integrator author facilitates implementations that do not want to integrate into the environment of their exploiters other than providing data.

The *Discovery Library Adapter* is an author that is also responsible for generating books for the Discovery Library. The Discovery Library Adapter builds book using the IdML Production API. The author can also use the IdML Production API to help create a book. The Discovery Library adapter API offers common interfaces for its exploiters to exercise command and control as Requesters. Each adapter provides an ability to accept configuration information. You can launch the Discovery Library Adapter from a command line interface to enable command and control support for scheduling technologies such as `cron`. Authors should implement the interfaces and degree of control that match their abilities and the requirements of their exploiting solutions. Figure C-4 on page 395 shows the author types.

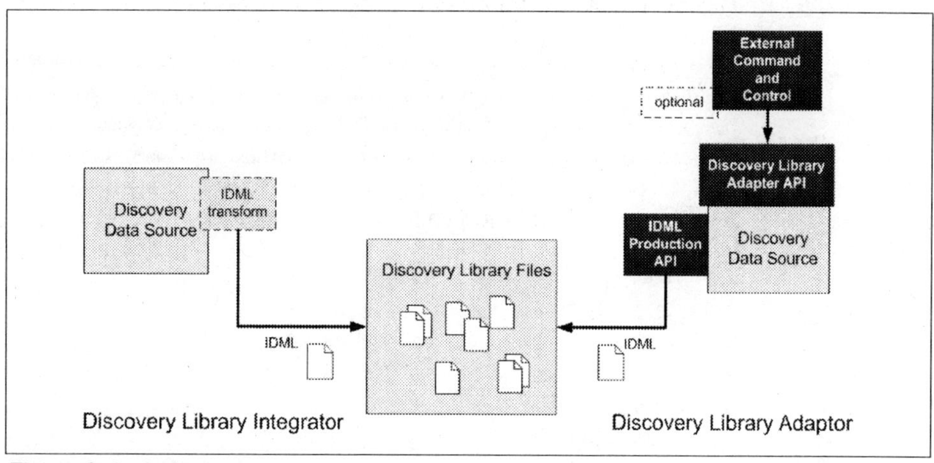

Figure C-4 Author types

C.2.2 Readers

When IdML files, or books, are placed in the Discovery Library they are available for readers to read. There is no infrastructure in the Discovery Library infrastructure to ensure that books are well-formed against the IdML schema. The reader copies the book from the Discovery Library.

Readers of the Discovery Library File Store access the information in either a pull or push method. Readers that pull information from the Discovery Library File Store at regular intervals, identify any new books that arrive and automatically load them. Other readers wait for the Discovery Library File Store to push the book to the reader and then load the book. Refer to the individual adapter guides to learn how the reader accesses the Discovery Library File Store.

To gain access to the books in the Discovery Library, a reader must have the appropriate access to the Discovery Library File Store. The Discovery Library does not provide an additional way to access the Discovery Library File Store. Use the a standard file system method of accessing files. Readers must adapt the IdML files to their environment.

The Discovery Library does not provide an impulse mechanism (notification or event infrastructure) to prompt authors to create a Discovery Library book or a reader to read a Discovery Library book. If a use case requires an author or reader receive an impulse, that must occur outside the Discovery Library. When reading books, use a common file I/O mechanism such as File Transfer Protocol (FTP) or local disk read/write.

C.2.3 IdML book files

A Discovery Library Book is self-contained. It uniquely identifies the author of the discovery data, when the data was generated, and the resources and relationships specified in the book that have sufficient identifying information that a reader can render into its own representation. A book is represented as one XML file in the Discovery Library. A Discovery Library book carries time stamp information to chronologically sequence multiple files from an author.

A Discovery Library book can describe either complete or delta discoveries. A complete discovery constitutes a declaration by the author that the set of instances and relationships in the book are the full set of entities that are in the authors domain at the time of discovery with the constraints of the authors observation algorithm. Therefore, a complete discovery can be used by a reader to compare to a previously read complete discovery from the author to determine which entities the author believes no longer exist in the domain. This is the Refresh tag. See C.2.6, “IdML Schema” on page 399 for details on the cdm:refresh operation.

A delta discovery can include operations to delete or modify previously announced instances and relationships. A delta discovery carries sufficient time stamp information so that it is clear what previous state it has changed from.

The IdML-schema-compliant data files contain the information that readers can process for their domain-specific purposes. Each file represents the view of the resources and relationships at a particular point in time for a single discovery adapter. Readers of the Discovery Library data integrate these views into the context of their environment for relevant information.

C.2.4 File naming conventions

All files in the Discovery Library use a specific book name format to name the book. This section describes the naming conventions for the files in the Discovery Library File Store. The information contained within the file name includes the unique identity of the author and a time stamp that represents the date the book was created. All files in the Discovery Library File Store are appended with the .xml extension.

The following example shows a book listed in the Discovery Library:

```
BWMv5.3.0.1.drknow.raleigh.ibm.com.2005-03-07T12.05.00Z.xml
```

author
: Each author and author version holds a unique application code, for use in the file name of books that come from each author type. This application code consists of up to the first 10 characters of the file name. Authors have a unique identity associated with each instance. This identity is stored in the IdML file under the

idml:source tag in each book. Because the identity string can exceed the maximum file name length, or contain characters not valid in a file name, the file name contains a unique code specific to an application type, application version, and the hostname of the running instance. You can perform a search by using this application code to list all books created by a specific author type. Books exist in the Discovery Library File Store from multiple authors of data. The Discovery Library book name (file name) aids in the ability to determine which book belongs to which author.

hostname
: The host name in the file name corresponds to the host name of the machine on which the management application, or author, is installed. Search by the hostname to list all books created by authors that exist on a particular hostname. Search by application code and hostname to return a list of all books created by a specific author running on a particular machine.

timestamp
: The author must store the time stamp in UTC (Universal Time Coordinated) according to ISO8601 with an exception. The time stamp in the file name corresponds to the UTC in which the book was written. Most file systems consider the colon (:) a restricted character, so a period (.) substitutes a colon in the time stamp.

Any book that contains the cdm:refresh operation must include the word refresh in the file name after the time stamp of the book. See "IdML Schema" on page 399 for details on the cdm:refresh operation. The following example shows a book listed in the Discovery Library that contains a refresh operation

```
BWMv5.3.0.1.drknow.raleigh.ibm.com.2005-03-07T12.05.00Z.refresh.xml
```

Readers must know when files from the authors are ready to read books from the Discovery Library File Store. Discovery Library authors that support versions 0.7 and higher of the IdML schema must implement the following two-step naming convention process. This naming convention enables readers to know when files are ready. Readers must consider that earlier versions of books follow this naming convention and must take appropriate action to prevent errors. The process is as follows:

1. Using the naming example above, when an author begins to write or copy a file to the Discovery Library File Store, the author writes the file with the following name:

   ```
   BWMv5.3.0.1.drknow.raleigh.ibm.com.2005-03-07T12.05.00Z.xml.partial
   ```

2. After the author completes writing or copying a file to the Discovery Library File Store, the file name is updated as in the following example:

   ```
   BWMv5.3.0.1.drknow.raleigh.ibm.com.2005-03-07T12.05.00Z.xml
   ```

C.2.5 Time stamp conventions

Information in the IdML files represents a point-in-time operation on one or more instances of which a particular author is aware. The operations are chronologically listed in the IdML file. This time stamp enables consuming applications to sort IdML files per author and preserve the chronology of the operations that occur between IdML files from a specified author. The Discovery Library books use the dateTime representation as defined in the W3C XML Schema Definition of Datatypes. The dateTime is a single lexical representation which is a subset of the lexical representations allowed by ISO 8601. This lexical representation is the ISO 8601 extended format. This format is:

```
CCYY-MM-DDThh:mm:ssZ
```

where:

CCYY Specifies the century and year. The CCYY field must have at least four digits. To accommodate year values greater than 9999 you can use additional digits to the left of this representation. Leading zeros are required if the year value is fewer than four digits. The year 0000 is prohibited.

MM Specifies the month with 2 digits.

DD Specifies the day with 2 digits. T Separates the date and time with 2 digits.

hh Specifies the hour.

mm Specifies the minutes.

ss Specifies seconds.You can optionally use additional digits to specify fractional seconds. For example, ss.ss...

Z You can append the specified time with a Z to indicate Universal Time Coordinated (UTC) or, to indicate the time zone, (the difference between the local time and Universal Time Coordinated) immediately followed by a sign (+ or -), followed by the difference from UTC represented as hh:mm (note that the minutes part is required). See ISO 8601 Date and Time Formats for details about legal values in the various fields. If the time zone is included, both hours and minutes must be present.

For example, to indicate 11:30:00.123 am on March the 7th 2005, the following examples show valid time stamps for operations:

```
2005-03-07T11:30:00-05:00 (for Eastern Standard Time)
2005-03-07T16:30:00Z (for Universal Time Coordinated)
2005-03-07T17:30:00.123+01:00 (for Central European Time)
```

C.2.6 IdML Schema

The XML Schema Definition (XSD) describe the operations necessary to take data about resource and relationship instances from an author and instantiate it into a readers repository. This schema defines the operations that occur on instances of resources and relationships. In order to facilitate future model versions and updates, this schema references an external schema, the Common Data Model, to define the resource and relationship instances. All files in the Discovery Library conform to the IdML schema. Books in the Discovery Library that do not validate against the IdML schema are in error, and are not consumed by readers. The IdML schema is designed to separate the operations from the model specification to enable the schema to handle updates to the model specification without modifying the IdML schema. Figure C-5 displays the a schema diagram.

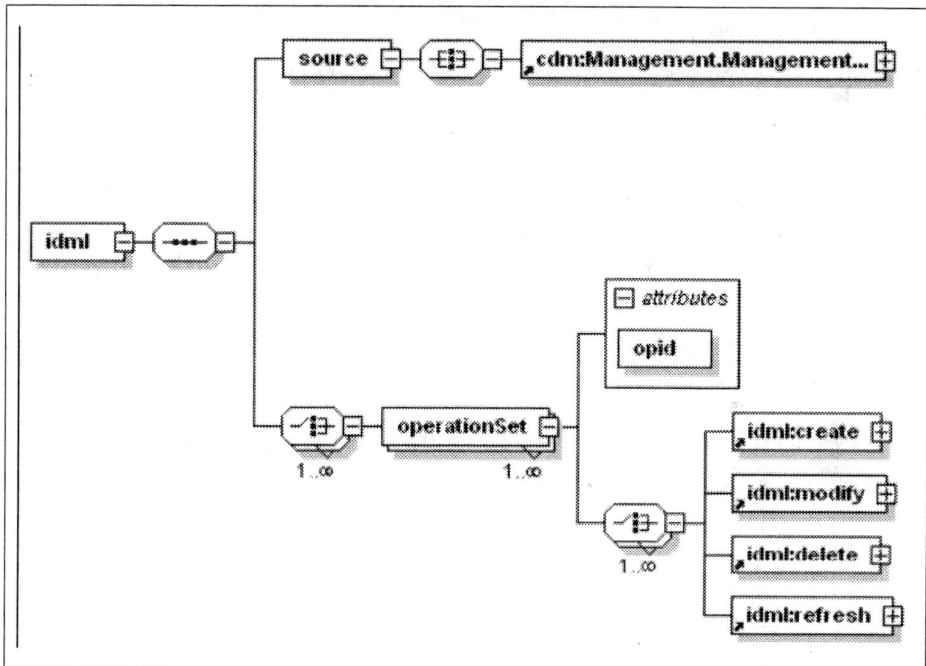

Figure C-5 Schema diagram

The reader treats the individual elements within the operations as a transaction. In this circumstance, the reader ignores the single resource or relationship instance that is in error.

The following lists and describes the IdML Schema elements:

- Data Source Definition

  For each file, a well-formed element, idml:source, representing a Management Software System (cdm:Management.ManagementSoftwareSystem) is required. The element defined here represents the application instance that is the authority of the information contained within the file, and is treated as such by any reader of the file.

- Base Operations - Operation Set

  Base operations are called operation sets (idml:operationSet). An operation set is the outer container for a set of operations. Many operations on resources can exist within an operation set. Readers should treat the contents of an operation set according to the attributes defined for the operation set. Each operation has two optional attributes (timestamp, endTimestamp).

  timestamp Used to denote when the operation occurred in the discovery domain. This is helpful to readers that want to understand a chronology of when the operation began.

  endTimestamp Used to denote when the operation ended in the discovery domain. This is helpful to readers that want to understand if the operation occurred within a particular span of time.

  For each operation set, the following attribute is required:

  opid A unique operation ID. This identifier is to differentiate one particular operation set from another. The uniqueness of the identifier is limited to the book.

  The following list includes elements that are permitted within the operation set:

  - idml:create

    Container element for the creation of instances. A reader should treat elements contained within this operation as a request to create these instances. One or more instances can be specified within this operation. Since authors can be knowledgeable of the information that they have reported in previous books, they might (or might not) provide idml:create operations for all resources and relationships in every discovery book.

Readers should treat a second idml:create operation from an author for an already existing resource as an idml:modify operation.

- idml:modify

  Container element for the update of instances. A reader should treat elements contained within this operation as a request to update these instances with the information provided. One or more instances can be specified within this operation. If a reader encounters an instance to modify a resource that does not exist in its domain, the reader should ignore the modify operation on that resource.

- idml:delete

  Container element for the deletion of instances. A reader should treat elements contained within this operation as a request to delete these instances. One or more instances can be specified within this operation

- idml:refresh

  Container element for the creation of instances, with an additional semantic. When an author environment is updated, the author can use the refresh element to suggest that the reader replace all existing author content pertaining to the author with the new content provided. The refresh element infers that a resource or relationship of a previous book from that author no longer exists and that the reader can delete or mark the resource or relationship as no longer found. Only idml:create operations are permitted within this operation. One or more instances of the idml:create operation can be specified within this operation.

  When an authors environment is updated, the author can use the refresh element to suggest the reader replace all existing author content pertaining to the author with the new content provided. The refresh element infers that a resource or relationship of a previous book from that author no longer exists and that the reader can delete or mark the resource or relationship as no longer found.

Within each of the operations, you can choose which model you want to use within the IdML operations. The following list describes what each base element includes:

- cdm:ManagedElement

  A book can contain any number of cdm:ManagedElement elements, and cdm:relationship instances within an operation. The cdm:ManagedElement element contains the necessary attributes for a reader to uniquely identify that class type instance. The set of attributes required for identity is determined though modeling the author data to the Common Data Model. The following

attributes Within each cdm:ManagedElement element the following attributes are allowed:

id Required. Specifies a unique identifier within the scope of a single book for the instance, of type string. The id attribute links an instance of a cdm:ManagedElement element to a reference within a relationship instance as a source or target. The value of the id attribute must be unique across all cdm:ManagedElement instances within a book.

superior Optional. Specifies an instance of id that references another cdm:ManagedElement instance within the book. In certain cases, cdm:ManagedElement instances require another cdm:ManagedElement instance in order to uniquely identify it. The set of cases that require the use of superior is a data modeling activity, and is contained within the Common Data Model naming rules document.

sourceToken Optional. Specifies a unique identifier for the instance, of type string. This attribute is available for use by authors to store a locally (to the author) unique identifier for cdm:ManagedElement instances. Authors should provide a unique identifier within the authors environment when using the sourceToken attribute.

sourceContactInfo Optional. A string attribute used for communicating directly with the author. This attribute is referenced by readers who support the ability to communicate back to the author directly about an instance. The contents of this attribute contain the necessary contact information to communicate with the author about a particular cdm:ManagedElement instance. The content of this attribute is a Uniform Resource Identifier (URI).

- cdm:relationship

  Prior to the creation or deletion of a relationship, the book must create or modify the resources participating in the relationship, and then create or delete the relationship. The structure of the current model schema is set up so that each operation, class type (cdm:ManagedElement) instances must be present prior to any relationship type (cdm:relationship) instances. Within a book, the class type instance can be present in another operation, as long as the operation precedes one that contains the relationship type (cdm:relationship) instance in the file. The book is not well formed if, within an operation, a relationship (cdm:relationship) instance is present before a class type (cdm:ManagedElement) instance. A relationship cannot be modified, as nothing is available in the relationship to modify.

C.2.7 Ownership of data

This section describes an example of a relationship between Management Software Systems and the source of their data. The example illustrates how to implement the ownership concept. In the example, the Management Software System has an *owns* relationship between the instance data for two resources and one relationship. The owns relationship is not explicitly stated in a book, as the relationship between the Management Software System and the instance data is implied. The implicit relationship is valid because the Management Software System (MSS) is the entity providing the book, and therefore is the owner of the instance data.

Figure C-6 shows relationship examples between Management Software Systems and the source of their data.

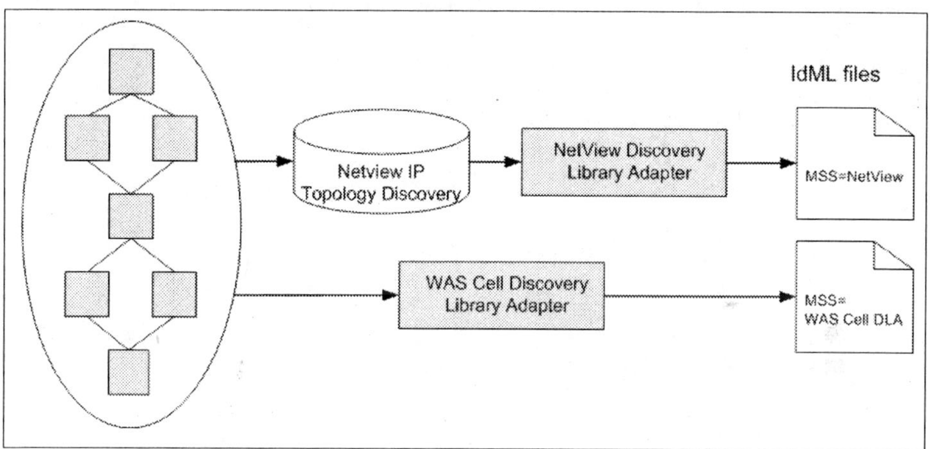

Figure C-6 Relationship examples

C.2.8 Example XML file

The following example shows the required content in the IdML format to create the two resources and one relationship shown in Example C-1.

Example: C-1 IdML example creating two resources an one relationship

```
<?xml version "1.0" encoding="UTF-8"?>
<idml:idml
  xmlns:idml="http://www.ibm.com/xmlns/swg/idml"
  xmlns:cdm="http://www.ibm.com/xmlns/swg/cdm"
```

```
  xmlns:xsi="http://www.w3.org/2001/XMLSchema-instance"
  xsi:schemaLocation="http://www.ibm.com/xmlns/swg/idml idml.xsd">
  <idml:source>
    <cdm:Management.ManagementSoftwareSystem>

<cdm:Name>ibm-cdm:///CDM-ManagementSoftwareSystem/Hostname=palmtree.raleigh.ibm
.com,Feature=IBMBWM</cdm:Name>
      <cdm:Caption>IM Tivoli Monitoring for Traction Performance</cdm:Caption>
      <cdm:Label>ITMTP 5.3</cdm:Label>
      <cdm:PrimaryOwnerName>Jacob Yackenovski</cdm:PrimaryOwnerName>
      <cdm:PrimaryOwnerContact>jyackeno@us.ibm.com</cdm:PrimaryOwnerContact>
    </cdm:Management.ManagementSoftwareSystem>
  </idml:source>
  <idml:operationSet opid="1" type>
    <idml:create timestamp="2005-03-07T15:30:00Z">
      <cdm:CDM-ER-Specification>
        <cdm:IPProtocolEndpoint id="15">
          <cdm:IPv4Address>9.27.134.4</cdm:IPv4Address>
          <cdm:SubnetMask>255.255.255.128</cdm:SubnetMask>
        </cdm:IPProtocolEndpoint>
        <cdm:IPProtocolEndpoint id="20">
          <cdm:IPv4Address>9.42.28.116</cdm:IPv4Address>
          <cdm:SubnetMask>255.255.255.0</cdm:SubnetMask>
        </cdm:IPProtocolEndpoint>
        <cdm:connectsTo source="20" target="15" />
      </cdm:CDM-ER-Specification>
    </idml:create>
  </idml:operationSet>
</idml:idml>
```

C.2.9 Discovery Library scenario: XYZ Corporation

This section describes a Discovery Library scenario flow from author to reader and provides an example of typical Discovery Library usage. In the following scenario, XYZ Corporation is the author of the data and application ABC is the reader. Table C-1 describes a single example flow. Many possible flows can occur through the Discovery Library.

Table C-1 XYZ Corporation flow example

Activity	Description
Data delivery agreement	XYZ Corporation is an author of data with an agreement to provide instance data to the Discovery Library. The data delivery agreement includes terms and conditions that specify the following: ► The frequency with which books can be delivered to the Discovery Library. ► The type of discovery that can occur. ► The type of instances that books can include. Because XYZ Corporation is a Discovery Library integrator, application control is outside the scope of the Tivoli management domain. Therefore XYZ Corporation cannot accept or digest any external command and control functions.

<table>
<tr><th>Activity</th><th>Description</th></tr>
<tr><td>Generating books</td><td>

After running for a number of days, XYZ Corporation generates the following books in the Discovery Library:

- **XYZGPSv2.0.gps.outsideco.com.2005-03-07T12.01.00Z.xml**
- **XYZGPSv2.0.gps.outsideco.com.2005-03-08T12.09.00Z.xml**
- **XYZGPSv2.0.gps.outsideco.com.2005-03-09T12.06.00Z.xml**
- **XYZGPSv2.0.gps.outsideco.com.2005-03-12T12.13.00Z.xml**
- **XYZGPSv2.0.gps.outsideco.com.2005-03-13T12.08.00Z.xml**

The following XML text displays an example of the contents of each book produced by XYZ Corporation:

```
<?xml version "1.0" encoding="UTF-8"?>
<idml:idml
  xmlns:idml="http://www.ibm.com/xmlns/swg/idml"
  xmlns:cdm="http://www.ibm.com/xmlns/swg/cdm"
  xmlns:xsi="http://www.w3.org/2001/XMLSchema-instance"
  xsi:schemaLocation="http://www.ibm.com/xmlns/swg/idml idml.xsd">
  <idml:source>
    <cdm:Management.ManagementSoftwareSystem>

<cdm:Name>ibm-cdm:///CDM-ManagementSoftwareSystem/Hostname=gps.outsid
eco.com,Feature=XYZGPS</cdm:Name>
      <cdm:Caption>XYZ GPS</cdm:Caption>
    </cdm:Management.ManagementSoftwareSystem>
  </idml:source>
  <idml:operationSet opid="1">
    <idml:create timestamp="2005-03-13T12:08:00Z">
      <cdm:CDM-ER-Specification>
        <cdm:Mchine id="15">
          <cdm:Mnufacturer>IBM</cdm:Mnufacturer>
        </cdm:Mchine>
        <cdm:AssetTag>12:23'18".327932-RDUW-X7A1</cdm:AssetTag>
        <cdm:OtherInfo>123 yellow brick road, land of
oz</cdm:OtherInfo>
        <cdm:BuildingNumber>200</cdm:BuildingNumber>
        <cdm:ComputerSystem id="101">

<cdm:PrimaryHostName>scarecrow.somewhere.com</cdm:PrimaryHostName>
        </cdm:ComputerSystem>
      </cdm:CDM-ER-Specification>
    </idml:create>
  </idml:operationSet>
</idml:idml>
```

</td></tr>
<tr><td>Reading the books</td><td>The Discovery Library books are named in chronological order according to author. Application ABC determines in what order to read the books. Application ABC reads the information related to the resources and relationships that were identified by XYZ Corporation.</td></tr>
</table>

Activity	Description
Incorporating the books	After reading the book, Application ABC determines whether to incorporate it into the application. Application ABC saves its read history locally.
Updating application ABC with new books in the Discovery Library	ABC must be updated as XYZ continues to generate more books: 1. Application ABC cross-references the books it already read with new books in the Discovery Library 2. Application ABC reads a new book and the process continues. 3. Books continue to populate from XYZ Corporation into the Discovery Library.
Deleting books	The administrator of the file store that holds the Discovery Library determines the amount of space to allocate to the Discovery Library. The administrator sets up a job to delete books after one year. After the books are deleted from the Discovery Library, they are removed from the file system and are no longer available to readers. readers do not have access to the knowledge of the life cycle of books.

C.3 Installation and configuration

This section describes Discovery Library installation issues, including:

- Configuration
- Compatibility
- Coexistence
- Upgrading
- Interaction with other Tivoli products

In addition, best practices for administrator tasks on the Discovery Library, including installing, uninstalling and deleting books from the Discovery Library File Store are covered.

Note: This section does not include best practices for upgrading, deploying, undeploying, and finding the various Discovery Library adapters. Refer to the individual Discovery Library adapter installation for those instructions.

When writing books, use a simple, common file I/O mechanism such as File Transfer Protocol (FTP) or local disk read/write. After the definitions (access and location) of the Discovery Library are complete by the customer, it is the responsibility of the customer to provide those definitions to all authors and readers of the Discovery Library. This information allows all authors and readers to be aware of the Discovery Library File Store, as the Discovery Library contains no mechanism to persist this information. The responsibility of finding the Discovery Library is outside the scope of the Discovery Library.

The customer defines the following attributes automatically during the Discovery Library installation or manually after the installation:

- The host that contains the Discovery Library File Store.
- The path name of the Discovery Library File Store.
- The security credentials to read and write to the Discovery Library File Store.

After defining the Discovery Library access and locations, the customer must provide those definitions to all authors and readers of the Discovery Library. An author's task is complete when it placed its book in the Discovery Library File Store. After books are placed in the Discovery Library they are available for readers to read. A book cannot be modified after it is written.

Each product that exploits the Discovery Library must produce a design document that addresses deployment, configuration and management of Discovery Library modules appropriate to their environment. The Discovery Library XML schemas are backwards compatible between full versions of the schema.

The Discovery Library API is compatible with previous full versions of the Discovery Library schema. Versions of the Discovery Library XML (IdML) schema might require an upgrade to the Discovery Library API since the Discovery Library XML schema and APIs are tightly integrated. The Discovery Library APIs and schema support compatibility between major version releases. For example, version 1.9 is compatible to version 1.8 and earlier. Version 2.0 is not compatible to any 1.x version.

More than one instance of the Discovery Library can exist within the customer environment, however the Discovery Library instances are disparate, and there is no data correlation between library instances.

The Discovery Library administrator performs uninstallations. The administrator uninstallation includes the following responsibilities:

- Determining if books must be deleted from the Discovery Library during uninstallation.
- Removing all access to the Discovery Library File Store.
- Informing all authors and readers that the Discovery Library was uninstalled.

When uninstalling, the administrator might perform the following functions:

- Archive and delete files
- Refresh files
- Back up files
- Restore files

For more information, see C.3.2, "Archiving and deleting files" on page 411.

C.3.1 Integration with other products

This section describes a scenario demonstrating how the Discovery Library interacts with Tivoli Business Systems Manager 3.1. For details on how authors and readers intend to exploit the Discovery Library, refer to the pertaining author or reader design document.

In this scenario, Tivoli Business Systems Manager views the Discovery Library as a conduit for acquiring resource instance and relationship information that it can use to provide improved business systems management to its users. The Discovery Library includes a recommended discovery process to Tivoli Business Systems Manager that is independent of the Tivoli Enterprise Console (TEC) event flow. In addition, the additional relationships provided through the Discovery Library enhance the ability of Tivoli Business Systems Manager to dynamically build business system representations.

TBSM is the reader or interacts with the reader. Table C-2 describes a scenario in which the Discovery Library interacts with Tivoli Business Systems Manager.

Table C-2 Discovery Library interaction scenario

TBSM action	Description
Design translation mapping	A design time effort to determine exactly how to map between the IdML Model and the TBSM model, especially in the areas of where to consolidate multiple IdML model instances into a TBSM model instance.
Map and translate schemas	The use of XSLT transforms to map and translate between the IdML Model schema employed in the Discovery Library and the schema used by the TBSM Common Listener component.
Communicate translated schema	The communication of the translated XML data to the Tivoli Business Systems Manager Common Listener component through the use of the Tivoli Business Systems Manager XML Toolkit utilities or something that provides a similar mechanism.

TBSM action	Description
Check the read history stored locally	Check which Discovery Library books were already read in order to facilitate ongoing interaction with the Library as well as to separate itself from administrative issues regarding when and how the Discovery Library is cleaned up.
Determine which books to read	Determine which types of Discovery Library books to read.
Determine which classes to filter	Determine which types of Tivoli Business Systems Manager classes can be filtered after a translation into Tivoli Business Systems Manager XML occurs.
Resynchronize Discovered data	Resynchronize discovery loads with one or more Discovery Library authors. This behavior might include loading of a previously processed complete discovery book and its subsequent delta books.
Verify interactions were successful.	Register the success or failure of the interactions listed in this table. This can enhance Tivoli Business Systems Manager Health Monitor depending on the implementation of the solution.

Note:

1. Within the deployment of a Tivoli Business Systems Manager instance and Discovery Library, a component must implement the roles provided by the requestor.
2. Discovery and event flows are separated when Tivoli Business Systems Manager uses the Discovery Library. To properly align those data in each of the flows, you must add change the central Tivoli Business Systems Manager installation as well as distributed Tivoli Business Systems Manager implementations. Details of the required changes are captured in the Tivoli Business Systems Manager documentation.

   The main task of associating status flows with discovery flows involves identification of identity resolution of resource instances between the Discovery Library and the exploiter. In many cases the use of the Tivoli Common Data Model identity support aids this mapping, but mapping require careful development are required in instances where preexisting resource models are in place.

C.3.2 Archiving and deleting files

When removing the Discovery Library, the customer must perform the following activities:

- Deactivate all current Discovery Library Adapters so they no longer provide books.
- Remove the security permission information.

The Discovery Library File Store is a simple file system that is the same as a directory or folder on a disk. Before deleting or archiving books from the Discovery Library File Store, review the file contents and "File naming conventions" on page 396. Do not delete refresh files with the word refresh in their name. You can archive or remove books prior to the book that contains a refresh operation. In the following example the book that contains the refresh operation includes all information contained in the previous books. You can delete or archive the first three books in the following list but do not delete the book that includes refresh in its name or in the file that follows it.

```
BWMv5.3.0.1.drknow.raleigh.ibm.com.2005-03-07T12.05.00Z.xml
BWMv5.3.0.1.drknow.raleigh.ibm.com.2005-03-08T12.00.00Z.xml
BWMv5.3.0.1.drknow.raleigh.ibm.com.2005-03-09T13.05.00Z.xml
BWMv5.3.0.1.drknow.raleigh.ibm.com.2005-03-10T12.00.00Z.refresh.xml
BWMv5.3.0.1.drknow.raleigh.ibm.com.2005-03-11T12.01.00Z.xml
```

For more information about refresh files, see the refresh section in C.2.6, "IdML Schema" on page 399.

Avoid archiving or deleting all books that form a particular author instance. Saving at least one book in the Discovery Library File Store for each author can help you troubleshoot problems with the Discovery Library author or reader.

Archive or delete books in chronological order. Start with book file names with the earliest time stamp to prevent information loss between the Discovery Library authors and readers.

Avoid archiving or deleting files from the Discovery Library File Store more often than every seven days to allow the different types of readers enough time to consume the information in the Discovery Library File Store. Refer to the individual Discovery Library adapter guides on how an Administrator can identify when a reader consumes books from the Discovery Library File Store.

Current backup technologies used by the customer can backup the contents in the Discovery Library File Store. Files with the extension .xml are safe to backup. Do not backup any files appended with the extension .partial. These files are still being written to the Discovery Library File Store.

Current restore technologies used by the customer are able to restore the contents in the Discovery Library File Store. Upon restoration of the Discovery Library File Store, you might need to adjust the readers so they are aware of the restored books. Refer to the individual Discovery Library adapter guides on how an Administrator should modify the reader upon Discovery Library File Store restoration.

C.3.3 Extending the CDM.xsd file

This section describes how to update the CDM.xsd file to extending its attributes. Extending the CDM.xsd enables the book to be verified using the Schema Validator and enables the book to be loaded through the CMDB Bulk loader functionality. After updating the CDM.xsd file, store it in the directory with the IdML book.

> **Note:** Extending the CDM.xsd file is supported only for version 1.x of the Common Data Model. You can reference the header of the CDM.xsd file to determine the version of the Common Data Model.

The following steps describe a scenario in which an Administrator extends the CDM.xsd file:

1. Add a simple type information about the attribute. For example:

```
</xs:simpleType>
<xs:simpleType name="New_Attribute">
<xs:annotation>
  <xs:documentation xml:lang="en">
  This is just a test of adding new   attributes to the common data model.
</xs:documentation>
</xs:annotation>
<xs:restriction base="xs:string">
</xs:restriction>
</xs:simpleType>
```

2. Add the new attribute as an element of a complex type. The text in bold font shows the new attribute added to ComputerSystem in the following example:

```
<xs:element name="ComputerSystem" substitutionGroup="cdm:ManagedElement">
<xs:complexType>
<xs:all>
<xs:element name="PrimaryFQHostname" type="cdm:PrimaryFQHostname"
minOccurs="0"/>
....more elements....
<xs:element name="New_Attribute" type="cdm:New_Attribute" minOccurs="0"/>
</xs:all>
...attribute info....
```

```
</xs:complexType>
</xs:element>
```

3. (Optional.) Add data to a sample book. The bold text shows the data added to the sample book in the following example:

```
<cdm:ComputerSystem id="6898" >
<cdm:SerialNumber>KB5AN6Kcdm:SerialNumber>KB5AN6K>
cdm:Manufacturer>IBM</cdm:Manufacturer>
<cdm:PrimaryMACAddress>00096BB2504Acdm:PrimaryMACAddress>00096BB2504A>
<cdm:Label>KB5AN6Kcdm:Label>KB5AN6K>
<cdm:Model>IBM 679221Gcdm:Model>IBM 679221G>
<cdm:New_Attribute>Blah<cdm:New_Attribute>Blah>
</cdm:ComputerSystem>
```

C.4 Use Cases

Use Cases cases are the types of interaction that can occur between an actor and the Discovery Library. The purpose of system level use cases is to identify the anticipated usage of the Discovery Library in terms of the roles that interact with the library and the broad categories of functions these roles perform. The specification of a use case does not imply that the Discovery Library implementation provides the functions contained in the use case. Some of the use cases are stated to inform Discovery Library exploiters of functions that are not provided, and for which the exploiters must implement functions according to their own requirements. Each system level use case is described by a set of more detailed use cases, called subsystem use cases.

C.4.1 Put Book use cases

The Put Book use case captures all interaction between the author and the Discovery Library that are involved with adding content from the domain of the author. A Discovery Library adapter is the instance representation of an application participating in the author role. Figure C-7 lists the subsystem level uses for the “Put Book” system level use case.

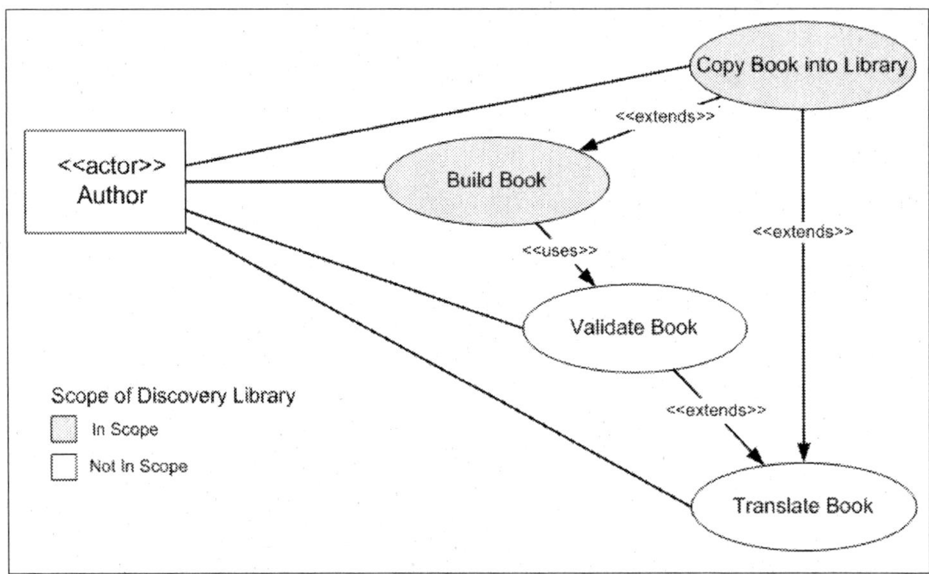

Figure C-7 Put Book Discovery Library use case

The following list describes the subsystem level use cases for the Put Book use case.

Copy Book Into Library
: Enables an author to copy a prebuilt book into the library. The author of a prebuilt book controls its construction and does not use the Build Book or Translate Book use cases. The Copy Book Into Library use case is also an extension of the Build Book and Translate Book use cases because the most common step after these two operations is to copy the resulting book into the library.

Build Book
: Describes the process by which the author constructs a book in the IdML format without having to understand the IdML schema, for example using an API.

Validate Book
: Used directly by the author to validate a prebuilt book. The Validate Book use case is an extension of the Translate Book use case because Translate Book ensures that the output is well-formed and does not validate the contents. Validate Book is also used by the Build Book use case because an author using Build Book should not be able to construct an book that is not valid. A book is valid if it is well-formed against the IdML schema. This form of validation is the equivalent of syntax checking.

Translate Book — Describes the process by which the author constructs a book in the IdML format, in which the author has already produced content that can be translated into the IdML format, for instance, using an XSLT transformation.

C.4.2 Get Book use cases

The Get Book use case describes how books and information about books are retrieved from the library. The Get Book use case is an interaction between the reader and the Discovery Library. The author does not communicate with this use case because it is based on content that is in the library at the time the use case is carried out. The following list and describes the subsystem level use cases for the Get Book use case. Figure C-8 on page 415 lists the subsystem use cases for the system level "Get Book" use case.

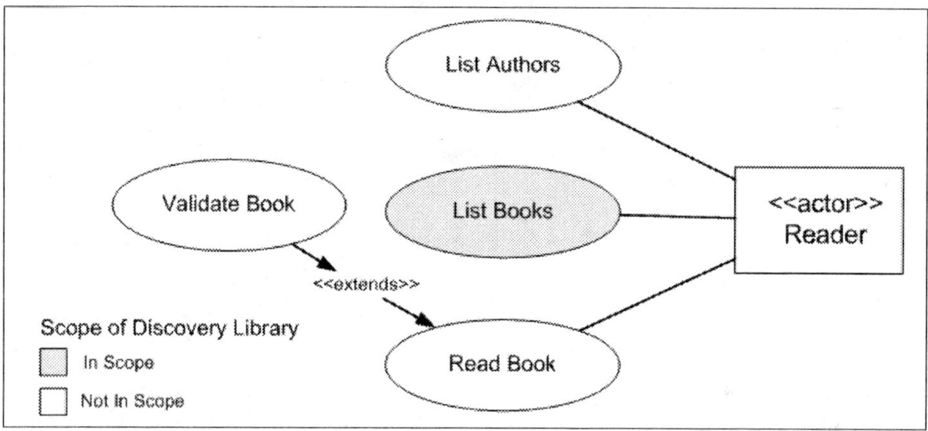

Figure C-8 Get Book Discovery Library use case

List Authors — Provides the reader with the set of distinct authors that placed books in the library.

List Books — Provides the reader with the set of books currently in the library that match reader-specified criteria such as the author and the time of discovery. The available information to list the books is restricted to the attributes of the XML files that are in the file system.

Read Book — Describes how the reader retrieves a known book from the library. Read Book is the fundamental retrieval use case.

Validate Book — Extends the Read Book use case. The reader can optionally validate the books contents according to the schema used to generate the book. A reader must validate any book before reading it to ensure that the book is valid. A book is valid if it is well-formed against the IdML schema. This form of validation is the equivalent of syntax checking. If a book is not valid, a reader cannot understand the book.

C.4.3 Request Discovery use case

The Request Discovery use case captures the communication between the requester and the author. Request Discovery has one support use case and three subsystem uses cases in which both author and requester directly participate. The requester owns the content of the scheduling-based use cases. Figure C-9 on page 416 shows the Request Discovery use case and subsystem use cases.

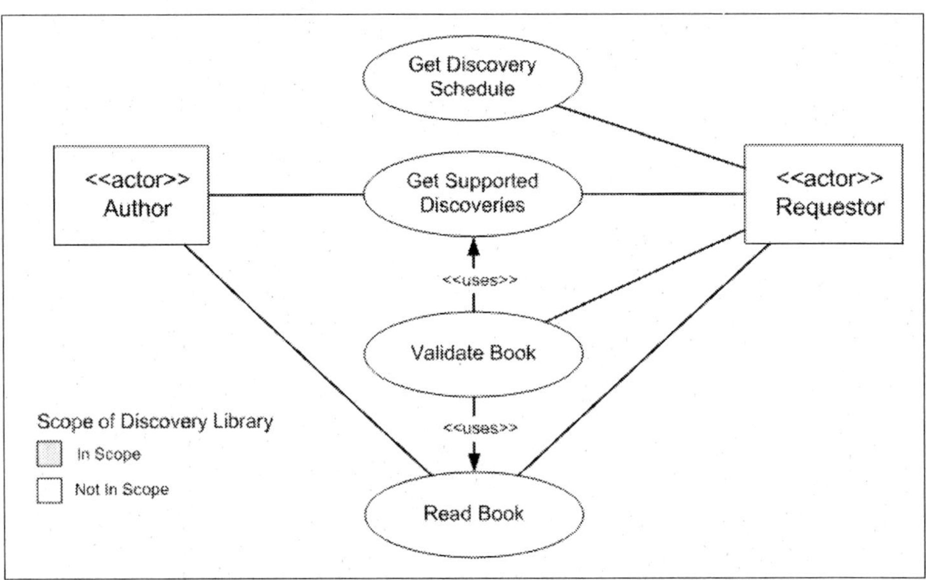

Figure C-9 Request Discovery Library use case

Get Discovery Schedule — Retrieves the set of scheduled discovery requests. Get Discovery Schedule is a query initiated by the requester.

Get Supported Discoveries — Communicates between the requester and the author to determine if the capabilities of the author with regard to the types of discoveries the author supports. For example, this use case allows the Requester to determine whether an author supports delta discoveries.

Schedule Discovery	The Requester initiates this use case to specify a discovery that is performed on a scheduled basis, either at a specified future time, or on a repeating basis.
Discover On-demand	This use case is initiated by the Requester, and fulfilled by the author. It expresses a request for the author to perform an immediate discovery of some type.

An application in the Requester might use the Request Discovery use case to orchestrate multiple Discovery Library authors. For example, an application in the Requester role might launch an inventory scan discovery on a collection of nodes. Then it would use the results of that discovery to launch specific component discoveries such as a WebSphere Application Server cell discovery or an Message Queuing queue manager discovery against specific nodes in the collection with WebSphere Application Server or Message Queuing components. The application in the Requester role uses information from one Discovery Library Adapter to direct additional Discovery Library Adapters in the environment. This behavior typically requires additional infrastructure in the environment.

C.4.4 Administer use case

The Administer use case describes how the Discovery Library is maintained. The Administer use case covers all functions not described by the previous use cases. The Administer use cases include three basic categories:

- Library-level functions
- Managing Discovery Library adapters
- Managing the data in the Discovery Library

You can introduce Manage Library, Manage Adapters, and Manage Books use cases to represent these categories. Figure C-10 shows all sets for maintaining only one level of subsystem use case diagrams.

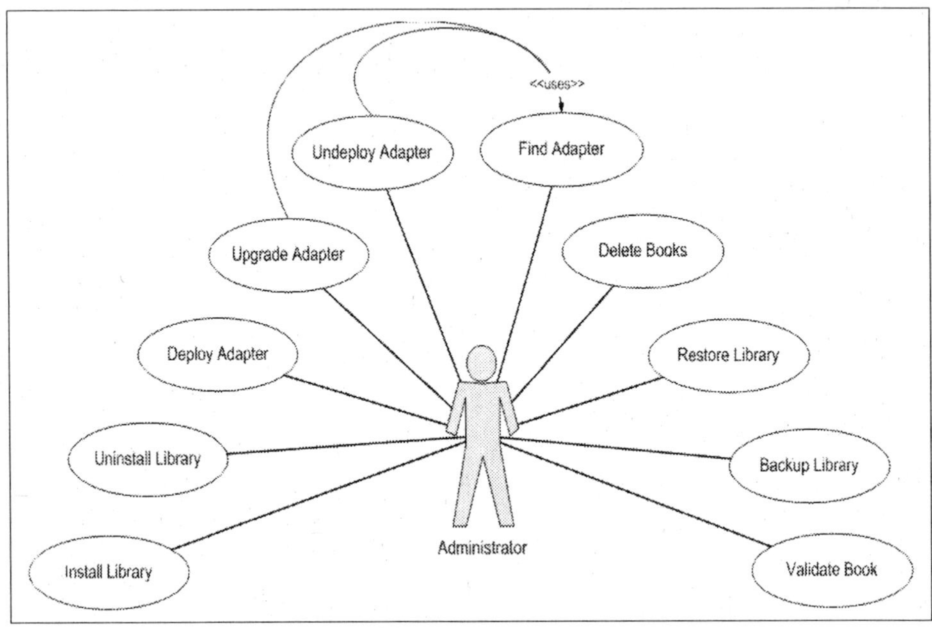

Figure C-10 Administer Discovery Library use case

Install Library	Describes how instances of the Discovery Library are installed into an environment.
Uninstall Library	Describes how instances of the Discovery Library are uninstalled from an environment.
Deploy adapter	Describes the behavior of installing new Discovery Library adapters into an environment.
Upgrade adapter	Describes how previously deployed adapters are upgraded.
Undeploy adapter	Describes how previously deployed adapters are removed from the environment.
Find adapter	Describes how the set of adapters deployed within an environment is retrieved. The Administrator uses the Find adapter use case which is also used indirectly by the Upgrade adapter and Undeploy adapter use cases.
Delete Books	Describes how books are removed from the library. Backup Library Describes how data in the Discovery Library is backed up. Restore Library Describes how data in the Discovery Library is restored.

Validate Book	Describes how the Administrator uses a commonly available schema validation tool to validate the contents of a book to conform to the IdML schema.

C.5 Discovery Library Security

The section lists Discovery Library security information.

Encryption/Cryptography	The Discovery Library API contains books that are not encrypted. The Discovery Library architecture has no facilitator to encrypt/decrypt books.
Authentication	Authentication to use the Discovery Library is addressed through governing access to the file system that contains the Discovery Library. Authentication of usage of the Discovery Library is not within the Discovery Library architecture.
Authorization	Authorization of access to use the Discovery Library is addressed through authorization to the file system that holds the Discovery Library File Store. Authorization is not within the Discovery Library architecture.

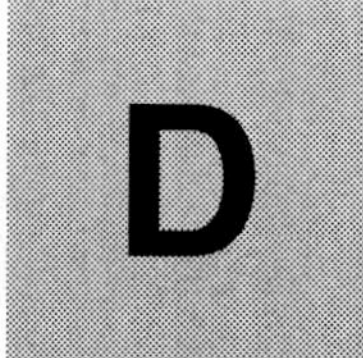

Supported sensors

Table D-1 lists the sensors that (at the time of writing) are delivered with IBM Tivoli Change and Configuration Management Database Configuration Discovery and Tracking v1.1:

Note: This list was compiled by extracting data from the ${COLLATION_HOME}/etc/discovery-sensors directory on the Configuration Discovery and Tracking server.

Table D-1 Sensors provided by Configuration Discovery and Tracking v1.1

Sensor	Gathers configuration information from
ActiveDirectory	Windows Active Directory
AixComputerSystem	AIX Computer systems
AlteonPort	Alteon network equipment (port information)
AlteonSnmp	Alteon network equipment (SNMP information)
AlteonVlan	Alteon network equipment (vlaninformation)
Anchor	Anchor hosts
ApacheServer	Apache Web Servers such as IBM HTTP Server
BigIPPort	BigIP network equipment (port information)

Sensor	Gathers configuration information from
BigIPSnmp	BigIP network equipment (SNMP information)
BigIPVlan	BigIP network equipment (vlaninformation)
BridgeSnmp	Generic network bridge - basic SNMP information
BridgeSnmp2	Generic network bridge - detailed SNMP information
Cdp	Cisco Discovery Protocol sensor
Checkpoint	CheckPoint Firewalls
CheckpointSnmp	CheckPoint Firewalls (SNMP information)
CiscoPort	Cisco network equipment (port information)
CiscoTelnet	Cisco network equipment (using the TelNet protocol)
CiscoVlan	Cisco network equipment (vlan information)
CiscoWorks	CiscoWorks sensor
CiscoWorksFile	CiscoWorks File sensor
CiscoWorksFileUDS	CiscoWorks File Universal Data Service sensor
CiscoWorksUDS	CiscoWorks Universal Data Service sensor
CustomAppServer	Servers identified by a Custom Server template defined in the Configuration Discovery and Tracking database
CustomComputerSystem	Computers identified by a Computer System template defined in the Configuration Discovery and Tracking database
Db2	IBM DB2 UDB
Dns	Domain Name Servers
EntityMIB	Basic SNMP information from any device
ExtremeVlan	Extreme network equipment (vlan information)
GenericComputerSystem	Any computer in the infrastructure
GenericServer	Any Server in the infrastructure (defined by having an active listening port)
HostResources	Hardware resources in a computer

Sensor	Gathers configuration information from
HpUxComputerSystem	Computers running a HPUX operating system
IlsWebService	Microsoft Internet Information Server
IpDevice	Any IP device in the infrastructure (
IpInterface	Any IP interface defined in the infrastructure
IPlanetServer	SUN IPlanet Java Servers
IpRange	Any IP device within the scope
IPSOComputerSystem	SOC IP discovery
JBoss	JBoss Application Servers
LanManagerSnmp	Lan Manager SNMP discovery
Ldap	LDAP based directory servers such s IBM Directory Server
LinuxComputerSystem	Any computer running a Linux distribution
LotusDominoDetail	Lotus Domino Server (detailed information)
LotusDominoDomain	Lotus Domino Server (domain information)
LotusDominoInitial	Lotus Domino Server (basic information)
NetscreenSnmp	Netscreen firewall SNMP sensor
NFSServer	Network File Server servers
NokiaSnmp	Nokia network equipment (SNMP information)
OpenVmsComputerSystem	Computers running an OpenVMS operating system
Oracle	Oracle database servers
OracleApp	Oracle Application Servers
Ping	IP Interface (status information)
Pix	Cisco PIX Firewall sensor
PortScan	Open ports on any IP Device
Session	Listening-port session information
SMBServer	Server Message Block File servers such as Windows file servers and Linux Samba servers
SMIS	Storage Management Initiative Specification

Sensor	Gathers configuration information from
SMS	Microsoft Windows Systems Management Server
SMSFile	Microsoft SMS files
SMSFileUDS	Microsoft SMS files Universal Data Service sensor
SnmpMib2	Detailed SNMP information
SqlServer	Generic relational database servers
Storage	Computers (gathers information related to the storage subsystem)
SunSparcComputerSystem	Sun SPARC Computer Systems
Sybase	Sybase database servers
SybaseIQ	Sybase databases
Weblogic	BEA Weblogic Application Servers
WebSphere	IBM WebSphere Application Servers
WebSphereCell	IBM WebSphere Application Servers (cell information)
WindowsComputerSystem	Computers running a Windows operating system

Top DB2 performance tips

The appendix is a reproduction of the information found at the following Web site:

`http://www.ibm.com/developerworks/db2/library/techarticle/hayes/0102_hayes.html`

The original material was created by Scott Hayes (scott@database-guys.com), President, Database-Guys Inc., and first published in the Spring 2001 issue of the *DB2 Magazine*.

We have reprinted this information here with permission from the Spring 2001 issue of the DB2 Magazine Copyright CMP Media.

To help DB2 database administrators avoid performance fires and achieve high performance on their own, we have summarized a troubleshooting process for our clients, customers, and fellow DB2 professionals. This appendix includes the top 10 performance tips for e-business OLTP applications in DB2 UDB for UNIX, Windows, and OS/2® environments.

E.1 Monitor switches

Make sure the monitor switches are turned on. If they are not, you will not have access to the performance information that you need. To turn on the monitor switches, issue the command:

```
db2 update monitor switches using
lock ON sort ON bufferpool ON uow ON
table ON statement ON
```

E.2 Agents

Make sure there are enough DB2 agents to handle the workload. To discern this point, issue the command:

```
db2 get snapshot for database manager
```

Look for the following lines:

```
High water mark for agents registered = 7
High water mark for agents waiting for a token = 0
Agents registered= 7
Agents waiting for a token= 0
Idle agents= 5
Agents assigned from pool= 158
Agents created from empty Pool = 7
Agents stolen from another application= 0
High water mark for coordinating agents= 7
Max agents overflow= 0
```

If you find either Agents waiting for a token or Agents stolen from another application, increase the number of agents available to the database manager (MAXAGENTS and MAX_COORDAGENTS as appropriate).

E.3 Maximum open files

DB2 tries to be a good citizen within the constraints of operating system resources. One of its "good citizen" acts is putting a ceiling, or upper limit, on the maximum number of files open at any one time. The MAXFILOP database configuration parameter stipulates the maximum number of files that DB2 can have open concurrently. After it reaches that point, DB2 will start closing and opening its tablespace files (including raw devices). Opening and closing files slows SQL response times and burns CPU cycles. To discern if DB2 is closing files, issue the command:

```
db2 "get snapshot for database on DBNAME"
```

Look for the line that reads:

```
Database files closed = 0
```

If files are being closed, increase the value of MAXFILOP until the opening and closing stops. Use the command:

```
db2 "update db cfg for DBNAME using MAXFILOP N"
```

E.4 Locks

The default value for LOCKTIMEOUT is -1, which means that there will be no lock time-outs - a situation that can be catastrophic for OLTP applications. Nevertheless, I all too frequently find many DB2 users with LOCKTIMEOUT = -1. Set LOCKTIMEOUT to a very short value, such as 10 or 15 seconds. Waiting on locks for extended periods of time can have an avalanche effect on locks.

First, check the value of LOCKTIMEOUT with this command:

```
db2 "get db cfg for DBNAME"
```

Look for the line that includes this text:

```
Lock timeout (sec) (LOCKTIMEOUT) = -1
```

If the value is -1, consider changing it to 15 seconds by using the following command (be sure to consult with the application developers or your vendor first to make sure the application is prepared to handle lock time-outs):

```
db2 "update db cfg for DBNAME using LOCKTIMEOUT 15"
```

You should also monitor the number of lock waits, lock wait time, and amount of lock list memory in use. Issue the command:

```
db2 "get snapshot for database on DBNAME"
```

Look for the following lines:

```
Locks held currently= 0
Lock waits= 0
Time database waited on locks (ms)= 0
Lock list memory in use (Bytes)= 576
Deadlocks detected= 0
Lock escalations= 0
```

```
Exclusive lock escalations= 0
Agents currently waiting on locks= 0
Lock Timeouts= 0
```

If the Lock list memory in use (Bytes) exceeds 50% of the defined LOCKLIST size, then increase the number of 4 K pages in the LOCKLIST database configuration.

E.5 Temporary tablespaces

Temporary tablespaces should have at least three containers on three different disk drives in order to help DB2 perform parallel I/O and improve performance for sorts, hash joins, and other database activities that use TEMPSPACE.

To discern how many containers your temporary tablespace has, issue the command:

```
db2 “list tablespaces show detail”
```

Look for the TEMPSPACE tablespace definition similar to this example:

```
Tablespace ID= 1
Name= TEMPSPACE1
Type= System managed space
Contents= Temporary data
State= 0x0000
Detailed explanation:Normal
Total pages= 1
Useable pages= 1
Used pages= 1
Free pages= Not applicable
High water mark (pages)= Not applicable
Page size (bytes)= 4096
Extent size (pages)= 32
Prefetch size (pages)= 96
Number of containers= 3
```

Notice that Number of containers has the value 3, and that Prefetch size is three times Extent size. For best parallel I/O performance, it is important for Prefetch size to be a multiple of Extent size. The multiple should be equal to the number of containers.

To find the definitions for the containers, issue the command:

```
db2 “list tablespace containers for 1 show detail”
```

The 1 refers to tablespace ID #1, which is TEMPSPACE1 in the example just given.

E.6 Sort memory

OLTP applications should not be performing large sorts. They are too costly in terms of CPU, I/O, and elapsed time and will slow down any OLTP application. Therefore, the default SORTHEAP size of 256 4 K pages (1 MB) should be more than adequate. You should also know the number of sort overflows and the number of sorts per transaction.

Issue the command:

```
db2 get snapshot for database on DBNAME
```

Look for the following lines:

```
Total sort heap allocated= 0
Total sorts = 1
Total sort time (ms)= 8
Sort overflows = 0
Active sorts = 0
Commit statements attempted = 3
Rollback statements attempted = 0
Let transactions = Commit statements attempted + Rollback
statements attempted
Let SortsPerTX= Total sorts / transactions
Let PercentSortOverflows = Sort overflows * 100 / Total sorts
```

If PercentSortOverflows—(Sort overflows * 100) / Total sorts)—is greater than 3 percent, there might be serious and unexpected sort problems in the application SQL. Because the very presence of overflows indicates that large sorts are occurring, finding zero sort overflows, or at least a percentage less than one, would be ideal.

If excessive sort overflows are present, the "band aid" solution is to increase the size of SORTHEAP. However, doing so only masks the real performance problem. Instead, you should identify the SQL that is causing the sorts and change the SQL, indexes, or clustering to avoid or reduce the sort cost.

If SortsPerTX is greater than 5 (as a rule of thumb), the number of sorts per transaction might be high. Some application transactions perform dozens of small composite sorts (which do not overflow and have very short durations), but consume excessive CPU. When SortsPerTX is high, my experience indicates that these machines are typically CPU bound. Identifying the SQL that is causing the sorts and improving the access plans (through indexes, clustering, or SQL changes) is paramount to improving transaction throughput rates.

E.7 Table access

For each table, identify how many rows DB2 is reading for each transaction. You must issue two commands:

```
db2 get snapshot for database on DBNAME
db2 get snapshot for tables on DBNAME
```

After you issue the first command, determine how many transactions have occurred (by taking the sum of Commit statements attempted plus Rollback statements attempted, see E.8, "Tablespace analysis" on page 431).

After issuing the second command, divide the number of rows read by the number of transactions (`RowsPerTX`). OLTP applications should typically read one to 20 rows from each table per transaction. If you discover that hundreds or thousands of rows are being read for each transaction, scans are taking place and indexes might need to be created. (Sometimes simply running **runstats** with distribution and detailed indexes all provides a cure.)

Sample output from "get snapshot for tables on `DBNAME`" follows:

```
Snapshot timestamp = 09-25-2000
4:47:09.970811
Database name= DGIDB
Database path= /fs/inst1/inst1/NODE0000/SQL00001/
Input database alias= DGIDB
Number of accessed tables= 8
Table List
  Table Schema= INST1
  Table Name= DGI_
SALES_ LOGS_TB
  Table Type= User
  Rows Written= 0
  Rows Read= 98857
  Overflows= 0
  Page Reorgs= 0
```

A high number of Overflows probably means you need to reorganize the table. Overflows occur when DB2 must locate a row on a suboptimal page due to a change in a row's width.

E.8 Tablespace analysis

A tablespace snapshot can be extremely valuable to understanding what data is being accessed and how. To get one, issue the command:

```
db2 "get snapshot for tablespaces on DBNAME"
```

For each tablespace, answer the following questions:

- What is the average read time (ms)?
- What is the average write time (ms)?
- What percentage of the physical I/O is asynchronous (prefetched) versus synchronous (random)?
- What are the buffer pool hit ratios for each tablespace?
- How many physical pages are being read each minute?
- How many physical and logical pages are being read for each transaction?

For all tablespaces, answer the following questions:

- Which tablespaces have the slowest read and write times? Why? Containers on slow disks? Are container sizes unequal?
- Are the access attributes, asynchronous versus synchronous access, consistent with expectations? Randomly read tables should have randomly read tablespaces, meaning high synchronous read percentages, usually higher buffer pool hit ratios, and lower physical I/O rates.

For each tablespace, make sure that the prefetch size is equal to the extent size multiplied by the number of containers. Issue the command:

```
db2 list tablespaces show detail
```

The prefetch size can be altered for a given tablespace if necessary. Container definitions can be checked by using the command:

```
db2 list tablespace containers for N show detail
```

in which N is the tablespace ID number.

E.9 Buffer pool optimization

All too often, one finds DB2 UDB sites where the machines have 2, 4, or 8 GB of memory, yet the DB2 database has one buffer pool, IBMDEFAULTBP, which is only 16 MB in size.

If this is the case at your site, create a buffer pool for the SYSCATSPACE catalog tablespace, one for the TEMPSPACE tablespace, and at least two more buffer pools: BP_RAND and BP_SEQ. Tablespaces that are accessed randomly should be assigned to a buffer pool with random objectives, BP_RAND. Tablespaces that are accessed sequentially (with asynchronous prefetch I/O) should be assigned to a buffer pool with sequential objectives, BP_SEQ. You can create additional buffer pools depending on performance objectives for certain transactions; for example, you could make a buffer pool large enough to store an entire "hot," or very frequently accessed, table. When large tables are involved, some DB2 users have great success placing the indexes for important tables into an index, BP_IX, buffer pool.

Buffer pools that are too small result in excessive, unnecessary, physical I/O. Buffer pools that are too large put a system at risk for operating system paging and consume unnecessary CPU cycles managing the over allocated memory. Somewhere between "too small" and "too large" lies the size that is just right. The right size exists where the point of diminishing returns is reached. If you are not using a tool to automate the diminishing returns analysis, you should scientifically test buffer pool performance (hit ratios, I/O times, physical I/O read rates) at incremental sizes until an optimum size is reached. Because businesses constantly change and grow, the "optimum size" decision should be reevaluated periodically.

E.10 SQL cost analysis

One bad SQL statement can ruin your whole day. Time and time again one sees a single, relatively simple SQL statement bring a finely tuned database and machine to its knees. For many of these statements, there isn't a DB2 UDB configuration parameter under the sun (or in the doc) that can make right the high cost of an errant SQL statement.

Making matters worse, the database administrator's hands are frequently tied: You cannot change the SQL can because it is provided by an application vendor (such as SAP, PeopleSoft, or Siebel). This leaves the database administrator three courses of action:

1. Change or add indexes
2. Change clustering
3. Change catalog statistics

What is more, today's robust applications are made up of hundreds or thousands of different SQL statements. These statements are executed at varying rates of frequency depending on application functionality and the business needs of the day. A SQL statement's true cost is the resource cost to execute it once multiplied by the number of times it is executed.

The monumental task that confronts each database administrator is the challenge of identifying the SQL statements with the highest "true cost," and working to reduce the costs of these statements.

You can learn the resource cost to execute a SQL statement once from native DB2 Explain utilities, a number of tools from third-party vendors, or the DB2 UDB SQL Event Monitor data. However, the frequency of statement execution can only be learned through careful and time-consuming analysis of DB2 UDB SQL Event Monitor data.

In researching problem SQL statements, the standard procedure used by database administrator's is:

1. Create an SQL Event Monitor, write to file:

   ```
   $> db2 "create event monitor SQLCOST for statements write to ..."
   ```

2. Activate the event monitor (be sure ample free disk space is available):

   ```
   $> db2 "set event monitor SQLCOST state = 1"
   ```

3. Let the application run.
4. Deactivate the event monitor:

   ```
   $> db2 "set event monitor SQLCOST state = 0"
   ```

5. Use the DB2-supplied db2evmon tool to format the raw SQL Event Monitor data (hundreds of megabytes of free disk space might be required depending on SQL throughput rates):

   ```
   $> db2evmon -db DBNAME -evm SQLCOST   > sqltrace.txt
   ```

6. Browse through the formatted file scanning for unusually large cost numbers, a time-consuming process:

   ```
   $> more sqltrace.txt
   ```

7. Undertake a more complete analysis of the formatted file that attempts to identify unique statements (independent of literal values), each unique statement's frequency (how many times it occurred), and the aggregate of its total CPU, sort, and other resource costs. Such a thorough analysis could take a week or more on just a 30-minute sample of application SQL activity.

To reduce the time it takes to identify SQL statements with high costs, you can consider many sources of available information:

From E.7, "Table access" on page 430, be sure to compute the number of rows read from each table per transaction. If the resulting number seems high, the DBA might be able to identify problem statements by searching the SQL Event Monitor formatted output for the table name in question (this will narrow the search, and possibly save some time).

From E.8, “Tablespace analysis” on page 431, be sure to compute the asynchronous read percentage and physical I/O read rates for each tablespace. If a tablespace has a very high asynchronous read percentage and way above average physical I/O read rates, one or more of the tables in the tablespace is probably being scanned. Query the catalog and discern which tables are assigned to the suspect tablespaces (one table per tablespace provides the best performance instrumentation), then search the SQL Event Monitor formatted output for the tables. This, too, might help narrow the search for costly SQL statements.

Try to look at DB2 Explain information for each of the SQL statements being executed by the application. However, I've found that high frequency, lower-cost statements often rob a machine of its capacity and ability to provide desired performance.

If analysis time is short and maximum performance is critical, consider vendor tools that can quickly automate the process of identifying resource intensive SQL statements. The SQL-GUY tool from Database-GUYS Inc. provides an accurate, real-time, proportional, cost rank analysis of SQL statements.

E.11 Staying in tune

Optimum performance requires not only eliminating high cost SQL statements, but also making sure that appropriate physical infrastructures are in place. Peak performance results when all the tuning knobs are set just right, memory is allocated to pools and heaps effectively, and I/O is evenly balanced across disks. Although it takes time to measure and make adjustments, the DBA who performs these 10 suggestions will be very successful at satisfying internal and external DB2 customers. As e-businesses change and grow, even the best-administered database will need regular fine-tuning. The DBA's job is never done!

E.12 The Top 10 at a glance

At a glance, the top 10 DB2 performance tips include:

1. Use sufficient agents for the workload.
2. Do not allow DB2 to needlessly close and open files.
3. Do not allow extended lock waits.
4. Ensure parallel I/O capabilities to the database `TEMPSPACE` tablespace.
5. Manage DB2 sort memory conservatively and do not mask sort problems with large `SORTHEAP`s.

6. Analyze table access activity and identify tables with unusually high rows read per transaction or overflow counts.
7. Analyze the performance characteristics of each tablespace, and seek to improve the performance of the tablespaces with the slowest read times, longest write times, highest physical I/O read rates, worst hit ratios, and access attributes that are inconsistent with expectations.
8. Create multiple buffer pools, and make purposeful assignments of tablespaces to buffer pools such that access attributes are shared.
9. Examine DB2 UDB SQL Event Monitor information to discover which SQL statements are consuming the largest proportions of computing resources, and take corrective actions.
10. Re-evaluate configuration and physical design settings after high cost SQL is eliminated.

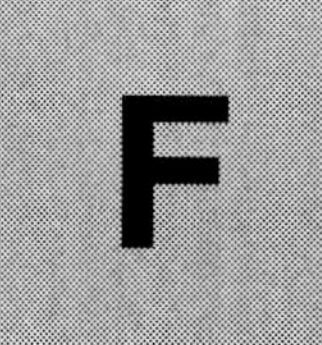

Solving WMI Access Denied errors

This appendix includes a reproduction of the information that is found at:

http://www.fair-computer.de/download/pdf/WMI-Troubleshooting.pdf

The original material was created by Fair Computer Systems GMBH, Nurenberg, Germany.

F.1 WMI Access Denied

The most common error reported by the operating system for WMI problems is `Access Denied`. There are many causes for this error message. The following list is a quick run-down of some of the more common reasons:

1. If reading data from another computer in the network, make sure that the user and password you have supplied for each feed corresponds to and administrator or valid WMI account on the target computer. That account MUST have a non-blank password.
2. Check the WMI remote access on the target by using the `wbemtest` program locally on the system from which you wish to gather WMI data from remote system(s). The `wbemtest` program is always available if WMI has been installed. Follow these steps:
   a. Execute `wbemtest` from a command line.
   b. Click **Connect**.
   c. Enter the monospacing for the target system.
   d. Enter a user ID and password. If you are using domain or Active Directory authentication, supply the user ID in the form `<domain>\<userid>`.
   e. Check different impersonations and authentication levels if the standard settings prove to be not successful.
3. Make sure that DCOM is enabled on both the calling and called (target) systems. On both systems the registry value `EnableDCOM` of the registry key `HKLM\Software\Microsoft\OLE` should be set to `Y`.
4. Make sure that WMI is installed. WMI is by default present in all flavors of Windows 2000 and later operating systems from Microsoft, however, on Windows NT4 it must be installed manually.

   To check for the presence of WMI, enter the `wbemtest` command from a command line. If the `WMI Tester` application starts, then WMI is present, if not, you must install WMI.
5. Ensure that WMI permissions have been set. Specifically, the account used for reading must have full permissions of the Root WMI namespace. To check this, view the properties for WMI through the Computer Management Console.

   Open the Computer Management Console, and switch to the `Security` tab. Then select **`Root`**, and click **Security**. Now, check that `Allow` it selected for all permissions under the account for which you are verifying WMI access.
6. If using the Windows XP Professional operating system, ensure that remote logins are not being coerced to the GUEST account - by having the

ForceGuest option enabled (this is the default on systems, which are not connected to a domain). The steps you have to complete to verify this are:

a. Open the Local Security Policy editor, by issuing the secpol.msc command from a command line.
b. Expand the Local Policies, and select **Security Options**.
c. Find the setting named Network access: Sharing and security model for local accounts and verify that the value is not Guest Only. If this is the case, chance the value to Classic - and restart the computer.

7. If using the Windows XP Professional operating system running SP2, configure the firewall to allow remote administration by issuing the netsh firewall set service RemoteAdmin from a command line.

8. If you have a third-party firewall installed, make sure that it is not blocking attempts to read the Event Log. The easiest - but least secure - way to do this, is to configure the firewall to allow all internal network traffic.

   A more secure alternative is to "punch-a-hole" in the firewall for internal WMI messages. This is complicated by the fact, that the DCOM - the core technology on which WMI is build - uses dynamic TCP port allocation. In other words, it is a moving target. Fortunately, it is possible to constrain the DCOM port allocation to a specific range. The following outlines on way to achieve this:

   a. Open the regedt32 registry editor.
   b. Navigate to the HKEY_LOCAL_MACHINES\Software\Microsoft\Rpc registry key.
   c. Create the subkey named Internet, if it does not already exist.
   d. In the Internet subkey, create a REG_MULTI_SZ parameter named Ports. Each line should specify a range of ports available to DCOM. For example, if you add a single line that reads 3000-3010 you allow only ports in this range to be used by DCOM.
   e. Add a new REG_SZ parameter named PortsInternetAvailable, and set the value to Y.
   f. Add a new REG_SZ parameter named UseInternetPorts, and set the value to Y.
   g. In your firewall, open TCP port 135 to internal traffic - it might also be necessary to open port 135 fro UDP traffic.
   h. In your firewall, open the DCOM port range defined in the previous step d.

   It is highly recommended that you reAd the following Microsoft articles for more detailed information:

   – http://msdn.microsoft.com/library/default.asp?url=/library/en-us/dndcom/html/msdn_dcomfirewall.asp
   – http://support.microsoft.com/default.aspx?scid=kb;en-us;154596

Even if you are not knowingly running any firewall software, remember that Microsoft XP systems have their own build-in firewall, which is more than capable of blocking WMI traffic. Additionally, many popular anitvirus solutions often contain their own firewall functionality. If such software is not properly configured to allow WMI traffic, this might be the cause of the Access Denied problem.

9. Ensure that no remote access or WMI related services have been disabled. On Microsoft XP systems, the following services should be running - or at lease be allowed to be started on demand:
   - COM+ Event System
   - Remote Success Auto Connection Manager
   - Remote Success Connection Manager
   - Remote Procedure Call (RPC)
   - Remote Procedure Call (RPC) Locator
   - Remote Registry
   - Server
   - Windows Management Instrumentation
   - Windows Management Instrumentation Driver Extensions
   - WMI Performance Adapter
   - Workstation

10. There is a known problem that results in an `Access Denied` error when connecting from an Windows NT4 based to a Windows XP based system. On request, a patch is available from Microsoft. Please the following Microsoft Knowledge Base article for more details:
   - `http://support.microsoft.com/default.aspx?scid=kb;EN-US;q282949`

G

Service management and the IT Infrastructure Library

There are various components and definitions behind service management in Information Technology Infrastructure Library terms. Anyone who is involved in the service level management (SLM) process will find this appendix to be a helpful reference.

G.1 The IT Infrastructure Library

The IT Infrastructure Library (ITIL) is a series of documents that are used to aid the implementation of a framework for IT service management. This customizable framework defines how service management is applied within an organization.

The ITIL was originally created by the Central Computing and Telecommunications Agency (CCTA), a United Kingdom (UK) Government agency (now known as the Office of Government Commerce (OGC)). It is now is becoming more popular and has been adopted and used across the world as the standard for best practice in the provision of IT service. Although the ITIL covers many areas, its main focus is on IT service management.

The ITIL's IT service management is organized into a series of sets, which are divided into two main areas: service support and service delivery. Each area contains several disciplines, which stipulate the ITIL practices or requirements.

- *Service support* is the practice of those disciplines that enable IT services to be provided effectively.
- *Service delivery* covers the management of the IT services themselves. It involves many management practices to ensure that IT services are provided as agreed upon between the service provider and the customer.

Refer to the following Web sites for details about what ITIL is and what it can provide:

- IT systems management forum Web site

  `http://www.itsmf.com`
- Official ITIL Web site

  `http://www.itil.co.uk`
- Official OGC Web site

  `http://www.ogc.gov.uk`

G.2 Service management

Today, the service management revolution is well on its way. Almost every IT organization is moving toward business-oriented service delivery. IT is being called upon to participate as a partner in the corporate mission, which requires their functioning as a proactive group that is responsive to their customers.

Adopting this mind set is difficult for internal service providers, who face an increasingly less captive audience. The corporate IT organization is now challenged to operate as a stand-alone business, without corrective forces that profit orientation and that the threat of losing customers presents for companies operating in a free market. In the absence of these forces, IT organizations are embracing a new competitive mindset: *service level management*.

Through the process of establishing a service level management (SLM) orientation, IT organizations can engage customers, as though they were driven by market forces. SLM is a means for the lines of business (LOB) and IT organization to explicitly set their mutual expectations for the content and extent of IT services. It also allows them to determine in advance what steps to take if these conditions are not met. The concept and application of SLM allows IT organizations to provide a business-oriented, enterprise-wide service by varying the type, cost, and level of service for the individual LOB.

For the IT organization to make and use the service level agreements (SLAs) with the LOBs as a tool for decision making, the IT organization must organize itself accordingly and establish internal procedures that support SLA management. SLM is not an isolated activity. It interacts with, and draws upon, all the other disciplines that are part of the IT infrastructure management.

There is no point in agreeing to deliver a service if the basic tools and processes needed to deploy, manage, monitor, correct, and report the service level achieved are not established. All of these activities are grouped into two major disciplines (Figure G-1): service delivery and service support.

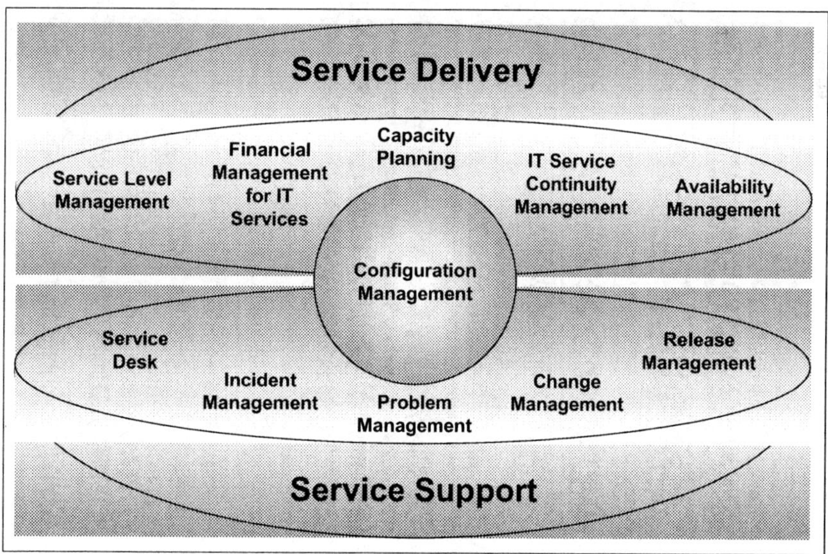

Figure G-1 The service management disciplines

G.2.1 Service delivery

The primary objective of the service delivery discipline is proactive. It consists of planning and ensuring that the service is delivered according to plan and, in turn, to the SLA. The tasks that you must accomplish to make this happen are:

- Service level management

  This involves managing customer expectations and negotiating service delivery agreements. It involves determining the customers' requirements and how you can meet them the best way possible within the agreed-upon budget.

  Working together allows IT disciplines and departments to plan and ensure the delivery of services. This involves setting measurable performing targets, monitoring performance, and taking action where targets are not met.

- Financial management for IT services

  You must register and maintain cost accounts related to the usage of IT services. You must also deliver cost statistics and reports to SLM to assist in obtaining the right balance between service cost and delivery. And you must assist in pricing the services in the service catalog and SLAs.

- Capacity management

  This involves planning and ensuring that adequate capacity with the expected performance characteristics is available to support the service delivery. It also entails delivering capacity usage, performance, and workload management statistics, and trend analysis to SLM.

- IT services continuity management

  This requires you to plan and ensure the continuing delivery, or minimum outage, of the service by reducing the impact of disasters, emergencies, and major incidents. You do this work in close collaboration with the company's business continuity management, which is responsible for protection of all aspects of the company's business, including IT.

- Availability management

  This entails planning and ensuring the overall availability of the services. It also requires you to provide management information in the form of availability statistics, including security violations, to SLM. This discipline might include negotiating underpinning contracts with external suppliers, and defining maintenance windows and recovery times.

G.2.2 Service support

The disciplines in the service support group are reactive and concerned with implementing the plans and providing management information regarding the levels of service achieved.

- Service desk

  This is an essential function to effective service management that acts as the main point-of-contact for the users of the service. You register incidents, allocate severity, and coordinate the efforts of the support teams to ensure timely and correct resolution of problems.

  Escalation times are noted in the SLA and are, as such, agreed upon between the customer and the IT department.

  This discipline also requires you to provide statistics to SLM to demonstrate the service levels achieved.

- Incident management

  This goal of this discipline is to restore services to their normal operational levels as soon as possible, ensuring service levels are maintained. You must maintain meaningful records of all reported incidents that causes, or might cause, interruption or degradation of quality of IT services. You must also provides investigation and diagnosis of incidents, as well as incident ownership, monitoring, and tracking.

- Problem management

  For this discipline, you must ensure that resources are prioritized to resolve problems in the most appropriate order based on business needs. A *problem* is the unknown cause of one or more incidents. When the root cause is known and a temporary work-around or a permanent fix is determined, the problem becomes a *known error*.

  You must also agree on escalation times internally with SLM during the SLA negotiation. And you must provide problem resolution statistics to support SLM.

- Change management

  In the change management discipline, you must ensure that the impact of a change to any component of a service is well known, and the implications regarding service level achievements are minimized. This includes changes to the SLA documents and the service catalog, as well as organizational changes and changes to hardware and software components.

- Release management

  For release management, manage the master software repository, named the Definitive Software Library (DSL), and deploy software components of services. You must also deploy changes upon the request of change management. And you must provide management reports regarding deployment.

- Configuration management

  With configuration management, your must register all components in the IT service, including customers, contracts, SLAs, hardware and software components, and more. Plus, you must maintain a repository of configurable attributes and relationships among the components.

Figure G-2 shows the key relationships among the disciplines.

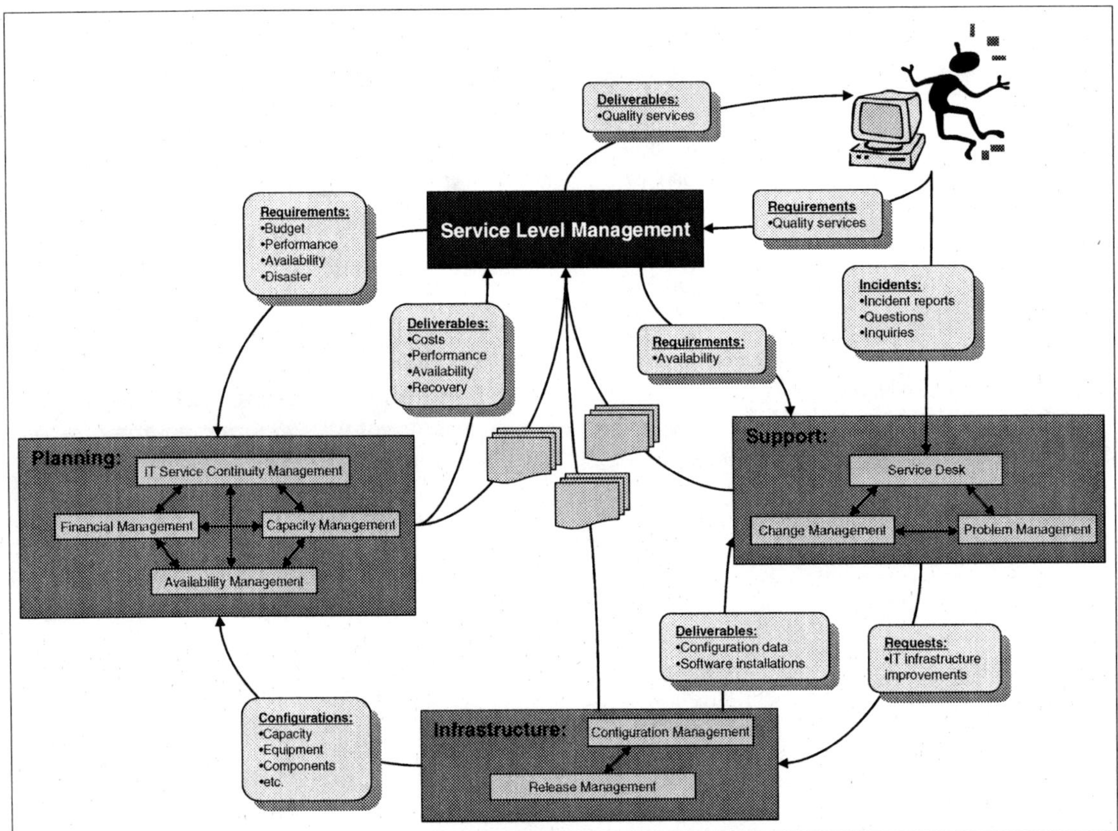

Figure G-2 Key relationships among service management disciplines

To fully understand the responsibilities of each of the disciplines and the relationships among them, the following sections discuss both the service support and the service delivery disciplines.

G.3 Service support disciplines

The purpose of the disciplines grouped in the service support group is to provide a means of implementing and monitoring the plans defined by the service delivery disciplines. Even though an IT organization might not have embraced the idea of SLM, it certainly has parts of most of the disciplines, in the service support group, in place. It is simply a prerequisite for managing client/server systems and the vast amount of desktop computers found in any business today.

Depending on many factors, size being one of the major ones, the disciplines might or might not be fully implemented. Also the same persons within the IT organization might have roles and responsibilities from more than one discipline. Take these factors into account when designing the procedures governing the incident, change, and problem management processes and, especially, the interfaces between each of the disciplines.

Having more caps makes it easy to skip the defined procedures. And implementing workflow tools to ensure compliance with the defined processes might be too rigid to make the daily work flow smoothly.

Because of the dramatic impacts that outages of IT services might have on a business, it is important that you define, document, and follow the processes well. These processes must be in line with the priorities of the business. Strict compliance with the rules might not always be required. However, if something goes wrong, it is better if you closely follow the rules and regulations.

During the life cycle of an IT service, it passes through the following phases:

- Planning
- Deployment
- Usage
  - Monitoring
  - Correction
  - Verification
- Disintegration

You can regard each of these phases as a change to the existing environment. Although the term *change* might apply mostly to the activities that occur inside the usage phase, it still applies to all of the phases. In each of them, there is a need for information regarding the environment, components, status, operational attributes, users, and so on. Likewise, there is a need to know where the roles and responsibilities of different activities involved with service support are placed within the support organization.

During all the phases of the life cycle, the IT organization as a whole should be able to answer the question: Who does what to which component: where, when, why, how, and authorized by whom?

Providing the answer requires contributions from all the disciplines in the service support group:

- **Configuration management**: Answers the *where* and *which*
- **Service desk**: Should be in a position to answer *why*
- **incident and problem management**: Are responsible for the *what* and *how*
- **Change management**: Takes care of the *when* and *whom*
- **Release management**: Depends upon the nature of the change; *who* is often placed here

Change requests can originate from sources other than incident management, problem management, and service desk. For example, if a request to increase the size of a file system is issued from capacity management, the change request is passed directly to change management without the knowledge of service desk. However, each change request should be registered with and governed by configuration management. This enables the service desk to find the answer to why, even though the change did not address a specific incident received by the service desk.

G.3.1 Configuration management

For day-to-day incident, problem, and change handling, as well as deployment of new services, information about all the components that are related to delivery of a service is vital. Configuration management is responsible for providing and maintaining this information because it is, perhaps, one of the toughest tasks related to service management.

Configuration management, as a discipline of service support, is not restricted to the configuration management aspects of development. If it applies to the specific environment, development aspects are included. But configuration management includes all of the components within the IT infrastructure that are related to delivery of a service. Configuration management should be applied throughout the organization and should not be restricted to IT-related items.

The four main activities of configuration management are:

- *Identification*: This involves identifying all the configuration items (CIs) in the IT infrastructure, as well as defining the information to hold each of the CIs and the relationships between them. Additionally, it entails defining baselines and identifying variants.

  To summarize, this task is responsible for defining the policies regarding the type and level of information that is maintained in the organization. Not only can identifying, gathering, and storing the information initially require a huge effort, but maintaining the information might be even worse.

  The basic principles for identifying the CIs are as follows:

  - CIs must be uniquely identified.
  - The indoctrination must be prominent and clearly visible.
  - Identities must be as meaningful as possible.
  - Versioning must be supported.
  - Growth must be catered to.

- *Control*: This activity handles maintenance, updates, and access to the configuration repository, called the Configuration Management Database (CMDB). Many of the other service management disciplines support this effort, but it requires adequate control procedures to be in place:

  - Specifications of CIs are agreed upon and frozen.
  - Only changes authorized through predefined change management procedures are allowed.

- *Status accounting*: Because the CMDB is used by all system management disciplines, it is vital that the information is correct and timely. The CMDB holds active and historical configuration data. Therefore, attributes must be defined and maintained to track the configuration of CIs over time. These attributes must support the state of acquisition, development, testing, or implementation of the CIs and must be recorded as soon as they happen.

  Another way of expressing the responsibilities of this activity is to record and report all current and historical data for all CIs. Some useful reports are:

  - The number of incidents from a particular CI in a particular period
  - The change history for a CI in a particular period
  - The total amount spent with a particular supplier over a particular period

- *Verification*: It is important to audit the contents of the CMDB, that is, verify them to make sure that the repository reflects the actual configuration of the IT infrastructure. The configuration management staff themselves can accomplish this, or some of the operational procedures (for example, related to incident reception in the service desk) might assist. Review the consistency of the CMDB regularly.

The accuracy of the CMDB might be easier if:

- The CMDB is active rather than passive.
- The CMDB is updated automatically whenever possible.
- Configuration management activities are integrated into other relevant operational procedures.
- Automatic audits are built into the system.

Configuration and configuration items

The ITIL documentation describes a configuration as a configuration is anything within the IT infrastructure that needs to be controlled. According to this definition, such configurations are:

- Hardware
- Software
- Networks
- People
- Relationships
- Documentation and contracts
- Incidents, problems, solutions, and changes
- Policies and procedures
- Anything else that needs to be controlled

However, a configuration, much like a service, is usually a self-contained cohesive collection of components that are called configuration items (CI).

Configuration item attributes

All CIs are identified uniquely within the CMDB, and, for each CI, several attributes are recorded. An attribute is an item of information that can be recorded about a CI. Only attributes that are relevant to a specific organization should be recorded.

For all of the different types of configurations, configuration management must identify and manage all the attributes needed to manage the configuration. Obviously, this is a cumbersome task. Within the IT infrastructure, there is a large number of configurations, each with different attributes, that are needed to support different management processes. The service desk might, for example, be interested in information regarding capacity and free space of a personal computer (PC) used by the person who calls. However, change management needs to know the physical characteristics (size, energy consumption, and so on) of the hard disk, as well as the manufacturer and serial number, to replace it in case of a failure. But it does not need the free space information in the case of hard disk failure.

You should record at least four basic attributes for every CI:

- *ID*: A unique identification. To ensure uniqueness and easily differentiate different types of CI from one another, you must develop a naming standard for CI IDs that supports type. This naming standard for the CIs should not include elements of information that can change over time. Therefore, avoid location and owner information because it might change, requiring the CI to assume a new ID.
- *Location*: Record the location where the CI might be found to assist all other service management disciplines. In particular, the impact analysis of the change management process relies on this piece of information.

  When discussing mobile computers, it might not make sense (or it might be difficult) to determine the physical location of the CI. Each individual organization must be determined within itself, if the efforts to maintain the physical location are too high to take on this task.
- *Owner*: To charge services, monitor SLA achievements for different LOBs, determine maintenance policies, and so on, it is necessary to connect the CI to an owner or user. Linking this information to the organizational structure, which is also recorded in the CMDB, the CI can be associated to a specific group or department, providing the key to the desired information.
- *State*: The state of the CI is vital to track the CI through its life cycle to ensure that each CI is made to cost, on time, complete, to specification, authorized, and more. During each state, you can track responsibilities, progress, and problems.

The information needed to manage a configuration varies as a function of the type of configuration and the management task performed. In the previous example, free space is an attribute of the configuration of type PC, and the serial number is an attribute of a configuration of type hard disk.

When you break down the IT infrastructure into configurations and configuration items, you must follow these three principles:

- Break down CIs only to the level at which they can be changed or amended independently.
- The level of CI breakdown and the attributes stored for each CI vary depending upon the individual organization and the purposes for which control is exercised.
- The cost of gathering and storing information must never exceed the value of the information.

Besides attributes, you might also use relationships to associate CIs with one another. This might be the most obvious way to break down CIs for tangible components, such as hardware. However, defining the CI structure for software and organizational configurations becomes more complicated. The CMDB must be able to handle relationships between:

- Hardware and hardware
- Hardware and software
- Software and subsystems
- Applications, hardware, and software
- Hardware, software, and operating systems
- Networks
- All of the previous items and their users
- Incidents, problems, solutions, and change requests

The configuration management database

Configuration management is not a discipline that arose with the use of IT. In particular, the building and manufacturing industries have used configuration management for as long as these industries have been around. Configuration management has been used to manage bill-of-materials of the components produced and to track which components were used in which assemblies and when. For manufacturers of airplanes, automobiles, and trains, and so on, this information is vital, especially when a failing component is identified and must be replaced on all products where it was used.

All of the information needed to support the service management disciplines is properly available within the organization. However, chances are that it is scattered all over the installation, is not based on a common data model, and is stored in a variety of formats on different media.

The CMDB does not necessarily have to be implemented according to an all-encompassing data model. Nor are there any requirements to store the data in a specific database management system (DBMS), but it helps. If neither a common data model nor a common DBMS systems is used, the CMDB is likely to be full of duplication and with a build-in potential for inconsistency. Furthermore, exchanging information between applications and extracting meaningful management information from all these sources of information is extremely difficult.

You must diminish these inconveniences by using a common data model and the same DBMS. It might be impractical to change all the applications that provide data to the CMDB, but extracting the required information and transforming it to fit the CMDB data model can prove beneficial to any organization in these ways:

- Avoids duplication
- Avoids inconsistencies
- Identifies relationships
- Allows corporate access to data
- Generates management information

This list is by no means complete. More benefits will be obvious for each specific discipline.

Configuration management and other disciplines

Since configuration management is the owner of the CMDB, this discipline interacts with all the other service management disciplines. Whenever data is requested, the request must be authorized by configuration management. And of course, configuration management must also be in control when it comes to updates and additions to the CMDB.

For the most part, the other disciplines primarily request data from the CMDB. However, especially within the service support group of the disciplines, service desk, problem management, change management, and release management, the repository is used as a means of communication when handling incidents and problems as described in the following sections.

For the service delivery disciplines, the CMDB is primarily a databank where information, related to such specific areas as cost, capacity, and performance, can be found. These disciplines contribute to the repository by adding SLA-specific information, updates, and additions to the service catalog.

G.3.2 Service desk

The service desk provides a main point of contact for users of the services. Whenever users experience problems, have questions, or need information regarding the use of services, they should contact the service desk. The service desk is also responsible for notifying users about disruptions in service, planned outages, and availability of new functions. It serves as a two-way conveyer of information between the service users and the staff supporting the service. This section focuses on the one-way information flows from user to staff (Figure G-3 on page 455).

Providing quality service requires processes and procedures to detect and rectify problems as quickly as possible. Detection is either done by programs that monitor specific resources of the hardware and software components of the IT infrastructure or by the users of the service. When an issue is reported, it is recorded centrally with the service desk as an incident. This central incident control is required, partly to ensure that the issue is handled and partly to ensure that the same issue is handled only once, even though more incidents might have been opened against the issue.

When the issue is reported, the service desk must provide a solution to it. The service desk might (but is not required to), through incident management processes, identify, test, and apply the solution. It must also keep track of the incident to ensure that the issue is solved within the time agreed in the SLA and to escalate the issue if necessary.

If a service desk cannot identify a solution to the issue on its own, the incident is recorded as a problem, which is stored in the CMDB. Now, problem management assumes responsibility to provide a solution for the problem by accepting the problem. When the root cause of the problem is known and a temporary work-around or permanent fix is identified, it is recorded as a known error.

When a solution is available, it might require changes to the CI for which the incident was opened or another CI within the infrastructure on which the failing CI relies. The service desk is now required to open a request for change in order for change management to access the impact and authorize the change. Once authorized, release management might take over to perform the actual implementation of the change.

During this process, each service support discipline is responsible for recording status information in the CMDB. The service desk must also keep the user informed through all the stages in the life cycle of the incident. It must also confirm that the issue has been resolved, record the solution to the known error, and close the incident.

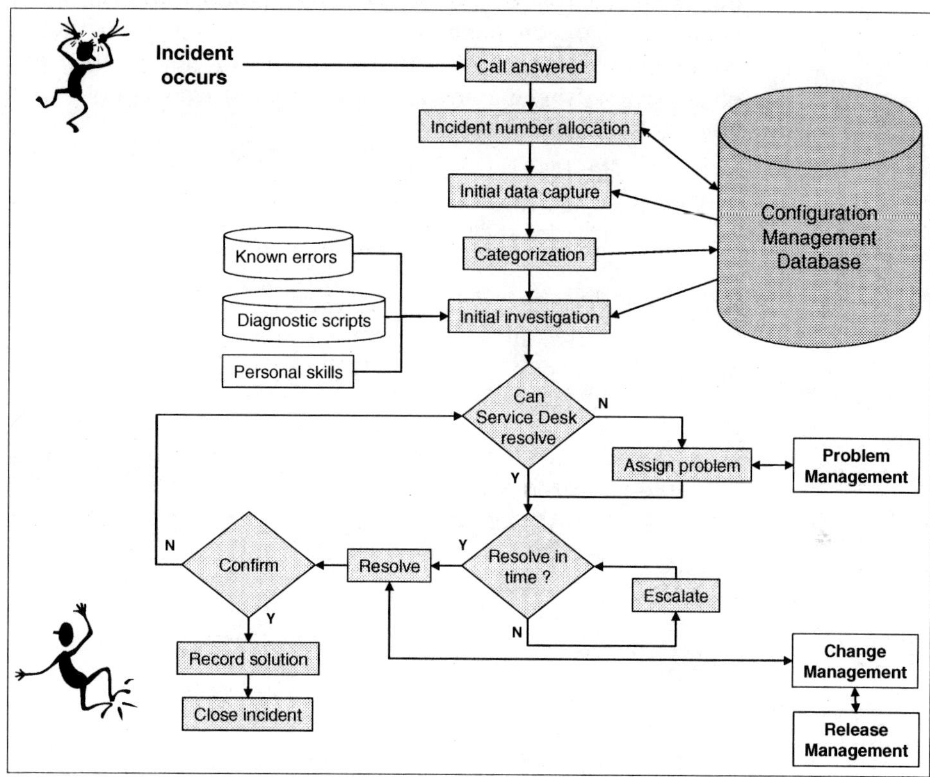

Figure G-3 Service desk activities

Service desk and other disciplines

Since the service desk is the "front office" of incident and problem management, there is a close collaboration between the three. However, since the service desk is responsible for tracking and following an incident through its entire life cycle, it must also interact with change management through incident management, once a solution is identified and must be implemented. Again, the service desk uses the CMDB to keep track of the status of an incident, the related problems, and changes.

Interfacing to configuration management (through the CMDB) is also vital to service desk. Ask the user a few simple questions, such as: What is your name or personnel number? Are you using your own workstation? Are you in your own office? Then using the answers as keys for searching the CMDB, the following information is available:

- Equipment held
- Software accessible
- Diagnostic aids available
- Problem history
- Change history
- Service level agreement
- Training and experience records
- Personal information

Since the service desk is the function, which has the most interaction with users, procedures might be established to assist configuration management to keep track of CIs and verify their attributes. It is common that the service desk asks the user questions related to the equipment and applications available to the user and records deviations from the expected values shown in the CMDB.

Finally, service desk provides statistics to SLM in order for it to verify that each LOB gets the required level of support from the service desk.

G.3.3 Incident management

As described earlier in this appendix, incident management has as a goal to restore services to their normal operational levels as soon as possible, to ensure that service levels are maintained. The service desk plays a key role in incident management. When an issue is reported, the service desk captures the data needed to open a new incident. This data must include an ID of the person (or proxy) who submitted the issue report, and the ID of the CI suffering the impact. With this information, service desk can query the CMDB to investigate whether the CI exists in the CMDB, and whether any outstanding problems, changes, or other incidents are active for that particular CI. It should also be determined if the particular issue was reported earlier.

If there are no indicators showing that the issue is being handled, the incident must be categorized. A type and an impact code are assigned to the incident. Do not confuse this with priority, urgency or severity, as defined here:

- **Impact**: Impact of the incident on the achievement of business objectives
- **Severity**: Impact of an incident on service provision
- **Urgency**: Determines the speed with which an incident must be resolved
- **Priority**: Order of handling incidents, based on a combination of impact, severity, urgency, and availability of resources to address the incident

Using these definitions, it is clear that an incident can have a high impact on the achievement of business objectives and yet have an insignificant impact on the provision of the service (and vice versa). The priority primarily depends on the impact on the business and secondly on the impact on the service. However, since the business relies on the service, incidents with a high service impact quickly affect the business as well.

The priority of the incident is determined from both a business and a service perspective as shown in Figure G-4.

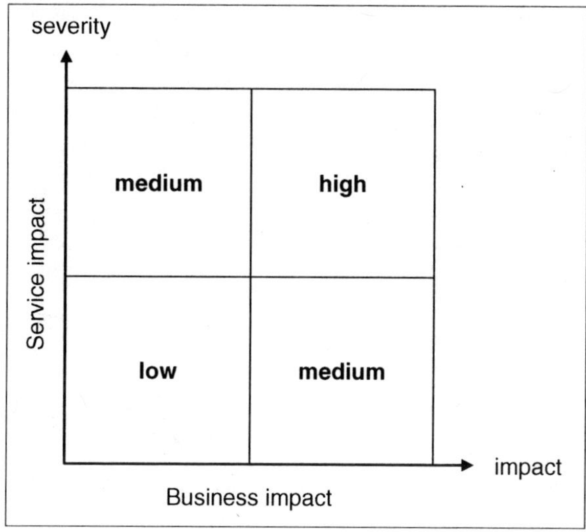

Figure G-4 Incident priority

Having categorized the incident, an initial investigation might be carried out using incident management processes. This involves searching the CMDB for similar or related issues to identify the cause of the incident as a known error. If this is the case, the service desk can inform the user of the status of the problem, when to expect the issues to be fixed, or any actions the user can take to circumvent the issue.

If no immediate solution can be found, the incident becomes a problem, and a solution must be provided by the problem management discipline. When the service desk passes the problem to problem management, the responsibility of managing the problem still lies with the service desk. The service desk is now responsible to keep the user informed about the progress and escalate the problem if the times for problem resolution set out in the SLA cannot be met.

G.3.4 Problem management

The activities performed by problem management are similar to those of the service desk. Problems are received, accepted, diagnosed, and assessed for severity. This is known as *problem control*. Then, solutions are developed or identified, tested, verified, and recorded, which is all part of the error control process.

The problem control process is concerned with identifying the real causes of incidents to prevent future recurrences. This process is made up of five phases:

1. Initially investigating the nature of the problem
2. Accepting the problem
3. Assigning priority (impact on service delivery and business objectives)
4. Allocating support effort
5. Performing further investigation and diagnosis

After the problem is accepted and a work-around or permanent fix is identified, it is recorded in the CMDB as a known error. There are two types of known errors:

- Accepted problems that are not yet rectified (Root cause analysis has been done, solution has been identified, but not implemented.)
- Accepted problems for which a resolution or circumvention is available

Allocating the support effort to find a solution to a problem is important. Depending on the nature of the problem, the impact, urgency, and the severity, it might prove more productive to the business as a whole to live with the problem rather than using all available support staff and all the budget for external support to diagnose and rectify it. Making a decision such as this requires detailed impact analysis and acceptance from the service level manager as well as the sponsor. It might lead to renegotiation of the SLA.

When the cause of the problem is identified and a decision to provide a solution is approved, *error control* takes over. The primary objective of this function is to eliminate all known errors by providing solutions to the problems and ensuring that they are implemented on all CIs where the problem has occurred or might occur. To meet this objective, error control and change management go hand-in-hand since change control is responsible for approving any changes made to any CI. See Figure G-5 on page 459.

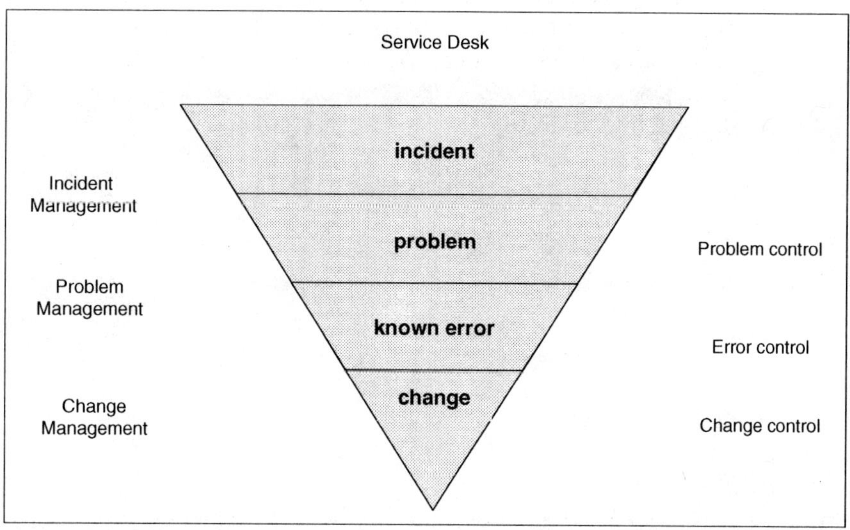

Figure G-5 Interrelationships of incidents, problems, and known errors

The verification of solutions is especially important. First, you must verify that the proposed solution targets the source of the problem rather than removing the symptoms. Secondly, you must ensure that implementation of the solution does not result in any undesired side effects. If this is the case, the solution implementation might lead to other (even worse) problems that will harm the overall service delivery.

All of the disciplines in service support should work together to avoid the vicious circle of change. Much too often, solutions, changes, and implementations are rushed through without proper testing, leading to even more severe incidents of higher impact. This requires even quicker resolution, so the solution is not tested properly and new incidents are the result. This is depicted on the left side in Figure G-6 on page 460.

On the right side of Figure G-6 on page 460, error control has had enough time to assess the impact of the solution. Change management also has had adequate time to assess the impact of the change, and the implementation had exactly the foreseen implications. The source of the problem was eliminated, and the technical support staff can start working on the next problem.

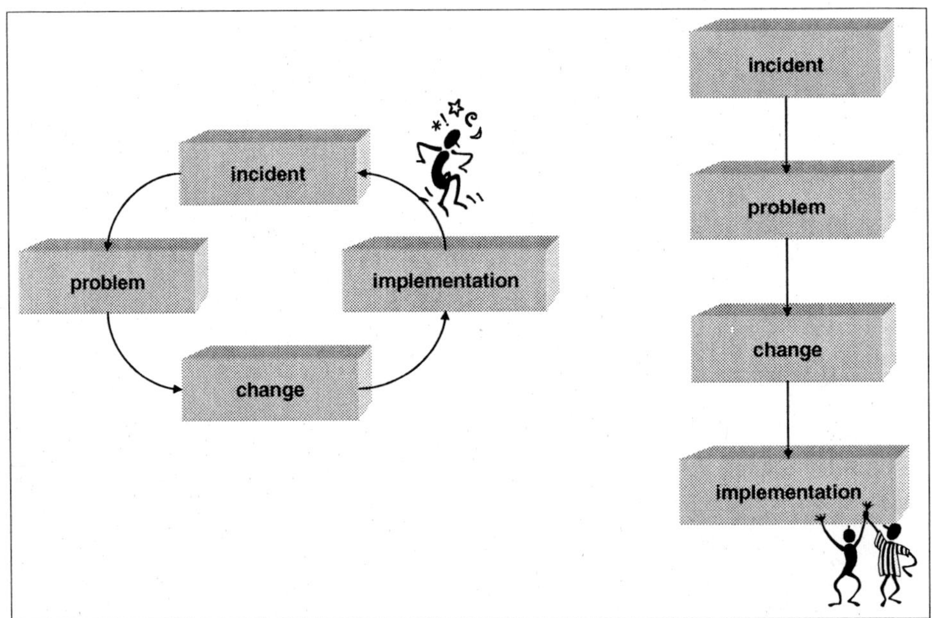

Figure G-6 The vicious cycle of change

Problem management and other disciplines

Having a front office to filter out irrelevant requests, such as a service desk, and a back office processes in place, such as incident management and change management, the problem management staff can focus only on problems. They interact primarily with the service desk function, incident management, and change management processes. They use the CMDB to gather information necessary to perform the following tasks:

- Automatic escalation
- Logging problems
- Highlighting trends: Incident and problem history
- Matching problems
- Listing known errors
- Identifying outstanding problems
- Identifying relationships
- Creating a Request for Change (RFC) to be performed
- List recent changes
- Identify responsibilities
- Assess impact
- Comparison of cost of fix with cost if no fix

You might wonder what the differences are between incident management and problem management processes. The objective of incident management is to restore services that support the business as quickly as possible, performing tasks such as researching the CMDB for known errors, while problem management focuses on determining the root causes of incidents, their resolutions, and prevention.

G.3.5 Change management

After configuration management, change management is the most important to continue delivering quality service. The responsibility of change management is to manage changes to the configuration items such as:

- Hardware
- Software
- Communication equipment and software
- Production application software
- All documentation, plans, and procedures relevant to running, supporting, and maintaining the production systems
- Environmental equipment
- People

By using the term *production*, it is indicated that changes to equipment and applications used for development and test purposes are normally not the responsibility of change management.

The processes that are used to manage changes involve:

1. Change initiation
2. Change reception: Logging and filtering
3. Initial change prioritization
4. Change assessment and scheduling
5. Change building
6. Change testing
7. Change implementation
8. Change review

To support the processes, several players must be involved. In the typical IT organization, a dedicated change manager is appointed. The change manager must receive, access, approve, and manage the changes.

To assist the change manager, a *change advisory board (CAB)* is appointed. This board consists of members from all the support groups within the organization, such as service desk, networking, space management, platform support, and representatives of the business. The board is responsible for assessing proposed changes for impact and estimating the resource requirements needed to design, build, test, implement, and review a change. The

CAB also advises the change manager in change acceptance matters and assist in scheduling changes.

The CAB can be divided into subcommittees that handle changes in specific areas as shown in Figure G-7. The LOB representative from finance does not have to attend the meeting when changes to the production control software are discussed. Also, the presence of the representative for networking is not always required when changes to the central disk configuration are handled.

A super-committee, the CAB/emergency committee (CAB/EC), is also appointed. The purpose of this committee is to meet to authorize urgent changes on short notice. Because of the size of the change advisory board, it is impractical to convene a full meeting to handle urgent changes. The change manager can be authorized to accept some urgent changes, but we do not recommend doing so without considering other key personnel. The CAB/EC, for example, can be made up of the change manager and key staff members from the CAB. It acts as the safety net, or sparring partner, of the change manager. The selection of members of the CAB/EC is a matter of preference and the nature of the change, but the change manager should always be a born member.

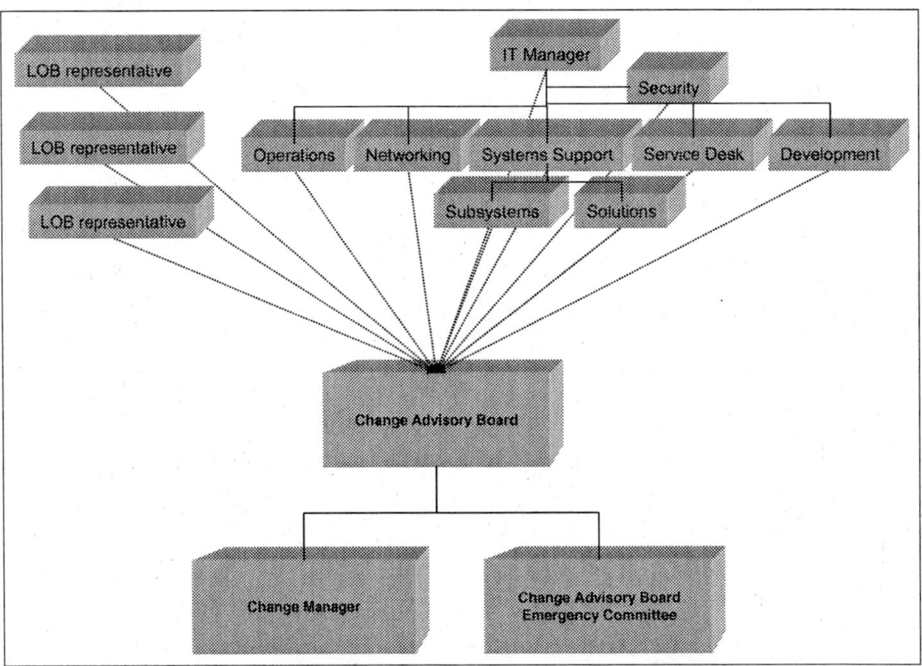

Figure G-7 CAB and CAB/EC

Managing normal changes

In day-to-day work, the change manager authorizes and manages all changes that apply to the IT infrastructure. In large and medium size installations, this is an enormous task. Therefore, the change manager can pre-approve standard changes and delegate the responsibility to others, such as the service desk.

For nonstandard and major changes, which are the concern of the change manager, follow the procedure shown Figure G-8. This includes the steps outlined in G.3.5, "Change management" on page 461.

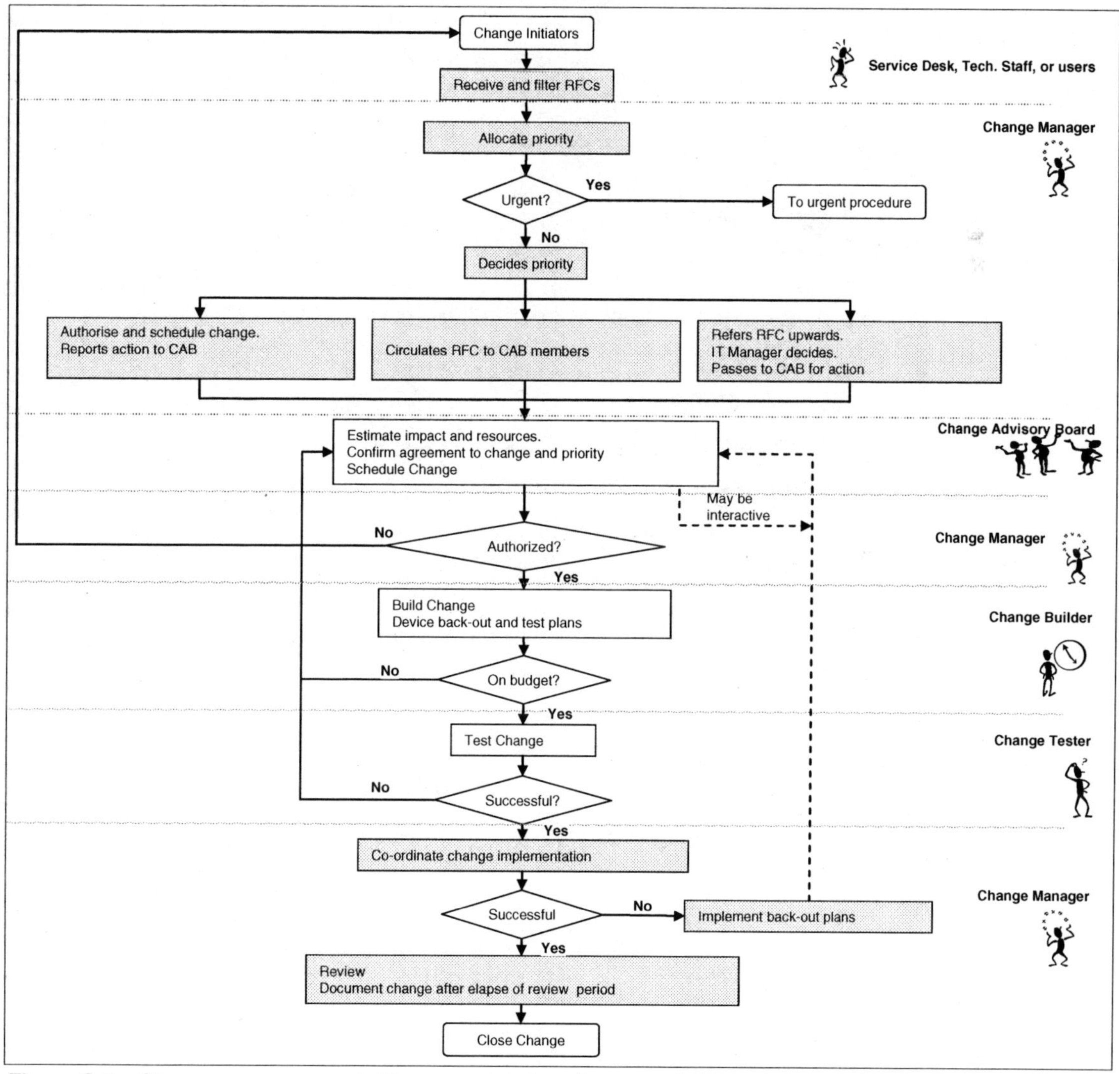

Figure G-8 Change management: Change procedure for normal changes

Change initiation

Usually, changes can be requested by any technical staff member in the organization. Users should also be allowed to submit RFC, but to provide initial filtering and coordination, user RFCs require approval of a LOB manager.

Change reception: Logging and filtering

Log all change requests as RFCs. Give each RFC a unique number and store it in the CMDB. If the change is suggested to resolve a problem, create a relationship between the incident and the change.

Having logged the request, the change manager should reject requests that are impractical, undesirable, repetitive, and so on. An appeal process should be in place for change initiators to dispute the verdict of the change manager.

Initial change prioritization

The first action that the change manager takes after receiving an RFC is to allocate an initial priority to the change. This initial priority indicates the urgency of the change. The change manager is solely responsible for allocating the correct priority, even though the change initiator can be consulted during this process. Urgent changes should be handled through special procedures as explained in “Managing urgent changes” on page 465.

For normal (non-urgent) changes, the change manager places the RFC into one of the following categories:

- **A: Minor impact and few additional resources needed**

  The change manager is delegated the authority to approve and schedule changes, although they should be reported to the CAB. If there are any doubts about authorizing these changes, the CAB should be consulted.

- **B: More than a minor impact or significant resources needed**

  The RFC must be discussed at the next regular CAB meeting. Prior to this, the change manager must circulate the RFC to the CAB members or to a wider audience if necessary (for impact and resource assessment).

- **C: Major impact or major resource requirements**

  The IT manager must refer these requests upward. Approved changes must be passed back to the CAB for scheduling and implementation.

Change assessment and scheduling

Each RFC is assessed in terms of impact on the business and availability of resources. At this point, you must consider several business and technical factors. It is more than likely that the change manager has to consult the business and technical support staff to fully assess the impact and requirements.

- **Change building**: If the change is authorized, the appropriate technical group is given the task of building the change and devising a test plan. Create backout plans to enable the implementation team to revert to a known trusted state in case problems arise during the implementation of the change.
- **Change testing**: An independent testing authority should test both the change and backout procedures prior to implementation. The change cannot be allowed to be implemented before satisfactory tests have been completed.
- **Change implementation:** Upon completion of testing, the change manager coordinates the implementation of the change. Advise all relevant staff in advance of the planned implementation, perhaps through the service desk. If anything fails, execute the backout plans and remove the change.
- **Change review**: To ensure that the desired effects are achieved and to assess whether the resource estimates are accurate, review all changes after a predefined period of time. This also helps to improve future estimates.

Managing urgent changes

Requests for urgent changes are bound to appear at the desk of the change manager. Typically, these are the result of component failures or unforeseen incidents, but urgent RFCs have been observed as the result of poor or missing planning. To avoid the panic of urgent changes, perform the disciplines of service delivery, primarily capacity management and availability management, with an equal focus on long-term and short-term issues.

Reception and prioritizing of urgent RFCs follow the same processes as for normal RFCs. After the change manager decides that the change is urgent, for business or IT service delivery reasons, the CAB emergency committee is called for an urgent meeting or conference call.

The urgency, the impact of the change, and the resources needed to create and implement the change are all assessed. Also the need for testing is determined. Figure G-9 on page 466 shows the urgent change procedure. Just as for a normal RFC, but hopefully a little faster, the change is built, and backout plans are created. If time allows, the change and backout plans are tested, and, with no further delay, the implementation takes place.

Of course, urgency is a matter for this type of RFC. Therefore, deviation from the normal requirements for thorough documentation throughout change processing might apply. The change manager has to make up for this when the implementation of the change proves to be satisfactory. The CMDB needs to be updated with all relevant information regarding the change.

Finally, the change is reviewed and properly documented as is the case if a normal RFC was handled.

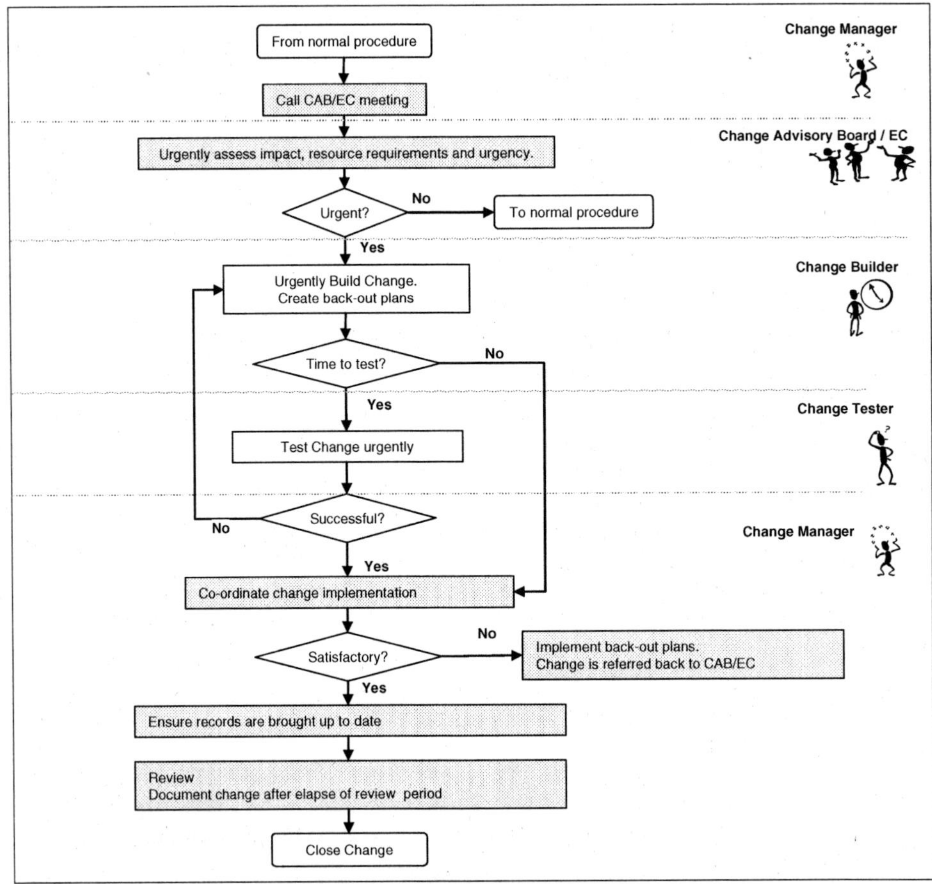

Figure G-9 Change management: Urgent change procedure

Change management and other disciplines

Change management is a key discipline for delivering high availability services. Naturally, there is a tight relationship between change management, problem management, incident management, and the service desk. Refer to "Problem management and other disciplines" on page 460. Change management often relies on release management for implementation, and, as usual, the main transfer of information between the cooperating disciplines is the CMDB.

However, the discipline that most depends on the services of change management is configuration management. The two disciplines mutually depend on each other. There can be no control over CIs in an organization if they are not subject to change control. At the same time, there can be no meaningful change control if there is no idea of what CIs are in the organization and what their functions are.

This interdependence leads to:

- Configuration management tasks to update the configuration repository should be prompted in several ways, a large number of which fall within the scope of change management. Some of these are:
  - When new CIs are added to the IT infrastructure
  - When the status of CIs changes
  - When the owners of CIs change
  - When the location of CIs changes
  - When relationships between CIs change
  - When old CIs are removed
  - When a unregistered CI is found or information regarding a CI is inaccurate
  - When a change is requested

    Change management should assess that change's impact on the business and identify other CIs that could possibly be affected. If the CMDB is not up to date, this affects the way in which the change is treated.
- Any change request is made using a RFC, which is reflected in the CMDB. Unless this is done, it is difficult to track progress and trace problems in the IT infrastructure back to previous changes.
- Unless change management is functioning effectively, the CMDB cannot reflect the current status of specific CIs in the organization.
- If changes fail, the CMDB can be used to indicate what state the CI should be reverted to. If that is out of date, time is wasted trying to remember what the CI looked like before the work started.

G.3.6 Release management

Because configuration management is responsible for managing the logical aspects of CIs (including software and hardware CIs), release management is responsible for the physical aspects. Release management is involved whenever a significant hardware or software rollout takes place. In relation to software, the main types that are to be controlled are:

- Application programs developed in-house
- Bought-in application software and utilities
- System software provided by suppliers

All of this software must be stored in a common secure software library, called the *Definitive Software Library*. This library contains all the definitive quality-controlled versions of all the software CIs defined in the configuration repository.

The DSL is one single library, separate from other parts of the environment. At least, the DSL, logically, is single, but it might be practical to use more physical locations, formats, and backup storage as part of the contingency plan.

For hardware control, set aside an area for the secure storage of approved hardware components, named *Definitive Hardware Store (DHS)*. Similarly to all the approved software, record all details that relate to the hardware components in the CMDB.

The tasks performed by release management are:

- Planning and overseeing the successful rollout of new and changed software and hardware and associated documentation
- Physical storage, protection, distribution, and implementation of all approved software and hardware
- Control of access to authorized versions and support of change control in releasing software for distribution for further work
- Ensuring that only correctly-released and authorized versions of software are in use
- Distributing software to remote locations
- Implementing (or bringing into service) approved software and hardware
- Managing the organization's rights and obligations regarding software and hardware

The release management processes include elements that are concerned with development and other elements that are concerned with the production environment. Both are managed to ensure that the required standards are met when the service is delivered and to control the way the software is being used in the production environment. This is why release management is considered a service management discipline.

Figure G-10 on page 469 shows the details of the release management process. The left part of the figure shows the tasks that are related to verifying and ensuring the functionality and quality of the new software CIs, which are developed in-house or bought-in. This is the control part of release management. After the required specifications are met, the software, along with its attributes, are registered in the CMDB and stored in the DSL.

The right part of the figure shows the functions that are related to distribution. The software is copied from the DSL and built. The build process can be a simple copy or a complete (or partial) compilation and linkage. The main issue is to test and verify that the output from the build process can be distributed and implemented successfully. This must be tested before initiating any distributions and implementations.

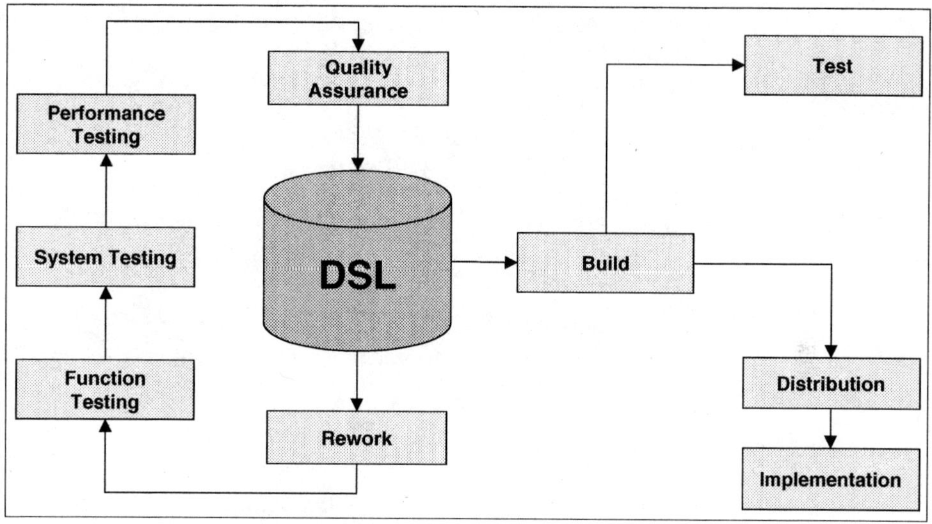

Figure G-10 Release management: DSL

Release management and other disciplines

Despite that fact that, for service management purposes, release management is the extended arm of change control, it also interacts with configuration management by maintaining the CMDB throughout the life cycle of the software and hardware CIs. Configuration can help release management achieve the following tasks:

- Recording location of software and hardware
- Code control
- Building releases
- Identifying who needs new releases
- Implementation
- Software and hardware auditing
- Determining license fees
- Identifying unused software and hardware
- Recovering software
- Recovering from data loss or corruption

In addition, release management must also provide reports to SLM regarding implementations.

G.4 Service delivery disciplines

If service support is the hands of the service management body, service delivery is the mind of service management. Service delivery is a discipline that needs to be mastered in most enterprises. One way or another, every enterprise provides services to its customers, either as the main business idea or as a supplement to the goods provided by the company. Even though services from various industries differ, all providers of services must answer two questions before they initiate service delivery:

- What is the service that will be delivered?
- How will the service be delivered?

To support the answering process, you must address a lot of related questions, such as:

- Why are we delivering the service?
- Why will customers buy the service?
- Where and when will the service be delivered, in what quantities, and at what level of quality?
- What resources are needed to deliver sufficient quantities of service of the desired quality, at the place or places and time or times of usage?
- What is the cost of delivering sufficient quantities of the service of the desired quality at the place or places and time or times of usage?
- How is service delivery assured?
- How is unauthorized use of the service assured?
- Who will support the delivery?
- What is the price customers have to pay to make use of the service?

Many services are standard off-the-shelf services that are well-defined and apply to a large number of different customers. Other services share the same attributes but can be tailored to the specific geographies, industries, businesses, or types of customers. Yet other services are highly customized to meet the needs of specific customers.

In general, IT services are grouped into three categories of service. Each reflects the need for particular adjustments to fulfill the requirements of the users:

- **Off-the-shelf**: Standard; no adjustment
- **Volume customization**: Standard versions; adjusted to fit similar groups of customers
- **One-of-a-kind**: Made to order to fit the unique needs of one particular customer

The cost of delivering a *one-of-a-kind* service properly is much higher than the cost of delivering a *standard* service. The price that the customer pays reflects the cost. To determine the cost, and thereby predefine the price that the customer must pay, you must answer all of the questions concerning who, why, what, where, when, and how. That is you must define the service in such detail that there can be no misinterpretations about:

- The deliverable
- Quantities and quality of the deliverable
- Prerequisites and requirements for the delivery
- Division of roles and responsibilities between customer and provider
- How, where, and when the delivery takes place
- The penalties for not delivering
- Benefits/penalties for increased delivery

And finally, when all these items are defined, you must determine the price.

Discussing SLM in the context of IT services typically applies to volume-customization and one-of-a-kind services. Within the enterprise, the IT organization provides the same basic services to all LOBs (mail, office applications, Internet access, etc.). It fulfills particular needs for each LOB by providing specialized services designed solely for this purpose (for example, accounts payable/receivable, payroll, procurement, and so on). Likewise, an external network service provider wants to sell similar networking services to many customers and perhaps design special services for customers with special needs.

In the service management organization, SLM is responsible for defining services. It is also responsible for managing customer demand and negotiating the SLAs. After the services are established and delivery has begun, service providers need to assure that the service is delivered as expected. They must also ensure continued delivery, which is also the responsibility of SLM.

To do this, SLM needs assistance from other disciplines that focus on various aspects of the service delivery processes and the overall mission of the IT department:

- **Capacity management**: Deals with the daily monitoring and reporting of workloads, resource usage, and component performance. It is also responsible for capacity planning by identifying trends and predicting future needs.
- **Availability management**: Ensures that the services are available to the users that are authorized to use those services, when they are needed. This is primarily achieved by ensuring the availability of each of the components that is part of the service.

- **Financial management of IT services**: Manages the IT budgets and negotiates contracts with suppliers. It also plays a key role in determining the cost of a service (often based on resource usage), therefore assisting SLM with pricing the service.
- **IT service continuity management**: Ensures that the IT services delivery might continue, or be re-established quickly, after a disaster. IT services are often required to perform business transactions, so the IT organization must have completed and tested plans and procedures for disaster recovery and related subjects.

The following sections explore these four disciplines and their association with SLM.

G.4.1 Capacity management

Insufficient capacity often leads to bottlenecks, performance problems, and loss of availability, all of which contribute to degrading service delivery. Looking at a typical client/server service, it is evident that, since more components make up the service as it is perceived by the end user, the capacity of each individual component must balance with the capacity of the other components.

In the IT community, more capacity is often synonymous with new technology. Capacity is an attribute of the hardware components that make up the service or the amount of hardware resources available to software components. Therefore, capacity management is often seen as managing procurement of new advanced technology. Too often, new technology is procured when performance or capacity problems are experienced, and then the capacity management function becomes reactive rather than proactive. This tends to happen in a very complex environment where many components are a part of more services and are tied together in a giant web.

Considering capacity as the maximum performance or output of a component, we can say that, to manage capacity of a service, it is important to manage the workloads of the service to forecast the need for capacity. It is also important to know what workloads run where and when, and under what circumstances.

In general, this means that the objective of capacity management is to ensure that the *appropriate technology* is used in the best way possible. The word *appropriate* is determined by the level of service that is to be provided to the business at all times. Also, the phrase *best way* is determined by how well any given technology supports the business requirements of the users.

Ensuring that the right technology is used to provide the best support for the business is like trying to hit a moving target that varies in size. Not only does the business environment change constantly, but technology changes happen so fast these days, that ordered devices might be obsolete before they are received. The rapid development of new technologies might even pose new possibilities and opportunities for the business leading to business changes driven by the availability of new technology. The e-revolution is one of the best examples of technology-driven business changes. Some of the questions that change management helps to answer are:

- How will the new technology affect the way business is conducted?
- How can we make the best use of these technologies?
- Will they really save us money?
- Are they going to make us more productive?

To answer these questions, capacity management draws upon data of the past environment where the variables are known. It compares this date to current projected future variables. Data about the past and present environment also helps to optimize current performance, estimate future needs and demands, and take steps to be ready to meet them when required.

To overcome all this, capacity management is divided into the following subdisciplines, each covering different aspects of capacity management.

- **Capacity management database**: Maintains the data related to capacity management
- **Performance management**: Monitors and optimizes the performance of the existing components
- **Workload management**: Identifies, understands, and forecasts workloads
- **Application sizing**: Predicts service levels, as well as cost and resource implications of future applications or major modifications to existing applications
- **Modeling**: Predicts systems performance under given volumes and varieties of work
- **Resource management**: Understands the IT infrastructure to ensure that the organization uses the available technology that best suits the business
- **Demand management**: Prioritizes customer demand for use of component resources without adding more capacity
- **Capacity planning**: Predicts when components reach their saturation point and identifies the action to be taken to prevent this

Capacity management database

The central tool used by capacity management is a repository of information relevant to capacity management. This repository is unlikely to reside in a single database but can exist in several physical locations and contain several types of data.

The type of information that is stored in the capacity management database is technical, business, and cost data required by capacity management to produce technical and management reports showing usage and trends.

Performance management

The objective of performance management is to ensure that the agreed-upon service level is maintained. In addition, performance management is responsible for ensuring that each hardware, software, and networking component delivers the expected capacity.

This is a day-to-day task that involves monitoring the capacity delivered to quickly identify problems or bottlenecks. The information gathered for monitoring purposes is stored in the capacity management database to keep historical information and help determine trends.

SLM delivers the required service levels to be achieved for performance management. These are in the form of thresholds for each component that must be met to provide the agreed-upon level of service. If these thresholds are not met or if indicators show that they will not be met in the near future, performance management investigates the reason, identifies actions to tune the systems to meet the thresholds, and implements the tuning activities shown in Figure G-11 on page 475.

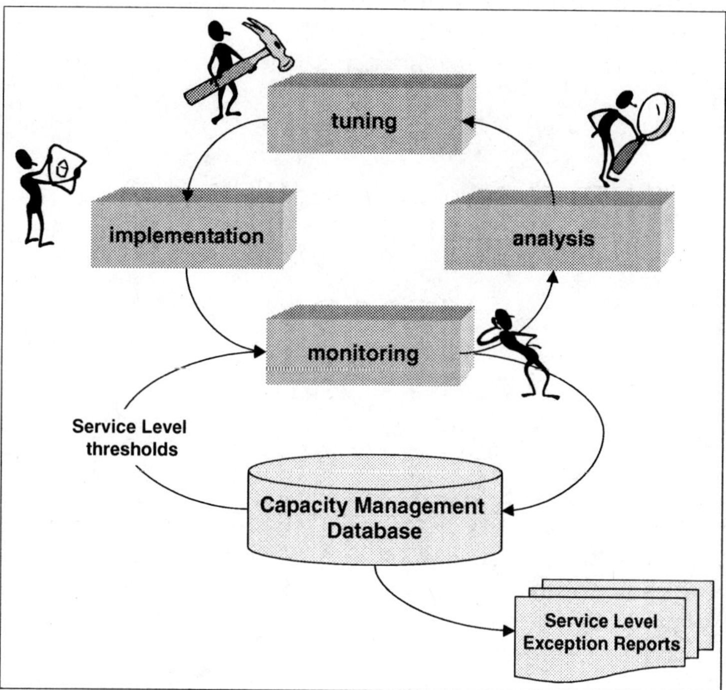

Figure G-11 Performance management activities

All the activities of performance management are conducted in close contact with configuration, problem, and change management.

Workload management

Workload management has three objectives:

- Understand and document all workloads
- Establish interfaces with relevant parties in the IT department for interchange of information
- Implement an effective workload forecasting system

Breaking down a service into individual workloads that execute on one or more components in the IT infrastructure is crucial to understanding and defining the capacity needs for any one component. Furthermore, workloads often depend on one another to form a hierarchy in which one workload must be completed before the next one occurs.

All the workloads, and the relationships between them, must be defined and categorized in the workload catalog, which is part of the overall capacity management database, as shown in Figure G-12 on page 476.

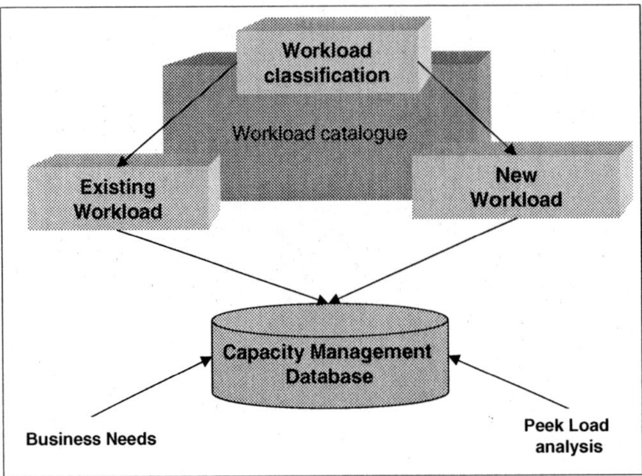

Figure G-12 Workload management activities

In addition to the existing workloads, capacity management must understand new workloads to estimate future capacity needs. The metrics used for this estimation are obtained from the application sizing and modeling tasks of capacity management.

Application sizing

The objectives of this task are to establish a means of predicting the service level, resource, and cost implications of new applications and major changes to existing applications. Application sizing is of particular interest in the early stages of the life of a service. Part of determining the cost of providing the service is a clear picture of the required capacity. Capacity management, therefore, supports SLM through the application sizing activities in the preliminary cost and business implications analysis.

Modeling

The modeling activities involve estimating or predicting the performance of a system under a given volume and variety of work. Modeling is the application sizing of hardware and networking components.

You can perform modeling with more or less accuracy. The most accurate method is benchmarking, where a load is run on a given system and the performance is measured. This is the most expensive way of modeling (Figure G-13 on page 477).

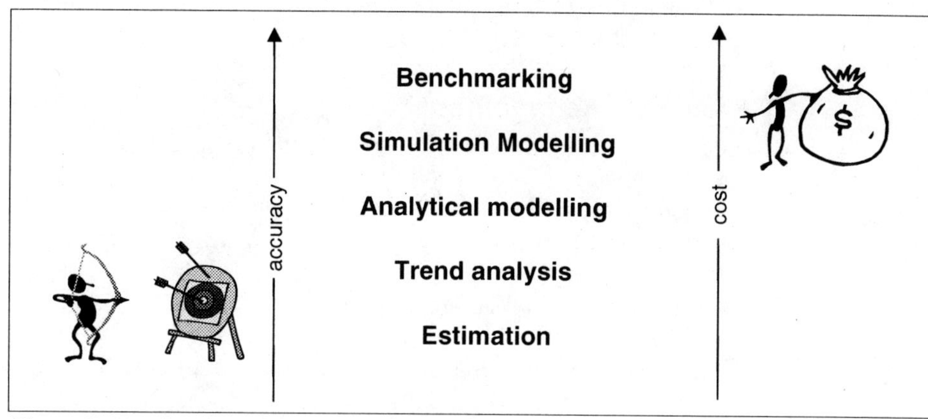

Figure G-13 Capacity management modeling

At the other end of the scale is estimation. Based on historical performance data and known variables, the performance of a workload is estimated. This is the most inaccurate way of modeling, but also the cheapest.

Between estimation and benchmarking are:

- **Trend analysis**: More historical data representing different workloads on different systems is compared with the expected workload on a new system.
- **Analytical modeling**: Statistical methods are brought into play to provide a more detailed workload and system models.
- **Simulation modeling**: A subset of a workload is run on the new system to obtain data that can be extrapolated to provide the expected performance figures.

Analytical models and even the equipment needed to run simulation and benchmarking tests might be provided by the hardware supplier. However, internally in the IT department, the most commonly found types of modeling are estimation, trend analysis, and common sense.

Modeling must be regarded as a tool that is available to all the tasks of capacity management since it is equally important and applicable to each of them.

Resource management

Resource management works together with the availability and configuration management disciplines. It helps to provide an understanding of the organization's hardware, software, infrastructure, and other resources and to ensure that the organization is aware of changes in technology. This information is vital when evaluating the business implications of acquiring new technology. It is also important when suggesting the application of new technologies to solve business challenges.

Demand management

Capacity management must also manage customer demand for IT resources of limited capacity. (*Limited*, in this sense, means that the available capacity cannot be increased for technical, financial, or business reasons.) Such a situation might occur when a component fails completely or when decreased capacity of exceptionally high demand is experienced. The capacity constraints might even be the result of a deliberate business decision not to invest in the full capacity needed to provide full service to all LOBs during peek hours. In a situation with limited capacity available, customers compete for service, and there is an evident need for prioritizing the tasks.

Demand management is related to capacity management and prioritizes competing demands based on business reasons rather than technical or other reasons. In this capacity, change management has to make some unpopular decisions, such as stopping or decreasing the service delivered to some users while others receive the usual high service level. However, since the decisions are based on business reasons, chances are that they are supported by senior management. And capacity management certainly needs that support when prioritizing.

Capacity planning

Using all the other capacity management disciplines, the foundation to create a capacity plan has been established. The ITIL defines the capacity plan as a plan that predicts when components will reach their saturation point and identify actions to prevent saturation.

Often, the capacity management discipline is perceived as creating and maintaining the capacity plan. In this definition, it is implied that all the other tasks (performance, workload, resource, and demand management as well as application sizing and modeling) are accomplished to provide all the information necessary to create the capacity plan. Figure G-14 on page 479 illustrates capacity planning.

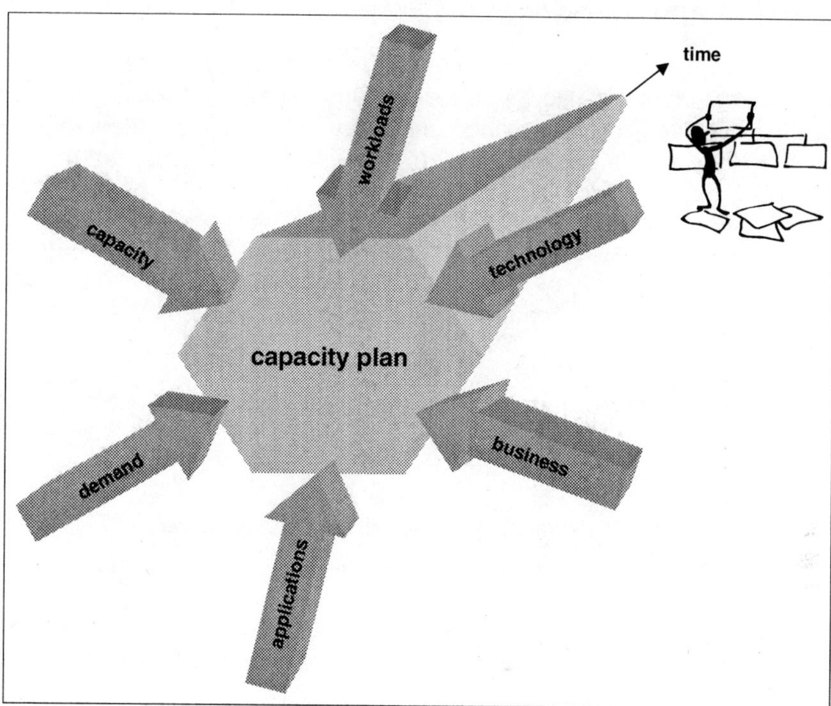

Figure G-14 Capacity planning

The capacity plan is by no means a static plan. Since both the business and technological environments change over time, demand, available capacity, service levels to deliver, and business priorities change accordingly, affecting the capacity plan.

Capacity management and other disciplines

Capacity management is a key discipline in service delivery. Since capacity management has the overview of the infrastructure, resources and capacities needed to support the services, knowledge about available technology and even business priorities, it interacts with all the other disciplines of service delivery.

The primary collaboration is between capacity management and SLM. When negotiating new SLAs (or renegotiating existing ones), SLM consults capacity management to assess the capacity needs to accommodate the customer requirements. After the SLA is negotiated, SLM sets the targets for capacity management to deliver, and capacity management reports performance and throughput achievements back to SLM.

G.4.2 Availability management

Sometimes, availability management can be regarded as part of capacity management. However, the responsibilities of availability management include planning, implementation, management, and optimization of IT services so that they can be used where and when the business requires.

Availability management, as defined by the ITIL, is involved with much more than system availability. Availability management focuses on entire services and ensures that the services are available where and when they are needed. Doing this, availability management is heavily influenced by the following factors:

- The complexity of the services
- The reliability of the IT components and environmental services
- The level of maintenance provided by suppliers or elements of self-maintenance
- The infrastructure on which the services are built
- The configuration of the infrastructure used to provide the service

When conducting availability management, you must observe the key elements (combined for all the components that are part of the service) in the following sections.

Availability

Availability is one of the main attributes of the quality of service delivery perceived by users. The availability of components to meet user requirements as stipulated in the SLA (expressed as a percentage) depends on these factors:

- The reliability of components
- The resilience to failure
- The quality of maintenance and support
- The quality of operating procedures

To optimize the availability of the service, you must take into account all of these factors for all components of the service. In this context, it is important to remember that the user's perception of the service is depends on the availability of the hardware, software, and networking components as well as the availability of the data that is used.

A service that meets the required availability can be characterized as a service that has minimal interrupts yet, when an incident occurs, is recovered quickly and efficiently.

Reliability

From a quality service point of view, reliability can be defined as freedom from operational failure. It is often measured as the *mean time between failure (MTBF)*, the mean time between system incidents (MTBSI), or the number of breaks in a period. All of these values help determine the reliability of a component to perform a required function under the stated conditions for a stated period of time.

The reliability of a service is partly determined by the amount of resilience built into the service and partly by the pervasive management applied with the aim of preventing failures from occurring. The resilience of a service is the ability of the service to continue providing an operation service when components of the infrastructure are non-operational.

Maintainability

Maintainability defines the ability of an IT service to be maintained in or restored to a satisfactory operational state. Maintaining or restoring a service involves five separate stages:

- Anticipating failures
- Detecting failures
- Diagnosing failures
- Resolving failures
- Recovering from failures

Serviceability

As used by the ITIL, serviceability defines the reliability, maintainability, and maintenance support of components for which external suppliers are responsible. When an external party assumes complete responsibility for an entire IT service and its support (as when a service is outsourced), availability is equivalent to serviceability.

Security

Availability management has the responsibility of the last letter in the basic security CIA principle:

- *C*onfidentiality
- *I*ntegrity
- *A*vailability

From the perspective of availability management, among the security considerations that you must address are:

- Services must only be available to authorized personnel.
- After failure, services must be recoverable without compromising confidentiality and integrity.

- Services must be recoverable without contravening IT security policies.
- Access for contractors to hardware and software should be clearly identifiable.
- Data must only be available to authorized personnel and only at agreed-upon times as specified in the SLA.

Figure G-15 shows the availability management perspective of the relationships between users, the IT organization, and external suppliers of services and the agreements/contracts that govern these relationships.

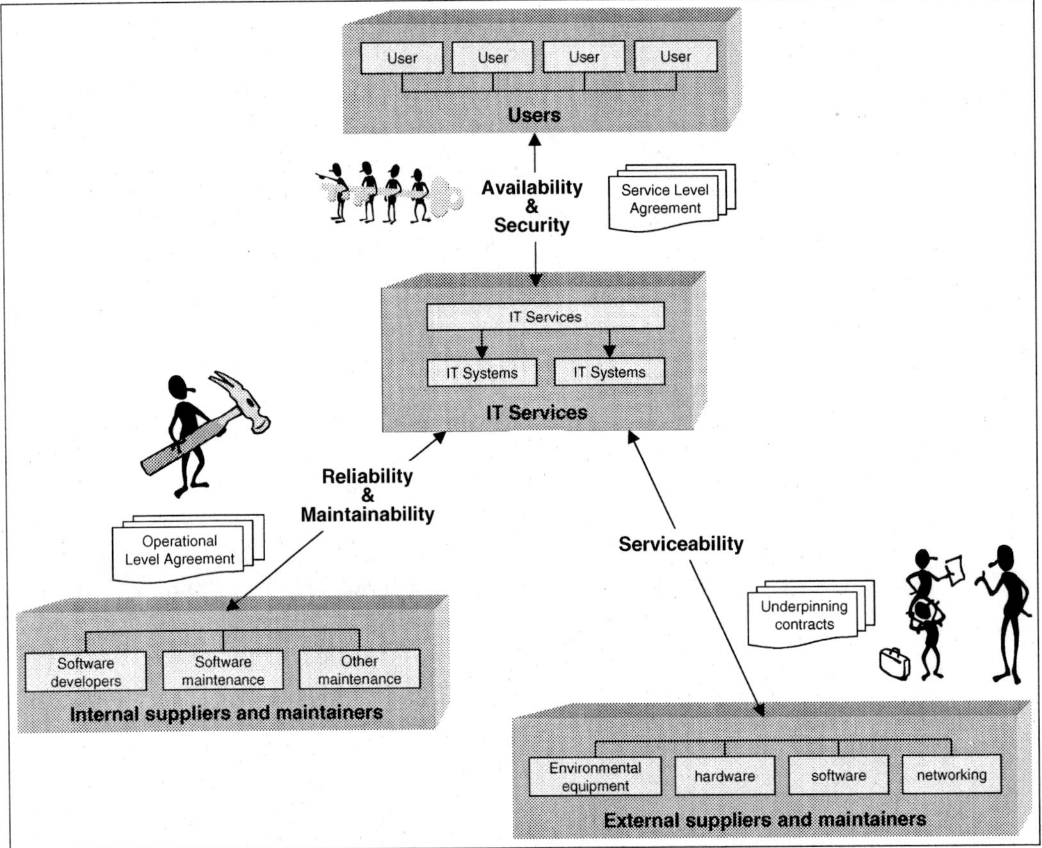

Figure G-15 Key elements of availability management

Availability management and other disciplines

Not surprisingly, availability management works most closely with configuration management, capacity management, SLM, incident and problem management, and service desk.

Configuration management provides information about the components to manage. Capacity management provides information about the availability of the hardware and software components (based on performance monitoring). Service desk and problem management alert availability management in case of user-discovered availability problems. Finally, service desk needs the help of availability management when user access to services needs to be modified and in case of authentication problems or violations.

Like all the other disciplines, availability management also provides reports and statistics to SLM that show the availability of the services delivered.

G.4.3 Financial management for IT services

While IT services are seen as essential in many organizations, the cost of providing these services is realized only by a small number of people. This might lead to accusations that IT is not providing value for the money spent. This might occur while the users demand a higher level of service, which requires more capacity, which, in turn, leads to a higher cost of providing the service.

The objective of financial management for IT services is to break this vicious circle by:

- Identifying all costs necessary to provide the service
- Establishing a fair means of recovering these costs from the business

This places IT in line with the rest of the business making users aware that they pay their fair price for the services they receive.

The tasks performed by financial management for IT services are:

- *Costing*: Identifies and accounts for the costs of running the IT department and providing IT services
- *Charging*: Recovers the costs of IT service provision in a fair and equitable way related to how the services are used

The objective of costing is to provide detailed information about where and why money is spent to provide IT services. The objectives of charging are:

- To recover the costs of providing IT services from the users of those services
- To create, maintain awareness of costs of IT service provision among users
- To provide an incentive for IT staff to deliver the agreed-upon level of service
- To shape customer behavior in conjunction with capacity management

Charging should be implemented only after careful consideration has been made. It might work as a double-edged sword. While providing money to the IT department, it might scare off users so seriously that they refuse to deal with their internal IT service provider and seek services from external providers. This can lead to higher costs for the remaining users, giving them more incentives to go to external providers, and, before long, the entire IT department can be outsourced. Figure G-16 illustrates the vicious charging cycle.

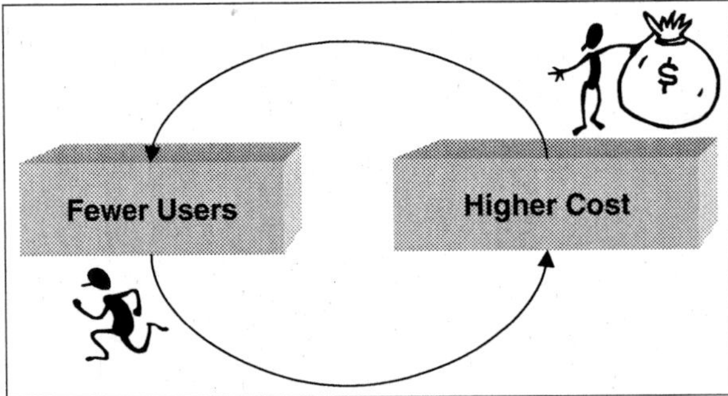

Figure G-16 The vicious charging cycle

For these reasons, you might consider using *notional charging* instead of *hard charging*. This creates user awareness of the costs involved in the service provision without affecting their budgets. However, notional charging is effective only if the normal financial management for IT services processes are functional and effective so the users have a realistic idea of the cost of a service.

Implement charging only when it will give a clear value to the organization. An environment that is ready for charging has these characteristics:

- Budgetary control by users
- Charging exists for other resources
- Freedom of choice
- Commercial flexibility
- Adequate monitoring capabilities

The reasons for charging might include:

- Improved cost consciousness
- Better utilization of resources
- Allows comparisons
- Demand management
- To recover IT costs in an equitable manner
- Inform users how changes are derived, so they can influence usage/charges
- Raise revenue

The costing and charging mechanisms used to align the IT infrastructure more closely to the business objectives is referred to as the *cost management system*.

This must be an integral part of the overall financial management system of the organization. The objectives for the cost management system are to:

- Provide assistance in developing a sound investment strategy that evaluates the options available from technology in the light of business strategy and objectives
- Set targets for financial performance and measure that performance in terms of budgeted versus actual costs
- Provide a basis for prioritizing resource usage
- Ensure sound stewardship of all assets employed in the organization
- Provide information for management's decision making and planning requirements
- Provide a flexible and fast response to changing business circumstances

The way financial management for IT services meets these objectives varies slightly depending on the nature of the IT department whether it is a profit center or a cost center. Following the ITIL, the two can be defined as a profit center or cost center.

- *Profit center*: A *computer services business center* that operates as a separate business entity, but with its business objectives set by the organization. It provides clearly-identified products that are sold to a market. Each of the provided services carries a price tag.
- *Cost center*: A *utility cost center* that provides services to other cost centers. Performance is not measured in terms of projected or anticipated return but on how effectively and efficiently it provides services to its users.

The major difference between the two models is the extent to which they charge the users. The profit center must charge in order to generate a profit, where the cost center might charge primarily to raise cost awareness among the users. Both need to estimate and measure the costs of service provision.

In its simplest form, cost estimation begins by identifying the IT services to be provided and then estimating the total resources needed to provide them. The cost of the resources is then broken down into costs per unit of output.

The aim of cost estimation is to understand (on a user-by-user level) the proportion of the IT resources being used. To do this, it is necessary to break costs down into cost units that can be measured according to workloads used by individual users. The cost estimation is based on the following areas:

- **Cost units**: A way to accumulate and classify costs for the purpose of calculating a rate. Typical cost units include:
  - Software
  - Equipment
  - Accommodation
  - Transfer
  - Organization
- **Cost classification**: Breaking down costs into units is not enough. There is still no way to determine how much a cost or resource is related to a particular user or group. Cost accounting can assist by further cost classification as:
  - Direct
  - Indirect
  - Capital
  - Operational
  - Fixed
  - Variable
- **Workload estimation and forecasting**: A way to calculate how each service is going to be used. Input is typically provided by capacity management.
- **Standard cost calculation**: A standard cost is a carefully predetermined unit cost that can be used as a basis for total cost calculations or the measure of financial performance.
- **Standard cost units**: Are used to determine the overall budget estimates. During the year, standard costs are monitored, and updated forecasts are made. A comparison of standard costs to actual costs enables financial management for IT services to assess the need for cost reduction or price increases.
- **Cost monitoring**: The identified costs are monitored on a regular basis to enable more effective financial planning and capacity planning. Monitoring is also a prerequisite to implement charging. Monitoring should be automatic.

Pricing

Any pricing policy must take the into account the objectives of charging, the direct and indirect costs, the demand for the commodity, the size of the market and the nature of the competitors. Based on the type of IT department (cost or profit center), charging can now be performed according to one or more of the following methods:

- **Direct charging**: Customers are charged directly upon receiving a service, such as charging for the delivery of a PC.
- **Resource usage**: Charges are based on the use of specific IT components or resources, such as disk space or CPU seconds.
- **Output related**: Customers are charged for specific printouts or reports.
- **Appointment**: The costs of shared facilities are split up between the users of that facility or resource.
- **Market related**: Customers are charged based on what other organizations are charging.

Financial management for IT services and other disciplines

It is evident that financial management for IT services is an important player in planning and conducting service management. Capacity and availability management provide input related to current and future needs for capacity that needs to be produced. Configuration management is an invaluable partner when categorizing and charging costs.

Financial management for IT services delivers information about financial performance to SLM. It also helps to shape customer behavior through the applied charging policies.

G.4.4 IT Service continuity management

It is essential that IT services can quickly recovered and delivered to the agreed quality, even if disaster strikes the IT infrastructure. IT service continuity management undertakes this by reducing the impact of major incidents, emergencies, and disasters. When a disruption affects critical business processes, the consequences can be severe and include substantial financial loss, embarrassment, and loss of credibility or goodwill for the organization concerned. The consequential damage can extend much further and impact staff welfare, customers, suppliers, taxpayers, shareholders, and the general public.

IT service continuity management is considered a part of overall Business Continuity Management (BCM), which is the responsibility of senior management in any organization. Both IT service continuity management and BCM are concerned with managing risks to ensure that an organization can, at all times, continue to operate to at least a predetermined minimum level. The risks that are addressed by BCM and IT service continuity management are those that could result in a sudden and serious disruption to the business, for example:

- Damage or denial of access to premises, possibly as a result of terrorism, fire, flood, or other disasters
- Loss of critical underpinning services, such as telecommunications and power
- Failure or non-performance of critical suppliers, distributors, or other third parties, particularly where key business functions have been outsourced
- Human error and technical or environmental breakdown
- Fraud, sabotage, extortion, or commercial espionage
- Infiltration of IT systems by viruses and other forms of malicious users
- Industrial action or other unavailability of key staff

The three objectives of IT service continuity management and BCM are:

- To reduce or avoid identified risks
- To plan for the recovery of business processes if the business is disrupted
- To transfer all or part of the risk to a third party

All business units or LOB within an enterprise should develop and maintain plans to continue business in case of a disaster. Figure G-17 shows the typical process model for business continuity.

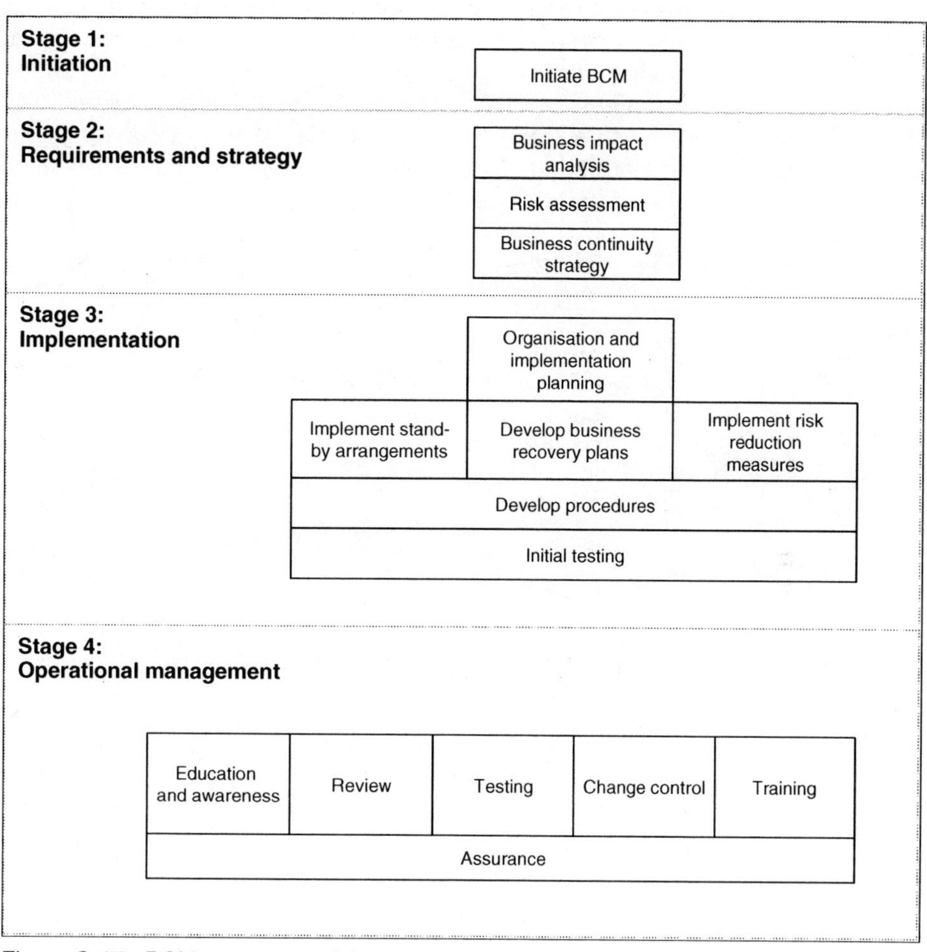

Figure G-17 BCM process model

Because the LOBs rely on IT services to perform their business, the IT department is heavily involved in this process. As is the case with any other business unit, the IT department should develop and maintain a set of plans to use in case of an emergency.

While the CEO is responsible for business continuity planning for the whole enterprise, the IT manager is responsible for the overall plan for the IT department. The IT manager is responsible for defining the strategy and organization to use for business recovery (stages 1 to 2). The responsibility to develop, test, verify, and maintain plans and procedures for recovery of the individual services is often delegated to the team leaders.

Meanwhile tactical stages 1 and 2 of the BCM process focus on proactive measures, to prevent the emergency from occurring, and the reactive measures. Operational stages 3 and 4 focus mainly on the reactive aspects. In stage 3, the product support teams are brought in to develop, document, and test emergency procedures. In stage 4, the procedures are tested with the users and maintained. Stage 4 must be repeated periodically to keep an awareness of what to do should anything happen.

The plans must be maintained and updated whenever major changes to the infrastructure or services are implemented. Figure G-18 on page 491 shows the typical content of business continuity plans.

Each plan describes specific roles and responsibilities as well as activities to perform. It also contains supporting data, such as addresses and telephone numbers, for different phases of an emergency. These phases are best illustrated using an example of a fire in an office building of a small company as follows:

1. **Emergency response and salvage**: Call the fire brigade, and, if possible, prevent the fire from spreading and secure vital assets; evacuate the building.
2. **Crisis management**: While the fire is being handled, inform senior management, employees, families, customers, and suppliers, and maybe the media. Put stand-by accommodations and equipment on alert.
3. **Stand-by invocation**: After the fire is extinguished, Assess the damage and decide what action to take. Invoke standby arrangements if necessary.
4. **Recover business processes**: Re-establish the basic IT services and business processes in intermediate offices. Provide accommodations and transportation for employees if necessary.
5. **Plan return to normal**: Arrange for the normal office to be cleaned and redecorated, re-establish IT infrastructure. Make plans for move back to the normal office and normal business procedures.
6. **Return to normal**: Place move-back plans into effect.

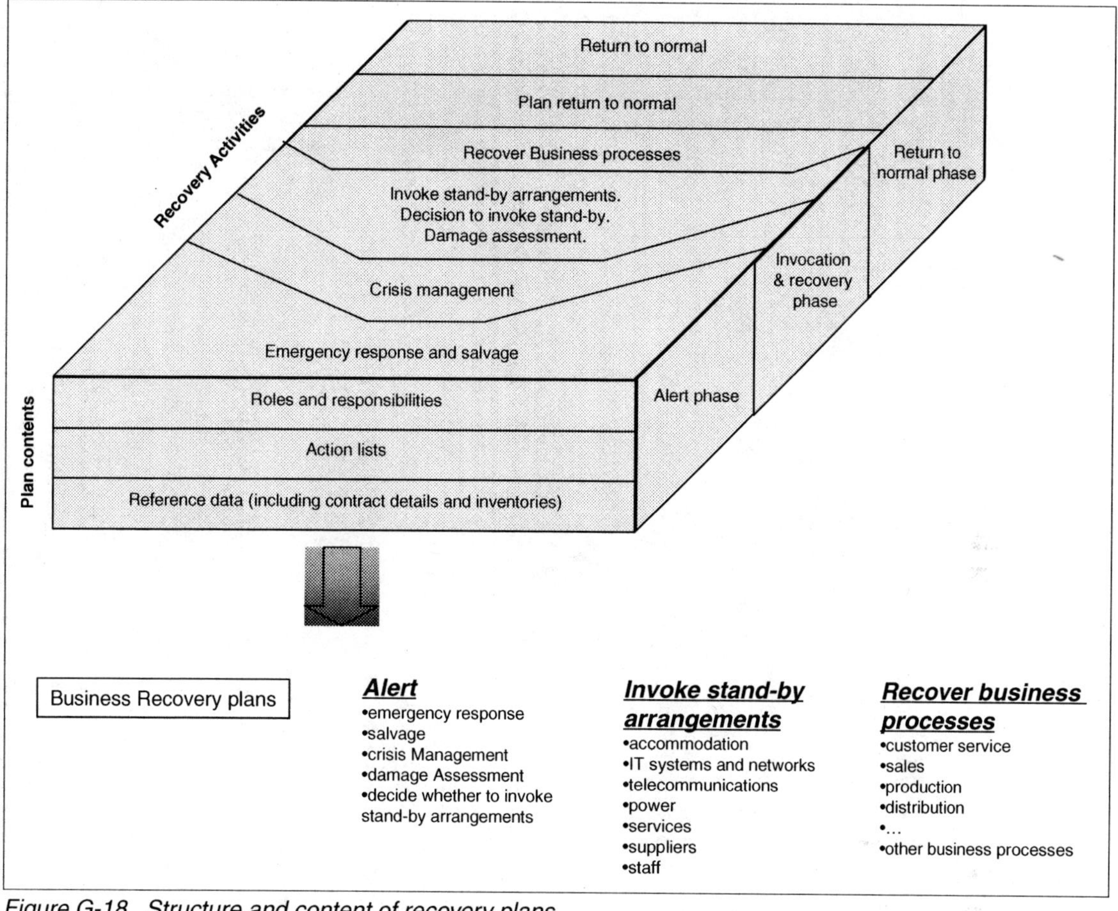

Figure G-18 Structure and content of recovery plans

Before you establish the individual recovery plans for each business unit, you must develop and agree on a framework for the business recovery plans. This framework should include:

- A master plan to coordinate the overall recovery effort
- A series of other plans for activities that might need to be coordinated across the organization
- Plans for each key support function
- Plans for each critical business process

Figure G-19 on page 492 shows a template framework.

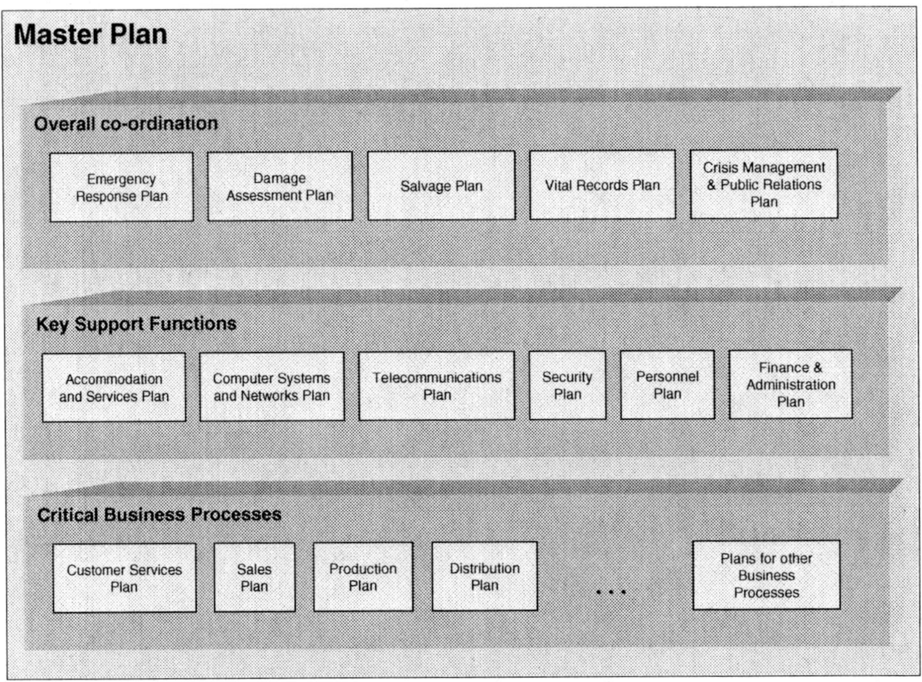

Figure G-19 Typical set of integrated business recovery plans

IT service continuity management and other disciplines

IT service continuity management involves all the other disciplines in service management, especially since each discipline must provide plans and procedures for handling an emergency. The capacity, availability, and configuration management areas are vital to the ability to develop and maintain valid plans. These disciplines provide input to the negotiations related to establishing and using the standby facilities.

Address IT service continuity management in every SLA, both internal and external. Even though nobody expects the disaster, a company that outsources its IT operation is depends almost 100 percent on the service provider's ability to deliver. If the supply of service is cut off, chances are that the company pays a very high price, perhaps even going out of business.

G.4.5 Service level management

Conducting SLM does not in itself guarantee high quality in the service delivery. It should be clear that several disciplines must be in place and working satisfactory to support SLM. They must provide information necessary to define and plan the service and the levels of service that must be delivered and provide feedback to indicate what levels of service have been achieved.

But what is high quality? Some users of a service might feel that they are receiving the best service ever while other users are dissatisfied with the same quality of service, even thought the IT department providing the service feels that the quality delivered is satisfactory. In most companies, the quality of service is an arbitrary issue. Therefore the judgement of the quality of service becomes a subjective matter based on personal (often short-term) criteria. This is why customers can be satisfied one week and demand the resignation of the entire IT department the next.

Before going into SLM, let's look at service quality and customer satisfaction.

Measuring service quality

Obviously, quality is an issue that closely related to expectations. Figure G-20 on page 494 illustrates the relationship between the actual performance (in terms of quality) of an IT department as opposed to the way their performance is perceived by its customers. It clearly shows that sustained improvements in the quality of service delivered increase the quality perceived by the users even more than the improvements made. This goes on until the users feel that they receive a higher quality of service than what is actually delivered.

From Figure G-20 on page 494, you can deduce that, even if the quality of service delivered remains the same and no improvements are made, users perceive the quality as being degraded.

Providing quality service is not enough. The service must consistently be of the same high quality both in actual delivery and in the eyes of the users. To fulfill this quality goal, quality must be defined. In the ITIL context, quality is a long-term strategic issue that defines exactly what *standards* to use to *measure IT's contribution* to the business.

On a day-to-day, week-to-week and year-to-year basis, quality is measured in terms of operational levels of service provided by the IT department. Therefore, in the short term, *quality* is expressed as the achievement of specified levels of service.

Following this definition of quality, a *quality service* is one that meets the specified levels of service, not high levels or low levels, but the levels specified by the customers during the SLA negotiations. The IT department simply has to provide the quality of service demanded by customers. However, customer demands and customer expectations are two different (often incompatible) issues.

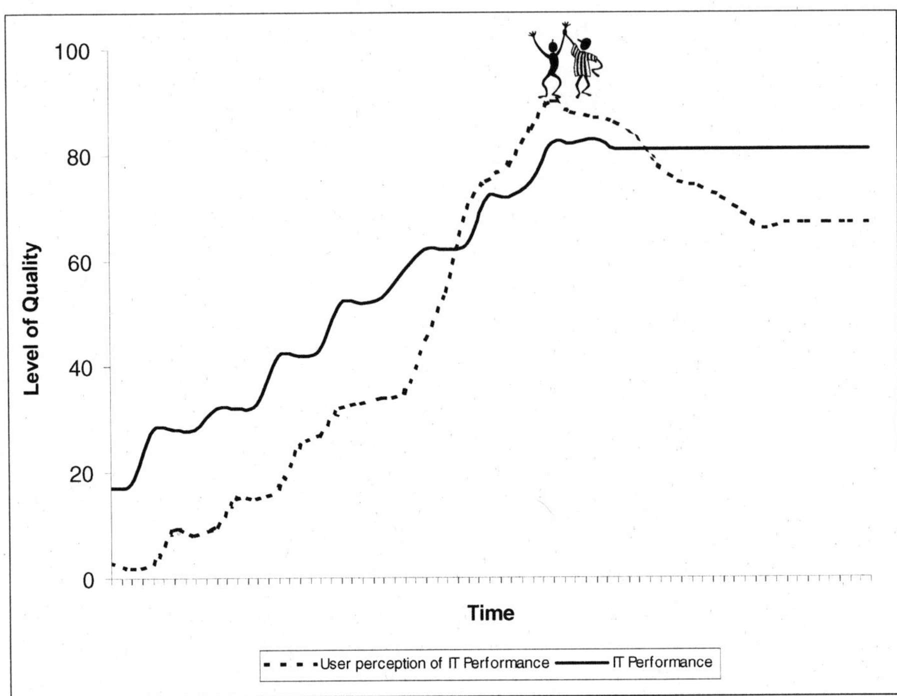

Figure G-20 Actual versus user-perceived service delivery performance

Service levels and customer satisfaction

Consistent delivery of the quality of service defined might lead to unhappy customers, since they perceive the service as degrading. One way to keep customers happy is to keep them satisfied. Constant high customer satisfaction means that the service is good, but it does not reveal anything about the quality of service.

Figure G-21 on page 495 shows how customer satisfaction of a delivered service might be grouped:

- *Generic*: The most basic service. All services of this type can be easily recognized because they are all based on the same generic type.
- *Expected*: This is the level of service that the customer has come to expect from a specific supplier or chain.
- *Generous*: This level of service offers more than the customer expects, often for the same price or less than is normally the case.
- *Total*: This level of service is of such a standard that it is impossible to improve it further.

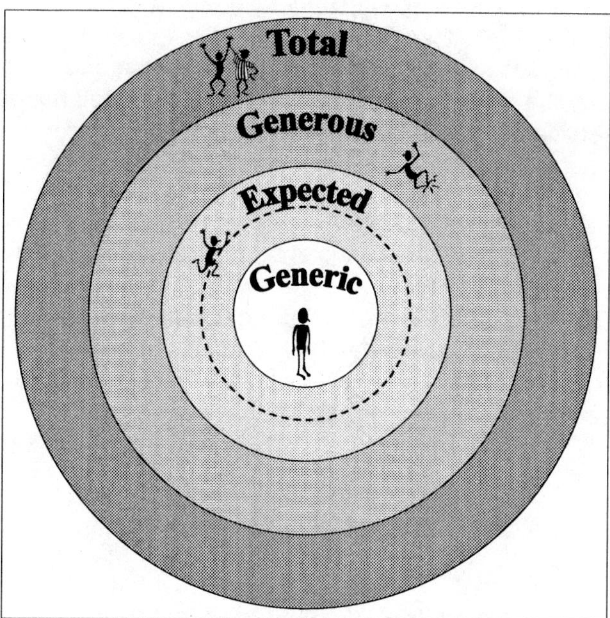

Figure G-21 Levels of service and customer satisfaction

Determining the right level to deliver is part of SLM. Working with intangibles, such as expectations, makes it a difficult task.

From a service provider point of view, the challenge is to keep customer satisfaction as high as possible while keeping costs down. Usually, higher quality means higher costs. Since the service provider is paid only to deliver to expectations, the optimum level of service to be delivered is in the expected range. This gives the service provider a small level of flexibility to deliver a service of a slightly higher or lower quality than what is expected. This depends on such factors as customer loyalty, delivery cost, and available capacity. The service provider can choose to divert from this (typically, by providing higher quality than expected) to promote services or to cater for specific LOBs.

Determining the right level to deliver is part of SLM. Again working with intangibles, such as expectations, makes it a difficult and tricky task.

Who is the customer

Chances are that the service provider is paid to meet the expected level of service. However, it is not always a level of service that is perceived as satisfactory by customers. In ITIL terms, the *customer* is the recipient of an IT service, who is responsible for the cost of IT either directly through a charge-out system or indirectly in terms of demonstrated business necessity.

According to this definition, the customer can use and pay for the service. In business organizations, it is not practical to negotiate service delivery on a person-by-person basis. Services are typically delivered to departments or LOB and paid for by the organization, and the one paying does not necessarily have to use the service. In this case, the one responsible for the cost is the *customer*, and those who are not financially responsible are called *users*

Usually, during negotiations between the customer and the provider, service quality is adjusted to meet the needs of both parties. This adjustment often leads to degradations in both service quality and service price without a readjustment of users' expectations. When the provider delivers the agreed-upon level of service, the users are disappointed because they receive a lower level of service than expected. However, customer satisfaction is as expected because the sponsor receives the expected level of service.

The role of service level management

From the previous sections, you can see that SLM is concerned with managing the customers' expectations to the IT department. In this external role, SLM tries to determine the customer's requirements and meet these within the budgetary constraints of the business.

SLM also has an internal role to work together with all IT disciplines and departments to ensure that these levels of service can be delivered. This involves setting measurable performance targets, monitoring performance, and taking action when targets are not met.

In the internal role, SLM works to make every person involved with service provision aware of what is expected of them and to ensure business success. This means that every member of the IT team is aware of what they need to do to perform well and how their individual performance might affect the overall business.

Consequently, SLM works to build recognition by all parties supplying and receiving services. This is achieved through preparation, agreement, and maintenance of formal SLAs that document all the relevant details of the service. In this way, SLM bridges customers and suppliers by:

- Identifying and integrating the elements that make up service provision
- Packaging these into an easy-to-understand service
- Expressing that service in terms that the customer can understand, for example, in business terms

The responsibilities of SLM can, in many ways, be compared to those of a cruise director on a cruise liner as shown in Figure G-22 on page 497. The customers see all of the ship above the waterline, while the technical mechanisms that are used to achieve all the services are out of sight below the waterline. SLM's task is to manage the technical assets and support business needs while keeping the technical aspects out of the customer's sight. The customers are more concerned with *what* is being delivered rather than *how* it is delivered.

Figure G-22 SLM: Cruise director comparison

Service level management objectives

SLM is the process of negotiating, defining, and managing the levels of IT service that are required and cost-justified. As such, it is an integral part of the overall goal of IT service management, which is the delivery of cost-effective IT services that are of known quality, are quantity-based, and meet or exceed customer expectations.

The service management goal is important because it emphasizes the quantification of services. Therefore, when defining the objectives for the SLM processes, specify the deliverables in quantifiable terms. Examples of such objectives are:

- IT services are catalogued.
- IT services are quantified in terms that both customers and IT providers understand.
- Internal and external targets of IT services are defined and agreed upon.
- Service targets are agreed upon.

The quantification of objectives applies to all three parts of the scope of the SLM process, which involves the management of IT services between:

- The customer organization and the IT services organization
- The IT services organization and its external suppliers
- The IT services organization and its internal departments

Of course, all of these objectives must be aligned with the overall business objectives as shown in Figure G-23 on page 498.

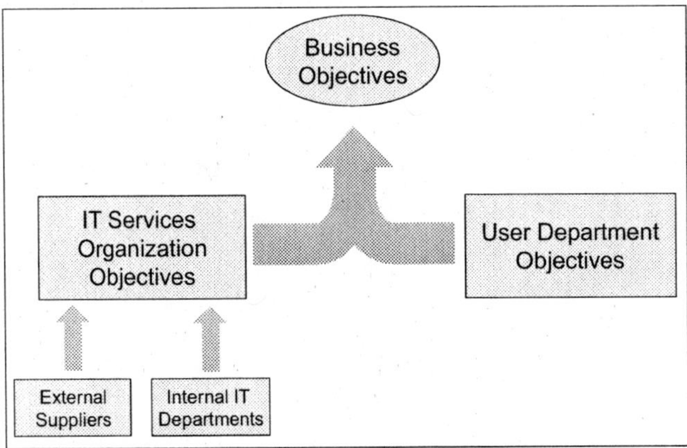

Figure G-23 Alignment of objectives

Quantifying IT services

A key to the success of SLM is correctly quantifying the services that are being provided. Unless there is an agreed-upon method of how services are to be measured, there is no way of knowing whether targets have been met. SLM is responsible for understanding and documenting customer requirements and translating them into a set of understandable measures.

Figure G-24 on page 499 illustrates the service design process, which consists of four steps:

1. **Understanding and documenting customer requirements**

   The basis for any service is to understand the customer's demands and requirements. Through this process, SLM acquires detailed knowledge about the customer environment and requirements. This understanding is a prerequisite for defining the service, estimating the capacity needs, and defining the measurements needed to support service delivery.

2. **Specifying external standards**

   With a basic understanding of the customer's requirements and demands, SLM can define the external standards. These specify the planned deliverables (both in terms of functionality and capacity) and the measurements that are used to quantify these to the customer, using customer terminology.

   Before completing the external standards, SLM must negotiate them with the customer. The external standards specify the functions and capacities that are delivered and the way in which they are measured. All of these must be accepted by the customer. The external standards, however, cannot be finalized without consent from all the teams in the IT department that are going to deliver on the promise. This consent is obtained by SLM using the internal standards.

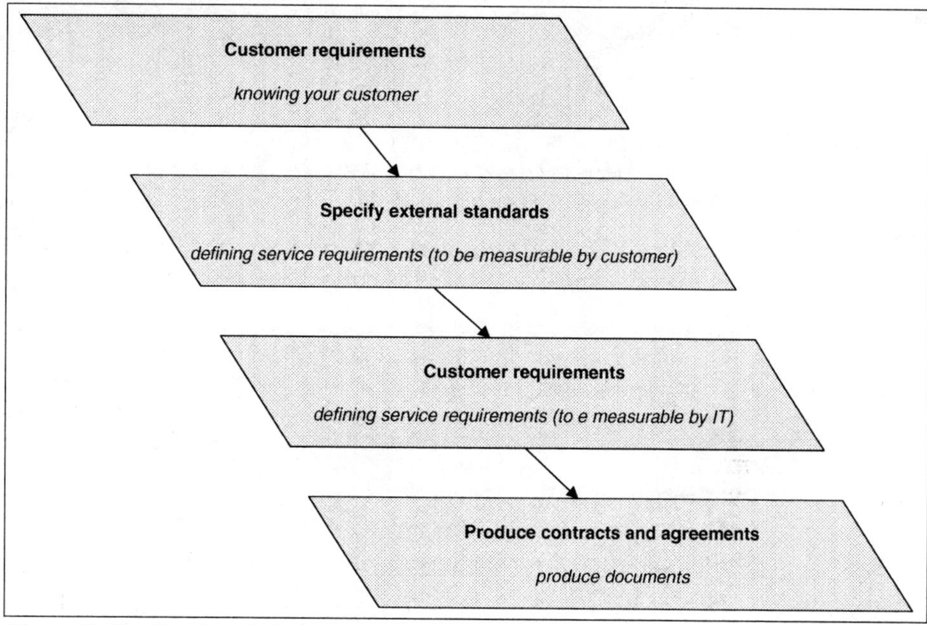

Figure G-24 Service design process

3. **Translate to internal standards**

   After the external standards are defined, or, rather, during the specification and negotiation processes, you must translate them into a set of standards to be used internally by the IT department.

   The internal standards specify, in IT terms, the functional and capacity-related requirements that the IT department must fulfill to support the delivery and the ways the delivery are measured and optionally charged. These specifications are negotiated between SLM and the other disciplines of service management. Each of the other disciplines is committed to providing the specified levels of service.

   The internal standards are produced by SLM and must be revised and renegotiated when the external standards change.

4. **Produce contracts and agreement**

   Finally, when both the internal and the external negotiations are finalized, the external and internal standards are used to create the final documents: contracts and agreements. SLM produces a set of contracts and agreements aimed at the customer. This set includes (for internal use):

   - Service level requirements
   - External specifications
   - Service level agreement
   - Service catalog

   There is another set of contracts and agreements produced to be used with external suppliers. In this set, the following items are found:

   - Service quality plan
   - Internal specifications
   - Operational level agreement
   - Underpinning contracts

Specifying service levels

When the customer's expectations are identified (through the service level requirements), the next logical step is to specify the detailed requirements to met those expectations. The goals for this specification are:

- An unambiguous and detailed description of an IT service and its components
- Specification of how the service is to be delivered to meet the agreed targets
- Specification of the quality control measures to consistently meet the specified demands, thereby, achieving customer satisfaction

Figure G-25 on page 501 illustrates the service specification process. During this process, you must keep the internal and external documents. *External documents* refer to targets that agreed upon with the customer. They provide the input for the internal documents. *Internal documents* refer to targets within the IT organization that must be met to comply with agreed upon customer requirements.

Another benefit of separating external and internal documents is that SLM does not have to bother the customer with unnecessary technical details. Yet it still maintains comprehensive documentation for both business and IT staff.

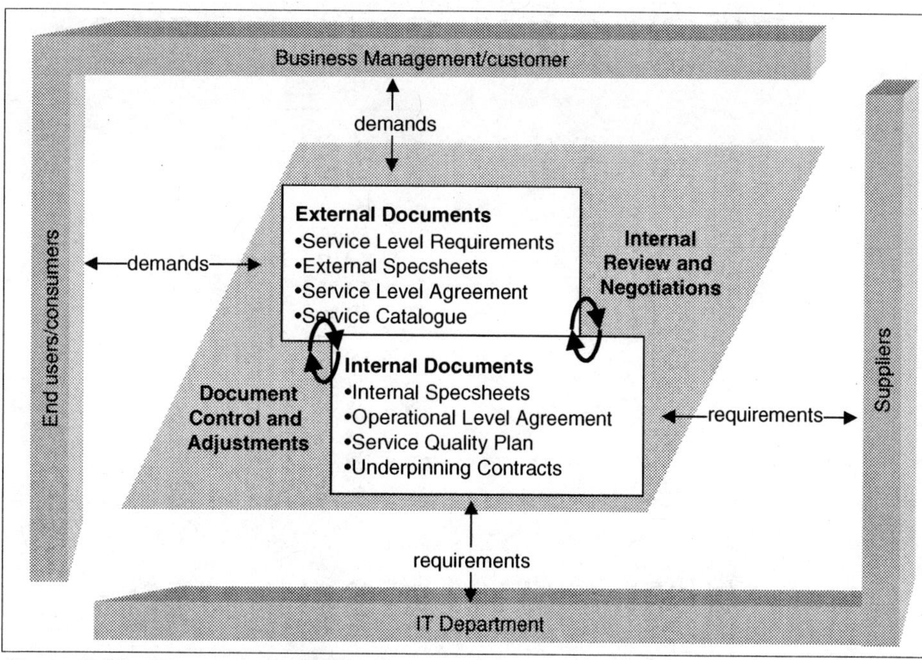

Figure G-25 The service specifications process

The use of *specsheets* is helpful to the SLA design process. The purpose of a specsheet is to specify, in detail, what the customer wants (external) and what consequences this has for the service provider (internal). Specsheets do not require signatures, but they are subject to document control.

The SLA and the service catalog are built from specsheets. When a service level requirements document is changed, the specsheets must be updated. This in turn leads to rebuilding the SLA. Therefore, you can use the specsheets to keep internal quality targets in line with the external demands. Figure G-26 on page 502 illustrates the use of external and internal specsheets.

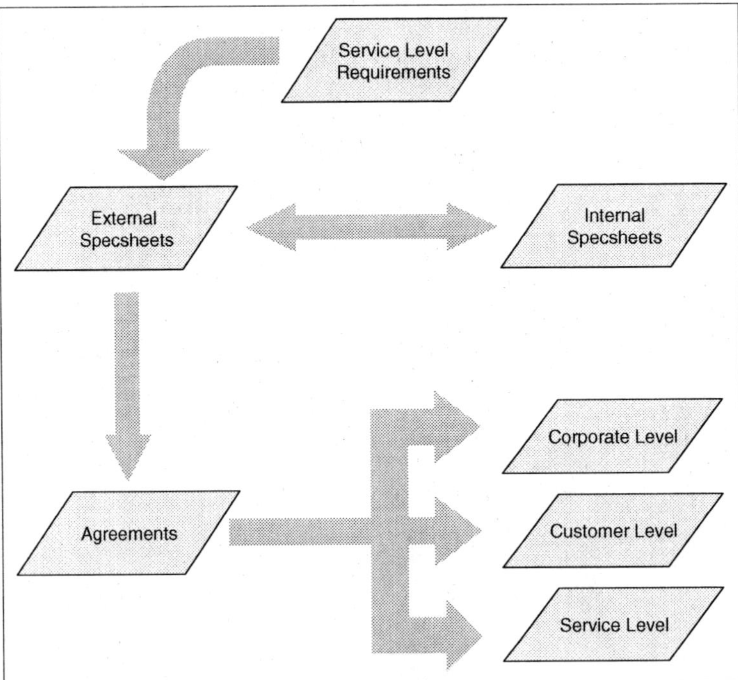

Figure G-26 Internal and external specsheets

Seven types of documents are generated and maintained by the service specification process:

- **External specsheet**: The external specsheet contains information about customer demands, which are quantified as measurable targets. It also defines responsibilities for delivery and the assurance of the quality of service.
- **Internal specsheet**: The internal specsheet contains all the information related to the building, control, and monitoring of the components that make up the service. After completion of the specsheets, the business demands should be successfully transformed into IT deliverables. It is now possible to draft the formal SLM documents:
- **Service catalog**: This document provides an overview of the services that are available to the customers of the IT organization. As a marketing tool, the service catalog presents a profile of the IT organization as a service provider and shows customers exactly what the IT organization can do. This also helps the IT organization manage the expectations of business more effectively.

  The design of the document should be consistent with its marketing purpose. This means that it should use information that is interesting to the customer, and expressed in non-technical language. Also the layout should be professional and interesting.

- **Service level agreement**: The format of each SLA depends on several factors, including the physical, cultural, and business aspects of the organization. Where the organization consists of several fairly independent business units, these should be seen as independent customers.

  Often, SLAs are divided into parts: a part specific to the customer that specifies responsibilities, terms, and conditions; a general part that describes the service; and several optional appendixes specific to the actual agreement.

- **Operational level agreement (OLA)**: The OLA is an internal document that is used only by the IT department. It serves as the internal SLA, specifying the service, responsibilities, terms, and conditions in IT terms rather than business terms.

- **Underpinning contracts**: Review all underpinning contracts regularly, both to accommodate changing service level requirements and as a routine measure. Underpinning contracts must be easily accessible for all participants in the SLM processes.

  Underpinning services supplied in-house are also vital to the service. It is important for you to review these and introduce OLAs (if they are not already in place) to safeguard the supporting services.

- **Service Quality Plan**: After the SLA is negotiated and signed, the difficult task of delivering on the promise begins. Even more difficult is the ongoing monitoring and review of the services delivered to the customer. This can only be accomplished with a full understanding of the total IT service delivery situation in terms of:

  - The capabilities of the IT service
  - Agreed-upon service levels
  - The demands for internal and external suppliers

  This information is contained in a comprehensive Service Quality Plan, which aims to balance the customer requirements with the IT organization. The Service Quality Plan achieves this in the following ways:

  - Specification of process parameters
  - Specification of required management information
  - Specification of key performance indicators

  The Service Quality Plan document is the written definition of the internal targets, responsibilities, and delivery times that are necessary to live up to the agreed upon service levels.

G.5 Bringing it all together

To enable service management and all the disciplines within service support and service delivery, you must consider three important factors:

- Organization
- Processes
- Tools

To make service management work successfully, these three ingredients have to be mixed in adequate proportions. They must all constantly undergo modifications to adapt to the needs and requirements of the company and to support the current and future IT infrastructure.

The key ingredients are interrelated so that both the organizational changes and the tools used might affect the processes. The processes might require a certain organizational structure and specialized tools. Also the tools can call for changes in the organization and impose limitations on the processes. Figure G-27 illustrates this relationship.

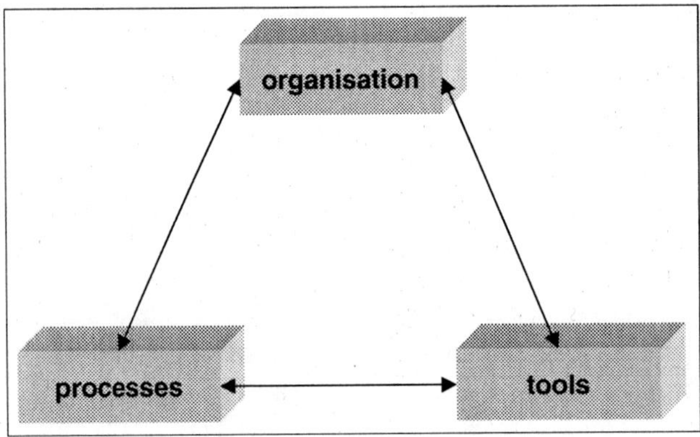

Figure G-27 Key ingredients of service management

G.5.1 Organization

While the organization, roles, and responsibilities are covered in previous sections, it is important to emphasize that the ITIL model is only a suggestion. When organizing the service management organization, you might adjust the model to fit the specific needs and policies of a particular company. Chances are that, when transforming the current IT organization into a service management organization, many of the disciplines are already, at least partially, implemented. Use this as the starting point for the service management organization.

It is equally important not to implement all of the disciplines at one time. This can create too great a disturbance for the entire organization and, most probably, can lead to a chaotic situation that threatens the welfare of the entire company.

Implementing service management is a gradual process of taking small steps and implementing the disciplines that provide the most benefit to the company first. In most situations, the two most obvious candidates are SLM and configuration management.

Configuration management is one of the most difficult disciplines to implement. It requires a lot of hard work and discipline to combine many data repositories (often, with a lot of built-in redundancy) into one all-encompassing repository and to build the processes around it that ensure data consistency and integrity. Furthermore, the benefits are more long term.

More immediate results are realized by implementing SLM. Doing this helps to shift the focus of the entire IT department to be much more business-oriented than if no SLM was in place. This shift in focus also helps to create an atmosphere in which the need for discipline and processes supporting the other service management disciplines is nurtured.

G.5.2 Processes

Processes are the bread and butter of service management. Where the organization defines roles and responsibilities (who does what), the processes define the achievements and procedures (inputs, outputs, and how to). Without processes, there can be no service management.

In a highly-dynamic environment, such as the IT world, the organization, tools, and processes might change. The technology undergoes constant changes, and organizations are constantly aligned to the businesses. People move from one job to another and from company to company. Also companies are acquired and sold (almost at the speed of light) to the benefit of the overall business.

In the middle of the chaotic structure that forms business today, the processes are the most stable of the three, despite having to be adjusted to support both the organizations and the underlying technology. In most cases, changes in technology or organization do not affect the nature (inputs and outputs) of the processes. Of course, processes need to be aligned to business requirements and company policies. They must also be constantly monitored for relevance and optimum efficiency.

The success of service management relies more on processes than any other discipline. The execution of the processes ensures delivery of services according to the SLA. The processes ensure that incidents and problems are raised and that solutions are identified and implemented when the service delivery is in jeopardy. Also processes ensure consistency of the data in the configuration repository. Processes are everything. Tools are merely there to assist.

G.5.3 Tools

Applying tools and technology alone will solve any of the challenges of service management. The basis of a successful service management operation is well-defined processes that ensure that everyone knows what their responsibilities are, what deliverables they are supposed to provide and in what quality, and why they are doing it.

You must realize that tools are necessary to help the processes work, to automate processes where possible, and to handle the volumes. In some cases, monitoring system resources being the most obvious example, tools are a necessity to make the process work.

The two most important parameters in deciding what tools are needed to support service management are *integration* and *openness*. How well the tools integrate and enable interdisciplinary processes and data usage is the key to a successful implementation. Using tools that are open (enabling integration into the current IT infrastructure and customization to support the specific organization and its processes) is a must. Failing to do so results in *islands of management* that are difficult, and even impossible, to bridge. This in turn, leads to a loss of business focus, autonomous sub-optimization for specific needs, and loss of control.

G.6 Constant improvement is a must

Continuous improvement is a key element of providing high quality services and is used to empower staff to drive improvements that benefit the business and the user of services. As discussed in “Measuring service quality” on page 493, sustained improvements in the quality of service delivered increase the quality perceived by the users, improving customer satisfaction and loyalty.

Even high quality service management processes need to go through an improvement process overtime. The service manager must ensure that corrective actions progress to address any shortfalls in the process in meeting the levels of services required and expected by the business.

This ongoing improvement process can, for example, be achieved by periodically performing the following tasks:

- Monitoring and reporting on service achievements

  Incorporate details of performance against all SLA targets, together with details of any trends or specific actions being undertaken to improve service quality, into the periodic report.

- Holding service review meetings with customers

  Hold periodic review meetings on a regular basis with customers (or their representatives) to review the service achievement.

- Implement a formal Service Improvement Program

  The Service Improvement Program (SIP) is a project that the organization establishes to continuously identify improvements in customer satisfaction and service quality as delivered by IT. When the analysis of service levels and achievement reports identifies issues that impact, or might impact, service quality, SLM in conjunction with problem management and availability management can initiate a SIP to identify and implement actions to overcome the issues and restore service quality.

- Maintenance of SLAs

  Keep current all SLAs that are in place to ensure that the services covered and the targets for each are still relevant and represent the need of the customers.

As shown in Figure G-28 on page 508, all of the disciplines within service management encompass four distinct activities:

- Planning
- Delivery or deploying
- Measurement and act based on measurements
- Calibration and changes for improvement

At the outset, the IT organization and its customers plan the nature of the service to be provided. Next, the IT organization delivers according to the plan. It takes calls, resolves problems, manages change, monitors inventory, opens the service desk to end users, and connects to the network and systems management platforms. The IT organization then measures its performance to determine whether it is delivering superior service based on the explicit needs of the LOB. Finally, the IT organization and the LOB continually reassess their agreements to ensure that those agreements meet changing business needs.

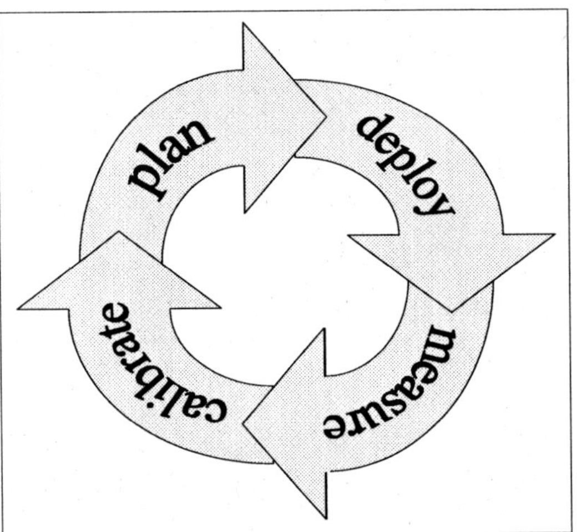

Figure G-28 Constant improvement of IT services

G.6.1 Planning

During the planning phase, IT and the LOB determine what services will be provided, at what levels, and for what ends. This effort leads to the establishment of SLAs, or contracts, that specify the who, what, when, and how of IT service.

The most effective SLAs focus on key issues, such as:

- The needs of the LOB
- Business system availability
- Device and service quality
- Device usage and maintenance

SLAs succeed when they are simple, clearly stated, and measurable. Clear and concise SLAs form an IT organization's SLM foundation, matching the LOB's need with IT service as well as cost. For example, consider an organization that has highly-skilled, relatively self-sufficient engineers who can deal with a four-hour response time during normal business hours. That organization should not have to pay the same for their IT service as a customer-billing organization with less experienced staff running real-time, important applications that require a one-hour response time 24 hours a day.

SLAs, while conceptually simple, can quickly become complex. When specifying the term of the agreement, we recommend that you offer several basic levels of service rather than tailoring one for each organization. In this way, the total number of service options stays at a manageable level, and IT's ability to monitor them effectively is greatly enhanced.

G.6.2 Delivery

Comprehensively delivering service at a competitive cost as outlined and mutually agreed upon in the plan is a difficult task. As shown in the previous sections, delivery involves many separate disciplines that span the IT functional groups, such as network operations, application development, hardware procurement and deployment, software distribution and training, and that support all these elements. It also involves incident and problem resolution, configuration management, service request and change management, end-user empowerment, and the complete spectrum of network and systems management. Successful service delivery requires these functions to be integrated seamless.

G.6.3 Measurement

How can an IT organization determine whether it is meeting the service levels established with its customer? Much of the measurement step is built around monitoring those terms outlined in the SLAs.

Therefore, an IT organization relies on technologies to actively monitor these service levels through the various delivery stages. These stages include the service delivery, monitoring of LOB assets, ensuring the health of LOB networks and systems, and managing changes to the LOB infrastructure. Two types of technologies support this measurement: real-time reporting tools and static historical reporting tools.

For example, two calls might come to the service desk simultaneously. One call is covered under an agreement that entitles the caller to a one-hour resolution, while the second is entitled to a four-hour resolution.

The service desk technology presents this information to the technician, who prioritizes the calls to ensure that both callers receive timely support. These technologies also include intelligent escalation utilities, operating in real time, to alert service desk management when agreements are in danger of being breached. Real-time reporting technologies enable management to initiate corrective action before service deteriorates.

In addition to these real-time metrics, it is important for the service desk to monitor other key performance indicators including first-call resolution rates, SLA thresholds, high-priority open problems, problem time open, and call queue by analyst. Historical reporting is also vital to management for planning purposes. The data generated by these reporting tools substantiates the discussion that IT and LOBs have when they determine the appropriate level of service required. It also assesses the effectiveness of the service delivered.

G.6.4 Calibration

The process of planning, delivering, and measuring the delivery of customized IT support to its LOB is continuous because competitive pressures, technologies, capabilities, and needs change over time. Planning is the foundation of SLM. Calibrating the plan keeps IT responsive to the continually-changing conditions throughout the entire organization.

To calibrate the service delivered, successful IT organizations employ a combination of historical reporting tools and a decision support framework. While the real-time monitoring tools described earlier assist IT in running the day-to-day operations, decision support tools provide a framework for exploring data more completely to make better-informed decisions. These tools, often built around multidimensional analysis techniques, enable IT management to see relationships in the volumes of data generated by one or more operational systems-relationships that are rarely apparent in real time or static reporting methodologies.

For example, as an IT manager, you are tasked with managing your organization efficiently and effectively. This means that you need to use the best means to support the LOB in your company, and the best means are not always the same for each LOB. For instance, let's return to the earlier example of highly technical users, such as engineers, and less technical users, such as customer billing representatives. The engineers are relatively self-sufficient while the billing representatives relatively depend on your support. Given this, IT will likely support these two groups differently. By analyzing problem and usage data, service desk management determines how best to support each group or user, whether by telephone, e-mail, Web, voice mail, or a combination of these.

The true power of decision support frameworks and static reporting technologies is to ensure that IT remains in sync with the LOB it supports. The calibration step of SLM is an explicit reminder for IT and LOBs to constantly evaluate the effectiveness and appropriateness of the service delivered.

G.7 The power of integration

The real power in managing your IT infrastructure as a business-oriented service is only realized when the core processes and tools used by service management are seamlessly integrated. Incidents, problems, events, changes, capacity, cost, and configuration items are all interrelated.

If an end user reports a problem with a faulty asset, service desk technicians know if a service call has been ordered for that asset. Because the problem was reported, the service desk can initiate that service request immediately. If a repair technician is dispatched and determines that the asset needs to be replaced, the technologies generate the appropriate change order and initiate that process. When the change is approved and executed, the asset discovery tools confirm the work, close the change request, and report the new status in the asset management system. Finally, if the same end user initiates a second call, the service desk technician sees the updated inventory and a history of the change.

In addition to the disciplines mentioned in the previous example, network and systems management integration encompass other enterprise IT technologies. These include technologies for software distribution, event management, systems management, applications management, remote control, and security. The seamless integration of these technologies can reduce the burden for many labor-intensive IT operations.

Related publications

We consider the publications that we list in this section to be particularly suitable for a more detailed discussion of the topics that we covered in this IBM Redbook.

IBM online resources

These Web sites and URLs are relevant as further information sources:

- Portal page to access all IBM resources related to IBM Tivoli Change and Configuration Management Database Configuration Discovery and Tracking v1.1:

  `http://www.ibm.com/software/tivoli/features/it-serv-mgmt/index.html`

- IBM Tivoli Change and Configuration Management Database v1.1 Information Center:

  `http://publib.boulder.ibm.com/infocenter/tivihelp/v10r1/topic/com.ibm.ccmdb.doc/ccmdb_welcome.htm`

- IBM Tivoli Change and Configuration Management Database v1.1: Release Notes:

  `http://publib.boulder.ibm.com/infocenter/tivihelp/v10r1/topic/com.ibm.ccmdb.doc/rnotes/c_rnotes_bucket.html`

- IBM Tivoli Change and Configuration Management Database v1.1: Planning Guide

  `http://publib.boulder.ibm.com/infocenter/tivihelp/v10r1/topic/com.ibm.ccmdb.doc/install/c_ccmdb_planning.html`

- IBM Tivoli Change and Configuration Management Database v1.1: Installing the Configuration Discovery and Tracking feature:

  `http://publib.boulder.ibm.com/infocenter/tivihelp/v10r1/topic/com.ibm.ccmdb.doc/cmdb_admin/c_cmdb_installing.html`

- IBM Tivoli Change and Configuration Management Database v1.1: Configuring Configuration Discovery and Tracking:

  `http://publib.boulder.ibm.com/infocenter/tivihelp/v10r1/topic/com.ibm.ccmdb.doc/cmdb_admin/c_cmdb_postinstalladmin.html`

- IBM Tivoli Change and Configuration Management Database v1.1: Administering the Configuration Discovery and Tracking feature:

  http://publib.boulder.ibm.com/infocenter/tivihelp/v10r1/topic/com.ibm.ccmdb.doc/cmdb_user/c_cmdb_administeringcmdb.html

- IBM Tivoli Application Dependency Discovery Manager 4.1: Technical Architecture Overview

  http://catalog.lotus.com/wps/portal/topal?NavCode=1TW10CC0A

- Agent versus Agentless Application Dependency Discovery

  http://catalog.lotus.com/wps/portal/topal?NavCode=1TW10PM02

How to get IBM Redbooks

You can search for, view, or download Redbooks, Redpapers, Hints and Tips, draft publications and Additional materials, as well as order hardcopy Redbooks or CD-ROMs, at this Web site:

ibm.com/redbooks

Help from IBM

IBM Support and downloads

ibm.com/support

IBM Global Services

ibm.com/services

Abbreviations and acronyms

API	Application Program Interface
ASP	Application Service Provider
BCM	Business Continuity Management
CAB	Change Advisory Board
CAB/EC	CAB/Emergency Committee
CCMDB	Change Configuration Management Database
CCTA	Central Computing and Telecommunications Agency
CDM	Common Data Model
CDT	Configuration Discovery and Tracking
CI	Configuration Item
CIM	Common Information Model
CLI	Command Line Interface
CMDB	Configuration Management Database
COTS	Custom Off The Shelf
CPU	Central Processing Unit
CVS	Comma Separated Value
DB2	IBM Database 2™
DBMS	Database Management System
DHS	Definitive Hardware Store
DLA	Discovery Library Adapter
DMTF	Distributed Management Task Force
DNS	Domain Name Server
DNS	Domain Name Server
DSL	Definitive Software Library
EJB	Enterprise Java Bean
FTP	File Transfer Protocol
GUI	Graphical User Interface
GUID	Globally Unique Identifier
IBM	International Business Machines Corporation
IDE	Integrated Development Environment
IdML	International Development Markup Language
IP	Internet Protocol
IT	Information Technology
ITIL	IT Infrastructure Library
ITSM	IT Service Management
ITSMF	IT Service Management Forum
ITSO	International Technical Support Organization
J2EE	Java 2 Enterprise Edition
J2SE	Java 2 Standard Edition
JMX	Java Management Extensions
JRE	Java Runtime Environment
LDAP	Lightweight Directory Access Protocol
LOB	Line Of Business
MIB	Management Information Block
MSP	Management Service Provider
MSS	Management Software System
MTBF	Mean Time Between Failure
MTBSI	Mean Time Between System Incidents
NSF	Network File System
NSM	Network and Systems Management

OGC	Office of Government Commerce
OLA	Operational Level Agreement
OLTP	On Line Transaction Processing
OPAL	Open Process Automation Library
PC	Personal Computer
PMIP	Process Management Integration Platform
RAM	Random Access Memory
RFC	Request For Change
SCP	Secure Copy Program
SDK	Software Development Kit
SIP	Service Improvement Program
SLA	Service Level Agreement
SLM	Service Level Management
SLO	Service Level Objective
SMB	Server Message Block
SMS	Systems Management Server
SNMP	Simple Network Management Protocol
SOA	Service Oriented Architecture
SQL	Structured Query Language
SSH	Secure Shell
TCO	Total Cost of Ownership
UDB	Universal Database
UI	User Interface
UML	Unified Modelling Language
URI	Universal Resource Identifier
URL	Universal Resource Locator
UTC	Universal Time Coordinated
WBEM	Web Based Enterprise Management
WMI	Windows Management Interface
WSDL	Web Services Description Language
WSH	Windows Scripting Host
XML	Extended Markup Language
XQuery	an XML Query Language
XSL	Extensible Stylesheet Language
XSLT	Extensible Stylesheet Language Transformations

Index

D